SOMETHING ABOUT THE AUTHOR®

Something about
the Author *was named
an "**Outstanding
Reference Source,**"
the highest honor given
by the American
Library Association
Reference and Adult
Services Division.*

SOMETHING ABOUT THE AUTHOR®

Facts and Pictures about Authors
and Illustrators of Books for Young People

volume 143

GALE®

Detroit • New York • San Diego • San Francisco • Cleveland • New Haven, Conn. • Waterville, Maine • London • Munich

Something About the Author, Volume 143

Project Editor
Scot Peacock

Editorial
Katy Balcer, Shavon Burden, Sara Constantakis, Anna Marie Dahn, Alana Joli Foster, Natalie Fulkerson, Arlene M. Johnson, Michelle Kazensky, Julie Keppen, Joshua Kondek, Thomas McMahon, Jenai A. Mynatt, Judith L. Pyko, Mary Ruby, Lemma Shomali, Susan Strickland, Maikue Vang, Tracey Watson, Thomas Wiloch, Emiene Shija Wright

Research
Michelle Campbell, Barbara McNeil, Tamara C. Nott, Gary J. Oudersluys, Tracie A. Richardson, Cheryl L. Warnock

Permissions
Margaret Chamberlain

Imaging and Multimedia
Dean Dauphinais, Robert Duncan, Leitha Etheridge-Sims, Mary K. Grimes, Lezlie Light, Dan Newell, David G. Oblender, Christine O'Bryan, Kelly A. Quin, Luke Rademacher

Composition and Electronic Capture
Carolyn A. Roney

Manufacturing
Stacy L. Melson

LIBRARY OF CONGRESS CATALOG CARD NUMBER 62-52046

ISBN 0-7876-5215-6
ISSN 0276-816X

Printed in the United States of America
10 9 8 7 6 5 4 3 2 1

Contents

Authors in Forthcoming Volumes

Below are some of the authors and illustrators that will be featured in upcoming volumes of *SATA*. These include new entries on the swiftly rising stars of the field, as well as completely revised and updated entries (indicated with *) on some of the most notable and best-loved creators of books for children.

*Floyd Cooper ▌ Winner of three Coretta Scott King Honor Awards for illustration, Cooper has brought to life many stories, poems, songs, and works of nonfiction detailing centuries of African-American experience. He has illustrated nearly fifty picture books by writers from Nikki Grimes to Amy Littlesugar to Jane Yolen to Margaret Wise Brown; additionally, Cooper has also penned several of his own picture books with strong African-American themes. In 2003 he illustrated *Mississippi Morning* by Ruth Vander Zee.

*Jamie Lee Curtis ▌ Curtis made her film debut in a series of low-budget horror films and—by sheer determination—moved from those into comedy and action-adventure hits alongside such big-name stars as Kevin Kline, John Travolta, and Arnold Schwarzenegger. in 1993 Curtis began to forge yet another career as a children's storybook author with *When I Was Little: A Four-Year-Old's Memoir of Her Youth.* That book made it to the *New York Times* bestseller list and has since sold almost a million copies. Curtis has published four more children's books since then, including the 2002 work *I'm Gonna Like Me: Letting Off a Little Self-Esteem.*

*David Gerrold ▌ Author or editor of over forty books and numerous television scripts, Gerrold is considered an inventive science fiction writer. Gerrold's award-winning novels include *When Harlie Was One, The Man Who Folded Himself, Yesterday's Children,* and *Moonstar Odyssey,* as well as the books that comprise his enterprising and entertaining "War against the Chtorr" series. For a young adult audience, he has also written a science fiction trilogy, the *Dingilliad* series, including *Jumping off the Planet, Bouncing off the Moon,* and *Leaping to the Stars.* Additionally, Gerrold has written of his experiences as the single father of an adopted son in the popular 2002 novel *The Martian Child: A Novel about a Single Father Adopting a Son.*

Emily Jenkins ▌ Novelist, essayist, and picture book writer Jenkins has written widely for children and adults. Her work for adults includes essays and articles for mainstream and not-so-mainstream periodicals as well as the novel *Mister Posterior and the Genius Child.* Jenkins's picture book debut, *Five Creatures,* received a *Boston Globe-Horn Book* Honor Award and was a Notable Children's Books selection by the American Library Association.

Elizabeth Mann ▌ A former schoolteacher and cofounder of Mikaya Press, Mann writes nonfiction works targeted to young readers. The books focus on man-made wonders, including the Great Pyramid, the Great Wall of China, the South American Inca city of Ma-

chu Picchu, and the Hoover Dam. Her work *The Panama Canal* was named a Notable Children's Book in the Field of Social Studies by the National Council for the Social Studies/Children's Book Council. In 2002 Mann published *Tikal: The Center of the Maya World.*

*Toni Morrison ▌ Nobel laureate Morrison has a central role in the American literary canon. Through works such as *The Bluest Eye, Song of Solomon,* and *Beloved,* Morrison proves herself to be a gifted teller of stories in which troubled characters seek to find themselves and their cultural riches in a society that warps or impedes such essential growth. Morrison has also proved herself to be an able creator of children's books, working in collaboration with her son Slade Morrison. Together the two writers have produced the rhyming parable *The Big Box* and *The Book of Mean People,* a child's eye view of the world—as seen by a rabbit. They have also collaborated on the "Who's Got Game?" series of retellings of Aesop's fables.

*Mary Pope Osborne ▌ A popular, prolific author for children and young adults, Osborne is considered a versatile writer who has contributed successfully to many of the genres encompassed by juvenile literature. Directing her works to an audience that ranges from preschool through high school, she has written picture books, realistic fiction, historical fiction, young adult novels, nonfiction, and retellings, and has edited collections of stories, poetry, and songs. Osborne is perhaps best known for writing the "Magic Tree House" books, a best-selling, multi-volume collection of time-travel fantasies for primary graders. In *New York's Bravest,* a book dedicated to the New York City firefighters who gave their lives on September 11, 2001, Osborne draws on both legends and published accounts to create her version of a larger-than-life volunteer fireman.

*Barbara Rogasky ▌ After working for nearly twenty-five years in the publishing field with such prestigious firms as Macmillan and Harcourt Brace Jovanovich, Rogasky moved to rural New England and began a career in freelance editing and ghostwriting. The daughter of Eastern-European Jews, Rogasky has preserved her Jewish heritage in several works. *The Golem* won the National Jewish Book Award, and her revised version of *Smoke and Ashes: The Story of the Holocaust* was selected as a Sydney Taylor Honor Book by the Association of Jewish Libraries in 2002.

Barbara Saffer ▌ Born in Germany, Saffer grew up in New York City. After earning doctorates in biology and geology, and teaching college courses, she delved into children's literature. Since the mid-1990s, she has produced a steady stream of nonfiction articles and books, including a handful of science "question and answer" and hands-on experiment books. Her work *ABC Science Riddles* was named an Outstanding Science Trade Book selection by the National Science Teachers Association/Children's Book Council.

*Arthur Yorinks ▌ Author of two dozen picture books and numerous stage plays, Yorinks is known for his outrageous and sometimes surreal stories which are frequently accompanied by the carefully composed, realistic illustrations of Richard Egielski, David Small, and Maurice Sendak. From *Sid and Sol,* in which a small man stands up to a formidable giant, to *Company's Coming* and its

2001 sequel, *Company's Going,* in which a woman graciously invites aliens to dinner, Yorinks's bizarre tales are told with deadpan humor that delights readers. Yorinks published *Quack!: To the Moon and Home Again* in 2003.

Introduction

Something about the Author (*SATA*) is an ongoing reference series that examines the lives and works of authors and illustrators of books for children. *SATA* includes not only well-known writers and artists but also less prominent individuals whose works are just coming to be recognized. This series is often the only readily available information source on emerging authors and illustrators. You'll find *SATA* informative and entertaining, whether you are a student, a librarian, an English teacher, a parent, or simply an adult who enjoys children's literature.

What's Inside *SATA*

SATA provides detailed information about authors and illustrators who span the full time range of children's literature, from early figures like John Newbery and L. Frank Baum to contemporary figures like Judy Blume and Richard Peck. Authors in the series represent primarily English-speaking countries, particularly the United States, Canada, and the United Kingdom. Also included, however, are authors from around the world whose works are available in English translation. The writings represented in *SATA* include those created intentionally for children and young adults as well as those written for a general audience and known to interest younger readers. These writings cover the entire spectrum of children's literature, including picture books, humor, folk and fairy tales, animal stories, mystery and adventure, science fiction and fantasy, historical fiction, poetry and nonsense verse, drama, biography, and nonfiction. Obituaries are also included in *SATA* and are intended not only as death notices but also as concise overviews of people's lives and work. Additionally, each edition features newly revised and updated entries for a selection of *SATA* listees who remain of interest to today's readers and who have been active enough to require extensive revisions of their earlier biographies.

Autobiography Feature

Beginning with Volume 103, *SATA* features two or more specially commissioned autobiographical essays in each volume. These unique essays, averaging about ten thousand words in length and illustrated with an abundance of personal photos, present an entertaining and informative first-person perspective on the lives and careers of prominent authors and illustrators profiled in *SATA*.

Two Convenient Indexes

In response to suggestions from librarians, *SATA* indexes no longer appear in every volume but are included in alternate (odd-numbered) volumes of the series, beginning with Volume 57.

SATA continues to include two indexes that cumulate with each alternate volume: the Illustrations Index, arranged by the name of the illustrator, gives the number of the volume and page where the illustrator's work appears in the current volume as well as all preceding volumes in the series; the Author Index gives the number of the volume in which a person's biographical sketch, autobiographical essay, or obituary appears in the current volume as well as all preceding volumes in the series.

These indexes also include references to authors and illustrators who appear in *Gale's Yesterday's Authors of Books for Children, Children's Literature Review,* and *Something about the Author Autobiography Series.*

Easy-to-Use Entry Format

Whether you're already familiar with the *SATA* series or just getting acquainted, you will want to be aware of the kind of information that an entry provides. In every *SATA* entry the editors attempt to give as complete a picture of the person's life and work as possible. A typical entry in *SATA* includes the following clearly labeled information sections:

PERSONAL: date and place of birth and death, parents' names and occupations, name of spouse, date of marriage, names of children, educational institutions attended, degrees received, religious and political affiliations, hobbies and other interests.

ADDRESSES: complete home, office, electronic mail, and agent addresses, whenever available.

CAREER: name of employer, position, and dates for each career post; art exhibitions; military service; memberships and offices held in professional and civic organizations.

MEMBER: professional, civic, and other association memberships and any official posts held.

AWARDS, HONORS: literary and professional awards received.

WRITINGS: title-by-title chronological bibliography of books written and/or illustrated, listed by genre when known; lists of other notable publications, such as plays, screenplays, and periodical contributions.

ADAPTATIONS: a list of films, television programs, plays, CD-ROMs, recordings, and other media presentations that have been adapted from the author's work.

WORK IN PROGRESS: description of projects in progress.

SIDELIGHTS: a biographical portrait of the author or illustrator's development, either directly from the biographee—and often written specifically for the *SATA* entry—or gathered from diaries, letters, interviews, or other published sources.

BIOGRAPHICAL AND CRITICAL SOURCES: cites sources quoted in "Sidelights" along with references for further reading.

EXTENSIVE ILLUSTRATIONS: photographs, movie stills, book illustrations, and other interesting visual materials supplement the text.

How a *SATA* Entry Is Compiled

A *SATA* entry progresses through a series of steps. If the biographee is living, the *SATA* editors try to secure information directly from him or her through a questionnaire. From the information that the biographee supplies, the editors prepare an entry, filling in any essential missing details with research and/or telephone interviews. If possible, the author or illustra-tor is sent a copy of the entry to check for accuracy and completeness.

If the biographee is deceased or cannot be reached by questionnaire, the *SATA* editors examine a wide variety of published sources to gather information for an entry. Biographical and bibliographic sources are consulted, as are book reviews, feature articles, published interviews, and material sometimes obtained from the biographee's family, publishers, agent, or other associates.

Entries that have not been verified by the biographees or their representatives are marked with an asterisk (*).

Contact the Editor

We encourage our readers to examine the entire *SATA* series. Please write and tell us if we can make *SATA* even more helpful to you. Give your comments and suggestions to the editor:

Editor
Something about the Author
The Gale Group
27500 Drake Rd.
Farmington Hills MI 48331-3535

Toll-free: 800-877-GALE
Fax: 248-699-8054

Something about the Author **Product Advisory Board**

The editors of *Something about the Author* are dedicated to maintaining a high standard of excellence by publishing comprehensive, accurate, and highly readable entries on a wide array of writers for children and young adults. In addition to the quality of the content, the editors take pride in the graphic design of the series, which is intended to be orderly yet inviting, allowing readers to utilize the pages of *SATA* easily and with efficiency. Despite the longevity of the *SATA* print series, and the success of its format, we are mindful that the vitality of a literary reference product is dependent on its ability to serve its users over time. As literature, and attitudes about literature, constantly evolve, so do the reference needs of students, teachers, scholars, journalists, researchers, and book club members. To be certain that we continue to keep pace with the expectations of our customers, the editors of *SATA* listen carefully to their comments regarding the value, utility, and quality of the series. Librarians, who have firsthand knowledge of the needs of library users, are a valuable resource for us. The *Something about the Author* Product Advisory Board, made up of school, public, and academic librarians, is a forum to promote focused feedback about *SATA* on a regular basis. The nine-member advisory board includes the following individuals, whom the editors wish to thank for sharing their expertise:

Eva M. Davis
Youth Department Manager,
Ann Arbor District Library,
Ann Arbor, Michigan

Joan B. Eisenberg
Lower School Librarian,
Milton Academy,
Milton, Massachusetts

Francisca Goldsmith
Teen Services Librarian,
Berkeley Public Library,
Berkeley, California

Harriet Hagenbruch
Curriculum Materials Center/Education Librarian,
Axinn Library,
Hofstra University,
Hempstead, New York

Monica F. Irlbacher
Young Adult Librarian,
Middletown Thrall Library,
Middletown, New York

Robyn Lupa
Head of Children's Services,
Jefferson County Public Library,
Lakewood, Colorado

Eric Norton
Head of Children's Services,
McMillan Memorial Library,
Wisconsin Rapids, Wisconsin

Victor L. Schill
Assistant Branch Librarian/Children's Librarian,
Harris County Public Library/Fairbanks Branch,
Houston, Texas

Caryn Sipos
Community Librarian,
Three Creeks Community Library,
Vancouver, Washington

Acknowledgments

Grateful acknowledgment is made to the following publishers, authors, and artists whose works appear in this volume.

ADA, ALMA FLOR. ▌ Cartwright, Reg, illustrator. From an illustration in *Three Golden Oranges,* retold by Alma Flor Ada. Atheneum Books for Young Readers, 1999. Illustrations © 1999 Reg Cartwright. Reproduced by permission of Atheneum Books for Young Readers, an imprint of Simon & Schuster Children's Publishing Division./ Tyron, Leslie, illustrator. From an illustration in *With Love, Little Red Hen,* by Alma Flor Ada. Atheneum, Books for Young Readers, 2001. Illustrations copyright © 2001 by Leslie Tyron. Reproduced by permission of Atheneum Books for Young Readers, an imprint of Simon & Schuster Children's Publishing Division./ Ada, Alma Flor, photograph. Reproduced by permission of the author.

BOYDEN, LINDA. ▌ Boyden, Linda, photograph by John Boyden. Reproduced by permission.

BURCHARD, PETER DUNCAN. ▌ Burchard, Peter, illustrator. From an illustration in his *Jed: The Story of a Yankee Soldier and a Southern Boy.* E.M. Hale and Company, 1960. © 1960, 1988 by Peter Burchard. Reproduced by permission of Coward-McCann, a division of Penguin Young Readers Group, A Member of Penguin Group (USA) Inc., 345 Hudson St., New York, NY 10014. All rights reserved./ Truth, Sojourner (ca. 1797-1883). Carte de visite by unidentified photographer, n.d. MHS image number 30. As found in *Lincoln and Slavery* by Peter Burchard. Atheneum Books for Young Readers, 1999. Reproduced by permission of the Massachusetts Historical Society./ Burchard, Peter Duncan, photograph by Judith Saunders. Reproduced by permission of Peter Burchard.

CAMPOY, F. ISABEL (CORONADO). ▌ Dewey, Ariane and Jose Aruego, illustrators. From an illustration in *Rosa Raposa,* by F. Isabel Campoy. Gulliver Books, 2002. Illustrations © 2002 by Jose Aruego and Ariane Dewey. Reproduced in the UK by permission of the Sheldon Fogelman Agency, Inc., in the rest of the world by permission of Harcourt, Inc. All right reserved./ Benitez, Roberto, artist. From an illustration in *Blue and Green,* by Alma Flor Ada and F. Isabel Campoy. Santillana, 2000. © 2000 Santillana USA Publishing Company, Inc. Reproduced by permission./ From a photograph in *Béisbol en los barrios,* by Henry Horenstein, translated by Alma Flor Ada and F. Isabel Campoy. Harcourt, 1997. Reproduced by permission of the author./ Campoy, F. Isabel, photograph. Reproduced by permission.

CAPPO, NAN WILLARD. ▌ Cappo, Nan Willard, photograph by Ellen Cappo. Reproduced by permission of Nan Willard Cappo.

COLLICOTT, SHARLEEN. ▌ Collicott, Sharleen, illustrator. From an illustration in *Which Witch is Which?,* by Judi Barrett. Simon & Schuster, 2001 Illustrations © 2001 by Sharleen Collicott. Repro-

duced by permission of Atheneum Books for Young Readers, an imprint of Simon & Schuster Children's Publishing Division./ Collicott, Sharleen, illustrator. From an illustration in *Toestomper and the Caterpillars,* by Sharleen Collicott. Houghton Mifflin, 1999. Copyright © 1999 by Sharleen Collicott. Reproduced by permission of the Houghton Mifflin Company./ Collicott, Sharleen, photograph. Reproduced by permission of Sharleen Collicott.

DURBIN, WILLIAM. ▌ Jokinen, Walfrid J., photographer. From a photograph in *The Journal of Otto Peltonen: A Finnish Immigrant,* by William Durbin. Scholastic, 2000. Photograph courtesy of University of Minnesota, Immigration Research Center. Reproduced by permission./ Archambault, Matthew, illustrator. From a cover of *Wintering,* by William Durbin. Yearling Books, 2000. Reproduced by permission of Random House Children's Books, a division of Random House, Inc./ Durbin, William, photograph. Reproduced by permission.

DUSSLING, JENNIFER. ▌ From a jacket of *Bugs! Bugs! Bugs!,* by Jennifer Dussling. Dorling Kindersley Books, 1998. Reproduced by permission./ Thornburgh, Rebecca, illustrator. From an illustration in *The 100-Pound Problem,* by Jennifer Dussling. The Kane Press, 2000. © 2000 by The Kane Press. Reproduced by permission.

EVANS, GREG. ▌ From an illustration in *Passion! Betrayal! Outrage! Revenge!* written and illustrated by Greg Evans. Rutledge Hill Press, 1999. Copyright © 1999 by GEC Incorporated. Reproduced by permission of United Media Syndicate, Inc./ From an illustration in *Passion! Betrayal! Outrage! Revenge!* written and illustrated by Greg Evans. Rutledge Hill Press, 1999. Copyright © 1999 by GEC Incorporated. Reproduced by permission of United Media Syndicate, Inc./ *Luann,* October 29, 1997, comic strip by Greg Evans. Reproduced by permission of United Feature Syndicate, Inc./ *Luann,* August 30, 1997, comic strip by Greg Evans. Reproduced by permission of United Features Syndicate, Inc./ Evans, Greg, photograph. Reproduced by permission of United Feature Syndicate, Inc./Greg Evans.

FLEMING, CANDACE. ▌ Potter, Giselle, illustrator. From an illustration in *Gabriella's Song,* by Candace Fleming. Aladdin Paperbacks, 2001. Illustrations © 1997 by Giselle Potter. Reproduced by permission./ Schindler, S.D., illustrator. From an illustration in *A Big Cheese for the White House: The True Tale of a Tremendous Cheddar,* by Candace Fleming. DK Publishing, 1999. Illustration copyright © 1999 by S.D. Schindler. Reproduced by permission./ Fleming, Candace, photograph. Reproduced by permission of Candace Fleming.

FUERST, JEFFREY B. ▌ Fuerst, Jeffrey B., photograph. Reproduced by permission.

GARDNER, SCOT. ▌ Gardner, Scot, photograph. Reproduced by permission.

GEOGHEGAN, ADRIENNE. ▌ Gale, Cathy, illustrator. From an illustration in *All Your Own Teeth,* by Adrienne Geoghegan. Dial Books for Young Readers, 2002. Pictures © 2001 by Cathy Gale. Reproduced in the UK by permission of Bloomsbury Publishing PLC, in the rest of the world by permission of Dial Books for Young Readers, a division of Penguin Young Readers Group, A Member of Penguin Group (USA) Inc., 345 Hudson St., New York, NY 10014. All right reserved./ Johnson, Adrian, illustrator. From an illustration in *There's a Wardrobe in My Monster!,* by Adrienne Geoghegan. Carolrhoda Books, 1999. Illustrations © 1999 by Adrian Johnson. Reproduced in the UK by permission of Bloomsbury Press, in the rest of the world by permission of The Lerner Publishing Group./ Geoghegan, Adrienne, photograph. Reproduced by permission.

GORBACHEV, VALERI. ▌ Gorbachev, Valeri, "Hrusha the Pig," illustration. © 2003 Valeri Gorbachev. Reproduced by permission./ Gorbachev, Valeri "Nicky," illustration. © 2003 Valeri Gorbachev. Reproduced by permission./ All photographs © 2003 Valeri Gorbachev. Reproduced by permission of the author.

GURNEY, JOHN STEVEN. ▌ Gurney, John Steven, illustrator. From an illustration in *Trolls Don't Ride Roller Coasters* ("Bailey School Kids"), by Debbie Dadey and Marcia Thornton Jones. Scholastic Inc., 1999. Illustration copyright © 1999 by Scholastic, Inc. Reproduced by permission./ Gurney, John Steven, illustrator. From an illustration in *Werewolves Don't Go to Summer Camp* ("Bailey School Kids"), by Debbie Dadey and Marcia Thornton Jones. Scholastic, 1991. Illustrations © 1991 by Scholastic Inc. Reproduced by permission.

HAVELIN, KATE. ▌ Havelin, Kate, photograph. Reproduced by permission.

HILL, ELIZABETH STARR. ▌ Liu, Lesley, illustrator. From an illustration in *Chang and the Bamboo Flute,* by Elizabeth Starr Hill. Farrar, Straus, Giroux, 2002. Pictures © 2002 by Lesley Liu. Reproduced by permission of Farrar, Straus & Giroux LLC.

HUDAK, MICHAL. ▌ Hudak, Michal, illustrator. From an illustration in *The Shepherd and the 100 Sheep,* by Michal Hudak. Liturgical Press Books, 1999. © 1999 by The Order of St. Benedict, Inc. Reproduced by permission.

JENSON-ELLIOTT, CYNTHIA L(OUISE). ▌ From a photograph in *East Africa,* by Cynthia L. Jenson-Elliott. Lucent Books, Inc., 2002. Photograph © Corbis. Reproduced by permission.

KAYE, PEGGY. ▌ Howell, Dan, photographer. From a cover of *Games for Writing: Playful Ways to Help Your Child Learn to Write,* by Peggy Kaye. Farrar, Straus & Giroux, 1995. Reproduced by permission of Farrar, Straus & Giroux LLC.

KITAMURA, SATOSHI. ▌ Satoshi Kitamura, illustrator. From a cover of *Weblines,* by John Agard. Bloodaxe Books, 2000. Illustration © 2000 Satoshi Kitamura. Reproduced by permission./ Kitamura, Satoshi, illustrator. From an illustration in *A Boy Wants a Dinosaur,* by Hiawyn Oram. Farrar, 1991. Illustrations © 1990 by Satoshi Kitamura. Reproduced in the UK by permission Andersen Press, in the rest of the world by permission of Farrar, Straus and Giroux, LLC./ Satoshi Kitamura, illustrator. From an illustration in *Me and My Cat?,* by Satoshi Kitamura. Farrar, Straus, Giroux, 2000. © 1999 by Satoshi Kitamura. Reproduced in the UK by permission of Andersen Press, in the rest of the world by permission of Farrar, Straus & Giroux LLC.

KLINE, LISA WILLIAMS. ▌ Kline, Lisa Williams, photograph. Reproduced by permission.

KUSUGAK, MICHAEL (ARVAARLUK). ▌ Jacket of *Baseball Bats for Christmas,* by Michael Arvaarluk Kusugak. Annick Press Ltd., 1990. Reproduced by permission./ Krykorka, Vladyana Langer, illustrator. From an illustration in *Arctic Stories,* by Michael Kusugak. Annick Press Ltd., 1998. Illustrations © 1998 Vladyana Langer Krykorka. Reproduced by permission.

LAVENDER, WILLIAM D. ▌ Lavender, William D., photograph by Bill Edledge. Reproduced by permission.

LEGG, GERALD. ▌ Scrace, Carolyn, illustrator. From an illustration in *From Caterpillar to Butterfly,* by Dr. Gerald Legg. Franklin Watts, 1998. Reproduced by permission./ Bergin, Mark, illustrator. From an illustration in *Bears,* by Gerald Legg. Franklin Watts, 2002. Reproduced by permission.

LLEWELLYN, CLAIRE. ▌ Bricknell, Paul, photographer. From a cover of *My First Book of Time,* by Claire Llewellyn. Dorling Kindersley, 1992. Reproduced by permission./ Taylor, Myke, illustrator. From an illustration in *Some Plants Grow in Mid-Air: And Other Amazing Facts about Rainforests,* by Claire Llewellyn. Copper Beech Books, 1998. © Aladdin Books Ltd. 1998. Reproduced by permission./ Taylor, Myke, and Jo Moore, illustrators. From an illustration in *Spiders Have Fangs: And Other Amazing Facts about Arachnids,* by Claire Llewellyn. Copper Beech Books, 1997. © Aladdin Books Ltd. 1997. Reproduced by permission.

MALVASI, MEG GREENE. ▌ From a photograph in *The Russian Americans,* by Meg Greene Malvasi. Lucent Books, 2002. Photograph from the Library of Congress.

MODESITT, JEANNE. ▌ Modesitt, Jeanne, photograph. Reproduced by permission of Jeanne Modesitt.

MORPURGO, MICHAEL. ▌ Birmingham, Christian, illustrator. From an illustration in *The Silver Swan,* by Michael Morpurgo. Penguin Putnam Books for Young Readers, 2000. Pictures © 2000 by Christian Birmingham. Reproduced in the UK by permission of the illustrator, in the rest of the world by permission of Phyllis Fogelman Books, a division of Penguin Young Readers Group, A Member of Penguin Group (USA) Inc., 345 Hudson St., New York, NY 10014. All rights reserved./ DiCesare, Joe, illustrator. From a cover of *Waiting for Anya,* by Michael Morpurgo. Puffin Books, 1997. Cover illustration copyright © Joe DiCesare, 1997. Reproduced by permission of Puffin Books, A division of Penguin Young Readers Group, A Member of Penguin Group (USA) Inc., 345 Hudson St., New York, NY 10014. All rights reserved./ Rane, Walter, illustrator. From a cover of *Why the Whales Came,* by Michael Morpurgo. Scholastic, Inc., 1990. Cover illustration copyright © 1990 by Scholastic Inc. Reproduced by permission of Walter Rane./ Morpurgo, Michael, photograph by James Ravilions. Reproduced by permission of the Estate of James Ravilions.

MURPHY, KELLY. ▌ Murphy, Kelly, illustrator. From an illustration in *The Boll Weevil Ball,* by Kelly Murphy. Henry Holt and Company, 2002. © 2002 by Kelly Murphy. Reproduced by permission of Henry Holt and Company, LLC.

NELSON, THERESA. ▌ All photographs © 2003 Theresa Nelson. Reproduced by permission

NIX, GARTH. ▌ Rawlings, Steve, illustrator. From a cover of *The Fall,* by Garth Nix. Scholastic, 2000. Copyright © 2000 LucasFilm Ltd. & TM. All rights reserved. Reproduced by permission of LucasFilm Ltd. Unauthorized duplication is a violation of applicable law. /Nix, Garth, photograph by Janet Bradley. Reproduced by permission of Garth Nix.

PARKS, PEGGY J. ▌ From a photograph in *Teacher,* by Peggy J. Parks. KidHaven Press, 2003. Photograph © Corbis. Reproduced by permission./ Parks, Peggy J., pausing at Pere Marquette Beach, photograph. © 2002 Cathy Schroeder, Russell Photography. Reproduced by permission.

PASCAL, FRANCINE. ▌ Book covers photograph by St. Denis, from *Bad,* written by Francine Pascal. Pocket Books, 2001. Copyright © 2001 by Francine Pascal. Cover art copyright St. Denis.

Reproduced by permission./ St. Denis, photographer. From a cover of *Alone,* by Francine Pascal. Simon & Schuster, 2002. Cover photograph © 2002 by St. Denis. Cover © 2002 by 17th Street Productions, an Alloy, Inc. company. Reproduced by permission./ St. Denis, photographer. From a cover of *Before Gaia,* by Francine Pascal. Simon & Schuster, 2002. Cover photograph © 2002 by St. Denis. Cover © 2002 by 17th Street Productions, an Alloy, Inc. company. Reproduced by permission./ Pascal, Francine, photograph. Reproduced by permission of Francine Pascal.

RIORDAN, JAMES. ❚ Hall, Amanda, illustrator. From an illustration in *Stories from the Sea,* compiled by James Riordan. Abbeville Kids, 1996. Illustrations © 1996 by Amanda Hall. Reproduced by permission./ Lennox, Elsie, illustrator. From a cover of *A Treasury of Irish Stories,* edited by James Riordan. Kingfisher, 1995. Cover illustration © Elsie Lennox 1995. Reproduced by permission of Elsie Lennox.

ROLEFF, TAMARA L. ❚ Berman, Nina, photographer. From a cover of *Native American Rights,* by Tamara Roleff. Greenhaven Press, 1998. Reproduced by permission of Nina Berman/Sipa Press./ From an illustration in *Hate Groups,* by Tamara L. Roleff. Greenhaven Press, 2001. The Library of Congress./ Roleff, Tamara L., photograph. Reproduced by permission.

ST. JOHN, NICOLE. ❚ All photographs © 2002 Nicole St. John. Reproduced by permission.

SAMPSON, MICHAEL ❚ Raschka, Chris, illustrator. From an illustration in *I Pledge Allegiance,* by Michael Sampson and Bill Martin, Jr. Candlewick Press, 2002. Illustration copyright © 2002 Chris Raschka. Reproduced by permission of the publisher Candlewick Press, Inc., Cambridge, MA./ Rand, Ted, illustrator. From an illustration in *The Football That Won . . .,* by Michael Sampson. Henry Holt and Company, 1996. Illustration copyright © 1996 by Ted Rand. Reproduced by permission of Henry Holt and Company, LLC./ Sampson, Michael, photograph. Reproduced by permission of Michael Sampson.

SHANNON, GEORGE (WILLIAM BONES). ❚ Shannon, George, photograph. Reproduced by permission.

STEWART, SARAH. ❚ Small, David, illustrator. From an illustration in *The Gardener,* by Sarah Stewart. Farrar, Straus, Giroux, 2000.

Illustrations © 1997 by David Small. Reproduced by permission of Farrar, Straus & Giroux LLC./ Small, David, illustrator. From an illustration in *The Journey,* by Sarah Stewart. Farrar, Straus, Giroux, 2001. Illustrations © 2001 by David Small. Reproduced by permission of Farrar, Straus & Giroux LLC./ Small, David, illustrator. From an illustration in *The Library,* by Sarah Stewart. Farrar, Straus & Giroux, 1999. Pictures © 1995 by David Small. Reproduced by permission of Farrar, Straus & Giroux LLC./ Small, David, illustrator. From an illustration in *The Money Tree,* by Sarah Stewart. Farrar, Straus & Giroux, 1994. Pictures © 1991 by David Small. Reproduced by permission of Farrar, Straus & Giroux LLC.

TOLBERT, STEVE. ❚ Tolbert, Steve, photograph. © 2003 Steve Tolbert. Reproduced by permission.

WAYLAND, APRIL HALPRIN. ❚ Aurness, Craig, photographer. From a jacket of *Girl Coming in for a Landing: A Novel in Poems,* by April Halprin Wayland. Knopf, 2002. Jacket photograph © 2002 by Craig Aurness/Corbis. Reproduced by permission of Alfred A. Knopf, an imprint of Random House Children's Books, a division of Random House, Inc.

WELTON, JUDE. ❚ From a cover of *Impressionism,* by Jude Welton. Dorling Kindersley, 2000. © 2000 Dorling Kindersley Limited. Reproduced by permission.

WOOLDRIDGE, CONNIE NORDHIELM. ❚ Rogers, Jacqueline, illustrator. From an illustration in *When Esther Morris Headed West: Women, Wyoming, and the Right to Vote,* by Connie Nordhielm Wooldridge. Holiday House, 2001. Illustrations © 2001 by Jacqueline Rogers. Reproduced by permission./ Wooldridge, Connie Nordhielm, photograph. Reproduced by permission of Connie Nordhielm Wooldridge.

YEE, PAUL (R.) ❚ Chan, Harvey, illustrator. From an illustration in *Dead Man's Gold and Other Stories,* by Paul Yee. Groundwood Books, 2002. Illustrations © 2002 by Harvey Chan. Reproduced by permission./ Lin, Grace, illustrator. From an illustration in *The Jade Necklace,* by Paul Yee. Crocodile Books, 2002. Illustrations © Grace Lin 2002. Reproduced by permission./ McGaw, Laurie, illustrator. From a cover of *Breakaway,* by Paul Yee. Groundwood Books, 1997. Reproduced by permission of Groundwood Books/ Douglas & McIntyre./ Yee, Paul, photograph. © 2003 Paul Yee. Reproduced by permission.

something ABOUT the AUTHOR

ADA, Alma Flor 1938-

Personal

Born January 3, 1938, in Camagüey, Cuba; daughter of Modesto A. (a professor) and Alma (a teacher and certified public accountant; maiden name, Lafuente) Ada; married Armando Zubizarreta, 1961 (divorced, 1971); married Jörgen Voss, 1984 (divorced, 1995); children: (first marriage) Rosalma, Alfonso, Miguel, Gabriel. *Education:* Universidad Complutense de Madrid, received diploma, 1959; Pontificia Universidad Católica del Perú, M.A., 1963, Ph.D., 1965; Harvard University, postdoctoral study, 1965-67.

Addresses

Home—1459 18th St. #138, San Francisco, CA 94107-2801. *Office*—School of Education, University of San Francisco, 2130 Fulton St., San Francisco, CA 94117-1071.

Career

Colegio A. von Humboldt, Lima, Perú, head of Spanish department, 1963-65, 1967-69; Emory University, Atlanta, GA, associate professor of Romance languages, 1970-72; Mercy College of Detroit, Detroit, MI, professor, 1973-75; University of San Francisco, San Francisco, CA, professor of education, 1976—, and director of Center for Multicultural Literature for Children and Young Adults. University of Guam, Agaña, Guam, visiting professor, summer, 1978; University of Texas, El Paso, TX, visiting professor, summer, 1979, winter,

Alma Flor Ada

1991; Universidad Complutense, Madrid, Spain, visiting professor, summers, 1989, 1990, 1991; St. Thomas University, Houston, TX, visiting professor, summers, 1992, 1993; Fundación José Ortega y Gassett, Madrid, Spain, summers, 1996, 1997, 1998. Member of selection committee, Fulbright Overseas Fellowship Program, 1968-69, 1977-78; chairperson, National Seminar on Bilingual education, 1974, National Policy Conference on Bilingualism in Higher Education, 1978, and International Congress of Children's Literature in Spanish, 1978, 1979, 1981; publishing consultant, 1975-95; member of the board, Books for Youth and Children's Television Workshop's *Sesame Street* in Spanish; *Loose Leaf; Between the Lions; Journal of Latinos in Education;* founder and first editor-in-chief of *Journal of the National Association for Bilingual Education;* Reading the World annual conference, University of San Francisco, faculty advisor.

Member

International Reading Association; International Board of Books for Young Children (IBBY); National Association for Bilingual Education (founding member of the Michigan and Illinois branches); California Association for Bilingual Education.

Awards, Honors

Fulbright scholar, 1965-67; grants from Institute for International Education, 1965-67, Emory University, 1971, and Michigan Endowment for the Arts, 1974; Mary Bunting Institute scholar at Radcliffe College and Harvard University, 1966-68; University of San Francisco Distinguished Research Award from the School of Education, 1984; Marta Salotti Gold Medal (Argentian), 1989, for *Encaje de piedra;* University of San Francisco Outstanding Teacher Award, 1985; Christopher Award (ages eight-ten), 1992, and Notable Children's Trade Book in the Field of Social Studies, National Council for the Social Studies/Children's Book Council, both for *The Gold Coin;* Parents' Choice Honor Book, 1995, for *Dear Peter Rabbit;* Aesop Accolade from the American Folklore Association and American Booksellers "Pick of the List," both 1995, for *Mediopollito/Half-Chicken;* Simon Wiesenthal Museum of Tolerance Award, 1998, for *Gathering the Sun;* Gold Medal, *Parenting* magazine, 1998, for *The Lizard and the Sun;* Marta Salotti Award (Argentina), for *Encaje de piedra;* California PTA Association Yearly Award; Latina Writers' Award, José Martí World Award (Costa Rica), and San Francisco Public Library Laurate, all 2000; Purá Belpré Award, American Library Association, 2000, for *Under the Royal Palms.*

Writings

FOR CHILDREN

(With Maria del Pilar de Olave) *El enanito de la pared y otras historias* (title means "The Wall's Dwarf and Other Tales"), Editorial Arica (Lima, Peru), 1974.

(With Maria del Pilar de Olave) *Las pintas de la mariquitas* (title means "The Ladybug's Dots"), Editorial Arica (Lima, Peru), 1974.

(With Maria del Pilar de Olave) *Saltarín y sus dos amigas y otras historias* (title means "Springy and His Two Friends and Other Stories"), Editorial Arica (Lima, Peru), 1974.

(With Maria del Pilar de Olave) *La gallinita costurera y otras historias* (title means "The Little Hen Who Enjoyed Sewing and Other Stories"), Editorial Arica (Lima, Peru), 1974.

Amigos/Friends, illustrated by Barry Koch, Santillana USA Publishing (Miami, FL), 1989.

¿Quién nacera aquí?/Who's Hatching Here?, illustrated by Viví Escriv´, Santillana USA Publishing (Miami, FL), 1989.

Me gustaría tener/How Happy I Would Be, Santillana USA Publishing (Miami, FL), 1989.

El canto del mosquito/The Song of the Teeny-Tiny Mosquito, Santillana USA Publishing (Miami, FL), 1989.

Una extraña visita/Strange Visitors, Santillana USA Publishing (Miami, FL), 1989.

The Gold Coin, translated from the Spanish by Bernice Randall, illustrated by Neil Waldman, Atheneum (New York, NY), 1991, published as *La moneda de oro,* Turtleback Books (Madison, WI), 1996.

(With daughter, Rosalma Zubizarreta) *Despues de la tormenta/After the Storm,* illustrated by Viví Escriv´, Santillana USA Publishing (Compton, CA), 1991.

(With Rosalma Zubizarreta) *La piñata vacia/The Empty Piñata,* illustrated by Viví Escriv´, Santillana USA Publishing (Compton, CA), 1991.

(With Rosalma Zubizarreta) *La jaula dorada/The Golden Cage,* illustrated by Viví Escriv´, Santillana USA Publishing (Compton, CA), 1991.

(With Rosalma Zubizarreta) *Como nació el arco iris/How the Rainbow Came to Be,* illustrated by Viví Escriv´, Santillana USA Publishing (Compton, CA), 1991.

(With Rosalma Zubizarreta) *No quiero derretirme/I Don't Want to Melt,* illustrated by Viví Escriv´, Santillana USA Publishing (Compton, CA), 1991.

(With Rosalma Zubizarreta) *La hamaca de la vaca, o, Un amigo mas/In the Cow's Backyard,* illustrated by Viví Escriv´, Santillana USA Publishing (Compton, CA), 1991.

(With Rosalma Zubizarreta) *No fui yo . . ./It Wasn't Me,* illustrated by Viví Escriv´, Santillana USA Publishing (Compton, CA), 1991.

(With Rosalma Zubizarreta) *Rosa alada/A Rose with Wings,* illustrated by Viví Escriv´, Santillana USA Publishing (Compton, CA), 1991.

(With Rosalma Zubizarreta) *La sorpresa de Mamá Coneja/A Surprise for Mother Rabbit,* illustrated by Viví Escriv´, Santillana USA Publishing (Compton, CA), 1991.

(With Rosalma Zubizarreta) *¿Pavo para la Cena de Gracias? ¡No, gracias!/Turkey for Thanksgiving? No Thanks!,* illustrated by Viví Escriv´, Santillana USA Publishing (Compton, CA), 1991.

(With Rosalma Zubizarreta) *¿El susto de los fantasmas?/What Are Ghosts Afraid Of?,* illustrated by Viví Escriv´, Santillana USA Publishing (Compton, CA), 1991.

Los seis deseos de la jirafa, illustrated by Doug Roy, Hampton-Brown Books (Carmel, CA), 1992, translated by Shirleyann Costigan as *Giraffe's Sad Tale (with a Happy Ending),* Hampton-Brown Books (Carmel, CA), 1992.

Una semilla nada más, illustrated by Frank Remkiewicz, Hampton-Brown Books (Carmel, CA), 1992, translated by Shirleyann Costigan as *Just One Seed,* Hampton-Brown Books (Carmel, CA), 1992.

Serafina's Birthday, illustrated by Louise Bates Satterfield, translated from the Spanish by Ana M. Cerro, Atheneum (New York, NY), 1992.

(With Rosalma Zubizarreta) *El papalote/The Kite,* illustrated by Viví Escriv´, Santillana USA Publishing (Compton, CA), 1992.

(With Janet Thorne and Philip Wingeier-Rayo) *Choices and Other Stories from the Caribbean,* illustrated by Maria Antonia Ordonez, Friendship Press (New York, NY), 1993.

Barquitos de papel/Paper Boats, illustrated by Pablo Torrecilla, Laredo Publishing (Beverly Hills, CA), 1993.

Barriletes/Kites, illustrated by Pablo Torrecilla, Laredo Publishing (Beverly Hills, CA), 1993.

Canción de todos los niños del mundo (title means "Song of All Children of the World"), Houghton Mifflin (Boston, MA), 1993.

Días de circo, Laredo Publishing (Beverly Hills, CA), 1993, translation by Rosalma Zubizarreta published as *Circus Time,* Laredo Publishing (Beverly Hills, CA), 1993.

La tataranieta de cucarachita Martina/The Great-great-granddaughter of La Cucarachita Martina, illustrated by Ana López Escrivá, Scholastic (New York, NY), 1993.

Me gusta . . . (title means, "I Like . . ."), illustrated by Denise y Fernando, Houghton Mifflin (Boston, MA), 1993.

¡Me gusta jugar! (title means, "I Like to Play!"), illustrated by Jon Godell, McGraw Hill (New York, NY), 1993.

(With Rosalma Zubizarreta) *Olmo y la mariposa azul,* illustrated by Viví Escriv´, Laredo Publishing (Torrance, CA), 1992, translation by Rosalma Zubizarreta published as *Olmo and the Blue Butterfly,* Laredo Publishing (Beverly Hills, CA), 1995.

El pañuelo de seda, illustrated by Viví Escriv´, Laredo Publishing (Torrance, CA), 1993, translation by Rosalma Zubizarreta published as *The Silk Scarf,* Laredo Publishing (Beverly Hills, CA), 1995.

Pin, pin, sarabín, illustrated by Pablo Torrecilla, Laredo Publishing (Beverly Hills, CA), 1993.

Pregones, illustrated by Pablo Torrecilla, Laredo Publishing (Torrance, CA), 1993, translation by Rosalma Zubizarreta published as *Vendor's Calls,* Laredo Publishing (Beverly Hills, CA), 1995.

El reino de la geometría, illustrated by José Ramón Sánchez, Laredo Publishing (Torrance, CA), 1993, translation by Rosalma Zubizarreta published as *The Kingdom of Geometry,* Laredo Publishing (Beverly Hills, CA), 1995.

(Reteller) *The Rooster Who Went to His Uncle's Wedding: A Latin American Folktale,* illustrated by Kathleen Kuchera, Putnam (New York, NY), 1993, published as

El gallo que fue a la boda de su tio, PaperStar (New York, NY), 1998.

(With Rosalma Zubizarreta) *Dear Peter Rabbit,* illustrated by Leslie Tryon, Atheneum (New York, NY), 1994, published as *Querido Pedrin,* Turtleback Books (Madison, WI), 1997.

En el barrio/In the Barrio, illustrated by Liliana Wilson Grez, Scholastic (New York, NY), 1994.

(With Rosalma Zubizarreta) *El unicornio del oeste/The Unicorn of the West,* illustrated by Abigail Pizer, Atheneum (New York, NY), 1994.

Me encantan los sabados . . . and Saturdays too, illustrated by Michael Bryant, Atheneum (New York, NY), 1994, English translation published as *I Love Saturdays y Domingos,* illustrated by Elivia Savadier, Atheneum (New York, NY), 1998.

El ratón de la ciudad y el ratón del campo, Grosset & Dunlap (New York, NY), 1994.

Los tres gatitos, Grosset & Dunlap (New York, NY), 1994.

Y colorín colorado, Turtleback Books (Madison, WI), 1995.

(With Pam Schiller) *A Chance for Esperanza/La oportunidad de Esperanza,* McGraw Hill (New York, NY), 1995.

Bernice the Barnacle/Más poderoso que yo, illustrated by Viví Escriv´, McGraw Hill (New York, NY), 1995.

(With Rosalma Zubizarreta) *Mediopollito/Half-Chicken: A New Version of a Traditional Story* (bilingual edition), illustrated by Kim Howard, Doubleday (New York, NY), 1995.

Mi mamá siembra fresas/My Mother Plants Strawberries, illustrated by Larry Ramond, McGraw Hill (New York, NY), 1995.

El vuelo de los colibríes (title means "The Hummingbirds' Flight"), illustrated by Judith Jacobson, Laredo Publishing (Beverly Hills, CA), 1995.

Jordi's Star, illustrated by Susan Gaber, Putnam (New York, NY), 1996.

(With Rosalma Zubizarreta) *The Lizard and the Sun/La lagartija y el sol: A Folktale in English and Spanish,* illustrated by Felipe Dávalos, Doubleday (New York, NY), 1997.

El árbol de Navidad/The Christmas Tree (bilingual edition), illustrated by Viví Escriv´, Santillana USA Publishing (Miami, FL), 1997, new edition, illustrated by Terry Ybanez, Hyperion (New York, NY), 1997.

The Malachite Palace, illustrated by Leonid Gore, translation by Rosalma Zubizarreta, Atheneum (New York, NY), 1998.

Yours Truly, Goldilocks, illustrated by Leslie Tryon, Atheneum (New York, NY), 1998.

En la playa (title means "At the Beach"), illustrated by Roberta Ludlow, Harcourt (Orlando, FL), 1999.

Three Golden Oranges, illustrated by Reg Cartwright, Atheneum (New York, NY), 1999.

Daniel's Mystery Egg, illustrated by G. Brian Karas, Harcourt (San Diego, CA), 2000.

Friend Frog, illustrated by Lori Lohstoeter, Harcourt (San Diego, CA), 2000.

Daniel's Pet, illustrated by G. Brian Karas, Harcourt, (San Diego, CA), 2001.

En el mar (title means "In the Ocean"), illustrated by Richard Bernal, Harcourt (Orlando, FL), 2001.

In her retelling of a Hispanic folktale, Ada portrays three brothers who are sent on a quest to an enchanted castle in search of women who will be their perfect mates. (From Three Golden Oranges, *illustrated by Reg Cartwright.)*

With Love, Little Red Hen, illustrated by Leslie Tryon, Atheneum (New York, NY), 2001.

(With Douglas Hill) *Brujas y magos,* Santillana USA Publishing (Miami, FL), 2002.

Also author of *Así pasaron muchos años; Canción y alegría;* (with F. Isabel Campoy) *Cieto abierto; En un lugar muy lejano; Erase que se era; Letters; ¿Quieres que te cuente?; The New Hamster;* and *Y fueron felices.*

POETRY

Una vez en el madio del mar (title means "Once Upon a Time in the Middle of the Sea"), illustrated by Ulises Wensell, Escuela Española (Madrid, Spain), 1987.

A la sombra de un ala (title means "Under the Shade of a Wing"), illustrated by Ulises Wensell, Escuela Española (Madrid, Spain), 1988.

Abecedario de los animales (title means "An Animal ABC"), illustrated by Viví Escriv´, Espasa-Calpe (Madrid, Spain), 1990.

(With Rosalma Zubizarreta) *Gathering the Sun: An ABC in Spanish and English,* illustrated by Simón Silva, English Lothrop (New York, NY), 1997.

Coral y espuma (title means "Coral and Foam"), illustrated by Viví Escriv´, Espasa-Calpe (Madrid, Spain), 2003.

CHAPTER BOOKS

Encaje de piedra (title means "Stone Lace"), illustrated by Kitty Lorefice de Passalia, Editorial Guadalupe (Buenos Aires, Argentina), 1989.

El manto de pluma y otros cuentos (title means "The Feather Cloak and Other Stories"), illustrated by Viví Escriv´, Alfaguara (Compton, CA), 1990.

My Name Is María Isabel, translated from the Spanish by Ana M. Cerro, illustrated by K. Dyble Thompson, Atheneum (New York, NY), 1993, published as *Me llamo María Isabel,* Macmillan (New York, NY), 1994.

¿Quién cuida al cocodrilo? (title means "Who Will Keep the Crocodile?"), illustrated by Viví Escriv´, Espasa-Calpe (Madrid, Spain), 1994.

(With F. Isabel Campoy) *Ecos del pasado* (title means "Echoes from the Past"), Harcourt Brace (Orlando, FL), 1996.

PLAYS; WITH F. ISABEL CAMPOY

Primer Acto, Harcourt School Publishers (Orlando, FL), 1996.

Risas y aplausos, Harcourt School Publishers (Orlando, FL), 1996.

Escenas y alegrías, Harcourt School Publishers (Orlando, FL), 1996.

Actores y flores, Harcourt School Publishers (Orlando, FL), 1996.

Saludos al público, Harcourt School Publishers (Orlando, FL), 1996.

Ensayo general, Harcourt School Publishers (Orlando, FL), 1996.

Acto final, Harcourt School Publishers (Orlando, FL), 1996.

Rat-a-Tat, Alfaguara (Miami, FL), 2000, published as *Rat-a-Tat Cat,* Santillana USA Publishing (Miami, FL), 2002.

Roll 'n' Roll, Alfaguara (Miami, FL), 2000, published as *Roll 'n' Role,* Santillana USA Publishing (Miami, FL), 2002.

Top Hat, Alfaguara (Miami, FL), 2000.

Curtains Up!, Alfaguara (Miami, FL), 2000.

FOR CHILDREN; WITH F. ISABEL CAMPOY

Sigue la palabra, Harcourt School Publishers (Orlando, FL), 1995.

Imágenes del pasado, Harcourt School Publishers (Orlando, FL), 1995.

Música amiga (anthology of Hispanic folklore; includes tapes and teacher's guide), ten volumes, Del Sol (Westlake, OH), 1996-98.

Una semilla de luz (title means "A Seed of Light"), illustrated by Felipe Dávalos, Alfaguara (Madrid, Spain), 2000.

Tablado de Doña Rosita/Curtain's Up, Santillana USA Publishing (Miami, FL), 2001.

¡Feliz cumpleaños, Caperucita Roja!/Happy Birthday, Little Red Riding Hood! (bilingual edition), illustrated by Ana López Escrivá, Alfaguara (Miami, FL), 2002.

El nuevo hogar de los siete cabritos/The New Home of the Seven Billy Goats, illustrated by Viví Escrivá, Alfaguara (Miami, FL), 2002.

A New Job for Pérez the Mouse/Ratoncito Perez, Cartero, illustrated by Sandra López Escrivá, Alfaguara (Miami, FL), 2002.

One, Two, Three, Who Can It Be?/Uno, dos, tres: ¿Dime quién es?, illustrated by Viví Escrivá, Alfaguara (Miami, FL), 2002.

On the Wings of the Condor/En alas del condor, Alfaguara (Miami, FL), 2002.

Eyes of the Jaguar/Ojos del jaguar, Alfaguara (Miami, FL), 2002.

Friends from A to Z: A Glossary of the Hispanic World/ Amigos de la A a la Z: Un alfabeto del mundo hispánico, Santillana USA Publishing (Miami, FL), 2002.

The Quetzal's Journey/Vuelo del quetzal, illustrated by Felipe Davalos, Santillana USA Publishing (Miami, FL), 2002.

POETRY; IN SPANISH; WITH F. ISABEL CAMPOY

Gorrión, Gorrión, Harcourt School Publishers (Orlando, FL), 1996.

El verde limón, Harcourt School Publishers (Orlando, FL), 1996.

La rama azul, Harcourt School Publishers (Orlando, FL), 1996.

Nuevo día, Harcourt School Publishers (Orlando, FL), 1996.

Huertos de coral, Harcourt School Publishers (Orlando, FL), 1996.

Ríos de lava, Harcourt School Publishers (Orlando, FL), 1996.

Dulce es la sal, Harcourt School Publishers (Orlando, FL), 1996.

Canta la letra, illustrated by Ulises Wensell, Del Sol (Westlake, OH), 1998, with music by Suni Paz, 2003.

Caracolí, illustrated by Ulises Wensell, Del Sol (Westlake, OH), 1998, with music by Suni Paz, 2003.

Con ton y son, illustrated by Ulises Wensell, Del Sol (Westlake, OH), 1998, with music by Suni Paz, 2003.

Corre al coro, illustrated by Ulises Wensell, Del Sol (Westlake, OH), 1998, with music by Suni Paz, 2003.

¡Do, re, mi, sí, sí!, illustrated by Ulises Wensell, Del Sol (Westlake, OH), 1998, with music by Suni Paz, 2003.

El camino de tu risa, illustrated by Ulises Wensell, Del Sol (Westlake, OH), 1998, with music by Suni Paz, 2003.

El son de sol, illustrated by Ulises Wensell, Del Sol (Westlake, OH), 1998, with music by Suni Paz, 2003.

¡Qué rica la ronda!, illustrated by Ulises Wensell, Del Sol (Westlake, OH), 1998, with music by Suni Paz, 2003.

Sigue la música, illustrated by Ulises Wensell, Del Sol (Westlake, OH), 1998, with music by Suni Paz, 2003.

"HAGAMOS CAMINOS" SERIES; WITH MARIA DEL PILAR DE OLAVE

Partimos (title means "We Start"), illustrated by Ulises Wensell, Addison-Wesley (Reading, MA), 1986.

Andamos (title means "We Walk"), illustrated by Ulises Wensell, Addison-Wesley (Reading, MA), 1986.

Corremos (title means "We Run"), illustrated by Ulises Wensell, Addison-Wesley (Reading, MA), 1986.

Volamos (title means "We Fly"), illustrated by Ulises Wensell, Addison-Wesley (Reading, MA), 1986.

Navegamos (title means "We Sail"), illustrated by Ulises Wensell, Addison-Wesley (Reading, MA), 1986.

Exploramos (title means "We Explore"), illustrated by Ulises Wensell, Addison-Wesley (Reading, MA), 1986.

"GATEWAYS TO THE SUN" SERIES; WITH F. ISABEL CAMPOY

Smiles/Sonrisas (biographies of Pablo Picasso, Gabriela Mistral, and Benito Juarez), Alfaguara (Miami, FL), 1998.

Steps/Pasos (biographies of Rita Moreno, Fernando Botero, and Evelyn Cisneros), Alfaguara (Miami, FL), 1998.

Voices/Voces (biographies of Luis Valdez, Judith F. Baca, and Carlos J. Finlay), Alfaguara (Miami, FL), 1998.

Paths/Caminos (biographies of José Marti, Frida Kahlo, and Cesar Chavez), Alfaguara (Miami, FL), 1998.

Yo/I Am, Santillana USA Publishing (Miami, FL), 1999.

Rimas/Rhymes, Santillana USA Publishing (Miami, FL), 1999.

Poemas/Poems, Santillana USA Publishing (Miami, FL), 1999.

Palabras, Santillana USA Publishing (Miami, FL), 1999.

Mis relatos/My Stories, Santillana USA Publishing (Miami, FL), 1999.

Mis recuerdos, Santillana USA Publishing (Miami, FL), 1999.

Mambru, Santillana USA Publishing (Miami, FL), 1999.

Letras, Santillana USA Publishing (Miami, FL), 1999.

Lapices/Pencils, Santillana USA Publishing (Miami, FL), 1999.

Crayones/Crayons, Santillana USA Publishing (Miami, FL), 1999.

Colores/Colors, Santillana USA Publishing (Miami, FL), 1999.

Así soy/This Is Me, Santillana USA Publishing (Miami, FL), 1999.

Acuarela, Santillana USA Publishing (Miami, FL), 1999.

Blue and Green/Azul y Verde, Alfaguara (Miami, FL), 2000.

Brush and Paint/Brocha y pinchel, Alfaguara (Miami, FL), 2000.

Artist's Easel/Caballete, Alfaguara (Miami, FL), 2000.

Canvas and Paper/Lienzo y Papel, Alfaguara (Miami, FL), 2000.

(Selector) *Dreaming Fish/Pimpón* (poetry), Alfaguara (Miami, FL), 2000.

(Selector) *Laughing Crocodiles/Antón Pirulero* (poetry), Alfaguara (Miami, FL), 2000.

(Selector) *Singing Horse/Mambrú* (poetry), Alfaguara (Miami, FL), 2000.

(Selector and contributor) *Flying Dragon* (published in Spanish as *Chuchurumbé*), Alfaguara (Miami, FL), 2000.

TEXTBOOKS AND EDUCATIONAL PUBLICATIONS

Sale el oso ("Big Book, Rimas y Risas Green" series), illustrated by Amy Myers, Hampton-Brown Books (Carmel, CA), 1988.

¡Manzano, Manzano!, illustrated by Sandra C. Kalthoff, Hampton-Brown Books (Carmel, CA), 1989.

El oso mas elegante, illustrated by Sandra C. Kalthoff, Hampton-Brown Books (Carmel, CA), 1989.

Cassette Guide: Culture through Literature and Music (Spanish Elementary series), illustrated by Jan Mayer, Addison-Wesley (Reading, MA), 1989.

Sol Kit, Addison-Wesley (Reading, MA), 1989.

Whole Language and Literature: A Practical Guide, Addison-Wesley (Reading, MA), 1990.

Cinco pollitos y otras poesías favoritas: Tan Small Book Set ("Días y Días de Poesía" series), Hampton-Brown Books (Carmel, CA), 1991.

Classroom Set: Tan Set ("Días y Días de Poesía" series), Hampton-Brown Books (Carmel, CA), 1991.

El patio de mi casa ("Early Learning Packs" series), illustrated by Liz Callen, Hampton-Brown Books (Carmel, CA), 1991.

Caballito blanco y otras poesías favoritas: Green Small Book Set ("Días y Días de Poesía" series), Hampton-Brown Books (Carmel, CA), 1992.

Chart Set: Green Set ("Días y Días de Poesía" series), Hampton-Brown Books (Carmel, CA), 1992.

Classroom Set: Green Set ("Días y Días de Poesía" series), Hampton-Brown Books (Carmel, CA), 1992.

Días y días de poesía: Complete Program (available with small books or tapes), Hampton-Brown Books (Carmel, CA), 1992.

Bear's Walk ("ESL Theme Links" series), illustrated by Jan Myers, Hampton-Brown Books (Carmel, CA), 1993.

(With Violet J. Harris and Lee Bennett Hopkins) *A Chorus of Cultures: Developing Literacy through Multicultural Poetry* (anthology), illustrated by Morissa Lipstein, Hampton-Brown Books (Carmel, CA), 1993.

Hampton-Brown Pre-K Program, Hampton-Brown Books (Carmel, CA), 1993.

(Editor, with Josefina Villamil Tinajero) *The Power of Two Languages: Literacy and Biliteracy for Spanish-Speaking Students,* Macmillan/McGraw-Hill (New York, NY), 1993.

Actividades para el hogar, Santillana USA Publishing (Miami, FL), 2001.

Teatro del gato garabato, Santillana USA Publishing (Miami, FL), 2001.

Teatrín de Don Crispin, Santillana USA Publishing (Miami, FL), 2001.

Stories the Year 'Round/Cuentos para todo el año, Santillana USA Publishing (Miami, FL), 2001.

Cuentos para todo el año: Cuaderno de actividades, Santillana USA Publishing (Miami, FL), 2001.

Stories for the Telling/Libros para contar, Santillana USA Publishing (Miami, FL), 2001.

Guía del Maestro, Santillana USA Publishing (Miami, FL), 2001.

Escenario de Polichinela, Santillana USA Publishing (Miami, FL), 2001.

A Magical Encounter: Latino Children's Literature in the Classroom, Santillana USA Publishing (Compton, CA), 1994, 2nd edition, Allyn & Bacon (Boston, MA), 2003.

(With Pam Schiller) *DLM Pre-Kindergarten and Kindergarten Early Childhood Programs,* McGraw-Hill (New York, NY), 1995.

(With Colin Baker) *Guía para padres y maestros de niños bilingües,* Multilingual Matters (Clevedon, England), 2002.

(With F. Isabel Campoy and Rosalma Zubizarreta) *Authors in the Classroom: A Transformative Education Process,* Allyn & Bacon (Boston, MA), 2004.

Also author of *Transformative Family Literacy: Engaging in Meaningful Dialogue with Spanish-Speaking Parents.*

COMPILER

Poesía menuda (anthology; title means "Tiny Poetry"), Editorial Arica (Lima, Peru), 1970.

Poesía pequeña (anthology; title means "Little Poetry"), Editorial Arica (Lima, Peru), 1973.

Poesía niña (anthology; title means "Child Poetry"), Editorial Arica (Lima, Peru), 1973.

Poesía infantil (anthology; title means "Poetry for Children"), Editorial Arica (Lima, Peru), 1974.

Fabulas de siempre (title means "Everlasting Fables"), Editorial Arica (Lima, Peru), 1974.

Cuentos en verso (title means "Stories in Verse"), Editorial Arica (Lima, Peru), 1974.

Vamos a leer (title means "Let's Read"), Editorial Arica (Lima, Peru), 1974.

Adivina adivinador (title means "A Collection of Traditional Riddles"), Editorial Arica (Lima, Peru), 1974.

El nacimiento del Imperio Incaico (history; title means "The Origins of the Inca Empire"), Editorial Arica (Lima, Peru), 1974.

El descubrimiento de America (history; title means "The Discovery of the New World"), Editorial Arica (Lima, Peru), 1974.

El sueño de San Martín (history; title means "San Martin's Dream"), Editorial Arica (Lima, Peru), 1974.

Las aceitunas y la cuchara (plays; title means "The Olives and the Wooden Spoon"), Editorial Arica (Lima, Peru), 1974.

La condesita peregrina y la desposada del rey (plays; title means "The Wandering Countess and The King's Bride"), Editorial Arica (Lima, Peru), 1974.

El cuento del gato y otras poesías favoritas, Hampton-Brown Books (Carmel, CA), 1992.

(With F. Isabel Campoy) *Pío peep!: Traditional Spanish Nursery Rhymes* (bilingual edition), illustrated by Viví Escriv´, English adaptations by Alice Schertle, HarperCollins (New York, NY), 2003.

TRANSLATOR

Lucille Clifton, *El niño que no creía en la primavera,* illustrated by Brinton Turkle, Dutton (New York, NY), 1975 (originally published as *The Boy Who Didn't Believe in Spring*).

Evaline Ness, *¿Tienes tiempo, Lidia?*, illustrated by the author, Dutton (New York, NY), 1975 (originally published as *Do You Have Time, Lydia?*).

Norma Simon, *Cuando me enojo,* illustrated by Dora Leder, A. Whitman (Chicago, IL), 1976 (originally published as *When I Get Mad*).

Judith Vigna, *Gregorio y sus puntos,* illustrated by the author, A. Whitman (Chicago, IL), 1977 (originally published as *Gregory's Stitches*).

Barbara Williams, *El dolor de muelas de Alberto,* illustrated by Kay Chorao, Dutton (New York, NY), 1977 (originally published as *Albert's Toothache*).

Barbara Brenner, *Caras,* photographs by George Ancona, Dutton (New York, NY), 1977 (originally published as *Faces*).

Mary Garcia, *The Adventures of Connie and Diego/Las aventuras de Connie y Diego,* illustrated by Malaquis Montoya, Children's Book Press (San Francisco, CA), 1978.

Lila Perl, *Piñatas and Paper Flowers/Piñatas y flores de papel: Holidays of the Americas in English and Spanish,* illustrated by Victori de Larrea, Clarion Books (New York, NY), 1982.

Harriet Rohmer, *The Legend of Food Mountain/La leyenda de la montaña del alimento,* illustrated by Graciella Carrillo, Children's Book Press (San Francisco, CA), 1982.

Judy Blume, *¿Estás ahí, Dios? Soy yo, Margaret,* Bradbury Press (Scarsdale, NY), 1983 (originally published as *Are You There, God? It's Me, Margaret*).

Judy Blume, *La ballena,* Bradbury Press (Scarsdale, NY), 1983 (originally published as *Blubber*).

Donald Charles, *El año de gato Galano,* illustrated by the author, Children's Book Press (San Francisco, CA), 1985 (originally published as *Calico Cat's Year*).

Judith Viorst, *Alexander y el día terrible, horrible, espantoso, horroso,* illustrated by Ray Cruz, Macmillan (New York, NY), 1989 (originally published as *Alexander and the Terrible, Horrible, No Good, Very Bad Day*).

Judith Viorst, *Alexander, que era rico el domingo pasado,* illustrated by Ray Cruz, Macmillan (New York, NY), 1989 (originally published as *Alexander, Who Was Rich Last Sunday*).

Robert Baden, *Y domingo, siete,* edited by Judith Mathews, illustrated by Michelle Edwards, A. Whitman (Chicago, IL), 1990.

Watty Piper, *La pequeña locomotora que si pudo,* illustrated by Doris Hauman, Putnam (New York, NY), 1992 (originally published as *The Little Engine That Could*).

Ruth Heller, *Las gallinas no son las unicas,* Grosset & Dunlap, 1992 (originally published as *Chickens Aren't the Only Ones*).

Val Willis, *El secreto en la caja de fosforos,* illustrated by John Shelley, Farrar, Straus (New York, NY), 1993 (originally published as *The Secret in the Matchbox*).

(With Rosalma Zubizarreta) Harriet Rohmer, *Uncle Nacho's Hat/El sombrero del tío Nacho,* illustrated by Mira Reisberg, Children's Book Press (San Francisco, CA), 1993.

Karen Ackerman, *Al amanecer,* illustrated by Catherine Stock, Atheneum (New York, NY), 1994 (originally published as *By the Dawn's Early Light*).

Keith Baker, *¿Quíen es la bestia?,* Harcourt (San Diego, CA), 1994 (originally published as *Who Is the Beast?*).

Kristine L. Franklin, *El niño pastor,* illustrated by Jill Kastner, Macmillan (New York, NY), 1994 (originally published as *The Shepherd Boy*).

James Howe, *Hay un dragón en mi bolsa de dormir,* illustrated by David S. Rose, Atheneum (New York, NY), 1994 (originally published as *There's a Dragon in My Sleeping Bag*).

Lynne Cherry, *El gran capoquero,* Harcourt (San Diego, CA), 1994 (originally published as *The Great Kapok Tree*).

Nancy Luenn, *El cuento de Nessa,* illustrated by Neil Waldman, Atheneum (New York, NY), 1994 (originally published as *Nessa's Story*).

Barbara Shook Hazen, *Fue el gorila,* illustrated by Ray Cruz, Atheneum (New York, NY), 1994 (originally published as *The Gorilla Did It*).

Barbara Shook Hazen, *¡Adiós! Hola!,* illustrated by Michael Bryant, Atheneum (New York, NY), 1995 (originally published as *Goodbye! Hello!*).

Nancy Luenn, *La pesca de Nessa,* illustrated by Neil Waldman, Atheneum (New York, NY), 1995 (originally published as *Nessa's Fish*).

Carolyn S. Bailey, *El conejito que queria tener alas rojas,* illustrated by Jacqueline Rogers, Putnam (New York, NY), 1995 (originally published as *The Little Rabbit That Wanted to Have Red Wings*).

Margery Williams, *El conejito de pana,* illustrated by Florence Graham, Putnam (New York, NY), 1995 (originally published as *The Velveteen Rabbit*).

Ann Hayes, *Te presento a la orquesta,* illustrated by Karmen Thompson, Harcourt (San Diego, CA), 1995 (originally published as *Meet the Orchestra*).

Carol Snyder, *Uno arriba, uno abajo,* illustrated by Maxie Chambliss, Atheneum (New York, NY), 1995 (originally published as *One Up, One Down*).

Judith Viorst, *Alexander que de ninguna manera—¿le oyen?—¡lo dice en serio!—se va a mudar,* illustrated by Robin Preiss Glasser, Libros Colibri (New York, NY), 1995 (originally published as *Alexander Who Is Not—Do You Hear Me?—Going—I Mean It!—to Move*).

Judith Viorst, *Alexander se muda,* Atheneum (New York, NY), 1995 (originally published as *Alexander Moves*).

Audrey Wood, *La casa adormecida,* illustrated by Don Wood, Harcourt (San Diego, CA), 1995 (originally published as *The Napping House*).

Julie Vivas, *La Natividad,* Harcourt (San Diego, CA), 1995 (originally published as *The Nativity*).

Sue Williams, *Sali de paseo,* Harcourt (San Diego, CA), 1995 (originally published as *I Went Walking*).

Jane Yolen, *Encuentro,* illustrated by David Shannon, Harcourt (San Diego, CA), 1996 (originally published as *Encounter*).

Cynthia Rylant, *Henry y Mudge: el primer libro de sus aventuras,* illustrated by Suçie Stevenson, Aladdin (New York, NY), 1996 (originally published as *Henry and Mudge*).

Cynthia Rylant, *Henry y Mudge con barro hasta el rabo: segundo libro de sus aventuras,* Suçie Stevenson, Aladdin (New York, NY), 1996 (originally published as *Henry and Mudge in Puddle Trouble*).

Cynthia Rylant, *Henry y Mudge y el mejor día del año,* illustrated by Suçie Stevenson, Aladdin (New York, NY), 1997 (originally published as *Henry and Mudge and the Best Day of All*).

Pat Hutchins, *El paseo de Rosie,* Aladdin (New York, NY), 1997 (originally published as *Rosie's Walk*).

TRANSLATOR; WITH F. ISABEL CAMPOY

Lois Ehlert, *Plumas para almorzar,* illustrated by the author, Harcourt (San Diego, CA), 1996 (originally published as *Feathers for Lunch*).

Lois Ehlert, *A sembrar sopa de verduras,* illustrated by the author, Harcourt (San Diego, CA), 1996 (originally published as *Growing Vegetable Soup*).

Gary Soto, *¡Que montón de tamales!,* illustrated by Ed Martinez, PaperStar (New York, NY), 1996 (originally published as *Too Many Tamales*).

Ellen Stoll Walsh, *Salta y brinca,* Harcourt (San Diego, CA), 1996 (originally published as *Hop Jump*).

Henry Horenstein, *Béisobol en los barrios,* Harcourt (New York, NY), 1997.

Mem Fox, *Quienquiera que seas,* illustrated by Leslie Staub, Harcourt (San Diego, CA), 2002 (originally published as *Whoever You Are*).

Gerald McDermott, *Zomo el conejo: un cuento de Africa occidental,* illustrated by the author, Harcourt (San Diego, CA), 2002 (originally published as *Zomo the Rabbit*).

Peter Golenbock, *Compañeros de equipo,* illustrated by Paul Bacon, Harcourt (San Diego, CA), 2002 (originally published as *Teammates*).

Lois Ehlert, *Día de mercado,* illustrated by the author, Harcourt (San Diego, CA), 2003 (originally published as *Market Day*).

FOR ADULTS; WITH F. ISABEL CAMPOY

Home School Interaction with Culturally or Language-diverse Families, Del Sol (Westlake, OH), 1998.

Ayudando a nuestros hijos (title means "Helping Our Children"), Del Sol (Westlake, OH), 1998.

Comprehensive Language Arts, Del Sol (Westlake, OH), 1998.

Effective English Acquisition for Academic Success, Del Sol (Westlake, OH), 1998.

OTHER

Where the Flame Trees Bloom (memoir), illustrated by Antonio Martorell, Atheneum (New York, NY), 1994, also published as *Alla donde florecen los flamboyanes.*

Under the Royal Palms: A Childhood in Cuba (autobiography), Atheneum (New York, NY), 1998, also published as *Bajo las palmas reales.*

A pesar del amor (novel for adults; title means "Love Notwithstanding"), Alfaguara (Miami, FL), 2003.

Escribiendo desde el corazón/Writing from the Heart (video), Del Sol Publishing (Westlake, OH), 1996.

Meeting an Author (video), Del Sol Publishing (Westlake, OH), 1996.

Aprender cantando I y II (sound recording; title means "Learning through Songs"), voice and music by Suni Paz, Del Sol Publishing (Westlake, OH), 1998.

Como una flor (sound recording; title means "Like a Flower"), voice and music by Suni Paz, Del Sol Publishing (Westlake, OH), 1998.

Also author of *Pedro Salinal: el diálogo creador,* and *Aserrin Aserran.* Author of introduction, Mayra Fernandez, *Barrio Teacher,* Sandcastle Publishing, 1992. Coauthor of "Cuentamundos" literature-based reading series, Macmillan/McGraw-Hill, 1993. Contributor to *In Grandmothers' House,* edited by Bonnie Christiensen, HarperCollins, 2003.

Adaptations

Andamos, Corremos, Exploramos, Navegamos, Partimos, and *Volamos* were adapted for audiocassette by Addison-Wesley, 1987; *Gathering the Sun, Coral y espuma,* and *Abecedario de los animales/An Animal ABC* were voiced by Suni Paz for audio recording and produced by Del Sol (Westlake, OH), 1998; many of the author's books were adapted for audiocassette by Santillana USA Publishing, 1999-2000.

Sidelights

Alma Flor Ada wrote in her 1994 Atheneum press release: "My grandmother taught me to read before I was three by writing the names of plants and flowers on the earth with a stick. Reading and nature became very intertwined for me." She continued, "My grandmother and one of my uncles were great storytellers. And every night, at bedtime, my father told me stories he invented to explain to me all that he knew about the history of the world. With all of these storytellers around me, it is not a surprise that I like to tell stories." Ada is not only a prolific storyteller, but a prime mover in the bilingual education movement. Most of her picture books are available in bilingual Spanish and English editions that promote literacy in both tongues. Ada has also translated into Spanish a significant number of picture books written in English.

As an educator, Ada promotes the use of quality literature as an integral part of the curriculum (her recent book, *A Magical Encounter,* is dedicated to this topic) and emphasizes that everyone—teachers, students, and their families—has important stories, life experiences, and thoughts that deserve to be written and shared. A recent book, cowritten with F. Isabel Campoy and Rosalma Zubizarreta (*Authors in the Classroom: A Transformative Education Process*), describes their extensive work in this field. Through her many books, Ada also serves as a cultural liaison: she retells traditional Latin American tales (*The Rooster Who Went to His Uncle's Wedding; Half-Chicken*), presents stories set in Latin

America (*The Gold Coin, Jordi's Star*), offers perspectives on life in Latin American countries (*Where the Flame Trees Bloom* and *Under the Royal Palms*), and describes the feelings of children as they confront cultural misunderstanding and learn to take pride in their heritage (*My Name Is María Isabel* and *I Love Saturdays y Domingos*). "My vocation as a writer started as a young child," Ada once told SATA. "I couldn't accept the fact that we had to read such boring textbooks while my wonderful storybooks awaited at home. I made a firm commitment while in the fourth grade to devote my life to producing schoolbooks that would be fun—and since then I am having a lot of fun doing just that!"

Ada was born in Camagüey, Cuba, in 1938. After studying at the Universidad Complutense in Madrid, Spain, she earned her doctorate in Peru. Postdoctoral studies at Harvard and at the Radcliffe Institute as an Institute fellow and a Fulbright scholar led to a teaching position at Emory University. She has spent the major part of her career at the University of San Francisco, as both a professor of education and the director for the Center for Multicultural Literature for Children and Young Adults. Ada is well known as a writer and translator of picture books and poetry for Spanish-speaking children and young adults. Her materials are often used in classrooms where both English and Spanish are taught, and she has done much to give Hispanic culture a wider representation through her nonfiction children's books. At the same time, she has written a series of children's books consisting of letters written by traditional storybook characters to one another (*Dear Peter Rabbit, Yours Truly, Goldilocks,* and *With Love, Little Red Hen*), which have garnered a devoted following among English-speaking children and have taken her work to a broader audience.

Ada's work as a scholar of romance languages—she is the author of a major study on the Spanish poet Pedro Salinas—has been a strong influence on her writing. Another major influence has been her active promotion of bilingualism and multiculturalism. At the same time, the author credits her children as a "constant source of inspiration." She once told SATA, "I was brought back to my childhood calling, when, in the midst of writing a very scholarly work, my daughter, who was three years old at the time, complained that I was writing very ugly books. One of my greatest joys is that my daughter has often collaborated with me in my work." Ada's daughter, Rosalma Zubizarreta, is an author in her own right and has translated many of her mother's books. Today, Ada's grandchildren continue to inspire and motivate Ada's writing, sometimes becoming characters in her books, just as their parents once did.

Ada created an "unusually appealing readaloud," according to a contributor to *Kirkus Reviews,* in *The Rooster Who Went to His Uncle's Wedding,* an English retelling of a traditional Latin American folktale. In this humorous cumulative tale, a rooster spends so much time grooming himself in preparation for his uncle's

wedding that he forgets to eat breakfast. On the way to the wedding, he cannot resist pecking at the kernel of corn he finds in a mud puddle. The rooster asks the grass to clean his muddy beak, but the grass will not help. A lamb refuses to eat the grass, and a dog refuses to bite the lamb . . . but at last the sun, who has always enjoyed the rooster's sunrise song, agrees to help the rooster. *School Library Journal* critic Lauralyn Persson recommended *The Rooster Who Went to His Uncle's Wedding* as a "solid addition to folklore collections."

In *The Three Golden Oranges,* a Spanish folktale, three brothers who wish to marry are instructed by a wise old woman to travel to a distant castle and return with three golden oranges. The two foolish older brothers refuse to follow the instructions they have received, but the faithfulness of the kind younger son is rewarded by marriage to Blancaflor, a beautiful princess, who helps the young man rescue his brothers. Reviewers detected a feminist twist in the ending, in which Blancaflor's sisters refuse to marry the foolish brothers, and praised Ada's simplified rendition of a fairly complex traditional tale.

Ada adapted a Mexican folktale for *The Lizard and the Sun/La lagartija y el sol,* published in a bilingual edition with the Spanish original on the left side of the page and the English translation by Zubizarreta on the right. The sun has disappeared, and everyone has gone out to search for him. Long after all the others have given up, Lizard continues to search, eventually finding the sun curled up inside a rock. "Readers will cheer Lizard as she find the Earth's source of light and warmth," observed Vianela Rivas in *School Library Journal.*

Ada adapted another Spanish folktale in *Mediopollito/ Half-Chicken: A New Version of a Traditional Story.* Set in colonial Mexico, the Spanish and English bilingual text tells the story of how the weathervane came to be. The story begins with the birth of Half-Chicken, whose unusual appearance—he was born with only one wing and one leg—makes him something of a celebrity in his small village. In search of greater fame, Half-Chicken travels to Mexico City to meet the Viceroy. Along his journey, he befriends a stream, fire, and wind, all of whom end up coming to his aid when the Viceroy's cook decides that Half-Chicken would make a tasty soup. The story is "brimming with silliness and the simple repetition that children savor," remarked Annie Ayres in *Booklist.*

Ada's original fairy tale *The Malachite Palace* features a lonely young princess who captures a songbird to be her friend. Yet when the songbird ceases to sing, she realizes she needs to release him. The bird helps the girl learn to venture out of her own cage and make friends with children her own age, regardless of their social differences. "Although the story is not highly original, youngsters will enjoy its gentle familiarity," remarked

Denise E. Agosto in *School Library Journal.* Another lonely character is at the center of *Jordi's Star,* another original picture book by Ada. Here Jordi tends a herd of goats on a barren hillside. In his loneliness, he comes to believe that a star's reflection in a pool of water is a fallen star which has come to befriend him. Jordi tends the star with care, decorating the place where it dwells until the barren landscape is transformed by his love. "Written with strong emotion and a sense of wonder, this story has the tone and resonance of a folktale," noted Joy Fleishhacker in *School Library Journal.* In a star review for *Booklist,* Susan Dove Lempke called the book a "touching, lyrically told story."

Ada's original picture book *The Gold Coin* was honored with a Christopher Award in 1992 and was named a Notable Children's Trade Book. While a thief looks on greedily through the window, Doña Josefa admires a gold coin and tells herself aloud that she must be the richest woman in the world. Juan, the thief, decides to steal the elderly woman's wealth, and lies in wait until she departs. Yet he finds no treasure when he ransacks her home, so he begins to pursue the old woman, intending to force her to give him her gold. Since he is asking for Doña Josefa, everyone assumes he must be her friend, and Juan is gradually transformed as he encounters the friendship and goodwill of all the people that Doña Josefa has helped. As Ann Welton remarked in *School Library Journal, The Gold Coin* "makes an important point" about the nature of true wealth and the consequences of greed. A critic for *Publishers Weekly* described the story as "unusual" and "rewarding," concluding that it is "worthy of repeated readings."

Where the Flame Trees Bloom, as Ada explains in the book's introduction, is based on her own childhood memories of Cuba. In the evenings, family members would reminisce, telling the stories from which these eleven vignettes are drawn. One of the short stories in this collection offers a portrait of Ada's grandfather, who was confronted at the same time with his wife's imminent death and the collapse of the economy. Another story recounts how Ada's blind great-grandmother crafted dolls for poor children. Ada also recalls the time when her uncle, a schoolteacher, feared for his students' lives when the school was struck by lightning, an experience that helped him realize the significance of his job as a teacher. According to a critic in the *Bulletin of the Center for Children's Books,* Ada's writing "evokes the warmth and character of her family," and *School Library Journal* contributor Marilyn Long Graham described Ada's writing as "elegant."

Under the Royal Palms is a companion volume to *Where the Flame Trees Bloom,* and is another celebration of Cuban life and culture in the 1940s. While in the first book, Ada recounts stories she remembers hearing in her childhood, in *Under the Royal Palms* she narrates her own childhood experiences. "At the core of the collection, there is a heartfelt portrayal of a quickly disappearing culture and a vastly beautiful land," observed a

When Little Red Hen moves her family to Happy Valley and plants a crop of corn, she has no idea she is putting her life in danger in **With Love, Little Red Hen,** *illustrated by Leslie Tryon.*

contributor to *Publishers Weekly.* The book received the Purá Belpré Award of the American Library Association in 2000.

Raising the self-esteem of Spanish-speaking children and children of Hispanic origin living in a society where Anglo culture dominates is the unstated goal of most of Ada's work, and several of her books take on this task explicitly. In *My Name Is María Isabel,* María Isabel's family has moved, and she must attend a new school. There are already two Marías in her class, so the teacher decides to call her "Mary Lopez" instead of María Isabel Salazar López. María Isabel has difficulty identifying herself as "Mary," which leads to some unhappy situations. Yet when María Isabel describes her difficulties in an essay she has been assigned, the teacher realizes her mistake and finds a way to remedy the situation. As Irvy Gilbertson wrote in *Five Owls,* the "link of María Isabel's name with her heritage is an important theme in this story," and various Spanish words are used to "expose the reader to a different culture."

Likewise, *I Love Saturdays y Domingos* makes "a strong statement about cultural diversity and the universality of love," remarked Ann Welton in *School Library Journal.* In this book, a little girl recounts with joy the pleasures she experiences on the Saturdays she spends with her Grandma and Grandpa, as well as the Sundays (*domingos*) she spends with her Abuelito and Abuelita. Both sides come together to celebrate her birthday, showing the girl the blessing of belonging to two worlds. Reviewers also noted that the bilingual format encourages easy adoption of Spanish-language terms, and a contributor to *Kirkus Reviews* remarked that "children eager to explore their own heritage will enjoy watching as the heroine embraces all the diversity in her life."

Ada received a Parents' Choice Honor Award for *Dear Peter Rabbit,* a fantasy that weaves together the tales of various storybook characters, including the Three Little Pigs, the Big Bad Wolf, Little Red Riding Hood, Peter Rabbit, and Baby Bear. Goldilocks is also included in this story, recast as the daughter of Mr. McGregor, the farmer who almost catches Peter Rabbit in the beloved Beatrix Potter stories. Through the letters that they send to one another, readers learn about their various adventures and misadventures. "Children will be enchanted by this opportunity to meet familiar faces in new settings," commented *School Library Journal* reviewer Joy Fleishhacker. Pointing out that Ada's book belongs to the genre of fairy tale parodies, Roger Sutton asserted in *Bulletin of the Center for Children's Books* that *Dear Peter Rabbit* "is as clever as most in the genre." In *Yours Truly, Goldilocks,* Ada and illustrator Leslie Tryon provided a sequel for fans of *Dear Peter Rabbit.* The fairy tale characters continue corresponding in preparation for a housewarming party at the Three Little Pigs' new, wolf-proof home. "This is fairy-tale fun at its best," wrote Beth Tegart in *School Library Journal.* Another sequel, *With Love, Little Red Hen,* portrays the arrival of the Little Red Hen in the enchanted forest that provided the setting for the first two books. "Lovers of fractured fairy tales will be amused by this further peek into the personal letters of familiar characters," predicted a contributor to *Kirkus Reviews.*

Due to Ada's talent and persistence, fewer children learning either Spanish or English will have to endure the boring textbooks or second-rate stories she bemoaned as a child. The author spoke of the benefits of this bilingual approach in her publicity release: "Nothing can surpass the inherent musicality of the [Spanish] language, the deep cultural values incorporated in it," she noted. "Yet [Spanish-speaking] children also need to read the literature that their peers are reading in English, so that their introduction to American culture occurs through the best medium the culture has to offer." One of Ada's successful ventures in providing bilingual education in a storybook format is *Gathering the Sun: An ABC in Spanish and English.* Ada wrote poems to celebrate aspects of farm laborers' lives for each letter of the alphabet, which were translated into English by Ada's daughter, Rosa Zubizarreta. The resulting book is more than a tribute to Cesar Chavez, hero of the migrant labor movement, noted Ann Welton in *School Library Journal;* "whether used to show the plight of migrant workers or the pride Hispanic laborers feel in their heritage, this is an important book," Welton concluded.

Ada is considered to have made a most important contribution to the education of both English and Spanish-speaking children in the United States since she began translating, adapting, and inventing stories for children in the 1970s. Her bilingual picture books are often credited as proof that bilingual education can be attractive and motivating for children while offering high aesthetic, literary, and human values. Ada's recent series, "Puertas al Sol/Gateways to the Sun," coauthored with F. Isabel Campoy, consists of a number of different genres, including poetry, theater, art, and biographies of cultural leaders. This collection offers children the opportunity to enjoy the various contributions that have shaped Hispanic culture. Given the significant population of Americans with Latin American origin, Ada's evident pride in the Latin American heritage is considered a valuable contribution to the literature enjoyed by children in the United States.

Biographical and Critical Sources

BOOKS

Children's Literature Review, Volume 62, Gale (Detroit, MI), 2000.
Notable Hispanic American Women, Book II, Gale (Detroit, MI), 1998.
Zipes, Jack, editor, *The Oxford Companion to Fairy Tales,* Oxford University Press (New York, NY), 2000, p.1.

PERIODICALS

American Book Review, November-December, 1997, George R. Bodmer, review of *Gathering the Sun: An ABC in Spanish and English,* pp. 12-13.
Booklist, March 1, 1991, review of *The Gold Coin,* pp. 1395-1396; March 1, 1993, Graciela Italiano, review of *The Rooster Who Went to His Uncle's Wedding,* p. 1231; June 1, 1993, Ilene Cooper, review of *My Name Is María Isabel,* p. 1828; May 1, 1994, Ilene Cooper, review of *Dear Peter Rabbit,* p. 1606; February 1, 1995, Isabel Schon, review of *La pesca de Nessa,* p. 1012; September 15, 1995, Annie Ayres, review of *Mediopollito/Half-Chicken: A New Version of a Traditional Story,* p. 165; December 1, 1996, Susan Dove Lempke, review of *Jordi's Star,* p. 652; April 15, 1997, Annie Ayers, review of *Gathering the Sun,* p. 1431; December 15, 1997, Julie Corsaro, review of *The Lizard and the Sun/La lagartija el sol,* p. 698; May 1, 1998, Ilene Cooper, review of *Yours Truly, Goldilocks,* p. 1520; May 15, 1998, Hazel Rochman, review of *The Malachite Palace,* p. 1629; November 15, 1998, Hazel Rochman, review of *Under the Royal Palms,* p. 582; May 15, 1999, Hazel Rochman, review of *The Three Golden Oranges,* p. 1698; September 15, 1999, review of *Under the Royal Palms,* p. 254; August, 2000, Isabel Schon, review of *Antón Pirulero,* p. 2154; July, 2001, Carolyn Phelan, review of *Daniel's Mystery Egg,* p. 2022; September 15, 2001, Lauren Peterson, review of *With Love, Little Red Hen,* p. 229; February 1, 2002, Annie Ayres, review of *I Love Saturdays y Domingos,* p. 944.

Book Report, May-June, 1995, Sherry York, review of *Where the Flame Trees Bloom,* p. 45.

Bulletin of the Center for Children's Books, April, 1994, Roger Sutton, review of *Dear Peter Rabbit,* p. 249; February, 1995, Susan Dove Lempke, review of *Where the Flame Trees Bloom,* p. 190; December, 1996, Amy E. Brandt, review of *Jordi's Star,* p. 126; June, 1997, Janice M. Del Negro, review of *Gathering the Sun,* pp. 348-349; October, 1997, Janice M. Del Negro, review of *The Lizard and the Sun,* p. 40; March, 1998, Pat Matthews, review of *The Malachite Palace,* pp. 234-235.

Five Owls, September-October, 1993, Irvy Gilbertson, review of *My Name Is María Isabel,* p. 14.

Horn Book, January-February, 1988, Laurie Sale, review of *The Adventures of Connie and Diego/Las aventuras de Connie y Diego,* p. 89; March-April, 1995, Martha V. Parravano, review of *Where the Flame Trees Bloom,* p. 218; November-December, 1995, Martha V. Parravano, review of *Mediopollito,* p. 749; January-February, 2002, Kitty Flynn, review of *I Love Saturdays y Domingos,* p. 65.

Horn Book Guide, July-September, 1992, Caroline Ward, review of *Serafina's Birthday,* p. 18; January-June, 1993, Marcia Cecilia Silva-Diaz, review of *The Rooster Who Went to His Uncle's Wedding,* p. 324; July-December, 1994, Martha V. Parravano, review of *Where the Flame Trees Bloom,* p. 72; spring, 1997, Maria B. Salvadore, review of *Jordi's Star,* p. 17; spring, 1998, Rebecca Mills, review of *The Lizard and the Sun* and *Gathering the Sun,* p. 116; fall, 1998, Marilyn Bousquin, review of *Yours Truly, Goldilocks,* p. 282, and Kitty Flynn, review of *The Malachite Palace,* p. 282; spring, 1999, Gail Hedges, review of *Under the Royal Palms,* p. 134; fall, 1999, Martha Sibert, review of *Three Golden Oranges,* p. 322.

Kirkus Reviews, January 1, 1991, review of *The Gold Coin,* p. 42; May 1, 1993, review of *The Rooster Who Went to His Uncle's Wedding,* p. 591; March 1, 1994, review of *Dear Peter Rabbit,* p. 297; July 15, 1995, review of *Mediopollito,* p. 1020; July 1, 1997, review of *The Lizard and the Sun,* p. 1026; December 15, 1997, review of *El arbol de Navidad/The Christmas Tree,* p. 1832; May 1, 1998, review of *The Malachite Palace,* p. 654; May 1, 1999, review of *The Three Golden Oranges,* p. 718; September 1, 2001, review of *Daniel's Mystery Egg,* p. 1284; October 1, 2001, review of *With Love, Little Red Hen,* p. 1418; December 1, 2001, review of *I Love Saturdays y Domingos,* p. 1680.

Language Arts, November, 1995, Miriam Martinez and Marcia F. Nash, review of *Where the Flame Trees Bloom,* pp. 542-543; March, 1996, review of *Me llamo María Isabel,* p. 207.

Library Journal, August, 2001, Lucia M. Gonzalez, review of *Abecedario de los animales-Animal ABC,* p. S26.

Publishers Weekly, April 22, 1983, review of *Piñatas and Paper Flowers,* p. 126; June-July, 1987, review of *The Adventures of Connie and Diego,* p. 82; January 11, 1991, review of *The Gold Coin,* p. 103; February, 1991, review of *Y domingo, siete* and *Amigos,* p. 102; April 19, 1993, review of *My Name Is María Isabel,* p. 62; April 26, 1993, review of *The Rooster Who Went to His Uncle's Wedding,* p. 76; February 21, 1994, review of *Dear Peter Rabbit,* p. 253; November 4, 1996, review of *Jordi's Star,* p. 75; March 31, 1997, review of *Gathering the Sun,* p. 76; October 6, 1997, review of *The Christmas Tree,* p. 54; May 4, 1998, Jennifer M. Brown, review of *The Malachite Palace,* p. 212; May 25, 1998, review of *Yours Truly, Goldilocks,* p. 89; December 7, 1998, review of *Under the Royal Palms,* p. 61; May 31, 1999, review of *Three Golden Oranges,* p. 93; December 10, 2001, review of *I Love Saturdays y Domingos,* p. 69.

Reading Teacher, September, 1993, Kathy G. Short and Kathryn Mitchell Pierce, review of *The Gold Coin,* p. 46; September, 1998, review of *The Lizard and the Sun,* p. 58.

School Library Journal, January, 1981, L. Michael Espinosa, review of *El niño que no creía en la primavera,* *Caras,* and *El dolor de muelas de Alberto,* p. 33; February, 1988, Louise Yarian Zwick, review of *Volamos, Partimos, Exploramos, Corremos, Andamos,* and *¡Manzano, Manzano!,* p. 92; February, 1990, review of *Alexander y el día terrible, horrible, espantoso, horroso* and *Alexander, que era rico el domingo pasado,* p. 120; August, 1990, Louise Yarian Zwick and Mark Zwick, review of *¿Quién nacera aquí?, Me gustaría tener . . . , Una extraña visita, El canto del mosquito,* and *Abecedario de los animales-Animal ABC,* p. 172; April, 1991, Ann Welton, review of *The Gold Coin,* p. 88; September, 1992, Alexandra Marris, review of *Serafina's Birthday,* p. 196; November, 1992, Rose Zertuche Trevino, review of *Olmo y la mariposa azul,* p. 133; April, 1993, Ann Welton, review of *My Name Is María Isabel,* p. 117; May, 1993, Lauralyn Persson, review of *The Rooster Who Went to His Uncle's Wedding,* p. 92; August, 1993, Rose Zertuche Trevino, review of *El secreto en la caja de fosforos,* p. 204; June, 1994, Jane Marino, review of *The Unicorn of the West,* p. 94; July, 1994, Joy Fleishhacker, review of *Dear Peter Rabbit,* p. 73; August, 1994, Rose Zertuche Trevino, review of *El unicornio del oeste,* p. 181; November, 1994, Rose Zertuche Trevino, review of *¿Quién es la bestia?* and *Querido Pedrin,* p. 130, and review of *La Natividad,* p. 131; February, 1995, Marilyn Long Graham, review of *Where the Flame Trees Bloom,* p. 96, and Rose Zertuche Trevino, review of *Hay un dragón en mi bolsa de dormir, Fue el gorila, Me llamo María Isabel,* and *Al amanecer,* p. 126; August, 1995, Rose Zertuche Trevino, review of *One Up, One Down* and *Good-Bye! Hello!,* p. 167; November, 1995, Graciela Italiano, review of *Mediopollito,* p. 87; February, 1996, Rose Zertuche Trevino, review of *Sali de paseo* and *Te presento a la orquesta,* pp. 128, 130; June, 1996, Cynthia R. Richey and Doreen S. Hurley, review of *The Gold Coin,* p. 54; August, 1996, Rose Zertuche Trevino, review of *Alexander que de ninguna manera—¿le oyen?—¡lo dice en serio!—se va a mudar,* p. 179; December, 1996, Joy Fleishhacker, review of *Jordi's Star,* p. 84; March, 1997, Ann Welton, review of *Gathering the Sun,* pp. 169-170; August, 1997, Vianela Rivas, review of *The Lizard and the Sun/La lagartija y el sol: A Folktale in English and Spanish,*

p. 180; October, 1997, Jane Marino, review of *The Christmas Tree,* p. 40; May, 1998, Denise E. Agosto, review of *The Malachite Palace,* p. 106; July, 1998, Beth Tegart, review of *Yours Truly, Goldilocks,* p. 64; December, 1998, Sylvia V. Meisner, review of *Under the Royal Palms,* p. 132; July, 1999, Sally Bates Goodroe, review of *Three Golden Oranges,* p. 83; October, 2001, Bina Williams, review of *With Love, Little Red Hen,* p. 104; January, 2002, Ann Welton, review of *I Love Saturdays y Domingos,* p. 89; February, 2002, Kathleen Simonetta, review of *Daniel's Mystery Egg,* p. 96.

OTHER

Ada, Alma Flor, "Alma Flor Ada" (publicity release), Atheneum (New York, NY), 1994.

Alma Flor Ada Web Site, http://www.almaada.com/ (April 8, 2002).

Houghton Mifflin Reading, http://www.eduplace.com/kids/ (April 8, 2002).

Little Chiles, http://www.littlechilies.com/ada.htm/ (April 8, 2002).

University of San Francisco, http://www.soe.usfca.edu/ childlit/ (April 8, 2002).

B

BANNOR, Brett 1959-

Personal
Born December 16, 1959, in Chicago, IL. *Education:* Southern Illinois University, B.S., 1981.

Addresses
Office—Zoo Atlanta, 800 Cherokee Ave. S.E., Atlanta, GA 30315. *E-mail*—brettbannor@aol.com.

Career
Zoo Atlanta, Atlanta, GA, zookeeper; also worked as a zookeeper in Miami, FL, and Orlando, FL.

Writings

Bighorn Sheep, Lucent Books (San Diego, CA), 2003.

Contributor of articles to scientific journals.

Work in Progress
Extensive research on wild animals and the law.

Sidelights
Brett Bannor told *SATA:* "People ask me why I am a zookeeper *and* a freelance writer. The answer is obvious, if you have ever tried to live on what you're paid for either of these professions alone.

"To anyone wishing to embark on a career as a writer, I advise the purchase of a computer, or at least pen and paper. Perhaps someday we will control mental telepathy, and then we will be able simply to project our thoughts into the readers' minds, thereby eliminating the need for keyboards, stationery, and, best of all, editors.

"[Good writing] is all in the preparation. The only way to write informative articles or nonfiction books is to do the research, and do it thoroughly. And for goodness sake, when you do research, go to a reliable source, preferably the first place where the relevant information was published. For instance, if you pick up the *New York Times* and read some article on the effects of a new artificial sweetener on mice bladders, remember two things. One: mice have very tiny bladders. They can't sit through a half-hour of *Friends* without having to leave the couch and visit the bathroom. And two: the study of these mouse bladders was not originally published in the *Times;* it was probably published first in the *New England Journal of Medicine* or something like that. Go to a good academic library and struggle through the original article so you are really well acquainted with rodent bladders and artificial sweeteners before you try to write about this fascinating topic yourself."

*   *   *

BOLTON, Elizabeth
See ST. JOHN, Nicole

*   *   *

BOYDEN, Linda 1948-

Personal
Born July 6, 1948, in Attleboro, MA; daughter of Ray and Marie (Dargis) Simmons; married John P. Boyden (an engineer), 1988; children: A. Rachel, Eámon, Maeve; (stepchildren) Luanne, John, Jr. *Ethnicity:* "Caucasian/Native American." *Education:* Framingham State College, B.S.Ed., 1970; University of Virginia, M.Ed., 1992. *Hobbies and other interests:* Volunteer work at Makawao Public Library, hiking in national parks, reading, sewing.

Addresses
Home—151 Alalani St., Pukalani, HI 96768. *E-mail*—lindadw@hawaii.rr.com.

Linda Boyden

Career

Self-employed storyteller and writer, specializing in American Indian stories. Elementary schoolteacher, 1970-97; teacher of writing at a private middle school on the island of Maui, Hawaii; gives readings from her works. United Lumbee Nation, enrolled member; Intertribal Council of Hawaii, member of Maui chapter.

Member

Society of Children's Book Writers and Illustrators, Wordcraft Circle of Native American Writers and Storytellers, Children's Literature Hawaii, Maui Live Poets Society.

Awards, Honors

New Voices Award, Lee & Low Books, 2000, for *The Blue Roses.*

Writings

The Blue Roses, illustrated by Amy Córdova, Lee & Low Books (New York, NY), 2002.

Work represented in anthologies, including *Through the Eye of a Deer,* Auntlute Books, 1999; and *Woven on the Wind,* Houghton Mifflin (Boston, MA), 2001.

Work in Progress

Several picture-book manuscripts; three middle-reader manuscripts; a picture-book biography of Sarah Winnemucca; poetry for adults and children.

Sidelights

Linda Boyden told *SATA:* "For as long as I can remember, I have loved words. Before I could read, I told myself stories to fall asleep or stories for my dolls to enact. The first most important discovery of my life was learning how to read. It changed everything! I still loved to make up my own stories, but now I could enjoy what others had imagined, too.

"Sometimes in my storytelling jaunts, though, important adults misunderstood me. To be good, they pointed out, I must learn the difference between telling the truth and telling lies. As I grew older and emerged as a writer, I discovered one of the truths of fiction writing: readers *approve* of the 'lies'! This is definitely for me, I decided.

"But I also wanted to teach, and I did for over twenty years. During snow days or when I was an at-home mom with my own babies, I wrote at every opportunity. When circumstances moved my husband and me to Maui in 1997, I abandoned teaching and began to try to market my writings in earnest.

"After many, many rejections, one of my manuscripts, *The Blue Roses,* hit the jackpot by winning the Lee & Low Books first New Voices Award in 2000. A traditional Cherokee myth says that the first stories came to people in dreams. My first book is based on a dream I had after my maternal grandfather passed on. I was thirty at the time, about to have my third child, and I couldn't travel the long distance to my grandfather's funeral. I was heartbroken. One night, Grandpa came to me in a dream. He stood in a beautiful garden (gardening had been his life-long hobby). Grandpa told me he was happy and to stop my carrying-on. It sounds strange, but I awoke with a new-found sense of contentment.

"Until then, death had terrified me. Seeing how happy he was changed that. Later I thought how poorly death is explained to most children. Wouldn't gardening be a great metaphor to help kids understand, to give them comfort and hope? These thoughts led to my book.

"Kids are still as hungry for good books as I was. Leading them to their own literacy is what I enjoy doing most, next to writing. Children have stories to tell. Teaching them to express their words aloud or on paper and to enjoy the written words of others empowers them and enriches the world."

Biographical and Critical Sources

PERIODICALS

Kirkus Reviews, April 1, 2002, review of *The Blue Roses,* p. 486.
School Library Journal, March, 2001, "New Voice in Children's Literature Honored," p. 22; June, 2002, Kathy Piehl, review of *The Blue Roses,* p. 88.

BURACK, Sylvia K. 1916-2003
(Sylvia K. Kammerman)

OBITUARY NOTICE—See index for *SATA* sketch: Born December 16, 1916, in Hartford, CT; died February 14, 2003, in Boston, MA. Editor, publisher, and author. Burack was best known as the former publisher of the advice magazine *The Writer.* She was a graduate of Smith College, where she received a B.A. in 1938. In 1941 she went to work for her husband as an associate editor for Writer, Inc., and Plays, Inc., in Boston, and took over the publishing companies in 1978, when her husband died; she retired in 1999. *The Writer* was designed to teach aspiring writers the mechanics of good writing and offer advice on how to get published, and Burack became highly respected among both aspiring and established authors for her good advice and encouragement. Burack also published *Drama Magazine for Young People,* from 1978 to 1999, which was all about plays for young audiences. In addition to her work as an editor and publisher, she was the author of numerous books about writing, some under her maiden name of Kammerman, including *Writing the Short Story* (1942), *Writing and Selling the Romance Novel* (1983), *Writing Mystery and Crime Fiction* (1985), *How to Write and Sell Mystery Fiction* (1990), *How to Write and Sell Your Articles* (1997), *Writing for Children and Young Adults* (2000), and the annual *The Writer's Handbook;* she also edited numerous collections of plays for children such as *The Big Book of Holiday Plays* (1990) and *The Big Book of Skits* (1996).

OBITUARIES AND OTHER SOURCES:

BOOKS

Who's Who in America, 56th edition, Marquis (New Providence, NJ), 2001.

PERIODICALS

Boston Herald, February 16, 2003, p. 32.
New York Times, March 17, 2003, p. A23.

* * *

BURCHARD, Peter Duncan 1921-

Personal

Born March 1, 1921, in Washington, DC; son of Russell Duncan (a lawyer) and Ethel (Brokaw) Burchard; married Elizabeth Chamberlain, March 23, 1946 (marriage ended); married Lucy Edwards (marriage ended); married Linda Wemyss Carman (marriage ended); children: (first marriage) Lee, Peter Jr., Laura. *Education:* Philadelphia Museum School of Art, graduate, 1947. *Politics:* Democrat. *Hobbies and other interests:* Sailing, tennis, skiing.

Addresses

Home—118 Church St., Apt. 0-2, Williamstown, MA 01267.

Peter Duncan Burchard

Career

Freelance illustrator, 1947—, writer, 1956—, and photographer, 1975—. Member of panel of advisers, George Polk awards, 1983—. *Exhibitions:* Author's work was exhibited at the Anne Fuller Gallery, 1978. *Military service:* U.S. Army Signal Corps, 1943-46, convoy duty, North Atlantic.

Member

International PEN.

Awards, Honors

Boys Club of America Award, 1955, for illustrating *Squanto: Friend of the White Man;* Nancy Bloch Award, 1963, and Lewis Carroll Shelf Award, 1964, both for illustrating *Roosevelt Grady;* Lewis Carroll Shelf Award, 1966, for *Jed: The Story of a Yankee Soldier and a Southern Boy;* Guggenheim fellowship, 1966; *Bimby* named to *Horn Book* honor list, 1968; Christopher Award, 1972, for illustrating *Pocahontas and the Strangers;* Western Writers award, 1975, for photographs illustrating *Ride 'Em Cowgirl;* Edgar Allan Poe award nomination, Mystery Writers of America, 1978, for illustrating *Night Spell;* Parents' Choice Award, 2003, for *Frederick Douglass: For the Great Family of Man.*

Writings

(And illustrator) *The River Queen,* Macmillan (New York, NY), 1957.
(And illustrator) *The Carol Moran,* Macmillan (New York, NY), 1958.
(And illustrator) *Balloons: From Paper Bags to Skyhooks,* Macmillan (New York, NY), 1960.
(And illustrator) *Jed: The Story of a Yankee Soldier and a Southern Boy,* Coward (New York, NY), 1960.
North by Night, Coward (New York, NY), 1962.

One Gallant Rush: Robert Gould Shaw and His Brave Black Regiment, St. Martin's Press (New York, NY), 1965, published as *Glory,* 1989.

Stranded: A Story of New York in 1875, Coward (New York, NY), 1967.

(And illustrator) *Bimby,* Coward (New York, NY), 1968.

Chito, illustrated with photographs by Katrina Thomas, Coward (New York, NY), 1969.

Pioneers of Flight: From Early Times to the Wright Brothers, St. Martin's Press (New York, NY), 1970.

(And illustrator) *Rat Hell,* Coward (New York, NY), 1971.

A Quiet Place, Coward (New York, NY), 1972.

The Deserter: A Spy Story of the Civil War, Coward (New York, NY), 1973.

Harbor Tug, Putnam (New York, NY), 1974.

(And illustrator) *Whaleboat Raid,* Coward (New York, NY), 1977.

(And photographer) *Ocean Race: A Sea Venture,* Putnam (New York, NY), 1978.

(And illustrator) *Chinwe,* Putnam (New York, NY), 1979.

Digger, Putnam (New York, NY), 1980.

First Affair, Farrar, Straus (New York, NY), 1981.

(And illustrator) *Sea Change,* Farrar, Straus (New York, NY), 1984.

(And photographer) *Venturing: An Introduction to Sailing,* Little, Brown (Boston, MA), 1986.

"We'll Stand by the Union": Robert Gould Shaw and the Black 54th Massachusetts Regiment, Facts on File (New York, NY), 1993.

Charlotte Forten: A Black Teacher in the Civil War (biography), Crown (New York, NY), 1995.

Lincoln and Slavery, Atheneum (New York, NY), 1999.

(And illustrator) *Frederick Douglass: For the Great Family of Man,* Atheneum (New York, NY), 2003.

Contributor of stories, articles, and reviews to magazines, including *Boy's Life, Interplay,* and *Connoisseur.*

Burchard's work is included in the Kerlin Collection.

ILLUSTRATOR

Marie McSwigan, *Our Town Has a Circus,* Dutton (New York, NY), 1949.

Franklin Folsom, *The Baby Elephant,* Wonder Books (New York, NY), 1950.

Phyllis Rowand, *The Cats Who Stayed for Dinner,* Wonder Books (New York, NY), 1951.

Jed: The Story of a Yankee Soldier and a Southern Boy, *a self-illustrated work by Burchard, was inspired by his grandfather's stint in the Union Army during the U.S. Civil War.*

Virginia Haviland, *William Penn,* Abingdon (Nashville, TN), 1952.

Hildreth T. Wriston, *Show Lamb,* Abingdon (Nashville, TN), 1953.

Clyde Robert Bulla, *Down the Mississippi,* Crowell (New York, NY), 1954.

Grace Tracy Johnson and Harold N. Johnson, *Courage Wins,* Dutton (New York, NY), 1954.

Clyde Robert Bulla, *Squanto: Friend of the White Man,* Crowell (New York, NY), 1954, published as *Squanto: Friend of the Pilgrims,* 1969.

Margaret Glover Otto, *Tiny Man,* Holt (New York, NY), 1955.

Alf Evers, *Treasure of Watchdog Mountain,* Macmillan (New York, NY), 1955.

Marian Cumming, *Clan Texas,* Harcourt (New York, NY), 1955.

William L. Brown and Rosalie Moore, *The Boy Who Got Mailed,* Coward (New York, NY), 1957.

Harold Keith, *Rifles for Watie,* Crowell (New York, NY), 1957.

Clyde Robert Bulla, *Pirate's Promise,* Crowell (New York, NY), 1958.

Wilma Pitchford Hays, *The Fourth of July Raid,* Coward (New York, NY), 1959.

Wilma Pitchford Hays, *Easter Fires,* Coward (New York, NY), 1960.

Louisa R. Shotwell, *Roosevelt Grady,* World Publishing (New York, NY), 1963.

Earl S. Miers, *Pirate Chase,* Holt (New York, NY), 1965.

Peggy Mann, *The Street of Flower Boxes,* Coward (New York, NY), 1966.

Lonzo Anderson, *Zeb,* Knopf (New York, NY), 1966.

Clyde Robert Bulla, *Pocahontas and the Strangers,* Crowell (New York, NY), 1971.

Lynn Haney, *Ride 'Em Cowgirl,* Putnam (New York, NY), 1975.

Robert Newman, *Night Spell,* Atheneum (New York, NY), 1977.

Illustrator of many other books.

Adaptations

One Gallant Rush, re-released as *Glory,* together with Lincoln Kirstein's *Lay This Laurel,* served as a historical source for the film *Glory,* released by TriStar Pictures in 1989, which won three Academy Awards.

Work in Progress

Paper Shoes, a novel for adults.

Sidelights

Author and illustrator Peter Duncan Burchard's long-time interests in both American history and maritime history are reflected in his many books for young readers. The U.S. Civil War in particular has been the focus of many of Duncan's most popular nonfiction titles, among them *One Gallant Rush: Robert Gould Shaw and His Brave Black Regiment* and *Lincoln and Slavery,* as well as several works of fiction.

Burchard was born in 1921, in Washington, D.C., where his father worked as a lawyer for the federal government. Raised in New Jersey, he developed a pronounced stutter as a child. Noting that "difficulties aren't always leaden weights around the necks of sufferers," Burchard declared in an essay for *Something about the Author Autobiography Series* (*SAAS*): "In compensating for my handicap, I triumphed in other ways." In his teens Burchard became a track star as well as a first-string halfback on his school's football team. Later, while attending a Connecticut boarding school, he continued to be a top athlete. As the novelist recalled: "My speech impediment kept me from becoming arrogant. It was, as one of my friends chose to put it, 'a great leveller.'"

Burchard's early interest in art was encouraged by his father, an amateur artist. "In our house," Burchard wrote in *SAAS,* "my father set aside a room where he put up an easel and sometimes, as he worked on a painting, I

In **Lincoln and Slavery** *Burchard shows how the sixteenth president's attitude toward slavery was influenced by the events and people of his day, including civil rights activist Sojourner Truth.*

Frederick Douglass, a former slave turned abolitionist and orator, is the subject of Burchard's biography Frederick Douglass: For the Great Family of Man.

sat close to him and did crayon drawings, most of them of fire engines rushing toward a blazing building." During his boarding school years he benefitted from the encouragement of teacher Paul Child, who suggested that Burchard study at the Philadelphia Museum School of Art, now called the University of the Arts.

When the United States entered World War II, Burchard had just begun his sophomore year at the Museum School of Art but in 1942 he decided to leave school temporarily and serve his country. Because his speech impediment initially disqualified him for military service, Burchard got a job as a draftsman, "doing detail and perspective drawings for designers of a cargo plane to be built for the Navy," as he explained in *SAAS*. In 1943 he was accepted by the U.S. Army and, after basic training in New Orleans, became a Signal Corps maritime radio operator assigned to the troop transport *Sea Robin*. He also contributed illustrations to *Yank* magazine. "Since childhood, I had loved the seashore—shallow waters, bright beaches, sounding waves," Burchard recalled, and the eighteen transatlantic crossings he made during the war instilled in him a love of deep water voyages. He later crewed on an ocean racing boat.

In March 1946 Burchard married Betsy Chamberlain; a month later he was discharged from the army. After

spending six months working on perspective drawings for a classified Navy project, he resumed his education at the Museum School of Art and earned his certificate in 1947. With his wife and their first child, Burchard moved to Rockland County, New York, and worked as a freelance children's book illustrator. After illustrating numerous books for other authors, he began writing his own books in 1957. *The River Queen,* his first self-penned work, is about a New Orleans river boat. Burchard's first YA historical fiction was published two years later, in 1960.

In 1959 Burchard's elderly mother gave him some papers that had once belonged to her father, who in 1861, at age sixteen, had joined the Union Army to fight in the Civil War. The letters and diaries written during his grandfather's stint in the Union Army inspired Burchard to write *Jed: The Story of a Yankee Soldier and a Southern Boy.* The first of several books Burchard would write about the Civil War, *Jed* quickly won recognition from critics and encouraged its author to continue along those lines. His next book about the Civil War, *North by Night,* begins in South Carolina's Sea Islands and involves a battle at the Confederate-controlled Fort Wagner. *Rat Hell,* another work of fiction focusing on the war, is the story of an escape from a Civil War military prison.

Burchard's family connection to the war between the states ultimately inspired his best-known and most popular book. Published in 1965, *One Gallant Rush: Robert Gould Shaw and His Brave Black Regiment* focuses on the heroism of the Massachusetts 54th, the Union's first black regiment, which led an attack on Fort Wagner under the command of wealthy, white, Harvard-educated Colonel Shaw. The book was popular with critics and eventually inspired film producer Freddie Fields to make the 1989 motion picture *Glory.* In 1993 Burchard again made Shaw the focus of his writing in *"We'll Stand by the Union": Robert Gould Shaw and the Black 54th Massachusetts Regiment,* which *Booklist* contributor Carolyn Phelan noted "includes a history of the regiment after his [Shaw's] death and assesses the impact of black soldiers on the course of the war." While detailing the history of the 54th, *"We'll Stand by the Union"* is primarily a biography of Shaw, a man who, according to *Voice of Youth Advocates* contributor Sherry Hoy, "began with prejudices of his own, expressing astonishment 'at the general intelligence these darkies display'" and whose life "provides an interesting study in contrasts." Noted Burchard in *SAAS:* "I am happy to have played a minor role in the restructuring of the history of our country, to have helped give Robert Gould Shaw and his officers and men the prominence they deserve."

Other works of biography that focus on mid-nineteenth-century America include *Charlotte Forten: A Black Teacher in the Civil War* and *Frederick Douglass: For the Great Family of Man,* a biographical account of the slave-turned-abolitionist whose memoirs serve as the basis of Burchard's account. *Lincoln and Slavery* examines the president's developing understanding of the conditions endured by African Americans, an understanding that did not evolve until Lincoln was in his thirties. Burchard takes an unusual position, according to a *Horn Book* reviewer: "That Lincoln's ignorance about African Americans . . . for most of his early life led him to make decisions and take actions" that stand in stark contrast to his eventual anti-slavery stance. The *Horn Book* reviewer praised the readability of *Lincoln and Slavery,* adding that Burchard fills his book with "descriptions of specific incidents, quotations, and anecdotes that add color and detail." Under Burchard's pen Lincoln "emerges as a real human being with some flaws," according to a *Kirkus* reviewer, "but also with enormous maturity, wisdom, and compassion."

In addition to mining the U.S. Civil War for topics of interest to young readers, Burchard has found book ideas in other areas. *Bimby,* published in 1968, tells the story of a young black boy born into slavery who is driven to escape. *Whaleboat Raid,* published in 1977, is about the Revolutionary War, and is based on an episode that took place in 1777. 1979's *Chinwe* is about a young African woman who is captured and put aboard a slave ship bound for Cuba. Chinwe and her fellow captives stage a successful mutiny, but in the end spend their lives in slavery in America. 1984's *Sea Change* focuses on how three teenagers living in different eras of the twentieth century each deal with the transition from child to adult.

Burchard has also written two books about sailing. Living near the ocean for much of his adult life, he began ocean racing in 1976, and has crewed in over twenty major races. His first sailing book, 1978's *Ocean Race,* has been followed by *Venturing: An Introduction to Sailing,* published in 1986. In addition to communicating Burchard's passion for the sea, *Venturing* provides novice sailors with advice on sail handling, helmsmanship, and basic navigation skills.

Biographical and Critical Sources

BOOKS

Something about the Author Autobiography Series, Volume 13, Gale (Detroit, MI), 1990, pp. 55-70.

PERIODICALS

Booklist, February 15, 1994, Carolyn Phelan, review of *"We'll Stand by the Union": Robert Gould Shaw and the Black 54th Massachusetts Regiment,* pp. 1068-1069.
Book Report, September-October, 1995, Brenda B. Little, review of *Charlotte Forten: A Black Teacher in the Civil War,* p. 47.
Bulletin of the Center for Children's Books, April, 1995, Elizabeth Bush, review of *Charlotte Forten,* p. 266.
Horn Book, July, 1999, review of *Lincon and Slavery,* p. 480.
Kirkus Reviews, May 15, 1999, review of *Lincoln and Slavery,* p. 797; November 15, 2002, review of *Frederick Douglass: For the Great Family of Man,* p. 1688.
School Library Journal, September, 1995, Gerry Larson, review of *Charlotte Forten,* p. 205; July, 1999, Mary Mueller, review of *Lincoln and Slavery,* p. 104.
Voice of Youth Advocates, June, 1994, Sherry Hoy, review of *"We'll Stand by the Union,"* p. 105.

C

CAMPOY, F. Isabel (Coronado) 1946-

Personal

Born June 25, 1946, in Alicante, Spain; daughter of Juan Diego Campoy (a professor of English) and Maria Coronado Guerro (a homemaker). *Ethnicity:* "Hispanic." *Education:* Universidad Complutense, Madrid, B.A. and M.A. (English philology); Reading University, M.A. (dialectology); doctoral studies in applied linguistics at University of California, Los Angeles. *Politics:* "A defender of justice and peace." *Hobbies and other interests:* Painting, collecting art, observing children and nature.

Addresses

Home—10 Walnut St., Mill Valley, CA 94941. *Office*—38 Miller Ave., No. 181, Mill Valley, CA 94941. *E-mail*—fisabelcampoy@yahoo.com.

Career

Poet, playwright, storyteller, and editor. Mangold & Santillana Publishing, Madrid, Spain, editor, 1971-78; Houghton, Mifflin, Boston, MA, senior acquisitions editor, 1981-93; freelance writer and lecturer on educational and multicultural matters. Transformative Education Services, president. Member of board of directors, Children's Book Council, 1998—, and San Francisco Public Library Foundation, 1997—.

Member

National Council of Teachers of English, International Reading Association, CABE, NABE, Association of Spanish Professionals in the U.S.A. (president, 1994-96), various national and regional bilingual education associations.

Awards, Honors

Fulbright scholar, 1979-81; Friends and Foundation of San Francisco Public Library Laureate Award, 2003.

F. Isabel Campoy

Writings

(Adaptor) *Rosa Raposa,* illustrated by Ariane Dewey and Jose Aruego, Harcourt (New York, NY), 2002.

FOR CHILDREN; WITH ALMA FLOR ADA

Tablado de Doña Rosita/Curtain's Up, Santillana USA Publishing (Miami, FL), 2001.

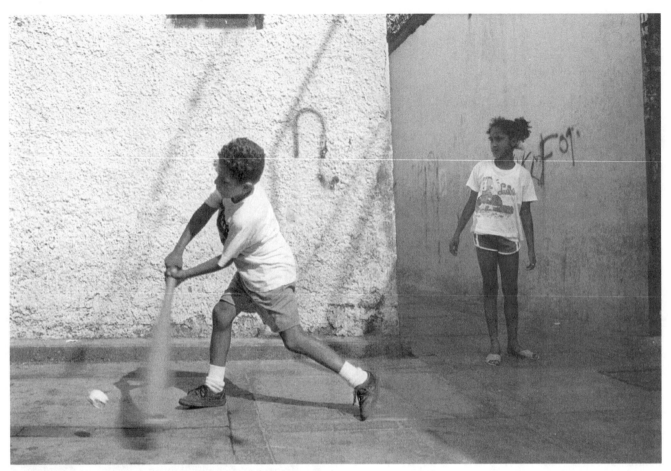

Fifth-grader Hubaldo's life in Venezuela centers around his country's most popular sport in Henry Horenstein's work **Béisbol en los barrios,** *translated by Alma Flor Ada and Campoy.*

¡Feliz cumpleaños, Caperucita Roja!/Happy Birthday, Little Red Riding Hood! (bilingual edition), illustrated by Ana López Escrivá, Alfaguara (Miami, FL), 2002.

El nuevo hogar de los siete cabritos/The New Home of the Seven Billy Goats, illustrated by Viví Escrivá, Alfaguara (Miami, FL), 2002.

A New Job for Pérez the Mouse/Ratoncito Perez, Cartero, illustrated by Sandra López Escrivá, Alfaguara (Miami, FL), 2002.

One, Two, Three, Who Can It Be?/Uno, dos, tres: ¿Dime quién es?, illustrated by Viví Escrivá, Alfaguara (Miami, FL), 2002.

On the Wings of the Condor/En alas del condor, Alfaguara (Miami, FL), 2002.

Eyes of the Jaguar/Ojos del jaguar, Alfaguara (Miami, FL), 2002.

The Quetzal's Journey/Vuelo del quetzal, illustrated by Felipe Davalos, Santillana USA Publishing (Miami, FL), 2002.

Friends from A to Z: A Glossary of the Hispanic World/ Amigos de la A a la Z: Un alfabeto del mundo hispánico, Santillana USA Publishing (Miami, FL), 2002.

(Compiler) *Pío peep!: Traditional Spanish Nursery Rhymes* (bilingual edition), illustrated by Viví Escriv´, English adaptations by Alice Schertle, HarperCollins (New York, NY), 2003.

Also translator of children's books into Spanish, including works by Louis Ehlert, Gary Soto, Kathleen Krull, and Gerald McDermott.

Works also published in Spanish translation.

"GATEWAYS TO THE SUN" SERIES; WITH ALMA FLOR ADA

Smiles/Sonrisas (biographies of Pablo Picasso, Gabriela Mistral, and Benito Juarez), Alfaguara (Miami, FL), 1998.

Steps/Pasos (biographies of Rita Moreno, Fernando Botero, and Evelyn Cisneros), Alfaguara (Miami, FL), 1998.

Voices/Voces (biographies of Luis Valdez, Judith F. Baca, and Carlos J. Finlay), Alfaguara (Miami, FL), 1998.

Paths/Caminos (biographies of José Marti, Frida Kahlo, and Cesar Chavez), Alfaguara (Miami, FL), 1998.

Yo/I Am, Santillana USA Publishing (Miami, FL), 1999.

Rimas/Rhymes, Santillana USA Publishing (Miami, FL), 1999.

Poemas/Poems, Santillana USA Publishing (Miami, FL), 1999.

Palabras, Santillana USA Publishing (Miami, FL), 1999.

Mis relatos/My Stories, Santillana USA Publishing (Miami, FL), 1999.

Mis recuerdos, Santillana USA Publishing (Miami, FL), 1999.

Mambru, Santillana USA Publishing (Miami, FL), 1999.

Letras, Santillana USA Publishing (Miami, FL), 1999.

Lapices/Pencils, Santillana USA Publishing (Miami, FL), 1999.

Crayones/Crayons, Santillana USA Publishing (Miami, FL), 1999.

Colores/Colors, Santillana USA Publishing (Miami, FL), 1999.

Así soy/This Is Me, Santillana USA Publishing (Miami, FL), 1999.

Acuarela, Santillana USA Publishing (Miami, FL), 1999.

Blue and Green/Azul y Verde, Alfaguara (Miami, FL), 2000.

Brush and Paint/Brocha y pinchel, Alfaguara (Miami, FL), 2000.

Artist's Easel/Caballete, Alfaguara (Miami, FL), 2000.

Canvas and Paper/Lienzo y Papel, Alfaguara (Miami, FL), 2000.

(Selector) *Dreaming Fish/Pimpón* (poetry), Alfaguara (Miami, FL), 2000.

(Selector) *Laughing Crocodiles/Antón Pirulero* (poetry), Alfaguara (Miami, FL), 2000.

(Selector) *Singing Horse/Mambrú* (poetry), Alfaguara (Miami, FL), 2000.

(Selector and contributor) *Flying Dragon* (published in Spanish as *Chuchurumbé*), Alfaguara (Miami, FL), 2000.

Series published in Spanish translation as "Colleccion Puertas al Sol."

POETRY; IN SPANISH; WITH ALMA FLOR ADA

Gorrión, Gorrión, Harcourt School Publishers (Orlando, FL), 1996.

El verde limón, Harcourt School Publishers (Orlando, FL), 1996.

La rama azul, Harcourt School Publishers (Orlando, FL), 1996.

Nuevo día, Harcourt School Publishers (Orlando, FL), 1996.

Huertos de coral, Harcourt School Publishers (Orlando, FL), 1996.

Ríos de lava, Harcourt School Publishers (Orlando, FL), 1996.

Dulce es la sal, Harcourt School Publishers (Orlando, FL), 1996.

Canta la letra, illustrated by Ulises Wensell, Del Sol (Westlake, OH), 1998, with music by Suni Paz, 2003.

Caracolí, illustrated by Ulises Wensell, Del Sol (Westlake, OH), 1998, with music by Suni Paz, 2003.

Con ton y son, illustrated by Ulises Wensell, Del Sol (Westlake, OH), 1998, with music by Suni Paz, 2003.

Corre al coro, illustrated by Ulises Wensell, Del Sol (Westlake, OH), 1998, with music by Suni Paz, 2003.

¡Do, re, mi, ¡sí, sí!, illustrated by Ulises Wensell, Del Sol (Westlake, OH), 1998, with music by Suni Paz, 2003.

El camino de tu risa, illustrated by Ulises Wensell, Del Sol (Westlake, OH), 1998, with music by Suni Paz, 2003.

El son de sol, illustrated by Ulises Wensell, Del Sol (Westlake, OH), 1998, with music by Suni Paz, 2003.

¡Qué rica la ronda!, illustrated by Ulises Wensell, Del Sol (Westlake, OH), 1998, with music by Suni Paz, 2003.

Sigue la música, illustrated by Ulises Wensell, Del Sol (Westlake, OH), 1998, with music by Suni Paz, 2003.

PLAYS; WITH ALMA FLOR ADA

Primer Acto, Harcourt School Publishers (Orlando, FL), 1996.

Risas y aplausos, Harcourt School Publishers (Orlando, FL), 1996.

Escenas y alegrías, Harcourt School Publishers (Orlando, FL), 1996.

Actores y flores, Harcourt School Publishers (Orlando, FL), 1996.

Saludos al público, Harcourt School Publishers (Orlando, FL), 1996.

Ensayo general, Harcourt School Publishers (Orlando, FL), 1996.

Acto final, Harcourt School Publishers (Orlando, FL), 1996.

Rat-a-Tat, Alfaguara (Miami, FL), 2000, published as *Rat-a-Tat Cat,* Santillana USA Publishing (Miami, FL), 2002.

Roll 'n' Roll, Alfaguara (Miami, FL), 2000, published as *Roll 'n' Role,* Santillana USA Publishing (Miami, FL), 2002.

Top Hat, Alfaguara (Miami, FL), 2000.

Curtains Up!, Alfaguara (Miami, FL), 2000.

Works published in Spanish translation.

IN SPANISH

¿Quieres que to cuente? Harcourt School Publishers (Orlando, FL), 1995.

En un lugar muy lejano, Harcourt School Publishers (Orlando, FL), 1995.

Erase que se era, Harcourt School Publishers (Orlando, FL), 1995.

Y fueron felices, Harcourt School Publishers (Orlando, FL), 1995.

Y colorín colorado, Harcourt School Publishers (Orlando, FL), 1995.

Así pasaron muchos años, Harcourt School Publishers (Orlando, FL), 1995.

(With Alma Flor Ada) *Sigue la palabra,* Harcourt School Publishers (Orlando, FL), 1995.

(With Alma Flor Ada) *Imágenes del pasado,* Harcourt School Publishers (Orlando, FL), 1995.

(With Alma Flor Ada) *Ecos del pasado,* Harcourt School Publishers (Orlando, FL), 1995.

(With Alma Flor Ada; and lyricist) *Música amiga* (anthology of Hispanic folklore; includes tapes and teacher's guide), ten volumes, Del Sol (Westlake, OH), 1996-98.

(With Alma Flor Ada) *Una semilla de luz,* illustrated by Felipe Dávalos, Santillana/UNICEF (Madrid, Spain), 2000.

Also coauthor, with Alma Flor Ada, of Spanish language-arts programs *Cielo abierto, Vamos de fiesta!* and *Trofeos,* Harcourt School Publishers (Orlando, FL), 1997, and of English-as-a-second-language programs.

TRANSLATOR; WITH ALMA FLOR ADA

Lois Ehlert, *Plumas para almorzar,* illustrated by the author, Harcourt (San Diego, CA), 1996 (originally published as *Feathers for Lunch*).

Lois Ehlert, *A sembrar sopa de verduras,* illustrated by the author, Harcourt (San Diego, CA), 1996 (originally published as *Growing Vegetable Soup*).

Gary Soto, *¡Que montón de tamales!,* illustrated by Ed Martinez, PaperStar (New York, NY), 1996 (originally published as *Too Many Tamales*).

Ellen Stoll Walsh, *Salta y brinca,* Harcourt (San Diego, CA), 1996 (originally published as *Hop Jump*).

Henry Horenstein, *Béisbol en los barrios,* Harcourt (New York, NY), 1997.

Mem Fox, *Quienquiera que seas,* illustrated by Leslie Staub, Harcourt (San Diego, CA), 2002 (originally published as *Whoever You Are*).

Gerald McDermott, *Zomo el conejo: un cuento de Africa occidental,* illustrated by the author, Harcourt (San Diego, CA), 2002 (originally published as *Zomo the Rabbit*).

Peter Golenbock, *Compañeros de equipo,* illustrated by Paul Bacon, Harcourt (San Diego, CA), 2002 (originally published as *Teammates*).

Lois Ehlert, *Día de mercado,* illustrated by the author, Harcourt (San Diego, CA), 2003 (originally published as *Market Day*).

FOR ADULTS

(With Alma Flor Ada) *Home School Interaction with Culturally or Language-diverse Families,* Del Sol (Westlake, OH), 1998.

(With Alma Flor Ada) *Ayudando a nuestros hijos* (title means "Helping Our Children"), Del Sol (Westlake, OH), 1998.

(With Alma Flor Ada) *Comprehensive Language Arts,* Del Sol (Westlake, OH), 1998.

(With Alma Flor Ada) *Effective English Acquisition for Academic Success,* Del Sol (Westlake, OH), 1998.

(With Alma Flor Ada and Rosalma Zubizarreta) *Authors in the Classroom: A Transformative Education Process,* Allyn & Bacon (Boston, MA), 2003.

Work in Progress

A nonfiction collection for ages five to eleven.

Sidelights

F. Isabel Campoy is the prolific author of bilingual materials for children of Hispanic heritage. Plays, poems,

The painting "Country Landscape" appears in **Blue and Green,** *an artbook cowritten by Alma Flor Ada and Campoy.*

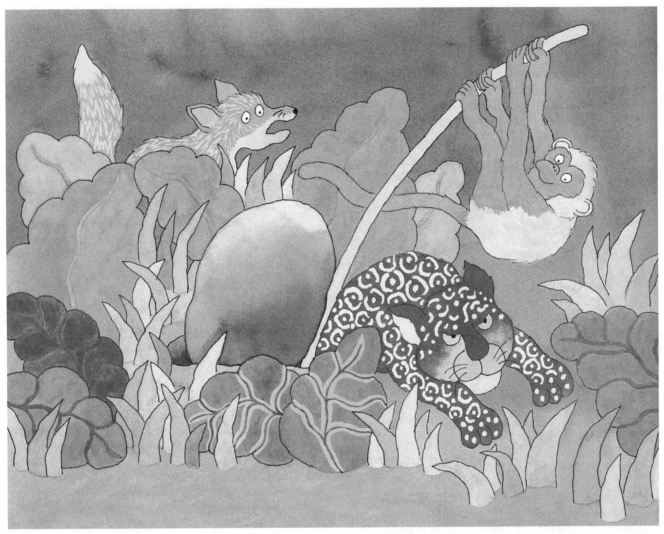

Three tricksters—Fox, Jaguar, and Monkey—match wits in **Rosa Raposa**, *adapted by Campoy and illustrated by Jose Aruego and Ariane Dewey.*

educational materials, picture books, biographies, and easy-readers all have issued from Campoy's fertile imagination, most of these works coauthored by Alma Flor Ada. In addition to stand-alone books, the collaborators have produced a number of book series, and several of their works have been included in the "Coleccion Puertas al Sol" series designed to introduce young readers to Hispanic culture. Their *Música amiga* anthology, published beginning in 1996, encompasses ten volumes of Hispanic folklore, along with original lyrics by Campoy, while other books, such as *Happy Birthday, Little Red Riding Hood!* "combine the charm of traditional tales with the surprise of the unexpected," according to *Booklist* reviewer Isabel Schon.

Books by Campoy and Ada that are part of the "Gateways to the Sun" series include the art books *Blue and Green* and *Brush and Paint,* as well as a four-book series of biographies of notable Hispanic men and woman titled *Smiles, Steps, Voices,* and *Paths.* Profiling such diverse individuals as artist Frida Kahlo, labor activist Cesar Chavez, and actress Rita Moreno, these books "briefly tell about the lives and achievements" of their

subjects, according to *Booklist* reviewer Schon, who praised the entire series as "a very appealing introduction" to Spanish-language culture.

In addition to her works with Ada, Campoy has authored the picture book *Rosa Raposa*. The book contains three stories adapted from Spanish trickster tales that take readers into the Amazon rain forest. In "A Cry for Help," "A Strong North Wind," and "The Green Dress" the clever little fox Rosa Raposa manages to outwit a hungry and bullying jaguar. While noting that the stories are "rather flat" in their narration, a *Publishers Weekly* contributor nonetheless praised *Rosa Raposa* for its lively watercolor illustrations. Julie Cummins was more enthusiastic in her *Booklist* review, noting that *Rosa Raposa* features a "well-paced text" that, with the rhyming conclusion to each story, "will make for lively read-alouds." Calling the book "delightful," *School Library Journal* contributor Judith Constantinides added that Campoy's stories do much to promote "the idea that brains are better than brawn."

Campoy told *CA:* "I was born by the Mediterranean Sea in a town called Alicante, an ideal vacation place in Spain both for national and international tourists, so during my childhood I was always in contact with people coming and going—family and friends from all over the world.

"That, and the fact that my father was a professor of English and wanted his children to become proficient in as many languages as possible, provided me with a great desire to travel and be in touch with other cultures very early on. My favorite books as a child were always full of adventure, from the medieval chivalric romances and the pirates of Sandocán to *Treasure Island, The Adventures of Tom Sawyer,* and *Alice's Adventures in Wonderland.* But perhaps my favorite of all times is *The Little Prince* by Antoine de Sainte-Exupéry.

"My curiosity for all things far and different was nurtured by my father's vast collection of *National Geographic* magazines that covered one side of our hallway from floor to ceiling, with copies that went back as far as 1924. Each picture was a promise of a new adventure, and I started writing about them in a huge accounting book my brother and I shared: on his end, the names of soccer players and winning teams; on mine, the products of my fertile imagination. My first published story was about a snowman. I was eleven, and I had never seen snow.

"At age sixteen, after a hard time convincing my mother and many competitive examinations, I won a scholarship as an exchange student to Trenton, Michigan. Finally, that winter, I saw snow—almost daily! I have the impression that I have been traveling ever since.

"In my twenties I crossed Europe and in Greece I fell in love with mythology. Years later I wrote down many legends of the Hispanic world.

"Morocco, Egypt, and Turkey were countries that fascinated me and inspired my research into the Arabic contributions to the history of Spain and Latin America.

"Whether in Asia or Micronesia, Africa or the Middle East, I have always found reason to admire other cultures and reflect on them. Perhaps that is why I write about Hispanic art, artists, theatre, poetry, and folklore: in the process of looking at other cultures, I discovered the beauty and richness of my own."

See sketch on Alma Flor Ada for more information.

Biographical and Critical Sources

PERIODICALS

Booklist, August, 2000, p. 2154; February 15, 2002, Isabel Schon, review of *Happy Birthday, Little Red Riding Hood!* and *The New Home of the Seven Billy Goats,* p. 1022; September 1, 2002, Julie Cummins, review of *Rosa Raposa,* p. 136.

Kirkus Reviews, August 15, 2002, review of *Rosa Raposa,* p. 1219.

Publishers Weekly, September 9, 2002, review of *Rosa Raposa,* p. 66.

School Library Journal, September, 2002, Judith Constantinides, review of *Rosa Raposa,* p. 181.

ONLINE

F. Isabel Campoy Web site, http://www.isabelcampoy.com/ (May 5, 2003).

OTHER

Path to My Word (videotape), Del Sol (Westlake, OH).

*   *   *

CAPPO, Nan Willard 1955-

Personal
Born March 5, 1955, in Traverse City, MI; daughter of Gradon F. (a chemical company executive) and Ellen (a nurse; maiden name, Connor) Willard; married Dirk F. Cappo (a financial consultant), 1983; children: Ellen, Emily, Mark. *Ethnicity:* "Caucasian." *Education:* University of Notre Dame, B.A., 1977; University of Pittsburgh, M.B.A., 1981; Wayne State University, M.A., 2003. *Religion:* Roman Catholic. *Hobbies and other interests:* Reading, movies, international politics.

Addresses
Home—Farmington, MI. *Agent*—Edite Kroll Literary Agency, 12 Grayhurst Park, Portland, ME 04102. *E-mail*—nancap@attglobal.net.

Career
Novelist, 2000—. IBM marketing representative, 1982-87; Oakland Community College, English teacher, 2002—; leader of various writing workshops; public speaker. Odyssey of Mind, coach, 1991-99.

Member
Society of Children's Book Writers and Illustrators, Detroit Women Writers (chair of Writers' Conference, 2002).

Awards, Honors
Judy Blume Contemporary Novel-In-Progress grant, Society of Children's Book Writers and Illustrators, 1992; nomination, Edgar Award for best young adult mystery, 2003, for *Cheating Lessons.*

Writings
Cheating Lessons (young adult novel), Simon & Schuster (New York, NY), 2002.

Nan Willard Cappo

Work in Progress

Natalie Wishbone, a young adult novel.

Sidelights

Nan Willard Cappo told *SATA:* "I always thought I'd be a writer someday, but until I quit my corporate job to stay home with my children, I never wrote fiction. Fortunately, a lifetime of reading had taught me more than I knew. The plot for *Cheating Lessons* came from my love of English literature, from coaching school teams in national competitions, and from my fascination with the difficulty most people, including me, have being honest all the time. As I wrote, the characters in the story began to remind me of people I knew. I changed their height and coloring to avoid libel charges and disinheritance. Bernadette is a bit like me at sixteen (though her memory is much better), and almost as smart as she thinks she is.

"My favorite review is the one in *Horn Book,* which calls Bernadette 'an adolescent who gains . . . friends when she learns to be a little less critical and who, while losing her naive confidence in adults, refreshingly maintains confidence in herself.' Bernadette's new tolerance for other people, now that she's seen how easy it is to do bad things for good reasons, is one of the things I like best about the book. Who doesn't face those temptations? Who doesn't wish the people you love could be a bit more lovable? But teenagers seem to like the scene where she hides in her teacher's closet while he takes off his shirt. Go figure.

"I have three teenagers of my own who supply me with plenty of material. Recently I began teaching college English, so my students, too, give me more ideas than they suspect. The best advice I have for young writers is to read like a writer. Try to figure out how authors did what they did, and then attempt the same thing, using your own material, of course. I pore over books by Anne Tyler and Jane Austen and Francine Prose—stories about things that matter, like courage and love and clever conversation. Some of my favorite writers for children are Anne Fine, Katherine Paterson, Nancy Farmer, Lynne Rae Perkins, and J. K. Rowling. For me, reading books I wish I'd written and trying to crack the code remains the best writing instruction in the world."

Biographical and Critical Sources

PERIODICALS

Horn Book, March-April, 2002, Jennifer M. Brabander, review of *Cheating Lessons,* p. 209.
Publishers Weekly, January 7, 2002, review of *Cheating Lessons,* p. 65.
School Library Journal, March, 2002, Susan Riley, review of *Cheating Lessons,* p. 226.
Teacher, May 1, 2002, review of *Cheating Lessons.*

* * *

CHAMBERS, Catherine E.
See ST. JOHN, Nicole

* * *

CHAMBERS, Kate
See ST. JOHN, Nicole

* * *

COLLICOTT, Sharleen 1937-
(Sharleen Pederson)

Personal

Born April 10, 1937, in Los Angeles, CA; married Con Pederson (a special effects designer; divorced, 1985); children: Eric. *Education:* University of California at Los Angeles, B.A., 1969.

Addresses

Home and office—2960 Bel Air Dr., Las Vegas, NV 89109-1581. *E-mail*—rubincolli@aol.com.

Career

Writer, illustrator, ceramist, sculptor, and educator. Duntog Foundation, artist-in-residence, 1983; Otis/Parson Design Institute, teacher, 1983; California State Univer-

Sharleen Collicott

sity, Long Beach, teacher, 1983-84. National Endowment for the Arts, panelist, 1985; affiliated with India Ink Galleries, 1985-86, and Every Picture Tells a Story (art gallery), 1991-95. Has also worked on special effects for motion pictures. *Exhibitions:* Exhibitor at galleries in Los Angeles, CA, including India Ink Gallery, 1983; Los Angeles City College, 1984; Every Picture Tells a Story, 1991, 1994; and Storyopolis, 1997.

Awards, Honors

Society of Illustrators, Los Angeles awards; Art Directors Club of Los Angeles awards; *Advertising Age* awards.

Writings

SELF-ILLUSTRATED

Seeing Stars, Dial (New York, NY), 1996.
Mildred and Sam, HarperCollins (New York, NY), 2002.
Toestomper and the Caterpillars, Houghton Mifflin (Boston, MA), 2002.
Toestomper and the Bad Butterflies, Houghton Mifflin (Boston, MA), 2003.

ILLUSTRATOR

(As Sharleen Pederson) Michael Hallward, *The Enormous Leap of Alphonse Frog,* Nash Publishing (Los Angeles, CA), 1972.

(As Sharleen Pederson) Suzanne Klein, *An Elephant in My Bed,* Follett (Chicago, IL), 1974.
Mouse, Frog, and Little Hen, DLM, 1990.
Sharon Lucky, *The Three Dinosaurs Dreadly,* DLM, 1991.
Karen Radler Greenfield, *The Teardrop Baby,* HarperCollins (New York, NY), 1994.
Laura Joffe Numeroff, *The Chicken Sisters,* HarperCollins (New York, NY), 1997.
Judith Barrett, *Which Witch Is Which?* Atheneum (New York, NY), 2001.

Also contributor of illustrations to *Elementary Math Series,* Addison-Wesley, *Frickles and Frackles,* DLM, and *Pattern Palace,* DLM. Contributor of illustrations to periodicals, including *Psychology Today, Westways, National Wildlife Federation, Human Behavior, Lady Bug,* and *Ranger Rick.*

Sidelights

Highly regarded illustrator Sharleen Collicott has been creating picture-book images since the early 1970s. After working for over twenty years teaching, illustrating the work of children's book authors, and exhibiting her paintings, sculpture, and ceramics at art galleries, Collicott decided to expand her creative talents even further. In 1996 she published *Seeing Stars,* the first of her works containing both original art and text. Her pictures—colorful, detailed paintings that range from intimate views to double-page spreads—characteristically feature fantastic animals and have been compared to such artists as Hieronymous Bosch for their imaginative quality and attention to detail.

Born in 1937, Collicott enjoyed drawing even as a child, and animals were among her favorite subjects. She graduated from the University of California, Los Angeles in 1969 with a degree in sculpture, then went to live in England for several years, where she worked on special effects for motion pictures. Although ceramics and welded steel were originally her artistic media of choice, she began to draw seriously during her stay in England when, because of rainy weather, she spent many days indoors at the London Zoo. In an interview with Marv Rubin in *Communication Arts,* Collicott explained that being at the zoo "put me much closer to the animals than I had ever been. That inspired me to try sketching in my notebook, and to discover how much I enjoyed it." Attending a centennial exhibit of nineteenth-century British illustrator Beatrix Potter's work convinced her "that drawing the things I imagined was indeed legitimate." After filling the pages of her notebook, she showed them to others, including director Stanley Kubrick, for whom she was sculpting alien creatures for the film *2001: A Space Odyssey.* Although Collicott's aliens were ultimately cut from the film, Kubrick encouraged her to add background to her animal sketches for exhibition or publication. She took his advice and has been illustrating ever since. "When I paint now," she told Rubin, "I'm revealing something from my imagination as realistically as possible."

Collicott began her new career as a professional artist by illustrating advertising copy, magazine articles, educational material, and record covers. One of her most recognizable works was the first wide-screen version of the "Columbia Lady," the image of a woman holding a torch that is featured at the beginning of movies produced by Columbia Pictures. Collicott has also taught art at the university level, served as an artist-in-residence in the Philippines, and formed affiliations with several Los Angeles art galleries. However, by the early 1990s she had decided to focus her efforts on illustrating and writing picture books.

Many of Collicott's initial book illustrations were done for educational publications, such as the easy-readers *An Elephant in My Bed* and *Mouse, Frog, and Little Hen.* The first children's picture book she contributed to was Karen Radler Greenfield's *The Teardrop Baby,* pub-

lished in 1994. In this original fairy tale, a childless couple meet a magical woman who creates a child for them from their tears. When the boy is seven, the old woman comes back to claim him and makes him her servant; after tricking the woman with a fortune baked into a loaf of bread, the boy returns to his parents. "Collicott's illustrations, with many-eyed flowers and a deliciously scary depiction of the edge of the world, realize and enhance Greenfield's cryptic tale," declared a contributor to *Publishers Weekly.* In a review for *School Library Journal,* Lisa Dennis called *The Teardrop Baby* an "unusual picture book" and noted that the illustrations "suit the fairy-tale flavor of the story." Collicott's "decision to paint eyes on the flowers creates a distinctly creepy atmosphere," concluded Dennis.

Collicott's 1996 work *Seeing Stars* marked her debut as a children's book author. The story describes how two

Collicott's gouache paintings complement the rhyming text in **Which Witch Is Which?,** *written by Judith Barrett.*

Befriending a group of baby caterpillars causes Toestomper to change his ways in **Toestomper and the Caterpillars,** *written and illustrated by Collicott.*

small animals, Motley and Fuzzball, build a makeshift spaceship out of parts found in a junkyard in an attempt to reach the stars in outer space. Through Collicott's illustrations, the reader knows exactly where the ship lands: in the ocean. However, the befuddled pair thinks they are in space and that the starfish are actually stars. Writing in *School Library Journal,* Jane Marino noted that "younger readers may forgive the lapses in the story to enjoy the beautiful illustrations and may even sympathize with these two wayward passengers." A *Publishers Weekly* reviewer found *Seeing Stars* "impressive for its eye-catching visuals," and noted that

Collicott "adroitly pulls off the kid-pleasing contrivance" of letting young readers in on a secret of which her characters are unaware.

As is characteristic in Collicott's books, animals take center stage in *Mildred and Sam,* the author/illustrator's 2002 easy-read chapter book. Mildred and Sam are fieldmice who make their home under a patch of daffodils, but the overwrought homemaker Mildred despairs of their tiny home ever being big enough for company. Although at first Sam is totally in the dark as to what his anxious mousewife means, he eventually understands when a litter of eight tiny mouse babies make their appearance. "A well-balanced narrative with plenty of judiciously repeated phrases" make *Mildred and Sam* "a fine choice for beginning readers," remarked a *Publishers Weekly* contributor, who also praised Collicott's "fetching graphics." Praising the book's "whimsical" illustrations, a *Kirkus* reviewer wrote that the book's "fanciful themes and vibrant illustrations make this an enjoyable romp to share as a read-aloud."

Collicott's self-authored *Toestomper and the Caterpillars* and its sequel, *Toestomper and the Bad Butterflies* feature a trio of bad-mannered rodents—Barfy, Basher, and Nightmare—who call themselves the Rowdy Ruffians and their leader, the bullying Toestomper, who suffers changes of heart when faced by small animals in peril. Actually, the peril in *Toestomper in the Caterpillars* is Toestomper himself; the uncouth rat crushes the bush a caterpillar family calls home before pangs of conscience kick in and he makes the homeless insects his friends. While a *Publishers Weekly* reviewer found the book's storyline "mediocre," the reviewer went on to dub Collicott's illustrations "cuddly" and the Rowdy Ruffians' behavior "funny."

In addition to illustrating her own texts, Collicott has continued to contribute highly praised illustrations to books by other authors. Among these are Laura Joffe Numeroff's 1997 work *The Chicken Sisters,* which features three sister hens whose hobbies—baking, knitting, and singing—annoy a neighboring wolf because of the talent (or lack thereof) of their practitioners. The story "comes brilliantly alive in Collicott's pictures," declared *Booklist* contributor Ilene Cooper, who added that the artist's work "is chock-full and pretty darn adorable." In *School Library Journal* Jane Marino commented that the illustrations for *The Chicken Sisters* "reinforce the text, giving personality to the feathered siblings," while a *Publishers Weekly* contributor predicted that toddlers would enjoy "the bright colors in Collicott's intricately detailed art." Collicott's contribution to Judith Barrett's *Which Witch Is Which?* were hailed by *Booklist* contributor Connie Fletcher as "eye-popping gouache paintings [that] deliver just the right kind of creepy-crawly landscapes" for Barrett's rhyming wordplay.

Collicott works from her artist's studio in Las Vegas, Nevada, where she has lived for several years. Although

when she began illustrating she used colored pencils, she has since expanded her medium to include water colors, egg tempera—a blend of ground pigment powder and egg yolk made using recipes and techniques dating from the Middle Ages—and gouache, an opaque form of water color. In her interview with Marv Rubin in *Communication Arts,* she explained that in individual illustrations every area is "equally important. I don't like empty areas or unimportant areas." Collicott spends almost as much time preparing for an illustration as she does painting it. "I plan the pictures and their 'stories' carefully," she explained to Rubin. "I 'cast' all the characters before I begin. I do research on them and on their settings. I know all about them."

Biographical and Critical Sources

PERIODICALS

Artist, October, 1994.
Booklist, May 1, 1997, Ilene Cooper, review of *The Chicken Sisters,* p. 1497; November 1, 2001, Connie Fletcher, review of *Which Witch Is Which?* p. 480.
Communication Arts, January/February, 1983, Marv Rubin, "Sharleen Pederson," pp. 66-70.
Crayola Kids, June/July, 1998.
Kirkus Reviews, May 1, 1997, review of *The Chicken Sisters;* September 14, 1999, review of *Toestomper and the Caterpillars,* p. 1498; November 15, 2002, review of *Mildred and Sam,* p. 1689.
Publishers Weekly, August 15, 1994, review of *The Teardrop Baby,* p. 95; April 29, 1996, review of *Seeing Stars,* p. 70; April 7, 1997, review of *The Chicken Sisters,* p. 90; September 27, 1999, review of *Toestomper and the Caterpillar,* p. 104; December 23, 2002, review of *Mildred and Sam,* p. 68.
School Library Journal, September, 1994, Lisa Dennis, review of *The Teardrop Baby,* p. 184; April, 1996, Jane Marino, review of *Seeing Stars,* p. 105; May, 1997, J. Marino, review of *The Chicken Sisters,* p. 109.
Today's Art, Volume 27, number 8.

OTHER

Collicott, Sharleen, interview in promotional piece, DLM Publishing.*

D

DRYDEN, Pamela
  See ST. JOHN, Nicole

*   *   *

DURBIN, William 1951-

Personal

Born February 17, 1951, in Minneapolis, MN; son of
Charles (a barber) and Dona (a bookkeeper) Durbin;
married October 14, 1971; wife's name Barbara (a
teacher); children: Jessica Durbin Froehle, Reid. *Education:* St. Cloud State University, B.S., 1973; Middlebury College, M.A. 1987. *Hobbies and other interests:*
Golf, canoeing.

Addresses

Home and office—2287 Birch Pt. Rd., Tower, MN
55790. *Agent*—Barbara Markowitz, 1505 Hill Dr., Los
Angeles, CA 90041. *E-mail*—Bill@williamdurbin.com.

Career

Writer and educator. Teacher of English in Minnesota
public schools, grades four through college, including
at Cook High School; speaker at writing conferences
and at schools and libraries.

Member

National Education Association, Society of Children's
Book Writers and Illustrators, Children's Literature
Network.

Awards, Honors

Great Lakes Booksellers Association Book Award, Minnesota Book Award, Bank Street College Children's
Book of the Year, and New York Public Library Books
for the Teen-Age selection, all 1998; New River Press
Poetry Competition finalist; Lake Superior Contemporary Writer's Series winner.

William Durbin

Writings

The Broken Blade, Delacorte (New York, NY), 1997.
Tiger Woods (biography; "Golf Legends" and "Black
 Americans of Achievement" series), Chelsea House
 (Philadelphia, PA), 1998.
Arnold Palmer (biography; "Golf Legends" series),
 Chelsea House (Philadelphia, PA), 1998.

Wintering (sequel to *The Broken Blade*), Delacorte (New York, NY), 1999.

The Song of Sampo Lake, Wendy Lamb Books (New York, NY), 2002.

Blackwater Ben, Wendy Lamb Books (New York, NY), 2003.

Contributor of poems, essays, and short stories to periodicals, including *English Journal, Great River Review, Milkweed Chronicle, Confrontation, North American Mentor, Canadian Author and Bookman, Boys Life, Loonfeather, Modern Haiku, Nebraska Language Arts Bulletin, Breadloaf News,* and *NCTE.*

Durbin's books have been translated into several languages, including Italian, and have been produced in Braille editions.

"MY NAME IS AMERICA" SERIES

The Journal of Sean Sullivan, a Transcontinental Railroad Worker: Nebraska and Points West, 1867, Scholastic (New York, NY), 1999.

The Journal of Otto Peltonen, a Finnish Immigrant: Hibbing Minnesota, 1905, Scholastic (New York, NY), 2000.

The Journal of C. J. Jackson, a Dust Bowl Migrant: Oklahoma to California, 1935, Scholastic (New York, NY), 2002.

Adaptations

The Broken Blade was adapted as a cartoon serial published in *Boys' Life* magazine.

Work in Progress

The Darkest Evening, scheduled for publication by Scholastic in 2004.

Sidelights

Making his home on the shores of Minnesota's Lake Vermilion, author and teacher William Durbin shares his enthusiasm and interests in history, golf, and canoeing in the pages of his books for young readers. In addition to biographies of golfing greats Tiger Woods and Arnold Palmer, he has penned a number of works of historical fiction that have been praised by reviewers.

Born in Minneapolis, Minnesota in 1951, Durbin attended St. Cloud State University before earning his master's degree at Middlebury College and spending a year at Lincoln College, Oxford, on a scholarship from the school's Bread Loaf School of English. Trained as a teacher, he worked for decades as a teacher and mentor to writers at Bread Loaf as well as for those students participating in writing projects sponsored by the National Council of Teachers of English. He was inspired to begin writing for young adults after speaking to author Gary Paulson during the award-winning young-adult writer's workshop appearance at Durbin's wife's school.

Durbin's first book, 1997's *The Broken Blade,* was inspired by his interest in the French *voyageur* fur traders who canoed the waters of the northern Midwest and Canada during the eighteenth and early nineteenth centuries. In the book, which takes place in 1800, Pierre LaPage's father supports his family as an oarsman for the North West Fur Company on the long, heavy voyageur canoes used by fur traders to transport pelts out of northern Canada. When his father is unable to make the trip after severing his thumb in an accident, thirteen-year-old Pierre leaves school, determined to take his place on the 1,200-mile trip from Montreal to Grand Portage that requires incredible physical strength and fortitude. Noting that Durbin fills the novel with action and describes in vivid detail the events that "transform . . . Pierre from classroom-softened boy to hard-muscled man," a *Bulletin of the Center for Children's Books* contributor Elizabeth Bush added that

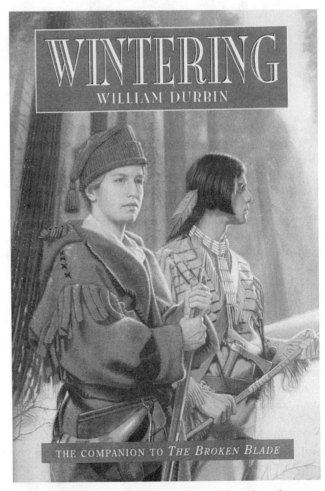

Pierre travels to northern Canada in **Wintering,** *the sequel to Durbin's* **The Broken Blade.** *(Cover illustration by Matthew Archambault.)*

Historical photographs, like this one showing immigrant Finnish children posing for their class photo, appear in Durbin's book **The Journal of Otto Peltonen, a Finnish Immigrant.**

The Broken Blade "should appeal to reluctant readers as well as adventure buffs." Dubbing the book "an impressive coming-of-age tale," a *Kirkus* reviewer added that "readers will embrace . . . [Pierre's] path to true bravery, strength of character, and self-reliance."

Wintering, which Durbin published in 1999, finds Pierre once again leaving his home in Montreal and heading north into the Canadian wilds, this time to work at the fur company's winter camp where he learns how to survive the region's brutal conditions with help from the native Ojibwa people. Dealing with the death of two close friends, as well as with the hardships of daily life, allow for a continuation of the coming-of-age theme, according to *Booklist* contributor Susan Dove Lempke, who noted that Durbin's use of period journals and diaries "gives the novel an authentic feel but doesn't overshadow the unfolding story of Pierre's growth and maturation." Dubbing *Wintering* an "engaging sequel," a *Kirkus* reviewer praised the novel as "well-written and atmospheric," and packed with "plenty of facts" about how the Native Americans of the Great Lakes region lived.

Durbin has produced several works of historical fiction for Scholastic's "My Name Is America" series. In *The Journal of Sean Sullivan, a Transcontinental Railroad*

Worker, he recounts the experiences of a fifteen-year-old Irish immigrant who works alongside his father on the Transcontinental Railroad in 1867. Traveling from state to state across the western territory, Sean writes of conflicts between the railroad, the Plains Indians, and cowboys, discrimination suffered by Chinese laborers, and extensive financial corruption, creating a narrative that "focuses on historic details to bring the Old West vibrantly alive," according to *Booklist* reviewer Roger Leslie, who dubbed *The Journal of Sean Sullivan* "a rollicking, atmospheric journey" into the past.

The Journal of Otto Peltonen, a Finnish Immigrant takes place in 1905 as fifteen-year-old Otto sails from Finland to America with his mother and sisters to join his father in the iron-rich lands of Minnesota. Working as a miner, Otto finds himself caught up in the early union movement, and joins other workers in a fight for safe working and living conditions in the company-owned shantytowns of Minnesota's Mesabi Iron range. "Historical notes and authentic photos round out this captivating, dramatic view of the past," maintained Leslie in his *Booklist* review. Durbin's third contribution to the "My Name Is America" series, *The Journal of C. J. Jackson, a Dust Bowl Migrant,* focuses on a thirteen year old forced to abandon the family farm during the devastating drought of the late 1920s that forced many Midwest farming families into lives of poverty as migrant workers. Noting that the novel would provide young readers with a good introduction to John Steinbeck's *The Grapes of Wrath,* School Library Journal contributor Ronni Krasnow added that *The Journal of C. J. Jackson* features a "likeable protagonist" and "effectively conveys the plight of Dust Bowl families."

Durbin's stand-alone historical novel *The Song of Sampo Lake* takes place at the turn of the twentieth century, as a Finnish farming family makes their new home in the author's home state of Minnesota. Matti, whose achievements are constantly overshadowed in the eyes of his father by those of his older brother, works as a store clerk and teaches English at the local one-room schoolhouse in addition to working on the family farm. Other works of historical fiction include *Blackwater Ben,* published in 2003.

In addition to writing and teaching, Durbin lectures to school and library groups as well as at writing conferences, and focuses his talk on topics such as how to begin a narrative, how to get published, writing and researching historical fiction, generating ideas through wordplay, and overcoming writers' block.

Biographical and Critical Sources

PERIODICALS

Booklist, February 15, 1999, Susan Dove Lempke, review of *Wintering,* p. 1061; October 15, 1999, Roger Leslie, review of *The Journal of Sean Sullivan, a Transcontinental Railroad Worker,* p. 428; October 1, 2000, Roger Leslie, review of *The Journal of Otto Peltonen, a Finnish Immigrant,* p. 332.

Bulletin of the Center for Children's Books, February, 1997, Elizabeth A. Bush, review of *The Broken Blade,* pp. 203-204; April, 1999, Elaine. A. Bearden, review of *Wintering,* p. 276.

Faces, January 2002, review of *The Journal of Otto Peltonen,* p. 46.

Kirkus Reviews, November 15, 1996, review of *The Broken Blade,* p. 1688; December 1, 1998, review of *Wintering,* pp. 1732-1733; October 1, 2000, review of *The Journal of Otto Peltonen,* pp. 1421-1422.

Kliatt, May, 2001, Deane A. Beverly, review of *Wintering,* p. 18.

St. Paul Pioneer Press (St. Paul, MN), November 2, 2000, Mary Ann Grossman, "Fictional Diary Mines the Tumultuous History of the Iron Range."

School Library Journal, September, 2000, Ronni Krasnow, review of *The Journal of C. J. Jackson, a Dust Bowl Migrant,* p. 220.

Voice of Youth Advocates, August, 2000, Nancy Zachary, review of *Tiger Woods,* pp. 202-203; December, 2000, Cindy Lombardo, review of *The Journal of Otto Peltonen,* p. 348.

OTHER

William Durbin Web site, http://www.williamdurbin.com/ (May 8, 2003).

A dust storm forces a man and his children to find shelter in **The Journal of C. J. Jackson, a Dust Bowl Migrant.**

DUSSLING, Jennifer 1970-

Personal

Born May 8, 1970, in Lima, PA; daughter of John and Ricky (Pfeifer) Dussling. *Education:* University of Delaware, B.A.; College of William and Mary, M.A.

Addresses

Home—Highland Park, NJ. *Agent*—c/o Kane Press, 240 W. 35th St., Suite 300, New York, NY 10001.

Career

Writer; children's book editor.

Awards, Honors

Big-Three Books Award, Nottingham City Libraries (Nottingham, England), 2003, for *A Very Strange Doll's House.*

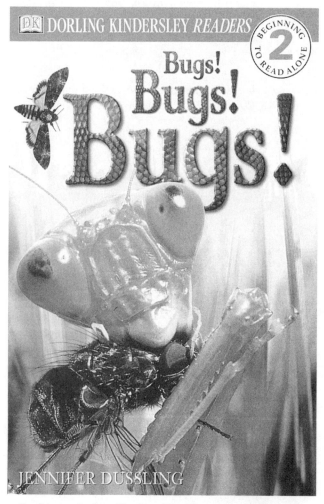

In this work, Jennifer Dussling visually immerses children into the world of insects. (Photograph by Kim Taylor/Warren.)

Writings

Finger Painting, illustrated by Carrie Abel, Grosset & Dunlap (New York, NY), 1995.

In a Dark, Dark House, illustrated by Davy Jones, Grosset & Dunlap (New York, NY), 1995.

Under the Sea, illustrated by Marcos Monteiro, Grosset & Dunlap (New York, NY), 1995.

Bossy Kiki, illustrated by Matthew Fox, Grosset & Dunlap (New York, NY), 1996.

Stars, illustrated by Mavis Smith, Grosset & Dunlap (New York, NY), 1996.

Kermit's Teeny Tiny Farm, illustrated by Rick Brown, Grosset & Dunlap (New York, NY), 1996.

Creep Show, illustrated by Jeff Spackman, Grosset & Dunlap (New York, NY), 1996.

A Very Strange Doll's House, Macmillan's Children (London, England), 1996, published as *A Very Strange Dollhouse,* illustrated by Sonja Lamut, Grosset & Dunlap (New York, NY), 1996.

Don't Call Me Names!, illustrated by Tom Brannon, Grosset & Dunlap (New York, NY), 1996.

The Princess Lost Her Locket, illustrated by Jerry Smath, Grosset & Dunlap (New York, NY), 1996.

Muppet Treasure Island, Grosset & Dunlap (New York, NY), 1996.

Top Knots: The Ultimate Bracelet and Hair-wrapping Kit, illustrated by Edward Heins, Grosset & Dunlap (New York, NY), 1996.

The Bunny Slipper Mystery, illustrated by Joe Ewers, Grosset & Dunlap (New York, NY), 1997.

A Simple Wish, Grosset & Dunlap (New York, NY), 1997.

Bug Off!, illustrated by Amy Wummer, Grosset & Dunlap (New York, NY), 1997.

The Dinosaurs of The Lost World, Jurassic Park, Grosset & Dunlap (New York, NY), 1997.

A Dozen Easter Eggs, illustrated by Melissa Sweet, Grosset & Dunlap (New York, NY), 1997.

Jewel the Unicorn, illustrated by Rebecca McKillip Thornburgh, Grosset & Dunlap (New York, NY), 1997.

Construction Trucks, illustrated by Courtney, Grosset & Dunlap (New York, NY), 1998.

Tall Tale Trouble, illustrated by Lyndon Mosse, Grosset & Dunlap (New York, NY), 1998.

Small Soldiers: The Movie Storybook, Grosset & Dunlap (New York, NY), 1998.

A Heart for the Queen of Hearts, illustrated by Lynn Adams, Grosset & Dunlap (New York, NY), 1998.

Slinky, Scaly Snakes, Dorling Kindersley (New York, NY), 1998.

The Magic Carpet Ride, illustrated by Jerry Smath, Grosset & Dunlap (New York, NY), 1998.

Bugs! Bugs! Bugs!, Dorling Kindersley (New York, NY), 1998.

Pink Snow and Other Weird Weather, illustrated by Heidi Petach, Grosset & Dunlap (New York, NY), 1998.

Gargoyles: Monsters in Stones, illustrated by Peter Church, Grosset & Dunlap (New York, NY), 1999.

The 100-Pound Problem, *written by Dussling and illustrated by Rebecca McKillip Thornburgh, helps youngsters with* *math concepts.*

Giant Squid: Mystery of the Deep, illustrated by Pamela Johnson, Grosset & Dunlap (New York, NY), 1999.

The 100-Pound Problem, illustrated by Rebecca McKillip Thornburgh, Kane Press (New York, NY), 2000.

Planets, illustrated by Denise Ortakales, Grosset & Dunlap (New York, NY), 2000.

Dinosaur Eggs, illustrated by Pamela Johnson, Scholastic (New York, NY), 2000.

(Adapter) L. M. Montgomery, *Anne of Green Gables,* illustrated by Lydia Halverson, Grosset & Dunlap (New York, NY), 2001.

Looking at Rocks, illustrated by Alan Drew-Brook-Cormack and Tim Haggerty, Grosset & Dunlap (New York, NY), 2001.

The Rainbow Mystery, illustrated by Barry Gott, Kane Press (New York, NY), 2002.

Lightning: It's Electrifying, illustrated by Lori Osiecki, Grosset & Dunlap (New York, NY), 2002.

Gotcha!, illustrated by John A. Nez, Kane Press (New York, NY), 2003.

Fair Is Fair!, illustrated by Diane Palimisciano, Kane Press (New York, NY), 2003.

Sidelights

Jennifer Dussling, a children's book editor for a New York City publishing house, is also a prolific author of children's picture books and early readers, with more than thirty titles to her credit since 1995. She has written movie storybooks based on such popular films as *Muppet Treasure Island* and *Small Soldiers,* as well as titles in the "All Aboard Reading" and "Science Solves It" series, an adaptation of the novel *Anne of Green Gables* for younger readers, and a number of stand-alone picture books.

While growing up outside of Philadelphia, Dussling read avidly, but dreamed of becoming an artist. In college she studied both art and English literature, paving her way to a career in children's book publishing. Among her titles are several books about insects, including *Bugs! Bugs! Bugs!* for the "Eyewitness Readers" series. According to Patricia Manning of *School Library Journal, Bugs! Bugs! Bugs!* is a "chatty" book with the visually interesting, "user-friendly format" made famous by Dorling Kindersley Publishing. Also in this series is Dussling's *Slinky, Scaly Snakes,* which Jackie C. Horne called a "good" beginner nonfiction book in her *Horn Book Guide* review. Another "bug book," this time part of the "Eek! Stories to Make You Shriek" series, is *Bug Off!* Several reviewers doubted the book's ability to make anyone "shriek," and in *Horn Book Guide* Maeve Visser Knoth termed the early reader merely "serviceable."

In the "All Aboard Reading" series Dussling is responsible for several titles, including *Planets,* a "satisfying" introduction to our solar system featuring "kid-friendly examples" to quote *Booklist* contributor Gillian Engberg. Another title in this series is *Gargoyles: Monsters in Stone,* about the fanciful waterspouts featured in Gothic architecture. Writing in *School Library Journal,* Lisa Smith thought the text somewhat "choppy" yet the work generally "adequate" overall, while *Booklist* reviewer Ilene Cooper deemed *Gargoyles* a "fine treatment of an intriguing topic" and gave the book a starred review. For the "Science Solves It" series, Dussling contributed *The Rainbow Mystery* in which Annie and her friend Mike discover the science secret behind the rainbows that form on Annie's wall when the sun shines. Praising

this work, Carolyn Phelan explained in her *Booklist* review that not only do the stories and illustrations appeal, they go over the top in showing the solve-the-mystery aspect of scientific investigation.

Biographical and Critical Sources

PERIODICALS

Booklist, October 1, 1999, Ilene Cooper, review of *Gargoyles: Monsters in Stone,* p. 365; December 1, 2000, Gillian Engberg, review of *Planets,* p. 735; September 15, 2002, Carolyn Phelan, review of *Rainbow Mystery,* p. 239.
Bulletin of the Center for Children's Books, July, 1996, p. 368.
Horn Book Guide, spring, 1998, Maeve Visser Knoth, review of *Bug Off!,* p. 55; spring, 1999, Danielle J. Ford, review of *Bugs! Bugs! Bugs!,* p. 110; fall, 1999, Jackie C. Horne, review of *Slinky, Scaly Snakes,* p. 344; fall, 2001, Harry Clement Stubbs, review of *Planets,* p. 354; fall, 2001, Carolyn Shute, review of *Anne of Green Gables,* p. 293.
School Library Journal, January, 1999, Patricia Manning, review of *Bugs! Bugs! Bugs!,* p. 114; August, 1996, pp. 121, 134; February, 1998, Gale W. Sherman, review of *Bug Off!,* p. 85; November, 1999, Lisa Smith, review of *Gargoyles,* p. 136.

ONLINE

Big Three Book Award, http://kotn.ntu.ac.uk/big3/ (May 14, 2003), "Jennifer Dussling."

E-F

EVANS, Greg 1947-

Personal
Born November 13, 1947, in Los Angeles, CA; son of Herman (an electrical inspector) and Virginia (a homemaker; maiden name, Horner) Evans; married Betty Ransom (a teacher and city council member), December, 1970; children: Gary, Karen. *Education:* California State University—Northridge, B.A., 1970. *Hobbies and other interests:* Movies, plays, writing music, golf.

Addresses
Office—c/o United Media, 200 Madison Ave., New York, NY 19916.

Career
High school art teacher in California and Australia, 1970-74; radio and television station promotion manager in Colorado Springs, CO, 1975-80; author of comic strip "Luann," 1985—. Participated in Cartoonists for Literacy campaign, 2001.

Member
National Cartoonists Society.

Awards, Honors
Reuben Award nomination, National Cartoonists Society, 1995 and 2002, both for "Luann."

Writings

SELF-ILLUSTRATED

Meet Luann, Berkeley (New York, NY), 1986.
Why Me?, Berkeley (New York, NY), 1986.
Is It Friday Yet?, Berkeley (New York, NY), 1987.
Who Invented Brothers Anyway?, Tor (New York, NY), 1989.

Greg Evans

School and Other Problems, Tor (New York, NY), 1989.
Homework Is Ruining My Life, Tor (New York, NY), 1989.
So Many Malls, So Little Money, Tor (New York, NY), 1990.
Pizza Isn't Everything but It Comes Close, Tor (New York, NY), 1991.
Dear Diary: The Following Is Top Secret, Tor (New York, NY), 1991.
Will We Be Tested on This?, Tor (New York, NY), 1992.
There's Nothing Worse than First Period P.E., Tor (New York, NY), 1992.
If Confusion Were a Class I'd Get an A, Tor (New York, NY), 1992.

High school student Luann DeGroot is the star of Evans's wildly popular comic strip Luann. *(From* Passion! Betrayal! Outrage! Revenge!, *written and illustrated by Evans.)*

School's OK If You Can Stand the Food, Tor (New York, NY), 1992.

I'm Not Always Confused, I Just Look That Way, Tor (New York, NY), 1993.

My Bedroom and Other Environmental Hazards, Tor (New York, NY), 1993.

Sometimes You Just Have to Make Your Own Rules, Rutledge Hill Press (Nashville, TN), 1998.

Luann, Rutledge Hill Press (Nashville, TN), 1998.

Passion! Betrayal! Outrage! Revenge!, Rutledge Hill Press (Nashville, TN), 1999.

Adaptations

The musical play *Luann* was adapted from Evans's comic strip by Eleanor Harder and published by Pioneer Drama Service (Denver, CO), 1985.

Sidelights

Cartoonist Greg Evans is the creative talent behind the popular comic strip "Luann," featuring the trials and traumas of an American high school student. "Simplistically drawn, *Luann* remains a sympathetic record of the changing lifestyles of contemporary youth," maintained essayist Dennis Wepman in *One Hundred Years of American Newspaper Comics.* "Teenagers of both sexes find in the strip much that is familiar and the reassurance that they are not alone."

Evans describes himself as quite similar to the title character of his comic strip, "Luann." "She's not exceptional in any way; she's just an average kid and I was very average all through school," Evans once commented to interviewer Deborah A. Stanley in *SATA.* A typical teen, Luann agonizes over her appearance, spends countless hours at the mall, fights with her older brother, and loves high school heartthrob Aaron Hill from afar. School is a source of endless frustration, but Luann takes solace in friends Delta and Bernice, guidance counselor Ms. Phelps, and Puddles, her dog, and they help her keep things in perspective. Of course, there is also Luann's classmate Tiffany, her snobby teen rival and source of much tension.

Born in Los Angeles, California, in 1947, Evans was a doodler since childhood and eventually studied art while a student at California State University—Northridge during the late 1960s. He began his career as an art teacher working with teens in both the United States and Australia. Other creative jobs included work as a

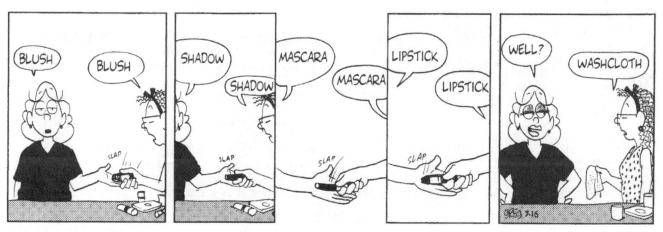

In this strip from the collection Passion! Betrayal! Outrage! Revenge!, *Evans captures the humor of adolescent behavior.*

Sibling rivalry is common between Luann and her older brother (and chief nemesis), Brad. (*From* Luann, *written and illustrated by Evans.*)

graphic artist and promotions manager for a Colorado television station and creating a promotional robot character for use at fairs and trade shows. Although he worked at developing saleable cartoon strips for years, nothing he submitted for publication ever caught the interest of editors; nothing until "Luann," that is.

Evans began to draw the "Luann" strip in 1985, after experimenting with several other comic-book characters. As he recorded on the United Media Web site, "I began developing comic strip ideas when I was in college. Over the years, I submitted a dozen or so strips, all rejected (for good reason: they were lousy). Finally, I came up with Luann and it was accepted." The character of Luann DeGroot began with Evans's observations of his daughter. As he shared in his interview with Stanley, "I was playing around with the idea of a strip about a saucy little five-year-old, because you know how little girls are at that age—they like to put on lipstick and Mom's big high-heeled shoes and clop around the house. As I was working around those lines, I began to realize that five was so young—you don't really have any life experiences—so I kept aging the character. Fi-

nally I said, 'Oh, I'll make her a teenager because I can remember being a teenager, and I'll have something to draw upon from my school teaching experiences.'"

The "Luann" strip has evolved over the years since its debut in 1985. "Part of that was intentional and part of it just happens over the years," Evans remarked to *SATA.* Some changes were the result of the artist's growing skill; others came from boredom or frustration with the material. "You'll suddenly say, 'I don't like the way I'm doing this. I'm going to figure out a better way,'" Evans explained. Luann's personality is one of several things that have changed. "In the beginning Luann was a little more cartoony and simpler, a caricature of a teenager," Evans recalled, noting that by the early 1990 she was a "much more authentic" thirteen year old. Timely topics introduced in the strip include drug abuse, the onset of menstruation, birth control, and teen drinking; Luann has also changed her hairstyle and had her ears pierced. In 1999, Luann aged three years, moving from junior high to high school. "I wanted her to have more adventures," Evans told interviewer Laura Groch in *Editor and Publisher,* although hastening to add that

Evans wittily addresses teen issues like body piercings in his comic strip. (*From* Luann.)

his popular character would never leave her teens. "She'll be getting her own car, so that opens up a whole can of worms."

A nationally syndicated cartoonist, Evans and fellow members of the National Cartoonists Society get together once a year to recognize the best among them with the Reuben Awards. "It's kind of like our version of the Academy Awards," Evans revealed. "The ballots go out to cartoonists around the world and we vote to nominate in various categories such as greeting card cartooning, animation, and comic strips. Then we all get together somewhere in the country and have a three-day bash and have the award ceremony. That's the place where most of the cartoonists see one another, which is nice because it's a very solitary profession. It's really good to get together with your peers and talk shop and just see everyone." In both 1995 and 2002, Evans was pulled from the crowd at the Reuben Awards reception as one of only four finalists for the as-yet-elusive honor.

While fellow artists provide a nudge to Evans's creativity, much of his inspiration has come from his children, who while growing into their teen years provided him with ready-made story lines acted out each day in his home. Before and since the home-grown teen was available, Evans relied on his and his wife's experiences as teachers. To continue to fuel "Luann," he remains a keen teen-watcher, and spends a lot of time observing teens at shopping malls and other popular hangouts. He summed up the guiding philosophy of "Luann" for interviewer Kenneth R. Shepherd, "It's tough being a teenager, but you will survive. Billions of people have survived it. Just try to have a sense of humor. And don't let anyone tell you these are the best years of your life."

Biographical and Critical Sources

BOOKS

Evans, Greg, in an interview with Deborah A. Stanley, *Something about the Author,* Volume 73, 1992, pp. 53-56.
Evans, Greg, in an interview with Kenneth R. Shepherd, *Authors and Artists for Young Adults,* Volume 23, Gale (Detroit, MI), 1998.
One Hundred Years of American Newspaper Comics, edited by Maurice Horn, Random House (New York, NY), 1996.

PERIODICALS

Editor and Publisher, October 16, 1999, David Astor, "Luann Ages Three Years in Twenty-four Hours," p. 42; March 27, 2000, Laura Groch, "Small Number of Comic Strips Have Plenty of New Wrinkles," p. 33.
Voice of Youth Advocates, August, 1997, p. 159.

ONLINE

United Media, http://www.unitedmedia.com/comics/ (April 5, 2003), "About the Artist: Greg Evans."*

FISHER, Aileen (Lucia) 1906-2002

OBITUARY NOTICE—See index for *SATA* sketch: Born September 9, 1906, in Iron River, MI; died December 2, 2002, in Boulder, CO. Author. Fisher was an award-winning author of over one hundred children's books. After attending the University of Chicago for two years, she completed a bachelor's degree in journalism at the University of Missouri in 1927. Fisher's involvement in journalism was brief, however. From 1928 to 1931 she directed the Women's National Journalistic Register in Chicago, followed by a year working as a research assistant at the Labor Bureau of the Middle West. Thereafter, she embarked on her successful career as a freelance writer of books for children. Fisher wrote in various genres, including poetry, plays, short stories, picture books, and biographies. Many of these works were selected by the American Library Association as notable books, including *Going Barefoot* (1960), *My Cousin Abe* (1962), *Listen, Rabbit* (1964), and *Valley of the Smallest: The Life Story of a Shrew* (1966), the last of which was also selected as a Hans Christian Andersen Honor Book. Fisher was especially praised for her verses for children, which often evoked her love for nature. She also wrote biographies, with Olive Rabe, on Emily Dickinson and Louisa May Alcott. Some of her most recent books include *Always Wondering: Some Favorite Poems of Aileen Fisher* (1991) and *The Story of Easter* (1997).

OBITUARIES AND OTHER SOURCES:

BOOKS

Cullinan, Bernice E., and Diane G. Person, editors, *The Continuum Encyclopedia of Children's Literature,* Continuum International (New York, NY), 2001.
Writers Directory, 17th edition, St. James (Detroit, MI), 2002.

PERIODICALS

Los Angeles Times, December 12, 2002, p. B15.
New York Times, December 9, 2002, p. A27.

*   *   *

FLEMING, Candace 1962- (Candace Groth-Fleming)

Personal

Born May 24, 1962; daughter of Charles (a superintendent) and Carol (a homemaker; maiden name, Price) Groth; married Scott Fleming (in commercial real estate), November 9, 1985; children: Scott, Michael. *Education:* Eastern Illinois University, B.A., 1985. *Religion:* Lutheran. *Hobbies and other interests:* Reading, collecting antiquarian books, camping, hiking, travel.

Addresses

Office—415 East Golf Rd., Arlington Heights, IL 60005; fax: 847-258-3154. *E-mail*—candymfleming@aol.com.

Candace Fleming

Career

Harper College, Palatine, IL, adjunct professor of liberal arts, 1997—.

Member

Authors Guild Midwest.

Awards, Honors

Highlights for Children history feature of the year, 1995, and patriotic feature of the year, 1996; best juvenile trade book of the year designation, Chicago Women in Publishing, 1996, for *Women of the Lights;* "notable book" citation, American Library Association, "best book of the year" citation, *Publishers Weekly,* and Parents' Choice Silver Honor Book, all c. 1997, all for *Gabriella's Song;* "notable children's book in the language arts" citation, National Council of Teachers of English, 1997, for *Gabriella's Song,* and 1998, for *The Hatmaker's Sign; Parenting* best book of the year designation, American Folklore Society Aesop Award, and International Reading Association Storytelling World Award, all 1998, and State of New York's Charlotte Book Award, 2000, all for *The Hatmaker's Sign;* listed among "one hundred books for reading and sharing," New York Public Library, and "best book" citation, *School Library Journal,* both 1999, both for *When Agnes Caws;* CCBC Choice designations, 2000, for *When Agnes Caws* and *A Big Cheese for the White House: The True Tale of a Tremendous Cheddar;* "best children's book" citation, Bank Street College of Education, 2000, for *A Big Cheese for the White House.*

Writings

(As Candace Groth-Fleming) *Professor Fergus Fahrenheit and His Wonderful Weather Machine,* illustrated by Don Weller, Simon & Schuster (New York, NY), 1994.

Women of the Lights, illustrated by James Watling, Albert Whitman (Morton Grove, IL), 1995.

Madame LaGrande and Her So High, to the Sky, Uproarious Pompadour, illustrated by S. D. Schindler, Alfred A. Knopf (New York, NY), 1996.

Gabriella's Song, illustrated by Giselle Potter, Atheneum (New York, NY), 1997.

Westward Ho, Carlotta!, illustrated by David Catrow, Atheneum (New York, NY), 1998.

The Hatmaker's Sign: A Story by Benjamin Franklin, illustrated by Robert Andrew Parker, Orchard Books (New York, NY), 1998.

A Big Cheese for the White House: The True Tale of a Tremendous Cheddar, illustrated by S. D. Schindler, D. K. Ink (New York, NY), 1999.

Who Invited You?, illustrated by George Booth, Atheneum (New York, NY), 2000.

Muncha! Muncha! Muncha!, illustrated by G. Brian Karas, Atheneum (New York, NY), 2001.

When Agnes Caws, Atheneum (New York, NY), 2002.

Boxes for Katje, illustrated by Stacey Dressen-McQueen, Farrar, Straus, (New York, NY), 2003.

This Is the Baby, illustrated by Maggie Smith, Farrar, Straus, (New York, NY), 2003.

Ben Franklin's Almanack: Being a True Account of the Good Gentleman's Life, Atheneum (New York, NY), 2003.

Gator Gumbo: A Spicy-Hot Southern Tale, illustrated by Sally Ann Lambert, Farrar, Straus (New York, NY), in press.

Contributor to magazines, including *Boys' Life* and *American Baby.*

Work in Progress

Smile, Lily, for Atheneum (New York, NY), 2004; picture books; nonfiction projects; a series of early chapter books.

Sidelights

Candace Fleming is the author of several children's picture books that weave elements of history and tradition within fanciful tales often featuring animal protagonists. In *Muncha! Muncha! Muncha!* she echos the childhood classic "Peter Rabbit" tales with a story of three rabbits poised to raid the garden of Mr. McGreely, whose efforts to preserve his beautifully maintained vegetable garden may all be for naught. In *School Library Journal* Lisa Gangemi Krapp dubbed *Muncha! Muncha! Muncha!* "a hilarious hop through the garden," while Gillian Engberg praised Fleming's book as a "delightful offering" complete with "hilarious, slapdash problem solving and irresistible sounds." Fleming's counting book *Who Invited You?* was described as a "clever cumulative counting caper" by an enthusiastic *Publishers*

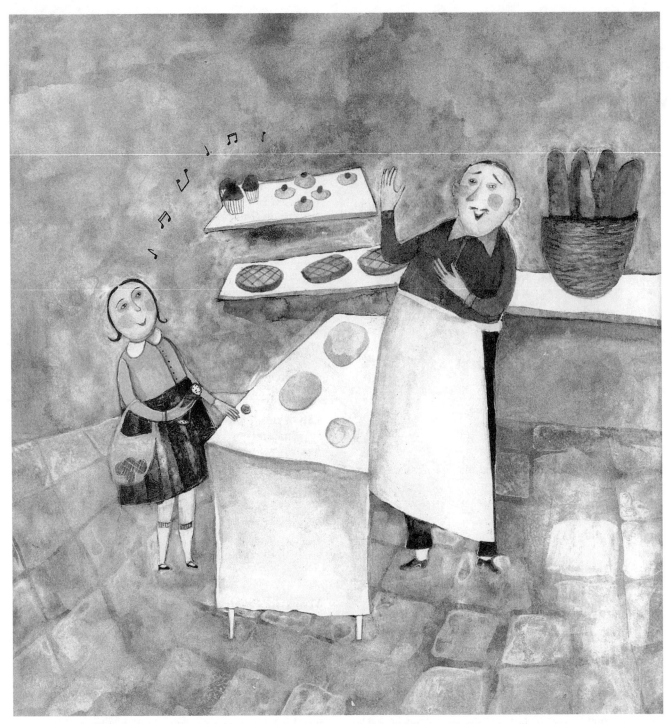

A young girl inspires others with her music in Fleming's **Gabriella's Song,** *illustrated by Giselle Potter.*

Weekly contributor. Her award-winning *The Hatmaker's Sign* retells a story first related by Benjamin Franklin, and in *A Big Cheese for the White House: The True Tale of a Tremendous Cheddar* the author mines U.S. history again, coming up with a humorous tale based on an actual 1801 newspaper headline from Cheshire, Massachusetts in which a 1,235 pound wheel of cheese took a trip south to Washington, D.C. as a gift for President Thomas Jefferson.

Fleming once commented: "I remember the day I discovered the music and magic of words. It was the day my second-grade teacher, Miss Johnson, held up a horn-shaped basket filled with papier-mâché pumpkins and asked the class to repeat the word 'cornucopia.' It sounded good. I said it again, and again, and I decided I loved that word. I loved its rhythm and cadence. I loved the way it felt on my tongue and fell on my ears. I skipped all the way home from school that day chanting 'Cornucopia! Cornucopia!' From then on, I really began listening to words—to the sounds they made, and the way they were used, and how they made me feel. I longed to put them together in ways that were beautiful, and yet told a story.

"Now, my family and close friends will tell you that I have always made up stories. My mother loves to tell of the time I regaled our next-door neighbor with tales of our family trip to Paris, France. So vivid were my descriptions of that romantic city that my neighbor believed every word I said. I can only imagine his chagrin when he learned I had never been beyond my home state of Indiana.

"I told many stories like this. My classmates heard the saga of my three-legged dog Tiger. My Sunday school teacher listened, wide-eyed, as I told the tale of the ghost in our attic. Lots of people heard my tall tales. Lots of people believed them.

"Technically, I suppose you could call this lying. Fortunately, I had parents who understood the difference between imagination and lies. They encouraged me to make up stories, but they strongly suggested that I not claim these stories as truth. Eventually, I took their advice.

"The result? My love of language and my need to tell a good story merged, and I became a writer. I filled notebook after notebook with my stories, poems, and plays. I couldn't stop the flow of words and ideas that rushed from my pencil, and I didn't try. Often, I arrived home from school, closed my bedroom door, and wrote for hours on end. When I wasn't writing, I was reading, and if something I read sparked my imagination, I would start writing all over again.

"I still have many of those notebooks today. I cherish them. They are a record of my writing life, from second grade to the present. In them I can see my struggle to tell a good and believable story. I can see my struggle to use musical language. I can't help but recognize that these are the same struggles I have as a writer today. They are also my goals. I want to tell you a good story. I want to tell it in a believable way. And I want to tell it with language that opens your ears to the music and magic of words."

Biographical and Critical Sources

PERIODICALS

Booklist, October 15, 1994, p. 434; March 15, 1996, p. 1258; July, 1996, p. 1829; May 1, 1998, Helen Rosenberg, review of *Westward Ho, Carlotta!,* p. 1520; February 15, 1999, Stephanie Zvirin, review of *When Agnes Caws,* p. 95; November 1, 1999, Hazel Rochman, review of *A Big Cheese for the White House: The True Tale of a Tremendous Cheddar,* p. 538; October 15, 2001, Shelley Townsend-Hudson, review of *Who Invited You?* p. 400; January 1, 2002, Gillian Engberg, review of *Muncha! Muncha! Muncha!,* p. 851.

Citizens from a small town in Massachusetts send an oversized wheel of cheese to President Thomas Jefferson in **A Big Cheese for the White House: The True Tale of a Tremendous Cheddar.** *(Illustrated by S. D. Schindler.)*

Horn Book, March-April, 1998, Mary M. Burns, review of
The Hatmaker's Sign: A Story by Benjamin Franklin,
p. 212; March, 1999, Susan P. Bloom, review of *When
Agnes Caws,* p. 188; September, 1999, Mary M.
Burns, review of *A Big Cheese for the White House,*
p. 594.

Kirkus Reviews, May 1, 1996, p. 687.

Publishers Weekly, October 3, 1994, p. 68; June 24, 1996,
p. 59; May 25, 1998, review of *Westward Ho, Carlotta!,* p. 88; December 21, 1998, review of *When
Agnes Caws,* p. 67; September 27, 1999, review of *A
Big Cheese for the White House,* p. 105; October 1,
2001, review of *Who Invited You?,* p. 61; December
10, 2001, review of *Muncha! Muncha! Muncha!,*
p. 69.

School Library Journal, January, 1995, p. 86; April, 1996,
p. 144; July, 1996, p. 59; April, 1998, Jack Hechtopf,
review of *The Hatmaker's Sign: A Story by Benjamin
Franklin,* p. 98; July, 1998, Steven Engelfried, review
of *Westward Ho, Carlotta!,* p. 74; February, 1999, Luann Toth, review of *When Agnes Caws,* p. 84; August,
1999, Amy Lilien-Harper, review of *A Big Cheese for
the White House,* p. 134; October, 2001, Linda Ludke,
review of *Who Invited You?,* p. 114; February, 2002,
Lisa Gangemi Krapp, review of *Muncha! Muncha!
Muncha!,* p. 100.

Smartkid, May, 1996, pp. 20, 45.*

* * *

FUERST, Jeffrey B. 1956-

Personal

Born February 17, 1956, in Paterson, NJ; son of Joel (a
business executive and college professor) and Paulette
(a teacher and librarian) Fuerst; married Marjorie Siegel
(an attorney), October 2, 1988; children: Jacob, Alexa.
Education: Oberlin College, B.A., 1978; Brooklyn College of the City University of New York, M.F.A., 1983.
Hobbies and other interests: Cooking, tennis, reading,
travel, cultural events.

Addresses

Home—95 Fairmont Ave., Hastings-on-Hudson, NY
10706. *E-mail*—jbfuerst@cs.com; jeff1st@optonline.
com.

Career

Phoenix Theater, worked as literary assistant; Medicine
Show Theater Ensemble, worked as booking manager,
publicist, and grant writer; script analyst for National
Playwrights Conference and Eugene O'Neill Festival;
American Stage Festival, Milford, NH, assistant artistic
director, 1979-81; Nederlander Television and Film Productions, writer and literary manager, 1983-84; Museum of Television and Radio, associate curator, 1984-
89; freelance writer and television producer, 1989-91;
Zillions: Consumer Report for Kids (magazine and Internet Web site), writer and editor, 1990-2001; freelance

Jeffrey B. Fuerst

writer and editor, 2002—. Consumers Union, educational programs editor, 2001-02. Creator of interactive
quiz series *Kat Man Doo Asks You, Guess What?, The
Bob Show,* and *Movie Mania with 2-XL,* 1987-88. Inter-
Village Continuing Education Program, member of advisory board, 2002—. State University of New York—
Westchester, adjunct instructor in television writing;
workshop presenter for schools, libraries, and community organizations; teacher of writing classes; public
speaker; judge of writing competitions. National Couch
Potato Olympix, creator, producer, and commissioner.

Member

Society of Children's Book Writers and Illustrators.

Awards, Honors

Distinguished Achievement Awards, Association of Educational Publishers, 1992, 1998.

Writings

Greetings from Nowheresville! (humor), Scott, Foresman
(Glenview, IL), 1999.

When in Rome (fiction), Scott, Foresman (Glenview, IL),
1999.

Pound Pals (fantasy), Scott, Foresman (Glenview, IL),
1999.

Hot Gobs: The Art of Glassblowing, Scott, Foresman
(Glenview, IL), 1999.

The Iditarod: Dogsled Race across Alaska, Wright Group (San Diego, CA), 2000.
Inside a Radio Station, McGraw-Hill (New York, NY), 2001.
African-American Cowboys: A True Tale of the Old West, Celebration Press (Parsippany, NJ), 2002.
The Kids' Baseball Workout: How to Get in Shape and Improve Your Game, illustrated by Anne Canevari Green, Millbrook Press (Brookfield, CT), 2002.
Funhouse Mirrors and Optic Tricks, Four Corners/Pearson Learning (Parsippany, NJ), 2003.
Explore the World: Earth Science Experiments, Four Corners/Pearson Learning (Parsippany, NJ), 2003.

PLAYS; FOR CHILDREN

The Perfessers (original skits and adaptations from children's literature), produced in Oberlin, OH, 1975.
It's a Dog's Life (based on the book *The Farmer Giles of Ham* by J. R. R. Tolkien), produced in Milford, NH, 1981.
Dr. Seuss on the Loose (based on the stories of Dr. Seuss), produced in Milford, NH, 1981.
What a Vacation!, Celebration Press (Parsippany, NJ), 2002.
The Substitute Tooth Fairy, produced, 2003.

PLAYS; FOR ADULTS

Never up, Never In, produced in Bloomington, IL, 1978.
The Imaginary Unit, produced in Oberlin, OH, 1978.
Boys Will Be Boys, produced in New York, NY, 1979.
The Plot beneath the Plot, produced in New York, NY, 1980.
Larry and His Old Lady, produced in New York, NY, 1981.
Wading for Cousteau, produced in New York, NY, 1983.
Beginner's Luck, produced in New York, NY, 1986.

OTHER

(With others; and associate producer) *Milton Berle: Mr. Television* (documentary television special), WNYC-Television, 1985.
D. J. Kat's Christmas Party (television special), Fox, 1990.
Kids-TV (educational television series), Showtime, 1990.
(With others; and producer) *Guide to New York City Housing Courts* (educational film), New York City Bar Association, 1990.

Contributor of articles and television reviews to periodicals, including *Scholastic Search, Writer's Digest, Animation, Cooking Light, Hartford Monthly, Instructor, Manhattan Spirit, Newsday,* and *Video Review.* Contributor to Internet Web sites, including *Nestle's Kids Corner* and *Juniornet.*

Work in Progress

Attack of the Googolplex: A Lone Integer Math Adventure; a musical play; a pilot for an animated cartoon series designed to "make learning math fun by spoofing super-hero comics and movie conventions."

Sidelights

Jeffrey B. Fuerst told *SATA:* "I like to make learning stuff fun. Whenever possible I try to infuse my nonfiction with humor. I call this the '3E' approach because my goal is to engage, entertain, educate. It is my hope that after kids read my work they will be inspired to go out and learn more on their own.

"I'm also a big believer in doing. When people say to me, 'Gee, I always wanted to be a writer' or 'Gee, I wish I could write,' I say don't think about it, just do it. Put the words on paper or the computer screen, or talk into a tape recorder. Don't be afraid to create. Go with it. Say what you want to say. It's always easier to crumple up paper or hit the delete button afterwards. The editing comes later in the writing process.

"After you write something, let it sit for awhile. Then look at it again. Read it aloud to yourself. Don't ask for too many opinions because in the long run, yours is the only one that really matters. You can listen to others, but trust yourself, and be willing to revise, revise, then revise some more. If it matters to you, you'll keep going, and you won't be afraid to work at it.

"I keep notebooks of ideas and have many projects in different stages of development at all times. I keep my projects in different folders and add to them as notions strike me, as character traits and plot points become apparent. As the stories or projects begin to take shape, I write a plot outline. The outline, or treatment, can go on for pages. When I think I know what the story is, I'll type up my notes and create a computer file. Then the hard work begins of actually writing. But it is also the fun work—invigorating. My favorite part is when characters start talking to each other. Even though I am their creator, it is as if I no longer exist except as a conduit for their thoughts, actions, reactions, feeling.

"I'm usually at my computer by nine o'clock in the morning on weekdays, just like someone with a 'real' job. This discipline I learned from having a staff writing job at a magazine for many years."

Biographical and Critical Sources

PERIODICALS

Booklist, September 1, 2002, Marta Segal Block, review of *The Kids' Baseball Workout: A Fun Way to Get in Shape and Improve Your Game,* p. 129.
School Library Journal, July, 2002, Blair Christolon, review of *The Kids' Baseball Workout,* p. 106.

ONLINE

J. B. Fuerst Web site, http://www.jbfuerst.com/ (April 21, 2003).

G

GARDNER, Scot 1968-

Personal

Born August 16, 1968, in Melbourne, Victoria, Australia; son of James (a drafter) and Joan (a diversional therapist; maiden name, Sloan) Gardner; married Robyn Grant (a natural therapist), June 2, 1995; children: Jennifer Ellen, Michelle Anne, Bryce James. *Ethnicity:* "Australian." *Education:* Holmsglen Tafe, gardening certificate, 1990; Melbourne School of Massage and Physical Culture, therapeutic massage certificate, 1997; Victorian School of Hypnotic Science, postgraduate diploma in psychotherapy, 1999. *Politics:* "Greens." *Religion:* "Pantheist." *Hobbies and other interests:* Nature photography, camping, riding mountain bikes, sailing, flying aircraft, stone sculpture, "building with earth."

Addresses

Home—Yinnar South, Victoria, Australia. *Office*—Karijan Enterprises, P.O. Box 8, Churchill, Victoria 3842, Australia. *Agent*—Pippa Masson, Curtis Brown Australia, P.O. Box 19, Paddington, New South Wales 2021, Australia. *E-mail*—scot@scotgardner.com.

Career

Morwell City Council, Morwell, Victoria, Australia, apprentice gardener, 1986-90; self-employed landscape gardener in Morwell, Victoria, Australia, 1990-97; self-employed therapeutic masseur in Morwell, Victoria, Australia, 1997-2000; freelance writer in Yinnar South, Victoria, Australia, 2000—. Victorian Writers' Centre, member, 2002—.

Member

Australian Society of Authors.

Writings

One Dead Seagull (young adult fiction), Pan Macmillan Australia (Sydney, Australia), 2001.

Scot Gardner

White Ute Dreaming (young adult fiction), Pan Macmillan Australia (Sydney, Australia), 2002.
Burning Eddy (young adult fiction), Pan Macmillan Australia (Sydney, Australia), 2003.

Contributor to *Earth Garden.*

Work in Progress

The Other Madonna, young adult fiction, for Pan Macmillan Australia, completion expected in 2004; *The*

Legend of Kevin the Plumber, general fiction, Pan Macmillan Australia, 2005; *The Chainsaw Prince,* general fiction, Pan Macmillan Australia, 2006.

Sidelights

Australian author Scot Gardner's *One Dead Seagull,* which Helen Purdie of *Magpies* called a "promising first novel," focuses on two boys who go head-to-head with some school bullies while coming to terms with personal tragedy, problems at school and at home, and confusing situations involving the opposite sex. As Gardner noted on his Web site: "I wrote parts of *One Dead Seagull* at Tarra Bulga National Park. Parts of the sequel, [*White Ute Dreaming,*] were written by gaslight in the Outback. The tools of the trade are simple—for me it's a pen and paper for the first draft then I take all the papers and stuff them into my computer. The technicians at Compaq said that 'damage caused by inserting hand-written manuscripts into a CD drive is not covered under warranty.'" As a result—and fortunately for fans of his books—Gardner has since learned how to type.

Biographical and Critical Sources

PERIODICALS

Magpies, July, 2001, Helen Purdie, review of *One Dead Seagull,* p. 39.

ONLINE

The Officious Scot Gardner Home Page, http://members. datafast.net.au/gmob/essgee/ (March 10, 2003).

*   *   *

GEOGHEGAN, Adrienne 1962-

Personal

Born March 4, 1962, in Dublin, Ireland; daughter of Noel and Marie (Woods) Haughney; married Ken Geoghegan, September 26, 1981 (divorced, 2001); married Mark Neiland (a photographer), May 17, 2002. *Education:* Kingston University, B.A. (graphic design/illustration; first class honours), 1993.

Addresses

Home and office—4 Provost Row, Palantine Square, Arbour Hill, Dublin 7, Ireland. *Agent*—Eunice McMullen, Low Ibbotsholme Cottage, Off Brick Lane, Troutbeck Bridge, Windemere, Cumbria LA23 IHV, England. *E-mail*—addieg@gofree.indigo.ie.

Adrienne Geoghegan

Career

Illustrator and writer. Dublin Institute of Technology, College of Marketing and Design, Dublin, Ireland, part-time lecturer, 1996—. *Exhibitions:* Solo exhibitions at Beint & Beint Gallery, London, England, 1993; TOSCA, Dublin, Ireland, 2000; and Linenhall Arts Centre, Castlebar, County Mayo, Ireland, 2000. Group exhibitions include Illustration '90, Riverside Centre, Dublin, 1990; Macmillan Prize Exhibition, Royal College of Art, London, 1992; Just Art '92, Crypt Gallery, London, 1992; Barbican Awards Show, Barbican Gallery, London, 1993; Images 19, Mall Galleries, London, 1994; Great Illustrations, The Ark, Dublin, 1997; and Celebrity Art Auction, Bank of Ireland Arts Centre, Dublin, 1997.

Member

Association of Artists in Ireland, Illustrators Guild of Ireland.

Awards, Honors

Just Art '92 exhibition winner, 1992; award from Barbican Awards Show, 1993; Irish Copyright Licensing Agency Award, for best illustrated children's book, 1996, for *Dogs Don't Wear Glasses;* Norway Arts Council ArtFlight award, 1997.

Martha is in for a surprise with her new pet monster in Geoghegan's book There's a Wardrobe in My Monster!, *illustrated by Adrian Johnson.*

Writings

PICTURE BOOKS

Six Perfectly Different Pigs, illustrated by Elisabeth Moseng, Hazar (London, England), 1993, Gareth Stevens (Milwaukee, WI), 1994.

(With John Cotton) *Oscar the Dog and Friends* (poetry), Longman (London, England), 1994.

(With Wendy Body and Ann Jungman) *Sally and the Booted Puss and Other Stories,* Longman (London, England), 1994.

(And illustrator) *Dogs Don't Wear Glasses,* Magi Publications (London, England), 1995, Crocodile Books (New York, NY), 1996.

There's a Wardrobe in My Monster!, illustrated by Adrian Johnson, Carolrhoda Books (Minneapolis, MN), 1999.

Who Needs Pockets, Hippo (London, England), 2000.

All Your Own Teeth, illustrated by Cathy Gale, Bloomsbury (London, England), 2001, Dial (New York, NY), 2002.

ILLUSTRATOR; "READ-ON BEGINNER BOOKS" SERIES BY WENDY BODY

When the Toy Shop Shuts, Longman (London, England), 1994, Sundance Press (Littleton, MA), 1997.

Our Play, Longman (London, England), 1994, Sundance Press (Littleton, MA), 1997.

The Toy Shop, Longman (London, England), 1994, Sundance Press (Littleton, MA), 1997.

In the Toy Shop, Longman (London, England), 1994, Sundance Press (Littleton, MA), 1997.

Special Friends, Longman (London, England), 1994, Sundance Press (Littleton, MA), 1997.

Can You Do This?, Longman (London, England), 1994, Sundance Press (Littleton, MA), 1997.

Who Am I?, Longman (London, England), 1994, Sundance Press (Littleton, MA), 1997.

In the Box, Longman (London, England), 1994, Sundance (Littleton, MA), 1997.

I'm Red, Longman (London, England), 1994, Sundance (Littleton, MA), 1997.

I Like Green, Longman (London, England), 1994, Sundance (Littleton, MA), 1997.

I Want a Red Ball, Longman (London, England), 1994, Sundance (Littleton, MA), 1997.

Where Is the Snake?, Longman (London, England), 1994, Sundance (Littleton, MA), 1997.

Where Is My Ball?, Longman (London, England), 1994, Sundance (Littleton, MA), 1997.

Our Play, Longman (London, England), 1994, Sundance (Littleton, MA), 1997.

I Don't Want That!, Longman (London, England), 1994, Sundance (Littleton, MA), 1997.

What's That?, Longman (London, England), 1994, Sundance (Littleton, MA), 1997.

I Can Make You Red, Longman (London, England), 1994, Sundance (Littleton, MA), 1997.

Come In!, Longman (London, England), 1994, Sundance (Littleton, MA), 1997.

I Want to Be, Longman (London, England), 1994, Sundance Press (Littleton, MA), 1997.

Can I Play?, Longman (London, England), 1994, Sundance Press (Littleton, MA), 1997.

Where Do You Live?, Longman (London, England), 1997, Sundance Press (Littleton, MA), 1998.

What Are You Making?, Longman (London, England), 1997, Sundance Press (Littleton, MA), 1998.

I Don't Want to Do That, Longman (London, England), 1997, Sundance Press (Littleton, MA), 1998.

It Wasn't Me!, Longman (London, England), 1997, Sundance Press (Littleton, MA), 1998.

I Like to Play, Longman (London, England), 1997, Sundance Press (Littleton, MA), 1998.

What Do I Want?, Longman (London, England), 1997, Sundance Press (Littleton, MA), 1998.

Can You Make a Bird?, Longman (London, England), 1997, Sundance Press (Littleton, MA), 1998.

But Where Is Jake?, Longman (London, England), 1997, Sundance Press (Littleton, MA), 1998.

I Want That!, Longman (London, England), 1997, Sundance Press (Littleton, MA), 1998.

Come and Play, Longman (London, England), 1997, Sundance Press (Littleton, MA), 1998.

I Like You, Longman (London, England), 1997, Sundance Press (Littleton, MA), 1998.

What's in the Box?, Longman (London, England), 1997, Sundance Press (Littleton, MA), 1998.

I Live Here, Longman (London, England), 1997, Sundance Press (Littleton, MA), 1998.

Where Is My Snake?, Longman (London, England), 1997, Sundance Press (Littleton, MA), 1998.

This Is Megan, Longman (London, England), 1997, Sundance Press (Littleton, MA), 1998.

Megan Went to Bed, Longman (London, England), 1997, Sundance Press (Littleton, MA), 1999.

One Duck, Two Ducks . . . , Longman (London, England), 1997, Sundance Press (Littleton, MA), 1999.

In the Backyard, Longman (London, England), 1997, Sundance Press (Littleton, MA), 1999.

I Like Red, Longman (London, England), 1997, Sundance Press (Littleton, MA), 1999.

It's Time for Bed, Longman (London, England), 1997, Sundance Press (Littleton, MA), 1999.

In the Garden, Longman (London, England), 1997.

One and One Make Two, Longman (London, England), 1997, Sundance Press (Littleton, MA), 1999.

Is She with You?, Longman (London, England), 1997, Sundance Press (Littleton, MA), 1999.

Did You Do That?, Longman (London, England), 1997, Sundance Press (Littleton, MA), 1999.

Let's Make a Cake, Longman (London, England), 1997, Sundance Press (Littleton, MA), 1999.

One for You, Longman (London, England), 1997, Sundance Press (Littleton, MA), 1999.

Let's Play with My Dog, Longman (London, England), 1997, Sundance Press (Littleton, MA), 1999.

I Do, Too!, Longman (London, England), 1997, Sundance Press (Littleton, MA), 1999.

Jake's Poem, Longman (London, England), 1997, Sundance Press (Littleton, MA), 1999.

ILLUSTRATOR; OTHER

Tony Bradman, *Pushchair Polly,* Picture Ladybird (Loughborough, England), 1996.

Tessa Krailing, *The Battle of Waterloo Road,* Oxford University Press (Oxford, England), 2001.

Contributor of illustrations to periodicals, including London *Guardian, Economist, Irish Times,* and Dublin *Independent.*

Adaptations

The characters from Geoghegan's *Dogs Don't Wear Glasses* were used in a televison advertising campaign for Jacob's Kimberly Mikado biscuits, 1999.

Sidelights

Irish illustrator and author Adrienne Geoghegan has seen success on both sides of the Atlantic, creating artwork for newspapers and book publishers in Dublin, London, and Massachusetts and exhibiting her work at group and solo art shows. From 1994 to 1997 she illustrated the "Read-on Beginner Books" series by Wendy Body, which numbers some forty books, each made up of eight pages of rudimentary text. Beginning in the mid-1990s Geoghegan began authoring her own picture-book texts, one of which, *Dogs Don't Wear Glasses,* she also illustrated. A hallmark of Geoghegan's work is humor, which a *Kirkus* reviewer, in an appraisal of *Dogs Don't Wear Glasses,* described as "satisfying silliness." The humor in *Dogs Don't Wear Glasses* lies in the actions of the visually imparied Nanny Needles, who has a number of accidents but blames them on her dog Seymour. Finally, thinking that Seymour cannot see well, she buys him glasses. At home Granny puts the glasses on herself, to see how they look, and discovers how much better she can see. Geoghegan's "bright and lively" crayon with watercolor-wash illustrations earned the praise of *Booklist* contributor Carolyn Phelan, although they were deemed "awkward" by a critic in *Publishers Weekly.*

The picture book *There's a Wardrobe in My Monster!,* which Sue Sherif of *School Library Journal* called "predictable but fun," revolves around the antics of Martha's new pet, a small green fellow who eats only wood. As the monster grows, its appetite increases until it has literally eaten a wardrobe. Finally, in this "romp of a tale to read aloud," to quote a *Kirkus* critic, Martha is forced by the monster's voracious appetite to return it to the pet shop for an exchange. *There's a Wardrobe in My Monster!* is a "quirky take on a tried-and-true pet story," concluded a *Publishers Weekly* contributor.

In the same vein of dry humor is Geoghegan's *All Your Own Teeth,* about would-be painter Stewart, who rather than realize he has no talent, searches for the perfect model from among the animals of the jungle. After rudely turning down an elephant, cheetah, giraffe, and hippopotamus who have answered his advertisement for a "Hansum wild animal" with his "own teeth and nice big smile," Stewart meets a crocodile. Stewart thinks the crocodile is just right and the crocodile, thinking Stewart is just right, gobbles up the nasty boy, a climax that *Booklist*'s Connie Fletcher thought might make this "rollicking morality tale" too intense for very young listeners. On the other hand, a critic for *Kirkus Reviews* predicted that "children will chuckle over this archly-delivered cautionary tale." Wendy Lukehart pointed out the work's "alliteration and letter play," dubbing the tale "perfectly preposterous" in her *School Library Journal* review, and in *Publishers Weekly* a contributor summed up *All Your Own Teeth* as an "odd but visually enticing parable."

Biographical and Critical Sources

PERIODICALS

Booklist, April 1, 1996, Carolyn Phelan, review of *Dogs Don't Wear Glasses,* p. 1371; March 1, 2002, Connie Fletcher, review of *All Your Own Teeth,* p. 1141.

Kirkus Reviews, April 1, 1996, review of *Dogs Don't Wear Glasses,* p. 529; September 15, 1999, review of *There's a Wardrobe in My Monster!* pp. 1499-1500; February 1, 2002, review of *All Your Own Teeth,* p. 181.

Publishers Weekly, March 4, 1996, review of *Dogs Don't Wear Glasses,* p. 64; August 16, 1999, review of *There's a Wardrobe in My Monster!* p. 82; December 24, 2001, review of *All Your Own Teeth,* pp. 63-64.

School Library Journal, January, 1995, Patricia Pearl Dole, review of *Six Perfectly Different Pigs,* p. 86; May, 1996, Susan Garland, review of *Dogs Don't Wear Glasses,* p. 91; November, 1999, Sue Sherif, review of *There's a Wardrobe in My Monster!* p. 116; April, 2002, Wendy Lukehart, review of *All Your Own Teeth,* p. 110.*

In **All Your Own Teeth,** *Stewart travels to the jungle to find the perfect wild animal to paint.* (Illustrated by Cathy Gale.)

GESNER, Clark 1938-2002
(John Gordon)

OBITUARY NOTICE—See index for *SATA* sketch: Born March 27, 1938, in Augusta, ME; died of a heart attack July 23, 2002, in Manhattan, NY. Composer, lyricist, actor, and author. Gesner is best remembered for his biggest theatrical success, *You're a Good Man, Charlie Brown,* based on the "Peanuts" comic strip by Charles M. Schulz. He studied at Princeton University, where he began acting in the Triangle Club and earned his bachelor's in 1960. For the next three years, he was in the U.S. Army Special Services. Gesner then took a job as a writer for the children's programs *Captain Kangaroo* and *Mister Mayor,* and he also worked as a freelance writer, composer, and lyricist for film and television. During this time, he had the idea of turning Shulz's popular comic strip into a theater production. He obtained permission from Schulz to make the adaptation, and the first production was staged in 1967 at Theater 80 in New York. The play was a huge success and saw over 1,600 performances. But although *You're a Good Man, Charlie Brown,* which he released under the pseudonym John Gordon, did well off Broadway, it only survived on Broadway briefly in 1971 and again in 1999. Despite this, Gesner did well enough with this one play to support himself for the rest of his life, during which he continued to write songs and plays. For television, he worked on the *Sesame Street* and *The Electric Company* children's programs, and he wrote such plays as *Finnerty Flynn and the Singing City* (1969) and the music and lyrics to *The Utter Glory of Morrissey Hall* (1976).

OBITUARIES AND OTHER SOURCES:

PERIODICALS

Los Angeles Times, July 29, 2002, p. B8.
New York Times, July 27, 2002, p. A24.
Washington Post, July 28, 2002, p. C6.

*   *   *

GOODHUE, Thomas W. 1949-

Personal

Born March 5, 1949, in Montebello, CA; son of Wallace T. and Mary Virginia (Gray) Goodhue; married Karen Pohlig (a yarn shop owner), May 13, 1975. *Ethnicity:* "Gringo." *Education:* Stanford University, B.A. (cum laude), 1971; Union Theological Seminary, M.Div., 1975; City College of the City University of New York, M.S., 1982. *Politics:* "Neo-liberal/progressive." *Religion:* Christian.

Addresses

Office—Long Island Council of Churches, 1644 Denton Green, Hempstead, NY 11550. *E-mail*—tgoodhue@suffolk.lib.ny.us.

Career

Pastor of United Methodist churches in Kailua, HI, 1975-77, and Kahaluu, HI, 1977-78; teacher at church-sponsored school in New York, NY, 1978-85; pastor of United Methodist churches in Island Park, NY, 1985-92, and Bay Shore, NY, 1992-99. Long Island Council of Churches, Hempstead, NY, presenter of weekly radio commentary, 1988-91, vice president, 1991-94, president, 1994-97, executive director, 1999—. United Methodist Center of Far Rockaway, vice president, 1985-92; Long Island Multi-Faith Forum, member; Building Bridges (interfaith education program), creator; Long Island Interfaith Disaster Response, founder, 2001. Windward Coalition of Churches, clergy coordinator, 1975-77; Hawaii Council of Churches, member of executive committee, 1977-78; member of board of directors, Health and Welfare Council of Long Island, 1999—, Fight for Families Coalition, 2000—, and United Way of Long Island, 2002—. Member, board of directors, Long Island Housing Partnership; WLIW-TV, member of community advisory board.

Member

Phi Beta Kappa.

Awards, Honors

Columbia University School of International Affairs, international fellow, 1974-75; Catholic Book Award; Educational Press Association Award.

Writings

Kaahumanu: Queen of Hawaii, Women of Courage, 1985.
Stories for the Children of Light, Sunday Publications (Lake Worth, FL), 1986.
Sharing the Good News with Children (collected writings), St. Anthony Messenger Press (Cincinnati, OH), 1992.
Curious Bones: Mary Anning and the Birth of Paleontology, Morgan Reynolds (Greensboro, NC), 2002.

Contributor of articles, essays, and reviews to periodicals, including *Anglican and Episcopal History, Northeastern Geological and Environmental Sciences, Journal of Ecumenical Studies, Momentum, Share, Christian Century, Midstream, Newsday, Education Week,* and *New Republic.*

Work in Progress

A longer biography of Mary Anning, *Fossil Hunter: The Life and Times of Mary Anning,* for Academic Press; a biography of Hawaiian queen Kaahumanu.

Sidelights

Thomas W. Goodhue told *SATA:* "I first became fascinated with Mary Anning while teaching kindergartners at the Riverside Church Weekday School in New York. Sharing the enthusiasm of five year olds for prehistoric creatures, I loved reading to them about dinosaurs and fossil hunters. I kept noticing references to the teenage girl who started the first dinosaur craze. Unable to find any factual account of her life—or any other books for children about female paleontologists—I started researching and writing a short summary of her life. This led to an article for the teachers' magazine *Instructor* in 1985, a children's sermon published in my collection *Sharing the Good News,* and a lasting obsession to learn more about this remarkable woman.

"What I find most fascinating about Anning are the paradoxes of her life. She was working class but formed friendships with wealthy fossil collectors and scholars. She had no formal education but helped shape the development of geology, biology, and paleontology. She was deeply pious herself, but her discoveries rattled the beliefs of millions of people. She could not vote herself, but she helped overturn the corrupt, aristocratic political machine that had dominated her town."

*   *   *

GORBACHEV, Valeri 1944-

Personal

Born June 10, 1944, in U.S.S.R. (now Ukraine); immigrated to the United States, 1991; son of Gregory and Polina (Koishman) Gorbachev; married; wife's name, Victoria (a librarian), October, 1970; children: Konstantin (son), Shoshana Alexandra (daughter). *Education:* Attended Academy of Art, Kiev, U.S.S.R. (now Ukraine).

Addresses

Home—1440 East 14th St., Apt. F-5, Brooklyn, NY 11230.

Career

Artist; author and illustrator of children's books.

Awards, Honors

Parent's Guide Children's Media Award and Kansas State Reading Recommended List citation, both for *Nicky and the Big, Bad Wolves.*

Writings

SELF-ILLUSTRATED JUVENILES

The Three Little Pigs: Full-color Sturdy Book, Dover (New York, NY), 1995.
Arnie the Brave, Grosset & Dunlap (New York, NY), 1997.
(With Warren Longmire) *The Flying Ship,* Star Bright (New York, NY), 1997.
Fool of the World and the Flying Ship, Star Bright (New York, NY), 1998.
Nicky and the Big, Bad Wolves, North-South (New York, NY), 1998.

Valeri Gorbachev

Where Is the Apple Pie?, Philomel (New York, NY), 1999.
Nicky and the Fantastic Birthday Gift, North-South (New York, NY), 2000.
Peter's Picture, North-South (New York, NY), 2000.
Chicken Chickens, North-South (New York, NY), 2001.
Goldilocks and the Three Bears, North-South (New York, NY), 2001.
Nicky and the Rainy Day, North-South (New York, NY), 2002.
One Rainy Day, Philomel (New York, NY), 2002.
Chicken Chickens Go to School, North-South (New York, NY), 2003.
The Big Trip, Philomel (New York, NY), 2004.
Whose Hat Is It?, HarperCollins (New York, NY), 2004.

ILLUSTRATOR

Joy N. Hulme, *What If? Just Wondering Poems,* Boyds Mills (Honesdale, PA), 1993.
Laurie A. Jacobs, *So Much in Common,* Boyds Mills (Honesdale, PA), 1994.
Pamela J. Farris, *Young Mouse and Elephant: An East African Folktale,* Houghton Mifflin (Boston, MA), 1996.
Miriam Kosman, *Red, Blue, and Yellow Yarn: A Tale of Forgiveness,* Hachai Publications (Brooklyn, NY), 1996.
Patricia Blanchard and Joanne Suhr, *There Was a Mouse,* Richard C. Owens (Katonah, NY), 1997.
Carol Roth, *Little Bunny's Sleepless Night,* North-South (New York, NY), 1999.
Judy Sierra, *Silly & Sillier: Read Aloud Tales from Around the World,* Knopf (New York, NY), 2002.
Carol Roth, *Who Will Tuck Me in Tonight?,* North-South (New York, NY), 2003.

Author and illustrator of several dozen books published in Russian. Contributor to children's magazines, including *Highlights for Children* and *Lady Bug.*

Work in Progress

More picture books.

Sidelights

Since arriving in America at the end of the Cold War, Valeri Gorbachev has established himself as a popular author and illustrator of children's books. Where once he worked primarily as an illustrator of other's works, he now writes and illustrates his own American titles, as he did in the former Soviet Union. This is all the more remarkable in light of the fact that he did not know any English when he came to the United States.

Gorbachev likes to draw "animals endowed with bold personalities," according to a *Publishers Weekly* reviewer. This penchant was an established part of his repertoire in the Soviet Union, where he created a best-selling series around a lively pig. In America his characters have included the "chicken chickens," who must bolster their courage to try new things, and Pig and Goat, a pair who can't quite trust each other's versions of events. *Booklist* reviewer Ellen Mandel noted that Gorbachev "etches humor and delight into each droll illustration."

Similarities and differences among people is the theme of Laurie A. Jacobs's book *So Much In Common,* a 1994 work that Gorbachev illustrated. Philomena Midge, a hippo, and Horace Abercrombie, a goat, are two friends who share different interests. The pair, however, easily acknowledge what they enjoy about each other—Philomena enjoys Horace's sense of humor while Horace savors Philomena's cooking. Other friends tell the hippo and goat that they have nothing in common, but the duo only grow closer. The story ends by promoting acceptance and diversity between the characters. Gorbachev adds to the theme with "cheerful pen-and-ink and watercolor drawings of the animal village," said *School Library Journal* reviewer Janet M. Bair. A *Publishers Weekly* contributor noted that the illustrator's drawings "bring the characters playfully to life."

Young Mouse and Elephant: An East African Folktale by Pamela J. Farris is another well-known children's book that includes Gorbachev's drawings. The humorous folktale focuses on Young Mouse, who claims to be the strongest animal on the African plains. Mouse's grandfather bruises his ego when he disagrees and states that Elephant is the strongest. Young Mouse goes out looking to challenge Elephant, proclaiming that he will "break Elephant apart and stomp her to bits." According to *School Library Journal* reviewer Jennifer Fleming, Gorbachev perfectly pairs his drawings to the folktale by making them "full of mischief and fun" and a "delightful match for this clever retelling." *Booklist* contributor Annie Ayres adds that the "sprightly ink-and-watercolor illustrations should amuse the small and swaggering."

Gorbachev's *Nicky and the Big, Bad Wolves,* is a picture book about a small bunny named Nicky who awakens one night terrified by a nightmare he has had. As Nicky relates his dream to his mother and four siblings, Gorbachev "wrings every last ounce of humor from the action" with his "particularly droll" pen-and-ink and watercolor illustrations, according to a reviewer for *Publishers Weekly.* The same commentator concluded that *Nicky and the Big, Bad Wolves* has a "fresh, friendly sensibility" that will "keep little ones coming back for more."

In *The Chicken Chickens,* two baby chicks make their first trip to the playground, where they are terrified by the play equipment. With the help of a kindly beaver, the two overcome their fears and learn to master the slide. Judith Constantinides in *School Library Journal* commended Gorbachev for endowing the animals with human expressions, "all in a simple and lively style." A *Publishers Weekly* critic felt that the book "takes a familiar preschool scenario and spins it out with gusto."

Gorbachev is equally at home illustrating established folktales from this country and others. His version of *Goldilocks and the Three Bears* was described by Sheilah Kosco in *School Library Journal* as "a perfect version for preschoolers." A contributor to *Publishers Weekly* liked the "snug interiors" that "conjure a cozy and comforting world." Another *Publishers Weekly* reviewer thought that Gorbachev's illustrations in *Silly & Sillier: Read-Aloud Tales from Around the World* "reflect the international settings and reinforce the playfulness of the tales."

Gorbachev once told *SATA:* "I arrived in the United States in 1991 with my wife, my two children, my suitcases, and dozens of characters I had created. Since then I have illustrated five books by American writers. In my native Ukraine, I illustrated forty children's books, half of which I also wrote. They have been translated into Finnish, German, and Spanish, and I have participated in many exhibitions of children's books in the former Soviet Union and abroad. I have also had solo exhibitions in Moscow and St. Petersburg. For many years government officials denied me the right to leave the country. The demise of communism at last cleared the way for me and my family to move to the United States.

"When I illustrate a book, the drawings and the text become one, and it is not really possible for me to separate the drawings from the text. I love to draw for children and to create books when I am both author and illustrator. I think that my work in children's magazines helped me to connect with the reading audience. Now I am enjoying my work with American magazines. I also love American children's books because they have strong visual appeal, and the connection between author and illustrator is close. Often the author and artist are the same person. That is how I understand children's literature. I hope that American children will love my books as much as Russian children do. My characters will take on nuances of American culture, but the basic qualities of the characters show the similarities among people all over the world."

Gorbachev's books have been translated into numerous foreign languages and have been published in Europe, Japan, and South America. He lives and works in New York City.

Biographical and Critical Sources

PERIODICALS

Booklist, May 1, 1996, Annie Ayres, review of *Young Mouse and Elephant: An East African Folktale,* p. 1509; July, 2001, Gillian Engberg, review of *Goldilocks and the Three Bears,* p. 2013; September 1, 2001, John Peters, review of *Chicken Chickens,* p. 114.

Publishers Weekly, June 21, 1993, p. 104; June 13, 1994, review of *So Much in Common,* p. 63; April 13, 1998, review of *Nicky and the Big, Bad Wolves,* p. 74; June 1, 1999, Ellen Mandel, review of *Little Bunny's Sleepless Night,* p. 1844; February 15, 2000, Ilene Cooper, review of *Where Is the Apple Pie?,* p. 1117; April 15, 2000, Marta Segal, review of *Peter's Picture,* p. 1550; May 7, 2001, review of *Goldilocks and the Three Bears,* p. 245; June 25, 2001, review of *Chicken Chickens,* p. 71; September 30, 2002, review of *Silly & Sillier: Read-Aloud Tales from Around the World,* p. 71.

School Library Journal, August, 1993, p. 158; December, 1994, Janet M. Bair, review of *So Much In Common,* p. 76.; April, 1996, Jennifer Fleming, review of *Young Mouse and Elephant: An East African Folktale,* p. 124; June, 2000, Sue Sherif, review of *Peter's Picture,* p. 112; June 2001, Sheilah Kosco, review of *Goldilocks and the Three Bears,* p. 116; August, 2002, Doris Losey, review of *One Rainy Day,* p. 156; September, 2001, Judith Constantinides, review of *Chicken Chickens,* p. 189.

Autobiography Feature

Valeri Gorbachev

My career as a children's book writer and illustrator started in Ukraine a long time ago. The Ukrainian Republic was a part of the former Soviet Union.

From my childhood I liked drawing. I used to draw all day long. Once my Uncle Eugene arrived at our home and took a quick look at my pictures. He told my mother, "Pauline, look at these sketches. Your son is a true artist." Uncle Eugene was a poet, his poetry was published; his appreciation meant a lot. From that time on I thought of my pictures as being special, unlike any other drawings by kids.

I sketched everything. I retrieved objects from memory, improvised, and did portraits of my sister. Not always could my poor sister recognize herself in my drawings. At fourteen I went to art school, at seventeen I became an art college student.

My parents' attitude to my plans for becoming an artist was ambivalent. My father's background was far from the arts. Early in his life he was drafted into military service. He participated in two wars; the Russo-Finish, in 1939, and World War II with Germany. During the latter he was wounded in the leg, and it was amputated. He wished me to master a solid profession that would result in stability. He wanted me to become

Valeri in his studio in Kiev, Ukraine

an engineer. But I was infected by art. If you are sick with art you can never recover. You rush forward and nothing can stop you. In the long run, my parents were proud of what I accomplished. However, my father always noted: "It should be brighter. People like when the pictures are bright."

Money-making necessity drove me into caricatures. Still in college, I took a full time cartoonist job for a satiric magazine, *Pepper.* It was a famous periodical, very popular in Ukraine. I would draw caricatures and write captions for them. The usual topics for caricatures were everyday life matters. They were reinforced by humorous dialogs.

During our meetings, we discussed illustrations for upcoming issues. Often my chief editor would announce, "Now let's see new sketches from our life Valeri came up with." For such assignments I used my life observations and along with drawings developed a knack for witty dialogs.

When I entered the children's book field, I realized how that helped. Playful interaction between images and words is imperative for an illustrated book. My creative experience at the magazine was indispensable.

The ratio between the books I had written and illustrated on my own, and the books by other authors where I participated only as an illustrator was approximately one to four. In the Soviet Union I had illustrated about forty books, ten of which I had authored.

Soon I felt that creation of a book from beginning to the very end, single-handedly, had grown into a burning desire. I craved to write the plot and dialogs, design layout, direct scenes, as if they were not books but productions in a theater or movies. Not surprisingly, my greatest success was achieved in this exact direction. I came up with the book series based on the protagonist Hrusha the Pig. It acquired intense popularity among kids. The series was reminiscent of American picture books as I can see it now. At the same time, it was quite different.

In Russia we existed behind the Iron Curtain. Few expositions took place. Occasionally, I visited Moscow book festivals. However, it is different to live and to work inside this atmosphere, and to watch it as a bystander. In terms of composition and concept, my books were vastly unlike those conventionally published in America.

It might sound ridiculous but my character Hrusha was brought to life by the propaganda demand. All of a sudden, my editor grabbed me into his office and asked me to write a book on frugality. He told me that the book was in need by the highest authorities. As most guidelines in the Soviet Union, the order was political rather than commercial. Because of the poor economy, propaganda had set a goal for children to live in thrifty ways without complaint. The publishing house had only one means to meet the penny-pinching initiative. They were to issue the book and I was to write it. The offer was too luring to neglect. I was glad to create a book with my own characters. The odds of such a book being accepted were minuscule. On the other hand, if you wrote on the suggested topic acceptance was more or less guaranteed.

With son Kostya and daughter Alexandra, 1975

I created the book about Hrusha, the little pig, with great enthusiasm. The topic turned out not so political but rather a common life subject: how you save bread, water, and forests. I had a plan. I did not want to create an ideal pig. My pig was to behave like a real kid, often in the wrong way. It would happen not because of wrongdoings but due to his temperament, curiosity, and personality, something all children have in common.

In Hrusha's character I reflected my son, Kostya. My character spoke with many words borrowed from my son. The book was saturated with humor. I like humor excessively (don't forget that for many years I had carried the proud title of a professional humorist, and got paid for cracking jokes). For the first time in my artistic career, I obtained an opportunity to create a character whose looks and words were both the product of my imagination. Working, I obtained the miraculous sensation of how everything in a book is tangled together. Prior to this, I had been given the text and my goal was just to illustrate it. Now that I became the master of the situation, the miracles started happening. If I improved the sketch, the text was automatically improved. If I enhanced the text, the pictures became better. I was delighted with the depth of interaction between art and words when you create a book.

The book became a big success. The publisher asked me to continue it as a series like they did in Europe and America but never before in Russia. Of course I gladly agreed. I know the character, I said. I got used to it. I can predict his behavior. I know what he will say under different circumstances. I can create two, four, ten books on Hrusha. . . .

In five years I produced ten books. From Ukrainian they were translated into Russian and published by the Moscow Publishing House. Hrusha the Pig had started his own life. Finland bought it. I had an expo with Hrusha's images in Moscow and Leningrad. It attracted children; kids had already read my books and knew about the funny pig.

Children's books were extremely cheap in the USSR. The government financed the publishing business and if the book was successful, millions of copies were put in print. For example, my book *How to Make Friends with a Little Dragon* had been published and sold in several million copies. For an American author it would have meant a fortune.

In 1991 my wife, two children, and I immigrated to the United States. I hoped to continue my career as a children's book author and illustrator. However, I was quite unconfident due to the language barrier. This obstacle is known to create a serious problem for any nonspeaking English author arriving in the USA. Having made the decision to live in America, I knew practically no English.

Speaking honestly, since my arrival in America I put all possible efforts to apply my skills and to demonstrate my talent. I had created a portfolio, which I carried with me to publishing houses. The editors accepted it with great interest. Unfortunately, I could not communicate with them without an interpreter's assistance. The lack of American experience was also quite obvious. As a result they did not rush to commission me to illustrate books.

In Manhattan I met Kent L. Brown, the publisher for Boyds Mills Press and the magazine *Highlights for Children.* Many generations have been educated on this magazine. It has been in business for a long time. Kent Brown expressed interest in my work. He sent a chauffeur to drive me to Honesdale for an appointment.

I went to Honesdale with my daughter. It was a great trip. Till that time, I lived in New Jersey, visited New York a few times, and had not seen America. When Frank the driver was driving us to Honesdale for 3.5 hours, I felt wonderful. It was like a foreshadowing of something new that would happen to me.

The tidiness and care with which American land was treated impressed me to a great extent. Especially by contrast to Russian and Ukrainian soil, where the nature is openly wild and the land is scarcely cultivated by humans. The small towns and villages that we passed were truly amazing.

My next wonders were with American roads. I used to read about highways in America; still I had never suspected they were so grand. Honesdale turned out to be a little town, provincial and dazzling. Frank drove us right to the publishing house.

We got familiar with the staff and seized the opportunity to watch them in the midst of their activities. The actions were familiar and reminded me of a Soviet publishing house. People were reading, writing, using computers. Still, there was something else. What it was specifically I could not discern. Only when I started working for the house did it become obvious. The tension was much higher.

Russian publishing business exists in a more relaxed atmosphere. In Moscow and Kiev, I could freely walk into my editor's office in the middle of the day, and we could have a cup of coffee together. Russians are not paranoid about losing their jobs and respectively are less industrious. In America, the author cannot casually drop by a publishing house without a scheduled appointment. This holds true for all New York editors.

I was impressed when my daughter and I were invited to stay in a big guesthouse, which was located in the woods far away from the town. There were almost too many rooms to count and inside it was delightful and neat.

After work, editors and art directors arrived at the house to look at my portfolio. I felt like it was a birth-

The author with his wife, Victoria, and children, ten years before immigrating to the United States

day party. Kent L. Brown invited an interpreter to join us at the dinner table. Barry Rubin, a New York University professor, knew Russian almost as well as me. He taught comparative literature classes. The professor did a good job; he made clear the nuances my daughter had difficulties to translate.

My family and I were staying with my friends in New Jersey when Kent Brown sent a letter to my friend's address. The friend ran into the living room and broke the news: "Kent Brown offers you a position as a staff artist."

"I've always said that Russian artists in America were given tremendous opportunities," Ken Brown emphasized in his note. "Now I intend to prove this using Valeri Gorbachev as an example."

It was well put and provided me with a source of great inspiration. The trip to Honesdale was triumphant. I got a job, my first job in America. I started gaining American experience.

I was lucky to find myself in the midst of the children's book manufacturing business.

The circumstances were tough; at times the pressure was unbearable. Upon coming home from work I frequently fell asleep. The work was familiar, but relentless guesses of what had been said by my colleagues made me feel nervous and uneasy. I have to admit that the staff was very helpful; they were nice people who expressed their interest in my work and my personality.

In Honesdale everything was new. I got my first paycheck and my first car. In Russia the range in salary between people was not that big. All made equal amounts of money and nobody stood out. Money was not an indicator of your success. In the United States, the money you make is the only measure of your accomplishments.

The language problem remained a top priority. Kent Brown held a meeting where he said, "Valeri is a Russian artist, and a good one, but he does not even have elementary knowledge of English." "It does not matter," the art director Jeff George, responded. "Valeri and I have a language in common. This is the language of art." If I could not grasp the task, he would illustrate the assignment. Two artists, we communicated by means of pencil and paper. Like ancient people we used picture language.

My first English phrases came to me in Honesdale. Coming to America, I started learning English but could not focus on it since I was preoccupied with job searching. To tell the truth, I am not a very capable student. I can do only what I love to do, paint, draw, and write books. Arriving in Honesdale I knew just a few words. When my colleague, her name was Mary, the girl sitting next to my desk, sneezed, I did not know what to say. She was so sympathetic, she wrote, "God bless you" on a paper and hung the note on a board. In a while, the notes with English expressions filled up the entire board. That was how Mary taught me English.

The author presenting his portfolio to editors, with daughter Alexandra translating

The town had sent me a tutor. She used to come once a week, we would sit together and talk. She gave me assignments that I attempted to complete. That was difficult, especially when I was coming from work dreadfully tired.

Honesdale blessed me with my first American friends. They barely understood what I mumbled; in return I could not make out what they were saying. Nevertheless the zeal to understand was so huge that our efforts resulted in sincere friendship that lasted till this day. They come to New York, I go to Honesdale, and we call each other. I remember how my art director Jeff George called up magazines with the announcement, "We got a great Russian artist. Would you be interested in his works?" Jeff kindly acted as my volunteering agent.

At a party in Honesdale I met Michael Grejniec. My friendship with Michael Grejniec is one of my fortunate events in America.

By the time I arrived in Honesdale, he had lived in America for nine years. Michael is a talented artist from Poland, possessing a sincere and open personality. When we met he was making one book after the other. As passionate about children's books as me, he rented a

The Gorbachev family in Honesdale, NY

house from Kent Brown in the mountains. After work I took my car and went to his place. We discussed books and talked about art. His excellent knowledge of American children's books was priceless. Also, his book collection was special and greatly reflected his personality.

He collected books meticulously, according to his taste and views. For hours he could talk about leading American artists. His views impacted my attitude and my concept of a children's book. He was the first to tell me of North-South Books; he worked with Marc Cheshire, the highly professional editor for this publishing house. It was a story about a remarkable and practically European publishing house. The owners lived in Switzerland; the American affiliate was only a branch. He showed me catalogs that were different from American catalogs. First, they were printed in colors, second, their very style was unmistakably European. Michael remarked that there were very few American artists working for North-South, the house mostly distributed books in Europe. His speech was full of useful hints. I tried to memorize each word. Now more than ever, I am thankful to Michael for his stimulating information about North-South.

Today, Michael lives and works in Japan, we call each other and talk for hours. I am sorry that Michael is far from me; in America we could have visited each other and communicated more often. When two artists work in one field they always find mutual topics.

It happened later that my books were published by North-South Books. They were also translated and printed in Japan. Being interviewed for a magazine I told that the first person to tell me of North-South Books was Michael Grejniec. After the Japanese publisher had read my interview he told Michael, "Thanks to you Valeri Gorbachev became aware of North-South Books. As a result, we publish Gorbachev's books in Japan to our mutual profits and pleasure. Thank you very much for giving us Valeri." When Michael described this conversation on the phone I came to the conclusion that Ken Brown was right when he wrote about America being a country of great opportunities. Could I imagine in

Russia, that my book written in the United States would be reprinted in Japan and a Japanese publisher would thank my newly acquired Polish friend for his recommendations? Such implausible sequence of events might have taken place only in an open society.

In Russia I had never driven a car. My Honesdale friends would give me lifts when I needed. Yet this was time consuming. I could not visit everyone I wanted. I felt uneasy and dependent. After my first paycheck, Frank the publishing house driver took me to a lot where I bought my first car. It was cheap and used but it was my car. The editors were taking turns giving me driving lessons. I obtained a permit, passed the road test, and became a genuine American—that meant a person on wheels. Now I was able to go to another city, pay visits to friends, and even go to the lake with my wife and children.

My kids left for New York to study and work. There my daughter got married. My wife remained in Honesdale with me but could not find a job and eventually also moved to New York. It was another reason for me to move.

While in Pennsylvania I illustrated two children's books, drew scores of hidden pictures, and worked for other publishing houses and magazines as a freelancer. This list includes *Cricket, Lady Bug, Turtle,* and *Playmate.* Magazine assignments were of great importance to me; they gave me necessary hints, answered various questions, and firmly directed my way to American children's literature.

I am grateful to my providence and will never forget that my fortunate beginning in America is due to the small town of Honesdale, to Kent L. Brown, and to his wonderful staff.

There is more to add regarding my first job in America. Every fall, I return to this place to attend the illustrators' party. This is the best time of the year. When I approach the town I get the feeling of a resident returning to his home.

Years have passed; I live in New York and work for numerous publishers. Whatever comes and goes in my life, I maintain a warm relationship with my Honesdale friends, and continue to collaborate with *Highlights for Children.* I draw covers, illustrations, and hidden pictures for them. Hidden pictures could serve as a hallmark for *Highlights for Children* since they outnumber those found in other magazines.

When I came to New York I started to regularly visit libraries to find out more about children's books. Libraries in America are a startling phenomena. They became my real universities. Thanks to New York libraries, I had acquired a full-sized, panoramic view of American children's literature. It advanced my knowledge and accelerated my involvement in the publishing mainstream.

In New York I expected to start my career from scratch. As a matter of fact I didn't have to, the first steps had already been made.

I was eager to work for magazines. From my experience in the USSR I knew that magazines shortened the path to children's books. When editors see illustrations in magazines they notice the author. Another reason was that magazine work is a quick process; a few pages and a spread are not a thirty-two page book. And magazine work is released in three months as opposed to a year. You have a chance to see flaws and correct them.

Mostly I worked for *Lady Bug* magazine. There I produced stories of Jinny and Bootsy. Jinny was a girl and Bootsy was a cat. I named the girl Jinny after my tutor. You might ask where "Bootsy" came from? I already knew that American cats conventionally aren't named like Russian cats. On my request, the editor created a list with a dozen cat names. I picked Bootsy. He told me that Jinny-Bootsy sounded like a good combination, and it did. The publisher loved my characters. I used to draw three or four magazines annually.

In *Turtle* I was occupied with the adventures of a small turtle. She was amiable, had friends, and was somewhat analogous to my Hrusha. Compared to Hrusha, the turtle was calm, balanced. I based its character on a turtle's temper. She was slow, demanding, and intelligent. I drew turtle stories for seven or eight years. They appeared in every release, starting from the single spread and reaching four or five pages in the last issues.

The stories helped me out in several ways. First, they gave me a clear idea of establishing connections with American children. If you are asked to draw a story every month, it means that the editors and kids have accepted it; that means you are on the right track. Second, the stories served as groundwork for my future books.

Lady Bug had published my profile, where I answered questions on my artistic background before coming to America. From this profile some publishers already knew about Valeri Gorbachev being a children's book author in addition to an artist.

Lady Bug is a magnificent, highly professional magazine considered by many to be the best children's magazine in America and possibly worldwide. It is ex-

ceptionally popular. When you get published often, which I did, the editors note you, pay attention to you as a creative artist. Thanks to *Lady Bug* I got my first commission in New York. Editors had spotted my work, called me, and I got an offer to illustrate a book for Houghton Mifflin Company, *Young Mouse and Elephant* by Pamela J. Farris.

The book topic was an African story of a little mouse and an elephant. I liked the contents because the author gave me the opportunity to draw what I liked to draw: African landscapes, storms, and exciting characters. The very mood of the book was congenial; it wound me up. I took the offer passionately. The book had grown into a pivotal point of my American career.

Another unexpected event happened that played a significant role in my creative life. One lucky day . . .

I met the publisher and the editor for North-South Books, Marc Cheshire. I knew of him from my Honesdale friend Michael Grejniec. Michael used to work with Marc and appreciated his professional qualities. Marc Cheshire liked my work. He was especially excited about me being an author and an artist since his publishing house had been searching for people of that kind. It had always had a number of brilliant author-artists such as Hans de Beer, Marcus Pfister, Lisbeth Zwerger, and others who brought success to the house. He expressed the desire to work together someday but there was no position for me at the moment. Mr. Cheshire was sure that sooner or later there would be.

Now that *Young Mouse and Elephant* was published and got good reviews, Cheshire gave me a call, and offered to meet. We met in his office at North-South.

"I like your book, Valeri," he said. "We could have started working together. Unhappily, I don't have a suitable manuscript. I have read your profile in *Lady Bug,* and know of you not only as an artist but as a writer as well. If you came up with something it would be cool." "I have an idea," I said, "but I don't know how to explain it. The idea sits entirely in my head." "Here is the paper." Marc said. "Take a pencil. Try to explain." I did. That is how *Nicky and the Big, Bad Wolves* was brought to light.

When I received an advanced incorrect proof for *Nicky* I found a cheerful note from Marc inside the book.

I was not aware if I would continue with North-South. The beginning was great but the rest was lost in the mist. It lasted till the moment I got a new call from Marc Cheshire.

"I've got two pieces of news for you, Valeri. One is good and the other is bad. Which one do you want me to relate first?" "Start with the bad one," I said cautiously. "I will start with the good one," Marc said. "Your book has been bought, it will be printed in German, French, Italian and Netherlands languages. Now the bad news follows: the French publisher does not like your cover; he wants to replace it."

Illustrating demonstration in bookstore

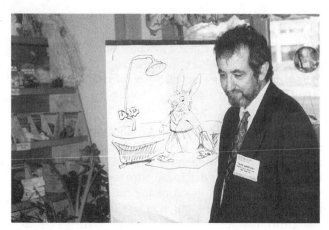

". . . and now let us draw a rabbit . . ."

My cover for the book was very dramatic. In it, Nicky was running away from pirates, there were boats, sea, night. Publishers in France wanted it simple: Nicky in bed, scared. The effect of fear should have been achieved by the formal methods like light, color, shapes, not at the cost of the plot. I worked intensely for ten days, then sent them my sketches. It is one of my best covers. No surprise they printed it as a poster.

Nicky is one of my most warmly accepted books. After so many countries have published it, I have a problem to list all of them without an error: Germany, Italy, France, Netherlands, Denmark, Japan, Brazil . . . Five years have passed, but yesterday I received mail from the French publishers with the fourth edition. It looks wonderful. It means my book is needed.

After the book was printed in Brazil I received a letter from the publisher. "I love your book *Nicky and the Big, Bad Wolves.* We ask your pardon for publishing it as a paperback. Our economy is poor and we cannot afford hardcover manufacturing." It was very poignant, especially taking in consideration that the paperback was manufactured excellently.

There were good evaluations, two starred reviews; and I got two awards for *Nicky,* the Parent's Guide Children's Media Award and the Kansas State Reading Recommended List. Still the most important consequence of the book was another offer from North-South Books.

North-South author Carol Roth had written *Little Bunny's Sleepless Night,* the next book I illustrated. It was another success, and again my publishers issued a poster. An illustration from *Little Bunny* became the cover for a North-South Books catalog.

Terrific times had started for me. I felt confident and reassured. *Little Bunny's Sleepless Night* also was quickly published in many countries. It received excellent reviews and awards.

The prominent stage in my artistic and human life began. I was deluged with ideas. One great idea replaced another. Frequent meetings with Marc Cheshire and Julia Amper, the editor of my books, were enormously productive.

Then I illustrated *Peter's Picture.* I made two other books with the character that had brought me big success, *Nicky and the Fantastic Birthday Gift* and *Nicky and the Rainy Day.*

Chicken Chickens was born out of a small idea that I had first implemented a while ago in the *Turtle* magazine. It took up two pages. Marc asked if I could expand it into a picture book. "This may not be an easy task, thirty-two pages." Mark said, "Why don't you give it a try?" That is how *Chicken Chickens* was born.

I am an artist who creates books for the smallest, for the youngest. When parents come to the bookstore with their kids, they look around. And they want to look at some books and don't want to look at the others. Why does it happen this way?

When I design a book I never pursue everyone's admiration as a goal. I conceive it, elaborate, and finish following only my personal emotions. If success comes, what can I say? I am happy.

How is a book born? At times you have just a general concept, an appealing situation, an image. A book could be started from a captivating spread or derive from the characters' relationship. The character can influence and modify the plot. The story line you begin from might disappear or grow into another story line. I love the moment when the book is setting up.

I begin by drawing small sketches on blueprint paper, usually thirty-two graphics, spreads, and the text. I write words in English, sometimes in Russian or in both languages. So if someone looked at the storyboard he might well think I was crazy.

My wife helps me with my work. She is a children's librarian. Her English is good, she works for Brooklyn Public Library. I appreciate her advice. In addition, she gives proper appearance to manuscripts so that I am not ashamed to show them in the publishing houses. She is my secretary and my translator. She prints the text, I clip and glue it to a dummy.

My wife and my children are my first spectators and critics. My children are also artists, so I listen to their opinion with interest.

At meetings, the soon-to-be book looks like rows of tiny pictures running down a cardboard. You bring the embryo of your creation, you think it is great; you love it, while an editor looks at it from a different perspective. Due to the editor's "help" a book often dies during the very early stages. At the same time, if an editor likes the story the work begins. I create a dummy, I work on the text. Finally, the originals and the art appear.

"Hrusha the Pig" illustration

You sit home, you visit no one, and no one visits you. You wake up at six and live with a book tête-à-tête. You don't care about the weather and the seasons. Finally, you bring the book to the publishing house, and see the impatient eyes of the editors.

Goldilocks and the Three Bears came next. That was another of Marc's ideas.

Marc Cheshire considers it a necessity for an artist to illustrate classic literature. It is a real challenge, the challenge across generations. You compete with the great authors of the past, you show your own interpretation. The act is full of significance. *Goldilocks* was chosen for an original art exposition, the annual display of the best children's books. I was part of the exhibition for three consecutive years.

Working with Marc and Julia results in immense pleasure. As well as being highly professional, they are exceptionally talented people. Our meetings are flamboyant and productive. Someone comes up with plot suggestions, another changes dialogs on the move, the third switches layouts. I hope that the enjoyment I am getting at our meetings is mutual. These are truly magnificent moments in children's book design.

It is not a yes-or-no situation. An editor is not only the decision-maker, the person that knows what is good and what is not. The dangerous editor is the one who sniffs out everything that is bad. Usually he cannot catch the particle of good in the pile of bad. The best editor is the one who can retrieve it and give possibility to the author to elaborate it and make a book out of it.

Marc Cheshire is an ideal publisher. His admiration for the artist's work serves as an authentic inspiration. He likes to compliment, of course, if he likes what you do. To each meeting he tries to bring something special. He says, "Here is the proof, a wonderful review." Or, "Here is the poster sketch for your book." As if for every meeting he prepares a present. I am so grateful to Marc for that. It contributes additional joy to the creative process. I consider it a very good style for a publisher.

The children's book kingdom is the entire universe. From an author, it requires unlimited imagination and semantic recognition. Children act on an intuitive level. Complex reasoning and high ideas wouldn't be understood in their minds. In Russia I tried to express sophisticated ideas in children's books. In fact, in one of my books, Hrusha does the impossible, since he is not aware of the impossibility. An intelligent and rational Fox, on the other hand, cannot comprehend how it happens. In real life, so-called reasonable people never do such things, since they know of its impossibility. They won't even try. I received letters from adults, they enjoyed what I said, they liked the idea. However, the kids, as I realize now, accept only images and plain ideas rendered in vivid form or enveloped in bright wrappings. In America I became convinced of complex thoughts in a children's book being futile. Only a limited number of values are needed, such as love for parents and pets, or friendship. I am saddened by the inability to express convoluted thoughts in children's books. At the same time, I fell in love with and believe in the American concept of children's books.

After *Nicky,* the offers from other publishing houses started flooding in. There was only one problem. I was so busy with North-South that I practically refused to work for anyone else.

Extraordinary people work for publishing houses. One of them is Patricia Lee Gauch, a publisher and senior editor for Philomel Book. I met her in Honesdale while attending an illustrator party. She invited me to show my portfolio. After Patty Gauch and Cecilia Yung, the art director, went through it they said, "Valeri we have only one question for you, how soon can you start."

When *Nicky and the Big, Bad Wolves* was issued, Patricia Gauch gave me a call. We met, she was excited and exclaimed: "Valeri, I want a book like *Nicky,* do it for me. I like the feeling of the book and I want exactly the same feeling. Do you understand what I mean by that?"

She was not sure with my English that I grasped what she said. She wanted me to preserve the intensity and richness of emotions expressed in *Nicky.* I got an idea for the new book. The book had to be named *Where Is the Apple Pie?,* with two characters, Goat and Pig. Patricia liked the plot and offered me a contract. The only trouble was with an ending. For several weeks I kept sending her faxes, each with a new version of the conclusion. With her assistance, I found a great story ending.

Patty Gauch is an extraordinary writer and a wonderful editor. She helped me to invent the rhythm of the story. The book was done, it got good reviews, and the French publisher Pepin bought it. The French published the book in quite a new design. When I glanced at it the first time, I could not recognize it. Brilliant designers, they used the title as a cover, and the cover as a title, while changing the format. It looked like a brand new book. When I showed it to my wife she exclaimed: "Oh, it is a very French book!" Design is a very powerful element in book manufacturing.

"Nicky" illustration

When I finished *Apple Pie,* Patricia said, "Valeri, I want another one. I would like you to make a book about rain. I consider your technique to be particularly beneficial for depicting rain." These words inspired me, and I asked if she agreed that we would use the same characters.

Thus, I made another book for Philomel. The plot is based on Pig's character. Pig is emotional, unruly, and he comes home all wet. His buddy Goat meets him on a threshold. Goat is phlegmatic, he thinks logically about everything. He wants to know why Pig got wet. Pig starts a long story how he hid from the rain. Goat cannot make out why Pig, having successfully hidden himself from the rain, got all wet. At this point, a remarkable climax occurred to me, a climax that is very understandable for Pig, who likes walking through puddles. After the rain was over, Pig rushed home (crossing all the puddles on his way) to tell everybody what had happened this rainy day.

I used numerals to count animals that were standing next to Pig under the tree: ten elephants, nine rhinoceros and so on. It was a list of animals and a story narration at the same time.

In music, there is a term *tutti.* It comes from Italian *tutto* that means "all." It indicates a passage of ensemble music that ought to be executed by all performers simultaneously. *Tutti* is used at the end of a symphony and gives the listeners a feeling of a strong climax.

The idea to put all animals under the single tree creates a feeling of culmination, an artistic *tutti.* It is an advantage for the sketch since in an enlarged spread a child can see all the animals at once, little Pig also included in this number. The publishing house had appreciated the spread and printed it as a poster.

With Patty Gauch, I keep working for Philomel Books. It will continue the story of Pig and Goat, and their humorous relations.

I love when I finish a book and bring it to the publishing house, spread it over long tables in a conference room. Many people come; almost the entire staff and guests. Then Marc from North-South or Patricia from Philomel walks along the tables while describing the plot of the book. I see people's faces and I am happy. I see that two or three months of hard work were not spent in vain.

Meeting the readers is my long-term habit. In Russia I was often invited to schools and kindergartens where I spoke of my characters and how I created books. In America, North-South Books asked me to participate in the American Library Association Annual Conference. It is a big book show where each publishing house has its booth. I was part of it twice, in Philadelphia and in Washington. You sit at a high stool, your books and posters are around you. It is a kind of conclusion, the final stage of your work. The long line of people, mostly professionals, librarians, publishers, and editors winds towards you. I remember well, the first book I signed was *Nicky and the Big, Bad Wolves.* I memorized the moment because my main problem was to recognize names by ear. What I did was this: I had each buyer write his name on paper so I could copy it without misspelling. If time and energy admitted I also drew a picture along with the inscription. Believe me, it was an enormous pleasure.

I used to sign books in bookstores as well. There is a famous bookstore in Pennsylvania. We went there together with North-South staff. Some people bought three or four books, often several copies of the same book. One woman asked me to inscribe the book to a baby who had yet to be born! Picture this, there is a book at someone's home on a shelf with my scribble, that says, "To the newborn baby from Valeri Gorbachev."

I am lucky. Practically all the people I work with are the best. While living in the USSR I also used to work in a children's publishing house with good editors. They were talented but most of them lacked the understanding of children's books that I found in American publishers and art directors. It is closely connected to the fact that New York and American publishing houses are the center of the children's book business.

When I appeared in New York years ago Isabel Warren-Lynch, an art director for Alfred A. Knopf, praised my portfolio, promised to keep me in mind, and find something for me. As it often happens she did not have a proper manuscript, and in time I had been completely forgotten.

One day, it sounds ridiculous, after nine years had passed, I got a buzz from her. Isabel Warren-Lynch spoke to me as to her old acquaintance. I could not recognize her. As it turned out, she had preserved the memory of my works, and followed my career closely. I got an invitation to the publishing house. Isabel and Janet Schulman, a very famous editor, who back in time worked with Dr. Seuss and many classical writers

Signing posters at American Library Association conference

in this genre, kept many books written and illustrated by me in America. They asked me to illustrate *Silly and Sillier,* a book of fools tales from different countries written by Judy Sierra.

The assignment was huge, eighty-six pages full of drawings. To tell the truth, at the beginning I was unconfident. Isabel created a wonderful design. I took enjoyment from drawing my pictures inside her splendid frame. Again, it was a great collaboration with great people. Janet Shulman said, "You have a wonderful team in North-South and in Philomel. We want to become your good team as well."

Alfred A. Knopf had manufactured a large beautiful lap book and made a fantastic poster for it. The poster is circular. It contains different pictures fetched from many stories. They fill up the poster's perimeter. The design is magnificent. I generally like posters, for they bring in new sensations. A poster is the quintessence of a book.

In terms of posters I am again a lucky artist. North-South, Philomel, and Alfred A. Knopf often create posters with my pictures. North-South prints calendars, postcards, and bookmarks. It gives plenty of pleasure, contributes to my budget, and serves as an advertisement for my work. *Silly and Sillier* was issued and had good responses and decent sales then and now.

I want to comment on the Easy Reader Book series. This genre is very attractive to me, since I like to invent stories, the stories that are long and saturated with events. The Easy Reader Book division in *HarperCollins Publishers* is one of a kind. They had collaborated with such tremendous artists as Arnold Lobel, whose books with Frog and Toad characters have been in print for decades. Or Maurice Sendak, one of the greatest living children's book artists. I have started my first book with HarperCollins.

A picture book, as Patricia Gauch puts it, is an artist's album. First of all, the pictures are looked upon, and only then the text. In an Easy Reader Book the text holds top priority. It is the first book a child can read on its own.

During my ten American years I had accumulated gigantic experience, which perfectly fit for Easy Reader Books. For over eight years, in every issue of *Turtle* magazine, I published stories. They were accepted pretty well. Even now, when I no longer work for the *Turtle,* the magazine repeats my old work in each issue. Those were small drawings, the ideas that developed the stories using a minimal number of words. There was no place for long captions. It was an excellent training. I use it abundantly now while writing a book for Easy Reader. At the same time I love the picture book, and will eventually work in both fields.

I have plenty of ideas and plans. I consider my creative pathway in America to be very successful. I came to this country with my own experience, my own view of the children's book; this view might have been harmful for my career. My understanding was different from the American, and I could have remained on a sidewalk. It would have been sad, since my creativity and my work is the bottom line of my personality, it is my main possession.

I am full of plans and I am interested in their implementation. I keep working with Marc Cheshire; I attend meetings where we discuss new books. I work with Patty Gauch, and I plan to continue my work with Janet Schulman and Isabel Warren-Lynch.

I am happy with my destiny. Leaving Russia, I was not sure whether American children would need me as an author. While immigrating and crossing the border I presented my book to the customs officer as a souvenir. He said: "Oh, you are my daughter's favorite artist. She knows all your books about Hrusha." Tears appeared in my eyes.

I think that the profession of an illustrator or the author of children's books is a gift from above. This is the best possible life that could be, at least for myself. Every night when I go to bed I impatiently wait for the morning to come in order to get sooner to my workshop and start writing, drawing, and thinking again and again, of my passion, children's books.

P.S. When I read over this manuscript it occurred to me that my life is not very rich with events. You get up in the morning at six, sit down at the table, and start working. Often your working hours last till midnight. Weekends or vacation days are very rare. It used to be in Russia, and I continue this habit in America. However, this is not true. The artist's life is very rich with events; these events are in his books, in his work. You place lots of your feelings, concerns, and personal achievements in your occupation, and it is a journey. Creative process is a voyage that sometimes goes well, and sometimes not. All of a sudden you make a discovery. Or the new way opens in front of you, and you produce marvelous stuff that never existed before. The artist's existence, no matter how quiet on the surface, is extremely intense and full of depth.

You write the book, you bring it to the publishing house, spread it over the long table and give thanks to God that editors often like it. The book is published. You see it in a bookstore. Then reviews come, then the statements of how much money you get. All these are stages that carry tons of pleasure.

*

FRIENDS

Throughout my ten years in American children's books, there were other friends—professionals like Lindsey George, Leonid Gore, John O'Brien, Michael Garland. I like all of them as artists, as friends, as people, and this is again my good luck in America.

MY CHILDREN

My own children became professional artists. My daughter, Alexandra, has illustrated a few books. My son, Konstantin, works in the 3-D animation field. I believe that occupation by arts develops soul and reveals breathtaking features in humans. I always supported their aptitude. I am looking forward to some of my grandchildren also being artists. However, my father was absolutely right, the artist's profession is shaky.

POSTCARDS

In Russia, on the New Years' eves, I used to draw postcards for my friends and editors. I had drawn them on watercolor paper, a genuine piece of art for each addressee, expressing by this my respect and being happy to draw anything without purpose and assignment, just for my and someone else's pleasure. I keep drawing postcards in America. I enjoy seeing my postcards in editors' offices, framed and on walls.

LIBRARIES

As I already told, American libraries became my universities. Today, when I come to the library and see my books on shelves I realize that the circle has been closed. I am part of American children's books, and I am proud of this fact.

APPETITE

An enormous craving for work possesses me. Every new idea triggers my work appetite.

HOPES

My hopes are inseparable from my creations. They are simple. I hope that American children fall in love with my books.

GORDON John
   See GESNER, Clark

*   *   *

GREENE, Meg
   See MALVASI, Meg Greene

*   *   *

GROTH-FLEMING, Candace
   See FLEMING, Candace

*   *   *

GURNEY, John Steven 1962-

Personal

Born January 11, 1962, in Lancaster, PA; son of Allan B. (a market research consultant) and Caroline E. (a hydrologic technician; maiden name, Whiteside) Gurney; married Kathleen Gatto (a dancer and choreographer), September 20, 1987; children: two. *Education:* Pratt Institute, B.F.A., 1984; attended New York Academy of Fine Art and Stevenson Academy of Traditional Painting. *Politics:* Democrat. *Religion:* Roman Catholic.

Addresses

Home and office—710 Western Ave., Brattleboro, VT 05301. *E-mail*—jsgurney@adelphia.net.

Career

Illustrator. *Exhibitions:* Work has been exhibited by the Society of Illustrators, the Society of Publication Designers, and numerous galleries in the New York City metropolitan area.

Member

Children's Book Illustrators Group (officer).

Writings

(Self-illustrated) *Dinosaur Train,* HarperCollins (New York, NY), 2002.

ILLUSTRATOR

William F. Buckley, Jr., *The Temptation of Wilfred Malachy,* Workman Publishing (New York, NY), 1985.
(Contributor) *The Classic Mother Goose,* Running Press (Philadelphia, PA), 1987.

The Bailey School kids wonder if their camp director is a werewolf in Werewolves Don't Go to Summer Camp, *written by Debbie Dadey and Marcia Thornton Jones, and illustrated by John Steven Gurney.*

Dan Elish, *The Worldwide Dessert Contest,* Orchard Books (New York, NY), 1988.
(Co-illustrator) Della Rowland, *A World of Cats,* Contemporary Books (Chicago, IL), 1989.
Clement Clarke Moore, *The Night before Christmas,* Scholastic (New York, NY), 1989.
(Contributor) *The Classic Treasury of Children's Poetry,* Running Press (Philadelphia, PA), 1990.
Dayle Ann Dodds, *On Our Way to Market,* Simon & Schuster (New York, NY), 1991.
Brothers Grimm, *Hansel and Gretel,* Andrews & McMeel (New York, NY), 1991.
Lydia Maria Child, *Over the River and through the Woods,* Scholastic (New York, NY), 1992.
The Jumbaroo, Wright Group (San Diego, CA), 1992.
SuAnn Kiser, *The Hog Call to End All!,* Orchard (New York, NY), 1995.
Patricia Hermes, *Turkey Trouble,* Scholastic (New York, NY), 1996.
Patricia Hermes, *Christmas Magic,* Scholastic (New York, NY), 1996.

Bill Wallace, *Upchuck and the Rotten Willy: Running Wild,* Minstrel (New York, NY), 2000.

Carol and Bill Wallace, *Chomps, Flea, and the Gray Cat (That's Me),* Minstrel (New York, NY), 2001.

Carol and Bill Wallace, *Bub Moose,* Minstrel (New York, NY), 2001.

Bill Wallace, *Bub Moose and the Burley Bear Scare,* Minstrel (New York, NY), 2002.

John Peel, *Double Disaster,* Aladdin (New York, NY), 2002.

Nikki Wallace, *Stubby and the Puppy Pack to the Rescue,* Simon & Schuster (New York, NY), 2002.

Joanne Sherman, *Because It's My Body!,* S.A.F.E. for Children Publishing, 2002.

Carol and Bill Wallace, *The Meanest Hound Around,* Simon & Schuster (New York, NY), 2003.

Also illustrator of "Kermit Tales" series of story cards, Jim Henson Productions, 1989-91; and of book covers for Ace, Berkley, Atheneum, Pocket Books, and Orchard Books. Illustrator for magazines, advertisements, greeting cards, and puzzles.

Illustrator of book series by Debbie Dadey and Marcia Thornton Jones, published by Scholastic (New York, NY), including "Adventures of the Bailey School Kids," 1990—, "Mrs. Jeepers," 1997—, and "Bailey School Monsters," c. 1999—.

Illustrator of "A to Z Mysteries" series by Ron Roy, published by Random House (New York, NY), 1997—.

Sidelights

Artist and illustrator John Steven Gurney worked for many years as an illustrator before breaking into picture-book writing. A graduate of New York's Pratt Institute, Gurney got his start as an illustrator after being "discovered" when his contest-winning poster design for a brand of ale was published in *Rolling Stone.* His detailed illustrations have complemented the work of many authors and he has spent much of his time creating black-and-white interior illustrations for multi-book series.

Born in 1962, Gurney was raised in Bucks County, Pennsylvania, where he came under the spell of the films of Walt Disney and the humor of *Mad* magazine. "When I was ten years old I attended a class where the students created illustrations while listening to selected

In **Trolls Don't Ride Roller Coasters,** *written by Debbie Dadey and Marcia Thornton Jones, the Bailey School kids must discover if a T-shirt vendor is an evil troll.* **(Illustrated by Gurney.)**

stories read by the teacher, artist Jean Burford," Gurney once recalled to *SATA*. "I knew then that I wanted to be an illustrator."

In addition to discovering the illustrations of noted New York artist N. C. Wyeth during his early teens, Gurney studied at the Philadelphia College of Art on the weekends, in between tennis and high school wrestling matches and practicing the saxophone. At one point during his teens he studied with noted illustrator William A. Smith. A scholarship to study illustration at the prestigious Pratt Institute followed, funded in part by a summer job in which Gurney drew caricatures of tourists walking the boardwalk in nearby Atlantic City, New Jersey. He graduated from Pratt with top-notch credentials in 1984, then hitchhiked through Europe, exploring the social scene as well as European museums and galleries.

While still a student at Pratt Institute, Gurney had entered a poster contest for Molson's Golden Ale. As the contest's winner, his poster illustration gained national exposure when it ran as part of a Molson advertisement published in *Rolling Stone* magazine. Recalled Gurney: "The exposure led to my first illustrated children's book, *The Temptation of Wilfred Malachy,* written by the noted columnist William F. Buckley, Jr."

Since publishing his first book illustrations, Gurney has gone on to specialize in creating artwork for children's books, among them titles in the "Bailey School Kids" and "A to Z Mysteries" series. The "Bailey School Kids" books, which numbered over forty volumes by 2002, feature Liza, Eddie, Howie, and Melody as they keep each other safe from suspected vampires, witches, monsters, and the occasional genie lurking in their small town. The "A to Z Mysteries" by Ron Roy find junior sleuths Josh, Dink, and Ruth Rose indulging their curiosity and winding up with trouble on their hands. Reviewing the 1999 installment *The Goose's Gold* for *Booklist,* Shelley Towsend-Hudson maintained that Gurney's pen-and-ink illustrations help maintain reader interest in Roy's "predictable but readable story."

Gurney expanded his creative output in 2002 when he decided to add "picture-book author" to his list of accomplishments. His first solo effort, *Dinosaur Train* follows a pajama-clad young boy named Jesse as he is whisked from his bedroom for a midnight ride aboard an amazing train occupied by dapper dinosaurs of all shapes and sizes. Fortunately for the dinosaurs, Jesse is an expert with trains, and when the train jumps the tracks after its weighty passengers all crowd to one side to watch a volcano eruption, he is able to help put it back on course. Hailing the book as a "brisk, bright solo debut," a *Kirkus* reviewer praised Gurney for combining the "two near-universal obsessions" of young boys into a story whose "towering prehistoric passengers" are given "a friendly look." Gurney's illustrations, which *School Library Journal* reviewer Marian Drabkin praised as "brilliantly colored and lovingly detailed," "mine a deep well of childhood enthusiasm for a Jurassic cast," according to a *Publishers Weekly* contributor who dubbed the book "a fabulous fantasy ride."

For Gurney, in creating his detailed illustrations "preparation is as important as the painting." As he once explained to *SATA:* "I took photographs from precarious rooftop heights to obtain interesting 'flying reindeer' angles for *The Night before Christmas.* I revisited my rural childhood surroundings for *On Our Way to Market.* And I had to track down a one-horse open sleigh to pose models for *Over the River and through the Woods.*" Many of his illustrations are based on photographs taken of friends who posed in costume for him; he exhibits these photographs alongside the completed illustration when he visits schools to speak with children about the book-illustration process.

Working in New York City for many years, Gurney left the city for a quieter life in northern New England in 1997. He lives in Vermont with his wife and two children and continues to devote much of his time to illustrating children's books.

Biographical and Critical Sources

PERIODICALS

Booklist, October 15, 1999, Shelley Towsend-Hudson, review of *The Goose's Gold,* p. 446; November 15, 2002, Diane Foote, review of *Dinosaur Train,* p. 610.
Kirkus Reviews, July 15, 2002, review of *Dinosaur Train,* p. 1031.
Publishers Weekly, September 19, 1992, review of *The Hog Call to End All!,* p. 69; September 30, 2002, review of *Dinosaur Train,* p. 70.
School Library Journal, December, 2002, Marian Drabkin, review of *Dinosaur Train,* p. 97.

ONLINE

John Steven Gurney Web site, http://www.author-illustr-cource.com/ (March 11, 2003).
Porfolios.com, http://www.portfolios.com/ (March 11, 2003), "John Steven Gurney."*

H

HARRIS, Lavinia
See ST. JOHN, Nicole

*   *   *

HAVELIN, Kate 1961-

Personal
Born January 23, 1961, in Bryn Mawr, PA; daughter of Dudley W. (a banker) and Marie (a nurse; maiden name, Doherty) Havelin; married Leo Timmons (an Internet director), June 30, 1990; children: Max Timmons, William Havelin. *Ethnicity:* "Caucasian." *Education:* Macalester College, B.A., 1983. *Politics:* "Liberal progressive." *Hobbies and other interests:* Running, including marathons, reading, travel, politics.

Addresses
Home and office—2028 Ashland Ave., St. Paul, MN 55104. *E-mail*—khavelin@aol.com.

Career
KTCA-TV, St. Paul, MN, administrative assistant, 1983-84; *Forum,* Fargo, ND, copy editor, 1984-85; WCCO-TV, Minneapolis, MN, producer, 1985-96; freelance writer, 1996—. Professional Editors Network, co-coordinator. Million Mom March, board member of Twin Cities chapter.

Kate Havelin

Writings

Imagine You Are a Secret Service Agent, Imaginarium (Edina, MN), 1999.

Imagine You Are an ER Doctor, Abdo Publishing (Edina, MN), 1999.

Assertiveness: How Can I Say What I Mean?, LifeMatters (Mankato, MN), 2000.

Child Abuse: Why Do My Parents Hit Me?, LifeMatters (Mankato, MN), 2000.

Dating: What Is a Healthy Relationship?, LifeMatters (Mankato, MN), 2000.

Family Violence: My Parents Hurt Each Other!, LifeMatters (Mankato, MN), 2000.

Incest: Why Am I Afraid to Tell?, LifeMatters (Mankato, MN), 2000.

Parents: "They're Driving Me Crazy!," LifeMatters (Mankato, MN), 2000.

Peer Pressure: How Can I Say No?, LifeMatters (Mankato, MN), 2000.
Sexual Harassment: "This Doesn't Feel Right!," LifeMatters (Mankato, MN), 2000.
Queen Elizabeth I, Lerner Publishing Group (Minneapolis, MN), 2002.
Andrew Johnson, Lerner Publishing Group (Minneapolis, MN), in press.
Ulysses S. Grant, for Lerner Publishing Group (Minneapolis, MN), in press.

Work in Progress

John Tyler, Lerner Publishing Group (Minneapolis, MN), 2005.

Sidelights

Kate Havelin told *SATA:* "I grew up in a family that loved reading and history. My mom's idea of a great vacation was visiting presidents' homes, and growing up in the Philadelphia area meant I had lots of lively historic places to visit close to home. So it's probably no surprise that I've ended up writing biographies of presidents and other historical figures.

"In college, I majored in anthropology and am still interested in different cultures and countries. I love to travel, to read, to run, and to spend time with my family."

Biographical and Critical Sources

PERIODICALS

School Library Journal, February, 2000, Katie O'Dell, review of *Parents: "They're Driving Me Crazy!,"* p. 130; May, 2000, Sally Bates Goodroe, review of *Child Abuse: Why Do My Parents Hit Me?* and *Family Violence: My Parents Hurt Each Other!,* p. 182; July, 2002, Kathleen Simonetta, review of *Queen Elizabeth I,* p. 136.

* * *

HILL, Elizabeth Starr 1925-

Personal

Born November 4, 1925, in Lynn Haven, FL; daughter of Raymond King (a science-fiction novelist) and Gabrielle (Wilson) Cummings; married Russell Gibson Hill (a chemical engineer), May 28, 1949 (died 1999); children: Andrea van Waldron, Bradford Wray. *Ethnicity:* Caucasian. *Education:* Attended Finch Junior College, 1941-42; attended Columbia University, 1970-73. *Politics:* Independent. *Religion:* Episcopalian. *Hobbies and other interests:* Music, theatre, art.

Addresses

Home—Langford Apartments, P.O. Box 940, Winter Park, FL 32790. *Agent*—Wendy Schmalz Agency, P.O. Box 831, Hudson, NY 12534.

Career

Freelance writer. Former actress in radio and summer-stock productions. Adult education teacher at Princeton Adult School. Painter, with work exhibited in metropolitan New York.

Member

University Club of Winter Park.

Awards, Honors

Notable Children's Book citation, American Library Association, 1967, for *Evan's Corner;* Pick-of-the-Lists citation, American Book Association, 1992, for *Broadway Chances;* award for outstanding achievement in children's books, Parent's Guide to Children's Media, and Parent's Choice gold Medal award, both 1999, both for *Bird Boy;* Parents' Guide to Children's Media award, for *Chang and the Bamboo Flute.*

Writings

The Wonderful Visit to Miss Liberty, illustrated by Paul Galdone, Holt (New York, NY), 1961.
The Window Tulip, illustrated by Hubert Williams, F. Warne (New York, NY), 1964.
Evan's Corner, illustrated by Nancy Grossman, Holt (New York, NY), 1967, revised edition illustrated by Sandra Speidel, Viking (New York, NY), 1990.
Master Mike and the Miracle Maid, Holt (New York, NY), 1967.
Pardon My Fangs, Holt (New York, NY), 1969, revised as *Fangs Aren't Everything,* illustrated by Larry Ross, Dutton (New York, NY), 1985.
Bells: A Book to Begin On (nonfiction), illustrated by Shelly Sacks, Holt (New York, NY), 1970.
Ever-after Island, Dutton (New York, NY), 1977.
When Christmas Comes, Penguin (New York, NY), 1989.
The Street Dancers, Viking (New York, NY), 1991.
Broadway Chances (sequel to *The Street Dancers*), Viking (New York, NY), 1992.
The Banjo Player, Viking (New York, NY), 1993.
Curtain Going Up! (sequel to *Broadway Chances*), Viking (New York, NY), 1995.
Bird Boy, illustrated by Lesley Liu, Farrar, Strauss (New York, NY), 1999.
Chang and the Bamboo Flute (sequel to *Bird Boy*), illustrated by Lesley Liu, Farrar, Strauss (New York, NY), 2002.

Contributor to *Encyclopaedia Britannica.* Contributor of stories and articles to periodicals, including *New Yorker, Reader's Digest, Harper's Bazaar, Seventeen,*

Woman's Day, Woman's Home Companion, Good Housekeeping, Collier's, Cricket, New World Writing, Faith Today, and other magazines in the United States, Britain, and France.

Adaptations

Evan's Corner was adapted as a film and produced by Stephen Bosustow in 1969.

Work in Progress

Wildfire! for Farrar Straus.

Sidelights

Although she is most well known as the author of the picture book *Evan's Corner,* Elizabeth Starr Hill has written books for young readers of a variety of reading levels. Including both fiction and nonfiction among her published works, Hill excels at creating believable characters who often grow in self-knowledge through their interaction with the natural world. "I find the natural world amazing, fascinating, endlessly absorbing—and people are as much a part of it as a tree or a chip-

munk," the author once commented to *SATA.* "There are stories in every country morning; and also in every city afternoon, and every frightened naptime. The important thing is to pay attention to life."

First published in 1967 and reissued with new illustrations in 1990, Hill's *Evan's Corner* focuses on an African-American boy who tries to find a quiet place in his family's noisy apartment. His mother gives him a subtle lesson in sharing after she allows him to claim a corner of the apartment as his own. Praising the story in *School Library Journal* Luann Toth noted that Hill presents young readers with a "sensitive and thoughtful" protagonist and shows the value of "the support and encouragement of a loving family" in learning that things gain in value when they are shared with others.

Beginning readers are the intended audience of Hill's *Bird Boy,* which takes place in China and focuses on a young mute boy named Chang. Living on a houseboat, Chang has developed a special love for water birds, and when his father helps him raise one of the cormorant chicks through which the family makes their living, Chang gains in self-confidence. In addition to introduc-

Chang's family battles a flood from their houseboat on the Li River in southern China in Chang and the Bamboo Flute, *written by Elizabeth Starr Hill and illustrated by Lesley Liu.*

ing readers to Chang's family's unique way of life, Hill "effortlessly weaves in multiple themes of courage, responsibility and friendship," explained a *Publishers Weekly* contributor. Praising the story for inspiring young readers with disabilities, Lauren Peterson added in her *Booklist* review that *Bird Boy* imparts an important lesson: that "friendship and trust must be given only to those who earn it." Praising Hill's "excellent little novel," Elaine A. Bearden noted in her review for the *Bulletin of the Center for Children's Books* that "readers will identify with Chang and his desire to do grownup things." Hill continues Chang's story in 2002's *Chang and the Bamboo Flute.*

Among Hill's novels for middle-grade readers is the three-book series that includes *The Street Dancers, Broadway Chances,* and *Curtain Going Up!.* The series focuses on a girl who lives an unsettled life due to her parents' theatrical careers. In *The Street Dancers* readers meet Fitzi Wolper, who lives in New York but is home-schooled because of the moves required by her parents' acting stints. Because the family's fortunes fluctuate with their ability to land roles on Broadway, nothing seems normal to the increasingly self-conscious teen, and normal is what Fitzi wants. Citing *The Street Dancers* for its "good balance of realism and glamor," *Bulletin of the Center for Children's Books* reviewer Kathryn Pierson Jennings added that Hill's "characters are believable." Calling the novel a "charming" tale that "grows out of the author's own stage experience," a *Kirkus* contributor praised the work for presenting a realistic picture of life behind the theater curtain.

Fitzi's teen years continue to be explored in the two sequels to *The Street Dancers.* In *Broadway Chances* Fitzi's grandfather lands a small role in a Broadway musical and her parent's are offered small roles as well. After she auditions for the child's lead and loses to an arch-rival, Fitzi nonetheless wins a dancer's role and helps to thwart a kidnaping between rehearsals. "Hill presents an enthralling look at a theatrical production," in the opinion of a *Kirkus* reviewer, and Jennings added in her *Bulletin of the Center for Children's Books* review that the author includes the requisite "good old Broadway happy ending." A love interest enters the picture in the series' conclusion, *Curtain Going Up!,* as Fitzi wins a dance solo in a Broadway show but loses her heart to Mark Hiller, the show's charismatic young lead.

Other novels Hill has written for middle-grade readers include *When Christmas Comes* and *The Banjo Player.* In *When Christmas Comes* a young girl named Callie attempts to come to terms with her parents' divorce, but is upset when the family breakup leaves her living in a trailer park with her father and his new wife. The fact that everyone is busy celebrating the approaching holiday season doesn't improve her mood, but when she and a friend find and care for an abandoned pup Callie finally begins to come to terms with the changes in her life. Praising the novel's characters, a *Kirkus* reviewer

noted that the stepmother, Fran, "is both creative and patient with her new charge," and praised the novel's ending as "satisfyingly heartwarming." Citing the relationship between Callie and her father and new step-mother as "well drawn," *Booklist* contributor Kay Weisman noted that young readers would find *When Christmas Comes* "a satisfying read." A work of historical fiction that focuses on the Orphan Trains of the late 1800s, *The Banjo Player* also features a teen protagonist in young Jonathan. Moving to New Orleans, the teen becomes a street musician, and later an actor on a showboat. Praising Hill's protagonist as commendable, *School Library Journal* contributor Bruce Anne Shook called *The Banjo Player* "upbeat reading" that "provides plenty of colorful details about the late 1800s in New Orleans and vicinity."

Describing her writing process, Hill once commented to *SATA:* "Story ideas are a combination of knowledge and imagination. I believe the use of our senses is as important to writing as the actual setting of pencil to paper. If we know—*really* know—how things look and sound and smell and feel, the daydreams that come to us will be rooted in life, recognizable to young readers.

"When I was a little girl, my mother told me, 'Learn to love nature. Then you'll always be happy.' It was good advice. Some of my happiest hours are spent in relative idleness, watching storms or butterflies or the coming of a new season. The wonder of growth and change never diminishes, and I try to express some of that wonder in my writing."

Biographical and Critical Sources

PERIODICALS

Booklist, November 15, 1989, Kay Weisman, review of *When Christmas Comes,* p. 668; October 1, 1992, Kay Weisman, review of *Broadway Chances,* p. 326; January 15, 1995, Ilene Cooper, review of *Curtain Going Up!,* p. 928; April 15, 1999, Lauren Peterson, review of *Bird Boy,* p. 1528; October 15, 2002, GraceAnne A. DeCandido, review of *Chang and the Bamboo Flute,* p. 405.

Books for Keeps, May, 1991, review of *Evan's Corner,* p. 29.

Bulletin of the Center for Children's Books, July, 1991, Kathryn Pierson Jennings, review of *The Street Dancers,* pp. 264-265; June, 1992, K. Jennings, review of *Broadway Chances,* pp. 263-264; March, 1995, Deborah Stevenson, review of *Curtain Going Up!,* pp. 237-238; July, 1999, Elaine A. Bearden, review of *Bird Boy,* p. 389.

Children's Book Review Service, May, 1985, Jeanette Cohn, review of *Fangs Aren't Everything,* p. 110.

Horn Book, September-October, 1991, Ethel L. Heins, review of *Evan's Corner,* p. 618.

Kirkus Reviews, August 15, 1989, review of *When Christmas Comes,* p. 1246; May 15, 1991, review of *The Street Dancers,* p. 672; May 15, 1992, review of

Broadway Chances, p. 671; July 1, 1993, review of *The Banjo Player,* p. 861; October 1, 2002, review of *Chang and the Bamboo Flute,* p. 1470.

Publishers Weekly, November 1, 1991, review of *When Christmas Comes,* p. 82; May 3, 1991, review of *The Street Dancers,* p. 73; May 18, 1992, review of *Broadway Chances,* p. 71; June 28, 1993, review of *The Banjo Player,* p. 78; April 10, 1995, review of *Curtain Going Up!,* p. 63; March 29, 1999, review of *Bird Boy,* p. 105.

School Library Journal, May, 1985, review of *Fangs Aren't Everything,* p. 90; March, 1991, Luann Toth, review of *Evan's Corner,* p. 173; June, 1991, Tatiana Castleton, review of *The Street Dancers,* p. 106; May, 1992, Jennifer Kraar, review of *Broadway Chances,* p. 114; July, 1993, Bruce Anne Shook, review of *The Banjo Player,* p. 85.

*   *   *

HUDAK, Michal 1956-

Personal

Born April 10, 1956, in Žilina, Slovakia; son of Michal (a Lutheran pastor) and Ludmila (a Lutheran pastor; maiden name, Mazakova) Hudak; married Annika Sjunnesson (a singer), 1996; children: Samuel. *Ethnicity:* "Slovak." *Education:* Studied architecture at Institute of Technology, Bratislava, Slovakia, 1975-78, and Royal Institute of Technology, Stockholm, Sweden, 1979-82; received master's degree, 1988. *Religion:* Christian.

Addresses

Agent—c/o Author Mail, Liturgical Press, St. John's Abbey, P.O. Box 7500, Collegeville, MN 56321-7500. *E-mail*—samhudek@spray.se.

Career

Lundquist & Carrier, Stockholm, Sweden, architect, 1985-88; Glimåkra FHS, Glimåkra, Sweden, teacher, 1994-97; artist and illustrator. *Exhibitions:* Works included in exhibitions throughout Scandinavia, including at Gallery of the Society of Graphic Artists, Stockholm, Sweden, 1984, Fagersta Town Art Gallery, 1995, and Hässleholm Town Art Gallery, 1997; work exhibited in "Project TRACK—Europe Ten Years after the Wall," Stockholms Länsmuseum, 2001, and Railway Museum Kristianstad, 2002, and "Landscapes for Johann Sebastian Bach," at Borgen, Gislaved, Sweden, 2001; work also exhibited in Japan and Poland. Work represented in private collections, including parish houses in Batizovce and Gerlachov, Slovakia, Lutheran churches in Svit and Dudince, Slovakia, and libraries in Tollarp and Kristianstad, Sweden.

Member

Swedish Artists National Organization, Swedish Society of Graphic Artists, Swedish Society of Illustrators.

In Michal Hudak's self-illustrated book The Shepherd and the 100 Sheep, *a shepherd leaves his flock to search for a lost lamb.*

Awards, Honors

Swedish Authors Foundation scholar in Greece, Israel, and Egypt, 1982, 1985, Iceland, 1988, and 1998 and 2001; Konstfrämjanet scholar, 1985; Swedish Fine Arts Society scholar, 1992; Swedish Illustrators scholar, 1999.

Writings

AND ILLUSTRATOR

Vem spelar i natten?, Verbum (Stockholm, Sweden), 1981.
Skeppet över Gamla Stan, Alfabeta (Stockholm, Sweden), 1988.
Skeppet och eldstenen, Alfabeta (Stockholm, Sweden), 1990.
Herden och den 100 fåren, Verbum (Stockholm, Sweden), 1998, published as *The Shepherd and the 100 Sheep,* Liturgical Press (Collegeville, MN), 1999.
Kalabaliken i Betlehem, Verbum (Stockholm, Sweden), 2001, translated as *The Uproar in Bethlehem,* Liturgical Press (Collegeville, MN), 2001.

Illustrator of books published in Swedish, including *Samtal med djävulen,* 1982, and *Sagor för stora och små,* 1984. Illustrations also represented in anthologies and textbooks.

Author's books have been translated into Norwegian, Danish, and Slovak.

Work in Progress

The Shepherd's Book, completion expected in 2004.

Biographical and Critical Sources

PERIODICALS

Children's Bookwatch, December, 2001, review of *The Uproar in Bethlehem,* p. 4.

J

JENSON-ELLIOTT, Cynthia L(ouise) 1962-

Personal

Born October 10, 1962, in Philadelphia, PA; daughter of William (a physician) and Norma (a homemaker) Jenson; married Chris Elliott (an engineer), July 24, 1993; children: Ronan (son), Ania. *Ethnicity:* "Caucasian." *Education:* Bowdoin College, B.A. (history), 1984; San Diego State University, M.A. (education), 1996. *Politics:* Democrat. *Religion:* "Contemplative." *Hobbies and other interests:* Gardening, reading, swimming, natural history.

Addresses

Home—San Diego, CA. *Agent*—c/o Author Mail, Lucent Books, 10911 Technology Pl., San Diego, CA 92127-1811. *E-mail*—cjensonelliott@aol.com.

Career

Writer and teacher. Cuyamaca Outdoor School, outdoor educator; Girl Scouts, USA, education program coordinator. Affiliated with International Center for Children and Families. Volunteer for Empty Cradle, San Diego Rescue Mission, Escondido Humane Society, La Jolla Quaker Meeting, and St. Mark's Preschool.

Member

Sierra Club, Young Men's Christian Association, Girl Scouts of America.

Writings

(With Linda C. Wood) *Cheetahs,* Creative Education (Mankato, MN), 1991.
East Africa, Lucent Books (San Diego, CA), 2001.
Southern Africa, Lucent Books (San Diego, CA), 2002.

Work in Progress

A young adult novel, various magazine articles.

Cynthia L. Jenson-Elliott's nonfiction work East Africa *examines the history, cultures, and lifestyles of the peoples in that region.*

Sidelights

Cynthia Jenson-Elliott told *SATA:* "Living with families in many East African tribes as a college student opened my eyes to the beauty of differences and the astonishing similarities of people all over the world. I love the people of Africa and their hope and strength in facing difficulties." With this attitude, it comes as no surprise that Jenson-Elliott has written about the people and land of Africa in such nonfiction titles as *East Africa* and *Southern Africa,* part of Lucent's "Indigenous Peoples of Africa" series. In these books she provides information on the geography of each area and the history, cultures, religions, and lifestyles of the peoples in eastern and southern Africa. She also comments on the problems faced by peoples in these regions and discusses possible solutions. Writing about *East Africa* for *School Library Journal,* Ajoke T. I. Kokodoko described the amount of information Jenson-Elliott supplies as "substantial," dubbing the work a "solid resource."

Although Jenson-Elliott has a distinct affinity for African people and culture, her interests are far ranging and include natural history and gardening. Though she has described herself as an "at-home mother" to her children, she remains active in her community as well. She has worked as an outdoor educator for the Cuyamaca Outdoor School and the Girls Scouts, USA, as well as with humanitarian organizations such as the Humane Society and the San Diego Rescue Mission. Jenson-Elliott explained to *SATA:* "As a generalist . . . interested in a variety of subjects, I hope to write about a range of subjects, from the sciences to parenting, to fiction."

Biographical and Critical Sources

PERIODICALS

School Library Journal, July, 2002, Ajoke T. I. Kokodoko, review of *East Africa,* p. 137.

*   *   *

JESSEL, Camilla (Ruth) 1937-

Personal

Born December 7, 1937, in Bearsted, Kent, England; daughter of Richard Frederick (a naval officer) and Winifred May (Levy) Jessel; married Andrzej Panufnik (a symphonic composer and conductor), November 27, 1963; children: Roxanna Anna, Jeremy James. *Education:* University of Paris, Sorbonne, degré supérieure, 1959. *Hobbies and other interests:* Music, theatre, art, ballet, literature, international politics.

Addresses

Home and office—Riverside House, Twickenham TW1 3JD, England. *Agent*—David Higham Associates Ltd., 5-8 Lower John St., London W1R 4HA, England.

Career

Photographer and author. Former vice chairperson of Home Welfare Committee; Save the Children United Kingdom child care committee, member and vice chairperson, 1969-84; Cranborne Chase School, Wiltshire, England, school governor; Park Lane Group (for young musicians), council member. *Exhibitions:* Work shown in group and solo photographic exhibitions in England at Royal Festival Hall, Arts Theatre Club, Photographers Gallery, and Royal Photographic Society.

Member

Royal Photographic Society (fellow).

Awards, Honors

Grant from Nuffield Foundation, 1972; Royal Photographic Society fellowship, 1980.

Writings

FOR CHILDREN; AND PHOTOGRAPHER

Manuela Lives in Portugal ("Children Everywhere" series), Hastings House (New York, NY), 1967.
Paul in Hospital, Methuen Children's Books (London, England), 1972.
Mark's Wheelchair Adventures, Methuen Children's Books (London, England), 1975.
Life at the Royal Ballet School, Methuen Children's Books (London, England), 1979, revised, 1985.
The Puppy Book, Methuen Children's Books (New York), 1980.
The New Baby, Methuen Children's Books (London, England), 1981.
Moving House, Methuen Children's Books (London, England), 1981.
Going to the Doctor, Methuen Children's Books (London, England), 1981.
Away for the Night, Methuen Children's Books (London, England), 1981.
Lost and Found, Methuen Children's Books (London, England), 1983.
At Playgroup, Methuen Children's Books (London, England), 1983.
Going to Hospital, Methuen Children's Books (London, England), 1983.
The Baby-sitter, Methuen Children's Books (London, England), 1983.
Learner Bird, Methuen Children's Books (London, England), 1983.
If You Meet a Stranger, Walker Books (London, England), 1990.
The Puppy Book, Walker Books (London, England), 1991, revised edition, 1993, Candlewick Press (Cambridge, MA), 1992.
The Kitten Book, Walker Books (London, England), 1991, revised edition, 1993, Candlewick Press (Cambridge, MA), 1992.
Ballet School: What It Takes to Make a Dancer, Hamish Hamilton (London, England), 1999, Viking (New York, NY), 2000.

"BABYDAYS" SERIES; AND PHOTOGRAPHER

Baby's Day, Methuen Children's Books (London, England), 1985.
Baby's Toys, Methuen Children's Books (London, England), 1985.
Baby's Bedtime, Methuen Children's Books (London, England), 1985.

Baby's Clothes, Methuen Children's Books (London, England), 1985.

Baby's Food, Methuen Children's Books (London, England), 1986.

Where Is Baby?, Methuen Children's Books (London, England), 1986.

PHOTOGRAPHER

Dorothy Shuttlesworth, *The Tower of London: Grim and Glamorous,* Hastings House (New York, NY), 1970.

Susan Harvey, *Play in Hospital,* Faber (London, England), 1972.

David Watkins, *Complete Method for the Harp,* Boosey & Hawkes (London, England), 1972.

Penelope Leach, *Baby and Child: A Modern Parent's Guide,* Knopf (New York, NY), 1978.

Sheila Kitzinger, *Pregnancy and Childbirth,* Knopf (New York, NY), 1980.

David Moore, *Multi-Cultural Britain* (booklet), Save the Children, 1980.

Miriam Stoppard, *Fifty-plus Life Guide: How to Ensure Fitness, Health, and Happiness in the Middle Years and Beyond,* Dorling Kindersley (London, England), 1983.

Esther Rantzen and Desmond Wilcox, *Baby Love,* Rainbird, 1985.

Contributor of photographs to newspapers.

OTHER

(Lyricist), Andrej Panufnik, *Thames Pageant* (cantata for children), Boosey & Hawkes (London, England), 1969.

(Lyricist) Andrej Panufnik, *Winter Solstice* (cantata), Boosey & Hawkes (London, England), 1972.

The Joy of Birth: A Book for Parents and Children, Dial Press (New York, NY), 1982.

Catching the Moment: Photographing Your Child, Dutton (New York, NY), 1985.

The Taste of Spain: Traditional Spanish Recipes and Their Origins, St. Martin's Press (New York, NY), 1990.

Birth to Three: A Parents' Guide to Child Development, Bloomsbury (London, England), 1990, published as *From Birth to Three: An Illustrated Journey through Your Child's Early Physical and Emotional Development,* Delta (New York, NY), 1991.

Sidelights

Photographer and author Camilla Jessel has enjoyed a career that allows her to explore her wide-ranging interests and share them with young children. Interested in child welfare and development, Jessel has created several series of toddler-sized books designed to assist youngsters in making connections, understanding abstract concepts, and learning the how-to's of life, while in photo-essays for older children and teens she explores personal health and safety issues. Among her many titles for children are *The Joy of Birth, The Puppy Book,* and *If You Meet a Stranger,* while *From Birth to*

Three: An Illustrated Journey through Your Child's Early Physical and Emotional Development presents parents with photographs that provide what *Booklist* contributor Tracie Richardson dubbed a "beautiful and convincing depiction . . . of a child's growth."

Jessel was born in Kent, England, in 1937. Because of her father's career in the Royal Navy, her family was required to move, and by the time she was a teen she was living in South India and would soon spend a year in Paris studying French literature and civilization. "At the age of twenty," Jessel once noted, "I went to America with about one hundred dollars and had twenty-six different temporary secretarial jobs in six cities in one year: Princeton, Washington, New York, New Orleans, Dallas, and San Francisco."

Jessel's illustration career began by chance, after she shot some promotional photographs for the organization Save the Children, where she worked. The organization's press officer "liked the amateur shots I'd done of the organization's work. These fund-raising photos were followed by lots of hard work and lucky breaks." Working as a freelancer, Jessel sold photo-essays to newspapers such as the *Times Educational Supplement,* and after two of her photographs made it to the pages of the London *Guardian,* she was offered her first book contract with Methuen, where she created *Manuela Lives in Portugal* for their "Children Everywhere" series.

Jessel's first books, as well as many of her books since, were inspired by her interest in child development. "Doing color slides for a lecture on the psychology of play of children in the hospital, I got the idea of doing a photographic book to overcome children's fears of the hospital," she once explained. After *Paul in Hospital* was published, Jessel was given a grant for *Mark's Wheelchair Adventures* a similar project that focuses on a young boy with a disability. Her 1982 work *The Joy of Birth: A Book for Parents and Children* features more than 100 photographs among its text outlining conception, birth, and the proper care of newborns. Praising Jessel's text as "well-written," a *Junior Bookshelf* contributor added that the "beautifully produced book" would be invaluable to parents seeking to educate their children about "the wonder and joy of motherhood." In *Booklist,* Denise M. Wilms praised *The Joy of Birth* as "a warm, realistic straighforward presentation" of "sensitive material."

Jessel's career as a photographer has allowed her to continue traveling, and assignments have taken her throughout both Africa and Europe. Her marriage in 1963 to an internationally known orchestra conductor and composer has also allowed her to explore parts of South America. Her love of music, art, and the dance also inspired her popular books *Life at the Royal Ballet School* and *Ballet School: What It Takes to Make a Dancer,* which features actual students of the dance. The more recent, *Ballet School,* takes readers on a year-long stay behind the scenes at England's Royal Ballet School, and reveals what a *Magpies* reviewer describes as "the dedication, passion and training required in becoming a professional ballet dancer." From the audition process through classes building dance technique and academic skills through recitals and performances, *Ballet School* "succinctly and honestly describes the unrelenting practice and commitment required to participate in the school's program," according to the *Magpies* contributor. A *Kirkus* reviewer praised Jessel's "brisk" text and "realistic attitude" about most students' chance of ultimate success in the field of professional dance, and recommended *Ballet School* as a top choice for parents to give to "the artistic aspirants they care about most deeply."

As Jessel explained, "Some books have just 'happened.'" 1980's *The Puppy Book,* for instance, was photographed when Saffy, her family's Labrador retriever, gave birth to nine puppies. Jessel's children also figure in the story, as they watch the pups develop and, as *School Library Journal* reviewer Carol Kolb Phillips noted, "sadly say goodbye when the animals leave for new homes." An accompanying volume, *The Kitten Book* focuses on a Burmese mother cat and her adorable litter. Praising both books for their "caring, supportive tone," a *Publishers Weekly* contributor added that Jessel's photographs are "captivating" and "well-composed," while Phillips dubbed *The Puppy Book* "truly charming."

Another book with its roots in Jessel's family is *Learner Bird,* which follows the fate of a baby thrush rescued by the photographer's then-eleven-year-old son. Citing Jessel's approach to the animal rescue as a "totally unsentimental and accurate" manner, a *Growing Point* reviewer noted that in *Learner Bird* the message for readers is that "wild birds are not pets." In her review for the *Times Educational Supplement,* Francesca Greenoak praised the factual information Jessel provides about the natural world, and pronounced *Learner Bird* "a super book."

In addition to building her own career as a successful photographer and illustrator, Jessel has also managed to raise her two children and work as her husband's business manager. "I enjoy being domestic—cooking, dressmaking—as well as having a career," she once noted. "I believe it's possible to be both liberated and a dedicated wife and mother."

Jessel's inspiration for her work is an "interest in children and my wish to use photography to combat prejudice and fear, such as the prejudice against the disabled or members of other races; I also want to use photography to educate children and to educate adults to be of more use to children. There is also my sheer enjoyment of photography and an attempt to heighten my own aesthetic standards."

Biographical and Critical Sources

PERIODICALS

Booklist, June 15, 1983, Denise M. Wilms, review of *The Joy of Birth,* p. 1340; Marcy 15, 1991, Tracie Richardson, review of *From Birth to Three: An Illustrated Journey through Your Child's Early Physical and Emotional Development,* p. 1439; October 15, 1991, Sally Estes, review of *The Taste of Spain,* p. 393; February 1, 1992, Stephanie Zvirin, review of *The Puppy Book* and *The Kitten Book,* p. 1032; January 1, 2000, Carolyn Phelan, review of *Ballet School,* p. 910.

Books for Your Child, autumn, 1986, review of *Life at the Royal Ballet School,* p. 14.

Daily Telegraph (London, England), August 24, 1979.

Growing Point, September, 1983, review of *Learner Bird,* pp. 4127-4128; May, 1990, review of *If You Meet a Stranger,* pp. 5353-5354.

Guardian (London, England), August 24, 1979.

Junior Bookshelf, February, 1983, review of *The Joy of Birth,* p. 27; December, 1983, review of *Lost and Found,* pp. 244-245; February, 1984, review of *Learner Bird,* p. 24; February, 1986, review of *Baby's Bedtime,* p. 24; April, 1990, review of *If You Meet a Stranger,* p. 86.

Kirkus Reviews, February 1, 1992, review of *The Kitten Book,* p. 185; December 15, 1999, review of *Ballet School,* p. 1958.

Magpies, May, 2001, review of *Ballet School,* p. 42.

Publishers Weekly, February 3, 1992, review of *The Puppy Book* and *The Kitten Book,* p. 81.

School Librarian, March, 1982, Cliff Moon, review of *Away for the Night,* p. 28; August, 1990, review of *If You Meet a Stranger,* p. 102.

School Library Journal, April, 1992, review of *The Kitten Book,* p. 106; July, 1992, Carol Kolb Phillips, review of *The Puppy Book,* p. 69; February, 2000, Ann W. Moore, review of *Ballet School,* p. 134.

Times Educational Supplement, March 9, 1984, Francesca Greenoak, review of *Learner Bird,* p. 54; October 25, 1985, Victoria Neumark, review of *Baby's Toys,* p. 31; March 7, 1986, Jenny Gilbert, review of *Baby's Clothes,* p. 25.

Times Literary Supplement, August 2, 1985, Frances Spalding, review of *Baby's Day,* p. 862.

Voice of Youth Advocates, December, 1983, Elizabeth Paddock, review of *The Joy of Birth,* p. 292.

Wilson Library Bulletin, May, 1992, review of *The Puppy Book* and *The Kitten Book,* p. 138.*

*   *   *

JOHNSTON, Norma
See ST. JOHN, Nicole

*   *   *

JOSHUA, Peter
See STONE, Peter

K

KAMMERMAN, Sylvia K.
See BURACK, Sylvia K.

*   *   *

KAYE, Peggy 1948-

Personal

Born March 27, 1948, in Philadelphia, PA. *Education:* Columbia University, B.A. (art history); Columbia University Teacher's College, M.A.

Addresses

Home and office—55 West 86th St., New York, NY 10024. *E-mail*—yggep1@aol.com.

Career

Author and illustrator of children's books. Former teacher in New York City public and private elementary schools; private tutor in reading and math; educational consultant.

Member

National Writers Union, National Council of Teachers of English, National Council of Teachers of Mathematics, International Reading Association.

Awards, Honors

Parents' Choice award, 1991, for *Games for Learning;* Distinguished achievement award, 2000, for column in *Sesame Street Parents.*

Writings

SELF-ILLUSTRATED

Games for Reading: Playful Ways to Help Your Child Read, Pantheon (New York, NY), 1984.

Games for Math: Playful Ways to Help Your Child Learn Math—from Kindergarten to Third Grade, Knopf (New York, NY), 1987.
Homework: Math, six volumes (with teachers' guide), American School Publishers (New York, NY), 1989.
Homework: Reading (with teachers' guide), American School Publishers (New York, NY), 1990.
Games for Learning: Ten Minutes a Day to Help Your Child Do Well in School—from Kindergarten to Third Grade, Farrar, Straus (New York, NY), 1991.
Games for Writing: Playful Ways to Help Your Child Learn to Write, Noonday Press (New York, NY), 1995.
Afterwards: Folk and Fairy Tales with Mathematical Ever Afters, 2 volumes, Cuisenaire (White Plains, NY), 1996-1997.
Games with Books: Twenty-eight of the Best Children's Books and How to Use Them to Help Your Child Learn—from Preschool to Third Grade, Farrar, Straus (New York, NY), 2002.

Series supervising author and author of volumes 1-3 of "Gifted Child Enrichment Reading Series," and volumes 1-2 of "Gifted Child Enrichment Math Series," illustrated by Doug Cushman, American Educational Publishing (Columbus, OH), 1995.

Contributor to periodicals, including *Slate, New York Times Book Review,* and *Tall;* columnist for *Creative Classroom,* 1989-95, and *Sesame Street Parents,* 1999.

Sidelights

Peggy Kaye is a teacher of English and mathematics whose personal battle to develop writing skills has given her insight into the hurdles many young students face in learning to read and write. Her popular series for parents that began in 1984 with *Games for Reading: Playful Ways to Help Your Child Read* has expanded into five volumes designed to harness children's natural ability to play to the task of developing academic skills. As Martin Zimmerman explained in his review of *Games for Writing: Playful Ways to Help Your Child Learn to Write* for the *Los Angeles Times Book Review,*

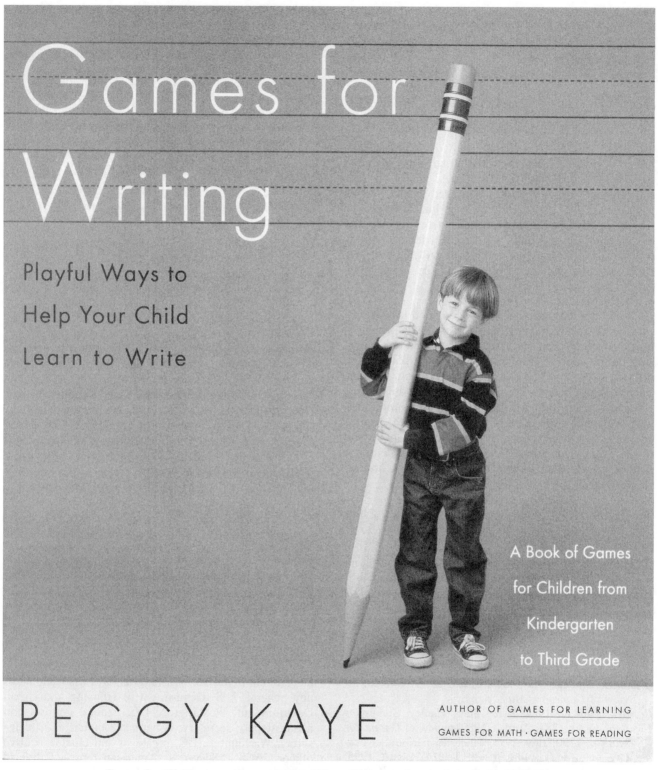

Games for Writing *provides more than fifty writing exercises and games for children.*

"There is method in her madness. . . . [Kaye's] games are designed to foster enthusiasm for learning, [and] to develop the mind-muscle that grows with the pleasure of learning new and challenging things." Praising *Games for Reading* in *Publishers Weekly,* a contributor described Kaye's book as a "cache of [seventy-five] very worthwhile activities," while in *Booklist* Karen Stang

Hanley commended the author's inclusion of clearly written instructions and dubbed the work "a welcome and unique addition to the parenting shelf."

The format in each of Kaye's "Games" books is similar. In *Games for Writing,* for example, she includes a host of word maps, word games, and even teaches a fun form of writing she calls "wribbling"—half writing, half scribbling. *Games for Math, Games with Books,* and *Games for Learning* round out Kaye's mix of play and learning. Denise Perry Donavin noted in her *Booklist* review that *Games for Writing* would "ward off writer's block in young children," while *Booklist* contributor Tracie Richardson described the seventy games included in *Games for Math* as "deceptively simple and fun to play."

Kaye told *SATA:* "I was the worst writer in my elementary school classes, high school classes, college classes, and graduate school classes. I despaired when I had to compose a paper. I suffered every time I needed to write a letter. When I had to write, pencils were my enemies, but when I drew, pencils were close friends. I drew constantly. I still draw constantly. I wasn't the best artist in my class, although I also wasn't the worst, but I didn't care. When I drew I was at peace.

"It would not have astonished my childhood friends and teachers to discover that I illustrate my books. Regarding my development as a writer of these books, one step led to another in a more-or-less straightforward fashion. It began when I decided to become a teacher. Then I started making up games to help children learn. I began sending home instructions for some of those games. Parents were grateful, enthusiastic even. I got a contract for a book of games. I published *Games for Reading,* and then *Games for Math,* and then *Games for Learning,* and then *Games for Writing,* and, finally, *Games with Books.*

"I still find writing difficult. Who doesn't? But sometime between the third and fourth 'Game' books, I began calling myself a writer and, better yet, I discovered that I enjoy writing."

Biographical and Critical Sources

PERIODICALS

Arithmetic Teacher, May, 1989, F. Alexander Norman, review of *Games for Math,* p. 32.

Booklist, May 15, 1984, Karen Stang Hanley, *Games for Reading,* p. 1281; April 1, 1989, review of *Games for Math* p. 1350; July, 1991, Tracie Richardson, review of *Games for Learning,* pp. 2015-2016; August, 1995, Denise Perry Donavin, review of *Games for Writing,* p. 1915.

Curriculum Review, November, 1997, review of *Afterwards: Folk and Fairy Tales with Mathematical Ever Afters,* p. 14.

Instructor, January, 1989, Theresa Denman, review of *Games for Math,* p. 89.

Library Journal, June 1, 1984, review of *Games for Reading* p. 1128; March 1, 1988, Joanne Troutner, review of *Games for Math,* p. 64; July, 1991, Linda Beck, review of *Games for Learning,* p. 111.

Los Angeles Times Book Review, June 3, 1984, Jonathan Kirsch, review of *Games for Reading,* p. B15; November 26, 1995, Martin Zimmerman, review of *Games for Writing,* p. 15; March 5, 2002, Bernadette Murphy, review of *Games with Books,* p. E3.

Publishers Weekly, April 13, 1984, review of *Games for Reading,* pp. 64-65; May 20, 2002, review of *Games with Books,* p. 69.

Teaching Children Mathematics, October, 1997, Janet Fuller, review of *Afterwards,* p. 125.

ONLINE

Peggy Kaye Web site, http://www.peggykaye.com/ (May 5, 2003).

* * *

KEATING, Frank 1944-

Personal

Born February 10, 1944, in St. Louis, MO; son of Anthony F. (a drilling contractor) and Anne (Martin) Keating; married Catherine Heller, November 17, 1972; children: Carissa Keating Leonard, Kelly Keating Hargett, Anthony Francis III. *Education:* Georgetown University, B.A., 1966; University of Oklahoma, J.D., 1969. *Politics:* Republican. *Religion:* Roman Catholic.

Addresses

Office—American Council of Life Insurers, 101 Constitution Ave. N.W., Washington, DC 20001.

Career

Federal Bureau of Investigation, Washington, DC, special agent, beginning c. 1969; worked as assistant district attorney of Tulsa, OK, until 1972; State of Oklahoma, member of House of Representatives, 1972-74, member of Senate, 1974-81, governor, 1995-2003; United States attorney for the northern district of Oklahoma, 1981-85; U.S. Department of the Treasury, Washington, DC, assistant secretary, beginning 1985; U.S. Department of Justice, Washington, DC, associate attorney general; U.S. Department of Housing and Urban Development, Washington, DC, general counsel and acting deputy secretary; American Council of Life Insurers, Washington, DC, president and chief executive officer, 2003—. Served as American representative to Interpol; Federal Law Enforcement Training Center, Glynco, GA, former chair. Interstate Oil and Gas Compact Commission, former chair.

Awards, Honors

William Booth Award, Salvation Army, for contributions to recovery after the 1995 bombing in Oklahoma City; Spur Award, Western Writers of America, 2003, for storytelling; Arthur Ross Award, Institute of Classical Literature and Classical America, 2003.

Writings

Will Rogers: An American Legend, illustrated by Mike Wimmer, Harcourt (San Diego, CA), 2002.

Contributor to periodicals, including *Washington Post.*

Work in Progress

A biography of Teddy Roosevelt.

Sidelights

Frank Keating, a two-term governor of his home state of Oklahoma and a long-time civil servant, made a contribution to children's literature with his 2002 biography *Will Rogers: An American Legend.* The story of one of America' most beloved twentieth-century humorist, *Will Rogers* also serves as Keating's profile of a fellow Oklahoman who became famous for the folksy, good-natured humor epitomized in his well-known statement "I never met a man I didn't like." *Will Rogers* was described by *Booklist* contributor Michael Cart as "affectionately impressionistic," while in *Publishers Weekly,* a reviewer praised Keating's emphasis on Rogers' "personality in place of much expository information."

Biographical and Critical Sources

PERIODICALS

Booklist, September 15, 2002, Michael Cart, review of *Will Rogers: An American Legend,* p. 236.
Publishers Weekly, July 22, 2002, review of *Will Rogers,* p. 178.
School Library Journal, November, 2002, Grace Oliff, review of *Will Rogers,* p. 145.

*   *   *

KITAMURA, Satoshi 1956-

Personal

Born June 11, 1956, in Tokyo, Japan; moved to England, 1983; son of Testuo (a retail consultant) and Fusae (Sadanaga) Kitamura; married Yoko Sugisaki (an interior designer), December 15, 1987. *Education:* Attended schools in Japan.

Addresses

Agent—c/o Farrar, Straus, 19 Union Square West, New York, NY, 10003.

Career

Freelance illustrator and author, 1975—.

Alex learns that having a dinosaur as a pet can be more trouble than it's worth in A Boy Wants a Dinosaur, *written by Hiawyn Oram and illustrated by Satoshi Kitamura.*

Awards, Honors

Mother Goose Award, Books for Children Book Club, 1983, for *Angry Arthur;* Signal Award, 1984, for *Sky in the Pie; What's Inside* was selected one of *New York Times* Notable Books, 1985; Children's Science Book Award (Great Britain) and Children's Science Book Award, New York Academy of Sciences, both 1987, both for *When Sheep Cannot Sleep.*

Writings

SELF-ILLUSTRATED

What's Inside?: The Alphabet Book, Farrar, Straus (New York, NY), 1985.
Paper Jungle: A Cut-out Book, A. & C. Black (London, England), 1985, Holt, Rinehart (New York, NY), 1986.
When Sheep Cannot Sleep: The Counting Book, Farrar, Straus (New York, NY), 1986.
Lily Takes a Walk, Dutton (New York, NY), 1987.
Captain Toby, Dutton (New York, NY), 1987.
UFO Diary, Andersen (London, England), 1989, Farrar, Straus (New York, NY), 1990.
From Acorn to Zoo, Andersen (London, England), 1991, published as *From Acorn to Zoo and Everything in between in Alphabetical Order,* Farrar, Straus (New York, NY), 1992.
Sheep in Wolves' Clothing, Andersen (London, England), 1995, Farrar, Straus (New York, NY), 1996.
Paper Dinosaurs: A Cut-out Book, Farrar, Straus (New York, NY), 1995.
Squirrel Is Hungry, Farrar, Straus (New York, NY), 1996.

Cat Is Sleepy, Farrar, Straus (New York, NY), 1996.

Dog Is Thirsty, Farrar, Straus (New York, NY), 1996.

Duck Is Dirty, Farrar, Straus (New York, NY), 1996.

Bathtime Boots, Andersen (London, England), 1997, Farrar, Straus (New York, NY), 1998.

A Friend for Boots, Andersen (London, England), 1997, Farrar, Straus (New York, NY), 1998.

Goldfish Hide-and-Seek, Farrar, Straus (New York, NY), 1997.

Me and My Cat?, Andersen (London, England), 1999, Farrar, Straus (New York, NY), 2000.

Comic Adventures of Boots, Farrar, Straus (New York, NY), 2002.

ILLUSTRATOR

Hiawyn Oram, *Angry Arthur,* Harcourt (New York, NY), 1982.

Hiawyn Oram, *Ned and the Joybaloo,* Anderson (London, England), 1983, Farrar, Straus (New York, NY), 1989.

Roger McGough, *Sky in the Pie* (poems), Viking (New York, NY), 1983.

Hiawyn Oram, *In the Attic,* Andersen (London, England), 1984, Holt (New York, NY), 1985.

The Flying Trunk (anthology), Andersen (London, England), 1986.

Pat Thomson, *My Friend Mr. Morris,* Delacorte (New York, NY), 1987.

Alison Sage and Helen Wire, compilers, *The Happy Christmas Book* (anthology), Scholastic (New York, NY), 1986.

Andy Soutter, *Scrapyard,* A. & C. Black (London, England), 1988.

A Children's Chorus (anthology), Dutton (New York, NY), 1989.

Hiawyn Oram, *A Boy Wants a Dinosaur,* Andersen (London, England), 1990, Farrar, Straus (New York, NY), 1991.

Hiawyn Oram, *Speaking for Ourselves* (poems), Methuen (London, England), 1990.

Carl Davis and Hiawyn Oram, *A Creepy Crawly Song Book,* Farrar, Straus (New York, NY), 1993.

Mick Fitzmaurice, *Morris Macmillipede: The Toast of Brussels Sprout,* Andersen (London, England), 1994.

Stephen Webster, *Inside My House,* Riverswift (London, England), 1994.

Stephen Webster, *Me and My Body,* Riverswift (London, England), 1994.

Richard Edwards, *Fly with the Birds: An Oxford Word and Rhyme Book,* Oxford University Press (Oxford, England), 1995, published as *Fly with the Birds: A Word and Rhyme Book,* Orchard Books (New York, NY), 1996.

Brenda Walpole, *Hello, Is There Anyone There?,* Riverswift (London, England), 1995.

Brenda Walpole, *Living and Working Together,* Riverswift (London, England), 1995.

John Agard, *We Animals Would Like a Word with You,* Bodley Head (London, England), 1996.

John Agard, *Points of View with Professor Peekaboo* (poems), Bodley Head (London, England), 2000.

John Agard, *Einstein, the Girl Who Hated Maths,* Hodder Wayland (London, England), 2002.

Kitamura's books have been translated into Spanish.

Adaptations

From Acorn to Zoo and Everything in between in Alphabetical Order was published in Braille and also made into a take-home literacy pack that includes an audiocassette and activity book. Several books have been translated into Braille, including *When Sheep Cannot Sleep* and Hiawyn Oram's *Ned and the Joybaloo.*

Sidelights

Praised for his ability to interweave Japanese and Western visual traditions within the engaging illustrations he has contributed to the works of numerous writers, Satoshi Kitamura has also become known as an author of children's books. With strong technical abilities and a gift for visual humor, Kitamura adds a whimsical, often unconventional touch to traditional children's book formats such as alphabet and counting books. He is widely recognized for his use of simplified, angular shapes and a rich palette of earth and sky tones. As David Wiesner noted in the *New York Times Book Review,* Kitamura's books "are suffused with both warmth and wit. . . . The simplicity of Mr. Kitamura's art is deceptive. A superb draftsman and colorist, he uses pen and brush to create remarkably lush and textured illustrations." Among the author/illustrator's most well-received titles are the award-winning counting book *When Sheep Cannot Sleep, Sheep in Wolves' Clothing,* and *UFO Diary,* a 1989 work that *School Librarian* contributor Sue Smedley praised as "a sophisticated book acknowledging that children deserve quality texts and illustrations."

"I am interested in different angles of looking at things," Kitamura once told *SATA.* "I find great potential in picture books where visual and verbal fuse to experience and [I also] experiment with these angles. Also, there is an advantage of universality of expression in this medium due to the clarity required for young readers."

Kitamura was born and raised in Tokyo, Japan. In 1983 he moved to England, making his permanent home in London. By the time he became a resident of Great Britain, Kitamura's first children's book illustration project, Hiawyn Oram's *Angry Arthur,* had already been published in both England and the United States. An award-winning book, *Angry Arthur* caused publishers to take notice of the young Japanese illustrator and his work; numerous projects were soon awarded Kitamura in quick succession.

In 1985 Kitamura published *What's Inside?: The Alphabet Book,* the first of his many solo children's book projects. Full of visual clues to help lead young pre-readers through alphabetically ordered pairs of lower-cased letters, *What's Inside* was dubbed "gloriously exuberant" by a *Junior Bookshelf* critic and praised by *School Library Journal* contributor Patricia Homer as a book "which will delight readers who are up to a verbal and visual challenge." Denise M. Wilms echoed such praise in *Booklist,* maintaining that the "imaginative quality" of Kitamura's full-color line and wash illustrations "make for a fresh, engaging display of letters that will stand up to more than one close look."

In another alphabet book, Kitamura builds young readers' vocabulary, one letter at a time. *From Acorn to Zoo* features pages chock-full of illustrated objects that begin with the same letter, allowing children's vocabularies to be "expanded almost painlessly and [their] capacity for observation sharpened," in the opinion of a *Junior Bookshelf* reviewer. Each illustration features energetic pen-and-ink renderings of an unusual assortment of animals and objects, richly colored and positioned on the page in ways readers will find humorous. For example, on one page a hefty hippo tests the strength of a hammock by sitting in it and playing his harmonica while a harp and coat hanger can be found nearby. In a similar vein, Kitamura tackles introductory mathematics by illustrating the quandary of an insomniac named Woolly in *When Sheep Cannot Sleep,* a 1-2-3 book. Rather than lay about in the dark, Woolly goes on a search for objects grouped first in pairs, then in threes, fours, and so on up to twenty-two before tiring himself out and falling asleep in an abandoned country cottage. But Kitamura does not make things any too easy for his

A witch's spell causes Nicholas to swap places with his cat for a day in Kitamura's self-illustrated Me and My Cat?

reader; on each page the object Woolly finds must also be discovered by the reader and its quantity totaled up. The work drew rave reviews. Calling *When Sheep Cannot Sleep* "a joy to look at," *Horn Book* contributor Anita Silvey added that Kitamura's "slightly primitive drawing style is delightful, making counting the objects or just looking at the book a great deal of fun." *Booklist* reviewer Ilene Cooper noted that the author/illustrator's "squared-off sheep has an endearingly goofy look that kids and adults will love," while Jane Doonan of the *Times Literary Supplement* dubbed *When Sheep Cannot Sleep* the "perfect picture book free from stereotype images, brimming with unforced humor." In *School Library Journal* Lorraine Douglas praised Kitamura for his "engaging and fresh approach." *School Librarian* reviewer Donald Fry also lauded *When Sheep Cannot Sleep*, concluding that no other such counting book is "so witty and enjoyable as this one."

Goofy looking sheep serve also as the focus of Kitamura's *Sheep in Wolves' Clothing*. Hubert, Georgina, and Gogol are sheep who hoof it on down to the seashore for one last dip in the ocean before the chill of winter sets in. Near the beach, they meet a group of wolves enjoying the fall afternoon by taking time off from work at their knitwear factory to take in a round of golf. The wolves generously offer to watch the sheep's warm wool coats while the seabound swimmers take their plunge; not surprisingly, neither wolves nor wool are anywhere to be found when the soaked sheep return. Fortunately, the sheep call in the services of Elliott Baa, a fully fleeced ace detective, who follows the woolly trail to its conclusion. "Younger children will delight in the climactic brouhaha and will also find [*Sheep in Wolves' Clothing*] a satisfying mystery story," according to *Horn Book* reviewer Margaret Bush.

In *Lily Takes a Walk* young readers get a look at an overactive imagination and the divergent perceptions of dog and child. While on their routine evening walk, Nicky scares up shadows of everything from vampires to monsters, yet owner Lily sees none of Nicky's concerns. Several reviewers of the book praised Kitamura's combination of scariness and humor, such as a *Kirkus* reviewer who called *Lily Takes a Walk* "understated, subtle, and delightful," and Kay E. Vandergrift, who dubbed the work a "clever idea with an appropriately humorous ending" in *School Library Journal*. In conclusion, a *Publishers Weekly* contributor deemed this walk "well worth taking."

Other books by Kitamura that showcase his vivid imagination and ability to capture a child's attention include *UFO Diary*, the observations of an outer-space visitor who accidentally lands on Earth and is befriended by a young boy. Although never depicted in Kitamura's colorful drawings, the alien provides readers with an opportunity to "see our planet's natural abundance and beauty with fresh eyes," according to John Peters, a *School Library Journal* contributor. Among the book's enthusiasts are Liz Brooks of the *Times Literary Supple-*

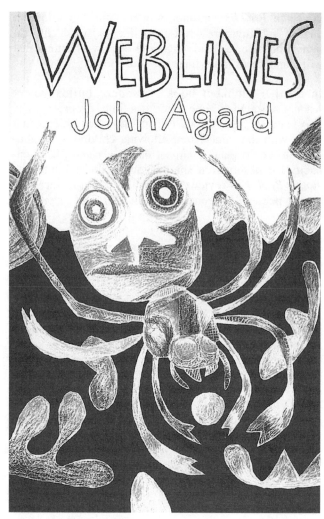

Kitamura has illustrated book covers, including this one for **Weblines,** *a poetry collection by John Agard.*

ment, who praised both Kitamura's artistry and simplicity, and Susan Perren of *Quill & Quire,* who noted that the illustrations "say it all." In the word's of *Horn Book* contributor Nancy Vasilakis, *UFO Diary* is an "unusual" work, one that constitutes a "beautiful, quiet, respectful reminder of who we are and whence we come."

The picture book *Captain Toby* is also unusual in showing the aplomb of a young boy who takes charge in his imagination after he becomes convinced that the storm raging outside his bedroom window has blown his house out to sea. According to *School Library Journal*'s Patricia Pearl, "a clever premise is carefully realized in the illustrations," yet she found the plot less successful, particularly its denouement. On the other hand, a *Publishers Weekly* contributor called *Captain Toby* a "nautical romp," a voyage in which the creator melds "sweet charm and raucous revelry." Likening the book to a film that scrolls from frame to frame, Margery Fisher described the book as a "complete and believable fantasy" in her *Growing Point* review.

Cats play an important role in a handful of Kitamura's picture books. For example, his *Me and My Cat?,* which

Booklist critic Amy Brandt described as "funny, frenetic, and insightful," revolves around the body-switch perpetrated by a witch's spell upon the boy Nicholas and his cat Leonardo. So while Leonardo in Nicholas's body goes off to school, Nicholas in Leonardo's body explores the varied activities of a cat with "high humor" and a "wickedly delightful twist at the end," to quote Ann Welton of *School Library Journal*. A reviewer for *Horn Book* also praised the book's humor, describing it as "dry" and the book as a whole as "farcical comedy." In addition, in *Goldfish Hide-and-Seek* a cat stalks a goldfish that has left his bowl in search of a missing playmate, in what Lynne Taylor of *School Library Journal* termed "original, playful, absurd, superlative, inspired." And finally, a cat stars in one of a quartet of cardboard books for toddlers. Since they are geared to the youngest book users, *Cat Is Sleepy, Squirrel Is Hungry, Dog Is Thirsty,* and *Duck Is Dirty* feature fewer words and use illustrations that employ somewhat heavier lines than Kitamura's standard fare. Applauding these books for their appropriate humor and plots, *School Library Journal* contributor Ann Cook added, "No cutesy, patronizing stuff here." In fact, each story shows how an animal hero solves a simple, but not trivial, problem. According to a *Kirkus* reviewer, even the artwork in this quartet demonstrates more sophistication than is expected in books for such young readers.

Also showing Kitamura's feline fancy, a cat named Boots figures prominently in his fictional world. *Bathtime Boots, A Friend for Boots,* and *Comic Adventures of Boots* introduce readers to a memorable feline. The first two works are board books for toddlers in which a round-eyed cat tries to evade the bath and to find a friend, respectively. This duo "will hit home with small children" a *Kirkus Reviews* writer noted, because of their simple plot lines and the expressively depicted characters. For an older readership, children in grades two through four, the *Comic Adventures of Boots* is a collection of three cat stories that, to quote *Booklist* reviewer Susan Dove Lempke, are "equally goofy and laugh-out-loud funny." The first story "Operation Fish Biscuit" shows how Boots gets back his best napping place, while in "Please to Meet You, Madam Quark" he takes swimming lessons from a duck, and in "Let's Play a Guessing Game" kittens play charades. The pages are broken up into panels like a comic book and use dialog balloons. This style elicited comment from Linda M. Kenton, who expressed concern in *School Library Journal* that some readers might be put off by such cluttered pages; even so she praised the humor as "simultaneously sly and outrageous." Sometimes, as a *Kirkus Reviews* writer pointed out, words are unnecessary because Kitamura "captures an astonishing range of expressions and reactions" in the cats' features.

In assessing Kitamura's contribution to children's literature for *Children's Literature,* Jane Doonan wrote: "Kitamura's work is notable . . . for the artist's material skills and for his distinctive relationship to the pic-

torial tradition of Japan. . . . In less than a decade Kitamura has made, and continues to make, a distinctive contribution to the art of the children's picture book. The fresh way of saying 'even something very commonplace' [to quote Maurice Sendak] is evident in all he does."

Biographical and Critical Sources

BOOKS

Children's Literature Review, Volume 60, Gale (Detroit, MI), 2000, pp 82-103.

PERIODICALS

Booklist, September 1, 1985, Denise M. Wilms, review of *What's Inside?: The Alphabet Book,* p. 64; October 1, 1986, Ilene Cooper, review of *When Sheep Cannot Sleep,* p. 273; April 15, 1991, Stephanie Zvirin, review of *A Boy Wants a Dinosaur,* p. 1651; July, 1992, Deborah Abbott, review of *From Acorn to Zoo,* p. 1943; May 1, 1996, p. 1512: March 1, 2000, Amy Brandt, review of *Me and My Cat?* p. 1250; October 1, 2002, Susan Dove Lempke, review of *Comic Adventures of Boots,* p. 326.

Books for Keeps, September, 1988, Liz Waterland, review of *When Sheep Cannot Sleep,* pp. 8-9; July, 1995, Wendy Cooling, review of *Sheep in Wolves' Clothing,* pp. 24-25, 28.

Children's Literature, Volume 19, 1999, Jane Doonan, "Satoshi Kitamura: Aesthetic Dimensions," pp. 107-137.

Growing Point, January, 1987, Margery Fisher, review of *When Sheep Cannot Sleep,* p. 4745; January, 1990, Margery Fisher, "Picture-Book Adventures," pp. 5269-5272; February, 1990, p. 5269.

Horn Book, November, 1986, Anita Silvey, review of *When Sheep Cannot Sleep,* pp. 736-737; March, 1990, Nancy Vasilakis, review of *UFO Diary,* pp. 190-191; May, 1992, Nancy Vasilakis, review of *From Acorn to Zoo,* p. 330; January, 1994, N. Vasilakis, review of *A Creepy Crawly Song Book,* p. 83; July, 1996, Margaret Bush, review of *Sheep in Wolves' Clothing,* p. 450; March, 2000, review of *Me and My Cat?* p. 187.

Horn Book Guide, July-December, 1997, Christine M. Heppermann, review of *Goldfish Hide-and-Seek,* p. 36; January-June, 1998, Christine M. Heppermann, review of *Bathtime Boots* and *A Friend for Boots,* p. 98.

Junior Bookshelf, October, 1982, A. Thatcher, review of *Angry Arthur,* p. 183; October, 1985, R. Baines, review of *What's Inside?,* p. 212; February, 1987, p. 21; August, 1989, p. 162; February, 1991, S. M. Ashburner, review of *Speaking for Ourselves,* p. 26.

Kirkus Reviews, May 15, 1985, review of *What's Inside? The Alphabet Book,* p. J26; November 1, 1987, review of *Lily Takes a Walk,* pp. 1575-1576; August 15, 1989, p. 1247; June 15, 1996, review of *Duck Is Dirty,* p. 906; June 15, 1997, review of *Gold Fish Hide-and-Seek,* p. 951; January 1, 1998, review of *Bathtime Boots,* p. 58; June 1, 2002, review of *Comic Adventures of Boots,* p. 806.

New York Times Book Review, June 16, 1985, Karla Kuskin, review of *What's Inside?,* p. 30; March 6, 1988, p. 29; May 21, 1989, John Cech, review of *Ned and the Joybaloo,* p. 41; May 19, 1991, Francine Prose, review of *A Boy Wants a Dinosaur,* p. 23; May 19, 1996, David Wiesner, review of "A Job for Elliott Baa, Private Eye," p. 27; May 14, 2000, David Small, review of *Me and My Cat?,* p. 21; June 1, 2002, review of *Comic Adventures of Boots,* p. 806.

Publishers Weekly, February 22, 1985, review of *In the Attic,* p. 158; September 11, 1987, review of *Lily Takes a Walk,* p. 92; June 24, 1988, review of *Ned and the Joybaloo,* p. 110; September 30, 1988, review of *Captain Toby,* p. 65; March 25, 1996, review of *Fly with the Birds: A Word and Rhyme Book,* p. 82; May 6, 1996, review of *Sheep in Wolves' Clothing,* p. 80; June 24, 1996, "Animal Pragmatism," p. 62; June 9, 1997, review of *Goldfish Hide-and-Seek,* p. 44; March 20, 2000, review of *Me and My Cat?,* p. 91; July 17, 2000, review of *Sheep in Wolves' Clothing,* p. 198.

Quill & Quire, October, 1989, Susan Perren, review of *UFO Diary,* pp. 17-18.

School Librarian, December, 1986, Donald Fry, review of *When Sheep Cannot Sleep,* p. 337; February, 1988, Margaret Meek, review of *Lily Takes a Walk,* p.16; November, 1989, Sue Smedley, review of *UFO Diary,* p. 145; November, 1990, Angela Redfern, review of *Speaking for Ourselves,* p. 156; February, 1991, Val Booler, review of *A Boy Wants a Dinosaur,* p. 20; August, 1992, I. Anne Rowe, review of *From Acorn to Zoo,* p. 97; November, 1997, Lynne Taylor, review of *Goldfish Hide-and-Seek,* p. 187.

School Library Journal, September, 1982, Holly Sanhuber, review of *Angry Arthur,* p. 110; August, 1984, Joan Wood Sheaffer, review of *Ned and the Joybaloo,* p. 63; September, 1985, Patricia Homer, review of *What's Inside?,* p. 120; December, 1986, Lorraine Douglas, review of *When Sheep Cannot Sleep,* pp. 90-91; November, 1987, Kay E. Vandergrift, review of *Lily Takes a Walk,* pp. 93-94; March, 1989, Patricia Pearl, review of *Captain Toby,* p. 164; January, 1990, John Peters, review of *UFO Diary,* p. 84; July, 1992, Mary Lou Budd, review of *From Acorn to Zoo,* p. 60; January, 1994, Jane Marino, review of *A Creepy Crawly Song Book* pp. 108-109; March, 1996, Sally R. Dow, review of *Fly with the Birds,* p. 173; August, 1996, Ann Cook review of *Cat Is Sleepy,* p. 124; August, 1996, Luann Toth, review of *Sheep in Wolves' Clothing,* p. 124; October, 1997, Karen James, review of *Goldfish Hide-and-Seek,* p. 100; March, 2000, Ann Welton, review of *Me and My Cat?,* p. 209; August, 2002, Linda M. Kenton, review of *Comic Adventures of Boots,* p. 159.

Times Educational Supplement, November 11, 1994, Mary Gribbin, review of *Inside My House,* p. 18.

Times Literary Supplement, November 28, 1986, Jane Doonan, review of *When Sheep Cannot Sleep,* p. 1345; July 7, 1989, Liz Brooks, "Picturing Pets," p. 757.*

KLINE, Lisa Williams 1954-

Personal

Born July 31, 1954 in Richmond, VA; daughter of George Patteson (a physics professor) and Alice (a guidance counselor and social studies teacher; maiden name, Verra) Williams; married Bradford Bailing Dyer (divorced); married Jeffrey Michael Kline (a veterinarian), June 1, 1985; children: (second marriage) Caitlin Eleanor, Kelsey Rebecca. *Education:* Duke University, A.B., 1975; University of North Carolina, M.A. (communications), 1976. *Politics:* Democrat. *Religion:* Unitarian. *Hobbies and other interests:* Theater, running, golf.

Addresses

Home—Mooresville, NC. *Agent*—Nancy Gallt, 273 Charlton Ave., South Orange, NJ 07079. *E-mail*—lisa73154@aol.com.

Career

UNC-TV, Chapel Hill, NC, writer/researcher, 1976-78; Arthur Andersen Video Training, Division, Elgin, IL, video training writer, 1978-81; Gaithersburg, MD, freelance writer, 1981—.

Member

Society of Children's Book Writers and Illustrators, North Carolina Writers' Network, Charlotte Writers' Club (vice president, programs, 2002-03; president, 2003-04).

Awards, Honors

Peregrine Prize second place, 1998, for "Webs"; first fiction prize, *Plum Review,* for "Under the Jello"; North Carolina Juvenile Literature Award, American Association of University Women, 2000, for *Eleanor Hill.*

Writings

Eleanor Hill, Front Street/Cricket Books (Chicago, IL), 1999.
The Princesses of Atlantis, Cricket Books (Chicago, IL), 2002.

Adaptations

Kline's short story "Under the Jello" was adapted as an audio recording by SIRS.

Work in Progress

Leeni Green and the Burning Unanswerable Questions of the Universe; an untitled sequel to *Eleanor Hill; The Summer of the Wolves.*

Lisa Williams Kline

Sidelights

Author Lisa Williams Kline came on the children's literature scene in 1999 with the publication of the well-received historical novel *Eleanor Hill,* based on the life of Kline's grandmother. A year later her contemporary novel *The Princesses of Atlantis* followed. Both novels contain a common element, as Kline explained to *SATA:* "Everything I write, whether for young people or adults, ends up being about the emotional lives of girls and women. I find fiction about inner conflict to be the most interesting both to read and to write."

Like many novelists, Kline began writing at an early age. "I started trying to write in second grade," she told *SATA.* "In my bedroom closet at home are 'The Adventures of Little Horse and Little Lamb,' one of my first series. I also wrote a novel in fourth or fifth grade about a brother and sister hiking barefoot through the North Carolina mountains in search of penicillin for a sick younger brother." Although she lost confidence in fiction-writing during middle school, Kline earned a college degree in communications. After graduation, she worked as a researcher and writer for a television station before striking out on her own as a freelance writer.

A chance event rekindled Kline's desire to write a middle-grade novel. "At the funeral of my grandmother, Eleanor Hill Verra, I learned that she was one of the first young women in New Bern, North Carolina, to learn to drive a car," Kline recalled to Joanne Spataro

at the *Fresh Air* Web site. "I was impressed—she probably learned to drive about 1912, a time when it wasn't really 'acceptable' for women to drive cars, and cars were also much, much harder to drive back then." Kline began to wonder what it was like to have been a teenager at the time her grandmother had been one. "Later, my mother gave me my grandmother's photo album from about 1914-1918 and the letters she had saved over the years." Kline pored over those photographs of her grandmother, wondering about the life she had led and about what gave her such an independent spirit, one that allowed her to buck the expectations for women of her era. *Eleanor Hill,* a novel about twelve-year-old Eleanor, a girl growing up in a small North Carolina town at during World War I, was the result.

Kline's debut novel caught the attention of reviewers, including a contributor to *Plays,* who found *Eleanor Hill* "engrossing," and *Booklist* reviewer Shelle Rosenfeld, who praised Kline's use of historical details as well as her "clear, descriptive prose, realistic dialogue" and "appealing, dimensional characters." *Voice of Youth Advocates* critic Nancy Zachary wrote, "*Eleanor Hill* is refreshing in its candor, emotion, and truly adventurous spirit." Reflecting on her grandmother, the real Eleanor Hill, Kline told Spataro: "I hope that by writing about her I could soak up some of that spirit and pass it on to a new generation of young women."

Kline's second novel is set in contemporary times. The dual narrative of *The Princesses of Atlantis* tells the separate stories of seventh-graders Carly and Arelene, whose friendship changes as boys come into the picture, and of the twin princesses of Atlantis who exist only in the fantasy novel the sixth-grade girls had been writing together. The novel elicited comment from several reviewers who commented on the girls' characterizations and the portrayal of their relationship. For example, Beth L. Meister praised the "realistic depiction of adolescence" in addition to both main characters and "clearly drawn supporting characters" in her *School Library Journal* review. A *Kirkus Reviews* critic called the idea behind *The Princesses of Atlantis* "appealing," the language "sharp and lovely," and the girls' friendship "nicely plotted." Writing in *Childhood Education,* Andrea Bartlett summed up *The Princesses of Atlantis* as "enjoyable" and a novel that "encourages many aspects of literacy."

Kline cites Katherine Paterson, Judy Blume, and Louis Sachar as her favorite children's book writers and Ann Tyler, Anita Shreve, and Elizabeth Berg as her favorite adult book writers. Offering advice to would-be writers, she told *SATA:* "I try to write for a couple of hours each day. I would advise aspiring authors to practice their writing as a musician would practice scales or a basketball player would practice free throws."

Biographical and Critical Sources

PERIODICALS

Booklist, February 15, 2000, Shelle Rosenfeld, review of *Eleanor Hill,* p. 1102; April 15, 2002, Sally Estes, review of *The Princesses of Atlantis,* p. 1401.

Childhood Education, winter, 2002, Andrea Bartlett, review of *The Princesses of Atlantis,* p. 110.

Kirkus Reviews, April 1, 2002, review of *The Princesses of Atlantis,* p. 494.

Plays, May, 2001, "Spotlight on Books," review of *Eleanor Hill,* p. 69.

School Library Journal, February, 2000, Lisa Prolman, review of *Eleanor Hill,* p. 122; February, 2002, review of *Eleanor Hill,* p. 122; July, 2002, Beth L. Meister, review of *The Princesses of Atlantis,* p. 122.

Voice of Youth Advocates, October, 2000, Nancy Zachary, review of *Eleanor Hill,* p. 266.

ONLINE

Fresh Air, http://www.families-first.com/ (March 12, 2003), Joanne Spataro, "Meet the Author: Lisa Kline."

*   *   *

KUSUGAK, Michael (Arvaarluk) 1948-

Personal

Born April 27, 1948, in Repulse Bay, Northwest Territories, Canada; married; four sons. *Ethnicity:* "Inuit." *Education:* University of Saskatchewan, B.A. (English literature).

Addresses

Home—P.O. Box 572, Rankin Inlet, Nunavut, Canada X0C 0G0. *E-mail*—mkusugak@arctic.ca.

Career

Storyteller and author of books for children. Worked as a civil servant in Canada for fifteen years; Arctic College, director of community programs. Member, National Library of Canada advisory board and Ranking Inlet Library board. Lecturer at schools and libraries; storyteller at festivals and other venues, including Kaleidoscope 6, Calgary, Alberta, 1996, Young People's Theatre, Toronto, Ontario, 1997, Wordfest, 1998, and Sunshine Coast Festival of the Written Arts, Sechelt, British Columbia, 2003.

Awards, Honors

Ruth Schwartz Children's Book Award, 1994, for *Northern Lights: The Soccer Trails.*

Writings

(With Robert Munsch) *A Promise Is a Promise,* illustrated by Vladyana Krykorka, Firefly Books (New York, NY), 1988.

Baseball Bats for Christmas, illustrated by Vladyana Krykorka, Firefly Books (New York, NY), 1990.

Hide and Sneak, illustrated by Vladyana Krykorka, Firefly Books (New York, NY), 1992.

Northern Lights: The Soccer Trails, illustrated by Vladyana Langer Krykorka, Firefly Books (New York, NY), 1993.

My Arctic 1, 2, 3, illustrated by Vladyana Langer Krykorka, Annick Press (Willowdale, Ontario, Canada), 1996.

Arctic Stories, illustrated by Vladyana Langer Krykorka, Firefly Books (New York, NY), 1998.

Who Wants Rocks?, Firefly Books (New York, NY), 1999.

A Promise Is a Promise has been anthologized in *Munschworks 3: The Third Munsch Treasury,* Firefly Books (New York, NY), 2000, and *The Munschworks Grand Treasury,* Annick Press (Willowdale, Ontario, Canada), 2001.

Adaptations

Northern Lights: The Soccer Trails was adapted as a CD-ROM, Discis Knowledge Research (Toronto, Ontario, Canada), 1995.

Sidelights

Michael Kusugak is a Canadian author who has broadened the spectrum of children's literature through his contribution of stories focusing on his Inuit heritage.

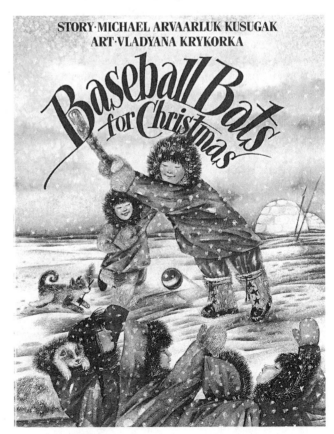

Baseball Bats for Christmas *by Michael Kusugak introduces readers to Inuit culture and life in the Arctic.*

Many of his titles, among them *Hide and Sneak, Baseball Bats for Christmas* and the short story collection *Arctic Tales* engage early elementary-grade readers with their crisp prose and unique subject matter. Reviewing *Baseball Bats for Christmas,* Kenneth Oppel remarked in *Quill & Quire* that Kusugak's "first-person narration is warm, energetic, and wonderfully humorous" as he tells the story of growing up in an Inuit fishing village.

Kusugak grew up in the small village of Repulse Bay, in Canada's Northwest Territories, and inherited his love of storytelling from his grandmother. As a child he spoke only Inuit, the language of his family, and his memories of those years, in which he lived in sod houses and igloos and traveled by dog team, has served as the basis of much of his fiction for young readers. By the time Kusugak was a teen the old Inuit way of life had gradually slipped away. He became one of the first Inuit in his region to graduate from a high school, a goal that required him to leave his home and become a boarding student during the school year. After college, although he worked for the Canadian government and for a local university, he always remained tied to his cultural roots and to Canada's Arctic region. As Jon C. Stott explained in an essay in *St. James Guide to Children's Writers,* by writing, "Kusugak set about to create stories that would combine elements of the old and modern worlds, would appeal to his own people as well as to larger audiences, and would catch the attention of children who were primarily interested in television and video games."

Written with coauthor Robert Munsch, whom Kusugak met when Munsch appeared at a northern Canada assembly, Kusugak's first published book, *A Promise Is a Promise,* is based on a childhood memory of going ice fishing. In the story, an Inuit girl named Allashua decides to disobey her parents' wishes and go fishing alone, but falls through the ice and is trapped by the Qallupilluit—creatures who dwell beneath the frozen sea. Released on her word that she will return to the Qallupilluit with her brothers and sisters, Allashua tricks the sea beasts with help from her mother. André Gagnon praised the story in his *Canadian Materials* review, commending its "suspense, magical moments, and . . . most satisfying ending." *A Promise Is a Promise* has been included in several anthologies of Munsch's stories.

Allashua returns in *Hide and Sneak,* and again gets herself into trouble with a magical being. This time the being is a Ijiraq, a small impish man who lures the young girl from her home but is thwarted in his kidnaping attempt when Allashua finds help from another source. Calling *Hide and Sneak* "a triumph," *Canadian Children's Literature* reviewer Stan Atherton praised Kusugak's preteen heroine as "credible, open, imaginative, and even slightly rebellious," while a *Bloomsbury Review* contributor dubbed the story "charming."

Kusugak's short story collection *Arctic Stories* was published in 1998 and also features a young female

Kusugak's **Arctic Stories,** *illustrated by Vladyana Langer Krykorka, contains three tales about Agatha, a young girl who lives in a small community in the Canadian Arctic.*

protagonist. Agatha is the focus of the three tales included, all of which take place during the late 1950s in a village along the Hudson Bay. Encounters with a U.S. Navy blimp and a large raven, as well as her adventures during her first year at boarding school, are recounted by Kusugak with what a *Publishers Weekly* contributor characterized as "clarity and dry humor." John Peters added in *Booklist* that *Arctic Tales* is a "combination of recognizable characters and exotic locale [that] will transport young readers effortlessly."

Also for novice readers, *Who Wants Rocks?* tells the story of Little Mountain, which exists in the Arctic region and leads a quiet life. With the coming of the Yukon gold rush, Little Mountain must contend with a strange man named Old Joe, who is determined to disrupt the mountain's surface and the creatures and plants making Little Mountain their home in his search for gold. Finally, Joe realizes that the true treasure lies elsewhere, and determines to make his home atop Little Mountain and enjoy the hillside's natural beauty. Praising the story as a good read-aloud choice due to its focus on environmental themes, Patty Lawlor commended *Who Wants Rocks?* in *Quill & Quire* for its "short sentences and simple, carefully worded descriptions" and noted that Kusugak recounts his tale in "traditional storytelling style."

In addition to writing stories, which he does in a shed next to his house, Kusugak enjoys telling his tales aloud to young listeners in much the same way that his grandmother used to tell stories to him. With only a single piece of string with which to bring to life his animal characters, he performs at schools and libraries around Canada, and in 1997 was featured on stage at Toronto's Young People's Theatre.

Biographical and Critical Sources

BOOKS

Jones, Raymond E., and Jon C. Stott, *Canadian Children's Books: A Critical Guide to Authors and Illustrators,* Oxford University Press (Toronto, Canada), 2000.

St. James Guide to Children's Writers, 5th edition, St. James Press (Detroit, MI), 1999, p. 615.

PERIODICALS

Bloomsbury Review, September, 1992, review of *Hide and Sneak,* p. 21.

Booklist, November 1, 1998, John Peters, review of *Arctic Stories,* p. 503.

Books in Canada, summer, 1992, Rhea Tregebov, review of *Hide and Sneak,* p. 36.

Canadian Children's Literature, Volume 72, 1993, Stan Atherton, review of *Hide and Sneak,* p. 84.

Canadian Materials, November, 1988, André Gagnon, review of *A Promise Is a Promise.*

Children's Book News, winter, 1999, Jeffrey Canton, review of *Arctic Stories,* p. 23.

Horn Book, May-June, 1991, Sarah Ellis, review of *Baseball Bats for Christmas,* pp. 366-368.

Publishers Weekly, November 30, 1998, review of *Arctic Stories,* p. 71.

Quill & Quire, October, 1990, Kenneth Oppel, review of *Baseball Bats for Christmas,* p. 14; February, 1991, Peter Cumming, "Inuit Writer Kusugak Thrives in Two Worlds," pp. 21, 23; March, 1992, Sarah Ellis, review of *Hide and Sneak,* p. 65; September, 1993, Linda Granfield, review of *Northern Lights: The Soccer Trails,* p. 67; September, 1999, Patty Lawlor, review of *Who Wants Rocks?* p, 69.

School Librarian, autumn, 1999, Jane Doonan, review of *Arctic Stories,* p. 145.

School Library Journal, February, 1989, Reva Pitch Margolis, review of *A Promise Is a Promise,* p. 74; September, 1995, LaVonne Sanborn, "Storyteller: Michael Arvaarluk Kusugak," p. 154; May, 1997, Roz Goodman, review of *My Arctic 1, 2, 3,* pp. 120-121; March, 1999, Mollie Bynum, review of *Arctic Stories,* p. 177.

ONLINE

Annick Press Web site, http://www.annickpress.com/ (March 12, 2003), "Michael Kusugak."

Michael Kusugak Web site, http://www.michaelkusugak. com/ (March 12, 2003).*

L

LAVENDER, William D. 1921-

Personal

Born 1921; son of Claud B. (a physician) and Maggie Mae (a homemaker; maiden name, Neel) Lavender; married Mary Bridget Kane (a research assistant); children: Debra, Larry, Randy. *Ethnicity:* "White." *Education:* Birmingham Southern Conservatory and College (Birmingham, AL), B. Music.; University of Southern California, M. Music.

Addresses

Home and office—4210 Carney Ct., Riverside, CA 92507. *Agent*—Barbara Markowitz, Los Angeles, CA. *E-mail*—maryl@pe.net.

Career

Writer. Formerly employed by a U.S. government documentary film agency, scoring films and working on sound recording.

Writings

Flight of the Seabird (adult novel), Simon & Schuster (New York, NY), 1977.
The Invisible People: A Musical Play, Anchorage Press (Louisville, KY), 2000.
Just Jane: A Daughter of England Caught in the Struggle of the American Revolution, Harcourt (San Diego, CA), 2002.

Author of several novels for adults.

Work in Progress

A historical novel set in San Francisco during the 1906 earthquake.

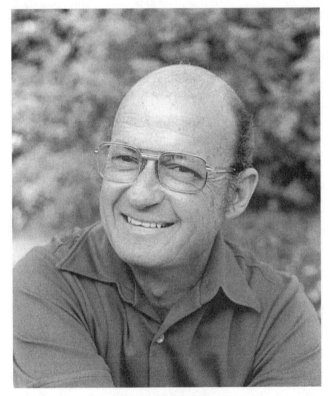

William D. Lavender

Sidelights

Author and composer William D. Lavender enjoyed several different careers—composing music, producing a musical show, and writing adult novels—before turning to writing fiction for children. After graduating from the Birmingham Southern Conservatory, Lavender worked for several years composing music to accompany documentary films made by the U.S. government. He then began to create for a more general audience, writing the book, music, and lyrics for *The Invisible People,* a musical fantasy for children and family audiences that was successfully mounted throughout the United States. As Lavender told *SATA,* "For years my wife and I made a sort of cottage industry out of promoting and handling the production arrangements of the play ourselves." Eventually Lavender offered *The Invisible People* for publication, and it appeared in print in 2000.

During the 1970s and 1980s Lavender wrote a handful of historical novels for adults, and one novel set in contemporary times. Although several of these novels were translated and brought out in foreign editions, by the turn of the millennium, all were out of print. Yet in the writing of them Lavender had honed his skills as a creator of historical fiction, a talent he was to put to good use in writing for children. "No longer feeling comfortable with the direction in which adult fiction was moving, I then discontinued writing for some time while engaging in other activities," he explained. "But recently I have returned to the novel form, now aiming my work at the Younger Reader genre." His 2002 offering, *Just Jane: A Daughter of England Caught in the Struggle of the American Revolution,* is Lavender's first novel for young readers, and as the title indicates, he returned to his favorite genre—historical fiction.

Lavender decided to base *Just Jane,* about an orphaned girl of noble English birth, in South Carolina, for as he continued, "Hardly any other American colony in rebellion against England saw the fabric of its everyday life so tragically torn apart as did South Carolina. The abundance of dramatic material collected was the basis of my decision to set my Revolutionary War story in that area." In the novel, Lady Jane Prentice, who drops her aristocratic title to become "just Jane," is forced to make choices about her own independence as well as her allegiance to the new nation or the old. Not only does the narrative involve Jane's decision making over a six-year period, it involves family feuds, political wrangling, and finally military action.

Like many writers of historical fiction, Lavender sets high value on the accuracy of his portrayal of past life. "Since historical accuracy is of enormous importance in this kind of writing, I consider myself extremely fortunate to have an outstandingly capable research assistant in my wife, Mary," Lavender explained. "For this project, as for others, she has gone all out to compile prodigious amounts of historical information, both from published materials and original sources. In collecting the background material for *Just Jane,* we spent an entire month in South Carolina, ranging from Charleston to remote locations in the back country." This attention to authenticity paid off for Lavender, as reviewers noted it in their comments on the novel's dialogue, characterizations, and subplots. In *School Library Journal,* Renee Steinberg called *Just Jane* "beautifully written" and praised Lavender's "vivid factual information," "rich prose," and "multilayered characters." Because the action of the novel takes place over a longer period than that in many novels for the young teen reading level, Lavender had to sometimes recap the action for readers, a technique that slows down the action. Yet according

to a *Kirkus Reviews* critic, "it's a lively story nevertheless," one that makes both the "personal and the political [choices] . . . real and immediate." *Booklist* contributor Carolyn Phelan predicted that historical fiction enthusiasts would find *Just Jane* "refreshing" for its unusual location.

Biographical and Critical Sources

PERIODICALS

Booklist, November 1, 2002, Carolyn Phelan, review of *Just Jane: A Daughter of England Caught in the Struggle of the American Revolution,* p. 485.
Kirkus Reviews, July 15, 2002, review of *Just Jane,* p. 1036.
School Library Journal, December, 2002, Renee Steinberg, review of *Just Jane,* pp. 143-144.

*   *   *

LEGG, Gerald 1947-

Personal

Born January 30, 1947, in Woodford Green, Essex, England; son of John Horace (a furniture shop owner) and Lilian Irene (a homemaker) Legg; married August 8, 1971; wife's name Patricia (a medical secretary); children: John Modupé, Michelle Joanne, Catherine Elizabeth Mary. *Education:* Received degree from South West Essex Technical College (biochemistry technology), 1968; attended University of Manchester, Ph.D., 1971. *Religion:* Anglican. *Hobbies and other interests:* Photography, scuba diving, microscopy, beekeeping, muzzle-loading rifle shooting, engineering.

Addresses

Office—c/o Booth Museum of Natural History, 194 Dyke Rd., Brighton, Sussex BN1 5AA, England. *E-mail*—gerald@natura.uklinux.net.

Career

Museum biologist, researcher, and nonfiction author. Fourah Bay College, University of Sierra Leone, Freetown, lecturer in zoology and researcher, 1971-74; Booth Museum of Natural History, Brighton, England, keeper of natural sciences, 1974—. British Arachnological Society, council member; Institute of biology, member.

Member

British Museums Association, British Ecological Society, Biological Curators Group, Society of Authors, Royal Entomological Society of London (fellow), Linnean Society of London, Zoological Society of London.

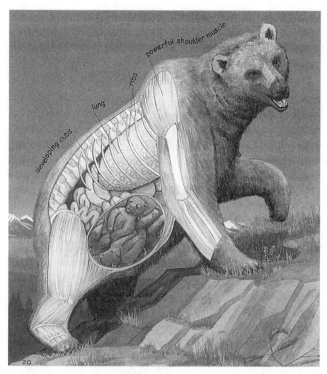

Gerald Legg's book Bears *dispels myths about various types of bears from grizzlies to pandas. (Illustrated by Carolyn Scrace and Mark Bergin.)*

Writings

FOR CHILDREN

Amazing Tropical Birds ("Eyewitness Juniors" series), photographs by Jerry Young, Knopf (New York, NY), 1991.

The X-Ray Picture Book of Amazing Animals, illustrated by David Salariya, F. Watts (New York, NY), 1993.

Minibeasts ("Puffin Factfinders" series), Puffin (London, England), 1993, Wright Group (Bothell, WA), 1994.

(With Kay Barnham) *Flyers Animals: Minibeasts,* F. Watts (London, England), 1994.

Monster Animals ("Puffin Factfinder" series), Puffin (London, England), 1994.

The X-Ray Picture Book of Incredible Creatures, illustrated by Carolyn Scrace, F. Watts (New York, NY), 1995.

(With Rupert Matthews) *Amazing Animal Facts,* Zigzag (Godalming, England), 1997.

Sharks ("Worldwise" series), illustrated by Elizabeth Branch and Jackie Harland, F. Watts (New York, NY), 1997.

Creepy Critters ("Factfinder" series), Smithmark (New York, NY), 1997.

Dragons ("Look and Wonder" series), illustrated by Carolyn Scrace, Macdonald Young Books (Hove, England), 1998.

Bugs ("Nature Watch" series), illustrated by Maggie Brand, Zigzag (New York, NY), 1998.

Find out about Minibeasts, Belitha (London, England), 2003.

Consultant to book series, including "Circle of Life," Franklin Watts, 1997, and other natural history titles.

"SCARY CREATURES" SERIES

Bears, illustrated by Carolyn Scrace and Mark Bergin, F. Watts (New York, NY), 2002.

Alligators and Crocodiles, illustrated by N. J. Hewetson, F. Watts (New York, NY), 2002.

Rats, illustrated by Mark Bergin and Bob Hersey, F. Watts (New York, NY), 2002.

"LIFECYCLES" SERIES

From Caterpillar to Butterfly, illustrated by Carolyn Scrace, F. Watts (London, England), 1997, F. Watts (New York, NY), 1998.

From Egg to Chicken, illustrated by Carolyn Scrace, F. Watts (London, England), 1997, F. Watts (New York, NY), 1998.

From Seed to Sunflower, illustrated by Carolyn Scrace, F. Watts (London, England), 1997, F. Watts (New York, NY), 1998.

From Tadpole to Frog, illustrated by Carolyn Scrace, F. Watts (London, England), 1997, F. Watts (New York, NY), 1998.

"HOW IT WORKS" SERIES

The World of Animal Life, illustrated by Steve Weston, Barnes & Noble Books (New York, NY), 1998.

The World of Plant Life, illustrated by Steve Weston, Horus Editions (London, England), 2000, Gareth Stevens (Milwaukee, WI), 2002.

The World of Insect Life, illustrated by Steve Weston, Horus Editions (London, England), 2000, Gareth Stevens (Milwaukee, WI), 2002.

OTHER

(With Richard E. Jones) *Pseudoscorpions (Arthropoda, Arachnida): Keys and Notes for the Identification of the Species* ("Synopses of the British Fauna" series), E. J. Brill (New York, NY), 1988.

Contributor of scientific papers, articles, and reviews to periodicals and journals.

Adaptations

Books by Legg have been adapted as CD-ROM products.

Work in Progress

More juvenile nonfiction natural history titles; research on various aspects of arachnid biology.

Sidelights

Gerald Legg is staff biologist at England's Booth Museum of Natural History, where as part of his job he presents the animal world in a way that captures the interest of young visitors. As an outgrowth of the displays and exhibition materials he has devised, as well as because of his personal interest, Legg has authored a number of titles focusing on animal biology. Among the books he has produced for both nonfiction series and stand-alone works of nonfiction are *The X-Ray Picture Book of Amazing Animals, Sharks,* and the four-volume "Lifecycles" series that includes the titles *From Caterpillar to Butterfly, From Egg to Chicken, From Seed to Sunflower,* and *From Tadpole to Frog.* Praising *The X-Ray Picture Book of Amazing Animals* as a "must have" for school libraries, *Science Books and Films* reviewer George Hennings noted that the "wealth of information, artistic skills, and fine editing" that went into the volume are commendable. Containing original illustrations revealing the anatomy of animals from snails to rats to tigers to whales in great—and sometimes even gross—detail, the book provides young researchers with what *School Library Journal* contributor Janet O'Brien characterized as "helpful and creatively presented bits of information."

In the four-volume "Lifecycles" series, Legg presents young readers with a detailed overview of natural processes. *From Seed to Sunflower* explains how a sunflower seed develops into a plant through germination, rooting, shooting, budding, and growth, and Legg's text is enhanced with brightly colored illustrations, a glossary, and a timeline. In *From Tadpole to Frog,* he also describes predators that can sometimes disrupt the growth cycle. Noting that the series is appropriate for very young students, *School Library Journal* contributor Anne Chapman commented that "these 'life stories' will be most appreciated" by fans of picture books such as Eric Carle's classic *The Very Hungry Caterpillar* "and who want to know more."

Legg told *SATA:* "As a postgraduate student in the zoology department of the University of Manchester, I started writing in the departmental magazine *Helix* on various aspects of natural history, and wrote a series of articles on British Pseudoscorpions for the magazine *Country Side.* After graduating, I eventually obtained the position of lecturer in zoology, with special reference to entomology, at the Fourah Bay College of the University of Sierra Leone. Here I continued publishing scientific papers and researched into aspects of tropical forest ecology and the biology of soil arachnids. It was only when I came back to England as a biologist in a museum that I became involved with writing children's books. Part of my work in the museum is making natural history available to the young—interpreting collec-

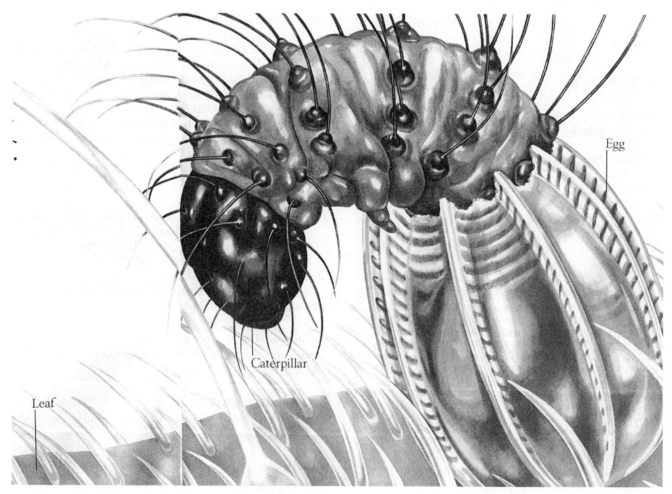

In **From Caterpillar to Butterfly,** *Carolyn Scrace's detailed illustrations enhance Legg's description of this creature's amazing transformation.*

tions and ideas. At the museum I have also edited, put together, and helped produce a number of publications. A number of years ago I was invited to work on a book for children and found the work stimulating and rewarding."

Biographical and Critical Sources

PERIODICALS

Appraisal, spring, 1992, Nancy R. Spence and Alison S. Jarvis, review of *Amazing Tropical Birds,* pp. 52-53.
Booklist, June 1, 1994, Carolyn Phelan, review of *The X-Ray Picture Book of Amazing Animals,* p. 1806.
School Librarian, February, 1994, John Feltwell, review of *Minibeasts,* p. 25; August, 1995, Wilfred Ashworth, review of *Incredible Creatures,* p. 114; summer, 1998, John Feltwell, review of "Lifecycles" series, p. 96.
School Library Journal, November, 1994, Janet O'Brien, review of *The X-Ray Picture Book of Amazing Animals,* p. 115; March, 1998, Anne Chapman and Eldon Younce, review of "Lifecycles" series, p. 197.
Science Books and Films, October, 1991, Edward I. Saiff, review of *Amazing Tropical Birds,* p. 211; October, 1994, George Hennings, review of *The X-Ray Picture Book of Amazing Animals,* p. 210.

*   *   *

LLEWELLYN, Claire 1954-

Personal

Born 1954, in Great Britain; married, 1979; children: one daughter, one son.

Addresses

Home and office—27 North Road Ave., Hertford, Hertfordshire SG14 2BT, England.

Career

Longman Publishers, editor, 1978-84; Macdonald Children's Books, commissioning editor, 1984—. Writer of children's books.

Awards, Honors

Times Educational Supplement Junior Information Book award, 1992, for *My First Book of Time.*

Writings

My First Book of Time, illustrated by Julie Carpenter, photographs by Paul Bricknell, Dorling Kindersley (New York, NY), 1992.
Trucks, illustrated by Nicholas Hewetson, F. Watts (New York, NY), 1995.

Disguises and Surprises, Candlewick Press (Cambridge, MA), 1996.
Wild, Wet, and Windy: The Weather—from Tornadoes to Lightning, Candlewick Press (Cambridge, MA), 1997.
The DK Picture Encyclopedia, Dorling Kindersley (New York, NY), 1997.
Our Planet Earth, Scholastic (New York, NY), 1997.
Cities, illustrated by Roger Stewart, Heinemann Interactive Library (Des Plaines, IL), 1998.
The Encyclopedia of Awesome Animals, illustrated by Chris Shields, Copper Beech Books (Brookfield, CT), 1998.
Animal Atlas, World Book (Chicago, IL), 1998.
The Best Book of Bugs, illustrated by Chris Forsey and others, Kingfisher (New York, NY), 1998.
The Big Book of Bones: An Introduction to Skeletons, Peter Bedrick Books (New York, NY), 1998.
The Earth Is like a Roundabout: A First Look at Night and Day, illustrated by Anthony Lewis, Macdonald Young Books (London, England), 1999.
The Best Book of Sharks, illustrated by Ray Grinaway and Roger Stewart, Kingfisher (New York, NY), 1999.
The Big Book of Mummies: All about Preserved Bodies from Long Ago, Peter Bedrick Books (Lincolnwood, IL), 2001, published as *The Complete Book of Mummies,* Wayland (London, England), 2001.
Kid's Survival Handbook, Scholastic (New York, NY), 2001.
Slugs and Snails, F. Watts (London, England), 2001.
Reptiles, Kingisher (New York, NY), 2002.
Who's Who in the Bible, Kingisher (New York, NY), 2002.
The Best Ears in the World (fiction), Smart Apple Media (North Mankato, MN), 2002.
Saints and Angels, Kingfisher (New York, NY), 2003.
The Sea, Smart Apple Media (North Mankato, IL), 2003.
Butterfly, illustrated by Simon Mendez, NorthWord Press (Chanhassen, MN), 2003.
Frog, illustrated by Simon Mendez, NorthWord Press (Chanhassen, MN), 2003.
The Moon, Smart Apple Media (North Mankato, IL), 2003.
Duck, illustrated by Simon Mendez, NorthWord Press (Chanhassen, MN), 2004.
Tree, illustrated by Simon Mendez, NorthWord Press (Chanhassen, MN), 2004.

Llewellyn's books have been translated into several languages, including Hebrew and Spanish.

"TAKE ONE" SERIES

Changing Clothes, Simon & Schuster (New York, NY), 1990.
Growing Food, Simon & Schuster (New York, NY), 1990.
Under the Sea, Simon & Schuster (New York, NY), 1990.
In the Air, Simon & Schuster (New York, NY), 1990.
Rubbish Simon & Schuster (New York, NY), 1990.
Bridges, Simon & Schuster (New York, NY), 1990.
Winter, Simon & Schuster (New York, NY), 1991.
Spring, Simon & Schuster (New York, NY), 1991.
Summer, Simon & Schuster (New York, NY), 1991.
Autumn, Simon & Schuster (New York, NY), 1991.

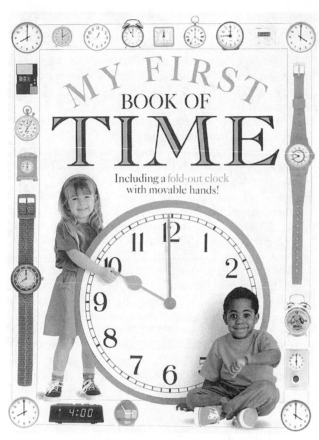

Claire Llewellyn's **My First Book of Time** *creatively shows children how to tell time. (Book cover photographs by Paul Bricknell.)*

"FIRST LOOK" SERIES

First Look at Clothes, Gareth Stevens Children's Books (Milwaukee, WI), 1991.
First Look in the Air, Gareth Stevens Children's Books (Milwaukee, WI), 1991.
First Look at Growing Food, Gareth Stevens Children's Books (Milwaukee, WI), 1991.
First Look under the Sea, Gareth Stevens Children's Books (Milwaukee, WI), 1991.

"MIGHTY MACHINES" SERIES

Tractor, Dorling Kindersley (New York, NY), 1995.
Truck, Dorling Kindersley (New York, NY), 1995.

"WHY DO WE HAVE" SERIES

Day and Night, illustrated by Anthony Lewis, Barron's (Hauppauge, NY), 1995.
Rivers and Seas, illustrated by Anthony Lewis, Barron's (Hauppauge, NY), 1995.
Rocks and Mountains, illustrated by Anthony Lewis, Barron's (Hauppauge, NY), 1995.
Wind and Rain, illustrated by Anthony Lewis, Barron's (Hauppauge, NY), 1995.
Towns and Cities, illustrated by Anthony Lewis, Rigby Interactive Library (Crystal Lake, IL), 1997.

Deserts and Rainforests, illustrated by Anthony Lewis, Rigby Interactive Library (Crystal Lake, IL), 1997.

"I DIDN'T KNOW THAT" SERIES

Some Birds Hang upside Down: And Other Amazing Facts about Birds, illustrated by Chris Shields and Jo Moore, Copper Beech Books (Brookfield, CT), 1997.
Some Bugs Glow in the Dark: And Other Amazing Facts about Insects, illustrated by Mike Taylor, Rob Shone, and Jo Moore, Copper Beech Books (Brookfield, CT), 1997.
Some Snakes Spit Poison: And Other Amazing Facts about Snakes, illustrated by Francis Phillipps, Copper Beech Books (Brookfield, CT), 1997.
Spiders Have Fangs: And Other Amazing Facts about Arachnids, illustrated by Mike Taylor and Christopher J. Turnbull, Copper Beech Books (Brookfield, CT), 1997.
Sharks Keep Losing Their Teeth: And Other Amazing Facts about Sharks, Copper Beech Books (Brookfield, CT), 1998.
Some Plants Grow in Midair: And Other Amazing Facts about Rainforests, illustrated by Mike Taylor and Christopher J. Turnbull, Copper Beech Books (Brookfield, CT), 1998.
Chimps Use Tools: And Other Amazing Facts about Animals, illustrated by Chris Shields and Jo Moore, Copper Beech Books (Brookfield, CT), 1999.
Only Some Big Cats Can Roar: And Other Amazing Facts about Cats, illustrated by Peter Barrett and others, Copper Beech Books (Brookfield, CT), 1999.

"WHAT'S FOR LUNCH" SERIES

Milk, Children's Press (New York, NY), 1998.
Peanuts, Children's Press (New York, NY), 1998.
Potatoes, Children's Press (New York, NY), 1998.
Chocolate, Children's Press (New York, NY), 1998.
Bread, Children's Press (New York, NY), 1998.
Eggs, Children's Press (New York, NY), 1999.
Oranges, Children's Press (New York, NY), 1999.
Peas, Children's Press (New York, NY), 1999.

"GEOGRAPHY STARTS" SERIES

Caves, Heinemann Library (Chicago, IL), 2000.
Coral Reefs, Heinemann Library (Chicago, IL), 2000.
Geysers, Heinemann Library (Chicago, IL), 2000.
Glaciers, Heinemann Library (Chicago, IL), 2000.
Islands, Heinemann Library (Chicago, IL), 2000.
Volcanoes, Heinemann Library (Chicago, IL), 2000.

The "Geography Starts" series was published as the "What Are . . ." series, Heinemann First Library (London, England), 2001.

"THE FACTS ABOUT" SERIES

Arthritis, illustrated by Tom Connell, Smart Apple Media (North Mankato, MN), 2001.

Diabetes, illustrated by Tom Connell, Smart Apple Media (North Mankato, MN), 2001.

Epilepsy, illustrated by Tom Connell, Smart Apple Media (North Mankato, MN), 2001.

"MATERIAL WORLD" SERIES

Plastic, F. Watts (New York, NY), 2002.
Rubber, F. Watts (New York, NY), 2002.
Silk, F. Watts (New York, NY), 2002.
Wood, F. Watts (New York, NY), 2002.
Concrete, F. Watts (New York, NY), 2002.
Glass, F. Watts (New York, NY), 2002.
Metal, F. Watts (New York, NY), 2002.
Paper, F. Watts (New York, NY), 2002.

"LETS RECYCLE" SERIES

Save Energy, Chrysalis Education (North Mankato, IL), 2003.

Stop Water Waste, Chrysalis Education (North Mankato, IL), 2003.

Fight Air Pollution, Chrysalis Education (North Mankato, MN), 2003.

Let's Recycle, Chrysalis Education (North Mankato, IL), 2003.

Protect Natural Habitats, Chrysalis Education (North Mankato, IL), 2003.

Sidelights

Claire Llewellyn is a prolific author of juvenile nonfiction whose books have been incorporated into numer-

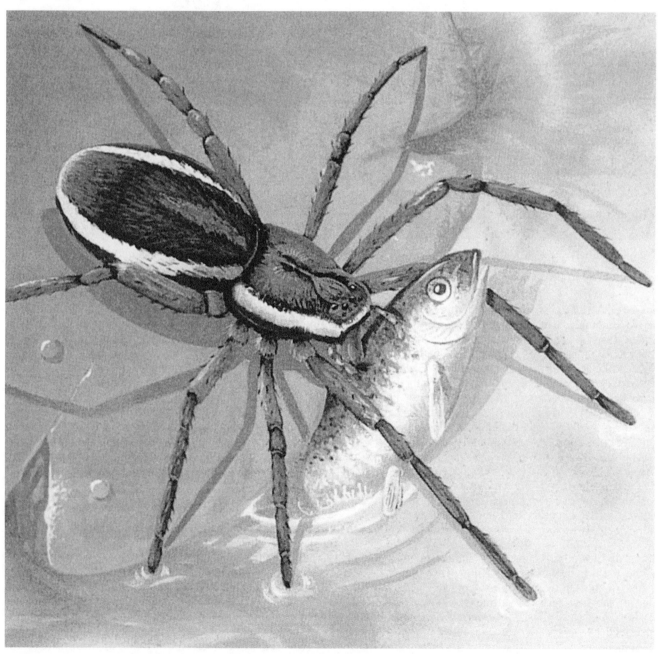

Llewellyn offers information in an interesting format in **Spiders Have Fangs: And Other Amazing Facts about Arachnids,** *illustrated by Mike Taylor and Christopher J. Turnbull.*

Some Plants Grow in Midair *is designed to excite young readers about the rainforest.* (*Book illustrations by Mike Taylor and Christopher J. Turnbull.*)

ous book series that, while originating in the author's native England, have also been released in the United States. One of her first books, *My First Book of Time* was highly praised by reviewers for its enthusiastic and clear explanation of time zones, seasons, fractions, and the history of timepieces. Dubbing it "comprehensive" in its scope, a *Publishers Weekly* contributor noted of *My First Book of Time* that Llewellyn covers the material "in exhaustive but never overwhelming detail." Other books by Llewellyn include *The Big Book of Mummies: All about Preserved Bodies from Long Ago, Our Planet Earth,* and *Some Plants Grow in Midair: And Other Amazing Facts about Rainforests,* and she has also utilized her organizational and research skills as well as her attention to detail to produce *The Encyclopedia of Awesome Animals* and *Animal Atlas.*

Some of Llewellyn's most popular books are included in the multi-author "I Didn't Know That" series, published in the United States by Copper Beech Books. One of the first series installments, *Some Snakes Spit Poison: And Other Amazing Facts about Snakes,* was described by *Science Books and Films* reviewer Edna DeManche as an "action-packed" "attention getter" of a book. In a text that speaks to kids in their own language, Llewellyn presents information on a variety of snakes, and adds quizzes and games to make the learning experience complete. Packed with information on everything from how spiders evolved, make webs, hunt, and communicate with each other, *Spiders Have Fangs: And Other Amazing Facts about Arachnids* is "loaded with fascinating facts and colorful drawings" that serve as a "fine starting point . . . for further learning," according to *School Library Journal* contributor Anne Chapman Callaghan. And in *Some Plants Grow in Midair,* the rainforest environment is described, along with information regarding its importance to the Earth's ecological health. Not only plants and animals, but also the human inhabitants of the Amazon region are discussed in a book that *School Library Journal* reviewer Ann G. Brouse dubbed "fresh and exciting." Each volume in the "I Didn't Know That" series contains an index, glossary, and projects, and is illustrated with drawings that afford curious readers the chance to explore in search of hidden objects.

Llewellyn covers a broad range of topics in her writing, and while most of them involve the world of plants and animals, some books, such as the three volumes in the "The Facts About" series, delve into medical matters. In the series installment titled *Diabetes* she describes in what *School Librarian* contributor James Donnelly termed "careful, unsentimental" terms, the causes, symptoms, and methods of treating the disease. Geared toward elementary-age children, each book in the series features a child who deals with the covered disease—other volumes deal with asthma, arthritis, and epilepsy—and the text relates their childlike concerns over their medical condition. Praising the series as "thorough and positive," Elizabeth Schleuther noted in her *Books for Keeps* review that Llewellyn mixes her clear, informative text with photographs, graphics, glossary, and information sidebars. Noting that the series will provide "reassurance to those who live with the condition" and also inform friends and family of a loved one's condition, Tom Deveson in *Times Educational Supplement* praised Llewellyn's "The Facts About" books for "perform[ing] a useful informative task without sentimentality and with laudable directness."

While most of Llewellyn's books for young researchers are organized into multi-volume series, several of her books serve as one-volume resources containing a wealth of detail on a single subject. In 2001's *The Big Book of Mummies*—published in England as *The Complete Book of Mummies*—Llewellyn discusses burial practices dating from 4,000 years ago in many different cultures, and explains why the study of mummies is so crucial to our understanding of the past. Noting that the book "lives up to its title," *School Librarian* reviewer Michael Kirby praised *The Big Book of Mummies* for its clear text, exemplary illustrations, and its graphically detailed description of Egyptian embalming rites. In fact, according to somewhat squeamish *Times Educational Supplement* contributor Paul Noble, "it is just too complete"; although Noble was deterred by the book's "revealing" photographs, he nonetheless agreed that *The Big Book of Mummies* is "a fine book."

Other single-volume books include *The Best Book of Bugs* a compendium of insects that a *Kirkus* reviewer described as a "radiantly illustrated" introduction to every bug from ants and bees to spiders and worms. Part of the Scholastic "First Encyclopedia" series, *Our Planet Earth* is organized in a topical format, providing readers with information regarding the Earth's surface, evolution, and life forms. Praising the book's short, "easy to understand" entries, *School Library Journal* reviewer Peg Glisson cited the volume as "an enjoyable browsing book," while in her appraisal for *American Reference Books Annual* Janet Hilbun noted that *Our Planet Earth* "has value as an overview" for budding Earth scientists.

Biographical and Critical Sources

PERIODICALS

American Reference Book Annual, Volume 30, 1999, Janet Hilbun, review of *Our Planet Earth,* pp. 417-418.

Appraisal, winter, 1999, Helen James and Leonard Garigliano, review of *Some Plants Grow in Midair,* pp. 53-54; spring, 2000, Barbara C. Sotto and Melvin S. Kaufman, review of *Chimps Use Tools,* pp. 150-151.

Booklist, October 15, 1991, p. 441; December 1, 1996, Hazel Rochman, review of *Disguises and Surprises,* p. 658; February 1, 1998, review of *Our Planet Earth,* p. 941; September 1, 1998, Karen Hutt, review of *The Big Book of Bones,* p. 116.

Books for Keeps, January, 1998, Ted Percy, review of *Wild, Wet, and Windy,* p. 19; November, 1999, Marget Mallett, review of *The Earth Is like a Roundabout,* p. 24; September, 2001, Elizabeth Schleuther, review of *The Facts about Epilepsy,* p. 26.

Bulletin of the Center for Children's Books, July, 1992, p. 299.

Horn Book, July, 1992, p. 468.

Junior Bookshelf, June, 1992, pp. 112-113; December, 1996, review of *Disguises and Surprises,* p. 254.

Kirkus Reviews, May 1, 1992, p. 613; June 1, 1997, review of *Some Snakes Spit Poison,* p. 876; March 15, 1998, review of *The Best Book of Bugs,* pp. 406-607.

Magpies, July, 1995, review of *Truck,* pp. 33-34.

Publishers Weekly, May 4, 1992, review of *My First Book of Time,* p. 55; May 20, 2002, review of *The Kid's Survival Guide,* p. 69.

School Librarian, August, 1995, Alasdair Campbell, review of *Truck,* p. 104; November, 1997, p. 205; spring, 1999, John Feltwell, review of *Animal Atlas,* p. 40; summer, 2001, Michael Kirby, review of *The Complete Book of Mummies,* p. 95; winter, 2001, James Donnelly, review of *The Facts about Diabetes,* p. 218; spring, 2002, Joyce Banks, review of *Slugs and Snails,* p. 19, and Shirley Paice, review of *Epilepsy,* p. 51.

School Library Journal, August, 1992, p. 152; February, 1998, Peg Glisson, review of *Our Planet Earth,* p. 138; August, 1995, John Peters, review of *How Things Work,* p. 168; February, 1997, Lisa Wu Stowe, review of *Disguises and Surprises,* p. 93; September, 1997, Jeffrey A. French, review of *Some Bugs Glow in the Dark,* and Kathy Piehl, review of *Deserts and Rainforests,* p. 204; March, 1998, Anne Chapman Callaghan, review of *Spiders Have Fangs,* p. 197; July, 1998, Christine A. Moesch, review of *The Big Book of Bones,* p. 108; July, 1998, Karen Wehner, review of *The Best Book of Bugs,* p. 89; August, 1998, Ann G. Brouse, review of *Some Plants Grow in Midair,* p. 178; September, 1998, Eldon Younce, review of *Potatoes,* p. 193.

Science Books and Film, October, 1995, James R. Hanley, review of *Tractor,* pp. 214-215; October, 1997, Edna DeManche, review of *Some Snakes Spit Poison,* p. 210; August, 1998, Katharine C. Payne, review of *Sharks Keep Losing Their Teeth,* p. 177; May, 2001, review of *Some Plants Grow in Midair,* p. 98.

Teaching Children Mathematics, September, 1994, David J. Whitin, review of *My First Book of Time,* p. 44.

Times Educational Supplement, April 6, 2001, Paul Noble, review of *The Complete Book of Mummies,* p. 22; April 13, 2001, review of "What Are" series, p. 22; November 16, 2001, Tom Deveson, review of "The Facts About" series, p. 22.*

LUSTED, Marcia Amidon 1962-

Personal

Born May 4, 1962, in Peterborough, NH; married Greg Lusted, 1985; children: three sons. *Education:* Bradford College, A.A., 1982; Keene State College, B.A., 1984, secondary education certification, 1985.

Addresses

Office—Hancock, NH. *Agent*—c/o Author Mail, Lucent Books, 10911 Technology Pl., San Diego, CA 92127. *E-mail*—mglusted@prexar.com.

Career

Writer.

Member

Society of Children's Book Writers and Illustrators.

Writings

Time's Passage (fiction), Writers Club Press (Lincoln, NE), 2000.
Building History: The Holy City of Jerusalem, Lucent Books (Detroit, MI), 2002.

Building History: Hoover Dam, Lucent Books (Detroit, MI), 2003.
Building History: The Canals of Venice, Lucent Books (Detroit, MI), 2003.

Sidelights

Marcia Amidon Lusted told *SATA:* "I have always been interested in history, and writing for the 'Building History' series was a perfect way to break into writing nonfiction. I enjoy doing research and finding the facts I need to produce a good reference book. Children's nonfiction writing is a growing field with a demand for new writers, and it is definitely the best way to become published in the competitive area of writing for children."

Biographical and Critical Sources

ONLINE

sffworld, http://www.sffworld.com/ (February 10, 2003), L. A. Solinas, review of *Time's Passage.*

M

MALVASI, Meg Greene
(Meg Greene)

Personal

Female. *Education:* Lindenwood College, St. Charles, MO, B.S., 1977; University of Nebraska—Omaha, M.A., 1980; University of Vermont, M.S., 1989.

Addresses

Home—13803 Sterlings Bridge Road, Midlothian, VA 23112. *E-mail*—malvasi@comcast.net.

Career

Center for Archaeological Research, College of William and Mary, architectural historian, 1997-99; freelance writer, 1994—.

Awards, Honors

Honor Book Award for social studies book, grades 7-12, Society of School Librarians International, 1999, for *Slave Young, Slave Long: A History of American Slavery; Buttons, Bones, and the Organ-Grinder's Monkey: Tales of Historical Archaeology* was named a Best Book for Teens, New York Public Library, 2001.

Writings

"GALAXY OF SUPERSTARS" SERIES; AS MEG GREENE

Lauryn Hill, Chelsea House (Philadelphia, PA), 1999.
Matt Damon, Chelsea House (Philadelphia, PA), 2000.
Will Smith, Chelsea House (Philadelphia, PA), 2002.

"BUILDING HISTORY" SERIES; AS MEG GREENE

The Russian Kremlin, Lucent Books/Gale (Detroit, MI), 2001.
The Eiffel Tower, Lucent Books/Gale (Detroit, MI), 2001.

"IMMIGRANTS IN AMERICA" SERIES; AS MEG GREENE

The Russian Americans, Lucent Books/Gale (Detroit, MI), 2002.
The Greek Americans, Lucent Books/Gale (Detroit, MI), 2004.
Polish Americans, Lucent Books/Gale (Detroit, MI), 2004.

NONFICTION; AS MEG GREENE (EXCEPT AS NOTED)

Legends of Ice Hockey: Peter Forsberg, Chelsea House (Philadelphia, PA), 1998.
Slave Young, Slave Long: The American Slave Experience, Lerner Books (Minneapolis, MN), 1999.
Your Government and How It Works: The DEA, Chelsea House (Philadelphia, PA), 2001.
Revolutionary War Heroes: Nathaniel Greene, Chelsea House (Philadelphia, PA), 2001.
Buttons, Bones, and the Organ-Grinder's Monkey: Tales of Historical Archaeology, Linnet Books (North Haven, CT), 2001.
Thaddeus Kosciuszko: Polish General and Patriot ("Revolutionary War Leaders" series), Chelsea House (Philadelphia, PA), 2002.
Famous Figures of the Civil War: Jeb Stuart, Chelsea House (Philadelphia, PA), 2002.
Jacques Cartier, Rosen Publishing (New York, NY), 2003.
Careers in the National Guards' Search and Rescue Units, Rosen Publishing (New York, NY), 2003.
U.S. Warplanes: The B-52 Stratofortress, Rosen Publishing (New York, NY), 2003.
(As Meg Green Malvasi) *Pope John Paul II: A Biography,* Greenwood Publishing Group (Westport, CT), 2003.
American Women: 1900-2000, Bluewood Books (San Francisco, CA), 2003.
Louis Sachar, Rosen Publishing (New York, NY), 2003.
Into the Land of Freedom: A History of Reconstruction, Lerner Books (Minneapolis, MN), 2004.

Contributing editor of "History for Children" at the *Suite101.com* Web site, "A Day in the Life" for the *PBS Kids!* and architectural articles for the *Bella Online* Web site. Contributor of articles to textbooks and refer-

Russian immigrants begin a new life in America. *(From* The Russian Americans, *written by Meg Greene Malvasi.)*

ence books, and to periodicals, including *The Southern Historian, North Dakota History, The Historian,* and *Women's Studies International Forum.*

Adaptations

Matt Damon was released on audiocassette by Recorded Books (Prince Frederick, MD), 2001.

Work in Progress

Primary Sources of World Culture: Japan, Rosen Publishing (New York, NY), 2004.

Sidelights

Meg Greene Malvasi has written widely under her maiden name Meg Greene. Listing biographies, history, architecture, and archaeology among the topics she has covered, her books include series titles as well as stand-alone works. She is also a frequent contributor to the renowned children's history magazine *Cobblestone.* Malvasi has penned biographies of such contemporary celebrities as actors Matt Damon and Will Smith, and novelist Louis Sachar; and biographies of such histori-cal figures as Catholic Pope John Paul II, explorer

Jacques Cartier and American Revolutionary war hero Thaddeus Kosciuzko. In addition, Malvasi has published a collective biography of twentieth-century women and contributed three books to the "Immigrants in America" series: *The Russian Americans,* with its "clear, lively text" to quote Diane S. Marton of *School Library Journal, The Greek Americans,* and *Polish Americans.*

Malvasi has also contributed one or more titles to several other series, including *The Eiffel Tower* and *The Russian Kremlin* to the "Building History" series. Two of Malvasi's stand-alone titles, the early title *Slave Young, Slave Long: The American Slave Experience* and *Buttons, Bones, and the Organ-Grinder's Monkey: Tales of Historical Archaeology,* not only caught reviewers' attention, but earned her accolades. *Slave Young, Slave Long,* which integrates narrative with many first-hand accounts of slaves and masters, earned the Honor Book Award for a high school social studies book for grades seven through twelve, while *Buttons, Bones, and the Organ-Grinder's Monkey,* about historical archaeology, was named a Best Book for Teens by the New York Public Library. *Booklist*'s Hazel Rochman found *Slave Young, Slave Long* an "excellent, accessible introduction" written in "quiet, direct prose." The latter book, with its colorful title, discusses how archaeological findings help historians assess history. Using a mystery format, the author describes how archaeologists work. She gives the following examples to illustrate their methods: locating the Jamestown Fort, retrieving the ship *LaBelle* from the bottom of the Texas Gulf, discovering slave artifacts at Thomas Jefferson's Monticello plantation, reassessing the events of the Battle of the Little Bighorn, and determining the true nature of the Five Points Neighborhood in New York City. Among enthusiasts of *Buttons, Bones, and the Organ-Grinder's Monkey* number *Booklist*'s Carolyn Phelan, who described it as "lively and informative" and in *Book Report* Kathy Fredrick praised the "snappy, concise style" with which Malvasi presents her information.

Biographical and Critical Sources

PERIODICALS

Booklist, April 1, 1999, Hazel Rochman, review of *Slave Young, Slave Long: The American Slave Experience,* p. 1404; October 1, 2001, Carolyn Phelan, review of *Buttons, Bones, and the Organ-Grinder's Monkey: Tales of Historical Archaeology,* p. 316.
Book Report, May-June, 2002, Kathy Fredrick, review of *Buttons, Bones, and the Organ-Grinder's Monkey,* p. 60.
School Library Journal, June, 2001, Ann W. Moore, review of *The Eiffel Tower,* p. 174; September, 2001, Elizabeth Talbot, review of *The Russian Kremlin,* p. 246; January, 2002, Kathleen Isaacs, review of *Buttons, Bones, and the Organ-Grinder's Monkey,* pp. 157-158; June, 2002, Marlene Gawron, review of *Thaddeus Kosciuszko: Polish General and Patriot,* pp. 158-159; July, 2002, Diane S. Marton, review of *The Russian Americans,* p. 129.

*   *   *

MARTON, Pierre
See STONE, Peter

*   *   *

McFARLAND, Henry "Hammer"
See McFARLAND, Henry O.

*   *   *

McFARLAND, Henry O. 1934-
(Henry "Hammer" McFarland)

Personal

Born March 4, 1934, in Concord, NH; son of Donald J. (a businessman) and Frances (a teacher and homemaker; maiden name, Morton) McFarland; married Nancy Norton, November 2, 1955; children: Susan M. McFarland Moynahan, Jay D. *Ethnicity:* "Anglo Saxon." *Education:* Middlebury College, B.A.; University of New Hampshire, graduate study. *Politics:* Independent. *Religion:* Protestant. *Hobbies and other interests:* Golf, skiing, crosswords, bridge.

Addresses

Home—12 Concord Point, P.O. Box 275, Rye, NH 03870. *Agent*—Patrika Vaughn, Advocate House, 888 Boulevard of the Arts, Suite 1503, Sarasota, FL 34236. *E-mail*—hankrye@aol.com.

Career

McFarland Ford Sales, Inc., president, 1955-2002; writer. Hampton Ford-Hyundai, Inc., treasurer.

Member

National Auto Dealer Association.

Writings

AS HENRY "HAMMER" MCFARLAND

Ralph's World, illustrated by Martha Gilfeather, A Cappella Publishing, 2002.
Ralph and Jimbo's Great Golf Adventure, illustrated by Martha Gilfeather, Advocate House (Sarasota, FL), 2002.

Work in Progress

It's a Dog's World, completion expected in 2003.

Sidelights

Henry O. McFarland worked as an automobile dealer for almost fifty years, but that was not his original intention. Until 1955 he intended to be a teacher or, perhaps, a writer. After a long and rewarding career in the automobile business, McFarland found himself remembering his college days as an American literature major and his early desire to teach.

When he became a grandfather, McFarland had an opportunity to explore that early dream by making up humorous children's stories that he hoped would entertain, educate, and tickle the imagination. By the time his fifth grandchild arrived, he had created Ralph and Jimbo.

Ralph is a young rhinoceros who lives on a small island with his parents. His best friend is an elephant named Jimbo. In the middle of the island is a magic volcano named Mount Hood, which erupts every afternoon. The remarkable thing about Mount Hood is that its daily eruption is in the form of ice cream. *Ralph's World* tells of the terrible, sad day when Mount Hood falls still and Ralph learns a lesson in life: there are more important things than ice cream.

In *Ralph and Jimbo's Great Golf Adventure,* humans have come to the island and constructed a golf course. The two friends observe these funny people and their antics with a ball and stick. When Ralph and Jimbo ask if they can play, too, the answer at first is "no animals allowed." The golfer reconsiders when he realizes that teaching a rhinoceros and an elephant to play golf would be a newsworthy achievement. Of course, no one could anticipate what happens next.

McFarland designed his stories for their entertainment value, hoping that they would also stimulate imagination. As the stories developed, however, he added subtle instructional messages and problem-solving opportunities that classroom teachers have declared to be useful. Letters to the author from his younger readers indicate their enjoyment of the stories, but they reveal far less enthusiasm for the idea of cauliflower-spinach ice cream, no matter how "good for you" it may be.

McFarland told *SATA:* "I love to write for recreation and intellectual stimulation. I mostly write about things in my life or, when writing children's books, I like to try to jump-start their imaginations.

"My writing process involves thinking about my project in its entirety, then filling in the details.

"The subjects I have written about until now involve writing imaginative children's stories and telling the life story of one of our pets from the animal's perspective."

Biographical and Critical Sources

ONLINE

The Ralph Books, http://www.ralph-jimbo.com/ (February 11, 2003).

*   *   *

MODESITT, Jeanne 1953-

Personal

Born August 2, 1953, in Long Beach, CA; daughter of George Edward (a physicist) and Lorraine Helen (Stasky) Modesitt; married Robin Thomas Spowart (a children's book illustrator), September 16, 1978. *Education:* University of California—Santa Cruz, B.A. (with honors), 1981; Oregon State University, M.A. (with honors), 1986. *Politics:* Natural Law Party.

Addresses

Home—2066 Wilton Dr., Cambria, CA 93428. *Agent*—Barbara Kouts, P.O. Box 560, Bellport, NY 11713.

Career

Writer.

Member

Society of Children's Book Writers and Illustrators.

Writings

FOR CHILDREN; PICTURE BOOKS

Vegetable Soup, illustrated by Robin Spowart, Macmillan (New York, NY), 1988.
The Night Call, illustrated by Robin Spowart, Viking Kestrel (New York, NY), 1989.
The Story of Z, illustrated by Lonni Sue Johnson, Picture Book Studio (Saxonville, MA), 1990.
Sometimes I Feel Like a Mouse: A Book About Feelings, illustrated by Robin Spowart, Scholastic (New York, NY), 1992.
(Compiler) *Songs of Chanukah,* illustrated by Robin Spowart, Little, Brown (Boston, MA), 1992.
Mama, If You Had a Wish, illustrated by Robin Spowart, Green Tiger Press (New York, NY), 1993.
Lunch with Milly, illustrated by Robin Spowart, Bridge-Water Books (Mahwah, NJ), 1995.

Jeanne Modesitt

It's Hanukkah!, Holiday House (New York, NY), 1999.

Little Bunny's Easter Surprise, illustrated by Robin Spowart, Simon & Schuster (New York, NY), 1999.

One, Two, Three Valentine's Day: A Counting Book, illustrated by Robin Spowart, Boyds Mills Press (Honesdale, PA), 2002.

Little Bunny's Christmas Tree, illustrated by Robin Spowart, Simon & Schuster (New York, NY), 2002.

Contributor of short stories to children's periodicals, including several for *Spider Magazine.*

Work in Progress

A collection of humorous stories for kids ages seven to ten.

Sidelights

Jeanne Modesitt has been writing children's stories for books and magazines since 1986. Working mostly with her husband, Robin Spowart, as illustrator, she has published ten picture books. Once she playfully told *SATA* about her enthusiasm for Spowart's work: "I am married to one of my favorite children's book illustrators, Robin Spowart. We like working together—maybe because we like each other (and each other's work) so much!"

Their first picture book, *Vegetable Soup,* which describes the successful efforts of two rabbits to make a meal with no carrots, earned the praise of a *Publishers Weekly* critic who called it "good company at anyone's

table." *Night Call,* which tells how two stuffed animals help return a fallen star to the sky, was recommended by Carolyn Polese in *School Library Journal* as an "appealing bedtime story." And *The Story of Z,* about the letter Z's attempts to form her own alphabet after becoming tired of always being last, received a good review from Ruth Semrau in *School Library Journal,* who described the book as a story of "unparalleled zest" in which "every page zings with zip."

In *Sometimes I Feel Like a Mouse,* different animals' expressions suggest various emotions, encouraging children to explore their own feelings. *Booklist*'s Stephanie Zvirin recommended the work, calling it "a fine way to introduce difficult concepts to young children." Similarly, *Mama, If You Had a Wish* deals with children's feelings. It assures a worried bunny in the mother bunny's words, "I love you just the way you are." A *Publishers Weekly* reviewer praised this book for achieving a "worthy purpose: promoting acceptance" and found the author's message "directly on target." A tale that complements *Vegetable Soup, Lunch with Milly* tells the story of a child who invites an adult to lunch but forgets to make dessert. When Milly shows her hostess how they can get dessert together, the tale ends on a high note. In her *School Library Journal* review, Carolyn Noah punned that "readers will find *Lunch with Milly* to be a quietly satisfying snack."

Among the couple's other books that deal with holidays are *It's Hanukkah!, One, Two, Three Valentine's Day: A Counting Book,* and *Little Bunny's Easter Surprise.* The first picture book, a "serviceable addition" to quote a reviewer of *School Library Journal,* uses rhyming couplets to tell how a family of mice celebrates the holiday. They light the menorah, eat latkes, and dance Jewish dances. *Little Bunny's Easter Surprise,* which a *Publishers Weekly* reviewer called an "affectionate holiday tale," revolves around Little Bunny's efforts to surprise his parents for a change. Like this "calming, comfortable" tale, to use a *Kirkus Reviews* contributor's words, about turning the tables on the adult rabbits, many of Modesitt's works involve humor because, as she told *SATA,* "I like writing funny stories most of all. That's because when I write them, I laugh, and I love to laugh. I also love to hear others laugh when they read my stories. Laughing is definitely one of my most favorite things in the world."

Reflecting on her career, Modesitt described her writing habits and the ups and downs of authorship. "I spend about four hours a day writing. I don't use a computer; I prefer writing with pencil and paper. For my final copy (the one I send to editors) I use a typewriter. Everybody tells me I will get a computer some day, but I don't think so. I like to keep my tools as simple as possible.

"I took two or three writing classes in college, but I don't remember much about them. Mostly, I wrote stuff for adults in the classes and didn't have much fun. I have much more fun now.

"One of the hardest things for me as a writer is the number of rejections I get from editors. 'Your story just doesn't work,' they say, or 'This story is supposed to be funny?! What are you, a nut or something?' Rejections hurt; but I never let rejections stop me from doing what I love.

"Sometimes people tell me I should write a book about what it was like for me to grow up in a family where there was abuse. But while I greatly respect those who write such books, I don't want to write one like that. I would feel very, very sad reliving certain memories. I much prefer to spend my time writing words that cheer me, that make me laugh, that make me want to hug the whole wide world."

Biographical and Critical Sources

BOOKS

Modesitt, Jeanne, *Sometimes I Feel Like a Mouse: A Book About Feelings,* illustrated by Robin Spowart, Scholastic (New York, NY), 1992.

PERIODICALS

Booklist, April 1, 1988, review of *Vegetable Soup,* p. 1352; November 1, 1989, review of *The Night Call,* p. 554; September 1, 1992, p. 63; October 1, 1992, Stephanie Zvirin, review of *Sometimes I Feel Like a Mouse: A Book About Feelings,* p. 337; July, 1993, p. 1975.

Horn Book, November-December, 1992, review of *Sometimes I Feel Like a Mouse,* p. 712.

Kirkus Reviews, December 15, 1998, review of *Little Bunny's Easter Surprise,* p. 1801.

Publishers Weekly, January 29, 1988, review of *Vegetable Soup,* 428; May 11, 1990, p. 57; November 2, 1992, p. 69; May 31, 1993, review of *Mama, If You Had a Wish,* p. 52; January 2, 1995, review of *Lunch with Milly,* p. 76; January 11, 1999, review of *Little Bunny's Easter Surprise,* p. 70; September 27, 1999, review of *It's Hanukkah!,* p. 52.

School Library Journal, January, 1990, Carolyn Polese, review of *The Night Call,* p. 86; January, 1991, Ruth Semrau, review of *The Story of Z,* p. 78; August, 1993, p. 148; February, 1995, Carolyn Noah, review of *Lunch with Milly,* p. 229; March, 1995, Carolyn Noah, review of *Lunch with Milly,* p. 184; October, 1999, M.M.H., review of *It's Hanukkah!,* p. 72.*

* * *

MORPURGO, Michael 1943-

Personal

Born October 5, 1943, in St. Albans, England; son of Tony Valentine Bridge (stepson of Jake Eric Morpurgo)

Michael Morpurgo

and Catherine Noel Kippe; married Clare Allen, 1963; children: three. *Education:* Attended Sandhurst; King's College, London, B.A., 1967.

Addresses

Home—Langlands, Iddesleigh, Winkleigh, Devon EX19 8SN, England. *Agent*—David Higham Associates, 5-8 Lower John Street, Golden Square, London W1R 4HA, England.

Career

Writer, teacher. Primary school teacher, 1967-75. Joint founder and director, Farms for City Children, 1976—; opened Nethercourt House farm, 1976, Treginnis Isaf, 1989, and Wick Court, 1998.

Awards, Honors

Runner-up, Whitbread Award, 1982, for *War Horse;* Runner-up, Carnegie Medal, 1988, for *King of the Cloud Forests;* Runner-up, *Guardian* Award, 1991, for *Waiting for Anya;* Silver Pencil Award, Holland; Best Books selection, *School Library Journal,* 1995, and Top of the List selection for Youth Fiction, *Booklist,* 1995, both for *The War of Jenkins' Ear;* Whitbread Award, 1995, for *The Wreck of the Zanzibar;* Smarties Gold Medal Award, 1997, for *The Butterfly Lion;* Editor's Choice, *Books for Keeps,* 1999, for *Cockadoodle-Doo, Mr. Sultana!* Awarded the MBE, 1999, for work in creating Farms for City Children.

Writings

FICTION; FOR CHILDREN

It Never Rained: Five Stories, illustrated by Isabelle Hutchins, Macmillan (London, England), 1974.

Thatcher Jones, illustrated by Trevor Ridley, Macmillan (London, England), 1975.

Long Way Home, Macmillan (London, England), 1975.

(Compiler with Graham Barrett) *The Story-Teller,* Ward Lock (London, England), 1976.

Friend or Foe, illustrated by Trevor Stubley, Macmillan (London, England), 1977.

What Shall We Do with It?, illustrated by Priscilla Lamont, Ward Lock (London, England), 1978.

Do All You Dare, photographs by Bob Cathmoir, Ward Lock (London, England), 1978.

(Editor) *All around the Year,* photographs by James Ravilious, drawings by Robin Ravilious, new poems by Ted Hughes, J. Murray (London, England), 1979.

The Day I Took the Bull By the Horn, Ward Lock (London, England), 1979.

The Ghost-Fish, Ward Lock (London, England), 1979.

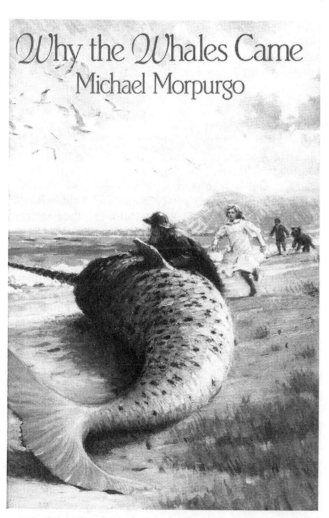

Friends work together to help save a group of beached whales in Morpurgo's story Why the Whales Came. *(Jacket illustration by Walter Rane.)*

Love at First Sight, Ward Lock (London, England), 1979.

That's How, Ward Lock (London, England), 1979.

The Marble Crusher and Other Stories, illustrated by Trevor Stubley, Macmillan (London, England), 1980.

The Nine Lives of Montezuma, illustrated by Margery Gill, Kaye and Ward (Kingswood, England), 1980.

Miss Wirtle's Revenge, illustrated by Graham Clarke, Kaye and Ward (Kingswood, England), 1981.

The White Horse of Zennor: And Other Stories from below the Eagle's Nest, Kaye and Ward (Kingswood, England), 1982.

The War Horse, Kaye and Ward (Kingswood, England), 1982, Greenwillow (New York, NY), 1983.

Twist of Gold, Kaye and Ward (Kingswood, England), 1983, Viking (New York, NY), 1993.

Little Foxes, illustrated by Gareth Floyd, Kaye and Ward (Kingswood, England), 1984.

Why the Whales Came, Scholastic (New York, NY), 1985.

Tom's Sausage Lion, illustrated by Robina Green, A. & C. Black (London, England), 1986, BBC Consumer Publishing, 2003.

Jo-Jo, the Melon Donkey, illustrated by Chris Molan, Simon & Schuster (New York, NY), 1987, illustrated by Tony Kerins, Heinemann (London, England), 1995.

King of the Cloud Forests, Viking (New York, NY), 1988.

My Friend Walter, Heinemann (London, England), 1988.

(With Shoo Rayner) *Mossop's Last Chance,* A. & C. Black (London, England), 1988.

Mr. Nobody's Eyes, Heinemann (London, England), 1989, Viking (New York, NY), 1990.

Conker, Heinemann (London, England), 1989.

(With Shoo Rayner) *Albertine, Goose Queen,* A. & C. Black (London, England), 1989.

(With Shoo Rayner) *Jigger's Day Off,* A. & C. Black (London, England), 1990.

Waiting for Anya, Heinemann (London, England), 1990, Viking (New York, NY), 1991.

Colly's Barn, Heinemann (London, England), 1991.

(With Shoo Rayner) *And Pigs Might Fly!,* A. & C. Black (London, England), 1991.

The Sandman and the Turtles, Heinemann (London, England), 1991, Philomel (New York, NY), 1994.

(With Shoo Rayner) *Martians at Mudpuddle Farm,* A. & C. Black (London, England), 1992.

The War of Jenkins' Ear, Heinemann (London, England), 1993, Philomel (New York, NY), 1995.

Snakes and Ladders, Heinemann (London, England), 1994.

(Editor) *Ghostly Haunts,* illustrated by Nilesh Mistry, Pavilion (London, England), 1994.

Arthur, High King of Britain, illustrated by Michael Foreman, Pavilion (London, England), 1994, Harcourt (San Diego, CA), 1995.

The Dancing Bear, illustrated by Christian Birmingham, Young Lion (London, England), 1994, Houghton (Boston, MA), 1996.

(With Shoo Rayner) *Stories from Mudpuddle Farm* (including the previously published *And Pigs Might Fly!, Martians at Mudpuddle Farm,* and *Jigger's Day Off*), A. & C. Black (London, England), 1995.

(With Shoo Rayner) *Mum's the Word,* A. & C. Black (London, England), 1995.

(Editor) *Muck and Magic: Tales from the Countryside,* forward by HRH The Princess Royal, Heinemann (London, England), 1995.

The Wreck of the Zanzibar, illustrated by Christian Birmingham, Viking (New York, NY), 1995.

Blodin the Beast, illustrated by Christina Balit, Fulcrum (Golden, CO), 1995.

Sam's Duck, illustrated by Keith Bowen, Collins (London, England), 1996.

The King in the Forest, illustrated by T. Kerins, Simon & Schuster (New York, NY), 1996.

The Butterfly Lion, illustrated by Christian Birmingham, Collins (London, England), 1996.

The Ghost of Grania O'Malley, Heinemann (London, England), 1996, Viking (New York, NY), 1996.

Robin of Sherwood, illustrated by Michael Foreman, Harcourt (San Diego, CA), 1996.

(Editor) *Beyond the Rainbow Warrior,* Pavilion (London, England), 1996.

The Marble Crusher (includes *The Marble Crusher, Colly's Barn,* and *Conker*), Mammoth (London, England), 1997.

Farm Boy, illustrated by Michael Foreman, Pavilion (London, England), 1997.

Red Eyes at Night, illustrated by Tony Ross, Hodder (London, England), 1997.

Wartman, illustrated by Joanna Carey, Barrington Stoke (Edinburgh, Scotland), 1998.

Escape from Shangri-La, Philomel Books (New York, NY), 1998.

Cockadoodle-Doo, Mr. Santana!, illustrated by Michael Foreman, Scholastic (New York, NY), 1998.

(Reteller) *Joan of Arc of Domremy,* illustrated by Michael Foreman, Harcourt Brace (San Diego, CA), 1999.

(Compiler) *Animal Stories,* illustrated by Andrew Davidson, Kingfisher (New York, NY), 1999.

Kensuke's Kingdom, illustrated by Michael Foreman, Heinemann (London, England), 1999, Scholastic (New York, NY), 2003.

The Rainbow Bear, illustrated by Michael Foreman, Doubleday (London, England), 1999.

Billy the Kid, illustrated by Michael Foreman, Pavilion (London, England), 2000.

Black Queen, Corgi Juvenile (London, England), 2000.

(Compiler) *The Kingfisher Book of Great Boy Stories: A Treasury of Classics from Children's Literature,* Kingfisher (New York, NY), 2000.

Wombat Goes Walkabout, illustrated by Christian Birmingham, Candlewick Press (Cambridge, MA), 2000.

The Silver Swan, illustrated by Christian Birmingham, Phyllis Fogelman Books (New York, NY), 2000.

From Hereabout Hill, Mammoth (London, England), 2000.

Who's A Big Bully Then?, illustrated by Joanna Carey, Barrington Stoke (Edinburgh, Scotland), 2000.

Mister Skip, Roaring Good Reads, 2000.

The King in the Forest, Hodder and Stoughton (London England), 2001.

Toro! Toro!, illustrated by Michael Foreman, Collins (London, England), 2002.

Out of the Ashes, illustrated by Michael Foreman, Macmillan (London, England), 2002.

Cool, HarperCollins Canada (Toronto, Ontario, Canada), 2002.

Because a Fire Was in My Head, Faber and Faber (London, England), 2002.

Beastman of Ballyloch, HarperCollins Canada (Toronto, Ontario, Canada), 2002.

Jim Davis: A High-Sea Adventure, Scholastic (New York, NY), 2002.

The Last Wolf, illustrated by Michael Foreman, Doubleday (London, England), 2002.

Sleeping Sword, Egmont (London, England), 2003.

Gentle Giant, Picture Lions (London, England), 2003.

Mairi's Mermaid, Crabtree, 2003.

OTHER

(Compiler with Clifford Simmons) *Living Poets,* J. Murray (London, England), 1974.

(Librettist) *Words of Songs,* music by Phyllis Tate, Oxford University Press (London, England), 1985.

Some of Morpurgo's books have been translated into Irish and Welsh.

Adaptations

Why the Whales Came was adapted for a movie titled *When the Whales Came,* 1989, by Golden Swan Films; *My Friend Walter* was adapted for a television movie by Portobello Films for Thames Television and WonderWorks, 1993; *Out of the Ashes* was adapted for a television movie.

Sidelights

"I write stories, not books," British author Michael Morpurgo told a school class in an interview for *Young Writer.* "And I write stories for me—for both the child and the adult in me. . . . My stories are about children, not for them, because I know children—they interest me, children of all ages, even adult ones." Morpurgo, since leaving childhood himself, has hardly spent a day out of the company of children: a father by twenty, he was a grandfather at forty-three; a teacher in primary schools for a decade, he has helped to run Farms for City Children—a venture that brings urban children to the countryside—since 1976. In his sixty-plus novels and picture books for young readers, Morpurgo has consistently demonstrated this knowledge of and appreciation for children.

"Undoubtedly a leading figure in the field of children's books," according to *Children's Fiction Sourcebook,* Morpurgo blends adventure, fantasy and moral drama in his lyrical yet always understated prose. Consistent themes for Morpurgo are the conquest of evil by good and the vindication of virtues such as loyalty, hard work and determination, things that might seem somewhat old-fashioned in the relativistic age of cyberspace. His books are generally uplifting and teach ethical lessons, but Morpurgo is never preachy; the story is primary in such books as *Why the Whales Came, War Horse, The*

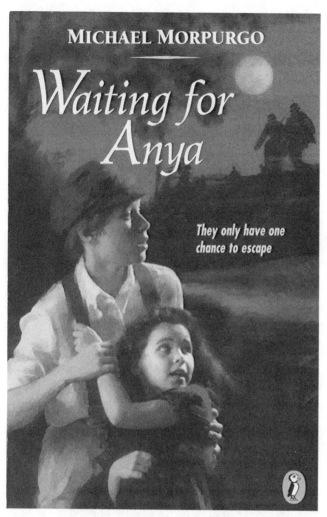

Jo risks his own life to help smuggle Jewish children to safety across the border of southern France to Spain in **Waiting for Anya.** *(Jacket illustration by Joe DiCesare.)*

War of Jenkins' Ear, Waiting for Anya, The Wreck of the Zanzibar, The Butterfly Lion, Escape from Shangri-La, Billy the Kid, and *Out of the Ashes,* although each propounds a moral dilemma. Much of Morpurgo's fiction is historical, set in the recent past, and in such exotic locales as the Scilly Islands, China, Renaissance Venice, and the Pyrenees. His subjects range from war to rural life, from the sea to the boarding school, and his writing combines stark realism with touches of fancy and magic.

Morpurgo was born on October 5, 1943, in St. Albans, England, into a country that had been at war for over four years. At the age of seven he went away to a grammar school in Sussex where he was introduced to "class war," as he told *Booklist*'s Ilene Cooper. "The schoolboys and the village boys had fights and difficulties; walking along cow paths, we'd hurl insults at each other. It was an indication that there were people out there who didn't like you because of the way you spoke, and we didn't like them either. And while things have changed since the 1950s, class still seems to me to be a cancer that riddles our society." As a young schoolboy

Morpurgo was thought of "as good at rugby and a bit stupid," he remarked in *Young Writer.* "As a child I think I lived up to that expectation. . . . I never liked writing as a child." It was not until much later that Morpurgo began to love reading, especially the novels of Robert Louis Stevenson, Paul Gallico, and Ernest Hemingway, and the poetry of Ted Hughes, a poet laureate of England and a close friend of Morpurgo's.

At age fourteen Morpurgo entered Kings School in Canterbury, graduating in 1962. The following year he married Clare Allen, daughter of the well-known publisher of Penguin books. They ultimately had three children together, two sons and one daughter. Graduating from King's College in London in 1967, Morpurgo became a teacher for a time after graduation, and also served as an army officer. It was during his teaching career that he determined to become a writer. "I had a notion I could tell a tale when the children I was teaching really seemed to want to listen to the tales I told them," Morpurgo noted in *Young Writer.* "An acid test." Reading Ted Hughes's *Poetry in the Making* influenced Morpurgo to think that he too could string words together rhythmically and literally got him writing. "No better invitation to write was ever written and I accepted," Morpurgo remarked in *Young Writer.* "I love the sound of words, the rhythm of a sentence."

Living in the countryside, Morpurgo also wanted to introduce city-born and bred kids to the wonders of nature. To that end, he and his wife started Farms for City Children in the 1970s. Under this program, kids come to stay at the farm and work and take care of animals for several weeks. So popular has the program become, that the Morpurgos operate three farms where more than two thousand children per year have the opportunity to get in touch with nature and themselves. In 1999, Morpurgo and his wife were honored in the Queen's Birthday List with the MBE for their work with Farms for City Children.

Much of Morpurgo's early work has not been published in the United States. This includes both short novels for ten-to twelve-year-olds, and picture books for younger readers. Already with this early work, however, Morpurgo was making a name for himself in England as a writer "successfully outside the mainstream," as Josephine Karavasil described his work in a *Times Literary Supplement* review of *Miss Wirtle's Revenge,* Morpurgo's tale about a little girl who competes successfully against a class full of boys. His 1980 *Nine Lives of Montezuma* is a short novel detailing nine narrow-escape adventures of a farmyard cat named Montezuma. Told from the cat's point of view, the book also details the farming year as a background story, with "continuity" being the theme of the book, according to Margery Fisher of *Growing Point.* When Montezuma dies, the cat knows that there is a descendant to take its place in the scheme of things on the farm. *Junior Bookshelf* critic D. A. Young noted that the story "is told without sentimentality, though not without sentiment," and concluded that the book could be "recommended with confidence to cat-lovers of any age."

This same characteristic—appealing writing about animals without sentimentality—was the hallmark of Morpurgo's first book to be published in the United States, *War Horse.* Inspired by a painting of a horse in the village hall near Morpurgo's home, the book is the story of the First World War seen through the eyes of Joey, a farm horse commandeered in 1914. Cavalry stood little chance against the mechanized horrors of modern war; Joey endures bombardment and capture by the Germans. He is set to work pulling ambulances and guns, worked by different masters but never forgetting young Albert, the kind son of his original owner back in England. In the end, persistence and courage pay off—Joey is reunited with Albert in Devon. Kate M. Flanagan, writing in *Horn Book,* noted that "the courage of the horse and his undying devotion to the boy" permeate this book, which she maintained was written with "elegant, old-fashioned grace." *Voice of Youth Advocates* contributor Diane G. Yates, noting that *War Horse* is based on a true story, commented: "The message about the futility and carnage of war comes across loud and clear. The characters, both human and animal, that die in the war are all the best and brightest of their generation." Margery Fisher of *Growing Point* highlighted similarities between *War Horse* and the classic, *Black Beauty,* and concluded her review by stating that Morpurgo's book "is a most accomplished piece of story-telling, full of sympathy for an animal manipulated by man but preserving its dignity." Warmly received on both sides of the Atlantic, *War Horse* helped win an international audience for Morpurgo.

Morpurgo's next book was *Twist of Gold,* set in both Ireland and the United States. When famine hits Ireland in the 1840s, Sean and Annie O'Brien set off for America to find their father, an adventurous journey that takes them first across the ocean and then across a continent by wagon train and river boat. A story of a childhood test, *Twist of Gold* is a "touching and inventive adventure story," according to Margery Fisher of *Growing Point.* Morpurgo's name became more widely recognized in the United States with the 1985 publication of *Why the Whales Came* and the book's subsequent adaptation for film. Set in 1914 on Bryher in the Scilly Islands off England's southwest coast, this is "a story full of compassion," according to *Children's Fiction Sourcebook.* Gracie and Daniel have been forbidden to associate with the strange old man on the far side of the island who is known as the Birdman to the locals. But soon the two youngsters learn that the old man is not some evil magician, but simply a person made lonely because of his deafness, and one who had to flee another of the islands as a youth because of a curse put on it. The three become fast friends with the war always hovering ominously in the background. Yet on Bryher there is a parallel war between the islanders and the sea and weather. When a whale washes ashore, the islanders must be convinced to help return it to the

sea rather than butcher it, for it was the destruction of sea life that brought the curse to the Birdman's original island. "The success of Morpurgo's novel comes . . . from its portrait of the two children and from its exploration of the blend of superstition and communal spirit existing in an isolated settlement," noted reviewer Marcus Crouch in *The Junior Bookshelf.* Cindy Darling Codell, writing in *School Library Journal,* commented that Morpurgo's language "is lean, yet lyrical," and that his descriptive paragraphs "let readers taste the salt of the sea and feel the grit of the islander's lives." Margery Fisher of *Growing Point* concluded her review by dubbing the book "a forceful and exciting narrative." Another Morpurgo novel that was adapted for film is *My Friend Walter,* a whimsical story about the ghost of Sir Walter Raleigh.

The Scilly Islands also provide a setting for Morpurgo's Whitbread Award-winning 1995 *Wreck of the Zanzibar,* the story of a childhood on Bryher Island as told through the diary of Laura, and of her secret treasure, Zanzibar, a wooden tortoise. Laura's narrative is the record of a harsh life, of adversity and the will to overcome. *Junior Bookshelf* reviewer Marcus Crouch commented that *The Wreck of the Zanzibar,* while a short book, is "by no means a slight one," and praised the "beautiful timing throughout." *Horn Book*'s Elizabeth S. Watson noted that "The slight book makes a solid impact on the reader, who will finish [it] with a satisfied smile." A further tale with an island setting is Morpurgo's *Ghost of Grania O'Malley,* a 1996 work set off the coast of Ireland and involving young Jessie, her American cousin Jack, and the ghost of the female pirate, Grania O'Malley, as they battle to prevent the ecological destruction of the island.

Morpurgo returned to an animal-centered story with *Jo-Jo, the Melon Donkey,* a picture book for older children set in 16th-century Venice. Jo-Jo is a bedraggled old donkey who is laughed at when attempting to sell melons in the main square. The Doge's (chief magistrate's) daughter, however, sees the plaintive look in the animal's eyes and decides to be his friend. When the Doge offers to give his daughter any horse in the kingdom, she opts for Jo-Jo, to her father's disgust. But when Jo-Jo helps to save the city from a flood, he becomes a hero and the Doge allows his daughter her wish. Amy Spaulding in *School Library Journal* noted that the "writing style follows that of the literary fairy tale, being at once simple and elegant," and a *Kirkus Reviews* critic commented: "With a nice blend of humor and sadness, Morpurgo brings to life the vibrancy of 16th-century Venice." Other Morpurgo picture books include the "Mudpuddle Farm" series with Shoo Rayner, and for older children, *Blodin the Beast* and *The Dancing Bear,* the latter being the story of young singer Roxanne and the orphaned bear cub she has raised. When a film crew comes to her remote village to make a video, Roxanne is lured by bright lights, and decides ultimately to leave with the group, pursuing fame and fortune as an entertainer. Her bear dies the following day.

As the narrator of the story, Roxanne's former teacher, says, "There's a lesson to be learned, if one just listens to my tale." *School Library Journal* contributor Kathy East, however, felt Morpurgo's lesson "likely to appeal more to adults, who will relate to the elderly narrator and his style, than to children."

Morpurgo has continued with picture books throughout his career, often teaming with Michael Foreman or with Christian Birmingham. Working with the former, Morpurgo wrote the 1999 *The Rainbow Bear,* about a polar bear who decides to hunt rainbows rather than seals. The book is "a fable about the folly of trying to become something that you naturally are not," according to Kate Kellaway, writing in London's *Observer.* Kellaway further noted that the book is "gracefully told and elegantly concluded." Another picture book collaboration with Foreman is *Cockadoodle-Doo, Mr. Sultana!,* about a rooster who refuses to be cheated out of a button it finds. For Mary Medlicott, writing in *School Librarian,* this tale "is rumbustiously full of life," with language "as rich as a plum pudding."

Working with Birmingham, Morpurgo has created a number of picture books, including *Wombat Goes Walkabout* and *The Silver Swan.* Catherine McClellan of *Magpies* felt that the story of a young wombat who becomes lost from its mother after digging a hole and then sitting in it to have a think is a "beautiful picture book." The hapless wombat meets up with a number of Australian animals as it searches for its mother, all of whom shake their heads at his digging and thinking skills. However, these are the very skills that ultimately save them all when they are threatened by a wildfire. In *The Silver Swan,* a swan is killed by a fox, breaking the heart of the boy who revered the dead animal. "Morpurgo writes compassionately and convincingly," commented Nikki Gamble in *School Librarian.* Gamble also praised Birmingham's "stunning artwork" in this "reflective story for quiet moments."

Morpurgo's love of animals finds its way into many of his novels for young adult readers, as well. The protagonist of *Little Foxes,* young Billy, feels attracted to the wildlife inhabiting land by a ruined church; the mythic Yeti save a lost boy in *King of the Cloud Forests;* Ocky the chimpanzee becomes a companion for Harry Hawkins in *Mr. Nobody's Eyes;* and giant turtles populate the dreams of Mike in *The Sandman and the Turtles.* In *King of the Cloud Forests,* young Ashley Anderson must make his way with a Tibetan Buddhist across China to India and safety, one step ahead of the invading Japanese. Crossing the Himalayas, he and his guide are separated. Lost and near starvation, Ashley is rescued by a band of the legendary Yeti, red-furred, ape-like creatures who revere the boy as a god. Ashley stays in their idyllic community for a time, but is finally reunited with his guide and ultimately makes it safely to England. Jacqueline Simms, writing in *Times Literary Supplement,* noted that "this marvelous adventure story . . . will surely become a perennial favourite,"

while Roger Sutton of the *Bulletin of the Center for Children's Books* thought that this "brief and dramatic novel . . . may woo reluctant readers back to the fold."

Two of Morpurgo's most compelling novels with child protagonists are *Waiting for Anya* and *The War of Jenkins' Ear. Waiting for Anya* relates the story of the plight of Jewish children in World War II France. The novel is set in the Pyrenees just after the surrender of the French forces, and its protagonist Jo, a young shepherd, becomes involved in a scheme to save the children when he discovers that a man named Benjamin is hiding them at a farm near the village of Lescun. Benjamin is smuggling the children across the border into Spain; he is also waiting for his own daughter to make her way to this safe house from Paris. Jo begins delivering supplies to the farm, a job made much riskier when the Nazis occupy Lescun and threaten to kill anyone aiding fugitives. Soon, however, the entire town of Lescun is helping to get the children across the border. Though Benjamin is captured and sent to die at Auschwitz, Anya does finally turn up at the farm and is saved at the end of this "gripping, clearly written story," as Ellen Fader described it in *Horn Book.* Marcus Crouch, in a favorable review for *The Junior Bookshelf,* commented that *Waiting for Anya* "is an intensely exciting story guaranteed to keep a sensitive reader on the edge of his chair." Crouch added that Morpurgo's story is "rich in the qualities which make for critical approval," concluding: "There have been many Second World War stories for the young, none which deals more convincingly with its perils and dilemmas."

The War of Jenkins' Ear is an English boarding school tale in which young Toby Jenkins meets a remarkable boy named Christopher who claims to be the reincarnation of Jesus. Christopher begins to develop a following before being betrayed by one of his friends and expelled from the school for blasphemy. *Quill and Quire* contributor Joanne Schott commented: "A strict school of 40 years ago makes a credible setting and gives scope for the complex relationships Morpurgo uses to examine questions of belief and credulity, deception and self-deception, loyalty and the pressure of doubt, and much more." Tim Rausch, writing in *School Library Journal,* called *The War of Jenkins' Ear* a book that "tackles provocative themes, dealing with the issues of hate, revenge, prejudice, and especially faith in an intelligent and fresh manner."

Morpurgo's 1996 novel, *The Butterfly Lion* is a blend of fantasy and fiction, a story within a story about a ten-year-old boy who runs away from his miserable school and ends up in a dusty house where an old widow shows him the figure of a giant lion cut into the chalk hillside. This woman tells the boy about her dead husband, Bertie, who, as a youth growing up in South Africa, had as his pet and only friend a white lion. When his father sold the lion one day, Bertie vowed to find him again. This he did during World War One and then brought the animal with him to England where it ultimately died.

Bertie thereafter spent forty years carving its likeness in the hillside, a figure visited by thousands of butterflies after the rains. Returning to school, the young boy learns that both Bertie and his widow had died many years before. "The story sounds hokey," noted *Booklist*'s Kathleen Squires, "but Morpurgo evocatively captures the South African landscape and presents young, lonely Bertie's heartbreak and blossoming friendship and love . . . with genuine emotion and tender passion." Reviewing the novel in *School Library Journal,* Gebregeorgis Yohannes concluded, "In addition to being a successful adventure story, the book demonstrates the value of character—of keeping promises, standing up for one's beliefs, and courage under fire." *The Butterfly Lion,* "at once marvelous and matter-of-fact," according to a writer for *Kirkus Reviews,* won England's prestigious Smarties Gold Medal Award in 1997. "This dreamlike story is suffused with a man's lifelong love for a rare, gentle animal friend," the critic for *Kirkus Reviews* concluded.

Morpurgo has also breathed new life into old legends. His retelling of the Arthurian tales in *Arthur, High King of Britain* is "the real thing—darkness and all," according to Heather McCammond-Watts in *Bulletin of the Center for Children's Books.* McCammond-Watts explained that the Arthur of Morpurgo's book, who rescues a young time-traveler from the modern era, "is a complex character: an impetuous youth, an august yet sometimes rash ruler, a jealous lover, and a tortured man trying to live up to his epic persona." *School Library Journal* contributor Helen Gregory concluded that Morpurgo's Arthur "stands with the best." With *Robin of Sherwood,* Morpurgo added twists to the old tale—an albino Marion for example—that creates an

"outstanding new version of the Robin Hood legend," according to Nancy Zachary in *Voice of Youth Advocates.* "Shelve this treasure alongside Howard Pyle's and Ian Serrailler's classic folktales," concluded Zachary. Similarly, *Booklist*'s Carolyn Phelan found the book to be a "fine, original piece of storytelling, faithful to the legend of Robin Hood."

Additionally, Morpurgo has tackled the legend of the Maid of Orleans in his 1999 *Joan of Arc of Domremy,* a tale that begins in the modern day when young Eloise Hardy moves with her family to Orleans, France and begins studying legends of Joan. Steeping herself in such lore, Eloise one day hears Joan's voice telling her the story of her life. "Morpurgo is an accomplished writer and storyteller," wrote Shirley Wilton in a *School Library Journal* review. "Facts and popular beliefs, history and legend are drawn upon to create an exciting tale." A reviewer for *Publishers Weekly* felt that Morpurgo's storytelling "is premised on faith," and concluded that the book's "polish and panoramic scope will lure and hold readers."

With *Farm Boy,* Morpurgo returned to the here and now to detail the memories of four generations of an English farming family. Set once again in Morpurgo's beloved Devon, the book tells on one level the story of a young boy who goes to visit his grandfather on the farm. His grandfather in turn enchants the boy with tales of how farming was done before mechanization, capturing the spirit of rural life before the internal combustion engine and agribusiness. "Morpurgo's storytelling style is unhurried," noted *School Library Journal*'s Lee Bock, "reflecting great skill at giving unique voices

A young farm boy follows the struggles of a family of swans. (*From* The Silver Swan, *illustrated by Christian Birmingham.*)

to his characters." Bock continued, "The memories of [Grandpa's] horse are particularly poignant, and readers will learn many details about life during the early part of this century and World War I." A critic for *Kirkus Reviews* called the book "a small gem" and an "expertly crafted reminder that stories can link generations."

Memories of World War II figure in *Escape from Shangri-La,* in which an old tramp, Popsicle, watching Cessie's house, turns out to be her long lost grandfather. When the old man has a stroke, he is put in the Shangri-La nursing home, but he is withering away there. Finally Cessie finds her grandfather's real home, an old lifeboat once used to evacuate the British forces from Dunkirk during the Second World War. From a photograph and news clippings, Cessie learns her grandfather took part in this heroic effort, and the sight of a faded photo of the Frenchwoman who hid him from the Germans when he fell off the boat rescuing others makes Popsicle recall the past. Cessie helps her grandfather and other residents of the home make a break for it; they head to France to track down this woman, only to discover she never returned from German arrest in 1940. Going back to England, the entire family is again happily reunited. "Readers will enjoy the climactic adventure and respond on a deeper level to the friendship between a spirited child and a lifelong loner," wrote John Peters in a *Booklist* review.

Morpurgo may well be one of the most versatile children's writers at work. Nearing his third decade of writing, his production and range have neither slowed nor narrowed. His themes and topics of books from the new millennium take readers from a Robinson Crusoe-type adventure yarn to a young girl recording the tragedy of the outbreak of disease on her farm, to the reminiscences of an old man. Morpurgo does not miss a beat as he changes from one era to another or from adventure to social commentary. In *Kensuke's Kingdom* he sets a young boy adrift on an island, on his own except for a dog and a mysterious old Japanese man, the Kensuke of the title, who slowly allows the boy—who fell overboard from the family boat—into his heart. "This must be ranked alongside Morpurgo's best," declared Linda Newbery in a *School Librarian* review, "and like several of his most successful stories, has the feel of a fable." Julia Eccleshore, reviewing the audiobook of the same title in *Books for Keeps,* also had praise for this "excellent adventure," noting that it is a "story full of insight and mood changes."

The reflections of age are conveyed in several other Morpurgo titles. *The Last Wolf* features an old man who is researching his family tree on the computer that his granddaughter has given him to use. While doing his research, he stumbles across a tale set during the Jacobite rebellion in Scotland in 1745, when a young boy whose parents had been killed found a similarly orphaned wolf pup. Together the two managed to escape to Canada and a new life. In *Toro! Toro!,* a grandfather

tells his grandson of how he once planned to save a bull from the bullfighting ring by setting the herd free. The very night he planned to do this, however, the horrors of the Spanish Civil War reached his village when bombs killed his entire family. A reviewer for the *Times Educational Supplement* called this an "elegantly told tale," while George Hunt, writing in *Books for Keeps* similarly noted that the book was both "moving and exciting." Another old man reflects on his life from boyhood to his years of soccer-playing as a youth, and then his time in the Second World War and his capture by and subsequent escape from enemy troops in *Billy the Kid,* a graphic novel in format with illustrations by Michael Foreman. Chris Brown, writing in *School Librarian,* noted that though the book was a "skeleton" of a novel, it was still a story of "tremendous life and liveliness." Brown praised Morpurgo's "masterly structure and telling," and found that the book had a profound emotional effect. "Inevitably the tale gets behind the eyes," Brown concluded.

More traditional in format is the novel *Out of the Ashes,* in which thirteen-year-old Becky Morley keeps a diary of the disastrous outbreak of hoof-and-mouth disease in England in 2001. Becky is a farmer's daughter, proud of her dad and loving her country life and her horse. All this changes as the epidemic reaches their Devon farm—as it did all three of Morpurgo's own farms in his Farms for City Children, forcing him to close down operations for a time. Within a matter of months the work of a lifetime has been destroyed for the Morleys and other farmers like them, but the novel does end on a positive note, giving hope for the future. Chris Brown, writing in *School Librarian,* felt that Morpurgo's book "leads us into the personal tragedies and awful aftermath of the foot and mouth epidemic." Brown also called Morpurgo a "master of his art." George Hunt, writing in *Books for Keeps* likewise found *Out of the Ashes* to be a "short novel powerfully told," while a contributor for the *Times Educational Supplement* dubbed it a "hard-hitting novel" as well as a "heartfelt account."

Morpurgo has, over the years, contributed original children's literature in historical fiction, animal stories, fantasies, picture books, easy readers, and retellings of legend and myth. Often employing the rural setting that he knows so well, he typically places his young male or female protagonist in challenging situations that call up the best in them—courage, loyalty, and self-confidence. Often praised for the simple elegance of his prose style, Morpurgo's works are "heartwarming and sensitive," according to Jennifer Taylor in *St. James Guide to Young Adult Writers.* Taylor further commented, "Morpurgo's imaginative empathy, whether writing about animals or people, makes for pure gold. His novels certainly open up horizons for young readers."

Biographical and Critical Sources

BOOKS

Authors and Artists for Young Adults, Volume 37, Gale (Detroit, MI), 2001, pp. 155-164.
Children's Literature Review, Volume 51, Gale (Detroit, MI), 1999, pp. 116-151.
Hobson, Margaret, Jennifer Madden and Ray Pryterch, *Children's Fiction Sourcebook: A Survey of Children's Books for 6-13 Year Olds,* Ashgate Publishing (Aldershot, Hampshire, England), 1992, pp. 154-155.
Taylor, Jennifer, "Morpurgo, Michael," *St. James Guide to Young Adult Writers,* 2nd edition, edited by Tom Pendergast and Sara Pendergast, St. James Press (Detroit, MI), 1999, pp. 603-605.

PERIODICALS

Booklist, February 1, 1984, p. 814; September 15, 1985, p. 137; July, 1988, p. 1814; November 1, 1989, p. 564; May 1, 1990, p. 1708; August, 1990, p. 2178; March 15, 1992, p. 1364; April 1, 1993, p. 1425; September 1, 1994, p. 44; September 1, 1995, p. 53; November 15, 1995, p. 560; January 1, 1996, Ilene Cooper, "The *Booklist* Interview," p. 816; March 15, 1996, p. 1282; October 1, 1996, Carolyn Phelan, review of *Robin of Sherwood,* p. 350; June 1, 1997, Kathleen Squires, review of *The Butterfly Lion,* p. 1704; September 15, 1998, John Peters, review of *Escape from Shangri-La,* p. 231.
Books for Keeps, September, 1997, Clive Barnes, review of *Sam's Duck,* p. 23; May, 1998, Gwynneth Bailey, review of *Red Eyes at Night,* p. 24; March, 1999, Rosemary Stores, review of *Cockadoodle-Doo, Mr. Sultana!,* p. 21; May, 1999, review of *The Rainbow Bear,* p. 6; July, 2001, Julia Eccleshore, review of *Kensuke's Kingdom* (audiobook), p. 24; January, 2002, George Hunt, review of *Out of the Ashes,* p. 23; March, 2002, George Hunt, review of *Toro! Toro!,* p. 22.
Bulletin of the Center for Children's Books, July-August, 1988, Roger Sutton, review of *King of the Cloud Forests,* pp. 234-235; March, 1991, p. 172; March, 1993, p. 221; May, 1995, Heather McCammond-Watts, review of *Arthur, High King of Britain,* p. 317; December, 1995, p. 135; May, 1996, pp. 309-10; January, 1997, p. 181.
Carousel, spring, 1997, p. 17.
Growing Point, November, 1980, Margery Fisher, review of *The Nine Lives of Montezuma,* p. 3776; November, 1982, Margery Fisher, review of *War Horse,* p. 3989; January, 1984, Margery Fisher, review of *Twist of Gold,* pp. 4183-4184; January, 1987, Margery Fisher, review of *Why the Whales Came,* p. 4749; November, 1989, pp. 5240-5245.
Horn Book, December, 1983, Kate M. Flanagan, review of *War Horse,* pp. 711-12; July-August, 1991, Ellen Fader, review of *Waiting for Anya,* p. 458; March-April, 1996, Elizabeth S. Watson, review of *The Wreck of the Zanzibar,* p. 198.

Junior Bookshelf, December, 1980, D. A. Young, review of *The Nine Lives of Montezuma,* p. 294; December, 1985, Marcus Crouch, review of *Why the Whales Came,* p. 279; August, 1988, pp. 179-80; December, 1989, pp. 298-299; February, 1991, Marcus Crouch, review of *Waiting for Anya,* pp. 35-36; June, 1992, pp. 113-14; August, 1995, Marcus Crouch, review of *The Wreck of the Zanzibar,* p. 148.
Kirkus Reviews, December 1, 1987, review of *Jo-Jo, the Melon Donkey,* p. 1677; April 15, 1997, review of *The Butterfly Lion,* p. 645; December 15, 1998, review of *Farm Boy.*
Magpies, November, 1999, Catherine McClellan, review of *Wombat Goes Walkabout,* p. 6.
Observer (London, England), October 24, 1999, review of *Wombat Goes Walkabout,* p. 13, Kate Kellaway, review of *The Rainbow Bear,* p. 13.
Publishers Weekly, May 12, 1997, pp. 76-77; February 12, 1999, review of *Joan of Arc of Domremy,* p. 95.
Quill and Quire, July, 1993, Joanne Schott, review of *The War of Jenkins' Ear,* p. 59.
School Librarian, February, 1997, p. 33; autumn, 1998, Norton Hodges, review of *Escape from Shangri-La,* p. 147; spring, 1999, Jam Cooper, review of *Joan of Arc of Domremy,* pp. 40-41; summer, 1999, Mary Medlicott, review of *Cockadoodle-Doo, Mr. Sultana!,* p. 79; winter, 1999, Linda Newbery, review of *Kensuke's Kingdom,* p. 192; spring, 2001, Chris Brown, review of *Billy the Kid,* pp. 47-48; summer, 2001, Nikki Gamble, review of *The Silver Swan,* p. 90; autumn, 2001, Chris Brown, review of *Out of the Ashes,* pp. 158-159.
School Library Journal, February, 1987, Cindy Darling Codell, review of *Why the Whales Came,* p. 82; September, 1987, p. 181; April, 1988, Amy Spaulding, review of *Jo-Jo, the Melon Donkey,* p. 87; September, 1988, p. 200; November, 1990, p. 117; April, 1991, p. 122; December, 1991, p. 31; February, 1993, p. 94; November, 1993, p. 156; July, 1995, Helen Gregory, review of *Arthur, High King of Britain,* p. 89; September, 1995, Tim Rausch, review of *The War of Jenkins' Ear,* p. 219; December, 1995, "SLJ's Best Books, 1995," p. 22; May, 1996, Kathy East, review of *The Dancing Bear,* p. 114; August, 1997, Gebregeorgis Yohannes, review of *The Butterfly Lion,* p. 158; March, 1999, Lee Bock, review of *Farm Boy,* p. 212; May, 1999, Shirley Wilton, review of *Joan of Arc of Domremy,* p. 128; April, 2001, Edith Ching, review of *The Kingfisher Book of Great Boy Stories,* p. 146.
Times Educational Supplement, January 14, 1983, p. 30; January 13, 1984, p. 42; June 6, 1986, p. 54; November 27, 1987, p. 48; February 5, 1988, pp. 54, 60; March 10, 1989, p. B16; November 24, 1989, p. 27; February 15, 1991, p. 32; May 24, 1991, p. 24; July 2, 1993, p. 11; November 4, 1994, p. 89; May 31, 1995, p. 15; February 8, 2002, review of *The Last Wolf, Toro! Toro!,* and *Out of the Ashes,* pp. 20-21.
Times Literary Supplement, March 26, 1982, Josephine Karavasil, "Matters of Rhythm and Register," p. 347; February 19, 1988, Jacqueline Simms, "Magic Man," p. 200.

Voice of Youth Advocates, April, 1984, Diane G. Yates, review of *War Horse,* p. 32; February, 1997, Nancy Zachary, review of *Robin of Sherwood,* p. 330; June, 1998, Kathleen Beck, review of *The War of Jenkins' Ear,* pp. 103-104.

ONLINE

Achuka, http://www.achuka.com/ (April 20, 2003), "Achuka's Special Guest #39: Michael Morpurgo."
Young Writer, http://www.mystworld.com/youngwriter/ (February 12, 2003), "Issue 12: Michael Morpurgo."*

* * *

MURHALL, J(acqueline) J(ane) 1964-

Personal

Born April 22, 1964, in London, England; daughter of Colin and Gwendoline (Goodwin) Murhall; partner of Michael Toumey (an actor, director, and playwright); children: Saoirse Ruby Murhall-Toumey. *Education:* Reigate School of Art and Design, degree in design. *Hobbies and other interests:* Reading, theatre, cinema, traveling, music, eating, dogs.

Addresses

Home—London, England. *Agent*—c/o Author Mail, Hodder Children's Books, 338 Euston Road, London NW1 3BH England; c/o Author Mail, Bloomsbury Children's Books, 38 Soho Square, London W1D 3HB England.

Career

Author of children's books. Worked for Virgin Records, London, England; former jewelry salesperson and dealer in vintage clothes from the 1950s and 1960s. Has appeared on television and radio programs in England, and at numerous writers' festivals. Became an ambassador for Reading Is Fundamental, U.K., 2000.

Awards, Honors

Series winner of a BAFTA and two prestigious awards at the "Cartoons on the Bay" animation festival held in Italy.

Writings

Eddie and the Swine Family, illustrated by Tony Blundell, HarperCollins (London, England), 1994.
Stinkerbell, illustrated by Tony Blundell, Bloomsbury (London, England), 1996.
Stinkerbell and the Fridge Fairies, illustrated by Tony Blundell, Bloomsbury (London, England), 1997.

Author of episode "You're My Hero" for Collingwood O'Hare animated television program *Eddie and the Bear,* CITV, 2002.

"MAGNIFICENT MISFITS" SERIES; ILLUSTRATED BY ELEANOR TAYLOR

The Great Mistake, Bloomsbury (London, England), 1998.
The Ghastly Ride, Bloomsbury (London, England), 1998.
Ride Again, Bloomsbury (London, England), 1998.
The Terrible Toddler, Bloomsbury (London, England), 1998.

Series has been translated into Italian.

"STAR PETS" SERIES; ILLUSTRATED BY ELEANOR TAYLOR

On Stage, Hodder Wayland (London, England), 1999.
Make It Big, Hodder Wayland (London, England), 1999.
On TV, Hodder Wayland (London, England), 1999.
In the Spotlight, Hodder Wayland (London, England), 1999.

"ST. MISBEHAVIOURS" SERIES; ILLUSTRATED BY MARTIN REMPHRY

Disco Inferno, Hodder Children's Books (London, England), 2001.
Roman Around, Hodder Children's Books (London, England), 2001.
Go Wild!, Hodder Children's Books (London, England), 2001.
No Surrender, Hodder Children's Books (London, England), 2001.

Series has been translated into Polish.

"HORSE FORCE" SERIES; ILLUSTRATED BY GARY SWIFT

Smash and Grab Squirrels, Hodder Children's Books (London, England), 2002.
Stick 'em Up, Bunny, Hodder Children's Books (London, England), 2002.
Riddle of a Rich Rat, Hodder Children's Books (London, England), 2002.

Work in Progress

A novel for adults; a novel for teenage girls; a book series for six to ten year olds.

Sidelights

Design-school graduate J. J. Murhall worked as a vintage clothing dealer before deciding to make the break and begin a writing career in 1990. With the popularity of her first book, 1994's *Eddie and the Swine Family,* her success as a children's author was assured, and she has gone on to publish many other titles, all which contain her irreverent humor and energetic, likeable characters. *Stinkerbell,* which Murhall published in 1996, features a dirty, ill-tempered fairy who lives in a garbage can and has to contend with a group of Elvis-lookalike goblins that are even more ill-tempered than she is. Describing Murhall's bewinged protagonist as a "punk fairy," a *Books for Keeps* contributor praised *Stinkerbell* as a "short and spicy book" that would captivate pre-teen readers.

Born in London in 1964, Murhall grew up reading books by Roald Dahl and C. S. Lewis, among others. She attended the city's Reigate School of Art and Design, where she earned a degree in surface decoration and three-dimensional design. After graduation, she traveled in Europe, at one point paying her way as a jewelry salesperson on a beach in the south of France. Returning to London, she worked for Virgin Records, then decided to start her own business selling clothing from the 1950s and 1960s in a market stall on London's trendy Portobello Road. Although Murhall had lots of ideas for books spinning around in her head, she never had the time to stop and write them down. Finally, in 1988 with the birth of her daughter, she found herself at home with some free time. *Eddie and the Swine Family* was the result, and HarperCollins publishers quickly snapped it up.

Eddie and the Swine Family is told from the point of view of the family's youngest member, who, despite his age, is left in charge of his less responsible siblings when his parents are away from home. Eddie is destined for life as an "astropig" according to his doting mother, while his sister idles away her time with dreams of soap-opera stardom and his brother plans small-scale criminal activities. Praising the book's "rich mixture of characters," a *Junior Bookshelf* contributor praised *Eddie and the Swine Family* as a humorous book that leads readers on a "bizarre journey" in a pizza delivery truck as Eddie thwarts his brother's latest criminal romp and helps his siblings make "at least part of their dreams come true."

Other books by Murhall include a sequel to *Stinkerbell,* titled *Stinkerbell and the Fridge Fairies.* Content to live in her grubby dustbin, Stinkerbell is not bad at heart, and is forced to come to the aid of a group of fridge-dwelling fairies when the dastardly goblin family—the Gobs—become too much to handle. Despite expressing some reservations about having "such a scruffy . . . thing as Stinkerbell as a role model" *School Librarian* reviewer Audrey Laski found *Stinkerbell and the Fridge Fairies* to be "great fun." Murhall has also penned a number of book series for older readers. In *Go Wild!,* part of her "St. Misbehaviours" series, Students at St. Saviour's School find their highly unconventional school threatened with closure and must come to the aid of their teachers when an undercover inspector from the "Department of Unnecessary Buildings"—or DOB—poses as a geography teacher in order to find reasons to close the building down. Praising Murhall's

"firm storyline" and good choice of vocabulary, Joan Nellist noted in her *School Librarian* review that despite being painted as quirky, "teachers are drawn quite sympathetically" and that *Go Wild!* would find many fans among reluctant readers.

Making her home in London with her partner, actor, director, and playwright, Michael Toumey, and daughter Saoirse Ruby—a "major fashion fiend"—Murhall cites her favorite pastime as writing. She told *SATA:* "I still love clothes and even though I don't sell them anymore I do continue to buy them avidly. I'm also a big music fan and listen to all types. I like going to the cinema, restaurants, and the occasional club to watch live bands play."

Regarding her work habits, Murhall told *SATA:* "I get up about 8:00 a.m. After three or four cups of coffee I finally start writing about 9:30 a.m. I try to write until about 1:00 p.m. and break for lunch. I then continue to write from about 2:00 p.m. until 6:00 p.m.

"I do sound like I am very disciplined, which obviously you do have to be in order to ever get anything written. However I, like a lot of writers I'm sure, will always find excuses not to sit down and actually make a start. Especially if I am about to embark on something new! Reasons can range from: 'The dog needs *another* walk' to 'Oh look. There's an episode of *The Loveboat* on TV this morning. I wonder if that's the original 1970s version that's really brilliantly bad and tacky! I might just have to watch it!'"

Murhall offered this advice to aspiring writers: "Read, read, read all the time. Write, write, write whenever you can. Believe in and care about the characters that you create and your readers will too. Don't waste time watching tacky 1970 television programmes!"

Biographical and Critical Sources

PERIODICALS

Books for Keeps, July, 1996, review of *Stinkerbell,* p. 7.
Junior Bookshelf, August, 1994, review of *Eddie and the Swine Family,* p. 138.
School Librarian, spring, 1998, Audrey Laski, review of *Stinkerbell and the Fridge Fairies,* pp. 35-36; spring, 2002, Joan Nellist, review of *St. Misbehaviours Go Wild!,* pp. 33-34.

ONLINE

Bloomsbury Magazine.com, http://www.bloomsbury magazine.com/ (February 12, 2003), "Jacqui Murhall."

MURPHY, Kelly 1977-

Personal

Born June 1, 1977, in Boston, MA. *Education:* Rhode Island School of Design, B.F.A., 1999.

Addresses

Home—Raynham, MA. *Agent*—c/o Author Mail, Candlewick Press, 2067 Massachusetts Ave., Cambridge, MA 02140. *E-mail*—kamurphy@lycos.com or kmurphy@montserrat.edu.

Career

Freelance illustrator of books, educational products, and films, 1999—; Montserrat College of Art, Beverly, MA, instructor, 2002—.

Member

Society of Children's Book Writers and Illustrators.

Awards, Honors

Society of Illustrators Student Scholarship Award, 1999.

Writings

(Self-illustrated) *The Boll Weevil Ball,* Henry Holt & Co. (New York, NY), 2002.
(Illustrator) Stephanie Bloom, *A Place to Grow,* Bloom and Grow Books, 2002.
(Illustrator) Dianna Hutts Aston, *Loony Little,* Candlewick Press (Cambridge, MA), 2003.

Work in Progress

A story about a bird who falls out of a nest and another about a traveling dog in search of friends.

Sidelights

Freelance author and illustrator Kelly Murphy has made a name for herself with her whimsical and expressive art in different areas of illustration, including children's books, educational products, and even the independent film *Little Erin Merryweather.* Murphy was born and raised in southeastern Massachusetts, and as she wrote at her personal Web site, "after failing a few gym classes and falling asleep during geometry," she decided she would be better off developing her artistic talent. While earning her bachelor of arts degree in illustration at the Rhode Island School of Design, she won the Society of Illustrators Student Scholarship Award, and after graduation she began teaching at the Montserrat College of Art, north of Boston.

Murphy began to get involved in children's book illustration while she was at the Rhode Island School of Design. "My illustration work, which is my true pas-

Redd, a very tiny beetle, is invited to a big dance in Kelly Murphy's self-illustrated The Boll Weevil Ball.

sion, had such a narrative quality to it," she explained to *SATA.* "I loved to create images that made the viewer come up with a story themselves, but through the persuasion of friends and family I started to write those stories on paper and lay them out. *The Boll Weevil Ball* was one of those first endeavors." Many more illustration projects came rapidly as Murphy's client list expanded to include the major New York-based children's book publishers, in addition to more local clients.

While many writers wish they had the artistic talent to illustrate their own picture books, Murphy finds writing to be the hard part of the picture-book making process. She remarked to *SATA* that because she does not "have a ton of confidence in that area just yet . . . I will put it off." Then she noted, "One day I sit down and force myself to get a story board idea down. Then I am golden. I do a lot of research, either for colors, animals, landscape, culture, or compositions. For me that's the most fun part. I love filling up sketchbooks of animal studies. And then comes the process of painting, which can take several days to finish just one page. My illustrations have several layers to them, making it tedious and slow going sometimes." Murphy is excited about recent developments in the world of graphic art, especially the increase in creativity that illustrators have been allowed to demonstrate in their works. "I see so much experimentation with medium and meaning that I have not seen before. And artists are more and more willing to involve a more raw approach to conceptual work that I am thrilled by," she explained. "Children's book are becoming so much more receptive to different styles and stories than before. I am glad for this openness."

When asked what she hopes to achieve through her books, Murphy told *SATA:* "Every book has a different meaning to me, I think. Some are based on the creatures and environments, the beautiful environments they're in; others are just merely entertaining tales. But on the whole, I'd like to create stories and characters that children can associate with and learn from. Something for them to have when they grow up, and something to look back on as a great part of their childhood."

Murphy offered the following advice to aspiring writers and illustrators: "The best piece of advice I give my students is to stick in there. Don't fold, and try not to let the negative critiques get to you. Find what it is that interests you and use that as your driving force. Also, being open to experimentation with your style and concepts will keep your noggin working."

Biographical and Critical Sources

PERIODICALS

Kirkus Reviews, July 15, 2002, review of *The Boll Weevil Ball,* p. 1039.

Publishers Weekly, September 2, 2002, review of *The Boll Weevil Ball,* p. 75.

School Library Journal, September, 2002, Kristin de Lacoste, review of *The Boll Weevil Ball,* p. 202.

ONLINE

Kelly Murphy Web Site, http://www.kelmurphy.com/ (February 14, 2003).

N

NELSON, Theresa 1948-

Personal

Born August 15, 1948, in Beaumont, TX; daughter of David Rogers, Jr. (an insurance executive) and Alice Carroll (a real estate agent; maiden name, Hunter) Nelson; married Kevin Cooney (an actor), September 26, 1968; children: Michael Christopher, Brian David, Errol Andrew. *Education:* University of St. Thomas, B.A. (magna cum laude), 1972. *Politics:* Democrat. *Religion:* Roman Catholic. *Hobbies and other interests:* "Singing, dancing, playing the piano. Most of all I love reading and going to movies and plays."

Addresses

Home—3508 Woodcliff Rd., Sherman Oaks, CA 91403. *E-mail*—tnelsonbooks@cs.com.

Career

Writer; speaker in schools, libraries, and literary groups, 1983—. Theatre under the Stars, Houston, TX, actress and teacher of creative dramatics, 1971-80; St. Mary's School, Katonah, NY, Glee Club director, 1983-90.

Member

Authors Guild, Authors League of America, Society of Children's Book Writers and Illustrators, Golden Triangle Writers Guild, Children's Literature Council of Southern California.

Awards, Honors

Best Book of the Year citation, *School Library Journal,* 1986, for *The 25 Cent Miracle;* Notable Children's Trade Book in the field of social studies citation, National Council for the Social Sciences-Children's Book Council, 1987, for *Devil Storm;* Washington Irving Children's Choice Award, 1988, for *The Twenty-Five Cent Miracle;* Notable Children's Book citation and Best Book for Young Adults citation from the American

Theresa Nelson

Library Association, Best Book of the Year citation from *School Library Journal,* Editor's Choice citation from *Booklist,* Fanfare citation from *Horn Book,* Pick of the Lists citation from *American Bookseller,* Books for Children citation from the Library of Congress/Children's Literature Center, Teacher's Choice citation from the International Reading Association, Books for the Teen Age citation from the New York Public Library, and Notable Children's Trade Book in the Field of Social Studies citation from the National Council for the Social Sciences-Children's Book Council, all for *And One for All;* Notable Children's Book citation and Best Book for Young Adults from the American Library Association, Best Book of the Year citation from *School*

Library Journal, Fanfare citation from *Horn Book,* Books for the Teen Age citation from the New York Public Library, and Children's Literature Center: Books for Children citation from the Library of Congress, all for *The Beggars' Ride;* Best Book of the Year citation, *School Library Journal,* 1994, Books for the Teen Age citation, New York Public Library, Child Study Children's Book Award, Bank Street College of Education, 1994, Honor Book selection, *Boston Globe-Horn Book* awards, 1995, Award for Distinguished Fiction, Children's Literature Council of Southern California, 1995, Best Book for Young Adults, Quick Picks for Young Adults, Notable Book, and Best of the Best citations, American Library Association, all for *Earthshine.*

Writings

The 25 Cent Miracle, Bradbury (New York, NY), 1986.
Devil Storm, Orchard (New York, NY), 1987.
And One for All, Orchard (New York, NY), 1989.
The Beggars' Ride, Orchard (New York, NY), 1992.
Earthshine, Orchard (New York, NY), 1994.
The Empress of Elsewhere, DK Publications (New York, NY), 1998.
Ruby Electric, Atheneum (New York, NY), 2003.

Author of "Andrew, Honestly," a short story included in *Don't Give up the Ghost,* Delacorte (New York, NY), 1993.

Sidelights

With several award-winning novels for young adults to her credit, Theresa Nelson has established a reputation as a creator of emotionally engaging and thought-provoking works. Nelson embraces such difficult topics as parents with AIDS and teenaged runaways, and—although she came from a stable and happy home herself—often portrays young teens struggling with tragedy on the home front. As a critic noted in the *St. James Guide to Young Adult Writers,* Nelson's work "provides fiction that has a refreshing combination of literary and social value. Focusing intentionally on themes or problems that are directly relevant to the lives of young adults, Nelson examines with care and compassion issues such as poverty, AIDS, homelessness, and myriad other issues, all detailed through the actions and insights of a cast of finely drawn characters."

For Nelson, writing is an act of the imagination, sometimes sparked by her own childhood memories and other times inspired by young people she meets. Her debut novel, *The 25 Cent Miracle,* introduces a girl named Elvira Trumbull. Elvira lives with her widowed, unemployed, and often inebriated father in a trailer park. An imaginative girl herself, Elvira finds refuge in the library. The librarian, Miss Ivy, helps her plant a garden and shows her how to tend roses. When Elvira's father attempts to send her to live with a wealthy aunt, Elvira

hatches an ill-fated plan to instill love between her father and Miss Ivy and then tries to run away. In the end, Elvira realizes that her father does love her, and he shows signs of changing for the better. Ellen Fader, writing for *School Library Journal,* commented that "Elvira is a splendidly realized character." The novel won a spot on the Best Book of the Year list of *School Library Journal* and a Washington Irving Children's Choice Award.

Nelson's next novel, *Devil Storm,* was based on the occurrence of a deadly storm that killed over six thousand Texans in 1900. Nelson's fictional characters are a family of watermelon farmers named the Carrolls who are mourning the death of their infant child. Walter and Alice, the older children in the family, ignore the warnings of their father and befriend and provide food for Tom, an outcast, wanderer, and ex-slave who is reputed to be the son of pirate Jean LaFitte. Tom, who appears almost magically at times, tells the children wonderful stories. When the hurricane threatens the state, and the children's father is away, Tom leads the family to shelter. Refusing rewards, he disappears after giving Alice his mother's locket to remember his stories.

Writing in *Voice of Youth Advocates,* Beth Anderson called *Devil Storm* a "fine story of decent people." More praise came from Ann A. Flowers, who wrote in *Horn Book* that Nelson's "writing is powerful, reflecting the force of the great storm." Diane Roback's review of the work in *Publishers Weekly* was especially complimentary of Tom's character, saying that "Nelson instills this character with mythical qualities." "Nelson's strong sense of place, poetic style and inspired characterization make this far more than just an enthralling adventure," said a reviewer for *Kirkus Reviews.* And Barbara Chatton wrote in the *School Library Journal,* "Once Nelson gets comfortably into the story . . . the characters take on real life, and the inherent drama of the tragedy takes over."

Nelson's novel *And One for All* centers on a sensitive social issue. The book recounts a story familiar to many Americans who fought in the Vietnam war. Relayed through the eyes of twelve-year-old Geraldine, the narrator tells of her brother Wing, who drops out of school to join the Marines and is eventually killed in the war. Geraldine blames her brother's friend Sam, who has decided to protest the war. As Frances Ruth Weinstein explained in *Voice of Youth Advocates,* each of the three young people "sees it [the war] in a different light." In the end, according to *School Library Journal* reviewer Gerry Larson, Geraldine's "grief and fury give way to understanding that Sam was always on Wing's side in trying to end the war." *Bulletin of the Center for Children's Books* critic Betsy Hearne described the novel as "moving" and a "thought-provoking probe of the past." *And One for All* was honored with several selections and awards, including a Notable Children's Book citation and a Best Book for Young Adults citation from the American Library Association.

The Beggars' Ride, as Diane Roback wrote in another *Publishers Weekly* review, is a "compelling and, sadly, relevant story." Twelve-year-old Clare steals money from her drunken mother's purse to leave home after she is sexually abused by her mother's boyfriend. When her hopes of tracking down her mother's previous boyfriend, Joey—a man who treated Clare with much more kindness—are destroyed, she finds herself shoplifting and even robbing with a group of runaways in Atlantic City. Nelson "skillfully crafts her plot to dramatize the plight of young teens with no recourse from either their families or a failed system," according to a *Kirkus Reviews* contributor. In *School Library Journal,* Trev Jones concluded that this "powerful story that's often painful and all too real" is bound "to keep readers on the edge of their seats until the final ride." The critic in the *St. James Guide to Young Adult Writers* concluded of *The Beggars' Ride:* "Though the book ends on a hopeful note, it is the despair and danger in the daily lives of these children that will remain with the reader long after the book is finished."

Nelson set her novel *Earthshine* on the West Coast, where she now lives. The tragic but uplifting tale unfolds through the eyes of twelve-year-old "Slim" McGranahan, whose actor father is dying of AIDS. Slim lives with her father and his companion, Larry, and she tries hard to keep her father's condition secret from her mother. An optimistic friend Slim meets at a support group convinces her that miracles can happen, and they set off together to save those they love from the fatal illness. The *St. James Guide to Young Adult Writers* essayist felt that *Earthshine* features Nelson's "best writing to date." The reviewer added that Nelson "almost never makes a false step in this wonderfully realized telling of a modern tragedy. The central characters are finely drawn and, as a group, are well balanced, but even the peripheral characters are strong and believable; there is hardly a stereotype to be found in the book." In her *Horn Book* review of the novel, Nancy Vasilakis praised the way Nelson commented upon homophobia and AIDS by illustrating the issues through the loving relationship between Slim and her father. "This social issue, brought painfully home, is what gives the story its amazing power," Vasilakis concluded.

Two lonely children forge a friendship in *The Empress of Elsewhere.* When Jim Harbert and his sister capture a runaway monkey and return it to its owner, she rewards them by allowing them to visit the monkey on her estate. There Jim meets J. D., a disaffected orphan who is bent upon escape herself. According to John Peters in *Booklist,* "Jim's lively, individual narrative voice, and a supporting cast that is energetically drawn from top to bottom will keep readers engaged." *Horn Book* contributor Terri Schmitz praised the "comic and heartrending" story for its depiction of characters with the "decency and courage to help a friend in need."

The heroine of *Ruby Electric* is struggling to make sense of her father's abandonment. She seeks solace in the movie scripts she writes in her head, and she fantasizes about restoring the concrete-encased Los Angeles River to its former wild glory. While these dreams never bear fruit, Ruby does learn to accept the real world through her association with two troublemaking classmates, Big Skinny and Mouse. Cindy Darling Codell in *School Library Journal* suggested that in *Ruby Electric* Nelson "is superb in covering serious topics . . . this novel will have wide appeal." A *Publishers Weekly* reviewer similarly concluded: "Smart and funny, Ruby will surely have the audience lined up for her next starring role."

Nelson's settings are drawn from places where she has lived herself: Atlantic City, Los Angeles, Texas, and New York among them. The critic for the *St. James Guide to Young Adult Writers* concluded that the author "uses the skill of the literary artist to take her young readers into meaningful encounters with characters who struggle with problems with which, unfortunately, many of the readers themselves also struggle. As good reading, as bibliotherapeutic tools, as aids to learning more about social problems and history, Nelson's books deliver and should be on the shelves of all serious young adult collections."

Biographical and Critical Sources

BOOKS

Authors and Artists for Young Adults, Volume 25, Gale (Detroit, MI), 1998.
St. James Guide to Young Adult Writers, 2nd edition, St. James (Detroit, MI), 1999.

PERIODICALS

Booklist, September 1, 1994, Mary Harris Veeder, review of *Earthshine,* p. 35; September 1, 1998, John Peters, review of *The Empress of Elsewhere,* p. 121.
Bulletin of the Center for Children's Books, January, 1989, Betsy Hearne, review of *And One for All,* p. 130.
Horn Book, November-December, 1987, Ann A. Flowers, review of *Devil Storm,* pp. 737-738; November-December, 1994, Nancy Vasilakis, review of *Earthshine,* p. 736; January, 1999, Terri Schmitz, review of *The Empress of Elsewhere,* p. 68.
Kirkus Reviews, June 1, 1987, review of *Devil Storm;* August 15, 1992, review of *The Beggar's Ride,* p. 1065.
Lambda Book Report, September-October, 1995, Nancy Garden, review of *Earthshine,* p. 30.
New York Times Book Review, October 22, 1989, review of *And One for All,* p. 35.
Publishers Weekly, June 26, 1987, Diane Roback, review of *Devil Storm,* p. 73; September 7, 1992, Diane Roback, review of *The Beggars' Ride,* p. 97; October 10, 1994, review of *Earthshine,* p. 71; September 28, 1998, review of *The Empress of Elsewhere,* p. 103; May 26, 2003, review of *Ruby Electric,* p. 71.

School Library Journal, May, 1986, Ellen Fader, review of *The 25 Cent Miracle;* June-July, 1987, Barbara Chatton, review of *Devil Storm*, pp. 111-112; February, 1989, Gerry Larson, review of *And One for All*, p. 102; November, 1992, Trev Jones, review of *The Beggars' Ride*, p. 97; June, 2003, Cindy Darling Codell, review of *Ruby Electric*, p. 148.

Voice of Youth Advocates, February, 1988, Beth Anderson, review of *Devil Storm*, p. 282; April, 1989, Frances Ruth Weinstein, review of *And One for All*, p. 30.

ONLINE

Theresa Nelson Home Page, http://www.theresanelson.net/ (June 18, 2003).

Autobiography Feature

Theresa Nelson

You don't have to come from an outsize Texas family to grow up dreaming outsize dreams.

But it probably doesn't hurt.

There were eleven of us Nelson children in the big house behind the President Clay azaleas, where our parents still live today. It's on 21st Street, in what was then—when we moved there in the early '50s—the spanking new Calder Place addition: City of Beaumont, Jefferson County.

In those days our neighborhood was still being carved out of the southeast Texas marshlands and piney woods. Our block was full of just-built houses and still-vacant lots, cut down the middle by a huge forbidden drainage ditch, where we naturally spent as much time as possible. Bulldozers had piled up big mounds of dirt on either side of it—the closest things to hills we flat-landers had ever seen. We dug them full of foxholes for our endless war games. We were all true Baby Boomers, children of the veterans who had just recently come home from winning what one of our confused classmates referred to as World War Eleven.

Bragging rights were hotly disputed—"My daddy's a bigger war hero than your daddy"—but we Nelson kids had a definite leg up there. Our father, David Rogers Nelson, Jr., was the genuine article.

Before we knew him, he'd been a Junior World Champion calf roper, the winner of the first-prize gold watch in the county-wide declamation contest, and the best and bluest-eyed tap dancer in his big sister Pat's dancing school. He was also very possibly the *only* tap dancer in the United States Marine Corps, which he joined in the fall of 1941, the day after seeing a patriotic movie. (Was it *Sergeant York,* Daddy?)

Just in time, as it turned out, for him to be among the first marines shipped to the South Pacific after Pearl Harbor. He fought in three of the bloodiest battles of the war—Guadalcanal, Tarawa, and Saipan—and was wounded twice, the second time almost fatally. "Nothing to worry about," he wrote his mother (Theresa Cullen Nelson) from the hospital ship *Bountiful.* And then again later, when he was truly out of danger: "Don't worry about your bachelor son. Just pick me out some brown-eyed beauty that doesn't mind waiting three or four years for a beat-up marine and write 'reserved' on her ticket."

Sure enough, when the war finally ended, he came home and found just what he'd ordered: Alice Carroll "Kissy" Hunter, the prettiest, most popular girl in Beaumont. She was a dancer, too, a ballerina with real promise. Her teacher (later also mine—Miss Judith of the Sproule School of Dance) wanted to take her to New York City, so she might become the next Pavlova.

But luckily—at least for us eleven—on February 8, 1946, the brown-eyed beauty stayed home and married the beat-up marine, instead.

My brother, David III, was born the following November. Ever anxious to tag along, I arrived on August 15, 1948, and was followed in turn by Frances, Hunter, Mary Pat, Carroll, Annie, Jane Cullen, James Keith (our "Bubba"), John Henry, and William.

My earliest memories are of stories: Daddy making up silly songs and adventures about my brothers and sisters and me, and Mama reading to all of us—wonderful books like *The Wind in the Willows, The Five Little Peppers and How They Grew,* and her favorite, *The Birds' Christmas Carol,* which she never once got all the way through, because it made her cry so hard. Books were magic, in my mother's hands; she could make them live and breathe. *"Read!"* I'd say, if she paused even for a second—never mind that there were ten other children vying for her attention. *"Read!"*

The author's father, David Rogers Nelson, Jr.

And oh, what a storyteller! When she told us all the legend of old Tom the Tramp, who back in 1900 had walked through the rising waters of the most monstrous hurricane in North American history, trying to save a family of children stranded on our own beloved Bolivar Peninsula, we could *hear* the thunder booming and *taste* the salt in the wind; we could *feel* the needle-sharp rain stinging our skin.

Small wonder, then, that before long I was making up stories of my own, and planning to be a writer, just like my two favorite heroines: Jo March in *Little Women* and Anne Shirley in *Anne of Green Gables*. I didn't have a garret for my scribbling, like Jo, and the drainage ditch was just a shade less romantic than Prince Edward Island, but that didn't stop me from churning out stories and dramatic poems by the bushel. Just recently I found a crumbling box full of them, with titles like "The Quest of Emerald," "The Witch in the Orchard," and "King Kang," which had nothing at all to do with giant apes. Not to mention "A Fairy Folk Fantasy" (I've always been a sucker for alliteration).

It didn't keep me from sneaking into my brother David's room, either, so that I could type my latest play on his magnificent new Tom Thumb typewriter. He caught me, of course, but decided against killing me once I explained that I had written the lead especially for him. After that, he always played the king, while my littler brothers and sisters and cousins and obliging neighbor children were assorted elves and gnomes and enchanted princesses or whatever the current script called for.

But I was always the witch. The wizened, withered, wicked old witch. Which passed for unselfishness on my part, but wasn't that bad, really, since the witch invariably got all the best lines.

And then in seventh grade I decided it was time to get *really* serious and start my first novel. "The Friends," I called it, a stirring domestic mystery/ adventure about a lost dog. Unfortunately, this effort coincided with what was also my first experience of writer's block—a particularly lethal case to which I succumbed after only three chapters.

Writing, it turned out, was going to be harder than I thought.

So I decided to become a movie star, instead. Or at least the toast of Broadway. And with that in mind . . .

I took a lot of dancing and music lessons and kept my eyes open for potential producers, beginning with the Bluebirds, who agreed to let me play the title role in "The Green Lady," a thrilling piece involving the liberal use of a bottle of food coloring and my mother's best cold cream. The critics didn't exactly rave ("That was the dumbest show I ever saw," said my brother Hunter), but I continued my career anyway, first at St. Anne's Elementary School—where I adapted a chapter of *Anne of Green Gables* and modestly gave myself the title role in that, too—then moving on to the Beaumont Little Theater and the drama club at Monsignor Kelly High School.

And then at the University of St. Thomas in Houston, during the second semester of my freshman year, I was cast as Little Mary in the musical, "Little Mary Sunshine." Little Mary, who—in the play—was supposed to be in love with Captain "Big Jim" Warington.

But in real life there was a really cute senior playing Corporal Billy Jester, the comic lead in the show. His name was Kevin Cooney, and he was by far the funniest guy in the whole school. The funniest guy, in fact, I had ever met.

So I married him—just a little more than a year later—on September 26, 1968. (And twenty is much too young to get married, and it was just sheer luck and God's own grace that it worked out, but when you're really good and ready, if you're looking for a keeper, try to find somebody who makes you laugh.)

Our timing wasn't the greatest. Nineteen sixty-eight was right in the middle of the Vietnam era, and by the time we got married, Kevin was in the army. He had already graduated from college and been drafted and gone to basic training, and we were waiting for his orders to come through and praying he wouldn't be sent overseas. But our chances were slim. That was a terrible year, even for newlyweds. Martin Luther King, Jr., and Robert Kennedy had both been killed; there was rioting in the inner cities, peace demonstrations turning violent in Washington, D.C. And still the war in Southeast Asia raged on.

Then, in March of 1969, we had a stroke of luck. Orders came through for Kevin's unit: Everybody whose last name started with a letter in the first half of the alphabet would be sent to Korea, where there was no fighting, at least at that time. Great news for Private First Class Kevin Cooney! Of course it still meant we'd be separated for a year. That was the hard part. But at least Kevin would be safe.

His best friend from basic training wasn't so lucky. James G. ("Greg") Brown had been on exactly the same track as Kevin when the two of them reported for duty back in June. Greg had even applied for leave to get married the same weekend Kevin and I did. But he was in a different unit now, and it didn't matter what letter his last name started with. Kevin and he wrote each other for a while, but within a few months after Greg was sent to Vietnam, one of Kevin's letters to him was returned, unopened, with a stamp that said only "Addressee Deceased." That was how we learned that Greg had died—in a fire fight, we heard later, trying to take some hill that ultimately mattered to no one.

I didn't want to believe it. I don't think I *did* believe it, deep down. War—even this strange new war that we watched in our family room on the nightly news—had no more substance in my mind than those old John Wayne movies my brothers loved. Just a bunch of trumped-up pictures on the television screen, right? Surely it couldn't be real.

My father knew better. He had the scars to prove it. He'd seen fellow marines blown up and shot down, had a friend from his old rugby team die in his arms, had hitchhiked across the country after VJ Day, visiting the families of the buddies he'd lost.

But in those days, Daddy's purple heart was still tucked away in his sock drawer. He wouldn't—couldn't—talk about *his* war for years to come.

So I pushed it all away for as long as I could: first the reality, then the memory of those troubled times. It wasn't until another twenty years had passed—when I

had sons of my own, and our eldest, Michael, started getting recruiting letters from the armed forces—that it all came pouring back.

But that was still in the unimaginably distant future; back in the spring of 1969:

Kevin did go to Korea. I was pregnant by this time and wasn't allowed to go with him, so I went back to Beaumont and lived at home for a year, during which Michael was born (just nine months after my mother gave birth to my youngest brother, Michael's "Uncle William"). Kevin got home for good in May of 1970, and for the next ten years we lived in Houston and acted in local theater at night and worked various dayjobs to pay the rent. I taught creative dramatics to children at Theater under the Stars; Kevin was a cost engineer. We also both went back to school. I graduated magna cum laude with a B.A. in English from University of St. Thomas in 1972—I know I'm bragging, but I'm still pretty proud of that—just six weeks after the birth of our second son, Brian. (Now *there's* something to brag about.) Meanwhile Kevin took graduate courses at the University of Houston and earned an M.A. in drama in 1974. But we kept our day jobs, just in case. And our night jobs, too. And our third beautiful son, Errol, was born in 1977.

And then in 1980, we turned in our respective two weeks' notice, packed up boys and books and frying pans, and hit the road for two and a half years, traveling all over the country with a theatrical touring company. It sounds nuts, I know. Looking back now, I guess it was a little nutty. But we all loved it. We homeschooled the guys, learned to cook spaghetti on a hotplate, drove from the Grand Canyon to the Golden Gate Bridge, and had the time of our lives.

This took us eventually to New York (where Kevin made his Broadway debut in 1981) and then—in March of 1983, just in time for the northeast's biggest blizzard in thirty years—to our new home in Katonah, Weschester County, about an hour's drive north of NYC. It was a great old place, a wonderful, rambling farmhouse that our dear actor/director friends and mentors, Peter Masterson and his wife, Carlin Glynn, had fallen in love with and invited us to share with them and their children (Lexie, Mary Stuart, and Peter, Jr.). It had a trout stream out back, woods to explore, apple trees for the kids to climb. Anne Shirley would have loved it. And it was there—I was thirty-four now—in a cozy little sun porch on the second floor, that I began writing again.

Well, not *again,* exactly. I'd never really stopped altogether. In all those years since getting that first case of writer's block with "The Friends," I'd written thousands—probably millions—of words: letters and nonsense rhymes and scribbles of all kinds, as well as a half dozen plays for my young theater students. But there was something about that house—which really could have been Green Gables, in a lot of ways—and somehow all the old dreams started resurfacing. . . .

The author's mother, Alice Carroll Hunter Nelson (far right), at the University of Texas, 1944

And they really *are* the same, in a sense—writing and dreaming. And sometimes—even at nine and ten—we really *do* know what we want to be when we grow up. . . .

So when two more dear old theater friends of ours (Will and Patsy Mackenzie) happened to come to town, and introduced us to great friends of theirs (the writer, Judie Angell, and her husband, Phil Gaberman), I took a deep, deep breath and told Judie about my dreams. And she suggested I take them—and some of my typed-up scribblings—to her editor and friend, Richard Jackson . . .

Who was (though I was too dumb to realize it at the time) only the smartest, kindest, funniest, most patient, and absolute *best* editor and friend in the world of children's literature—and any world, for that matter—as anyone who's ever worked with him will tell you.

He didn't publish any of those first efforts of mine. A good thing, I realize now, since I was trying and failing to be the new Dr. Seuss, even though—at the time—the old one was still alive and well. But fortunately I included the first twenty pages of a little chapter book I was working on, too, and Dick saw promise in those. Actually in just one paragraph, he told me much later.

Thank God for that one paragraph.

And so he encouraged me to keep trying, and trying again, and finally, in the fall of 1983, I began writing my first novel—or second, counting that failed seventh-grade attempt. To my surprise, it wasn't anything like the story I'd planned to write. (I'd thought, in the beginning, it would be about our family's years on the road with the touring company.) But that was okay. To paraphrase John Lennon, sometimes a book—like life—is what happens when you're busy making other plans.

There's a wonderful writer named Rumer Godden, whose books changed the world for me when I was in high school (especially her heartwrenching novel *An Episode of Sparrows,* which was first loaned to me by my beloved English and drama teacher, Sister Magdalena—now Sister Joanne Neuhaus, O.P.). In the preface to *Gone,* a collection of her short stories, Ms. Godden says that writers are like oysters. You know how it works: First an oyster gets a little grit of something—some bit of broken glass or a grain of sand, maybe—caught inside its shell. And that bothers the oyster, just a little at first, then more and more, until one day it just can't stand it any longer. So then it starts to coat that little whatever-it-is with layer after layer of its special, magical oyster juice, until finally that tiny bit of next-to-nothing has been transformed—wonder of wonders—into a pearl.

Well, Ms. Godden says that for a writer, a memory—an actual experience—is sometimes like that grit in the oyster's shell. You never know what it might

be or when or where it might happen; it's not always something you consciously *choose,* any more than you choose your dreams when you go to bed at night. But for some reason a particular face, or place, or river, or tree—it might be anything!—stays with you, prickles inside your memory and won't go away. It just keeps sticking there, bothering you, until eventually you can't stand it any longer, and you begin to coat that fragment of actual experience with layer after layer of imagining (the human brain's version of oyster juice). And finally, after months or even years, you might just end up with—well, not a pearl, necessarily. But maybe, if you're lucky—

A story.

Memory and imagination, Mark Twain once said, are the only tools a writer really needs.

I love how that sounds. But in my experience, a good eraser helps, too.

With my first book, I think the initial impetus for the story, that little grit that stuck in my shell and tickled until I couldn't ignore it, was a single image: a yellow rosebush struggling to grow in the rock-hard Texas dirt.

I'd had a rosebush just like that, when I was a little girl, growing outside my bedroom window. But it wasn't my own window, my own house, that I was picturing now; it was a trailer door in a scraggly block full of motor homes called the Happy Trails Trailer Park. There had been one just like it in Beaumont—the Alamo Courts, I think it was called—that I'd passed hundreds of times when I was growing up.

What was the rosebush doing there? I wondered. Who planted it? Why?

The answers didn't come right away. No such luck. But they did start coming, little by little, in fits and starts and notebook scribbles. (Like *Harriet the Spy,* I can't imagine life without notebooks.) Just bits of memories, mostly: a girl with a head full of dreams and a stuffed-up nose (like mine), plus a habit of reading the fine print on cereal boxes. A mother who had died of cancer (like my friend David Doty's mother). A father with an old football injury (like my friend Glenn Holtzman's), a knack for catching speckled trout (like my daddy's), and a lack of confidence in his own abilities as a single parent—

Which came from where, exactly?

I don't really know. It's been nearly twenty years now, and those hazy beginnings are all jumbled together in my head. But I do remember thinking a lot in those days about a boy I knew when I was eight or nine: a nice little guy named Willie, who had lived for a time at the Beaumont Children's Home. I don't know his last name, or his family circumstances, or what series of catastrophes had landed him in the orphanage. All I know is that my mother used to pick him up and take him with us on picnics, or to the movies, or just over to our house to play (it never crossed my mind, as a child, to wonder how she found the time), until Willie's family's situation improved, somehow, and he moved away and disappeared from our lives.

There was a story there, I felt sure. What had those days been like for Willie—an only child, as far as I knew—being suddenly immersed in our big, loud, cheerful mob of a family? What had happened to his own parents? Surely he missed them terribly—didn't he? Or did he even remember them? What if his history was a bit like my friend David's, whose father (a traveling salesman) had to farm out his children to various relatives after his wife's death?

I was finally starting to "catch fire," as the writer Ellen Gilchrist puts it, one idea igniting another, and then another. Beaumont became Calder, Texas. It was summer, and a storm was coming. Willie turned into the girl with the stuffed-up nose, planter of the rosebush and dreamer of dreams, living with her widowed father on what would have been the wrong side of the tracks— "if there had been any tracks in Calder, which there weren't."

Long before the sun rose on the morning of Elvira Trumbull's eleventh birthday, the smell of rain was in the air. . . . (*The 25 Cent Miracle*).

An actual beginning! My blood was racing; my heart was pounding; I was off and running at last! Dick read my first chapter, liked it, and asked for more.

This was followed by a year of total confusion.

In my earliest drafts—there were dozens of them— Elvira's dad, feeling less than adequate as a father, sent her to live with her aunt and uncle and their eleven children. (Eleven. Hmm. Exactly.) She was overwhelmed, angry, and painfully shy (all at once), but gradually she began to fit in and to get to know her cousins—*all* her cousins—one by one, chapter by painfully slow chapter.

"It's as if all your brothers and sisters are looking over your shoulder as you write," Dick told me, after he'd plowed through ten or twelve more chapters. "I can almost hear them talking to you: 'Make my part bigger.' 'Make me funnier.' 'I wouldn't say *that*, would I?'"

He was right, of course. I wasn't really writing fiction at all; I was just piling up my favorite family anecdotes and trying to corkscrew them into what *should* have been Elvira's story, all the while thinking ahead to the moment when my family would recognize themselves on my pages and love me for making every one of them so wonderful. Meanwhile poor Elvira mostly had to just sit around watching all the Nelsons (I called us the O'Learys, I believe) cavorting adorably around her. She was always *reacting*, Dick explained—never initiating one bit of the action herself. "Just let her *do* something," he advised me.

Like what? I wondered, bitterly disappointed. I had been pretty sure—until he informed me otherwise—that those first eighty pages were brilliant. Where in the world could I go from here?

Second-grade school photo

To other stories, that's where—or at least other *beginnings* of stories, which came tumbling into my head by the cartload, much faster than middles or endings. I put Elvira in a drawer and wrote all sorts of terrible openings: A messy cliché of a ghost story about two grumpy children visiting a spooky old house inhabited by their doddering great-aunt ("nattering," Dick called her). A comic novella made up entirely of dialogue spoken by two endlessly arguing teenage boys. (Dick: "I wish I could say I loved it, but I didn't.") And on and on and on, for months, though mercifully I can't really remember much about those feeble efforts. Only that there wasn't a glimmer of an idea among them that hadn't been used in a book already—and to much better effect, without exception—years before I ever came along.

The only sensible thing to do, of course, was to give up.

But I was born stubborn, if nothing else (hardheaded, my daddy calls it), and the idea of giving up made me sick to my stomach. I might not ever get anywhere, but I could sure as heck die trying.

"Go back to Elvira," Dick encouraged me. "You were on to something there."

Oh, Lord. "But I thought all those chapters about the eleven cousins were too long and boring and confusing!"

"She doesn't have to go live with a big family. Her aunt and uncle don't have to have eleven children; it doesn't have to be exactly like *your* family. Just use the facts as a springboard into your story."

A springboard? I didn't understand. "But aren't writers supposed to write what they know?"

"Well, sure. Of course they are," said Dick. (It was a wonder he was still talking to me.) "But this is fiction, remember? *Anything* is possible here. It's not just what you *know* that matters. It's what you can *imagine.*"

Oh. Right. Mark Twain again. Memory and imagination. I had it on a bookmark, too, come to think of it, in a quote from Anatole France: "To know is nothing at all. To imagine is everything."

But my imagination, at the moment, was a total blank. At least as far as Elvira Trumbull was concerned.

So . . .

I went to the library. A lot. The Katonah Village Library. I went there day after day, while the boys were at school, and read and read, and marveled at all those hundreds of shelves filled with books that other writers, *real* writers, had somehow miraculously managed to finish. I read and read and reread all my favorite books and piles of new ones, trying to see how on earth those authors had done it: not just all the *Anne* books and *Little Women* but dozens of others, too: *To Kill a Mockingbird, Jane Eyre, A Wrinkle in Time, The Great Gilly Hopkins, The Dark Is Rising, Freckle Juice*—everything from *Anna Karenina* to *Cloudy with a Chance of Meatballs.*

The library has always been my salvation. As a child I spent countless hours in the children's department on the top floor of the Tyrrell Public Library in downtown Beaumont, a marvelous old building that reminded me of the Witch's castle in *The Wizard of Oz.* My mother, who had worked there one summer as a teenager, had taught us all to love it as much as she did. It was the best of all secret hideaways, with its gray stone towers and turrets and great winding stairway, gateway to untold galaxies. And maybe because it had once been a church (it even *smelled* holy), there was an air of the sacred, of mystery, a hush even beyond the ordinary library hush hanging about it still, floating down with the dust motes in the great shafts of multicolored light that fell through its stained glass windows.

Oddly enough, my new refuge in Katonah had once been a church, too. It looked—and even smelled—like a somewhat smaller, slightly more Methodist sister of my dear old Tyrrell Public. And when I saw those blessedly familiar titles on the shelves, I knew I was home.

All that reading woke me up, somehow. I don't know how to explain it, except that it had something to do with my eventually discovering—for the very first time—*The Yearling,* by Marjorie Kinnan Rawlings, and

reading it, over and over, during the peculiar summer of 1984. Peculiar not only because of that book (which made me feel as if I were being lifted out of myself and transported to another world, chapter after gorgeous chapter), but because our family really did get transported to another world that summer: a surreal little planet called Atlantic City, New Jersey.

We loved it, mostly. Kevin had gotten a part in a musical that was being produced at the Claridge, one of the big casino-hotels, so the boys and I went along from July to Labor Day, spending our nights in a moldy little basement apartment in the Ventnor area, and our days playing on the beach or exploring the famous old Boardwalk.

Ventnor and Boardwalk—sound familiar? There was a Park Place, too, as well as an Illinois and an Indiana Avenue, not to mention a Baltic and Mediterranean. . . .

"Did they name all these streets after the Monopoly board?" I asked Kevin.

He explained that it was the other way around, of course. The guy who invented Monopoly had lived in Philadelphia, only about an hour from Atlantic City. So when he made up his get-rich-quick game (this was back in the thirties, during the Depression era), he modeled it after his favorite resort town. Sure enough, Boardwalk and Park Place really were in the high rent district, while Baltic and Mediterranean actually did cut right through some of the least expensive parts of town.

What a great setting for a story! I scribbled a couple of notebooks full of notes, so I wouldn't forget any of it: Peanut World, the ship-shaped mall, Boardwalk Roger's Famous Hot Dogs, the Miss America Food Court, fortune tellers and lounge singers and old guys in Bermuda shorts smoking fat cigars, slot machines ringing and roulette wheels turning, tourists spending money like there was no tomorrow.

Meanwhile, just down the Boardwalk—not five minutes from the glitzy, ersatz glamor of the casinos—there was shocking poverty: drugs and crime and long stretches of abandoned buildings covered with graffiti, where the homeless (some of them teenagers) camped out, scrounging to get by. Scruffy-looking panhandlers hung around outside every casino. A woman with no arms and no legs played a portable keyboard with her tongue. Her angry young companion shook a plateful of change at us, not so much asking for donations as daring us to pass.

It all went into my notebooks. Surely there were stories—hundreds of stories—staring me right in the face. But it was all still chaos to me then, just a collection of random images. I couldn't see how to connect the dots and make sense of a single one.

And all this time, that first chapter about Elvira Trumbull—the only one that Dick had really liked—was still waiting patiently beside my typewriter. I had lugged it to Atlantic City with me, along with my very own new copy of *The Yearling*. My brain—so cold and dull when I stared at the words "Chapter Two" typed at the top of an otherwise blank page—shot sparks when I read Ms. Rawling's prose. What was her secret, the magic she used to bind ordinary words into such extraordinary sentences and paragraphs?

I remember standing outside the door of some violently-colored boardwalk arcade one evening near the end of that summer, reading *The Yearling* yet again, while my three sons played all the latest ear-blasting, head-spinning games inside. Bells rang, battleships blew up, raucous music blared from giant speakers, but I scarcely noticed any of it. I was a thousand miles away in the Florida backcountry:

> He was addled with April. He was dizzy with Spring. . . . He was stabbed with the candle-light inside the safe comfort of the cabin; with the moonlight around it. . . . He went to bed in a fever and could not sleep. A mark was on him from the day's delight, so that all his life, when April was a thin green and the flavor of rain was on his tongue, an old wound would throb and a nostalgia would fill him for something he could not quite remember. A whip-poor-will called across the bright night, and suddenly he was asleep. (*The Yearling,* by Marjorie Kinnan Rawlings, Charles Scribner's Sons, 1970)

Oh, my. Even now, it makes me ache. I remember coming to the end of that chapter and looking up, and this is the moment that is still clear to me, nearly twenty years later:

For just a split second, there on the boardwalk, I didn't know where I was.

And then, of course, the moment passed. I was back in New Jersey again. To my left were the flashing lights of the arcade, the music and bells and exploding rockets; to my right, the moon was rising over the Atlantic Ocean. There was bubble gum stuck to my shoe, and I still didn't know how to write a book.

But something had shifted in my head—maybe only infinitesimally, but shifted, all the same. And the next morning (or maybe the one after that; I can't say for sure), I woke up at daybreak with my brain buzzing, while the rest of my family was still asleep, and rushed to the typewriter, and started banging out word after word. . . .

It still wasn't chapter two of my Elvira story. I didn't care. My synapses were firing; I wasn't *frozen* anymore! I typed until it was time to pack up to go home, happier than I'd been in months, and was still typing a week later, back in Katonah. So what if it was yet another beginning? Surely Dick would love this one—all about a boy and the older brother he worships: a young policeman who gets in trouble somehow, breaking the younger kid's heart, so that then there's this terrible rift in the family, and—

And then what?

I didn't know, exactly. Lord help me. But that was okay; it would come to me when I got there, right? My brain was *awake* again, that was what mattered. And in the meantime I had a thousand other things on my mind. The boys were back in school; there were uniforms and books and Crayolas to buy, Michael's birthday coming up, a pie to bake, so I certainly didn't have time to stand around worrying about—

Wait a minute.

A pie?

A lemon meringue pie.

What if—

What if Elvira bakes a pie? I wondered. Just like the one I tried to bake when I was eleven—when I thought "three eggs, separated" meant three eggs in three separate bowls?

What if . . .

What if her reason for baking the pie is to make it the crowning touch for the perfect dinner—the dinner that she cooks for her father and . . . and . . .

And the beautiful lady librarian Elvira meets when she goes to the Calder Public Library—that great old Gothic fortress of a building that makes her think of the witch's castle in *The Wizard of Oz*!

Because . . .

Because she *has* to go there, doesn't she? So that she can find books about growing roses, like the half-dead bush she's planted outside the trailer door?

And what if Elvira *doesn't* go live with her aunt and uncle, after all? What if she *refuses* to go, when her father tells her she has to, because in spite of everything, she doesn't want to leave him? What if her romantic dinner-cooking and pie-baking are all part of her attempt to play matchmaker for her dad and this library lady, who Elvira thinks will be the perfect new mother?

What if and what if and what if . . . ?

Kevin and Theresa on their wedding day, with Kevin's mother, September 26, 1968

Thank God.

I remember standing at the kitchen sink, shaking, holding on to the sides so I wouldn't fall down, ideas pouring into my head in a torrent, water pouring out of the faucet, unchecked. (I couldn't remember why I had turned it on in the first place.) Tears streamed down my cheeks. I felt as if I might faint. Or throw up. I could hardly breathe, I was so excited. After all these months—it had been a whole *year* now since I wrote that first chapter that Dick had liked—I could suddenly see it all, the shape of the entire story. Not every piece, of course, but the big ones, the really essential building blocks—what Elvira *wanted* and *why* she wanted it and what she was going to *do* about getting it. ("Just let her *do* something," I could still hear Dick saying.)

> It was then that it hit her. The inspiration. Pure-D inspiration—manna from heaven—the Holy Ghost Himself, maybe . . . Whatever it was, it hit her so hard that she almost fell down right there in front of the man with the Adam's apple, who was standing in the doorway of the trailer park office, blowing smoke rings. Elvira started trembling all over. Her heart was beating a mile a minute. Her eyebrows began to sweat. She wouldn't have been all that surprised if she had started speaking in tongues. . . . (*The 25 Cent Miracle*)

After that lightning flash, that lemon-pie revelation, I finished the story in about eleven weeks. Eleven beautiful, amazing weeks, like nothing I've ever experienced, before or since. It seems to me now, looking back on that time, that it was one long stretch of birds singing and blue skies blazing and red leaves falling outside my window, and that the sun shone every single day, and my children were pink-cheeked and perfectly behaved, and my husband never frowned, even once.

Maybe I'm wrong.

But I know it was the best autumn of my life, and that every morning I woke up happy, itching to get back to my old battered electric typewriter (the one with the overly-enthusiastic carriage return that shook the whole house and regularly knocked over my water glass, which for some reason I kept putting back in the same spot, anyway).

I typed the last words of my manuscript just before Christmas, 1984, wrapped it up (with shaking hands), and took it in to Dick's office in New York City.

A few weeks later, he called to say he liked it.

I named it *The 25 Cent Miracle* for a lot of reasons, but mostly because—to me, at least—it was one.

I could hardly wait to try for a second. Within a couple of months I was working on another story, one that had been giving me goose bumps since I was eight years old: my mother's tale of Tom the Tramp, the hero of the Great Storm of 1900.

We drove back to Texas in the summer of 1985, rented a beach house on the Bolivar Peninsula. I rode the ferry to Galveston every day to do research at the Rosenberg Library. There were stacks and stacks of books and newspapers from the time of the storm, hundreds of eyewitness accounts and interviews with the survivors.

But I could find virtually nothing about Tom himself.

Of course there was no end of material dealing with just about everybody else who had ever set foot on the Gulf Coast, including Jean Lafitte, the pirate, who had a camp on Galveston Island in the early 1800s. My daddy took me to Rollover Pass, through which Lafitte and the other pirates used to roll barrels of rum, to avoid the customs officials. I visited what's said to be his cabin boy's grave in a Bolivar burial ground. I discovered an old newspaper account of a crazy loner who used to roam the Galveston beaches, claiming to have sailed with Lafitte and to know where his treasure was hidden.

But though Tom the Tramp's grave is a famous one, too, not far from my grandparents' plot in Beaumont's Magnolia Cemetery, no one could tell me anything about the old man's real history. No one seemed to know where he had come from, or where his wanderings had taken him, or how, exactly, he had ended up in Bolivar on the fateful morning of September 8, 1900.

I might have given up, if Dick's words hadn't still been fresh in my ears: "It's not just what you know that matters. It's what you can *imagine*." So I started asking the "what ifs?" all over again. What if local rumor has it that Tom is the illegitimate son of Lafitte and a beautiful girl from one of the many slave ships he raided? What if, as an old man (a former slave himself), he's come back to Bolivar, looking for something—maybe even his father's long-lost treasure? What if a thirteen-year-old white boy named Walter and his sister Alice spy him on the beach, digging, and follow him, hoping to learn his secrets? And what if when the storm hits, and the children's father is away in Galveston on business, there's no one but old Tom to help them reach safety—old Tom, who has more than enough reason to let the whole white race go to the devil?

What if and what if and what if . . .?

Glory be.

It wasn't one long joyous blaze of creating this time, even after I could see the light shining—hazily—up ahead. It was more like purgatory, with occasional side trips to heaven, like every writing experience I've known since: dazzling bursts of clarity one day, agonizing dry spells the next three, sleepless nights, hopeful mornings, despairing noons. By the time I finished *Devil Storm* in May of 1986, I felt as if I'd drowned and been resuscitated at least fifty times over. But Dick liked that book, too, thank heaven.

I took a deep breath, and kept scribbling.

And One for All started life as *The Lover's Tree,* a title that came from a real tree we called by that name—an ancient copper beech that grew in the woods

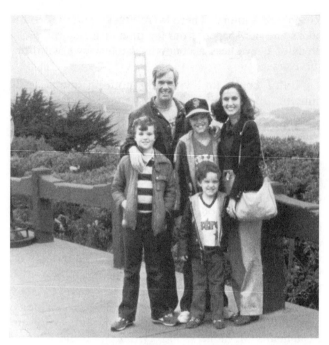

The author and her family at the Golden Gate Bridge, 1981. Clockwise, from right: Theresa, Errol, Brian, Kevin, Michael

behind our house in Katonah. It was carved all over with hearts and dates and initials, some so old we could barely make them out. The first time I saw it, I knew it belonged in a book—a wonderfully romantic book, I thought, in which each chapter would be a different story, inspired by all the different lovers who had carved their initials on that tree in the hundreds of years it had been growing there.

But then those letters started arriving in the mail—the ones from the armed forces, encouraging Michael to consider enlisting after he graduated from high school. And the image of my boy in uniform brought another boy's face swimming up from my subconscious, where I thought I'd buried it, two decades before. So in the end, only a single set of initials—from the 1960s, the Vietnam era—found its way into my story about the intertwining lives of three young people: three friends, driven apart by those troubled times, yet trying to honor the oath they had sworn as children:

I swear by the sacred Lover's Tree, eternal friendship and everlasting loyalty. All for one and one for all. . . .

(And One for All)

In the spring of 1987, while I was still struggling through the early stages of that manuscript, our landlord informed us that he wouldn't be renewing our lease; he wanted to take back the house for his own family's use. We were sick about it, but could hardly blame him. So we said good-bye to our Masterson buddies (and to dear old Kizzy, the neighbors' dog who

thought she was ours, and to "Three-Penny Rock" and "Danger Hill" and "Darkwood Forest"—all of which ended up in the story). And then we moved yet again, this time to another fine old farmhouse in Armonk, New York, about twenty minutes from White Plains.

In time we grew to love it, as well, but it took a while to settle in, and for months it seemed to me that I'd left not only my heart, but my *brain* in Katonah. Draft after draft of *And One for All* ended up in the trash. Still, eventually, I thought I'd got it right at last: a first person, present tense novel in three parts—covering nearly thirty years—all narrated by Geraldine Brennan, the youngest of the three main characters. I'd cried quarts over it, sweated blood (well, almost), certainly didn't see how I could make it any better. So in early December I worked up my courage again and sent it to Dick.

"Are you sitting down?" he asked me, when he called, a few days later.

I was pretty sure, from the sound of his voice, that he wasn't just saying this to make sure I wouldn't faint dead away when he told me how much he loved the book.

I was right.

It wasn't *all* terrible. There was a lot that he did love—pretty much all of Part Two, actually (he told me that right away, bless him). But the entire beginning—all of Part One—would have to go. If I were writing for adults, he said, they might (*possibly*) put up with forty pages told from the point of view of a six-year-old. My young audience wasn't about to. No way.

My heart sank. It had taken me six months to write those forty pages. Still, surely I could fix that. What else?

The ending wasn't there yet, Dick said. I'd skipped all the way from the emotional core of the book (a candlelight peace march in Washington, D.C.) to a letter, written in the '80s, which tried (and failed) to make sense of the entire aching sum of the friends' lives after the war. It left the reader feeling cheated, unsatisfied, floating in a narrative void.

Well, shoot. Of course he was right. Why hadn't I seen it before? My heart sank another foot or two. Still, that wasn't *impossible* to fix, either. Was it? Two more chapters—really *good* ones—in place of Sam's letter. I could do that.

But the first person point of view—that worked, didn't it? And the present tense, which I'd chosen to make the past seem more immediate—Dick liked that, didn't he?

"Well," he said (after just a hairbreadth of a pause), "none of that really bothered me."

Oh, dear. "You mean you think it might work better if it were third person, past tense?"

He did.

So I cried for a couple of days, and then I started all over again.

Six months later, in May of 1988, I sent him the new manuscript. And this time, when he called, he didn't ask if I was sitting down.

By the following fall, I was already trying to find my way into another story—*Everett Forever,* I called it—based loosely on a boy I had met in a special class taught brilliantly by my sister-in-law, Sheila Tybor. The real Everett was a funny, lovable little guy with a great grin and an irrepressible spirit—in spite of the fact that his dad had died (a fact he sometimes pretended away), his house had burned down (the dog had chewed through electrical wires), and his family was surviving on next to no money.

In my early drafts, Everett's father was a stunt man. I have no idea now where that came from. But maybe there were movie vibes in the air, because out of the blue one afternoon, some friends with Hollywood connections called, saying they'd read *Devil Storm* and thought it would make a great film. Would I be interested in writing the screenplay "on spec"?

That meant for free, basically, unless a producer could sell it later.

But who cared? I was thrilled! I'd always been crazy about the movies. And I already knew that story by heart, right? Surely I could whip out a fabulous screenplay in a couple of weeks, pick up my Oscar, and be back with Everett before I knew it.

A couple of months, was more like it. At least, for the first draft. Fifteen years later, I'm still rewriting it—along with a half dozen other scripts that have yet to be actually produced.

So Hollywood was a bust. No matter. It was 1989 now, and Everett was waiting. But for some reason I couldn't find my way back into his story, no matter how hard I tried. My words wouldn't sing; they just sat there on the page, croaking, like a bunch of tuneless toads.

And then the phone rang again. It wasn't Steven Spielberg this time, either; it was a woman with the New York prison system. She'd seen my name on a list of authors who made school visits, and she wanted to know if I might be willing to come to the Bedford Hills Women's Correctional Facility on the next visitor's day and tell stories to the inmates' children, who'd be there spending the morning with their mothers.

A few days later I found myself walking through clanging gates and metal detectors, with no idea what to expect. But once I was inside the big recreation room with the children and their moms, I felt silly to have worried. These were just kids, terrific kids, no different from thousands of others I'd met—just a bit younger than usual. So I told them my name, and they told me theirs, and I started telling stories. And before long we were all having a good time. Or so I thought.

Then I noticed a tall girl standing off to one side, away from the others, who plainly thought she was way too old and too cool to have to sit there listening to some dumb storyteller. She was tapping her toe, cracking her gum; she'd dressed herself up like a twenty-five-year-old punk rock star—skimpy little skirt, tons of makeup and costume jewelry, nose rings and belly button rings and tattoos everywhere. She'd done her hair punk-style, too—cut it short and spiked it up and dyed it orange and green and purple—every color of the rainbow. Talk about tough!

This girl was maybe twelve, thirteen at the outside. And no matter how tough she wanted me to think she was, when I looked in her eyes all I could see was hurt, and confusion, and little-girl vulnerability, great gray-green pools of wanting and never getting, and no clue why.

I don't think she told me her name. I never learned her story. I didn't know, that day in the women's prison, that she was going to stick with me the way she did—inside my mind, my heart, even my nightmares—another grit in the oyster's shell. What had happened in her life that made her feel she had to disguise herself that way, to face the world with such fierce bravado? It wasn't her fault that her mother had done whatever she had done and ended up in prison. My own life had been so safe, so idyllic, compared to whatever hell that kid had been through. Who knew what *I* might have done, or been, if the person I trusted most in the world had failed me the way that child's mom had failed her?

I didn't have the answers. But one half-awake afternoon, months later, when I was sitting in my bedroom (my family called it "The Cave") with my notebook in my lap, trying to concentrate on Everett, I saw that girl instead, spiky as ever. Only now—in my mind's eye—she wasn't slouching in the corner of the prisoners' recreation room in the Bedford Hills Women's Correctional Facility.

She was walking into the middle of a gang of teenage runaways, on the Boardwalk, in Atlantic City, New Jersey.

It took me three years to write *The Beggars' Ride.* Every book, every writing experience is strange—the way every dream is strange, a world unto itself. But *The Beggars' Ride* was the strangest, in many ways, so far removed was that child's precarious existence from anything I'd ever actually experienced.

Of course there are common themes that run through all my books, as in every writer's work. I guess for me it's a kind of stubborn hope, a yearning for connection, for family, that unquenchable thirst for love—no, more than that: the *assumption* of love, of every child's *right* to it—that's hardwired into every human heart. Not that I was the first to claim that territory, nor will I be the last! But this yearning plays itself out in as many unique ways as there are human beings on the planet, which is why it never works to repeat myself: to play it safe and fall back on what's worked before.

Not that I haven't tried.

Of course it's also true that those three years were strange anyway, with all sorts of other dramas playing out in my real world. Michael and Brian went off to college; I turned forty (egad!); Kevin was cast in another touring company. We pulled up stakes again and hit the road for twelve more months, home-schooling thirteen-year-old Errol—the best of all sports—until the summer of 1991, when we landed in Los Angeles (Sherman Oaks, to be precise), where we still live now.

But all that was a walk in the park, next to the dark world the child in my head was facing: Clare Frances Caldwell, my spiky, orange-haired heroine, "sharp as freshly-broken glass."

I've always been afraid of the dark.

You don't need to hear about all the false starts, the dead stops, the half-baked pages I sent to Dick—who, if he tore his hair, kindly tore it when I wasn't looking. My trusty old glass-knocking typewriter had traveled with me during that year on the road, but I never was

Errol and Brian at the Katonah house, winter 1987

much good, trying to write in hotel rooms. There were only isolated bits and pieces of the puzzle that would come to me at odd moments, including one long stretch of stream of consciousness typed in Cleveland—or was it Detroit?—that started with the words "GOD IS LOVE." (It seemed important to me, so I saved it, though I had no idea where it fit in.) But I never settled down and made real progress until I was unpacked and re-rooted and sitting in the spot where I'm sitting right now.

I worked steadily then, gratefully, in the fall of 1991, loving Clare and her strange new "family" so much it hurt: Cowboy, Thimble, Little Dog, Racer, silent Shoe (the last two—Racer in particular—bearing more than a passing resemblance to my old pal Everett). And finally, in February, 1992, I sent my finished manuscript off to Dick. He loved the first half, said it had "a kind of brilliance about it." But he thought I'd lost my way completely, midway through the story. I was devastated, cried for twenty-four hours, wondered why he couldn't be wrong, just once?

But somewhere in that black hole of a day, I remembered that peculiar piece of the puzzle, the "GOD IS LOVE" section I had written in Cleveland (or Pittsburgh?) more than a year before. It was like a life raft floating by after the *Titanic* went down; when I grabbed it, I could breathe again. I had to search through piles of discarded pages to find it; I'd never found a place for it in the book until that moment. But now I knew where it had to go—that it was at the very heart of Clare's story—and saw, in a flash, the whole crazy chain of events that had to happen in order for it to go there.

I called Dick back, read it to him, sobbing.

"Don't change a word," he said.

That was the good news.

The bad news: it was only two pages out of more than a hundred, nearly half a book that would have to be completely redone.

But I could see where I was going now, that was the main thing, and was in such a frenzy to get there that I finished that new second half in something like three weeks—

Which must have blown every last writing circuit in my poor old beat-up brain. For the next year and half, I could barely manage a shopping list.

The toads were back, croaking louder than ever.

They did pipe down—briefly—somewhere in there, long enough for me to write a short story called "Andrew, Honestly," which I dreamed up during a fit of homesickness for our old Katonah house. (It appeared in *Don't Give up the Ghost,* the Delacorte Book of Original Ghost Stories, edited by David Gale.) I dreamed a few more Hollywood dreams, too, and sweated over a few more screenplays, but the book I was supposed to be working on kept eluding me. All through the rest of 1992 and deep into 1993, I was mired in endless notebook scribbling: a thousand more beginnings—including forty pages of a manuscript that I sent to Dick, hoping he'd tell me it was better than I thought it was. (Ha!)

Then one morning, when I'd planned to jump up first thing and fix everything that was wrong with those forty pages, I woke up thinking about an old friend, instead: a Texas theater buddy named Patrick Hamilton, who had died of AIDS a year and a half before.

Pat was a wonderful guy—an actor, singer, comedian, writer, dancer—you name it; he could do it, and do it better than anybody else. He was the life of every party, the star of every show, the fellow we all counted on to make us laugh.

He was also the father of a beautiful daughter.

I hadn't seen Jenny since she was a little girl, watching in the wings, while her dad worked his magic on stage. But no one who'd ever seen those two together could forget how much they loved each other.

It wasn't the first time that the thought of them had tugged at me. They'd never been far from my mind, really, since we heard the news of Pat's death. But until that morning, it had never occurred to me to try to write about it.

Now, for some reason, I could think of nothing else.

The next time I spoke to Dick, while we were supposed to be discussing that other manuscript—the forty uninspired pages—I found myself talking about Pat and Jenny. I think I half-hoped he would let me off the hook, tell me that he was truly sorry about my friend, but there was no way anybody would want to read a book about a girl whose father dies of AIDS.

In my heart, I knew better.

"That's your story," he said. "That's the book you should be writing. Don't worry about what anybody else is going to think. Just *write.*"

"Lightning shining through the telephone wires," I wrote in my notebook, after that conversation. "Hallelujah."

Thank God for Dick.

I was still terrified, of course. Had no clue where to begin. Floundered for months, until November of 1993, when visits from two more old friends changed everything:

Ricky Carlson, first. Our dear, funny Ricky, who is battling for his life in a Houston hospital, even as I type these words. He wasn't sick back then, but he had just learned he was HIV-positive. And he told me about his new friend, Barbara Crofford, and the wonderful work she was doing with the Los Angeles Shanti Foundation,

and how much that work was helping him and countless other "PWAs" (People with AIDS) learn to cope with the myriad difficulties facing them.

The second old friend didn't come in person. But I was happy to see him, anyway, when he showed up in my head. Remember Everett? Sheila's former student? The boy with the great grin, who'd lost his dad and his house, and still managed to hang in there with his spirit intact, hoping for the best?

I've already mentioned that there was some of Everett in two of the characters—especially Racer—in *The Beggars' Ride.* And now he came to my rescue again, this time in the shape of an eleven-year-old prophet with Coke-bottle lenses, who believes that "death is a physical impossibility":

> Isaiah says if you leave L.A. before the morning smog burns off and head out the Five up to Hungry Valley, you can stop at the Miracle Man's for lunch and still make it home before dark. . . . (*Earthshine*).

Writing *Earthshine* was a joy, once Everett (Isaiah) showed up. I guess that might sound like an exaggeration, but it isn't. He made it *possible,* somehow, for me to begin, and for Slim to find her voice—Slim, the unbeliever, who wants so much and fights so hard to keep her irresistible, irreplaceable father alive.

I think our friend Pat was around, too, in that oddly joyful season I even dreamed about him one night, after one of those days when I was stumped and half nuts, with no clue where the story might go next. He was backstage, appropriately, getting ready for an entrance, gluing on an enormous handlebar moustache. I ran up to him, hugely relieved to see him. "Oh, Pat," I said, all in a rush, "thank God you're back, I'm trying to write this book, and it's fiction but it's real, too, sort of, it's about you and Jenny but not exactly and I don't know how, I don't know what's going to happen—"

"Don't worry, kiddo," he said, giving me a hug. "You're doing just fine."

And then he hurried off to make his entrance.

I finished *Earthshine* in late February, 1994. And Dick said it was just fine, too.

The toads had the upper hand for the next few years. A hundred more story beginnings, a few more stabs at the movies, but nothing that struck a single spark. Meanwhile, change was in the wind again: Kevin had been acting in television and film, but now he got a job back East in a Broadway show. It took two years to develop, two weeks to close. We burned up the cross-country red-eye miles. We also moved twice, as a result of the Northridge earthquake—from our house to an apartment for six months, then back again.

One morning during that apartment phase (it was on Dickens Street, which I hoped boded well, literarily), I was about to sit down at the breakfast table when a headline caught my eye. An upside-down headline, from where I stood: "The Czar of Elsewhere," I thought it said. What a wonderful title!

But when I turned the newspaper around, what it actually said was "The Czar of Elasera." I think that was it. I can't even remember what the article was about now, only that it wasn't at all the kind of story I was hoping for. So I read a bit, then put it down.

Still, my mistake stuck with me. "The Czar of Elsewhere." Or maybe not the czar—maybe the Emperor, or the Empress . . . *The Empress of Elsewhere*? I loved the sound of it, anyway. So I scribbled it in my notebook, even though I had no idea what it might mean. Something to do with the Los Angeles River, I thought (I passed its prison-like concrete walls nearly every day); something about a girl with a head full of stories, a girl whose family teased about living "elsewhere"—in her imaginary kingdom—far more vivid than the drab world around her.

Nearly a year and a million scribbles later, back in our house again, I woke one morning with a completely different picture in my head: not Los Angeles at all, but the East Texas of my childhood. I could see the old Phelan mansion, where my cousins' widowed grandmother used to live. I could see the heavy iron gate that was always closed before it. There was an angry girl on the inside, looking out; a lonely boy on the outside, looking in. And while I was wondering who in the world they were, in my mind's eye, a monkey came running.

> First time I ever laid eyes on the Empress, she was skittering out the south gate of the Monroe mansion with her crown on crooked and her tail in the air. . . . (*The Empress of Elsewhere*)

My Phelan cousins once had a monkey just like that, a little Capuchin named Nicky. I thought he was the most marvelous creature I'd ever seen. I begged for a monkey of my own, but my mother (in an uncharacteristic fit of unreasonableness) refused to get me one. Monkeys bite, I was informed. Even Nicky. He didn't really care much for anybody, except my Aunt Pat. He used to escape regularly into the trees in the back yard, and the only way she could catch him was to sit on the ground below with her baby in her lap and make loud kissing noises, which would enrage poor Nicky, filling him with such terrible jealousy that he would climb right down and try to push the baby away—whereupon Aunt Pat would grab him and put him back in his cage.

I never could stand cages.

Nobody would ever mistake any of this for *Great Expectations*. But maybe that flicker of a beginning in our Dickens apartment did have *some* subliminal effect on *The Empress of Elsewhere,* at least in one small respect. Remember the stories about Americans waiting on the docks for the ships from England, so they'd be the first to read the English newspapers with the latest installment of *The Old Curiosity Shop* or *Oliver Twist*? Well, Dick didn't have to wait at the dock, exactly, but he did spend a good bit of time listening for the fax machine to start ringing. Meanwhile, I typed (and re-typed, endlessly) each chapter until I was satisfied with it, then sent it off for his approval before I wrote the

The author's family at Brian's wedding, 1999. Left to right: Errol, Michael, Brian's wife Gina, Brian, Theresa, Kevin

next one. It wasn't our plan, exactly; it just happened that way—mostly because I was so far behind schedule—which meant both of us were on pins and needles, for months on end.

But in March of 1998, he read the last chapter. And approved it.

I tap-danced in the kitchen that morning.

It would be another three years before I really caught fire again, story-wise. Not that I wasn't writing. (As Ron Koertge puts it, when people ask him about his routine: "I write badly every day.") My piles of notebooks and rejected screenplays got taller and taller. I visited lots of schools, made some wonderful new friends, flew back to Texas for family crises and celebrations. Our son Brian met his dear Gina; they were married in April, 1999. And eventually, after dozens of bungled beginnings, I found myself back at the river again—or what passes for a river, here in Los Angeles: that "overblown cement gutter that couldn't hold a candle to the Wichita."

> But Mama took up for it. It wasn't always like this, she said—all boxed in, like some wild animal in a cage. Used to be this river ran free as the wind, when the San Fernando Valley was nothing but country. Used to be it had nice soft sand on its bottom and sides, not these rock-hard prison walls. And fish, too—well, sure, but not just *fish*. . . . (*Ruby Electric*)

It was Ruby Miller speaking—a twelve-and-a-half-year-old Texas transplant with a head full of stories. Only now her stories were larger than life, even more vivid than in their last tentative incarnation. Big enough to mend her broken family, she believes; big enough to solve all mysteries and bring her daddy home. Because this time—as I sat up in bed with my heart pounding and realized all at once, one sunny morning in April, 2001—this time Ruby was determined to be a screenwriter.

> Sure, you couldn't show any of this in a movie, because she's walking around just like regular, but the world is different now; *she's* different—all charged up, like a jillion-watt bulb. "She's small, but she's wiry," the doctor once said. (It worried her at the time; she had just seen *The Terminator.*) She pictures her insides, whirring and ticking. A tangle of live wires, shooting sparks.

> Introducing RUBY ELECTRIC!
> Better put on your rubber-soled shoes.
> She's got the POWER, man. . . .

(Ruby Electric)

And so it's happened, somehow or other, that I've come full circle. Back to the girl from a middle-size town in Texas, who dreamed in technicolor and was fiercely proud of her beautiful mama, and knew for a fact her daddy could do no wrong.

She never really grew up. She just moved to California.

Ruby Electric was published in June, 2003.

I'm grateful to be working on another story now—"inch by bloody inch," as Ruby would say—even though I still have lots of days when I'm just as blank and blocked and clueless as I was in the seventh grade. But now I know it's just part of the job, that's all, and that even *other* writers—writers who actually know what they're doing—go through this all the time. And keep going anyway.

Of course even on the good days, the ones we live for, it's really hard work. I'm not about to tell you it's a breeze. Chances are it won't make you rich, either—at least, not in dollars and cents.

But on those good days, when the stories are dreaming themselves along in my head, coming together in ways I never expected . . .

On those miracle days, when the characters start to *say* things and *do* things I never planned at all . . .

On those outsize days, when I'm typing like crazy, trying to keep up, and telling myself to "*write!* Just *write!*" . . .

Well, I guess there are less peculiar ways to spend your life. But on days like that, I can't help thinking—like Jimmy in *The Empress of Elsewhere*—"Maybe it ain't happily ever after, but it'll sure do for now."

NIX, Garth 1963-

Personal

Born 1963, in Melbourne, Victoria, Australia; married, 2000; wife's name, Anna; children: Thomas Henry. *Education:* University of Canberra, B.A., 1986. *Hobbies and other interests:* Traveling, fishing, bodysurfing, book collecting, reading, and films.

Addresses

Home—Sydney, Australia. *Agent*—c/o Author Mail, HarperCollins, 10 E. 53rd St., 7th Floor, New York, NY 10022. *E-mail*—garthnix@ozemail.com.au.

Career

Author, editor, publicist, public relations consultant, agent. Worked for the Australian government; worked in a Sydney, Australia, bookshop; senior editor for a multinational publisher; Gotley Nix Evans Pty. Ltd., Sydney, Australia, marketing communications consultant, 1996-98; part-time agent, Curtis Brown, Australia, 1999-2002. *Military service:* Served four years in the Australian Army Reserve.

Awards, Honors

Best Fantasy Novel and Best YA Novel, Aurealis Awards, 1995, Notable Book and Best Book for Young Adults, American Library Association (ALA), Notable Book, CBCA, Recommended Fantasy Novel, *Locus* magazine, Books for the Teenage, New York Public Library, 1997, shortlisted for six state awards in the United States, all for *Sabriel;* "Books in the Middle: Outstanding Titles" selection, *Voice of Youth Advocates,* 1996, for *Sabriel,* and 1997, for *Shade's Children;* shortlisted, Aurealis Award, 1997, Best Book for Young Adults, ALA, Pick of the Lists, ABA, Notable Book, CBCA, shortlisted for the Heartland Prize, the Pacific Northwest Reader's Choice Awards, the South Carolina Reader's Choice Awards, the Evergreen YA Award, and the Garden State Young Reader's Awards, all for *Shade's Children;* Adelaide Festival Award for Children's Literature, 2002, Best Book for Young Adults, ALA, Recommended Reading Fantasy Novel, *Locus* magazine, shortlisted for Young Adult and Fantasy Novel categories, Aurealis Awards, 2002, shortlisted for the 2002 Australian Science Fiction Achievement Award, all for *Lirael: Daughter of the Clayr.*

Garth Nix

Writings

FOR CHILDREN; EASY READERS

Bill the Inventor, illustrated by Nan Bodsworth, Koala Books (Sydney, New South Wales, Australia), 1998.
Blackbread the Pirate, Koala Books (Sydney, New South Wales, Australia), 1999.
Serena and the Sea Serpent, illustrated by Stephen Michael King, Puffin (New York, NY), 2001.

FOR CHILDREN; "THE SEVENTH TOWER" SERIES

The Fall, Scholastic (New York, NY), 2000.
Castle, Scholastic (New York, NY), 2000.
Renir, Scholastic (New York, NY), 2001.
Above the Veil, Scholastic (New York, NY), 2001.
Into Battle, Scholastic (New York, NY), 2001.
The Violet Keystone, Scholastic (New York, NY), 2001.

FOR YOUNG ADULTS

The Ragwitch, Pan Books (Sydney, New South Wales, Australia), 1990, Tor (New York, NY), 1995.
Shade's Children, HarperCollins (New York, NY), 1997.
The Calusari ("X Files" Series), HarperCollins (New York, NY), 1997.

"THE OLD KINGDOM" TRILOGY; YOUNG ADULT

Sabriel, HarperCollins (New York, NY), 1995.
Lirael: Daughter of the Clayr, HarperCollins (New York, NY), 2001.
Abhorsen, HarperCollins (New York, NY), 2003.

"VERY CLEVER BABY" SERIES

Very Clever Baby's First Reader: A Simple Reader for Your Child Featuring Freddy the Fish and Easy Words, Nix Books (Sydney, New South Wales, Australia), 1988.
Very Clever Baby's Ben Hur: Starring Freddy the Fish as Charlton Heston, Nix Books (Sydney, New South Wales, Australia), 1988.
Very Clever Baby's Guide to the Greenhouse Effect, Nix Books (Sydney, New South Wales, Australia), 1992.
Very Clever Baby's First Christmas, Text Publishing Co. (Melbourne, New South Wales, Australia), 1998.

OTHER

Mister Monday ("Keys to the Kingdom" series), Scholastic (New York, NY), 2004.

Also author of short stories and coauthor of shows for dinner theater. Nix's works have been translated into Dutch, Japanese, German, Portuguese, Finnish, Russian, Spanish, and several other languages.

Work in Progress

Additional books in the "The Keys to the Kingdom," a seven-book fantasy series for children nine to thirteen, for Collins; *A Confusion of Princes,* a young adult science fiction novel.

Sidelights

The author of over twenty books for children and young adults, Australian Garth Nix is best known for his fantasy novels in the "Old Kingdom" trilogy, including *Sabriel, Lirael,* and *Abhorsen.* Writing for a slightly younger audience, he has also penned a six-novel cycle, "The Seventh Tower" series, and is at work on another fantasy series, "The Keys to the Kingdom." Known for his engaging and finely detailed fiction, Nix told Kelly Milner Halls of *Teenreads* about the need for fantasy and magic in his own life that helps to fuel his popular fiction: "Like most fantasy authors, I would love to have magic in this world. It would be great to be able to fly, or summon a complete restaurant meal on a white tablecloth to a deserted beach, or to take the shape of an animal. But I wouldn't want the downside of most fantasy books—the enemies, evil creatures, and threats to the whole world—and my sense of balance indicates that you can't have the good without the bad." Nix has also explained the genesis of his novels on his own Web site. "Most of my books seem to stem from a single image or thought that lodges in my brain and slowly grows into something that needs to be expressed. That thought may be a 'what if?' or perhaps just an image. . . . Typically I seem to think about a book for a year or so before I actually start writing."

Born in 1963, in Melbourne, Australia, Nix grew up in Canberra with an older and a younger brother. His father worked in science, while his mother was an artist, working with papermaking. Both parents also wrote and read widely, so Nix had a firm foundation for his own future work. Nix has noted that his mother was reading J. R. R. Tolkien's *The Lord of the Rings* when she was pregnant with him, "so I absorbed this master work of fantasy *in utero,* as it were," he once commented. "I went all through school in Canberra," Nix remarked in an autobiographical sketch on his Web site, "but as with many authors, much of my education came from books. . . . My apprenticeship as an author began with reading." Nix grew up, as he once commented, in "a culture of reading," with books all over his home and with frequent trips to the local library. Early on he encountered the works of Ursula Le Guin, Robert Heinlein, Robert Louis Stevenson, John Masefield, Mary Stewart, Isaac Asimov, Madeleine L'Engle, and a variety of other fantasy and science fiction authors. He would much rather read a book than do his homework, but did well in school. "I was a smart and smart-mouthed kid," he remarked on his Web site, "but I got on pretty well with everyone, probably because my best friend was always the school captain in every school and he was friends with everybody."

At seventeen, Nix thought he might want to become an army officer, so he joined the Australian Army Reserve, serving for one weekend a month and one month per year in training. However, he discovered that he did not want to make the military his career, but enjoyed the part-time soldiering enough to stick with it, learning how to build bridges and then blow them up. He was also going to the University of Canberra during these years, and worked a paper-shuffling job with the government for a year. He saved enough money to go traveling for six months, hitting the roads in England. It was during this time away from Australia that he began writing, composing the short story "Sam, Cars and the Cuckoo" while on the road, but not learning of its sale until he was back in Australia and was contacted for reprint rights.

With this success, Nix decided he could become a professional writer. To that end, he earned a bachelor's degree in professional writing from the University of Canberra, and immediately took a job at Dalton's Bookshop in Canberra (not connected to the American chain of the same name). "I now believe that anyone who works in publishing should spend at least three months in a bookshop, where the final product ends up," he once commented. Nix spent six months at the job, and then went into publishing, working as a sales representative, publicist, and editor to gain knowledge of all ends of

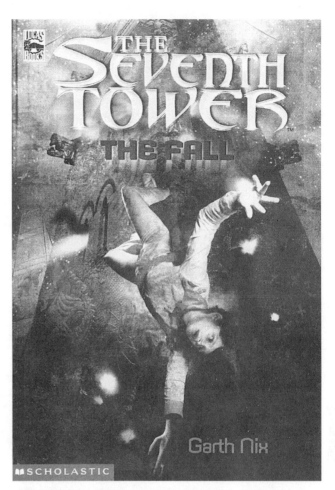

In Nix's **The Fall** *thirteen-year-old Tal must find a way to enter the spirit world of Aenir. (Jacket illustration by Steve Rawlings.)*

the publishing and writing industry. During the six years he spent in publishing, he also became a published novelist.

His earliest publications were far from fantasy, though they do include elements of the fantastical. His self-published "Very Clever Baby" books are parodies of an easy reader, exploring the wonders of Christmas or the movie *Ben Hur* featuring Freddy the Fish, but are not yet available outside of his homeland. "They're little books that I first made back in 1988 as presents for some friends expecting babies, on the basis that all parents think their babies are geniuses," Nix explained to Claire E. White on *Writers Write.* Greeting card sized, the little books are intended for adults rather than children.

If the "Very Clever Baby Books" were intended as a joke, there was nothing joke-like about his first published novel, *The Ragwitch,* which he had worked on as part of his degree requirement. Published in Australia in 1990, the novel tells the story of Paul and his sister Julia who are exploring a prehistoric garbage dump. There they find a nest that contains a rag doll that has the power to enslave others; and Julia becomes its first victim. Paul must then go into a bizarre fantasy world in order to save his sister. Reviewing this first novel, Ann Tolman, writing in *Australian Bookseller and Publisher,* felt that Nix "skillfully relates a magical tale which begins in a nice and easy way, but soon develops into a compelling and involving story of a journey through evil times." Tolman further noted that the book provides "good adult mystic escapism with considerable imaginative experiences for the reader." Similarly, Laurie Copping, writing in the *Canberra Times,* found *The Ragwitch* an "engrossing novel which should be enjoyed by true lovers of high fantasy."

Nix traveled in Turkey, Syria, Jordan, Iran, and Pakistan in 1993. During the trip, be began his next novel, *Sabriel,* finishing it upon his return to Australia. Also on his return, he left publishing for the public relations firm he helped to establish. *Sabriel,* a young adult novel, was the first of what ultimately became a trilogy. "A vividly imagined fantasy," in the words of *School Library Journal* contributor John Peters, it is the first of Nix's works to receive acclaim in the United States. Sabriel is a young woman who has been trained by her father, Abhorsen, a necromancer who, unlike others of his trade, is skilled at putting uneasy souls to rest instead of calling them to life. Sabriel is in her last year of boarding school when she receives Abhorsen's necromancing tools and sword and realizes that her father's life is in danger—he has left the Land of the Living. Sabriel leaves the safety of her school to return to the Old Kingdom, which her father was supposed to protect, in order to rescue him. As she travels to the world beyond the Land of the Living to the Gates of Death, Sabriel is joined by Mogget, a powerful being in the form of a cat who has acted as her father's servant, and a young prince named Touchstone, whom she has brought back from the dead. With their help, Sabriel battles her way past monsters, beasts, and evil spirits until she finally reaches her father, "only to lose him permanently in the opening rounds of a vicious, wild climax," as Peters explained. However, Sabriel—whom critics acknowledged as an especially sympathetic heroine—realizes that she is her father's successor and that the future of the Old Kingdom depends on her. Peters concluded, "This book is guaranteed to keep readers up way past their bedtime." Other reviewers also reacted favorably. "Rich, complex, involving, hard to put down," claimed a critic in *Publishers Weekly,* who added that the novel "is excellent high fantasy." *Booklist* reviewer Sally Estes, who compared *Sabriel* favorably to English writer Philip Pullman's fantasy *The Golden Compass,* stated, "The action charges along at a gallop, imbued with an encompassing sense of looming disaster. . . . A page-turner for sure." Writing in the *Horn Book Magazine,* Ann A. Flowers commented: "The story is remarkable for the level of originality of the fantastic elements . . . and for the subtle presentation, which leaves readers to explore for themselves the complex structure and significance of the magic elements." According to a critic for *Voice of Youth Advocates, Sabriel* is "one of the best fantasies of this or any other year."

After publication of *Sabriel,* Nix's publishers wanted him to capitalize on its popularity and continue the saga. Nix, however, had another darker book that he needed to write. *Shade's Children* is a science fiction novel for young adults that, according to a *Publishers Weekly* critic, "tells essentially the same story" as *Sabriel,* with its "desperate quest by a talented few." In this book, however, a psychic young boy, Gold-Eye, runs to escape the evil Overlords who use the body parts of children for their own insidious purposes. The novel is set in a future time when the earth has been taken over by the terrible aliens, who have destroyed everyone over fourteen; the only adult presence is Shade, a computer-generated hologram. Gold-Eye joins a group of teenagers who, working from Shade's submarine base, fight the Overlords. In addition to battling the aliens, the young people must deal with betrayal and with losing half their group; however, they learn about their special talents and achieve victory through their sacrifices.

Critical reception for this third novel was again positive. A *Publishers Weekly* reviewer concluded that while *Shade's Children* "lacks some of the emotional depth of Nix's first work, it will draw (and keep) fans of the genre." According to a critic in *Kirkus Reviews,* the book "combines plenty of comic-book action in a sci-fi setting to produce an exciting read. . . . [An] action-adventure with uncommon appeal outside the genre." Ann A. Flowers of *Horn Book* praised Nix's characterization of his young protagonists, adding: "The author leaves the reader to draw many conclusions from scattered evidence, hence capturing and holding the audience's attention all the way to the bittersweet ending. Grim, unusual, and fascinating." Donna L. Scanlon, writing in *Voice of Youth Advocates,* had further praise for the title, noting that through "a fast-paced combination of narrative, transcripts, chilling statistical reports, and shifting points of view, Nix depicts a chilling future." For Scanlon, however, Nix's grim futuristic view is also "laced with hope." *Reading Time* contributor Kevin Steinberger similarly enthused: "Exciting action, cracking pace and absorbing intrigue, all in a vividly imagined world, marks *Shade's Children* as one of the best adolescent reads of the year."

Following the publication of *Shade's Children,* Nix left his PR firm to devote his time to writing, and also met the woman who would become his wife. He quickly wrote the young adult *The Calusari,* a novelization of an episode from the television series, *The X-Files.* The work "really did not suit me," Nix told Claire E. White. As he set to work to complete the next novel in the "Old Kingdom" series, *Lirael: Daughter of the Clayr,* he also turned out several easy readers for young children, including *Bill the Inventor, Blackbread the Pirate,* and *Serena and the Sea Serpent.* Russ Merrin, reviewing *Blackbread the Pirate* in *Magpies,* felt it was "utterly delightful nonsense." *Serena and the Sea Serpent,* about a little girl who saves a town from a misunderstood vegetarian sea serpent, is a "great story," according to another *Magpies* contributor.

Nix also busied himself working part-time as a literary agent (a position he gave up for full-time writing in 2002), and with a six-part fantasy series for Scholastic and Lucas Films, "The Seventh Tower," a children's fantasy featuring young Tal, a Chosen one of Orange Order from the Castle of the Seven Towers and his adventures in search of the Sunstones which he needs to save not only his family but his future. Tal's world is in the dark, literally; the sun only shines above the mysterious Veil, high above in the atmosphere over the Seven Towers. Tal's father disappears in the first book of the series, *The Fall*, on the very day that Tal is ascending to the throne. And his father has taken the Sunstone, which Tal needs for the ascension. Without the Sunstone, Tal cannot bind himself to a Shadowspirit, and failing that, he will lose not only his Chosen status, but also will not be able to find a cure for his mother's illness. Joining Tal in much of his search is the young woman, Milla.

"I had to write these books fairly quickly, faster than I normally would," Nix told White. Basically, he turned out each novel in the series in two months. The books became popular with readers in the targeted age range of middle graders, reaching an older audience as well. The fourth book in the series, *Above the Veil*, even made a short appearance on the *New York Times* bestseller list and the series as a whole was on the *Publishers Weekly* children's bestseller lists, both in 2001. Reviewing *Above the Veil*, a contributor for *Publishers Weekly* praised Nix's creation of a "very complex world," and noted that fans of the series would enjoy "plenty of narrow squeaks, exciting chase scenes, and stunning revelations."

Nix published *Lirael*, the long-awaited sequel to *Sabriel*, in 2001. This book takes place fourteen years later, but the Old Kingdom is still facing dangers, this time from an evil necromancer who wants to free a terribly evil being. The book focuses on a group of clairvoyant women, the Clayr, who are gifted with what is called the "Sight." One of these, however, Lirael, does not have such powers, partly due to the mystery of her birth. Turning fourteen, she fears that she will never gain the Sight and become an adult. Yet she does have magic powers, and in the company of the Disreputable Dog, she is able to complete a quest that wins her the trust of her fellow Clayr. They thus entrust her with an even more dangerous and seemingly impossible mission. At the same time, similar doubts have infected Prince Sameth, son of King Touchstone and Sabriel, who feels he is not fit to perform the duties of office after battling with the evil necromancer, Hedge. Sameth and Lirael ultimately team up to battle the evil force attacking the Old Kingdom in a book "outstanding" for its "imaginative magical descriptions, plot intrigues, and adventure sequences," according to *Horn Book*'s

Anita L. Burkam. Similarly, Beth Wright, reviewing the novel in *School Library Journal*, praised the "fast-paced plot" as well as the intricacy of the "haunting and unusual, exhaustively and flawlessly conceived connections among . . . rulers and guardians, and the magic that infuses them all." *Booklist*'s Sally Estes also lauded the book, noting that "the characterizations are appealing," and that Nix "not only maintains the intricate world he created for the earlier book but also continues the frenetic pace of the action and the level of violence." Janice M. Del Negro, writing in *Bulletin of the Center for Children's Books*, commended Nix for a book "filled with hair-raising escapes, desperate flights, relentless pursuits, and magical duels, described in sensual language that makes the scenes live." And a reviewer for *Publishers Weekly* likewise found Nix's creation of the Old Kingdom "entrancing and complicated." The same reviewer noted that *Lirael* ends in a "cliffhanger," to be resolved in the third novel of the series.

That novel, *Abhorsen*, appeared in 2003. In this final installment, Sameth and Lirael continue to do battle with the forces of the dead, brought together by the evil Hedge. Again Disreputable Dog and Mogget are on hand to help out their respective companions. Lirael is now Abhorsen-in-Waiting and must travel into death to foil plans to release the Destroyer from an age-old prison. Secrets are revealed and ends tied up in this concluding novel of the trilogy, a book at once "breathtaking, bittersweet, and utterly unforgettable," as a critic for *Kirkus Reviews* described it. A reviewer for *Publishers Weekly* was also impressed by Nix's achievement, calling *Abhorsen* a "riveting continuation" of the saga, and further remarking that the novel was both an "allegory regarding war and peace and a testament to friendship." Estes, writing in *Booklist*, similarly held that the "tension throughout the story is palatable" and the conclusion was "satisfying." One and all, reviewers hoped, as did Sharon Rawlins in her *School Library Journal* review, that "this may not be the last story about the Old Kingdom."

In the course of his twenty books for young readers, Nix has created amazing and intricate worlds, a cast of characters that stick in the imagination, and lessons of friendship and loyalty that resonate. However, Nix does not see himself as a didactic writer, or that he is writing for a particular audience. "To be honest," he told White, in *Writers Write*, "most of the time I don't think about the fact that I am writing for children or young adults. I simply enjoy telling the story and the way I naturally write seems to work well for both young and older audiences. . . . Because my natural writing voice seems to inhabit the Young Adult realm, . . . I haven't had to change it." As for theme or message in his work, Nix told White, "I subscribe to the belief that 'if you want to send a message, use Western Union.' In other words, if the values or moral messages are too overt, the story will suffer and no one will read it. Children don't like to be preached to any more than adults do.

On the other hand, while I always try and tell a good story, I can't help but infuse my moral and ethical views into any book."

Biographical and Critical Sources

BOOKS

Authors and Artists for Young Adults, Volume 27, Gale (Detroit, MI), 1999, pp. 167-173.

Children's Literature Review, Volume 68, Gale (Detroit, MI), 2001, pp. 100-111.

St. James Guide to Young Adult Writers, 2nd edition, edited by Tom Pendergast and Sara Pendergast, St. James Press (Detroit, MI), 1999, pp. 632-633.

PERIODICALS

Australian Book Review, September, 1996, p. 63.

Australian Bookseller and Publisher, November, 1990, Ann Tolman, review of *The Ragwitch.*

Booklist, October 1, 1996, Sally Estes, review of *Sabriel,* p. 350; April 15, 2001, Sally Estes, review of *Lirael,* p. 1557; July, 2001, Jennifer Hubert, review of *Shade's Children,* p. 1999; January 1, 2003, Sally Estes, review of *Abhorsen,* p. 871.

Bookseller, February 21, 2003, "Latest Deals in Children's Publishing," p. 34.

Bulletin of the Center for Children's Books, December, 1996, p. 146; November, 1997, p. 95; May, 2001, Janice M. Del Negro, review of *Lirael,* pp. 348-349.

Canberra Times (Canberra, Australia), June 2, 1991, Laurie Copping, review of *The Ragwitch.*

Horn Book, January-February, 1997, Ann A. Flowers, review of *Sabriel,* pp. 64-65; September-October, 1997, Ann A. Flowers, review of *Shade's Children,* pp. 576-77; July-August, 2001, Anita L. Burkam, review of *Lirael,* p. 459; November-December, 2002, Kristi Beavin, review of *Sabriel* and *Lirael* (audiobooks), p. 790.

Kirkus Reviews, August 15, 1997, review of *Shade's Children,* pp. 1309-1310; December 15, 2002, review of *Abhorsen,* pp. 1854-1855.

Kliatt, January, 1998, Lesley S. J. Farmer, review of *Sabriel,* p. 17.

Magpies, September, 1998, Annette Dale Meiklejohn, review of *Bill the Inventor,* p. 33; September, 1999, Russ Merrin, review of *Blackbread the Pirate,* p. 28; March, 2001, review of *Serena and the Sea Serpent,* p. 29.

Publishers Weekly, October 21, 1996, review of *Sabriel,* p. 84; June 16, 1997, review of *Shade's Children,* p. 60; March 19, 2001, review of *Lirael,* p. 101; March 18, 2002, John F. Baker, "Garth Nix," p. 16; May 27, 2002, review of *Lirael,* p. 62; November 25, 2002, review of *Abhorsen,* p. 70.

Reading Time, November, 1997, Kevin Steinberger, review of *Shade's Children,* p. 35.

School Library Journal, September, 1996, John Peters, review of *Sabriel,* p. 228; May, 1998, review of *Shade's Children,* p. 52; May, 2001, Beth Wright, review of *Lirael,* p. 157; September, 2001, John Peters, review of *Above the Veil,* p. 231; February, 2003, Sharon Rawlins, review of *Abhorsen,* p. 146.

Voice of Youth Advocates, June, 1997, review of *Sabriel;* February, 1998, Suzann Manczuk and Ray Barber, review of *Shade's Children,* p. 366; June, 1998, Donna M. Scanlon, review of *Shade's Children,* p. 132.

ONLINE

Australian SF Online, http://www.eidolon.net/ (August 5, 2003).

Garth Nix Author Web site, http://www.garthnix.co.uk/ (August 5, 2003).

Offical Garth Nix Site, http://www.members.ozemail.com.au/ (April 21, 2003), Garth Nix, "How I Write: The Process of Creating a Book," and "A Biographical Whimsy."

Teenreads.com, http://www.teenreads.com/ (February 18, 2003), Kelly Milner Halls, "Garth Nix Interview."

Writers Write, http://www.writerswrite.com/ (July-August, 2000), Claire E. White, "A Conversation with Garth Nix."*

P

PARKS, Peggy J. 1951-

Personal

Born September 1, 1951, in Lansing, MI; daughter of Earl J. (a utility company executive) and Elaine Lynne (a bookkeeper) Wheeler; children: Jeff Kosloski, Becky Vollink, Amy Bayne. *Ethnicity:* "Caucasian." *Education:* Aquinas College, B.S. (magna cum laude). *Politics:* "Moderate/libertarian/green party." *Religion:* Christian. *Hobbies and other interests:* In-line skating, reading, cooking, creative writing, gardening, travel, Detroit Red Wings hockey.

Addresses

Home and office—1623 E. Harbour Towne Circle, Muskegon, MI 49441. *E-mail*—pj@pjparks.com.

Career

Freelance writer, 1995—. Volunteer Muskegon, formerly on board of directors and chairman of marketing committee; West Michigan's Cherry County Playhouse, pro bono public relations work; city of Muskegon, member of public relations/communications committee; volunteer at Muskegon Summer Celebration.

Peggy J. Parks

Writings

"CAREERS FOR THE TWENTY-FIRST CENTURY" SERIES

News Media, Gale/Lucent (Detroit, MI), 2002.
Music, Gale/Lucent (Detroit, MI), 2002.

"EXPLORING CAREERS" SERIES

Police Officer, Gale/Kidhaven (Detroit, MI), 2003.
Doctor, Gale/Kidhaven (Detroit, MI), 2003.
Computer Programmer, Gale/Kidhaven (Detroit, MI), 2003.

Teacher, Gale/Kidhaven (Detroit, MI), 2003.
Lawyer, Gale/Kidhaven (Detroit, MI), 2003.

"GIANTS OF SCIENCE" SERIES

Benjamin Franklin, Gale/Blackbirch (Detroit, MI), 2002.
Jonas Salk, Gale/Blackbirch (Detroit, MI), 2003.
Robert Fulton, Gale/Blackbirch (Detroit, MI), 2003.

"NATIONS IN CONFLICT" SERIES

Afghanistan, Gale/Blackbirch (Detroit, MI), 2003.
Iraq, Gale/Blackbirch (Detroit, MI), 2003.
North Korea, Gale/Blackbirch (Detroit, MI), 2003.

A special education teacher helps a student with a lesson in Parks's **Teacher,** *part of the "Exploring Careers" series.*

OTHER

Grand Rapids: The City That Works, Towery Publications, 1998.
Great Depression ("Daily Life" series), Gale/Kidhaven (Detroit, MI), 2003.
The Internet ("Science Library" series), Gale/Kidhaven (Detroit, MI), 2003.
Global Warming ("Our Environment" series), Gale/Kidhaven (Detroit, MI), 2003.
Aswan Dam ("Building World Landmarks" series), Gale/Blackbirch (Detroit, MI), 2003.
Global Warming ("Library of Science" series), Gale/Lucent (Detroit, MI), 2004.

Work in Progress

"Five books for Blackbirch Press's 'Yesterday and Today' series and five books for Kidhaven Press's 'Exploring Careers' series, as well as miscellaneous other Kidhaven titles."

Sidelights

Peggy J. Parks told *SATA:* "From the time I was very young, I knew I wanted to be a writer. I never realized that I would end up writing professionally, and I certainly never dreamed I would be an author. All I know is that I had a pen and paper in my hand from the time I was old enough to scribble on a tablet. I spent ten years in marketing and advertising, on the account side of the business, and then formed my own communications company in 1995. Building a writing portfolio was challenging, to say the least, because when you do not have professional writing experience, how do you get professional writing experience? So, I did what any self-respecting wannabe-writer does—I begged. I pleaded. And I eventually convinced people to let me write for them. Eight years have passed, and I am blessed with a successful career as a writer and author. I will always be grateful to those who believed in my talent enough to help me get started.

"As for writers who have influenced me, Alice Hoffman and Sally Mandel immediately come to mind. Also Pat Conroy. Because I have a very silly side, I love the humorous writings of Dave Barry, who makes me laugh out loud. I was fortunate enough to interview him and he is the featured writer in my "Exploring Careers" book on writers. Actually, there are too many authors to mention because for as long as I have been writing, I have also had my nose in a book. And in terms of writers who have inspired me, at the top of the list is my son, Jeff Kosloski, who is an immensely gifted writer.

"My current specialty is nonfiction, but down the road, I would love to write fiction. I have many ideas—in fact, I have more ideas than I do time to write all the books I want to write! I will say that future books will undoubtedly revolve around humor, because when I write with the purpose of making people laugh, I am at my most creative.

"What advice would I give to aspiring writers? Never, ever give up. Be a voracious reader. Write all the time. If writing is your dream, then follow that dream and do not let anything or anyone stop you."

Biographical and Critical Sources

PERIODICALS

Booklist, October 15, 2002, Roger Leslie, review of *The News Media,* p. 416.

ONLINE

PJ Parks Communications, http://www.pjparks.com/ (February 18, 2003).

*   *   *

PASCAL, Francine 1938-

Personal

Born May 13, 1938, in New York, NY; daughter of William and Kate (Dunitz) Rubin; married John Robert Pascal (a journalist and author), August 18, 1954 (died, 1981); children: Laurie, Susan, Jamie (daughter). *Education:* New York University, B.A., 1958. *Hobbies and other interests:* Travel, reading.

Addresses

Home—New York, NY, and France. *Agent*—Amy Berkower, Writers House, 21 West 26th St., New York, NY 10010.

Francine Pascal

Career

Writer and lecturer. Troy State University, writer-in-residence; Michael Stewart Foundation for Musical Theater, founder and director.

Member

PEN, Dramatists Guild, Authors Guild, Authors League of America, American Theatre Wing (Advisory Committee), Writers Guild of America (East).

Awards, Honors

New York Public Library books for the teenage citation, 1978-85, for *Hangin' out with Cici;* American Library Association best book for young adults citation, 1979, for *My First Love and Other Disasters;* Dorothy Canfield Fisher Children's Book Award, Vermont Congress of Parents and Teachers, *Publishers Weekly* Literary Prize list, both 1982, Bernard Versele Award, Brussels, and Milner Award, Atlanta Public Library, both 1988, all for *The Hand-Me-Down Kid.*

Writings

"VICTORIA MARTIN" SERIES

Hangin' out with Cici, Viking (New York, NY), 1977, paperback edition published as *Hangin' out with Cici; or, My Mother Was Never a Kid,* Dell (New York, NY), 1985.

My First Love and Other Disasters, Viking (New York, NY), 1979.

Love and Betrayal and Hold the Mayo!, Viking (New York, NY), 1985.

My Mother Was Never a Kid, Simon Pulse (New York, NY), 2003.

"SWEET VALLEY HIGH" SERIES

Double Love, Bantam (New York, NY), 1984.
Secrets, Bantam (New York, NY), 1984.
Playing with Fire, Bantam (New York, NY), 1984.
Power Play, Bantam (New York, NY), 1984.
All Night Long, Bantam (New York, NY), 1984.
Dangerous Love, Bantam (New York, NY), 1984.
Dear Sister, Bantam (New York, NY), 1984.
Heartbreaker, Bantam (New York, NY), 1984.
Racing Hearts, Bantam (New York, NY), 1984.
Wrong Kind of Girl, Bantam (New York, NY), 1984.
Too Good to Be True, Bantam (New York, NY), 1984.
When Love Dies, Bantam (New York, NY), 1984.
Kidnapped!, Bantam (New York, NY), 1984.
Deceptions, Bantam (New York, NY), 1984.
Promises, Bantam (New York, NY), 1985.
Rags to Riches, Bantam (New York, NY), 1985.
Love Letters, Bantam (New York, NY), 1985.
Head over Heels, Bantam (New York, NY), 1985.
Showdown, Bantam (New York, NY), 1985.
Crash Landing!, Bantam (New York, NY), 1985.
Runaway, Bantam (New York, NY), 1985.
Too Much in Love, Bantam (New York, NY), 1986.
Say Goodbye, Bantam (New York, NY), 1986.
Memories, Bantam (New York, NY), 1986.
Nowhere to Run, Bantam (New York, NY), 1986.
Hostage!, Bantam (New York, NY), 1986.
Lovestruck, Bantam (New York, NY), 1986.
Alone in the Crowd, Bantam (New York, NY), 1986.
Bitter Rivals, Bantam (New York, NY), 1986.
Jealous Lies, Bantam (New York, NY), 1986.
Taking Sides, Bantam (New York, NY), 1986.
The New Jessica, Bantam (New York, NY), 1986.
Starting Over, Bantam (New York, NY), 1987.
Forbidden Love, Bantam (New York, NY), 1987.
Out of Control, Bantam (New York, NY), 1987.
Last Chance, Bantam (New York, NY), 1987.
Rumors, Bantam (New York, NY), 1987.
Leaving Home, Bantam (New York, NY), 1987.
Secret Admirer, Bantam (New York, NY), 1987.
On the Edge, Bantam (New York, NY), 1987.
Outcast, Bantam (New York, NY), 1987.
Caught in the Middle, Bantam (New York, NY), 1988.
Pretenses, Bantam (New York, NY), 1988.
Hard Choices, Bantam (New York, NY), 1988.
Family Secrets, Bantam (New York, NY), 1988.
Decisions, Bantam (New York, NY), 1988.
Slam Book Fever, Bantam (New York, NY), 1988.
Playing for Keeps, Bantam (New York, NY), 1988.
Troublemaker, Bantam (New York, NY), 1988.
Out of Reach, Bantam (New York, NY), 1988.
In Love Again, Bantam (New York, NY), 1989.
Against the Odds, Bantam (New York, NY), 1989.
Brokenhearted, Bantam (New York, NY), 1989.

Teacher Crush, Bantam (New York, NY), 1989.
Perfect Shot, Bantam (New York, NY), 1989.
White Lies, Bantam (New York, NY), 1989.
Two-Boy Weekend, Bantam (New York, NY), 1989.
That Fatal Night, Bantam (New York, NY), 1989.
Lost at Sea, Bantam (New York, NY), 1989.
Second Chance, Bantam (New York, NY), 1989.
Ms. Quarterback, Bantam (New York, NY), 1990.
The New Elizabeth, Bantam (New York, NY), 1990.
The Ghost of Tricia Martin, Bantam (New York, NY), 1990.
Friend against Friend, Bantam (New York, NY), 1990.
Trouble at Home, Bantam (New York, NY), 1990.
Who's to Blame, Bantam (New York, NY), 1990.
The Parent Plot, Bantam (New York, NY), 1990.
Boy Trouble, Bantam (New York, NY), 1990.
Who's Who?, Bantam (New York, NY), 1990.
The Love Bet, Bantam (New York, NY), 1990.
Amy's True Love, Bantam (New York, NY), 1991.
Miss Teen Sweet Valley, Bantam (New York, NY), 1991.
The Perfect Girl, Bantam (New York, NY), 1991.
Regina's Legacy, Bantam (New York, NY), 1991.
Rock Star's Girl, Bantam (New York, NY), 1991.
Starring Jessica!, Bantam (New York, NY), 1991.
Cheating to Win, Bantam (New York, NY), 1991.
The Dating Game, Bantam (New York, NY), 1991.
The Long-Lost Brother, Bantam (New York, NY), 1991.
The Girl They Both Loved, Bantam (New York, NY), 1991.
Rosa's Lie, Bantam (New York, NY), 1992.
Kidnapped by the Cult, Bantam (New York, NY), 1992.
Steven's Bride, Bantam (New York, NY), 1992.
The Stolen Diary, Bantam (New York, NY), 1992.
Soap Star, Bantam (New York, NY), 1992.
Jessica against Bruce, Bantam (New York, NY), 1992.
My Best Friend's Boyfriend, Bantam (New York, NY), 1992.
Love Letters for Sale, Bantam (New York, NY), 1992.
Elizabeth Betrayed, Bantam (New York, NY), 1992.
Don't Go Home with John, Bantam (New York, NY), 1993.
In Love with a Prince, Bantam (New York, NY), 1993.
She's Not What She Seems, Bantam (New York, NY), 1993.
Stepsisters, Bantam (New York, NY), 1993.
Are We in Love, Bantam (New York, NY), 1993.
The Morning After, Bantam (New York, NY), 1993.
The Arrest, Bantam (New York, NY), 1993.
The Verdict, Bantam (New York, NY), 1993.
The Wedding, Bantam (New York, NY), 1993.
Beware the Babysitter, Bantam (New York, NY), 1993.
The Evil Twin, Bantam (New York, NY), 1993.
The Boyfriend War, Bantam (New York, NY), 1994.
Almost Married, Bantam (New York, NY), 1994.
Operation Love, Bantam (New York, NY), 1994.
A Date with a Werewolf, Bantam (New York, NY), 1994.
Beware the Wolfman, Bantam (New York, NY), 1994.
Jessica's Secret Love, Bantam (New York, NY), 1994.
Death Threat, Bantam (New York, NY), 1994.
Left at the Altar, Bantam (New York, NY), 1994.
Double-Crossed, Bantam (New York, NY), 1994.
Love and Death in London, Bantam (New York, NY), 1994.
Jessica's Secret Diary, Bantam (New York, NY), 1994.
College Weekend, Bantam (New York, NY), 1995.

The Cousin War, Bantam (New York, NY), 1995.
Jessica's Older Guy, Bantam (New York, NY), 1995.
Jessica Quits the Squad, Bantam (New York, NY), 1995.
Jessica the Genius, Bantam (New York, NY), 1995.
Meet the Stars of Sweet Valley High, Bantam (New York, NY), 1995.
The Morning After, Bantam (New York, NY), 1995.
Nightmare in Death Valley, Bantam (New York, NY), 1995.
The Pom-Pom Wars, Bantam (New York, NY), 1995.
She's Not What She Seems, Bantam (New York, NY), 1995.
"V" for Victory, Bantam (New York, NY), 1995.
The Treasure of Death Valley, Bantam (New York, NY), 1995.
When Love Dies, Bantam (New York, NY), 1995.
The Arrest, Bantam (New York, NY), 1996.
Beware of the Babysitter, Bantam (New York, NY), 1996.
Camp Killer, Bantam (New York, NY), 1996.
Dance of Death, Bantam (New York, NY), 1996.
Elizabeth's Rival, Bantam (New York, NY), 1996.
The High School War, Bantam (New York, NY), 1996.
In Love with the Enemy, Bantam (New York, NY), 1996.
A Kiss before Dying, Bantam (New York, NY), 1996.
Kiss of a Killer, Bantam (New York, NY), 1996.
Meet Me at Midnight, Bantam (New York, NY), 1996.
Out of Control, Bantam (New York, NY), 1996.
Tall, Dark, and Deadly, Bantam (New York, NY), 1996.
Cover Girls, Bantam (New York, NY), 1997.
Fashion Victim, Bantam (New York, NY), 1997.
Happily Ever After, Bantam (New York, NY), 1997.
Lila's New Flame, Bantam (New York, NY), 1997.
Model Flirt, Bantam (New York, NY), 1997.
Once Upon a Time, Bantam (New York, NY), 1997.
To Catch a Thief, Bantam (New York, NY), 1997.
Too Hot to Handle, Bantam (New York, NY), 1997.
The Big Night, Bantam (New York, NY), 1998.
Elizabeth Is Mine, Bantam (New York, NY), 1998.
Fight Fire with Fire, Bantam (New York, NY), 1998.
Picture Perfect Prom, Bantam (New York, NY), 1998.
Please Forgive Me, Bantam (New York, NY), 1998.
What Jessica Wants, Bantam (New York, NY), 1998.
Party Weekend, Bantam (New York, NY), 1998.

"SWEET VALLEY HIGH SUPER" EDITIONS

Perfect Summer, Bantam (New York, NY), 1985.
Malibu Summer, Bantam (New York, NY), 1986.
Special Christmas, Bantam (New York, NY), 1986.
Spring Break, Bantam (New York, NY), 1986.
Spring Fever, Bantam (New York, NY), 1987.
Winter Carnival, Bantam (New York, NY), 1987.
Falling for Lucas, Bantam (New York, NY), 1996.
Jessica Takes Manhattan, Bantam (New York, NY), 1997.
Mystery Date, Bantam (New York, NY), 1997.
Last Wish, Bantam (New York, NY), 1998.
Earthquake, Bantam (New York, NY), 1998.

"SWEET VALLEY HIGH SUPER THRILLER" SERIES

Double Jeopardy, Bantam (New York, NY), 1987.
On the Run, Bantam (New York, NY), 1988.
No Place to Hide, Bantam (New York, NY), 1988.

Deadly Summer, Bantam (New York, NY), 1989.
Murder on the Line, Bantam (New York, NY), 1992.
Beware the Wolfman, Bantam (New York, NY), 1993.
A Deadly Christmas, Bantam (New York, NY), 1994.
A Killer on Board, Bantam (New York, NY), 1995.
Murder in Paradise, Bantam (New York, NY), 1995.
A Stranger in the House, Bantam (New York, NY), 1995.
"R" Is for Revenge, Bantam (New York, NY), 1997.

"SWEET VALLEY HIGH SUPER STAR" SERIES

Lila's Story, Bantam (New York, NY), 1989.
Bruce's Story, Bantam (New York, NY), 1990.
Enid's Story, Bantam (New York, NY), 1990.
Olivia's Story, Bantam (New York, NY), 1991.
Todd's Story, Bantam (New York, NY), 1992.

"SWEET VALLEY MAGNA" EDITIONS

A Night to Remember, Bantam (New York, NY), 1993.
The Evil Twin, Bantam (New York, NY), 1993.
Elizabeth's Secret Diary, Bantam (New York, NY), 1994.

In Pascal's novel Bad, *a new boyfriend may not be enough to help Gaia forget her tragic past. (Cover photograph by St. Denis.)*

Jessica's Secret Diary, Bantam (New York, NY), 1994, as *Jessica's Secret Diary, Volume I,* 1996.

Return of the Evil Twin, Bantam (New York, NY), 1995.

Elizabeth's Secret Diary, Volume II, Bantam (New York, NY), 1996.

Jessica's Secret Diary, Volume II, Bantam (New York, NY), 1996.

The Fowlers of Sweet Valley, Bantam (New York, NY), 1996.

The Patmans of Sweet Valley, Bantam (New York, NY), 1997.

Elizabeth's Secret Diary, Volume III, Bantam (New York, NY), 1997.

Jessica's Secret Diary, Volume III, Bantam (New York, NY), 1997.

"SWEET VALLEY UNIVERSITY" SERIES

College Girls, Bantam (New York, NY), 1993.

Love, Lies, and Jessica Wakefield, Bantam (New York, NY), 1993.

What Your Parents Don't Know, Bantam (New York, NY), 1994.

Anything for Love, Bantam (New York, NY), 1994.

A Married Woman, Bantam (New York, NY), 1994.

The Love of Her Life, Bantam (New York, NY), 1994.

Home for Christmas, Bantam (New York, NY), 1994.

Good-Bye to Love, Bantam (New York, NY), 1994.

Behind Closed Doors, Bantam (New York, NY), 1994.

College Cruise, Bantam (New York, NY), 1995.

Deadly Attraction, Bantam (New York, NY), 1995.

No Means No, Bantam (New York, NY), 1995.

The Other Woman, Bantam (New York, NY), 1995.

Shipboard Wedding, Bantam (New York, NY), 1995.

Sorority Scandal, Bantam (New York, NY), 1995.

S.S. Heartbreak, Bantam (New York, NY), 1995.

Take Back the Night, Bantam (New York, NY), 1995.

Billie's Secret, Bantam (New York, NY), 1996.

Broken Promises, Shattered Dreams, Bantam (New York, NY), 1996.

Busted, Bantam (New York, NY), 1996.

Elizabeth's Summer Love, Bantam (New York, NY), 1996.

For the Love of Ryan, Bantam (New York, NY), 1996.

Here Comes the Bride, Bantam (New York, NY), 1996.

His Secret Past, Bantam (New York, NY), 1996.

Sweet Kiss of Summer, Bantam (New York, NY), 1996.

The Trial of Jessica Wakefield, Bantam (New York, NY), 1996.

Beauty and the Beach, Bantam (New York, NY), 1997.

The Boys of Summer, Bantam (New York, NY), 1997.

Elizabeth and Todd Forever, Bantam (New York, NY), 1997.

Elizabeth's Heartbreak, Bantam (New York, NY), 1997.

One Last Kiss, Bantam (New York, NY), 1997.

Out of the Picture, Bantam (New York, NY), 1997.

Spy Girl, Bantam (New York, NY), 1997.

The Truth about Ryan, Bantam (New York, NY), 1997.

Undercover Angels, Bantam (New York, NY), 1997.

Breaking Away, Bantam (New York, NY), 1997.

Elizabeth Loves New York, Bantam (New York, NY), 1998.

Escape to New York, Bantam (New York, NY), 1998.

Good-Bye Elizabeth, Bantam (New York, NY), 1998.

Have You Heard about Elizabeth?, Bantam (New York, NY), 1998.

Private Jessica, Bantam (New York, NY), 1998.

Sneaking In, Bantam (New York, NY), 1998.

The Price of Love, Bantam (New York, NY), 1998.

Love Me Always, Bantam (New York, NY), 1998.

Dropping Out, Bantam (New York, NY), 1999.

Don't Let Go, Bantam (New York, NY), 1999.

I'll Never Love Again, Bantam (New York, NY), 1999.

Fooling Around, Bantam (New York, NY), 1999.

Rush Week, Bantam (New York, NY), 1999.

Truth or Dare, Bantam (New York, NY), 1999.

You're Not My Sister, Bantam (New York, NY), 1999.

The First Time, Bantam (New York, NY), 1999.

Stranded, Bantam (New York, NY), 1999.

Summer of Love, Bantam (New York, NY), 1999.

Living Together, Bantam (New York, NY), 1999.

No Rules, Bantam (New York, NY), 1999.

Who Knew?, Bantam (New York, NY), 1999.

The Dreaded Ex, Bantam (New York, NY), 2000.

Elizabeth in Love, Bantam (New York, NY), 2000.

Secret Love Diaries: Elizabeth, Bantam (New York, NY), 2000.

Secret Love Diaries: Jessica, Bantam (New York, NY), 2000.

Secret Love Diaries: Sam, Bantam (New York, NY), 2000.

Secret Love Diaries: Chloe, Bantam (New York, NY), 2000.

"SWEET VALLEY UNIVERSITY THRILLER" EDITIONS

Kiss of the Vampire, Bantam (New York, NY), 1995.

Wanted for Murder, Bantam (New York, NY), 1995.

He's Watching You, Vol. 2, Bantam (New York, NY), 1995.

The House of Death, Bantam (New York, NY), 1996.

The Roommate, Bantam (New York, NY), 1996.

Running for Her Life, Bantam (New York, NY), 1996.

Dead before Dawn, Bantam (New York, NY), 1996.

Killer at Sea, Bantam (New York, NY), 1997.

What Winston Saw, Bantam (New York, NY), 1997.

Don't Answer the Phone, Bantam (New York, NY), 1998.

Channel X, Bantam (New York, NY), 1998.

Love and Murder, Bantam (New York, NY), 1998.

Cyberstalker: The Return of William White, Part I, Bantam (New York, NY), 1999.

Cyberstalker: The Return of William White, Part II, Bantam (New York, NY), 1999.

Loving the Enemy, Bantam (New York, NY), 1999.

Killer Party, Bantam (New York, NY), 2000.

Very Bad Things, Bantam (New York, NY), 2000.

Face It, Bantam (New York, NY), 2000.

"SWEET VALLEY" SAGAS

The Wakefields of Sweet Valley, Bantam (New York, NY), 1991.

The Wakefield Legacy: The Untold Story, Bantam (New York, NY), 1992.

"SWEET VALLEY TWINS" SERIES

Best Friends, Bantam (New York, NY), 1986.
Teacher's Pet, Bantam (New York, NY), 1986.
The Haunted House, Bantam (New York, NY), 1986.
Choosing Sides, Bantam (New York, NY), 1986.
Sneaking Out, Bantam (New York, NY), 1987.
The New Girl, Bantam (New York, NY), 1987.
Three's a Crowd, Bantam (New York, NY), 1987.
First Place, Bantam (New York, NY), 1987.
Against the Rules, Bantam (New York, NY), 1987.
One of the Gang, Bantam (New York, NY), 1987.
Buried Treasure, Bantam (New York, NY), 1987.
Keeping Secrets, Bantam (New York, NY), 1987.
Stretching the Truth, Bantam (New York, NY), 1987.
Tug of War, Bantam (New York, NY), 1987.
The Bully, Bantam (New York, NY), 1988.
Playing Hooky, Bantam (New York, NY), 1988.
Left Behind, Bantam (New York, NY), 1988.
Claim to Fame, Bantam (New York, NY), 1988.
Center of Attention, Bantam (New York, NY), 1988.
Jumping to Conclusions, Bantam (New York, NY), 1988.
Second Best, Bantam (New York, NY), 1988.
The Older Boy, Bantam (New York, NY), 1988.
Out of Place, Bantam (New York, NY), 1988.
Elizabeth's New Hero, Bantam (New York, NY), 1989.
Standing Out, Bantam (New York, NY), 1989.
Jessica on Stage, Bantam (New York, NY), 1989.
Jessica the Rock Star, Bantam (New York, NY), 1989.
Jessica's Bad Idea, Bantam (New York, NY), 1989.
Taking Charge, Bantam (New York, NY), 1989.
Big Camp Secret, Bantam (New York, NY), 1989.
Jessica and the Brat Attack, Bantam (New York, NY), 1989.
April Fool!, Bantam (New York, NY), 1989.
Princess Elizabeth, Bantam (New York, NY), 1989.
Elizabeth's First Kiss, Bantam (New York, NY), 1990.
War between the Twins, Bantam (New York, NY), 1990.
Summer Fun Book, Bantam (New York, NY), 1990.
The Twins Get Caught, Bantam (New York, NY), 1990.
Lois Strikes Back, Bantam (New York, NY), 1990.
Mary Is Missing, Bantam (New York, NY), 1990.
Jessica's Secret, Bantam (New York, NY), 1990.
Jessica and the Money Mix-Up, Bantam (New York, NY), 1990.
Danny Means Trouble, Bantam (New York, NY), 1990.
Amy's Pen Pal, Bantam (New York, NY), 1990.
Amy Moves In, Bantam (New York, NY), 1991.
Jessica's New Look, Bantam (New York, NY), 1991.
Lucky Takes the Reins, Bantam (New York, NY), 1991.
Mademoiselle Jessica, Bantam (New York, NY), 1991.
Mansy Miller Fights Back, Bantam (New York, NY), 1991.
The Twins' Little Sister, Bantam (New York, NY), 1991.
Booster Boycott, Bantam (New York, NY), 1991.
Elizabeth the Impossible, Bantam (New York, NY), 1991.
Jessica and the Secret Star, Bantam (New York, NY), 1991.
The Slime That Ate Sweet Valley, Bantam (New York, NY), 1991.
The Big Party Weekend, Bantam (New York, NY), 1991.
Brooke and Her Rock-Star Mom, Bantam (New York, NY), 1992.

The Wakefields Strike It Rich, Bantam (New York, NY), 1992.
Steven's in Love, Bantam (New York, NY), 1992.
Elizabeth and the Orphans, Bantam (New York, NY), 1992.
Barnyard Battle, Bantam (New York, NY), 1992.
Ciao, Sweet Valley!, Bantam (New York, NY), 1992.
Jessica the Nerd, Bantam (New York, NY), 1992.
Sarah's Dad and Sophia's Mom, Bantam (New York, NY), 1992.
Poor Lila!, Bantam (New York, NY), 1992.
The Charm School Mystery, Bantam (New York, NY), 1992.
Patty's Last Dance, Bantam (New York, NY), 1993.
The Great Boyfriend Switch, Bantam (New York, NY), 1993.
Jessica the Thief, Bantam (New York, NY), 1993.
The Middle School Gets Married, Bantam (New York, NY), 1993.
Won't Someone Help Anna?, Bantam (New York, NY), 1993.
Psychic Sisters, Bantam (New York, NY), 1993.
Jessica Saves the Trees, Bantam (New York, NY), 1993.
The Love Potion, Bantam (New York, NY), 1993.
Lila's Music Video, Bantam (New York, NY), 1993.
Elizabeth the Hero, Bantam (New York, NY), 1993.
Jessica and the Earthquake, Bantam (New York, NY), 1994.
Yours for a Day, Bantam (New York, NY), 1994.
Todd Runs Away, Bantam (New York, NY), 1994.
Steven and the Zombie, Bantam (New York, NY), 1994.
Jessica's Blind Date, Bantam (New York, NY), 1994.
The Gossip War, Bantam (New York, NY), 1994.
Robbery at the Mall, Bantam (New York, NY), 1994.
Steven's Enemy, Bantam (New York, NY), 1994.
Amy's Secret Letter, Bantam (New York, NY), 1994.
The Cousin War, Bantam (New York, NY), 1995.
Deadly Voyage, Bantam (New York, NY), 1995.
Don't Go in the Basement, Bantam (New York, NY), 1995.
Elizabeth the Seventh-Grader, Bantam (New York, NY), 1995.
Escape from Terror Island, Bantam (New York, NY), 1995.
It Can't Happen Here, Bantam (New York, NY), 1995.
Jessica's Cookie Disaster, Bantam (New York, NY), 1995.
The Mother-Daughter Switch, Bantam (New York, NY), 1995.
Romeo and Two Juliets, Bantam (New York, NY), 1995.
Steven Gets Even, Bantam (New York, NY), 1995.
The Battle of the Cheerleaders, Bantam (New York, NY), 1996.
The Beast Is Watching You, Bantam (New York, NY), 1996.
The Beast Must Die, Bantam (New York, NY), 1996.
Don't Talk to Brian, Bantam (New York, NY), 1996.
Elizabeth the Spy, Bantam (New York, NY), 1996.
The Incredible Madame Jessica, Bantam (New York, NY), 1996.
The Mysterious Dr. Q, Bantam (New York, NY), 1996.
Too Scared to Sleep, Bantam (New York, NY), 1996.
Twins in Love, Bantam (New York, NY), 1996.
Big Brother's in Love Again, Bantam (New York, NY), 1997.

Breakfast of Enemies, Bantam (New York, NY), 1997.
Cammi's Crush, Bantam (New York, NY), 1997.
Elizabeth Solves It All, Bantam (New York, NY), 1997.
Jessica's Lucky Millions, Bantam (New York, NY), 1997.
Pumpkin Fever, Bantam (New York, NY), 1997.
Sisters at War, Bantam (New York, NY), 1997.
The Twins Hit Hollywood, Bantam (New York, NY), 1997.
The Boyfriend Game, Bantam (New York, NY), 1998.
The Boyfriend Mess, Bantam (New York, NY), 1998.
Down with Queen Janet, Bantam (New York, NY), 1998.
Happy Mother's Day, Lila, Bantam (New York, NY), 1998.
If Looks Could Kill, Bantam (New York, NY), 1998.
Jessica Takes Charge, Bantam (New York, NY), 1998.
No Escape!, Bantam (New York, NY), 1998.

"SWEET VALLEY TWINS SUPER" SERIES

Class Trip, Bantam (New York, NY), 1988.
Holiday Mischief, Bantam (New York, NY), 1988.
The Big Camp Secret, Bantam (New York, NY), 1994.
The Unicorns Go Hawaiian, Bantam (New York, NY), 1994.
Lila's Secret Valentine, Bantam (New York, NY), 1994.
The Twins Take Paris, Bantam (New York, NY), 1996.
Jessica's Animal Instincts, Bantam (New York, NY), 1996.
Jessica's First Kiss, Bantam (New York, NY), 1997.
The Twins Go to College, Bantam (New York, NY), 1997.
The Year without Christmas, Bantam (New York, NY), 1997.
Good-Bye Middle School, Countdown to Junior High, Bantam (New York, NY), 1997.
Jessica's No Angel, Bantam (New York, NY), 1998.

"SWEET VALLEY TWINS MAGNA" SERIES

The Magic Christmas, Bantam (New York, NY), 1992.
A Christmas without Elizabeth, Bantam (New York, NY), 1993.
BIG for Christmas, Bantam (New York, NY), 1994.
If I Die before I Wake, Bantam (New York, NY), 1996.

"SWEET VALLEY TWINS SUPER CHILLER" SERIES

Jessica's Christmas Carol, Bantam (New York, NY), 1989.
The Carnival Ghost, Bantam (New York, NY), 1990.
Christmas Ghost, Bantam (New York, NY), 1990.
The Ghost in the Graveyard, Bantam (New York, NY), 1990.
The Ghost in the Bell Tower, Bantam (New York, NY), 1992.
The Curse of the Ruby Necklace, Bantam (New York, NY), 1993.
The Curse of the Golden Heart, Bantam (New York, NY), 1994.
The Haunted Burial Ground, Bantam (New York, NY), 1994.
The Secret of the Magic Pen, Bantam (New York, NY), 1995.
Evil Elizabeth, Bantam (New York, NY), 1995.

"SWEET VALLEY KIDS" SERIES

Surprise! Surprise!, Bantam (New York, NY), 1989.
Runaway Hamster, Bantam (New York, NY), 1989.
Teamwork, Bantam (New York, NY), 1989.
Lila's Secret, Bantam (New York, NY), 1990.
Elizabeth's Valentine, Bantam (New York, NY), 1990.
Elizabeth's Super-Selling Lemonade, Bantam (New York, NY), 1990.
Jessica's Big Mistake, Bantam (New York, NY), 1990.
Jessica's Cat Trick, Bantam (New York, NY), 1990.
Jessica's Zoo Adventure, Bantam (New York, NY), 1990.
The Twins and the Wild West, Bantam (New York, NY), 1990.
Starring Winston, Bantam (New York, NY), 1990.
The Substitute Teacher, Bantam (New York, NY), 1990.
Sweet Valley Trick or Treat, Bantam (New York, NY), 1990.
Crybaby Lois, Bantam (New York, NY), 1990.
Bossy Steven, Bantam (New York, NY), 1991.
Carolyn's Mystery Dolls, Bantam (New York, NY), 1991.
Fearless Elizabeth, Bantam (New York, NY), 1991.
Jessica and Jumbo, Bantam (New York, NY), 1991.
The Twins Go to the Hospital, Bantam (New York, NY), 1991.
Jessica the Babysitter, Bantam (New York, NY), 1991.
Jessica and the Spelling Bee Surprise, Bantam (New York, NY), 1991.
Lila's Haunted House Party, Bantam (New York, NY), 1991.
Sweet Valley Slumber Party, Bantam (New York, NY), 1991.
Cousin Kelly's Family Secret, Bantam (New York, NY), 1991.
Left-Out Elizabeth, Bantam (New York, NY), 1991.
Jessica's Snobby, Bantam (New York, NY), 1991.
Sweet Valley Clean-Up, Bantam (New York, NY), 1992.
Elizabeth Meets Her Hero, Bantam (New York, NY), 1992.
Andy and the Alien, Bantam (New York, NY), 1992.
Jessica's Unburied Treasure, Bantam (New York, NY), 1992.
Elizabeth and Jessica Run Away, Bantam (New York, NY), 1992.
Left Back, Bantam (New York, NY), 1992.
Caroline's Halloween Spell, Bantam (New York, NY), 1992.
The Best Thanksgiving Ever, Bantam (New York, NY), 1992.
Elizabeth's Broken Arm, Bantam (New York, NY), 1993.
Elizabeth's Video Fever, Bantam (New York, NY), 1993.
The Big Race, Bantam (New York, NY), 1993.
Good-bye, Eva?, Bantam (New York, NY), 1993.
Ellen Is Home Alone, Bantam (New York, NY), 1993.
Robin in the Middle, Bantam (New York, NY), 1993.
The Missing Tea Set, Bantam (New York, NY), 1993.
Jessica's Monster Nightmare, Bantam (New York, NY), 1993.
Jessica Gets Spooked, Bantam (New York, NY), 1993.
The Twins' Big Pow-Wow, Bantam (New York, NY), 1993.
Elizabeth's Piano Lessons, Bantam (New York, NY), 1994.
Get the Teacher!, Bantam (New York, NY), 1994.
Elizabeth, the Tattletale, Bantam (New York, NY), 1994.

Lila's April Fool, Bantam (New York, NY), 1994.
Jessica's Mermaid, Bantam (New York, NY), 1994.
Steven's Twin, Bantam (New York, NY), 1994.
Lois and the Sleepover, Bantam (New York, NY), 1994.
Julie and the Karate Kid, Bantam (New York, NY), 1994.
The Magic Puppets, Bantam (New York, NY), 1994.
Star of the Parade, Bantam (New York, NY), 1994.
The Halloween War, Bantam (New York, NY), 1995.
The Jessica and Elizabeth Show, Bantam (New York, NY), 1995.
Jessica + Jessica = Trouble, Bantam (New York, NY), 1995.
Jessica Plays Cupid, Bantam (New York, NY), 1995.
Lila's Birthday Bash, Bantam (New York, NY), 1995.
Lila's Christmas Angel, Bantam (New York, NY), 1995.
No Girls Allowed, Bantam (New York, NY), 1995.
Scaredy-Cat Elizabeth, Bantam (New York, NY), 1995.
The Amazing Jessica, Bantam (New York, NY), 1996.
And the Winner Is, Jessica Wakefield, Bantam (New York, NY), 1996.
Elizabeth's Horseback Adventure, Bantam (New York, NY), 1996.
A Roller Coaster for the Twins!, Bantam (New York, NY), 1996.
The Secret of Fantasy Forest, Bantam (New York, NY), 1996.
Steven's Big Crush, Bantam (New York, NY), 1996.
Class Picture Day!, Bantam (New York, NY), 1997.
Good-Bye, Mrs. Otis, Bantam (New York, NY), 1997.
Jessica's Secret Friend, Bantam (New York, NY), 1997.
The Macaroni Mess, Bantam (New York, NY), 1997.
The Witch in the Pumpkin Patch, Bantam (New York, NY), 1997.
Danger: Twins at Work!, Bantam (New York, NY), 1998.
Little Drummer Girls, Bantam (New York, NY), 1998.
Sweet Valley Blizzard!, Bantam (New York, NY), 1998.

"SWEET VALLEY KIDS SUPER SNOOPER" SERIES

The Case of the Secret Santa, Bantam (New York, NY), 1990.
The Case of the Magic Christmas Bell, Bantam (New York, NY), 1991.
The Case of the Haunted Camp, Bantam (New York, NY), 1992.
The Case of the Christmas Thief, Bantam (New York, NY), 1992.
The Case of the Hidden Treasure, Bantam (New York, NY), 1993.
The Case of the Million-Dollar Diamonds, Bantam (New York, NY), 1993.
The Case of the Alien Princess, Bantam (New York, NY), 1994.

"SWEET VALLEY KIDS SUPER SPECIAL" SERIES

Trapped in Toyland, Bantam (New York, NY), 1994.
Save the Turkey, Bantam (New York, NY), 1995.
A Curse on Elizabeth, Bantam (New York, NY), 1995.
The Easter Bunny Battle, Bantam (New York, NY), 1996.
Elizabeth Hatches an Egg, Bantam (New York, NY), 1996.

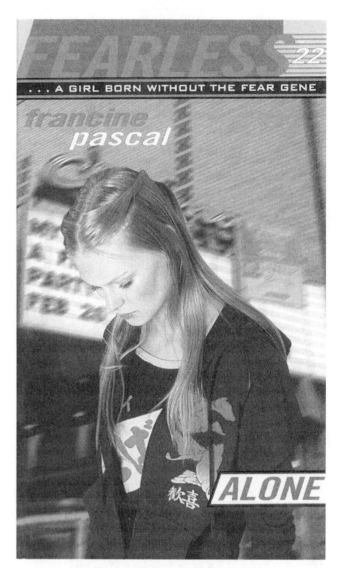

Alone, from the "Fearless" series, deals with the sometimes tumultuous relationships between a group of friends. *(Cover photograph by St. Denis.)*

"CAITLIN" SERIES; "THE LOVE" TRILOGY
Loving, Bantam (New York, NY), 1986.
Love Lost, Bantam (New York, NY), 1986.
True Love, Bantam (New York, NY), 1986.

"CAITLIN" SERIES; "THE PROMISE" TRILOGY
Tender Promises, Bantam (New York, NY), 1986.
Promises Broken, Bantam (New York, NY), 1986.
A New Promise, Bantam (New York, NY), 1987.

"CAITLIN" SERIES; "THE FOREVER" TRILOGY
Dreams of Forever, Bantam (New York, NY), 1987.
Forever and Always, Bantam (New York, NY), 1987.
Together Forever, Bantam (New York, NY), 1987.

"UNICORN CLUB" SERIES
Save the Unicorns, Bantam (New York, NY), 1994.
Maria's Movie Comeback, Bantam (New York, NY), 1994.
The Best Friend Game, Bantam (New York, NY), 1994.

Lila's Little Sister, Bantam (New York, NY), 1994.
Unicorns in Love, Bantam (New York, NY), 1994.
Unicorns at War, Bantam (New York, NY), 1995.
Too Close for Comfort, Bantam (New York, NY), 1995.
Kimberly Rides Again, Bantam (New York, NY), 1995.
Ellen's Family Secret, Bantam (New York, NY), 1996.
Lila on the Loose, Bantam (New York, NY), 1996.
Mandy in the Middle, Bantam (New York, NY), 1996.
Who Will Be Miss Unicorn?, Bantam (New York, NY), 1996.
Angels Keep Out, Bantam (New York, NY), 1996.
Five Girls and a Baby, Bantam (New York, NY), 1996.
Too Cool for the Unicorns, Bantam (New York, NY), 1997.
Bon Voyage, Unicorns!, Bantam (New York, NY), 1997.
Boyfriends for Everyone, Bantam (New York, NY), 1997.
The Most Beautiful Girl in the World, Bantam (New York, NY), 1997.
Rachel's In, Lila's Out, Bantam (New York, NY), 1997.
Snow Bunnies, Bantam (New York, NY), 1997.
In Love with Mandy, Bantam (New York, NY), 1997.
Jessica's Dream Date, Bantam (New York, NY), 1998.
Trapped in the Mall, Bantam (New York, NY), 1998.

"SWEET VALLEY SENIOR YEAR" SERIES

Boy Meets Girl, Bantam (New York, NY), 1999.
Broken Angel, Bantam (New York, NY), 1999.
Can't Stay Away, Bantam (New York, NY), 1999.
I've Got a Secret, Bantam (New York, NY), 1999.
If You Only Knew, Bantam (New York, NY), 1999.
Maria Who?, Bantam (New York, NY), 1999.
Say It to My Face, Bantam (New York, NY), 1999.
So Cool, Bantam (New York, NY), 1999.
Take Me On, Bantam (New York, NY), 1999.
The One That Got Away, Bantam (New York, NY), 1999.
Your Basic Nightmare, Bantam (New York, NY), 1999.
Bad Girl, Bantam (New York, NY), 2000.
Three Girls and a Guy, Bantam (New York, NY), 2000.
The It Guy, Bantam (New York, NY), 2000.
Split Decision, Bantam (New York, NY), 2000.
So Not Me, Bantam (New York, NY), 2000.
On My Own, Bantam (New York, NY), 2000.
All about Love, Bantam (New York, NY), 2000.
As If I Care, Bantam (New York, NY), 2000.
Backstabber, Bantam (New York, NY), 2000.
Falling Apart, Bantam (New York, NY), 2000.
Nothing Is Forever, Bantam (New York, NY), 2000.
It's My Life, Bantam (New York, NY), 2000.
Never Let Go, Bantam (New York, NY), 2000.
Straight Up, Bantam (New York, NY), 2001.
Too Late, Bantam (New York, NY), 2001.
Playing Dirty, Bantam (New York, NY), 2001.
Meant to Be, Bantam (New York, NY), 2001.
Where We Belong, Bantam (New York, NY), 2001.
Close to You, Bantam (New York, NY), 2001.
Stay or Go, Bantam (New York, NY), 2001.
Road Trip, Bantam (New York, NY), 2001.
Me, Me, Me, Bantam (New York, NY), 2001.
Troublemaker, Bantam (New York, NY), 2001.
Control Freak, Bantam (New York, NY), 2001.
Tearing Me Apart, Bantam (New York, NY), 2001.
Be Mine, Bantam (New York, NY), 2002.

Get a Clue, Bantam (New York, NY), 2002.
Best of Enemies, Bantam (New York, NY), 2002.
Never Give Up, Bantam (New York, NY), 2002.
He's Back, Bantam (New York, NY), 2002.
Touch and Go, Bantam (New York, NY), 2002.
It Takes Two, Bantam (New York, NY), 2002.
Cruise Control, Bantam (New York, NY), 2002.
Tia in the Middle, Bantam (New York, NY), 2002.
Prom Night, Bantam (New York, NY), 2002.
Sweet 18, Bantam (New York, NY), 2002.
Senior Cut Day, Bantam (New York, NY), 2002.

"SWEET VALLEY JUNIOR HIGH" SERIES

Boy Friend, Bantam (New York, NY), 1999.
Cheating on Anna, Bantam (New York, NY), 1999.
Get Real, Bantam (New York, NY), 1999.
Got a Problem?, Bantam (New York, NY), 1999.
How to Ruin a Friendship, Bantam (New York, NY), 1999.
Lacey's Crush, Bantam (New York, NY), 1999.
One 2 Many, Bantam (New York, NY), 1999.
Soulmates, Bantam (New York, NY), 1999.
The Cool Crowd, Bantam (New York, NY), 1999.
Too Popular, Bantam (New York, NY), 1999.
Twin Switch, Bantam (New York, NY), 1999.
Third Wheel, Bantam (New York, NY), 1999.
What You Don't Know, Bantam (New York, NY), 2000.
Wild Child, Bantam (New York, NY), 2000.
Whatever, Bantam (New York, NY), 2000.
True Blue, Bantam (New York, NY), 2000.
Three Days, Two Nights, Bantam (New York, NY), 2000.
She Loves Me . . . Not, Bantam (New York, NY), 2000.
Hands Off!, Bantam (New York, NY), 2000.
My Perfect Guy, Bantam (New York, NY), 2000.
Keepin' It Real, Bantam (New York, NY), 2000.
Invisible Me, Bantam (New York, NY), 2000.
I'm So Outta Here, Bantam (New York, NY), 2000.
Clueless, Bantam (New York, NY), 2000.
Drama Queen, Bantam (New York, NY), 2001.
No More Mr. Nice Guy, Bantam (New York, NY), 2001.
She's Back . . ., Bantam (New York, NY), 2001.
Dance Fever, Bantam (New York, NY), 2001.
He's the One, Random House (New York, NY), 2001.
Too Many Good-byes, Random House (New York, NY), 2001.

"ELIZABETH" SERIES

University, Interrupted, Bantam (New York, NY), 2001.
London Calling, Bantam (New York, NY), 2001.
Royal Pain, Bantam (New York, NY), 2001.
Downstairs, Upstairs, Bantam (New York, NY), 2001.
Max's Choice, Bantam (New York, NY), 2001.
I Need You, Bantam (New York, NY), 2001.

"FEARLESS" SERIES

Fearless, Pocket Books (New York, NY), 1999.
Sam, Pocket Books (New York, NY), 1999.
Run, Pocket Books (New York, NY), 2000.

Twisted, Pocket Books (New York, NY), 2000.
Kiss, Pocket Books (New York, NY), 2000.
Payback, Pocket Books (New York, NY), 2000.
Rebel, Pocket Books (New York, NY), 2000.
Heat, Pocket Books (New York, NY), 2000.
Blood, Pocket Books (New York, NY), 2000.
Liar, Pocket Books (New York, NY), 2000.
Trust, Pocket Books (New York, NY), 2000.
Killer, Pocket Books (New York, NY), 2000.
Bad, Pocket Books (New York, NY), 2001.
Missing, Pocket Books (New York, NY), 2001.
Tears, Pocket Books (New York, NY), 2001.
Naked, Pocket Books (New York, NY), 2001.
Flee, Pocket Books (New York, NY), 2001.
Alone, Simon Pulse (New York, NY), 2002.
Betrayed, Simon Pulse (New York, NY), 2002.
Blind, Simon Pulse (New York, NY), 2002.
Fear, Simon Pulse (New York, NY), 2002.
Lost, Simon Pulse (New York, NY), 2002.
Sex, Simon Pulse (New York, NY), 2002.
Twins, Simon Pulse (New York, NY), 2002.
Escape, Simon Pulse (New York, NY), 2003.
Chase, Simon Pulse (New York, NY), 2003.
Shock, Simon Pulse (New York, NY), 2003.
Gaia Abducted, Pocket Books (New York, NY), 2003.
Lust, Simon & Schuster (New York, NY), 2003.
Before Gaia, Simon & Schuster (New York, NY), 2003.
Freak, Simon & Schuster (New York, NY), 2003.

OTHER

(With husband, John Pascal, and brother, Michael Stewart) *George M!* (musical), produced on Broadway, 1968.
(With John Pascal) *George M!* (television special based on musical of same title), American Broadcasting Companies, Inc. (ABC-TV), 1970.
(With John Pascal) *The Strange Case of Patty Hearst,* New American Library (New York, NY), 1974.
The Hand-Me-Down Kid, Viking (New York, NY), 1980.
Save Johanna! (adult novel), Morrow (New York, NY), 1981.
If Wishes Were Horses, Crown (New York, NY), 1994.
(Reviser) *Mack & Mabel* (musical), music and lyrics by Jerry Herman and original book by Michael Stewart, first produced on Broadway at the Brooks Atkinson theater, January 10, 2002.

Also author, with Jon Marans and David Bryan, of *Fearless, The Musical.* Creator for television of *The See-through-Kids,* a live-action family series; adapter of television scripts; co-writer with John Pascal of television scripts for soap-opera serial *The Young Marrieds,* ABC-TV. Has contributed humor, nonfiction, and travel articles to *True Confessions, Modern Screen, Ladies' Home Journal,* and *Cosmopolitan.*

Adaptations

Hangin' out with Cici was filmed by ABC-TV and broadcast as "My Mother Was Never a Kid," an *ABC Afterschool Special,* 1981; *The Hand-Me-Down Kid* was filmed by ABC-TV and broadcast as an *ABC After-school Special,* 1983; the "Sweet Valley High" series began syndication as a television series in 1994. Books that have been recorded onto audiocassette and released by Warner Audio include: *Double Love, Secrets,* and *Playing with Fire,* all 1986, *All Night Long, Dangerous Love,* and *Power Play.*

Work in Progress

Games, an adult novel; Monthly plot outlines for various series. Creation of further series aimed at young adults readers.

Sidelights

With an estimated $15 million in net profits, Francine Pascal is one of the best-paid authors in the world. She has published over seven hundred books in her "Sweet Valley High" series alone, for which she is best known. "Sweet Valley High" is a series of books about a fictional California suburb and the youngsters who inhabit it. With two hundred and fifty million copies of her series books in print in over two dozen languages worldwide, Pascal has become a publishing phenomenon, making history in 1985 when *Perfect Summer,* the initial "Sweet Valley High" super edition, became the first young adult novel to make the *New York Times* bestseller list. Yet Pascal's achievement is even more amazing in light of the fact that she has written only a handful of books by herself. All of her series novels—for young adults and adolescents—are written by a team of ghostwriters who follow a thirty-page resource book Pascal created for the series. Chana R. Schoenberger, writing in *Forbes* magazine, noted that Pascal's team of writers follow the character and location details in the sourcebook, producing "up to five books a month, earning an estimated $5,000 per volume, about one-tenth of what Pascal grosses."

Although many critics maintain that the various "Sweet Valley" series are simplistic, unbelievable, and sexist, their popularity with young adults is undeniable. The various series revolve around Elizabeth and Jessica Wakefield, beautiful and popular identical twins with completely opposite personalities—while Elizabeth is sweet, sincere, and studious, Jessica is arrogant, superficial, and devious. The events in each story usually focus on relationships with boys or other personal issues, and adults are nearly nonexistent. "Sweet Valley is the essence of high school," asserted Pascal in a *People* interview with Steve Dougherty. "The world outside is just an adult shadow going by. The parents barely exist. Action takes place in bedrooms, cars, and school. It's that moment before reality hits, when you really do believe in the romantic values—sacrifice, love, loyalty, friendship—before you get jaded and slip off into adulthood."

With changing times and fashion, however, Pascal has tweaked her series books, adding younger and older spin-offs to the original, and since the inception of the

"Fearless" series in 1999, she has taken her teen women in totally new directions, away from ho-hum romance and into a darker world of New York chic and violence, with a heroine who, quite literally, knows no fear. "[Teenagers] like 'Fearless' because it's the graduation from 'Sweet Valley,' which is yesterday," Pascal told Schoenberger.

Born in New York City, Pascal moved from Manhattan to Jamaica, Queens, when she was five. Movies, adventure comics, and fairy tales were among Pascal's many passions, and because there was no young adult literature at the time, she read the classics. "I have always had a very active imagination—my retreat when things don't go right," Pascal once commented. "I realized early that this set me apart from most people. For example, it wasn't my habit to confide in others very much, particularly my parents. As far back as I can recall, I kept a diary. Important thoughts, imaginings, and events were recounted in my diaries, not to people."

Other forms of writing that Pascal attempted at an early age included poetry and plays. Her brother was a writer, so Pascal wanted to write too, but her parents did not take her writing as seriously as they did his. Her teachers and classmates encouraged her, though, and she even performed her plays, casting and directing her friends for neighborhood audiences. Moving from childhood into adolescence, Pascal, unlike her "Sweet Valley" characters, had a less than ideal high school experience. "Going to high school in the fifties, as I did, was not appreciably different from going to high school in the eighties," she once noted. "Both decades are conservative and full of nostalgia. Adolescence is pretty awful no matter when you go through it. And all of us think high school is wonderful for everyone else. The 'Sweet Valley' series come out of what I fantasized high school was like for everyone but me."

College, on the other hand, was something Pascal looked forward to and thoroughly enjoyed. It was a couple of days after her last class that she met her future husband, John Pascal, who was then a journalist working for a number of papers. "He was an excellent writer," Pascal recalled, "and in many ways my mentor. He loved everything I wrote and encouraged me unceasingly." In their early years together, Pascal's husband freelanced while she began her own writing career with articles for such magazines as *True Confessions* and *Modern Screen,* eventually moving up to *Ladies' Home Journal* and *Cosmopolitan.* They began working together as second writers for the soap opera *The Young Marrieds* in 1965, staying with the show until it moved to California. The musical *George M!* and the nonfiction work *The Strange Case of Patty Hearst* were among the other writings they collaborated on before Pascal turned her attention to the young adult audience.

The idea for Pascal's first young adult novel, *Hangin' out with Cici,* came to her early one morning while she was lying in bed. She had never written a novel before, and at the time had no idea what young adult novels were. Upon hearing her idea, Pascal's husband encouraged her to sit down and begin writing immediately, so she did. When the manuscript was finished she mailed it off to three agents, and the book sold within two weeks. *Hangin' out with Cici* introduces Victoria, a spoiled and selfish young girl who has just been caught smoking a joint during a weekend visit to her aunt. On the train ride home, Victoria somehow wishes herself back in time to 1944, where she makes friends with a girl named Cici. Even wilder than Victoria, Cici shoplifts and sneaks cigarettes before being caught trying to buy a science test with stolen money. Over time, Victoria realizes that Cici is really her mother as a young girl and urges her to confess to her crime. She then wakes up to find herself on the train, where she had been all along—everything was just a dream. From that point on, however, Victoria and her mother have a stronger relationship. Adapted for television as *My Mother Was Never a Kid,* Pascal's first novel for younger readers proved exceedingly popular. A critic for *Kirkus Reviews* felt that similar to her mother-daughter characters, Pascal "enjoys setting up wiggy situations but can't always handle the consequences." Other reviewers, however, found more to like in the book. "The story contains some funny episodes," commented Ann A. Flowers in *Horn Book,* adding that *Hangin' out with Cici* is "an amusing fantasy with realistic adolescent characters." Similarly, Diane Haas, reviewing the work in *School Library Journal,* praised the "several hilarious escapades" she found in the book.

A few other novels followed before Pascal came up with the idea for the "Sweet Valley High" series. *My First Love and Other Disasters,* published in 1979, follows the story of Victoria as she takes a summer job as a mother's helper on Fire Island to be close to her first love, the rather vacuous Jim. Soon she is overburdened with the children she is caring for, and one day decides to leave them in the care of their grandfather, with nearly fatal results. In this difficult time, however, she turns to steady Barry who is always there for her, finally realizing that Jim is too stuck on himself. This second novel about Victoria had a largely positive critical reception. Barbara Elleman, writing in *Booklist,* maintained that the novel is "wittily told in the first person vernacular of a 15-year-old" and "captures the kaleidoscopic complexities of living through a first love." Though Joyce Milton, writing in the *New York Times Book Review,* had doubts about Pascal's characterizations, she commended the author's "good comic timing" and creation of "a few truly funny scenes." And reviewing the novel in *School Library Journal,* C. Nordhielm Wooldridge remarked that Pascal "writes about teenage sex with candor and sensitivity." *My First Love and Other Disasters* was named a Best Book for Young Adults by the American Library Association.

Pascal reprised Victoria in *Love and Betrayal and Hold the Mayo!,* in which she is working at a summer camp with her best friend Steffi. When Steffi's boyfriend,

Robbie, shows up at the camp, Victoria proceeds to fall in love with him, then to cover up these feelings avoids both Steffi and her boyfriend. As if that is not complication enough, her waitressing job at the camp is also proving to be more difficult than she had ever expected. When Robbie finally makes a play for her, she has to decide between loyalty to Steffi and romance. *Booklist*'s Stephanie Zvirin praised Victoria's narrative voice and its "humorous portrayal of the impetuous infatuations of teenage life in the extreme." *School Library Journal*'s Catherine van Sonnenberg similarly commended the "exceptionally satisfying" resolution to this "compelling" story.

The Hand-Me-Down Kid, another solo juvenile offering, offers a younger protagonist. Eleven-year-old Ari Jacobs is the youngest child in her family, and has a distinctly negative view of life until she meets Jane, who is in the same position as herself, yet exudes positiveness. The two become friends, a boon for Ari, who needs such support; her brother and sister tease her mercilessly, and she is continually receiving their hand-me-down clothes and toys. When she borrows her sister's fancy ten-speed bike for the class bully to ride in a race, things go decidedly downhill. The bike is stolen and Ari finds herself making up stories for everyone—police included—just in order to avoid her sister's anger. From Jane, however, Ari finally learns to stick up for herself. "Narrated in the slightly skewed grammatical style typical of today's adolescent, the story is an amusing contemporary novel with an urban setting," wrote Mary M. Burns in *Horn Book.* Burns also felt that Pascal's novel "maintains a perspective on everything from training bras to older brothers and sisters and offers hand-me-down kids a believable example of assertiveness training." A critic for *Kirkus Reviews,* while finding the book "trendy and overdrawn," also thought that "anyone in Ari's fix might learn a thing or two from Jane's ripostes." Millicent Lenz, writing in the *Voice of Youth Advocates,* had further praise, noting that Ari is a "charming character," and that Pascal's novel is a "well told, humorous, absorbing tale [which] skillfully depicts [Ari's] confrontation with sibling rivalry." And Margery Fisher also lauded the novel in a *Growing Point* review. Noting the dangers of first-person narration, Fisher lauded Pascal for avoiding most such pitfalls to create a "firm, satisfying structure under which a shrewd picture of changing relationships is built on." As with *Hangin' out with Cici,* this novel was also adapted for television.

Pascal's husband died in 1981, shortly after the 1980 publication of *The Hand-Me-Down Kid.* "It seems unfair that he isn't alive to enjoy the success of my 'Sweet Valley' series," Pascal once commented. "He would have gotten a real kick out of it, and could have retired on the money I've made. The house is too quiet now." The idea for this incredibly successful series was not a completely new one. In the late 1970s, Pascal wanted to do something similar, but in the form of a television soap opera for teenagers. No one was interested, but a few years later one of Pascal's editors suggested she try a teenage book series instead, maybe something similar to the television show *Dallas.*

When this first attempt failed, Pascal examined the reasons why, coming up with the elements she thought must be present to make a teenage series work. "Each book, I concluded," Pascal once explained, "would have to be a complete story in itself, but with a hook ending to lead you to the sequel. The series would have to have vivid continuing characters. When I came up with the idea for Elizabeth and Jessica, the Jekyll and Hyde twins, I was off and running. I did a proposal over the course of several days, wrote about six pages and that was that." Bantam immediately bought the project and, with successful marketing and packaging, made it a publishing sensation. At the beginning of the series, Pascal presented Sweet Valley as a completely idealized fantasy world. But when she started getting letters from readers telling her how "real" the books were to them, Pascal decided to include some aspects of reality, such as minority characters. "I didn't intend Sweet Valley to be realistic," Pascal once noted, "so I'm a little puzzled. It is a soap opera in book form, after all. I guess what these readers mean is that there is emotional reality in the relationship between the characters." The stories in the series cover a wide range of subjects and genres, from mysteries to domestic problems to peer pressure and fads to the power of first love and the mutability of emotional ties.

Despite the success of the various "Sweet Valley" series, Pascal has received a great deal of criticism. Reviewing the fourth book in the series, *Power Play,* in *Voice of Youth Advocates,* Judy Mitchell, for example, noted, "This is formula fiction in its darkest hour, folks. The characters are both unbelievable and one dimensional; the plot depends upon a legion of cliches, and it is probably kinder to skip over conflict and theme." Mitchell further remarked, however, that her own thirteen-year-old "read and liked" the book, an example of the "cotton candy of young adult fiction." More such criticism came from Annette Curtis Klause, reviewing *Power Play* in *School Library Journal:* "A book for junior high school students should not appear as if it were written by one." Reviewing *Dangerous Love* in the *ALAN Review,* Sarah Simpson similarly complained that the "work fails to address the pressures and problems today's young adults have in their relationships with members of the opposite sex." Writing of *Showdown,* Myrna Feldman of *Voice of Youth Advocates* described Pascal's make-believe cosmos as a place where "all the guys and gals are just too beautiful and rich to be true, and where parents and homework are only vaguely in the picture."

Countering such criticism, Pascal argues that her "books encourage young people to read." As she once noted, "'Sweet Valley High' opened a market that simply didn't exist before. It is not that those millions of girls were not reading my books, they weren't reading any books.

I have gotten many, many letters from kids saying that they never read before 'Sweet Valley High.' If nine out of ten of those girls go on to read Judith Krantz and Danielle Steel, so be it, they are still reading. . . . The reality is that not everyone is able, or wishes to read great literature. There should be books for all types of readers. Reading time is precious; it's a time for privacy, fantasy, learning, a time to live in our imaginations. No one should be denied that."

Pascal also has her defenders. Writing in *Voice of Youth Advocates,* Tony Ling found *Alone in the Crowd* "readable as well as interesting." Ling also thought the book "could be enjoyed by men as well as young ladies." Writing in *School Library Journal,* Mary M. Huntwork noted the usual complaints about Pascal's series novels: "poor character development; weak writing; use of stereotypes; emphasis on superficial and materialistic values. . .; sexism. . .; and finally, a failure to reflect real life. . . ." However, after doing research on the "Sweet Valley High" books and romance series for

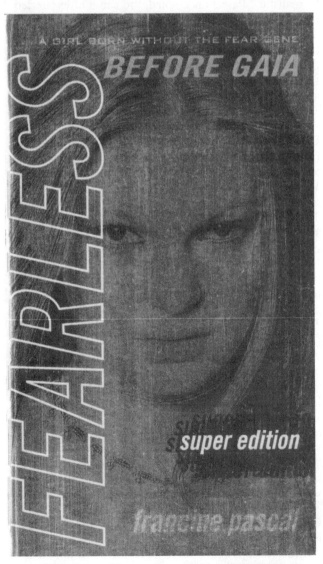

In this novel, Gaia searches for the truth behind the death of her mother. (Cover photograph by St. Denis.)

young readers, Huntwork found studies that "emphasized the satisfaction and pleasure romance readers receive from leisure reading." Huntwork, a school librarian, concluded that librarians should respect the needs and desires of their readers. "I . . . no longer view 'Sweet Valley High' as a threat. I will no longer be overly concerned if my daughter lingers there a while longer," Huntwork wrote, further noting that "not all teenagers identify with the characters of the heavier problem novels, [and] that some teenagers want to read about situations closer to their own."

The popularity of the "Sweet Valley High" series prompted a number of spin-off series, including "Sweet Valley Twins," which aims at younger readers by placing Elizabeth and Jessica in sixth grade, "Sweet Valley Kids," which presents the twins as six-year-olds, and "Sweet Valley High" super thriller series, which attempts to compete with other young adult mystery and horror writers. In a *Voice of Youth Advocates* review of *Best Friends,* from the "Sweet Valley Twins" series, Civia Tuteur noted the "identity crisis" the twins—now in middle school—were having after so many years of dressing alike and doing the same sorts of things. Tuteur found the book "fast-paced and easy to read," despite concerns about slight plot and character development.

In 1991, Pascal brought a new twist to the series with the publication of *The Wakefields of Sweet Valley.* This full-length novel covers one hundred years as it traces five generations of the Wakefield family. It begins in 1860 with the sea voyage of sixteen-year-old Alice Larson of Sweden and eighteen-year-old Theodore Wakefield from England, following the family through wagon trains, earthquakes, the Roaring Twenties, love, courage, and heartbreak.

Other new additions to the Sweet Valley stable include "Sweet Valley University," "Sweet Valley Junior High," "Sweet Valley Senior Year," and the edgier non-Sweet Valley series, "Fearless." Inaugurated in 1993, "Sweet Valley University" follows the twins to college. "It had to happen," announced a reviewer for *Publishers Weekly.* "Jessica and Elizabeth Wakefield, the darlings of Sweet Valley High, have graduated to swinging college life." The two experience the gambit of emotions and adventures of college-age girls in this series, while in "Sweet Valley Junior High" more adolescent scenarios come into play. Reviewing *Get Real,* an early title in the "Sweet Valley Junior High" series, Lisa Denton noted in *School Library Journal* that Pascal capitalizes on the "popular teen-soap genre," producing a book with "humorous moments, fast switches in narrative voices, and fun characters." All in all, Denton concluded, the book "has that quick-read quality sought after by many busy preteens."

More mature matters are dealt with in the "Sweet Valley Senior Year," such as the death of a classmate during an earthquake, as in *Can't Stay Away.* Karen Hoth of *School Library Journal* noted an "interesting break from standard [Sweet Valley High] style here in that there are 'diary' entries from the key players, in an attempt to create three-dimensional characters." Reviewing the same title in *Voice of Youth Advocates,* Holly Ward Lamb called the book and the series "great teen sudsy drama."

With her "Fearless" series, Pascal attempts to capture a more daring reader, using a New York city teenager, seventeen-year-old Gaia, who appears to have been born "without the gene for fear," according to *Booklist*'s Frances Bradburn. As Pascal explained to *Book*'s Kristin Kloberdanz, "I happened to see in the 'Science' section of the *New York Times* a little article about a woman who was baffling scientists because they gave her all kinds of tests and she didn't respond to fear physically or emotionally. And I thought that was absolutely fascinating." Pascal took this germ of an idea to create a series about the abandoned daughter of a terrorism expert for the CIA and a murdered Russian mother. Gaia Moore is a black belt in kung fu and trained in numerous other martial arts, who continually puts herself in harm's way to test herself. Bradburn felt "Pascal has created a fascinating, complex character," and that the lead book, *Fearless,* "is a winning set piece for this new series." Reviewing *Twisted,* the fourth book in the series, Bradburn noted in *Booklist* that readers "hooked on Gaia and her mixture of teen angst and the darkness that surrounds her" would keep "clamoring for the next book." In *Before Gaia,* the young protagonist attempts to trace the history of her parents' meeting and their courtship. Reviewing that title, *School Library Journal*'s Lynn Evarts remarked that the "Fearless" series "continues to give readers a strong female character, intense espionage excitement, and, in this Super Edition, the love-at-first sight romance of Gaia's parents." Evarts further called the entire series "stylish [and] exciting." Gillian Engberg, writing in the *Los Angeles Times Book Review,* also found the series "wildly popular."

With so many series in progress, Pascal's stable of ghostwriters has grown, with several contract writers providing the content for each series. However, each of the series has one author's name attached to it. For example, the 'Sweet Valley High' books are written by "Kate William," the "Sweet Valley Twins" by "Jamie Suzanne," and the "University" titles by "Laurie John." These names are fictitious, taken from the names of Pascal's family members. "It would be impossible to do [the series] without a stable of writers," Pascal once remarked. "They come out at the rate of one a month plus periodic super editions. I do all the plot outlines, descriptions of characters, time setting, and so forth. I love plot twists and the conflicts between the good and bad twin. Creating Sweet Valley was a real 'high.' I loved making up the history of the place, visualizing it in great detail. We have a stable of authors each of whom generally does one title every three months. I maintain artistic control over every aspect of these novels. I may not write every word, but they are very much mine."

Biographical and Critical Sources

BOOKS

Children's Literature Review, Volume 25, Gale (Detroit MI), 1991, pp. 175-182.
Contiuum Encyclopedia of Children's Literature, edited by Bernice E. Cullinan and Diane G. Person, Continuum (New York, NY), 2001, p. 610.
Drew, Bernard A., *The 100 Most Popular Young Adult Authors: Biographical Sketches and Bibliographies,* Libraries Unlimited (Englewood, CO), 1996, pp. 373-391.
Meet the Stars of Sweet Valley High, Bantam (New York, NY), 1995.
St. James Guide to Young Adult Fiction, edited by Tom Pendergast and Sara Pendergast, St. James Press (Detroit MI), 1999.

PERIODICALS

ALAN Review, spring, 1984, Sarah Simpson, review of *Dangerous Love,* p. 23.
Book, July-August, 2002, Kristin Kloberdanz, "Fear Factor," pp. 30-31.
Booklist, February 15, 1979, Barbara Elleman, review of *My First Love and Other Disasters,* p. 936; March 15, 1985, Stephanie Zvirin, review of *Love and Betrayal and Hold the Mayo!,* p. 1052; January 15, 1994, p. 901; February 1, 2000, Frances Bradburn, review of *Fearless,* p. 1016; April 1, 2000, Frances Bradburn, review of *Twisted,* p. 1451.
Boston Globe, October 14, 1994, Linda Matchan, "'Sweet Valley High': Cool Success."
Chicago Tribune, June 1, 1987.
Forbes, October 28, 2002, Chana R. Schoenberger, "A Valley Girl Grows Up," p. 114.
Growing Point, September, 1984, Margery Fisher, review of *The Hand-Me-Down Kid,* pp. 4311-4312.
Horn Book, September-October, 1977, Ann A. Flowers, review of *Hangin' out with Cici,* p. 541; May-June, 1980, Mary M. Burns, review of *The Hand-Me-Down Kid,* pp. 302-303.
Kirkus Reviews, February 1, 1977, review of *Hangin' Out with Cici,* p. 99; June 1, 1980, review of *The Hand-Me-Down Kid,* pp. 714-715.
Library Journal, June 15, 1981, pp. 1323-1324; January, 1994, p. 163.
Los Angeles Times, April 20, 1986, section 6, pp. 1, 10-11.
Los Angeles Times Book Review, June 10, 2001, Gillian Engberg, review of *Tears* and *Naked,* pp. 16-17.
New York Times Book Review, April 29, 1979, Joyce Milton, "All for Love," p. 38.
People, March 30, 1981; July 11, 1988, Steve Dougherty, "Heroines of 40 Million Books, Francine Pascal's 'Sweet Valley' Twins Are Perfection in Duplicate," pp. 66-68.
Publishers Weekly, January 8, 1979, p. 74; July 26, 1985; May 29, 1987, p. 30; September 27, 1993, review of *College Girls,* p. 64; November 29, 1993, p. 55.

School Library Journal, September, 1977, Diane Haas, review of *Hangin' Out with Cici,* p. 134; March, 1979, C. Nordhielm Wooldridge, review of *My First Love and Other Disasters,* pp. 149-150; September, 1980, p. 76; September, 1984, Annette Curtis Klause, review of *Power Play,* p. 136; September, 1985, Catherine van Sonnenberg, review of *Love and Betrayal and Hold the Mayo,* p. 148; March, 1990, Mary M. Huntwork, "Why Girls Flock to 'Sweet Valley High,'" pp. 137-140; February, 1999, Karen Hoth, review of *Can't Stay Away,* p. 111, Lisa Denton, review of *Get Real,* p. 111; January, 2003, Lynn Evarts, review of *Before Gaia,* p. 142.

Variety, August 7, 2000, p. 23.

Voice of Youth Advocates, October, 1980, Millicent Lenz, review of *The Hand-Me-Down Kid,* p. 27; August, 1984, Judy Mitchell, review of *Power Play,* p. 146; October, 1985, Myrna Feldman, review of *Showdown,* p. 264; December, 1986, Tony Ling, review of *Alone in the Crowd,* pp. 231, Susannah Neal, review of *Bitter Rivals,* pp. 231-232, Civia Tuteur, review of *Best Friends,* p. 232; June, 1987, Jennifer Harvey, review of *A New Promise,* p. 87; August, 1999, Holly Ward Lamb, review of *Can't Stay Away* and *Say It to My Face,* p. 181.

ONLINE

Sweet Valley High Web site, http://www.sweetvalley.com/ (August 7, 2003), "Meet Francine."

*   *   *

PEDERSON, Sharleen
See COLLICOTT, Sharleen

R

RIORDAN, James 1936-

Personal

Born October 10, 1936, in Portsmouth, England; son of William (an engineer) and Kathleen (a cleaner; maiden name, Smith) Brown; married Annick Vercaigne, July 4, 1959 (divorced, 1964); married Rashida Davletshina (a teacher), July 1, 1965; children: Tania, Nadine, Sean, Nathalie, Catherine. *Education:* University of Birmingham, B.S., 1959, Ph.D., 1975; University of London, certificate in education, 1960; University of Moscow, diploma in political science, 1962. *Politics:* Socialist. *Religion:* "Faith in people, not gods."

Addresses

Home—Portsmouth, England. *Office*—Department of Language and International Studies, University of Surrey, Guildford, Surrey GU2 5XH, England.

Career

Writer and educator. British Railways, Portsmouth, England, clerk, 1956-57; Progress Publisher, Moscow, USSR, senior translator, 1962-65; Portsmouth Polytechnic, Portsmouth, England, lecturer in Russian, 1965-69; University of Bradford, Bradford, England, senior lecturer and reader in Russian studies; University of Surrey, Guilford, England, professor of Russian studies and head of the department. *Military service:* Royal Air Force, 1954-56, served in Berlin, Germany; British Olympic Attache at Moscow Olympic Games, 1980.

Member

International Sports History Association (vice president).

Awards, Honors

Kurt Maschler Award runner-up, 1984, for *The Woman in the Moon and Other Tales of Forgotten Heroines;* NASEN Award and Whitbread Children's Book award shortlist, both 1998, both for *Sweet Clarinet.*

Writings

FOR CHILDREN

(With Eileen H. Colwell) *Little Grey Neck: A Russian Folktale,* illustrated by Caroline Sharpe, Kestrel, 1975, Addison-Wesley (Reading, MA), 1976.

(Reteller) *Beauty and the Beast,* illustrated by Annabel Large, Macdonald Educational (London, England), 1979.

(Reteller) *Sleeping Beauty,* illustrated by Carol Tarrant, Macdonald Educational (London, England), 1979.

The Three Magic Gifts, Kaye & Ward (London, England), 1980, illustrated by Errol le Cain, Oxford University Press (New York, NY), 1980.

The Secret Castle, illustrated by Peter Dennis, Silver Burdett (Morristown, NJ), 1980.

Flight into Danger, illustrated by Gary Rees, Silver Burdett (Morristown, NJ), 1980.

Changing Shapes, Macmillan (London, England), 1982.

The Little Humpback Horse, illustrated by Andrew Skilleter, Hamlyn (London, England), 1983.

(Reteller) *Peter and the Wolf,* illustrated by Victor G. Ambrus, Oxford University Press (New York, NY), 1986.

(Reteller) *The Wild Swans,* illustrated by Helen Stratton, Hutchinson (London, England), 1987.

(Reteller) *Pinocchio,* illustrated by Victor G. Ambrus, Oxford University Press (New York, NY), 1988.

Babes in the Wood, illustrated by Randolph Caldecott, Hutchinson (London, England), 1988, Barron's (Hauppage, NY), 1989.

(Reteller) *The Snowmaiden,* illustrated by Stephen Lambert, Hutchinson (London, England), 1990.

(Reteller) *Thumbelina,* illustrated by Wayne Anderson, Putnam (New York, NY), 1990.

(Reteller) *Gulliver's Travels,* illustrated by Victor G. Ambrus, Oxford University Press (New York, NY), 1992.

(Compiler) *A Book of Narnians: The Lion, the Witch, and the Others* (based on the work of C. S. Lewis), illustrated by Pauline Baynes, Collins (London, England), 1994, HarperCollins (New York, NY), 1995.

My G-r-r-reat Uncle Tiger, illustrated by Alex Ayliffe, Peachtree (Atlanta, GA), 1995.

(Reteller) *The Barnyard Band: A Story from the Brothers Grimm,* illustrated by Charles Fuge, Macmillan (London, England), 1996.

Grace the Pirate, illustrated by Steve Hutton, Oxford University Press (New York, NY), 1996.

The Twelve Labors of Hercules, illustrated by Christina Balit, Millbrook Press (Brookfield, CT), 1997.

Sweet Clarinet (novel), Oxford University Press (New York, NY), 1998.

Little Bunny Bobkin, illustrated by Tim Warnes, Little Tiger, 1998.

(Reteller) *King Arthur,* illustrated by Victor G. Ambrus, Oxford University Press (New York, NY), 1998.

(Adaptor) *The Coming of Night: A Yoruba Tale from West Africa,* illustrated by Jenny Stow, Millbrook Press (Brookfield, CT), 1999.

The Story of Martin Luther King (biography), illustrated by Rob McCaig, Smart Apple Media (North Mankato, MN), 2001.

The Story of Nelson Mandela (biography), illustrated by Neil Reed, Smart Apple Media (North Mankato, MN), 2001.

When the Guns Fall Silent (young adult novel), Oxford University Press (London, England), 2001.

War Song (sequel to *When the Guns Fall Silent*), Oxford University Press (London, England), 2002.

Match of Death, Oxford University Press (New York, NY), 2002.

Boxcar Molly: A Story from the Great Depression ("Survivors" series), Barron's Educational (Hauppage, NY), 2002.

The Enemy: A Story from World War II ("Survivors" series), Barron's Educational (Hauppage, NY), 2002.

(Reteller) Charles Dickens, *Great Expectations,* illustrated by Victor G. Ambrus, Oxford University Press (New York, NY), 2002.

COLLECTIONS FOR CHILDREN

(Adapter and translator) *The Mistress of the Copper Mountain: Tales from the Urals,* Muller, 1974.

Tales from Central Russia: Russian Tales, Volume I, illustrated by Krystyna Turska, Kestrel (New York, NY), 1976.

Tales from Tartary: Russian Tales Volume II, illustrated by Anthony Colbert, Kestrel (New York, NY), 1978.

A World of Fairy Tales, Hamlyn (London, England), 1981.

A World of Folktales, Hamlyn (London, England), 1981.

Tales of King Arthur, illustrated by Victor G. Ambrus, Rand-McNally (Chicago, IL), 1982.

Tales from the Arabian Nights, illustrated by Victor G. Ambrus, Hamlyn (London, England), 1983, Rand-McNally (Chicago, IL), 1995.

The Boy Who Turned into a Goat, illustrated by I. Ripley, Macmillan (London, England), 1983.

Petrushka and Other Tales from the Ballet, Stodder & Houghton (London, England), 1984.

Stories of the Ballet, illustrated by Victor G. Ambrus, foreword by Rudolf Nureyev, Hodder & Stoughton (London, England), 1984, published as *Favorite Stories of the Ballet,* Rand McNally (Chicago, IL), 1984.

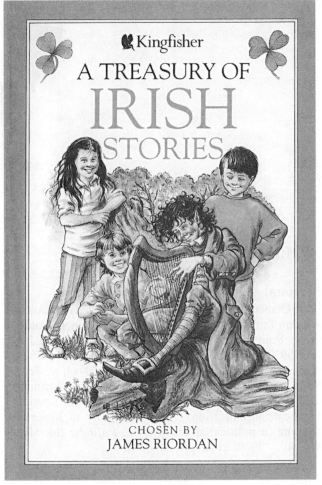

Riordan selected fourteen tales for this collection, illustrated by Elsie Lennox.

(Translator) *The Twelve Months: Fairy Tales by Soviet Writers,* illustrated by Fyodor Lemkul, Raduga (Moscow, USSR), 1984.

The Woman in the Moon and Other Tales of Forgotten Heroines, illustrated by Angela Barrett, Hutchinson (London, England), 1984, Dial (New York, NY), 1985.

A World of Myths and Legends, Hamlyn (London, England), 1985.

(Translator) Yefim Drutëtìs and Alexei Gessler, collectors, *Russian Gypsy Tales,* Canongate (Edinburgh, Scotland), 1986, Interlink Books (New York, NY), 1992.

(Reteller) *Korean Folk-Tales,* Oxford University Press, 1994 (New York, NY).

(With Brenda Ralph Lewis) *An Illustrated Treasury of Myths and Legends,* illustrated by Victor G. Ambrus, Hamlyn (London, England), 1987, Peter Bedrick Books (New York, NY), 1991.

(Collector and translator) *The Sun Maiden and the Crescent Moon: Siberian Folk Tales,* Canongate (Edinburgh, Scotland), 1991.

(Editor) *A Treasury of Irish Stories,* illustrated by Ian Newsham, Kingfisher (New York, NY), 1995.

Stories from the Sea, illustrated by Amanda Hall, Abbeville Press (New York, NY), 1996.

(Editor) *The Songs My Paddle Sings: Native American Legends,* illustrated by Michael Foreman, Trafalgar (New York, NY), 1996.

(Editor) *The Young Oxford Book of Football Stories,* Oxford University Press (Oxford, England), 1999.

(Editor) *The Young Oxford Book of Sports Stories,* Oxford University Press, 2000.

(Editor) *The Young Oxford Book of War Stories,* Oxford University Press, 2000.

Russian Folk-Tales, illustrated by Andrew Breakspeare, Oxford University Press (New York, NY), 2000.

The Storytelling Star: Tales of the Sun, Moon, and Stars, illustrated by Amanda Hall, Trafalgar Square (New York, NY), 2000.

NONFICTION

Sport in Soviet Society: Development of Sport and Physical Education in Russia and the USSR, Cambridge University Press (New York, NY), 1977.

(Editor) *Sport under Communism: The USSR, Czechoslovakia, the G.D.R., China, Cuba,* C. Hurst (London, England), 1978, revised second edition, 1981.

Soviet Sport: Background to the Olympics, Washington Mews Books (New York, NY) 1980.

(Adapter) George Morey, *Soviet Union: The Land and Its People,* MacDonald Educational (London, England), 1986, Silver Burdett Press (Morristown, NJ), 1987.

Eastern Europe: The Lands and Their Peoples, Silver Burdett Press (Morristown, NJ), 1987.

(Editor) *Soviet Education: The Gifted and the Handicapped,* Routledge (London, England), 1988.

(Editor) *Soviet Youth Culture,* Indiana University Press (Bloomington, IN), 1989.

Sport, Politics, and Communism, Manchester University Press (New York, NY), 1991.

(Editor and translator, with Susan Bridger) *Dear Comrade Editor: Readers' Letters to the Soviet Press under Perestroika,* Indiana University Press (Bloomington, IN), 1992.

(Editor) *Soviet Social Reality in the Mirror of Glasnost,* St. Martin's Press (New York, NY), 1992.

(With Victor Peppard) *Playing Politics: Soviet Sport Diplomacy to 1992,* JAI Press (Greenwich, CT), 1993.

(Editor with Igor S. Kon) *Sex and Russian Society,* Indiana University Press (Bloomington, IN), 1993, revised as *The Sexual Revolution in Russia: From the Age of the Czars to Today,* Free Press (New York, NY), 1995.

Russia and the Commonwealth of Independent States, Silver Burdett Press (Morristown, NJ), 1993.

(Editor with Christopher Williams and Igor Ilynsky) *Young People in Post-Communist Russia and Eastern Europe,* Dartmouth College/University Press of New England (Hanover, NH), 1995.

(Editor with Petar-Emil Mitev) *Europe, the Young, the Balkans* (conference proceedings), International Centre for Minority Studies and Intercultural Relations (Sofia, Bulgaria), 1996.

(Editor with Arnd Krüger) *The Story of Worker Sport,* Human Kinetics (Champaign, IL), 1996.

(Editor, translator, and contributor) Olga Litvinenko, collector, *Memories of the Dispossessed: Descendants of Kulak Families Tell Their Stories,* Bramcote Press (Nottingham, England), 1998.

(Editor with Pierre Arnaud) *Sport and International Politics: The Impact of Fascism and Communism on Sport,* E. & F. Spon (New York, NY), 1998.

Russia and the Commonwealth of Independent States, Silver Burdett Press (Morristown, NJ), 1999.

(Editor with Robin Jones) *Sport and Physical Education in China,* Routledge (New York, NY), 1999.

(Editor with Arnd Krüger) *The International Politics of Sport in the Twentieth Century,* Routledge (New York, NY), 1999.

Sidelights

British author and educator James Riordan, an expert in Russian language, folklore, and culture, has made a contribution to children's literature by translating and retelling folktales from Eastern Europe and Asia. From Russia, he brings young readers *The Three Magic Gifts* and *The Snowmaiden*), as well as many shorter folktales included in the collections *Tales from Tartary* and *Russian Folk-Tales.* Presenting each tale with what a *Publishers Weekly* reviewer characterized as "a storyteller's bravado," Riordan has also mined other regions of the world for traditional tales, which have been published in such books as *A Treasury of Irish Stories, Korean Folk-Tales,* and *The Woman in the Moon, and Other Tales of Forgotten Heroines.* In more recent years he has also begun to publish original works, including picture books such as *Little Bunny Bobkin* and novels for older readers that focus on World War II.

Born in 1936, Riordan spent his early childhood in Portsmouth, England. During World War II he was sent to live with his grandparents, an experience that proved influential. As he once recalled to *SATA*: "The household was big, twelve adults and me, very warm and friendly. Amid the doodle-bugs and air raid sirens (Portsmouth was blown to bits), the all-pervasive tang of soot in mouth and nose, and the massive picture of Lord Kitchener dominating our living room, my lasting attitudes of faith in ordinary people and hatred of war were being formed."

After finishing school Riordan "became successively a barman, a cratestacker in a brewery, commercial salesman (of 'unbreakable tea sets'), double-bass player in a dance band, postman, railway clerk and junior technician in the Royal Air Force." Determined to gain an education, he took classes at the universities of Birmingham, London, and Moscow, and "travelled and worked in various countries," including France, Germany, and the former Soviet Union. Spending five years in the USSR, Riordan gained a good understanding of both Russia's language and people. Beginning his teaching career in England in 1965, he worked as a lecturer of Russian at Portsmouth Polytechnic, and eventually worked his way up to professor of Russian studies at a university in Guilford.

Riordan published his first folk-story adaptations in 1975. *Little Gray Neck: A Russian Folktale,* a collaboration between Riordan and Eileen H. Colwell, is about a little duck with an injured wing. The duck, who cannot migrate with the other ducks as winter approaches, worries that she will be eaten by a fox. Instead, she is rescued by a man who takes her home for a pet.

Little Gray Neck marked the beginning of what has become a prolific career as a children's writer for Riordan, and among his many works have been retellings of traditional Russian tales. *The Three Magic Gifts,* described by a critic for *Junior Bookshelf* as an "excellent folktale," recounts the fate of an impoverished, good brother—Ivan the Poor—and a wealthy, bad one—Ivan the Rich. A *Booklist* contributor noted that "Riordan spices the text with brief verses," and in *Publishers Weekly* a reviewer maintained that *The Three Magic Gifts* "should entrance little readers." *The Snowmaiden,* a retelling described by a *Junior Bookshelf* contributor as "highly charged," tells the story of the daughter of Spring and Frost. She has been living with peasants for sixteen years, hidden from the god of the sun and keeping warmth from the land. When the Snowmaiden leaves the peasants who have raised her, spring returns to the earth. The Snowmaiden then finds herself loved by a shepherd boy. Disappointed because she lacks a heart and cannot love him back, she begs for one. After she gains the ability to love the shepherd, the Snow-

maiden remains too long in the sun; she melts away, and flowers grow on the spot where she once stood.

In *Tales from Central Russia* Riordan presents traditional Russian stories, his translations and retellings presented with "flavor and directness," in the opinion of *Horn Book* contributor Virginia Haviland. Praising the book's accessibility to children, a critic for *Junior Bookshelf* commented, "Here's treasure." *Tales from Tartary* is the product of months spent at the homes of friends and relatives of Riordan's Tartar wife, Rashida. Influenced by Asian culture, these tales come from Tartarstan, Siberia, and the Crimea, and show what a *Junior Librarian* contributor called Riordan's "deep respect for the traditions" of the Tartar people. A more broad-ranging collection, *Russian Folk-Tales* features ten stories that include "The Firebird" and a Baba Yaga tale as well as some more unfamiliar to Western readers. Noting that Riordan makes his selections carefully, *School Library Journal* contributor Denise Anton Wright noted that the stories included in *Russian Folk-Tales* "emphasize family relationships, clever main characters, magical gifts, and punishment for evil," and the authors retellings "beg to be shared aloud."

Riordan has not limited himself to collecting and retelling the stories of former Soviet societies. *The Songs My Paddle Sings: Native American Legends* contains twenty stories collected during Riordan's trip across the United States and presents the myths of the Apache, Blackfoot, Pueblo, and Salish, among others, all told in "stately language eminently suited to reading aloud," according to a *Kirkus Reviews* critic. *Korean Folk-Tales* provides twenty stories from Korea, and, in the words of a critic for *Junior Bookshelf,* provides "riches . . . for the oral storyteller." These stories are, in the words of *School Library Journal* contributor Diane S. Marton, "for the most part clearly and pleasantly told." *The Boy Who Turned into a Goat* contains six stories from different cultures written with "freshness and vitality," as a *Junior Bookshelf* reviewer remarked. *A World of Fairy Tales* contains stories from Australia, China, Africa, India, Russia, North and South America, and Europe. *The Coming of Night: A Yoruba Tale from West Africa* provides a fanciful explanation of how night was first created, and draws readers back to a time when the sun never set. According to the story—"written in a style rich with descriptive language and images" according to *School Library Journal* contributor Paul Kelsey—when a powerful chief named Oduduwa marries the daughter of the river goddess, his young bride leaves the waterbound home where Night dwells, but soon tires of the perpetual daylight. Her husband commands some animals to fetch Night from the river and bring it to his wife, but to be sure Night is kept in a sack as it will otherwise cause mischief. True to folktale form, the animals succumb to curiosity, open the sack, and release Night to overshadow a portion of each day.

In addition to collecting, translating, and retelling folktales, Riordan has made other contributions to children's

Stories from the Sea, *compiled by Riordan, includes folktales from around the world. (Illustrated by Ian Newsham.)*

literature. *Tales from the Arabian Nights* presents readers with a children's classic, retold in Riordan's own words with "sympathy and dramatic flair," according to a *Booklist* critic. *The Twelve Labors of Hercules* starts with the ancient hero's birth and goes on to tell how he incurred the wrath of the jealous goddess Hera, and how Hera caused him to go mad and kill his family, causing the labors meted out as his punishment. In Riordan's retelling, which is punctuated by what *School Librarian* reviewer Mary Medlicott described as "occasional touches of humor," Hercules' "personality comes through, especially his impulsiveness," according to *School Library Journal* contributor Pam Gosner. In *King Arthur*, Riordan presents an account of the famous king in a style that *Voice of Youth Advocates* contributor Rebecca Barnhouse characterized as "formal and distant, as befits a legend." Citing Riordan's effective mix of myth and history—he includes notes on the origins of the Arthur myth—Hazel Towson in *School Librarian* praised the retelling for being "well researched" and "lucidly told." *A Book of Narnians: The Lion, the Witch, and the Others* is a compilation which allows readers unfamiliar with the famous books of C. S. Lewis to get to know the series' characters. "The words are largely Lewis's own, though plucked selectively," noted *School Library Journal* contributor Nancy Palmer, who added that the "selection is skillfully done."

Riordan's original fiction includes several diverse works. In *Flight into Danger,* a pair of twins take a harrowing plane ride with their father, who falls ill during the flight. *The Secret Castle* follows the story of a boy and a girl who travel back in time to the Middle Ages, where they lead the lives of lord and lady. The picture book *Little Bunny Bobkin* appeals to the very young, as it presents simple counting through the experiences of a young rabbit. After no one in the family burrow wants to help him practice counting, little Bobkin wanders out into the forest, where a group of hungry foxes seem only too happy to humor the tasty bunny. Riordan has also contributed two original stories—*Boxcar Molly: A Story from the Great Depression* and *The Enemy: A Story from World War II*—to Barron's "Survivors" series for preteen readers.

World Wars I and II have figured not only in *The Enemy* but in several other works by Riordan, who himself has memories of the World War II years. He includes excerpts from poems, diaries, and fiction about war in his edited anthology *The Young Oxford Book of War Stories*, which also covers the Vietnam conflict in what *School Librarian* contributor Janet Fisher described as a "sombre tone" in keeping with the book's subject matter. The 1998 novel *Sweet Clarinet* introduces readers to Billy Riley, an English boy who is touched personally by World War II when he is disfigured by burns after German bombs hit an air-raid shelter and his mother is killed. Sent to a children's hospital, the orphaned Billy withdraws until he meets an injured soldier whose gift to the lonely boy—a clarinet—allows Billy to express his sadness and put his bitterness behind him. Praising Riordan for his use of accurate period detail, Sandra Bennett added in her *School Librarian* review of *Sweet Clarinet* that within Riordan's "simply told" story the young teen's "isolation and unhappiness are convincingly portrayed."

When the Guns Fall Silent and *War Song* are linking novels that focus on World War I. In *When the Guns Fall Silent* Jack Loveless is forced to relive his memories of the Great War during a trip with his grandson to France's war cemeteries. Noting that Riordan "is good at showing the dreadful chauvinism" that existed in Great Britain toward those of German heritage during the war years, Dennis Hamley noted in *School Librarian* that *When the Guns Fall Silent* is "a necessary, powerful, outspoken but ultimately healing book" that brings to life for modern readers the true horrors and disillusionment caused by war. Calling Riordan's text "as jagged and staccato as a fusillade" a *Books for Keeps* contributor also praised the book for recapturing the emotions visited upon Jack as a naive sixteen-year-old volunteer of the Great War. Equally poignant reading is *War Song,* which follows two sisters who, left at home, determine to help the war effort through working as a nurse and in a munitions factory. Noting the tension built up through the novel as the young women witness the tragedies visited upon friends and their own families, Eileen Armstrong praised *War Song* in her *School Librarian* review as a "compelling" and "accessible but uncomfortable, make-you-stop-and-think story that should not be missed."

Riordan credits his five children for helping him ensure that his stories and story collections are appropriate for ethnically diverse children, whether they are boys or girls. He explained to *SATA*, "I love children and test all my stories out on them before producing a final version; so I have to keep producing more children to keep up with my writing. My own multi-ethnic family (parts English/Irish/Tartar/Bashkir) is a useful touchstone for all my stories. And since I only have one son, I make sure that at least half the stories in all my collections are about girls (most folk and fairy tales have exclusively male heroes)."

Biographical and Critical Sources

PERIODICALS

Booklist, July 15, 1979, review of *Tales from Tartary,* p. 1629; March 1, 1981, review of *The Three Magic Gifts,* pp. 967-68; December 15, 1985, review of *Tales from the Arabian Nights,* p. 630; March 15, 1991, pp. 1494-1495; March 15, 1998, Karen Hutt, review of *The Song My Paddle Sings,* p. 1242; October 1, 1998, Carolyn Phelan, review of *King Arthur,* p. 330; February 15, 1999, Ilene Cooper, review of *The Coming of Night: A Yoruba Tale from West Africa,* p. 1072; April 1, 2001, Carolyn Phelan, review of *Russian Folk-Tales,* p. 1463.

Books for Keeps, March, 2001, George Hunt, review of *When the Guns Fall Silent,* p. 25.

Bulletin of the Center for Children's Books, February, 1983, p. 116; December, 1985, review of *The Woman in the Moon and Other Tales of Forgotten Heroines,* p. 76.

Horn Book, August, 1979, Virginia Haviland, review of *Tales from Central Russia* and *Tales from Tartary,* pp. 430-431.

Junior Bookshelf, February, 1977, review of *Tales from Central Russia,* pp. 24-25; December, 1978, review of *Tales from Tartary,* p. 320; April, 1981, review of *The Three Magic Gifts,* p. 60; December, 1982, review of *A World of Fairy Tales,* p. 226; October, 1983, review of *The Boy Who Turned into a Goat,* p. 210; February, 1985, review of *The Woman in the Moon,* p. 30; August, 1990, review of *The Snowmaiden,* p. 164; December, 1992, review of *Gulliver's Travels,* p. 262; February, 1995, review of *Korean Folk-Tales,* p. 43.

Kirkus Reviews, February 15, 1998, review of *The Song My Paddle Sings,* p. 273.

Library Journal, July, 1991, p. 106.

Magpies, March, 1993, review of *Gulliver's Travels,* p. 23.

New York Times Book Review, March 9, 1986, p. 37.

Publishers Weekly, December 12, 1980, review of *The Three Magic Gifts;* December 21, 1998, review of *Little Bunny Bobkin,* p. 66; March 19, 2001, review of *Russian Folk-Tales,* p. 101; November 4, 2002, review of *Boxcar Molly: A Story from the Great Depression,* p. 85.

School Librarian, spring, 1998, Mary Medlicott, review of *The Twelve Labours of Hercules,* p. 36; autumn, 1998, Hazel Towson, review of *King Arthur,* p. 148; spring, 1999, Sandra Bennett, review of *Sweet Clarinet,* pp. 47-48; spring, 2001, Dennis Hamley, review of *When the Guns Fall Silent,* p. 49; autumn, 2001, Janet Fisher, review of *The Oxford Book of War Stories,* p. 159; winter, 2001, Eileen Armstrong, review of *War Song,* p. 214.

School Library Journal, April, 1987, p. 89; June, 1991, p. 89; March, 1995, Diane S. Marton, review of *Korean Folk-Tales,* p. 218; October, 1995, Nancy Palmer, review of *A Book of Narnians,* pp. 148-149; February, 1998, Pam Gosner, review of *The Twelve Labors of Hercules,* pp. 122, 124; May, 1998, Lisa Mitten, review of *The Song My Paddle Sings,* p. 136; October, 1998, Carolyn Jenks, review of *Little Bunny Bobkin,* p. 112; April, 1999, Helen Gregory, review of *King Arthur,* p. 154; May, 1999, Paul Kelsey, review of *The Coming of Night,* p. 112; November, 2000, Nancy A. Gifford, review of *The Storytelling Star,* p. 148; July, 2001, Denise Anton Wright, review of *Russian Folk-Tales,* pp. 97-98; October, 2002, Patricia D. Lothrop, review of *Great Expectations,* p. 170.

Times Educational Supplement, November 5, 1999, "After the Fire," p. 11; April 20, 2001, review of *The Oxford Book of War Stories,* p. 20.

Voice of Youth Advocates, December, 1998, Rebecca Barnhouse, review of *King Arthur,* p. 368.*

*   *   *

ROBERT, Adrian
See ST. JOHN, Nicole

ROLEFF, Tamara L. 1959-

Personal

Born November 27, 1959, in Council Bluffs, IA; daughter of Richard A. Fahey (an engineer) and Linda E. Schoenrock (an attorney); married Keith W. Roleff (a U.S. Marine Corps officer), March 17, 1984. *Education:* Iowa State University, B.S., 1981. *Hobbies and other interests:* Golden retrievers, travel.

Addresses

Office—Greenhaven Press, 10911 Technology Place, San Diego, CA 92127. *E-mail*—orchids59@hotmail.com.

Career

Author and editor. Worked as a newspaper "Lifestyles" editor in New Bern, NC, 1991-93; Greenhaven Press, San Diego, CA, book editor, 1995—; nonfiction author.

Awards, Honors

Invited to enter *Inner City Poverty* for the 2002 Harry Chapin Media Award, sponsored by World Hunger Year.

Writings

EDITOR

The Atom Bomb ("Turning Points in World History" series), Greenhaven Press (San Diego, CA), 2000.

Sex ("Teen Decisions" series), Greenhaven Press (San Diego, CA), 2001.

America Under Attack: Primary Sources, Lucent (San Diego, CA), 2002.

Inner-City Poverty ("Contemporary Issues Companion" series), Greenhaven Press (San Diego, CA), 2003.

EDITOR; "OPPOSING VIEWPOINTS" SERIES

The Homeless, Greenhaven Press (San Diego, CA), 1995.

The Legal System, Greenhaven Press (San Diego, CA), 1996.

Abortion, revised edition, Greenhaven Press (San Diego, CA), 1997.

(With others) *Gun Control,* Greenhaven Press (San Diego, CA), 1997.

(With others) *Global Warming,* Greenhaven Press (San Diego, CA), 1997.

Sexual Violence, Greenhaven Press (San Diego, CA), 1997.

AIDS, Greenhaven Press (San Diego, CA), 1997, third edition, 2003.

Biomedical Ethics, Greenhaven Press (San Diego, CA), 1998.

Suicide, Greenhaven Press (San Diego, CA), 1998.

Tamara L. Roleff

Tobacco and Smoking, Greenhaven Press (San Diego, CA), 1998.
Immigration, Greenhaven Press (San Diego, CA), 1998, second edition, forthcoming.
War, Greenhaven Press (San Diego, CA), 1999.
(With others) *Hate Groups,* Greenhaven Press (San Diego, CA), 1999.
Civil Liberties, Greenhaven Press (San Diego, CA), 1999.
Pollution, Greenhaven Press (San Diego, CA), 2000.
Mental Illness, Greenhaven Press (San Diego, CA), 2000.
Crime and Criminals, Greenhaven Press (San Diego, CA), 2000.
Domestic Violence, Greenhaven Press (San Diego, CA), 2000.
Teen Sexuality, Greenhaven Press (San Diego, CA), 2001.
Censorship, Greenhaven Press (San Diego, CA), 2002.
(With others) *Extremist Groups,* Greenhaven Press (San Diego, CA), 2001.
Criminal Justice, Greenhaven Press (San Diego, CA), forthcoming.

EDITOR; "HISTORY FIRSTHAND" SERIES

The Vietnam War, Greenhaven Press (San Diego, CA), 2002.
The Holocaust: Death Camps, Greenhaven Press (San Diego, CA), 2002.
The World Trade Center, Greenhaven Press (San Diego, CA), 2003.

The American Frontier, Greenhaven Press (San Diego, CA), forthcoming.
Oklahoma City Bombing, Greenhaven Press (San Diego, CA), forthcoming.

EDITOR; "AT ISSUE" SERIES

Business Ethics, Greenhaven Press (San Diego, CA), 1996.
Gay Marriage, Greenhaven Press (San Diego, CA), 1998.
Sex Education, Greenhaven Press (San Diego, CA), 1999.
Guns and Crime, Greenhaven Press (San Diego, CA), 2000.
Teen Suicide, Greenhaven Press (San Diego, CA), 2000.
Teen Sex, Greenhaven Press (San Diego, CA), 2001.
Satanism, Greenhaven Press (San Diego, CA), 2001.
What Encourages Gang Behavior?, Greenhaven Press (San Diego, CA), 2002.
Police Corruption, Greenhaven Press (San Diego, CA), 2003.

EDITOR; "CURRENT CONTROVERSIES" SERIES

Genetics and Intelligence, Greenhaven Press (San Diego, CA), 1996.
Gay Rights, Greenhaven Press (San Diego, CA), 1997.
(With others) *Marriage and Divorce,* Greenhaven Press (San Diego, CA), 1997.
Native American Rights, Greenhaven Press (San Diego, CA), 1998.
The Rights of Animals, Greenhaven Press (San Diego, CA), 1999.
Police Brutality, Greenhaven Press (San Diego, CA), 1999.
Hate Crimes, Greenhaven Press (San Diego, CA), 2001.

EDITOR; "FACT OR FICTION" SERIES

Alien Abductions, Greenhaven Press (San Diego, CA), 2003.
Black Magic and Witches, Greenhaven Press (San Diego, CA), 2003.
Psychics, Greenhaven Press (San Diego, CA), 2003.

EDITOR; "CONTEMPORARY ISSUES COMPANION" SERIES

Extraterrestrial Life, Greenhaven Press (San Diego, CA), 2001.
Inner-City Poverty, Greenhaven Press (San Diego, CA), 2003.

Work in Progress

War on Drugs ("Opposing Viewpoints" series).

Sidelights

Tamara L. Roleff is a book editor and author who specializes in nonfiction titles. In her job for Greenhaven Press, she has contributed edited titles to several book series, among them Greenhaven's "Opposing Viewpoints," "History Firsthand," and "Current Controversies," which has allowed Roleff to research a number of hotly debated social issues. In her books for the "Current Controversies" series, for instance, she has edited the titles *Gay Rights, Native-American Rights,* and *Genetics and Intelligence.* Praising *Gay Rights* in her *School Library Journal* review, Sue A. Norkeliunas cited both the "well-selected articles" and "extensive list" of sources cited for students to contact, and praised the book as "an ideal research tool for short assignments" due to its "balanced coverage of emotional topics."

Most of Roleff's books are contained in the "Opposing Viewpoints" books, which *Kliatt* reviewer Claire Rosser praised as an "excellent" series that provides a "wonderful" opportunity for high school students to "improve . . . critical thinking skills." For titles such as *Suicide, Global Warming, Teen Sexuality,* and *Civil Liberties,* Roleff assembles a number of essays representing a diverse selection of views on the topic, as well as illustrations, a list of relevant organizations, and bibliographies for use in more in-depth study. In *Suicide,* an extensively revised version of a 1992 work, Roleff includes Pope John Paul II, physician Thomas Quill, and others, who debate issues such as whether suicide is a personal right, the reason for escalating suicide among

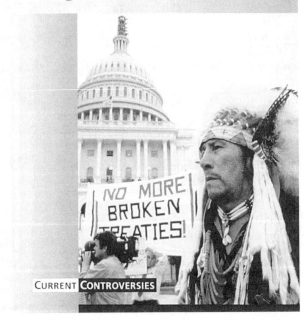

Native American Rights *is a collection of viewpoints on Native American issues. (Book cover photograph by Nina Berman.)*

adolescents, and the legalities of assisted suicide. *Hate Groups* includes essays authored by U.S. Senator Orin Hatch, David Kopel, U.S. Supreme Court Justice Thomas Scalia, and former president Bill Clinton that present several sides of the freedom-of-speech issues surrounding the treatment of hate crimes and the social effects of hate-group activity, providing both high school and college students with "excellent source material for debates or class discussion." Background material is presented by Roleff in what *Booklist* contributor Randy Meyer characterized as a "crisp, journalistic" style that "combines anecdotes and facts," as well as documents such as the Bill of Rights, relevant legislation, and actual hate-group propaganda pieces. In *Global Warming* maps and charts are included, along with contradictory views regarding whether the Earth's ecosystem is being threatened by industrialization and the destruction of the Amazonian rainforests. Information regarding the issue of global warming is presented in what R. M. Ferguson described in *Choice* as an "antagonistic format" in which the viewpoints of "well-known and articulate commentators, leading professionals, and . . . ordinary observers" are presented. As Rosser noted in a review of *Global Warming* and several other series installments for *Kliatt:* The "Opposing Viewpoints" series allows students to see that "issues have to be argued in a democracy, that compromise is probably the outcome of any legislation, and that it is important to be informed because policy affects us all."

Roleff told *SATA:* "When I went to college, my intention was to become a veterinarian. It wasn't long, however, before I discovered that I was baffled by organic chemistry, a requirement I needed to fulfil if I was to become a vet. I drifted along in school until forced to declare a major in my junior year. I had taken a lot of English literature classes, as I loved to read, and so I decided to major in English.

"After graduating, I didn't have a clue what I was going to do with my degree. I found out employers were not at all anxious to hire me simply because I had a college degree in English. I finally got a job entering orders for a mail-order printing company; I did proofreading for them as well, then customer service. After four years, I decided I needed to do something new in my life, so I tried to get a job in advertising. I ended up writing copy for another mail-order company that sold stamps and coins and collectibles. This was a great job for two years until the company had to lay off employees—including me.

"Then I started working for newspapers writing stories, and from there I got a job editing the 'Lifestyles' section of a small-town paper in North Carolina—my husband is in the military, so we moved around a lot. Just as I was getting tired of the deadlines of working for a newspaper, we moved to Okinawa, Japan, for a year. I took the year off and thought about what I wanted to do, and I decided I wanted to become an editor for a book publisher. I was lucky enough to move to San Di-

Members of the Ku Klux Klan, one of the groups discussed in Roleff's Hate Groups, *are depicted in this illustration from an 1868 newspaper.*

ego, California, which had a couple of publishing companies, and I got a job at one of them, where I've worked since. Book editors are expected to complete their books in eight weeks—or less! We learn a lot about our topic, and it's always interesting. It's definitely the best job I've ever had. When my husband's job forced us to move away from San Diego, I was lucky enough to be able to continue working for the same company on a freelance basis."

Biographical and Critical Sources

PERIODICALS

Booklist, January 1-15, 1997, Sally Estes, review of *Abortion,* p. 828; January 1, 1997, Sally Estes, review of *Abortion,* p. 828; April 1, 1997, Frances Estes, review of *Gay Rights,* p. 1321; July, 1997, F. Bradburn, review of *Sexual Violence,* p. 1810; November 1, 1997, Anne O'Malley, review of *Suicide,* p. 461; February 15, 1998, F. Bradburn, review of *AIDS,* p. 993; May 1, 1998, Roger Leslie, review of *Gay Marriage,* p. 1508; February 1, 1999, Karen Hutt, review of *Police Brutality,* p. 969; May 15, 1999, Roger Leslie, review of *Sex Education,* October 15, 1999, Roger Leslie, review of *The Rights of Animals,* p. 428; February 1, 2000, Roger Leslie, review of *Crime and Crimi-*

nals, p. 1013; November 15, 2000, Shelle Rosenfeld, review of *Domestic Violence,* p. 627; January 1, 2001, Roger Leslie, review of *Mental Illness,* p. 936; February 15, 2001, Roger Leslie, review of *Hate Crimes,* p. 1126; September 15, 2001, Roger Leslie, review of *Extremist Groups,* p. 214; January 1, 2002, Randy Meyer, review of *Hate Groups,* p. 838; April 1, 2002, Roger Leslie, review of *Censorship,* p. 1315; May 15, 2002, Roger Leslie, review of *Satanism,* p. 1590; November 1, 2002, Roger Leslie, review of *America under Attack: Primary Sources,* p. 483.

Book Report, March, 1999, Anitra Gordon, review of *Civil Liberties* and *Hate Groups,* p. 85; March-April, 2002, Mary Hofmann, review of *Teen Sex* p. 62.

Catholic Library World, March, 1999, Michael Dialessi, review of *Hate Groups* and *Civil Liberties,* p. 56.

Choice, February, 1998, R. M. Ferguson, review of *Global Warming,* p. 1028.

History: Review of New Books, winter, 2001, Thomas W. Judd, review of *The Atom Bomb,* p. 54.

Kliatt, May, 1996, Shelley A. Glantz, review of *Business Ethics,* p. 28; July, 1996, p. 32; March, 1997, Claire Rosser, review of *Abortion* and *Censorship,* p. 30; September, Rita M. Fontinha, review of *Marriage and Divorce,* p. 33; January, 1998, review of *AIDS,* p. 28; January, 1999, Claire Rosser, review of *Hate Groups,* p. 28; May, 1999, Claire Rosser, review of *Sex Education,* p. 39; September, 1999, Claire Rosser, review of *The Rights of Animals,* p. 38.

School Library Journal, February, 1997, Sue A. Norkeliunas, review of *Gay Rights,* p. 124; January, 1998, Sylvia V. Meisner, review of *Suicide,* p. 130; March, 1998, Darcy Schild, review of *Native American Rights,* p. 241; July, 1998, Edward Sullivan, review of *Gay Marriage,* p. 111; February, 2001, Katie O'Dell, review of *Teenage Sexuality,* p. 138; March, 2001, Marilyn Heath, review of *Hate Crimes,* p. 276; December, 2001, Pat Scales, review of *Censorship,* p. 156; March, 2002, Paula J. LaRue, review of *The Holocaust: Death Camps,* pp. 256-257; June, 2002, Edward Sullivan, "Teens and Sex," p. 160; July, 2002, Ann G. Brouse, review of *Satanism,* p. 141; September, 2002, Wendy Lukehart, review of *America under Attack: Primary Sources,* p. 251; February, 2003, Libby K. White, review of *Inner-City Poverty,* p. 168.

Teaching History, spring, 2002, Brian Boland, review of *The Atom Bomb,* p. 53.

Voice of Youth Advocates, June, 1996, Mary Jo Peltier, review of *The Homeless,* p. 117; December, 1996, Ann Welton, review of *Genetics and Intelligence,* pp. 286-287; June, 1999, Cindy Lombardo, review of *Civil Liberties,* p. 130.

*   *   *

RUEPP, Krista 1947-

Personal

Born August 16, 1947, in Cologne, Germany; daughter of Josef (an advertising manager) and Christl (a designer; maiden name, Röhrig) Wild; married Michel

Ruepp (a pharmacist), October 9, 1971; children: Kristian, Robin. *Education:* Attended Pädagogical University of Cologne. *Religion:* Catholic.

Addresses

Home—Remscheiderstrasse 210, 42855 Remscheid, Germany. *Office*—Alleestrasse 11, 42853 Remscheid, Germany. *Agent*—Jürgen Lassig, Braugasse 5, 85110 Kipfengerg-Arnsberg, Germany. *E-mail*—reupp@aar.de.

Career

Teacher in Neuss, Germany; WDR-School TV, Cologne, Germany, 1973-83; AAR-Pharma GMDH, Remscheid, Germany, marketing and advertising director, 1984.

Member

Geschichtsverein Remscheid, Astronomischer Verein Remscheid.

Awards, Honors

Citysen-Medaille, City of Remscheid, for activities for the historical city, 1985; Best Book of the Month, September, 2001, for *The Sea Pony.*

Writings

Midnight Rider, translated by J. Alison James, illustrated by Ulrike Heyne, North-South Books (Gossau, Switzerland), 1994.

Horses in the Fog (sequel to *Midnight Rider*), translated by J. Alison James, illustrated by Ulrike Heyne, North-South Books (Gossau, Switzerland), 1997.

The Sea Pony (sequel to *Horses in the Fog*), translated by J. Alison James, illustrated by Ulrike Heyne, North-South Books (Gossau, Switzerland), 2001.

Winter Pony, translated by J. Alison James, illustrated by Ulrike Heyne, North-South Books (Gossau, Switzerland), 2002.

Work in Progress

Island Friends about Charlie and Starbright, and *Winter Pony II,* about Anna and her pony Prince.

Sidelights

German author Krista Ruepp has enjoyed several careers. In addition to working for a children's television show for a decade, teaching German, history and art, and working for her husband's scientific company, she has written several early-reader books about horses. Prior to connecting with North-South Books at the international book fair in Bologna, Italy, Ruepp had been unable to place her work with a publisher, as she recalled to Jörg Isringhaus in the *Remscheider General-*

alanzeiger: "Before that I had nothing but rejections because I also illustrated my own work." Finally an editor at North-South Books recognized the value of her texts and chose Ulrike Heyne to illustrate them. Ruepp's debut novel, *Midnight Rider,* was translated into English and with a press run of 35,000 copies distributed in the United Kingdom, Australia, Tasmania, and the United States.

Although as a child Ruepp enjoyed writing stories, she put that interest aside for many years, until she had children herself. Eventually her sons Kristian and Robin, who inspired her to resume writing, became her first audience. She said to Isringhaus, "I always get to hear quite a bit from my children. They are the best first editors." Her books are early readers, which bridge the gap between picture books and chapter books, and revolve around the activities of children and their horses. The first three books take place on the island of Outhorn in the North Sea and feature a young girl named Charlie. In *Midnight Rider* Charlie, after her own horse dies, secretly visits the neighbors' horse Starbright, sereptitiously taking him on a fateful night-time ride. The book caught reviewers' attention. Writing in the *Bulletin of the Center for Children's Books,* Deborah Stevenson commented on the "poetic pleasure" of Charlie's midnight ride, though the critic thought the narrative somewhat predictable. *Booklist*'s Carolyn Phelan also dubbed this a "good story," one that would appeal to equine enthusiasts. The success of *The Midnight Rider* engendered two sequels. *Horses in the Fog* is about Charlie and her friend Mona, who get lost on horseback in the sea-fog after riding on a sandbar. This work elicited comment from Susan Dove Lempke, who described the girls as "appealingly realistic" and their horses as "alluring" in her *Booklist* review. So too, *The Sea Pony,* about how newcomer Philip and his horse Goblin learn to fit in, garnered praise for its poetic and "unfussy" prose, to quote Irene Babsky of *School Librarian.*

Unlike her earlier works, Ruepp's fourth early reader, *Winter Pony,* takes place in Iceland and revolves around the relationship of Anna and the foal Prince, who must leave the farm to graze in the summer pasture. Although her grandparents reassure Anna that Prince is going to be fine, the foal is challenged by a stallion and falls over a cliff. In the end, Prince proves his mettle and is accepted by the herd. When he returns to the farm, Anna is overjoyed. Several reviewers commented favorably on *Winter Pony,* including *School Library Journal*'s Carol Schene, who dubbed the work "pleasant but slight," and *Booklist*'s Ellen Mandel, who predicted horse lovers would "relish this spare" tale.

While horses are the ostensible topic, the themes of Ruepp's books are more complex. About her works the author told SATA: "Sometimes children can help other children and even the adults to manage problems like prejudice in *Midnight Rider,* anxiety in *Horses in the*

Fog, or homesickness in *The Sea Pony.* Here I show, that a home place can be where you have friends. In my new book *Winter Pony* friendship is growing, although the friends—Anna and Prince—have to go their own ways. Friendship is a feeling, which is always in your heart, and when you meet your friend, after being separated a long time, it is like you have seen him the day before." Ruepp's goal is "to show, that things mostly get better, that some problems, which are growing can be managed with courage, and that it is good to live in nature and with nature," she continued. "The relationship to a horse is a good example of this. But it can be any other animal, or it can be a tree or a flower for which a human being is responsible."

Reflecting on her books, Ruepp told *SATA:* "I want to mediate to children the joy of language and of painting, so that they are willing and able to write stories themselves and to paint. They shall send their works to me and I will send them back the stories and a letter which includes my wishes to encourage them. With my stories I want to show children how to manage problems and that it is better to be courageous than to be frightened. I try to encourage children with my stories and in the letters I write to them."

Biographical and Critical Sources

PERIODICALS

Booklist, December 1, 1995, Carolyn Phelan, review of *Midnight Rider,* pp. 636-637; February 1, 1998, Susan Dove Lempke, review of *Horses in the Fog,* p. 919; January 1, 2003, Ellen Mandel, review of *Winter Pony,* pp. 909-910.

Bulletin of the Center for Children's Books, October, 1995, Deborah Stevenson, review of *Midnight Rider,* p. 67.

Der Inselbot (Amrum and Föhr, Germany), July 22, 2002, "Kleine Wirbelwinde lauschten Geschichten vom 'Horelwinj.'"

Horn Book Guide, spring, 1998, Stephanie Loer, review of *Horses in the Fog,* p. 64; spring, 2002, Anita L. Burkam, review of *The Sea Pony,* p. 77.

Kirkus Reviews, October 1, 2002, review of *Winter Pony* pp. 1479.

Remscheider Generalanzeiger (Remscheid, Germany), August 12, 1995, Jörg Isringhaus, "Reiter in der Nacht," (Rider in the Night).

School Librarian, spring, 1998, Gillian Lathey, review of *Horses in the Fog,* p. 37; spring, 2002, Irene Babsky, review of *The Sea Pony,* p. 35.

School Library Journal, December, 1995, Charlene Strickland, review of *Midnight Rider,* pp. 90-91; December, 2002, Carol Schene, review of *Winter Pony* pp. 107-108.

S-T

ST. JOHN, Nicole
(Elizabeth Bolton, Catherine E. Chambers, Kate Chambers, Pamela Dryden, Lavinia Harris, Norma Johnston, Adrian Robert)

Personal
Born in Ridgewood, NJ; daughter of Charles Eugene Chambers and Marjorie Johnston. *Education:* Montclair University, B.A. (English); studied acting at the American Theatre Wing, New York, NY.

Addresses
Office—Box 299, 103 Godwin Ave., Midland Park, NJ 07432. *E-mail*—johnstonstjohn@keepingdays.com.

Career
Full-time writer, 1972—. Worked in fashion as buyer and display designer for mother's lingerie shop at the age of seventeen; buyer's assistant in Boston, MA, women's wear store; later opened own fashion boutique; designs jewelry and other collectibles. Worked in theater as producer's assistant, costume designer, and actress in summer theater and regional theater; producer in summer theater; co-founder and director of Geneva Players and founder, producer/director of Geneva Players, Inc., both interfaith drama companies. Advisory board member, Stepping Stone Theatre, Wilmington, Delaware. Worked in publishing as editorial assistant at fashion trade publication and book publishing company; freelance editor and ghostwriter for book publishers. Former council chair of Rutgers University Council on Children's Literature and former chair of its "One-on-One" writers conference. Speaker, teacher, and seminar leader.

Member
Authors Guild, Authors League of America, Mystery Writers of America, Sisters in Crime (organizer and former president of Midlantic Chapter).

Nicole St. John

Awards, Honors
New Jersey Institute of Technology award, 1964, for *The Wider Heart,* 1965, for *Ready or Not,* 1967, for *The Bridge Between,* 1983, for *Timewarp Summer,* 1989, for *Return to Morocco,* and 1990, for *The Delphic Choice;* Secondary Outstanding Merit Carter G. Woodson Book Award, National Council on Social Studies, 1995, for *Harriet: The Life and World of Harriet Beecher Stowe; The Wishing Star* was a Junior Literary Guild selection; *Pride of Lions: The Story of the House of Atreus* was a *Horn Book* honor list book; many of St.

John's books have been on the New York Public Library Best Books for the Teen-Age list; St. John's books have also been on many state honor book lists.

Writings

FOR YOUNG ADULTS

(As Norma Johnston) *The Wishing Star,* Funk & Wagnalls (New York, NY), 1963.

(As Norma Johnston) *The Wider Heart,* Funk & Wagnalls (New York, NY), 1964.

(As Norma Johnston) *Ready or Not,* Funk & Wagnalls (New York, NY), 1965.

(As Norma Johnston) *The Bridge Between,* Funk & Wagnalls (New York, NY), 1966.

(As Norma Johnston) *Of Time and of Seasons,* Atheneum (New York, NY), 1975.

(As Norma Johnston) *A Striving After Wind,* Atheneum (New York, NY), 1976.

(As Norma Johnston) *The Swallow's Song,* Atheneum (New York, NY), 1978.

(As Norma Johnston) *If You Love Me, Let Me Go,* Atheneum (New York, NY), 1978.

(As Norma Johnston) *The Crucible Year,* Atheneum (New York, NY), 1979.

(As Norma Johnston) *Timewarp Summer,* Atheneum (New York, NY), 1982.

(As Pamela Dryden) *Mask for My Heart,* New American Library (New York, NY), 1982.

(As Norma Johnston) *The Potter's Wheel,* Morrow (New York, NY), 1988.

(As Norma Johnston) *The Image Game,* BridgeWater Books (Mahwah, NJ), 1994.

(As Norma Johnston) *Feather in the Wind,* Marshall Cavendish (New York, NY), 2000.

MYSTERY AND SUSPENSE; FOR YOUNG ADULTS

(As Lavinia Harris) *Dreams and Memories,* Scholastic (New York, NY), 1982.

(As Norma Johnston) *Gabriel's Girl,* Atheneum (New York, NY), 1983.

(As Norma Johnston) *Watcher in the Mist,* Bantam (New York, NY), 1986.

(As Norma Johnston) *Shadow of a Unicorn,* Bantam (New York, NY), 1987.

(As Norma Johnston) *Whisper of the Cat,* Bantam (New York, NY), 1988.

(As Norma Johnston) *Return to Morocco,* Four Winds (New York, NY), 1988.

(As Norma Johnston) *The Delphic Choice,* Four Winds (New York, NY), 1989.

(As Norma Johnston) *The Time of the Cranes,* Four Winds (New York, NY), 1990.

(As Norma Johnston) *The Dragon's Eye,* Four Winds (New York, NY), 1990.

"THE KEEPING DAYS" SERIES; FOR YOUNG ADULTS AND ADULTS; AS NORMA JOHNSTON

The Keeping Days, Atheneum (New York, NY), 1973.
Glory in the Flower, Atheneum (New York, NY), 1974.
The Sanctuary Tree, Atheneum (New York, NY), 1977.
A Mustard Seed of Magic, Atheneum (New York, NY), 1977.
A Nice Girl like You, Atheneum (New York, NY), 1980.
Myself and I, Atheneum (New York, NY), 1981.

"THE CARLISLE CHRONICLES" SERIES; FOR YOUNG ADULTS; AS NORMA JOHNSTON

Carlisle's Hope, Bantam (New York, NY), 1986.
To Jess, with Love and Memories, Bantam (New York, NY), 1986.
Carlisles All, Bantam (New York, NY), 1986.

"DIANA WINTHROP" DETECTIVE SERIES; FOR YOUNG ADULTS; AS KATE CHAMBERS

The Secret of the Singing Strings, New American Library (New York, NY), 1983.
Danger in the Old Fort, New American Library (New York, NY), 1983.
The Case of the Dog Lover's Legacy, New American Library (New York, NY), 1983.
Secrets on Beacon Hill, New American Library (New York, NY), 1984.
The Legacy of Lucian Van Zandt, New American Library (New York, NY), 1984.
The Threat of the Pirate Ship, New American Library (New York, NY), 1984.

"THE COMPUTER DETECTIVES" SERIES; AS LAVINIA HARRIS

The Great Rip-Off, Scholastic (New York, NY), 1984.
Soaps in the Afternoon, Scholastic (New York, NY), 1985.
A Touch of Madness, Scholastic (New York, NY), 1985.
Cover Up!, Scholastic (New York, NY), 1985.

"PIONEER LIVING" SERIES; FOR MIDDLE-SCHOOL READERS; AS CATHERINE E. CHAMBERS

California Gold Rush: Search for Treasure, illustrated by Allan Eitzen, Troll Associates (Mahwah, NJ), 1984.
Daniel Boone and the Wilderness Road, illustrated by George Guzzi, Troll Associates (Mahwah, NJ), 1984.
Flatboats on the Ohio: Westward Bound, illustrated by John Lawn, Troll Associates (Mahwah, NJ), 1984.
Frontier Dream: Life on the Great Plains, illustrated by Dick Smolinski, Troll Associates (Mahwah, NJ), 1984.
Frontier Farmer: Kansas Adventure, illustrated by Len Epstein, Troll Associates (Mahwah, NJ), 1984.
Frontier Village: A Town Is Born, illustrated by Dick Smolinski, Troll Associates (Mahwah, NJ), 1984.

Indian Days: Life in a Frontier Town, illustrated by John Lawn, Troll Associates (Mahwah, NJ), 1984.

Log-Cabin Home: Pioneers in the Wilderness, illustrated by Allen Eitzen, Troll Associates (Mahwah, NJ), 1984.

Texas Roundup: Life on the Range, illustrated by John Lawn, Troll Associates (Mahwah, NJ), 1984.

Wagons West: Off to Oregon, illustrated by Dick Smolinski, Troll Associates (Mahwah, NJ), 1984.

OTHER MIDDLE-SCHOOL BOOKS

(As Pamela Dryden) *Riding Home,* Bantam (New York, NY), 1988.

(As Norma Johnston) *Lotta's Progress,* Avon (New York, NY), 1997.

(As Norma Johnston) *Over Jordan,* Avon Camelot (New York, NY), 1999.

EASY READER MYSTERIES; AS ELIZABETH BOLTON

Ghost in the House, illustrated by Ray Burns, Troll Associates (Mahwah, NJ), 1985.

The Secret of the Ghost Piano, illustrated by Gioia Fiammenghi, Troll Associates (Mahwah, NJ), 1985.

The Tree House Detective Club, illustrated by S. D. Schindler, Troll Associates (Mahwah, NJ), 1985.

The Case of the Wacky Cat, illustrated by Paul Harvey, Troll Associates (Mahwah, NJ), 1985.

The Secret of the Magic Potion, illustrated by Blanche Sims, Troll Associates (Mahwah, NJ), 1985.

EASY READER MYSTERIES; AS ADRIAN ROBERT

The "Awful Mess" Mystery, illustrated by Paul Harvey, Troll Associates (Mahwah, NJ), 1985.

My Grandma, the Witch, Troll Associates (Mahwah, NJ), 1985.

The Secret of the Old Barn, illustrated by Penny Carter, Troll Associates (Mahwah, NJ), 1985.

Ellen Ross, Private Detective, illustrated by T. R. Garcia, Troll Associates (Mahwah, NJ), 1985.

The Secret of the Haunted Chimney, illustrated by Irene Trivas, Troll Associates (Mahwah, NJ), 1985.

MYTHOLOGY NOVELS; FOR YOUNG ADULTS AND ADULTS; AS NORMA JOHNSTON

Strangers Dark and Gold, Atheneum (New York, NY), 1975.

Pride of Lions: The Story of the House of Atreus, Atheneum (New York, NY), 1979.

The Days of the Dragon's Seed, Atheneum (New York, NY), 1982.

NONFICTION; FOR YOUNG ADULTS AND ADULTS; AS NORMA JOHNSTON

Louisa May: The World and Works of Louisa May Alcott, Four Winds (New York, NY), 1992.

Harriet: The Life and World of Harriet Beecher Stowe, Four Winds (New York, NY), 1994.

Remember the Ladies: The First Women's Rights Convention, Scholastic (New York, NY), 1995.

SUSPENSE NOVELS FOR ADULTS; AS NICOLE ST. JOHN

The Medici Ring, Random House (New York, NY), 1975.

Wychwood, Random House (New York, NY), 1976.

Guinever's Gift, Random House (New York, NY), 1977.

OTHER

Contributor (as Nicole St. John) to nonfiction books for adults, including *Library Education & Leadership: Essays in Honor of Jane Anne Hannigan,* edited by Sheila S. Intner and Kay E. Vandergrift, Scarecrow Press, 1990, and *Cooking with Malice Domestic,* edited by Jean and Ron McMillen, Mystery Bookshop (Bethesda, MD), 1991. Also author of unpublished poems and dramas; author of columns about writing, and cooking and entertaining. Ghostwriter of fiction, mystery, biography, cookbooks, and books on reference, religion, patternmaking, and popular culture.

Work in Progress

Adapting *Guinever's Gift* for an IMAX film; *Touchstone,* the first in a planned series of detective/murder mystery series featuring Maris Crayle, a forensic antiquarian with a Ph.D. in Renaissance studies.

Sidelights

Nicole St. John's life has been packed with memorable times, and her fiction books—many of which are for young adults though she writes for readers ranging from middle-graders to adults—are largely drawn from her own experiences. Best known for her beloved "Keeping Days" series about a family in turn-of-the-century West Farms, New York, St. John has worked in the worlds of publishing, theater, and fashion and has taught art, English, writing, and acting. As with the "Keeping Days" books, many of the author's stories are based upon her family history and take place in historical settings.

Although she was an only child, St. John comes from a large extended family, as the families she writes about tend to be. On her mother's side she is descended from Dutch and English colonists who settled in what are now New York and New Jersey. This branch of the family tree is fictionalized in the "Keeping Days" series, and the English part of her family—Calvinist Separatists who settled in Massachusetts in 1630—later led to St. John's interest in Louisa May Alcott and Harriet Beecher Stowe, about whom she would eventually write biographies. The family in the "Carlisle Chronicles" series is based on her father's side of the family—English and Scottish colonists who settled in the Middle Atlantic region prior to the American Revolution.

St. John's primary role model in writing was Maud Hart Lovelace, with whom she began corresponding while writing the original draft of *The Wishing Star,* and who gave the budding writer a great deal of encouragement. *The Wishing Star* was eventually accepted by Funk & Wagnalls, which agreed to buy it if the author would cut one hundred pages from it. That was a valuable experience, for it forced St. John to reduce *The Wishing Star* to outline form in order to see what was really necessary and what was not. Since then, she has written all of her books from outlines.

Over the next few years St. John continued to publish about one book a year, while also working as assistant to an editor at a religious publishing house and directing the Geneva Players, an interfaith drama company she co-founded with a pastor of her church. The purpose of the dramatic group was to allow young actors to perform in classics and major Broadway plays as a means to helping them speak out on the issues and conflicts in their own lives. The first production put on by the group was Arthur Miller's *The Crucible.* It opened on the night of the assassination of John F. Kennedy. The events surrounding that unforgettable night became the basis of another of St. John's books, *The Crucible Year.* In that book, the protagonist is sixteen-year-old Elizabeth Newcomb, who has recently transferred from a private to a public school. In her new environment, Elizabeth struggles with many problems, new ideas, and new people. All of life seems to be taking unpredictable, disturbing new turns, and the murder of President Kennedy greatly increases Elizabeth's sense of confusion and disillusionment with the world.

Horn Book reviewer Karen M. Kleckner praised the author's probing questions about personal values, religion, prejudice, and stereotypes. Although Kleckner felt the book was written more to "recollect and understand" a troubled time in history than to develop a story, the reviewer noted that St. John has a "fluid style" and that the stage scenes where Elizabeth's personality blends with that of her character are "particularly effective." According to St. John, these excerpts were taken directly from her actual, real-life journal.

Several years after the events related in *The Crucible Year,* the publishing industry underwent a dramatic change: young adult books suddenly became popular, and St. John's life changed as well. The respiratory and arthritis problems that had plagued her since her youth became much worse, limiting her activities just as the demand for her books greatly increased. Her writing increased so much that she began publishing—for adults as well as young adults—under several different names, all taken from ancestors on various branches of the family tree that had inspired her best-loved series, "The Keeping Days." Although serious illness would usually be considered a drawback, St. John found it was in an odd way quite the opposite for her, especially since after "The Keeping Days" she was able to support herself completely from her writing. She wrote philosophically

about her health in *SAAS:* "If I hadn't been out of school so much when I was little, I wouldn't have read so much, I wouldn't have hung around so much with adults and had my horizons widened. I know I wouldn't have had as much empathy for others. Perhaps I wouldn't even have been a writer. . . . So this is something else I want to pass on through my characters—you can't control what life dishes out to you, but you can control how you react to it and what you do with it. You can use your gifts—if not one way, then another."

St. John's strong feeling for family traditions and her positive beliefs are always reflected in her writing. The "Carlisle Chronicles" series, which includes *Carlisle's Hope, To Jess, with Love and Memories,* and *Carlisles All,* revolves around the life of the large and loving Carlisle family. In these books, excitement and uncertainty comes from the father's job in the foreign service, which requires many moves around the world. Jess, the central character, looks for stability by clinging to her family history. In the first book in the series, Jess's security is challenged when she learns that her father was actually adopted—the family she has so revered is not, by blood, really hers to claim after all. By the end of the book, however, Jess has learned that family means more than blood ties.

In *Carlisles All,* which Katharine Bruner in *School Library Journal* called "a smoothly written and swiftly flowing, hold-on-tight tale of adolescent adventure," the Carlisles are enjoying an idyllic Christmas holiday together when their father is sent on an emergency trip to the Middle East. Mrs. Carlisle accompanies him, leaving the children home alone. The young Carlisles are horrified when they see that the embassy where their parents were scheduled to be is the target of a bomb attack. Again, Jess is the anchor of the story. Because her father's mission was a secret one, she must put up a charade for the public, pretending that her family is intact and enjoying the holidays. Meanwhile, she waits tensely to field phone calls from overseas that will reveal if her parents are dead or alive. The young Carlisles handle "everything with remarkable dexterity," while still remaining flawed and human enough "to bond with readers," noted Bruner.

The Middle East again provides the background in the novel *The Delphic Choice.* Like so many of St. John's books, this one carries a message about moral responsibility. A "Delphic choice" is a "choice between public and private duty," explained Linda L. Lowry in the *School Library Journal.* This is exactly what the heroine, seventeen-year-old Meredith Blake, faces in Istanbul, Turkey, where she has been acting as caretaker for her aunt's two children. Her uncle is kidnapped by terrorists, who want Meredith to deliver messages between them and the U.S. government. Cooperating with them might save her uncle, but could endanger many other lives. Lowry complained that some parts of the book become too "didactic," but admitted that St. John has created a strong heroine in Meredith. She also praised the author for weaving an exciting story full of Middle Eastern color: "Teens . . . will be intrigued by the excitement and mystery of the plot."

Return to Morocco combines St. John's taste for stories of espionage and suspense with her deep feeling for family relations. In this story, Tori Clay accompanies her genteel grandmother to the Mediterranean. Once there, Tori discovers that the woman she knows as Nannie was actually Nance O'Neill, former undercover agent for the OSS (forerunner of the CIA) who had worked with the French Resistance during World War II. The corpses, poisonous snakes, and other physical dangers that lie in wait for Tori are nothing compared to her struggle to understand and accept her grandmother's secret past.

Not all of St. John's mysteries are set overseas. *Shadow of a Unicorn* is a mystery, a horse story, and a romance all in one. It takes place in Kentucky bluegrass country, although the house is modeled on the beautiful New Jersey mansion where the author lived as a young girl. In the story, orphaned Sarah goes to live at Unicorn Farm, where thoroughbreds are raised and raced by her cousin Rowena. But the farm has been struck by one disaster after another, including the deaths of Rowena's parents and of several horses. Rumors arise that Unicorn Farm is cursed, but Sarah and Rowena dig deep to find out the truth. A *Publishers Weekly* contributor noted that the story is "lively" and "unfolds slowly and satisfyingly," while calling St. John "deft in evoking the Kentucky landscape."

The Time of the Cranes springs from St. John's involvement with acting, memories of one of her own teachers, and experiences in teaching and counseling teens in the process of directing plays. In the novel, Stacy's drama teacher passes away and names Stacy her sole beneficiary, much to the girl's surprise. In investigating the woman's death, Stacy finds it to be suspicious and eventually realizes that her teacher took an intentional overdose of painkillers. She must struggle to come to terms with this death and with the death of her mother. In doing so, she reaches a breakthrough point in her own acting. Susan F. Marcus, writing in *School Library Journal*, called *The Time of the Cranes* "a satisfying read for fans of fast-moving soap operas, acting enthusiasts, and mature readers who can grapple with the issue of elderly suicide."

Of all the author's writings, "The Keeping Days" series is the favorite both of readers and of St. John herself. It includes *The Keeping Days, Glory in the Flower, The Sanctuary Tree, A Mustard Seed of Magic, A Nice Girl like You,* and *Myself and I.* Tish Sterling is the narrator and central character in the first book, which is set in turn-of-the-century Bronx, New York. She, like her creator, is a precocious writer with a great sense of drama who thinks of herself as "sensitive and misunderstood." *Horn Book* reviewer Mary M. Burns noted the first book's debt to *Little Women* by Louisa May Alcott, but

assured potential readers that St. John's story was "by no means a carbon copy" of Alcott's. She called *The Keeping Days* "nostalgic but not sentimental" and a "fresh, compelling story told with perception and spontaneity" that captures the anxieties of adolescence.

The series continued into a new generation by the time it reached *A Nice Girl Like You,* set in 1917. The title character is Saranne Albright, a "nice girl" who falls in love with the neighborhood's "bad boy," Paul Hodge. Saranne's large and loving family provides her with all the comfort and warmth she could ask for, but her friends scorn her when she becomes involved with Paul. The boy has been unfairly accused of many things, and by the end of the book all have learned an important lesson about making hasty judgments. "The author is a fluent storyteller; the families are as full of vitality as ever, constantly caught up in turmoil or triumph," noted Ethel L. Heins in *Horn Book.* Saranne's romance is complicated and continued in the next book in the series, *Myself and I.*

More recently, St. John has published several nonfiction works for young adults and adults, including two biographies, *Louisa May: The World and Works of Louisa May Alcott* and *Harriet: The Life and World of Harriet Beecher Stowe,* and *Remember the Ladies: The First Women's Rights Convention,* a book that not only discusses the important 1848 convention held in Seneca Falls, New York, but which also helps young readers understand the history of the women's movement and which *Booklist* contributor Carolyn Phelan calls a "good resource for students of women's history." As with her fiction, St. John's desire to write her two well-received biographies stemmed from her interest in her family history, and her portraits of Alcott and Stowe describe not only the lives and backgrounds of these famous authors but also how these affected their written works, just as St. John's have affected hers. As Anne Larsen noted in her *Kirkus Reviews* assessment of *Louisa May,* "by depicting [Alcott's] real life in all its complexity while showing the many links with [her] fiction . . . [St. John] enriches understanding of Alcott's books." In another *Kirkus Reviews* article, Penny Kaganoff similarly remarked of *Harriet:* "[St. John] does a fine job of setting context and of showing how Harriet's Calvinist roots . . . played roles in the development of her ideas and writing."

St. John later returned to the life of Harriet Beecher Stowe as inspiration for a fictional story called *Over Jordan.* The protagonist, fourteen-year-old Roxana, is minding her family's Indiana farm (which, unbeknownst to Roxana, is a stop on the Underground Railroad) while her father is away. When Roxana discovers that her African-American maid, Joss, is actually a cousin and that Joss's fiancé Gideon is an escaped slave who is being tracked by bounty hunters, she decides to undertake a dangerous journey to take Joss and Gideon to relative safety in the house of Roxana's former teacher, Miss Hattie Beecher, in Cincinnati. Along the way, Roxana discovers how prejudiced she has been towards African-Americans. When they arrive at the Beechers' house their visit with that "contentious, brilliant" family conveys "a clear sense of the times, manners, attitudes, and widespread turbulence," John Peters noted in a review for *Booklist.*

Just as the lives of Alcott and Stowe affected their writings, so has St. John's fascination with the past affected hers. And it is the importance of the lives of those who are a part of our history that the author has striven to convey to her readers. As she once told *SATA,* "I write of our own American past because there is an enduring strength and source of nurture in our own taproots that we are very much in danger of forgetting. We have ceased to look on all our forebears as perfect saints, and that is good, but in recognizing their follies, their stupidities, and their downright cruelties, we must not overlook their very real accomplishments and the *American* ethnic strengths, which yet have much to give."

Biographical and Critical Sources

BOOKS

Authors and Artists for Young Adults, Volume 12, Gale (Detroit, MI), 1994.
Children's Literature Review, Volume 46, Gale (Detroit, MI), 1998.
Gallo, Donald R., editor, *Speaking for Ourselves: Autobiographical Sketches by Notable Authors of Books for Young Adults,* National Council of Teachers of Education (Urbana, IL), 1990.
Johnston, Norma, *The Keeping Days,* Atheneum (New York, NY), 1973.
Reginald, Robert, *Science Fiction & Fantasy Literature, 1975-1991,* Gale (Detroit, MI), 1992.
Something about the Author, Volume 89, Gale (Detroit, MI), 1997.
Twentieth Century Romance and Historical Writers, third edition, St. James Press (Detroit, MI), 1994.

PERIODICALS

Booklist, September 1, 1978, p. 39; March 15, 1980, p. 1058; December 15, 1986, p. 641; May 1, 1995, Carolyn Phelan, review of *Remember the Ladies: The First Women's Rights Convention,* p. 1570; December 15, 1999, John Peters, review of *Over Jordan,* p. 778.
Book Report, March-April, 1989, Jim Lauritsen, review of *Return to Morocco,* p. 35; May-June, 1991, Carol A. Burbridge, review of *The Dragon's Eye,* p. 46.
Bulletin of the Center for Children's Books, July, 1974, p. 179; September, 1975, p. 12; September, 1978, p. 11; December, 1978, p. 63; June, 1979, p. 177; July, 1980, p. 215; January, 1992, p. 130; October, 1994, pp. 50-51.
English Journal, November, 1987, Terry C. Ley, review of *Shadow of a Unicorn,* p. 95.

Horn Book, December, 1973, Mary M. Burns, review of *The Keeping Days,* p. 591; April, 1979, Karen M. Kleckner, review of *The Crucible Year,* p. 200; April, 1980, Paul Heins, review of *Pride of Lions,* p. 180; June, 1980, Ethel L. Heins, review of *A Nice Girl Like You,* pp. 306-7; April, 1983, review of *Timewarp Summer,* p. 171; October, 1983, Mary M. Burns, review of *Gabriel's Girl,* pp. 583-584.
Kirkus Reviews, July 15, 1966, p. 696; February 15, 1974, p. 192; September 1, 1976, p. 982; December 1, 1978, p. 1309; April 15, 1979, p. 456; October 15, 1991, Anne Larsen, review of *Louisa May: The World and Works of Louisa May Alcott,* p. 1344; June 15, 1994, Penny Kaganoff, review of *Harriet: The Life and World of Harriet Beecher Stowe,* p. 846.
Library Journal, November 15, 1966, p. 5761; March 15, 1974, p. 902.
New York Times Book Review, May 11, 1975.
Publishers Weekly, June 27, 1986, Diane Roback, review of *Carlisle's Hope,* p. 96; December 26, 1986, Diane Roback, review of *The Watcher in the Mist,* p. 61; p. 61; May 20, 1988, p. 93; May 29, 1987, review of *Shadow of a Unicorn,* p. 80; May 20, 1988, Kimberley Olson Fakih, review of *The Potter's Wheel,* p. 93; April 27, 1990, Diane Roback and Richard Donahue, review of *The Time of the Cranes,* p. 62; December 20, 1999, review of *Over Jordan,* p. 80; March 26, 2001, review of *Feather in the Wind,* p. 94.
School Library Journal, April, 1975, p. 66; November, 1975, p. 91; September, 1976, p. 134; September, 1977, p. 145; October, 1977, p. 124; May, 1978, p. 77; October, 1978, p. 156; March, 1979, p. 148; November, 1979, p. 88; May, 1980, p. 76; November, 1981, p. 106; September, 1983, p. 135; December, 1983, review of *Gabriel's Girl,* p. 85; August, 1986, Joyce Adams Burner, review of *Carlisle's Hope,* p. 101; December, 1986, Candy Bertelson, review of *To Jess, with Love and Memories,* p. 118; May, 1987, Katharine Bruner, review of *Carlisles All,* p. 112; October, 1987, Laura Dixon, review of *Shadow of a Unicorn,* p. 140; March, 1988, Catherine van Sonnenberg, review of *The Potter's Wheel,* p. 214; September, 1988, Merilyn S. Burrington, review of *Return to Morocco,* p. 200; May, 1989, Linda L. Lowry, review of *The Delphic Choice,* p. 126; May, 1990, Susan F. Marcus, review of *Time of the Cranes,* p. 122; February, 1992, Barbara Hutcheson, review of *Louisa May: The World and Works of Louisa May Alcott,* p. 114; October, 1994, Margaret B. Rafferty, review of *Harriet: The Life and World of Harriet Beecher Stowe,* pp. 153-154; September, 1997, Liza Bliss, review of *Lotta's Progress,* p. 218; December, 1999, William McLoughlin, review of *Over Jordan,* pp. 134-135.
Voice of Youth Advocates, December, 1982, p. 33; October, 1983, p. 203; February, 1987, p. 285.

ONLINE

Nicole St. John's Home Page, http://www.chipmunk crossing.com/ (April 2, 2003); and http://www.keeping days.com/.

Autobiography Feature

Nicole St. John

THE KEEPING DAYS OF MY LIFE

Once upon a time there was an insufferable brat. That's how I began my first college writing assignment. "Write me your autobiography," the professor said. "Make it short because none of you insufferable brats have lived long enough to have any experiences worth writing about . . . !" He didn't know me . . .

Who am I? I'm Nicole St. John, and also (in the order in which readers know me best) Norma Johnston, Lavinia Harris, Kate Chambers, Pamela Dryden, Catherine E. Chambers, Elizabeth Bolton, and Adrian Robert. I'm an author, editor, ghostwriter, entrepreneur, actress, director, designer, stylist, retailer, teacher, counselor, and (as some critics have said about me, and I'm proud of it) preacher. Those aren't merely job labels; they're who I am, how I live out the covenant to use the talents I've been given—because that we all *do* have talents of one kind or another, and that we all have a responsibility to use them for the common good, is one of the things in which I most surely believe.

That English professor didn't know any of this, and I didn't want him to. I was almost twice my classmates' age, intimidated by the teacher ("I eat freshmen for breakfast!" he said), and had already published several books—all of which could make me fair game for his celebrated put-downs. So in that writing assignment I hid behind a mask—and ended, as always, in finding that when we put on the mask of a character, we drop our own.

In that autobiography, I included everything *important*—things that had happened to me, and things I'd done; how they'd made me feel, and how they'd made me grow. I *showed* all of what I believed, what I lived for, what made me *me*—without ever *telling* any actual facts. Try it sometime, when you have to write. It's what every good fiction writer does, consciously or not.

I can't write a chronological resume, because my life has not been chronological. Everything overlaps; everything comes round, not full circle, but in spirals. Everything hooks back onto the center, then spins out again.

The circle of rocks on which the house of my life is built are these: my grandmother, and the family heritage I was born into. Books I've read and written; plays I've seen or been in or directed. My faith, and the church I became deeply involved in as a teenager—and

Ridgewood Secretarial School, where the author was born. "The house was also a 'character' in some of my books."

my theatre training, for in a weird and wonderful way these two interpreted and illumined each other and all the rest. My travels. And one other thing—but I'll get to that later.

Have you ever tried memorizing history just as a succession of dates? None of us remembers our life just as a one-after-the-other series of events. What we remember are *moments,* some enormous, some small, in which everything comes together—moments which (in our conscious or unconscious) remain with us forever. Like fleeting images in a music video, or the way sight and sound and taste and touch and smell suddenly stand out sharp and clear, for a brief instant, when we have a high fever, or are very very tired, or spaced out on medications. Those come together, make-a-memory moments are our Keeping Days.

> There are moments when everything's so sharp and bright it almost seems I cannot bear the pain and beauty of the world. But whenever I find myself thinking that way, I cross my fingers quick and take the wish back. Because if I wasn't sensitive, I would never have stumbled onto being a writer . . .

I found the first Keeping Day the summer I was ten. It was an August evening, and the dishes were done, and all the kids were playing Kick the Can in the street. When it started getting dark, we drifted down to Lathams' side lawn, the way everyone did that summer. [Somebody] had found a nest of baby rabbits, and my sister had the rabbits in her lap and was trying to feed them milk from a medicine dropper. When I looked up the sky behind the maple tree was purple. Lights were going on in windows, and from houses all down the street our mothers started calling . . . From far, far down the street came the sound of Mama's bell. All at once I could feel it all inside of me, the purple and silver, the shimmer of fireflies and flowers, the tender look in my sister's eyes, and the familiar silver tinkle of the bell. And I knew I had found a Keeping Day (from Norma Johnston, *The Keeping Days,* Atheneum (New York, NY), 1973).

That's from *The Keeping Days,* the first book in my best-loved series, and (with its sequel, *Glory in the Flower*—they were originally written to be one volume) my own favorite of the books I've written. I didn't have a sister, the girl with the rabbits was someone else. But otherwise the scene came straight out of my own memories, as has the major part of everything I've written.

The family in the "Keeping Days" series is definitely my family—that is, my maternal grandparents' family as I imagine them to have been from the stories my great-uncles told. The roots of my family tree stretch on my mother's side back to colonists from the Netherlands, the Messlers (originally *Metselaer*) and Van Zandts, who settled New Amsterdam in 1632 (and during the next hundred years settled New Jersey, too, making me "Jersey Dutch"), and the Pierces from Dorsetshire, England, who colonized Dorchester, Massachusetts, in 1630. On my father's side (see the "Carlisle Chronicles") I come from English and Scottish families who settled in the Middle Atlantic colonies prior to the American Revolution. All these strong-willed, Calvinist, fiercely independent (my grandmother called it *pigheaded*) men and women have been a major influence on me, and on my writing, through the anecdotes, values, and customs that were passed down from one generation to another.

The earliest Keeping Days that I can remember were when we lived at the school (that's the way I always thought of it) in Ridgewood, New Jersey, where I was born. (Ridgewood in 1920-21, the year my mother and grandparents moved there, is the setting for *If You Love Me, Let Me Go.*) The school was a beautiful Greek Revival mansion built sometime around the Civil War, and many years later I used that house as the mansion in both *Ready or Not* (I "moved" it to the Wyckoff, New Jersey, location where I actually lived while in high school) and *Shadow of a Unicorn:*

Whenever I remembered Unicorn Farm, I remembered sunlight. I could close my eyes and see it all again . . . White-pillared, gracious, with its spreading porches, three stories of tall windows, and a red mansard roof. And white wicker furniture . . . The carved front door, with its leaded glass fanlights and sidelights . . . carved

paneling and old Oriental rugs, the double parlors, the library [that] was an office now. Ledgers were piled on the big double desk . . . (from Norma Johnston, *The Shadow of a Unicorn,* Bantam (New York, NY), 1987).

That's the way I can still see the school. My grandparents' Ridgewood Secretarial School was on the ground floor, their apartment was on the second floor, and my parents' on the third, up under the mansard roof. My main Keeping Days memories from Ridgewood are of my mother teaching me to read and write when I was four (I've never stopped doing either of those things since!) . . . of memorizing "The Night before Christmas" to recite to Aunt Emma and Uncle Elmer on Christmas Day . . . of having the chicken pox while we were staying at a summer hotel in Asbury Park . . . of Fourth of July picnics on the spreading lawns, attended by aunts and uncles from both sides of the family, Pierce and Messler.

My grandmother, Margaret Messler Pierce, was a remarkable woman who was totally liberated because the idea that she wasn't never crossed her mind. In her opinion, if a thing mattered enough, you made it happen, and that was all there was to it. If you had brains and common sense and gumption and health, then you could do it.

"Grandmother Margaret Messler Pierce (Bronwyn in **The Keeping Days)** *in her wedding gown"*

What mattered to Nonnie was family, a high code of ethics, being a good businesswoman, and living well. She found no problems or conflicts in running a house and a business, being a great hostess, and raising a daughter, all at the same time. She was a very feminine woman, sharp as a tack, who believed you catch more flies with honey than with vinegar—but she kept the vinegar handy, just in case! It has always amused me that most people found her not only fascinating but also totally intimidating, which I never did. (My cousin Bolton, who as a career military and foreign-service officer was pretty intimidating himself, told me in a letter written for Nonnie's eightieth birthday, "Margie always scared the hell out of me!")

Nonnie was born in West Farms, Bronx, New York; she had two older brothers and two younger ones; and when she was twenty-one she married a widower thirty years older than she with a teenage son. The house she moved into when she married was her "dream house," one she'd walked past as a girl and longed to live in someday. That was long before she started "walking out" with Harris Pierce (my grandfather)—and *that* came about because her Kings' Daughters group at the Episcopal Church was having a girls-invite-the-gentlemen "basket party" and her girlfriends dared her to invite Harris. (He may have been pushing fifty, but according to photographs he had a dashing mustache and a devilish twinkle in his eye!) Having been brought up with four brothers, Nonnie wouldn't chicken out on a dare—and the rest is history. According to Nonnie, no one in either family (other than Aunt Emma Pierce, who became Aunt Kate in "Keeping Days") had any negative reaction when she and Harris announced they were getting married. I don't believe it.

What I do know is that the family agrees "Margie" was the only family member that *everyone* in both families got along with. (Got along with? They were crazy about her!) My grandparents' romance and marriage became the love story of Bronwyn Sterling and Mr. Albright in the "Keeping Days" books. But I gave my grandparents' secretarial school, and how and why it was founded, to Ma and Pa Sterling. The rest of Pa and Ma is the way I imagine them to have been from family stories. And Bronwyn (and Tish) lived in Nonnie's dream house before, not after, the marriage.

Having been born into a large and close-knit extended family, I was frequently dragged to family reunions. Fourth of July picnics were fun, but long car trips to visit Uncle Joe in Basking Ridge, New Jersey, and Uncle John in Katonah, New York, were *boring*. I liked my aunts and uncles, but there was nobody else in my particular age bracket, so from my perspective things got pretty dull. They livened up considerably after I discovered I could get my great-uncles to tell tales about each other; Uncle Elmer (Ben in "Keeping Days") and Uncle Joe were both newspapermen, and they and Uncle John knew how to tell good stories. My school compositions livened up after that, too. My grandmother had ten fits when I wrote about how John and Elmer

"My paternal grandmother, Catherine Dryden Chambers Johnston, with my father, Charles Eugene Chambers Johnston"

once got their father drunk on year-old cider as a sort of scientific experiment, but my eighth-grade classmates liked it fine. That story got recycled, of course, in "Keeping Days," and then my mother had the ten fits.

By the time I was collecting family skeletons, my grandmother had sold the school, which she'd run during Harris's old age and then her widowhood, and we'd moved (when I was a seven-year-old fourth grader) to a split-level three-generation house in the Ramsey Country Club Estates. *That* house became the home of Sidney Scott Webster in the "Computer Detectives" series, except that the "apartment" Sidney's lucky enough to have to herself in it was my grandmother's apartment. And "the club," transformed into a condominium community, is the setting—clubhouse, swamp, swans, and all—for *Dreams and Memories:*

A stone mansion stood upon rolling emerald lawns. The stones were those of the New Jersey fields, but the shape of the mansion was the style of Old England. A tower rose against the darkling sky . . . Angled steps led to verandas framed with arches. And on the lawns . . . My throat constricted and I could scarcely breathe. The white forms were so relaxed, so still, the swans' heads tucked beneath their wings. Why did I feel, so surely, that they were watching us?

The clubhouse steps led to a carved oak door that opened onto a great hall, L-shaped, covered with linen-fold paneling that looked hand-carved. You could roast a whole steer in the fireplace. Above its copper hood hung round bronze plaques—bas-relief portraits of a king and queen . . . I was dazzled by the building . . . the sunken dining room with its hand-painted mural of an English garden on the walls; the rose garden beyond it, framed by arbors . . . the scent of climbing roses was everywhere.

We walked across the road and down twin flights of steps into a sunken garden. *There* were the roses, and a pair of fountains, and matching peeled-wood gazebos at each end. Beyond a stone ledge the landscape dropped again to a maze, the golf course, and a large lake where swans were sailing. They [had] a nest at the far end . . . We saw tennis courts, the golf shop, the small low building that housed the bowling alley . . . (from Lavinia Harris, *Dreams and Memories,* Scholastic (New York, NY), 1982).

"The club" was a wonderful place for children and dogs to grow up in (both could wander at will, singly or in groups, all over the place, to everybody's houses, because all the families who lived there were friends). My elementary-school boyfriend, who used to love to go to Saturday-afternoon horror movies and then scare me to death telling me the stories as gospel truth, was the one who originally paralyzed me into horrified belief that there was a body hidden somewhere beneath the falls!

Elementary school was a mixed blessing. I was two years younger than everyone else in class; I was the littlest (obviously); I think they thought of me as a cross between a pet and a pest; *I* thought of myself as an adult, because I was used to hanging around with adults. As a result I showed off a lot (hiding behind the mask of the character I wished I were) and spent a lot of time indulging myself in feeling Misunderstood (with a capital M), just like Tish Sterling. Except that as the only child of an almost-only child (Mother's adored half-brother, my Uncle Bolton, was a teenager when she was born and so seemed like part of a different generation), I didn't have as good a sense of humor as Tish with her six brothers and sisters!

I've been told by people who know me well that it's because I was an only child that I've been writing ever since about the big family I never had. I do know my definition of "family" (ideal version) came from *Little Women* and Nonnie's stories (everything was *always* sweetness and light in them!); my experience of "family" (reality version) came from my uncles' unexpurgated versions of the stories (see "Keeping Days," except that Grandma and Grandpa Messier, Nonnie's

parents, never to my knowledge had the marital problems Ma and Pa Sterling had), and from my "kin of the spirit" families of church and theatre.

My main Keeping Days memories from Ramsey are the ones quoted earlier about the baby rabbits . . . holidays . . . going to movies and the theatre with my grandmother and her best friend (and my "other mother"), Gus (Augusta) Lamm . . . rainy afternoons when my mother made tea or hot chocolate and the neighborhood kids and/or she and I put puzzles together in our living room . . . nights when the same kids would start card games on our dining-room table, and eventually parents would come in search of them and stay to join the game . . . all the times Billy would scare the wits out of me with his horror stories and then gleefully pedal away, leaving me to walk home (in the twilight, past the swamp with its supposed slimy monsters) *alone.* And dance recitals. Those were the highlights of the year.

I "took ballet" from the time I was three, and my mother could make the most gorgeous costumes (so gorgeous that neighborhood kids would con her into making their costumes when we put on plays). I got to wear *rouge and lipstick.* The aunts and uncles came to stay all night, watch the performance, and *applaud.* I'd get *flowers,* handed up across the footlights—baskets of flowers from the aunts and uncles and my grandmother; an old-fashioned bouquet in a paper-lace collar from my father. Heaven on earth to an introverted, younger-than-the-others loner!

All through elementary school I wrote poetry, having started (according to my mother) when I was four. I was tone-deaf, and not allowed to sing in music class, so the music teacher took pity on me and let me read my poems aloud to the class (I danced in school assemblies, too, considerably more dramatically than my dancing teacher had intended). And the winter I was eleven, in eighth grade, I wrote my first book.

The whole of my eighth-grade year was a kind of extended Keeping Day, in the sense of how it was to affect my life. It was definitely a turning point, and most of my books revolve around turning points in the heroines' lives.

That eighth-grade winter I was sick, really sick, for a whole marking period. I'd always had coughs and colds and "sinus trouble" from the time I was very small; Mother always said the reason I missed most childhood diseases was because I was always home from school when they went through the classroom. I'd had to be carted down to the Jersey shore in the winter to "breathe the salt air." I was "allergic to everything" (I'll admit sometimes it made a great excuse). But all during eighth grade I kept coming down with cold/coughs/fever; I'd get better enough to go back to school, but in another week I'd be worse and home in bed again. Finally the doctor told my parents to keep me home the whole January/February marking period, in the hope I could lick whatever ailed me once and for all. My teachers gave me my tests over the phone; Billy used to bring my books and assignments over. And when I could breathe, when I wasn't coughing too hard, I read. And wrote.

That was the winter I read *Gone with the Wind* in one sitting, all eight-hundred-plus pages of it, finishing by flashlight under the covers during the night and ending up with the worst headache of my life. *My* book, a full-length book, was about an Abolitionist girl in the 1850s, living on a Maryland plantation that was a station on the Underground Railroad, who fell in love with a gorgeous young man who turned out to be the son of a slave-catcher!

I never showed the book to anyone, unless maybe Mrs. Cadman, my English teacher, but I still have it. I may do something with it yet someday. Eventually, I went back to school, but the cough still lingered, and after that I started getting pains in my chest.

At the end of my first year of high school my grandmother, my parents, and I moved to a big old brown-shingled house in Wyckoff, built in 1923 and perfect for

The author at age three months, held by her mother, Marjorie

parties. After that life was like the young-adult novels I'd been reading, my favorite of which was Maud Hart Lovelace's "Betsy-Tacy" series.

The first thing that changed was that (like Betsy) I started going to a different church and joined its Youth Fellowship. The Messlers had been Dutch Reformed back to the seventeenth century, except that Wyant Van Zandt turned Episcopal, the "English religion," and is buried in Trinity churchyard in New York (see *The Legacy of Lucian Van Zandt*). When my grandmother was a girl her family started "going Episcopal" in West Farms, and that's how I'd been raised. My mother was married, and I was baptized, in Christ Church, Ridgewood, New Jersey, the church the heroine goes to in *If You Love Me, Let Me Go*. By the time I was twelve I was very rational and skeptical and didn't believe in God. (See Ben Sterling, in *The Keeping Days,* for my thoughts on the subject then and what changed my mind.) In Wyckoff, *everybody* went to the Reformed Church. The really great kids in school went to the Youth Fellowship on Sunday nights (it was a direct model for the fellowship, and The Crowd, in *The Wishing Star).* So, of course, I went too, once I'd gotten somebody to "drag me there against my will"! And that made everything change.

What the minister at the Wyckoff Reformed Church said made sense to me. The church wasn't dark like churches I was used to; it was full of light. When a young seminarian came to be youth minister, membership in Fellowship shot up to more than fifty. Pretty soon our big house was the only house large enough to hold the meetings. Being an only child, with no cousins near my age and most of the aunts and uncles a good deal older, I'd never experienced "family" as my mother and grandmother knew it; now that youth group became my extended family. All this later went into my first book, *The Wishing Star.*

I had another crowd, too, the "art-class crowd." My graduating class at Ramsey High School (where Wyckoff sent its students in those days) was unique; we had a lot of highly creative students, and regardless of whether our field of creativity was art, we hung out in the art room. The art teacher was young, and had been second-grade teacher and Presbyterian Sunday-school teacher to most of the Ramsey kids, so they regarded her as more friend than teacher, an attitude the rest of us picked up on. We spent study-hall time in the art room, we spent lunchtime (when we could get away with it) in the art room, we did other homework, and daydreamed, and worked on *The Ram* (the school newspaper) in the art room. We were one of those rare classes in which the "creative crowd" was as respected as the "jocks."

A lot of that class have gone on to success in creative fields, though I'd like to bet that most of them, like me, were told it couldn't be done. But here we are today, living, breathing proof that, just as my grandmother told us, *yes, it can!* That's one of the major things I want to pass on through my books: It *is* possible to make things happen. It *is* possible to make it. Especially with the encouragement and faith of friends and family, of blood or of spirit.

I'm an author. I think one of my classmates is a newspaper writer somewhere. One's a packaging designer and corporate executive. Another, Stephen Bruce, is a nationally known restaurateur/entrepreneur who when he was twenty-one founded (with two friends) the "restaurant and general store" Serendipity III in New York City. It now has branches in other major cities, and many famous people go there. Connie Bond Ftera used to doodle horses in class; now she's a graphics artist who designed my Macmillan "international intrigue" book, *Return to Morocco*. Barbara Stegen Shear is an artist and designer. Her husband, David Shear, was the iconoclast of our class, clear back to elementary school; he has specialized in Third World development, working for the U.S. government and later for nongovernmental agencies, in both Africa and Washington, D.C. David's work in famine prevention won him a Rockefeller Foundation award.

I lost track of Barbara and Dave for several years, but one day after my first four books had been published she telephoned; the Shears were home from Africa on stateside leave, and she wanted to tell me that her daughters Liz and Jessica had brought my books home from their English-language school *in Africa*. "My stock went up considerably when they found out *I knew Norma Johnston!!!*" she told me, laughing. Which tickled me, because in elementary school Barbara had been one of the "in kids" I'd have given my eyeteeth to have hung around with!

The major Keeping Day of my junior year was when I was costumes chairman for our class play, *Our Hearts Were Young and Gay*. It was set in 1923, and Mother (who was and is a pack rat) had lots of beautiful Twenties clothes and accessories (many of which she'd made) in which I'd been dressing up for years. Practically everyone on stage was wearing things that belonged to her (not all of them borrowed with her permission) and what I hadn't been able to beg, borrow, or filch, I made. The cast party was held at my house afterwards. Everybody loved to come there for parties because (1) we had a huge sun porch where they could dance, play shuffleboard and games (cutthroat Chinese checkers was the rage one year); (2) my father would put red light bulbs in the ceiling fixture to make the sun porch look like a real ballroom (meaning dark; meaning kids could make out in relative privacy); (3) my mother always made her famous "party sandwiches" (girls could usually find the most desirable boys sitting in a circle around the kitchen table, eating the sandwich crusts as fast as Mother trimmed them off) and Nonnie made her famous Pierce family punch; (4) Mother felt a party that ended before 1:00 a.m. was some kind of failure, and a party that lasted till 3:00 (many of ours did) was even better. Parents liked having the kids hang out at our house, because they knew where to find them, and knew they were chaperoned.

The author as a baby, with her father, Gene

It was with that junior play, and then through my senior year in high school, when I was fifteen, that I began to believe I finally belonged. I was an officer in Fellowship and several other clubs, and Feature Editor of *The Ram*. I had a Canadian boyfriend who used to go with his family to the same summer hotel in Ocean Grove that Nonnie and I always went to (see *The Swallow's Song*). His mother was everything I wanted to be someday—except that she made a career of being a "company wife" and hostess in Montreal, and I knew by then I wanted to be a famous dress designer and author!

His mother and *my* grandmother took the two of us on a cruise to Bermuda as graduation presents (me from high school, he from university). That fall his mother "presented" me at the St. Mary's Hospital debutante ball in Montreal. (She didn't have a daughter, so I was her "honorary niece.") It was my first taste of being a celebrity, and I felt as if I'd stepped into the pages of one of my favorite books.

I'd never wanted to go to college, I wanted to study design at art school, but my parents felt sixteen was too young to commute to New York City. So I was staying home for a year—I made and sold hand-painted writing paper and other art items, as I'd been doing since I was twelve; I read a lot and went to lots of movies and plays; I did a lot of community service work through Fellowship and other organizations. I was invited to join the Village Players, the area's adult Little Theatre group. I made my debut. And I began writing my first "real" book. It was patterned on the format of Maud Hart Lovelace's "Betsy" books, and drew on a lot of things that had happened in my Crowd.

In late winter, most of us were in a charity revue that a local young man staged annually for the Lions Club. I threw a party after the last performance of that, too. And early the next morning we left for a trip to see the azalea gardens in Charleston, South Carolina—my parents, my grandmother, Stephen Bruce, and I.

And on the third morning, in Fayetteville, North Carolina, my father died.

We were sitting in a hotel coffee shop having breakfast, and laughing at my father taking his first taste of hominy grits, and he just fell over out of his chair onto the floor. He'd never had any heart trouble that anybody knew of, but he had a heart attack, and he died. If you want to know more details, hunt up a copy of *The Wider Heart,* because the death of the heroine's father in it is my father's death.

After that, the plan for me to go to art school was never mentioned again—to my relief, because I'd already decided I didn't want that anymore. I wanted to be a writer.

Everybody told me there was no future in it, but I wrote anyway. I finished my book, and entered it in a contest, and it came back. I gave it to one of my best friends to read, and she returned it (liking it but guessing wrong about which character was based on her!) while the Crowd was in our favorite hangout after Fellowship. The boys got ahold of the manuscript, and laughed themselves silly reading choice bits of a love scene out loud!

When I reread my journal for those first two years out of school, it seems I was always either sick, or writing, or working on plays, or all of those together. The chest pains and leg pains and cough and breathing problems were getting much, much worse. I taught art at the local Y's summer day camp, and then opened a Saturday School of Arts and Crafts on the sun porch during the school year. My mother opened a lingerie shop, and I did buying and displays and advertising for her. I went to the summer writers' conference at the University of Connecticut, and got really valuable advice, and rewrote my book. It was again rejected. Ann Freeman, the mother of one of my Saturday School students, was instrumental in my being hired to run the whole art program at her town's summer recreation program. Being me, I managed to write, produce, direct, and do most of the costumes for a historical pageant there as well. The following winter, through too much enthusiasm coupled with too little practical experience, I tried to teach drama and produce *A Christmas Carol* with the same junior highers. It was a disaster.

That experience taught me a lot. My grandmother always said if you want a job doing something, go out and *create* the job; start your own business. Now I knew (what she'd also told me but I hadn't heard) that first you had to know *how* to do what you wanted to do. You had to pay your dues. I started paying mine.

If I wanted to sell what I wrote so people other than just my friends could read it, I had to learn how to write professionally. If I wanted to do theatre, I had to learn how to act and direct professionally. I was accepted as a member of Tufts University Theatre summer theatre company, and signed up for a writing course at Tufts as well.

That was another disaster. The professor was an educator, not a writer, and the class's goals were not my goals. I wanted to write for and about young people, and work with them through drama, to help them understand themselves, just as I'd learned through identifying with the characters in good books and plays. I wanted to write the kind of books Mrs. Lovelace wrote. I'd been corresponding with Mrs. Lovelace for a year or so, and she'd encouraged me, insisting I should always write about what I really knew. The opening night of the first play, I was told by the professor that I'd *never* be a writer. After the performance I sat up the rest of the night writing to Mrs. Lovelace, asking her advice.

Her publisher forwarded the letter to Mankato, Minnesota (Deep Valley in her books), where she was guest of honor at a townwide celebration. She wrote back by return mail, for which I'll be forever grateful; she said I should *quit the class!!!* pleading bad health or something (which was no lie); never take lessons or advice from anyone who isn't a professional in the same field or isn't on the same wavelength with me; start another book right away! I've been passing that good advice on to others ever since.

My grandmother was my role model as a businesswoman, Maud Hart Lovelace was my mentor as a writer. Ann Freeman, who has a special gift for nurturing, was my mentor in learning how to use sensitivity constructively (as a bridge to understanding and helping others) and my role model of a woman with real soul. In the summer theatre company, I tried to do as she did: hold the circle together; help people defuse and believe in themselves again. At the end of summer, I was told I was wonderful at nurturing but would *never* be an actress or director.

In spite of that, I'd become so involved in theatre and with people that I moved back to Boston that fall. Because of my retailing experience, I was hired as a buyer's assistant in a Boston specialty store. I lived in a one-room apartment on Marlborough Street, and worked days at the store and nights and weekends at the theatre. It was rotten for my health but wonderful otherwise. I was so poor that the soles of my shoes had holes in them, and I went barelegged in snow-storms when I had no money to buy stockings, but I wouldn't give up.

I was very lucky in discovering the real theatre of toil and tears and sweat and glory which lies beneath the surface glamour. Every day I walked to work past a house with lavender windowpanes that later became the setting for my first gothic novel, *The Medici Ring.*

When I did move back to New Jersey, I was asked to become "book" director (and eventually costume designer) for fund-raising charity musicals. I wasn't getting much further with my writing (I was too afraid of rejection slips to send things out) but I had plenty of opportunities with regional theatre, and I knew enough now to know I needed to learn much more. So I auditioned and was accepted into the American Theatre Wing's Professional Training Program in New York.

I was lucky enough to have teachers who'd trained with each of the major acting "schools": Actors' Studio, Berghof Studio, Group Theatre, Moscow Art Theatre. *That* was how I really learned to write—when first Ellen Andrews and then Mme. Barbara Bulgakov taught us step by step how to break down scripts, find the main "spine" of the plot and of the character, understand (and *show,* not *tell*) the character's background and motives and objectives. How to include everything that was necessary, and nothing that was not. How to "hold something back," so that what the audience saw was only the tip of an iceberg, with the other eight-ninths merely sensed. How to make the audience "walk in the character's moccasins" and experience empathy. Above all, in Tennessee Williams's words from *The Glass Menagerie,* how to "give truth in the pleasant disguise of illusion."

All this was a revelation, because I could see instantly how the same method could be applied to writing books, and also how it linked with everything I had been taught in church and Fellowship about "not judging one's brother until one has walked for a moon in his moccasins" and about how doing so could help us gain a better understanding of ourselves, of others, and of the love of God.

That's something else I try to do in my writing— give readers the chance to walk in the footsteps of characters like and unlike themselves, and have the same kind of suddenly-seeing-in-a-mirror experience I've always had from books and theatre.

While I was at the Theatre Wing, I moved to New York, first to a walk-up studio apartment in a Murray Hill brownstone (that was haunted), and then to an apartment in Gramercy Park. Both of these settings, and other New York experiences as well, I used in my "Diana Winthrop" detective series. In addition to studying acting full-time at night, I also worked full-time days as an editorial assistant on a fashion trade publication put out by the legendary "Miss Tobe," who had literally created the occupation of fashion consultant. Miss Tobe and Mme. Bulgakov were two more inspiring role models for me.

"I started being theatrical very young!"

During the first summer at Theatre Wing I was producer's assistant, costumes and props person, and sometimes actress at a summer theatre in Pennsylvania operated by the man who'd produced those high-school-years reviews and the charity musicals. That was probably the most significant summer of my life. Everything I'd learned everywhere came together; I was no longer hiding behind masks or trying to be what others wanted me to be, or protecting myself from feeling or from being hurt. I was deeply emotionally involved with someone, and feeling responsibility for a few others, too, and those experiences are hidden between the lines in *The Crucible Year* and *Myself and I,* and in many other books as well.

The turning point of that crucible summer came (as it often does in any creative project) about two-thirds of the way through. I was doing too many jobs for which I had too little time and experience (we did a different play every week) and like everyone was having very little sleep. I was being a mother hen, crying towel, and advisor, often at the expense of my job responsibilities, and was trying to protect cast from crew and crew from cast, person from person, *everyone* from the director (he, too, ate novices for breakfast), and the company and producer from one another. With the best intentions in the world, I was building walls that separated people, instead of bridges that could have led to understanding.

Everything came to a head the day I had to drive into an Allentown torn up with road repairs, in the stage manager's old stick-shift car (I didn't know how to drive anything not automatic), to look for props instead of being at rehearsal. I was exhausted, in over my head, worried sick about the very lives of two people I cared for deeply but couldn't seem to help, and in a lot of pain, physically, emotionally, and spiritually. Suddenly I longed to be back home, on Ann's screened porch being comforted with tea and sympathy, or in the security of my Fellowship circle. But I wasn't a schoolgirl anymore. I couldn't run backwards in time, and I wouldn't have even if I could. I had taken on responsibilities; I cared about people and projects and my work; if I backed out I'd let people down, but nothing about how I felt would change.

I could not go home. I wasn't even sure where "home" was anymore. I felt like Tom Wingfield in *The*

Glass Menagerie, a wanderer, and like Laura Wingfield too. What I did do was go into a church and sit in a pew in the empty silence, just as I used to go sit in St. Patrick's when I got too swamped with psychic overload at Theatre Wing.

I kept a journal, as recommended by both Mrs. Lovelace and my acting teachers, almost constantly all that summer. But, astonishingly, I never wrote an account of that afternoon. It was too intense; it was too personal; I think I was afraid someone might see it and, what would be even more awful, laugh. What I do remember was how still everything was, and how peaceful, and how the place was filled with pale gray light. I remember starting to cry, and starting to shake, because I was so tired and so worried. And so angry, because nothing I tried to do seemed to be getting anywhere, not really. My book still wasn't selling. People I cared about were still hurting. *I* was hurting. I remember screaming to God inside my head: *Okay! I know everything's supposed to have a reason! I know our gifts and talents come from You! But what's the use of having them if they're not doing anybody one darn bit of good? What's the use of being one of the creative ones . . . having our nerves on the outside of our skins . . . if it's never going to accomplish anything?!?* Something like that.

I remembered how late one night another cast member had stormed that being sensitive was supposed to be an advantage in our art, but that really it was like being born with two heads; "One's fine, but who needs two!!!" I'd been so shocked when she'd said she almost hated being "creative," and I'd tried passionately to convince her there was some good reason for it. Now I found myself crying out silently, *God, if You want me to be like this, sensitive, feeling things so deeply, torn up with talents, tell me why! If there's a use for me going through all this, USE it. Otherwise take it away! If there is a purpose for it, I promise I'll always write, and do theatre, as a means of communication and of "passing on" the gifts and truths that I've been given—no matter how much it hurts. If there isn't, I promise I'll give up writing and theatre, and accept being one of the contented cows! Just tell me which I should do, go on or quit!*

I wasn't shaking anymore. I just felt drained. I got up and went back to the theatre. I didn't tell anybody. I didn't "get told" anything. But I think I did get shown. For one thing, I wasn't so torn up anymore—on the outside, yes, but not inside. For another, there's a long entry in my journal, written what I think was a few nights later, halfway through the run of *I Am a Camera,* the play on which the musical *Cabaret* is based. I was cast as Mrs. Watson-Courtneidge, the heroine's mother, and I was awful.

It was the strangest thing. I was sitting in the dressing room last night about halfway through the performance, when suddenly I closed my eyes and SAW her—Mrs. Watson-Courtneidge—there in front of me . . . I saw her sitting on the train

coming to Berlin, with her hands on her purse and her umbrella and valise beside her. And then I saw her earlier, in England, with her husband; in their country home outside of London. It was a very still quiet afternoon, about four o'clock. They were in a very airy high-ceilinged room with parquet floors and Georgian furniture, standing beside a high bowed window with small rectangular panes and crimson satin drapes looped back with dull gold knobs. The window ran from floor to ceiling sending a shaft of light into the quiet dimness and making golden patterns on the parquet floor. And outside the window there was a formal border that curved to follow the contours of the house—there were rhododendron bushes with very pale pink flowers, very neat outside the window, and beyond that rolling English lawn of pale green grass as far as eye could see; only low box hedges and tall thin poplars between it and a very bright blue sky that was strung with wispy clouds.

There was a sense of stillness and serenity, and of peace, that hung over it like a veil—that feeling that comes from a family's having known for centuries its place in life. . . . an island lost in time . . .

I saw the Watson-Courtneidges standing in the window talking and I could even hear what they were saying. She was wearing a blue crepe dress that matched her eyes, and pearls, and her hands were clasped and her little heels planted firmly on the floor, and she was saying, "Now you know very well that I can handle it. I shall be kind, but firm. You know perfectly well that if you should go you would doubtless do something quite violent." And I heard him sputtering, "Now, Cecily . . ." and somehow knew that was her name. And then I saw her pack her bag—including her hot water bottle, for she never goes anywhere without her hot water bottle. And I saw her crossing the Channel, and arriving in Berlin, and going into Fraulein Schneider's house. I even know what she was thinking as she went upstairs, and what the landing looked like, and where the plaster was cracked along the wall—

And then I opened my eyes and she was still with me—I looked in the mirror and it was not my face but Cecily's—I looked at my hands and knew how she would fold them, and knew how she would sit which was different from the way I sat—I went to hook my arm around the back of the chair the way I do, and could not, because Cecily could not—I looked around the room and saw everyone the way Cecily would see them: the tear in Schneider's dress, the cobwebs, the dust—suddenly I was reacting to it the way Cecily would . . .

I went onstage and saw the set not as it was but as it ought to be, and when I picked up Sally's red slip, which I always knew I had been doing wrong, I picked it up and dropped it without even thinking and suddenly knew that it was right. . . .

After the show everyone was laughing and talking and somehow I could not, somehow it was wrong because I was still Cecily. I wanted to be alone . . .

This was my first experience of what's called "the artist's duality"; of being in what scientists call "alpha state," in which the creative unconscious takes over, and yet at the same time having our conscious mind fully aware and "standing off observing." It's rather like an out-of-the-body experience. That's also the state in which I do most of my writing; certainly my best writing—the book I'm working on never comes alive until I "psyche in." (If you want to read the best definition of the creative process—and of the creative person's responsibility—I've ever seen, read the last page of choreographer Agnes de Mille's first autobiography, *Dance to the Piper.*)

That, for me, was the proof that "to everything there is a season" (which was the theme of *Of Time and of Seasons*), or perhaps more accurately, "to everything there is a reason." The "season" for being full-time professional author and theatre person didn't come till later. But I knew that I'd made a covenant about my gifts and talents. What other people knew was that something in me had changed and that now the magic started happening when I was onstage. And when I wrote. As an ex-GI classmate demanded bluntly when I got back to Theatre Wing, "What the —— happened to you this summer? You aren't the same person."

That fall I began to really understand Stanislavski Method acting, and how the actor's emotions (and everything of self and study the actor brings to a character) are not an end in themselves (any more than happiness, or being loved, etc., etc., can be achievable objectives, as many of my book heroines ultimately learn) but are means of making the audience (or the readers) "walk in the moccasins" of the character and wind up with a "wider heart." (The title of *The Wider Heart* comes from an Edna St. Vincent Millay poem.)

That winter at Theatre Wing, all the pieces began falling into place. The next summer, I couldn't bear to not do summer theatre, but neither I nor many of the others could afford to give up our jobs. Being the granddaughter of an entrepreneur I started my own summer theatre. I rented a red barn in Wyckoff that was used the rest of the year as a dance studio, and my mother made a sign saying *Bandbox Theatre.* I persuaded our speech teacher, Raymond Edward Johnson (who'd created the role of Thomas Jefferson in *The Patriots* on Broadway, and was famous for many years on radio), to take the job of director. Most of the cast members were Theatre Wing classmates, and a recent local high-school graduate phoned to ask if she could apprentice as stage manager; she is now an internationally known producer.

We rehearsed in apartments all over New York during the week, and performed in Wyckoff on the weekends. The cast, crew, and director lived at our house those weekends; the sun porch became the men's dorm and was wall-to-wall mattresses on the floor. My mother, while running a store six-plus days a week, rounded up props, delivered publicity to newspapers, and paid the grocery bills; my grandmother, who was in her late seventies, cooked the meals and ran the box office. We must have all been crazy! Because I was known locally from school days, and I was afraid I wouldn't be taken seriously, I produced under the name of my father's grandmother, Pamela Dryden.

After I completed studies at the Theatre Wing, I opened a dress shop in an old Victorian house in Wyckoff, and my mother moved her store into half the space. I had three months between when I resigned from Miss Tobe's and when the store would open, and during that time, in addition to vacationing at Rockport, Massachusetts, which much later became the setting for *Watcher in the Mist,* I reread and rewrote the book I'd written when I was sixteen. Only now the theme changed from "be like everybody else and you'll be liked" to "be true to yourself, your best self, even if it's hard and lonely." The title of the book was *The Wishing Star.*

I was so busy once my dress shop opened that I didn't finish rewriting the manuscript, particularly since I was staging a lot of fashion shows and directing a few plays locally. Once I did finish the rewrite, I wasn't sure what to do next. I knew the manuscript was too long. I knew I should "send it out" to publishers. But it's much easier to believe you'll be a successful author when you aren't risking receiving rejection slips!

Ever since sophomore year in high school, Lois Gaeta (my first friend in Wyckoff) and I had been critiquing each other's writing. I gave her the manuscript and asked her what to cut. She read it, said, "It's too long, but I don't know what you should take out. Send it out!" I protested. She said, "Get an agent!" I pointed out that was easier said than done. She said, "I know of an agency who handles stuff for somebody I know. [Lois was in advertising then; she's now an executive, writing and coproducing TV programs for continuing medical education.] Call them!" I said I couldn't. "*I* can," Lois said firmly, and marched into a phone booth in Rockefeller Center, with me protesting frantically that it wasn't protocol!

The agent sent *The Wishing Star* to Funk and Wagnalls, where the editor said she'd publish it if I cut a hundred pages. I had to reduce the book to an outline before I saw where to cut; since that experience I *always* work from outlines. I wrote *The Wider Heart* (based on an incident in our stores) and *Ready or Not* for Funk and Wagnalls, and consulted with Phyllis Whitney at a Syracuse University writers' conference, between when *The Wishing Star* was bought and when it came out. *The Wishing Star* was chosen as a Junior Literary Guild book club selection, and I closed my shop and sailed on my first of many trips to Europe.

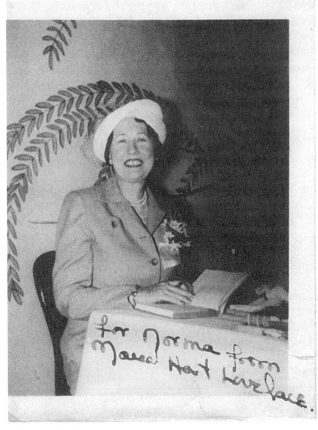

The author's mentor, Maud Hart Lovelace

Now all the different spirals of my different careers began to come together. Because of my school-newspaper and art-class training, I'd gotten the jobs I'd had already and working in my mother's store had also helped with the Tobe job. Now, because of those, plus my own published books, I became assistant to an editor in a religious publishing house. Because of *all* my various experiences I was asked to be a youth counselor at church, and one of the ministers and I founded Geneva Players, producing major Broadway plays and classics (like *The Miracle Worker, The Diary of Anne Frank, Romeo and Juliet*) as a platform on which teens could speak out (through the characters they played) on the issues and conflicts of contemporary life. Our aims were to comfort the troubled and trouble the comforted, and to get people to "walk in other people's moccasins" and broaden and deepen their angles of vision—not bad objectives for a writer, either.

The first Geneva Players production was Arthur Miller's *Crucible*, and it opened on the night of President John F. Kennedy's assassination.

For the rest of my life, I thought, I'll remember sitting here *[in the auditorium]* this afternoon, alone yet not alone, sewing on Danforth's cloak. I looked at the clock at that moment; I did not know why. The hands stood at exactly twenty to three. And all at once I realized that I was no more alone.

Gramps had come in . . . an odd cracked look on his old face . . .

"I just heard it on the car radio, driving over. The President's been shot."

At twenty to three, on the afternoon John Fitzgerald Kennedy died, I sat in the auditorium, sewing a costume for *The Crucible*, and the red fabric, fallen from my lap, lay on the floor like a pool of blood (from Norma Johnston, *The Crucible Year*, Atheneum (New York, NY), 1979).

Those lines in *The Crucible Year*, and much else in that book, came straight from my own journals.

Everything was coming full circle . . . everything in the Keeping Days of my life found its way into counseling, and teaching, and books, and plays. Because I was spending so much time teaching theatre, communication, how to find what's between the lines in books and plays, and how to write ("Miss J. *help!!!* I have a term paper due tomorrow! Yes, I *know* I should have started it sooner, but. . . . !!!") I decided to go to Montclair University and get my teaching certificate. I was still giving at least twenty hours a week to youth work and Geneva Players; I became a research assistant to my psychology professor; I edited a newsletter on a free-lance basis. I was no longer working at the publishing house but I did free-lance editing and also ghostwriting for that house and others. I finished *The Bridge Between* (set in the Revolutionary War farmhouse across the street from the split-level house in which I now lived) and began working on *The Keeping Days* while I was in college. After graduation, I taught eighth-grade English for two years. At that time the cofounder of Geneva moved away, and the members voted to dissolve the group rather than risk its being changed. Many of them joined Geneva Players, Inc., which I formed as an interfaith (the original Geneva had been, too, but unofficially) and intergenerational drama company.

Up till now I had only written one book a year. *The Keeping Days* and *Glory in the Flower* began as one book but became too long, and Jean Karl, the famous editor at Atheneum, could see how it could be divided into two. Much of the "Keeping Days" books came from my grandparents' youth; much came also from my own teaching experiences.

Suddenly the publishing market changed as paperback publishers discovered young-adult books. My life changed, too. I said earlier that there was one other major factor that has shaped my life. This was my health—or I should say, my lack of it! I'd had "breathing problems" from childhood; I'd had aches and pains ever since that bout of illness in eighth grade. While I was in college the aches and pains were identified as several forms (one offbeat) of arthritis. ("Is there anything about you that isn't offbeat?" my friends inquired.) It got much worse; the breathing problems got much worse.

At this same time, I began writing for several publishers at once, both hardcover and softcover, becoming one of the small percentage of authors who support themselves totally from their book writing. I write under eight different names, for different writing genres and different publishers; names all taken (in whole or in mixed combinations) from ancestors on both sides of the family. My father was an orphan when he met my mother, but there's a story and a half in the lives of *his* mother, Catherine Dryden Chambers Johnston, and her two husbands. (Read *Carlisle's Hope* and *To Jess, with Love and Memories*.)

I also give speeches and have taught writing and drama courses, and travel for personal appearances and for research. And I do free-lance editing and ghostwriting. With all those "different identities" being juggled, something had to give, and what did was my health. I found myself "working horizontal" (but with my head propped up so I could breathe) much of the time. I had to take high-school or college students with me on trips to help me. All of them are now themselves in creative fields. Karen Louise Hansen, my "almost daughter," is an editor: Susan Wilder is an art director. Elizabeth Lund is an actress and producer/director of a New York showcase theatre she founded; the old Band-box Theatre sign is now repainted to say *Stepping Stone Theatre*. My cousin Kimberley Pierce, who is my "horse books expert," is still in high school but a gifted writer. But even with a wonderful support network, I found it hard to keep up.

Two years ago my doctor shocked me. "Do you know that for the past two years you've been seriously ill and gasping for breath two months out of every three?" she demanded. "How do you get any books written? You're going to get much worse unless you stop pushing yourself so hard and find a breathing specialist who can pinpoint what's doing this to you." The antibiotics and cortisone were no longer working.

She was right. I almost collapsed during a public appearance that June and spent the summer struggling for breath. In the intervals when I could get off a respirator, Karen and Liz helped me move from my townhouse and office back into the split-level with my mother. Being allergic to the household pets—German shepherd Susie, mostly-sheltie Missy, and rooster Red—didn't help. I'd already given up acting and directing; now I had to cut down on other things as well and save my "functioning time" for writing.

But I've written half a dozen books since then. I'm able to work, part of most days, at least half the time. Just as I finally found a doctor who diagnosed and treated the arthritis, I've recently found one who diagnosed my lifelong respiratory troubles as severe chronic asthma-and-then-some, meaning that my respiratory system "dramatically overreacts" to *everything,* not just things to which I'm genuinely allergic. *Dramatically overreacts;* there's poetic irony there somewhere, considering my background! More important than putting a name to the condition, we've apparently put a stop to its getting worse.

I'm writing again. I'm still giving speeches and making personal appearances and teaching workshops. I belong to the Authors League and Mystery Writers of America and Sisters in Crime, and serve on the Rutgers University Council on Children's Literature. I'm still traveling, even if with cane and sometimes respirator and wheelchair. In fact I'm working on a book now for my Macmillan editor, Cindy Kane, which has a "handicapped" heroine and starts with a traumatic Keeping Day I had last summer.

If you've got brains and gumption, nothing can stop you, Nonnie used to say. *Don't fight it, use it!* Mme. Bulgakov would say, eyes snapping, when we came to class at Theatre Wing with excuses for why scenes did not go well. *Twist your troubles round and make them bless you,* Mrs. Lovelace wrote in *Betsy's Wedding,* making Betsy remember the story of Jacob wrestling with the angel. If I hadn't been out of school so much when I was little, I wouldn't have read so much, I wouldn't have hung around so much with adults and had my horizons widened. I know I wouldn't have had as much empathy for others. Perhaps I wouldn't even have been a writer. Being sidelined for *time-out* often gave me *time.* Even if I'm not well enough to write, I can lie around and read—and watch television; I watch about eleven hours a day (yes, even when I'm writing!) and get all kinds of plot ideas from news and science programs. So this is something else I want to pass on through my characters—you can't control what life dishes out to you, but you can control how you react to it and what you do with it. You can use your gifts—if not one way, then another.

Getting back to that college professor and his assignment:

Who am I? A Victorian. A cat curled by the fire (but I'm allergic to cats). An herb-and-flower garden. The color red. Old houses with low-ceilinged rooms, a teakettle on the hearth, and a fire burning bright. Caftans, antique rings and earrings, crosses on silver chains. Big-brimmed hats. Candlelight. Shakespeare, mythology, John Donne's poems, mysticism. Somebody in Geneva once described me as a total environment.

Why do I write? Because I have things that I must say, and I can no more hold them back than I can cease to breathe and still be alive. Because I believe, with Tennessee Williams, that writers of fiction can share real truths through the pleasant disguise of illusion.

As my grandmother said, "You catch more flies with honey than with vinegar." I write in a romantic, often gothic, style, because I know from my own reading and from theatre that when you draw people into the circle of a rosy glow, they become more open to the thrust of truth. I write about young people facing today's realities without flinching. I write mysteries and detective and suspense stories because deep down they're the age-old story of the struggle between good and evil—and besides, they're fun! I write about love—all the different meanings of the word—and about family, and all that word's different meanings.

Today I write a great deal about broken and blended and nonrelated families, because I see so much of that around me, and besides I've had them in my family and know they aren't the end of the world. My father was abandoned by his birth-father, and raised by a stepfather he was very fond of. My grandmother was a much-loved stepmother, and she married a man who'd had a stepmother himself. So adoption, divorce, death, remarriage—even desertion—appear in my books, from *The Keeping Days* to the "Carlisle Chronicles" and *The Potter's Wheel:*

> I was thinking about that word *home.* When Mother took off, I'd felt as if I no longer had one. That wasn't true. Not in the literal sense. It wasn't that I didn't *have* one, I didn't have *one.* Not just one. Home, I thought with satisfaction, was inside me. Home was wherever my heart was, wherever I had friends and kin. I had many homes. I was rich indeed (from Norma Johnston, *The Potter's Wheel,* Morrow (New York, NY), 1988.)

Like Laura in that quotation from *The Potter's Wheel,* I have several people in my family circle who

Portrait for the jacket of **The Medici Ring**

have no blood or legal ties to me. And as a result, my life has been enriched.

And so I write of the Keeping Days that remain in our memories forever; of the turning points in which we go from innocence to knowledge; of the abstract truths I believe to be unchanging in a changing world. And of facing change without feeling threatened by it. My grandmother used to say, "The world's going to keep turning whether you want it to or not, and you'd better go forward with it or you'll find yourself going backward!"

That essay that started out, "Once there was an insufferable brat," ended like this: "Call her a romanticist, but she still believes, in spite of everything, that man has at heart the potential for good as well as evil; that life is no mere accident or dirty joke but has meaning and purpose. To her, that's realism. Perhaps commitment's out of style these days. This artist is past the point of no return—and she's very glad she is!"

The Keeping Days of my life have been *wonderful!*

POSTSCRIPT

Nicole St. John contributed the following update to *SATA* in 2003:

Plus ça change, plus c'est la même chose . . . "The more that changes, the more that stays the same," or so I learned in high school French class. Or, to quote from a chancel drama I've directed, "Time does not come full circle; it moves in a spiral." It's now some fifteen years since I wrote "The Keeping Days of My Life" for this author biography series. The rocks on which I've built my life—writing, faith, family, friends (and pets)—remain, but life has changed.

My longtime agent and close friend Dorothy Markinko has retired. Some books listed in my earlier bibliography—*The Five Magpies, Such Stuff As Dreams Are Made Of, Summer of the Citadel,* and *A Small Rain*—were either not published, or published under other names. Check the updated bibliography for a correct list of all my published titles (and check on the Internet for copies of out-of-print ones being offered for sale).

My distinguished editor Jean Karl has died, as has my mentor Maud Hart Lovelace and her daughter, who told me I was MHL's only "official protégée." One of my favorite editors, Cynthia Kane, is no longer editing books for young readers. Publishing companies I wrote for merged with others; some went out of business. The whole field of children's/young adult book publishing has changed enormously—including the definition of what *young adult* means, and what they read. Mega-changes in computers, the Internet, films, music, and TV have impacted those of us who are or were writing for "young readers." The world in general, and the world of youth, has become more sophisticated, more knowledgeable, and more dangerous.

I've had ten more books published. *The Delphic Choice, The Dragon's Eye,* and *The Time of the Cranes* are all suspense stories, the plots of which Cindy Kane and I had great fun concocting over the phone. After them came two biographies of which I'm very proud: *Louisa May* is a biography of Louisa May Alcott, who with *Little Women* literally created the genre of young adult novels. While there have been notable books about her in the past, I'm the first of her biographers who actually *is,* like her, an author of fiction for and about young adults. My *Lotta's Progress* is a fictional story based on the actual German-refugee family that the Alcotts helped (and from whom "Beth"—Elizabeth Alcott—caught scarlet fever) that Louisa called the Hummels.*Harriet* is the biography of Harriet Beecher Stowe, who wrote *Uncle Tom's Cabin,* the novel about the evils of slavery that made Abraham Lincoln say to Mrs. Stowe, "So you're the little lady that started this great war." And that first book I wrote, when I was in eighth grade, that no one but my English teacher ever saw, became after major plot revisions *Over Jordan,* in which Harriet Beecher Stowe is a major character. (The moral in that is "Never throw anything out!" More on that later.)

Scholastic publishers' noted editor, Ann Reit, asked me to write *Remember the Ladies: The First Women's Rights Convention. The Image Game* is a high school story; the title says it all. *Feather in the Wind* is a modern-day suspense story (set in the 1780s house across the street from mine) about a teenage girl with strangely altered DNA, her astronaut grandfather whom NASA won't acknowledge exists, and the ghost of a Lenni Lenape youth who died while on his vision quest hundreds of years ago. Book design for *Feather* was done by my high school friend Constance Bond Ftera, who also designed *Return to Morocco.* Here at Chipmunk Crossing a great deal has changed. The owner of the *Feather in the Wind* house donated neighboring acres to the township as a garden in memory of his late wife; in spring and summer the roses there are beautiful. He has since died also, but his sons and their families still live on the land, one in the 1780s house and the other in a newer one. One sheep still lives there, too, and a lot of mallard ducks. My front lawn is now an English cottage garden of roses and lilies, tulips and daffodils. There are raised garden beds behind the house, too, and most of the gardens are named for my books. There's a Guinever's Garden of flowers from medieval tapestries, a Shakespeare Garden with plants and flowers from his plays, and a Wychwood Physick Garden of medicinal and potentially poisonous plants—monkshood, foxglove, and others that have played dangerous roles in my mysteries.

A lot of this floral extravaganza was because of a major flood. A mountain of snow, piled by plows at the end of the cul-de-sac on the street behind our house, turned into a mountain of ice. When the ground beneath the ice thawed, melting water ran under frozen snow on our back lawn, encountered a similar mountain at the top of our driveway, detoured under our garage door, up over the step into my office, across the hall, and down the cellar stairs. *Major* catastrophe—carpets and an antique Turkish rug ruined; ditto a lot of what had been stored in the cellar, and many old family things and books, including some of mine that are out of print.

While all this was happening my mother's health, physical and—as we realized finally, mental—was failing. She had inherited the family's creativity, artistic talent, "bad legs," and stubbornness (my grandmother called it "pigheadedness"). She was seeing things like wounded birds and animals in the back yard, and was furious when we checked and reported nothing there. She fell, and could not get up. She threatened to throw me out of the house if I called the volunteer ambulance corps. She crawled along the hall to the stairs, thinking she could pull herself up by holding the banisters. It didn't work. Finally, without her knowing, I explained the situation to the neighbor who has since moved, and asked if he'd "just drop in." Over he came with his two sons, all tall, bronzed, handsome in Bermuda shorts and shirts open to the waist. Immediately Mother reverted to being a teenage girl out of the silent movies of her youth, all smiles and giggles and flirtatious green eyes.

They got her back into bed. But not long afterwards she tried to get out again—another fall. I found her sitting on the stairs, being heartbreakingly polite like a good little girl, thinking she was in an office somewhere where she must "have to get back to work" and clearly not recognizing me at all. I left a message with my doctor, begging him to make a house call. He returned the call early the next morning to say "Call an ambulance; I'll see her at the hospital." I phoned my best friends Clare and Erik Hansen, whose daughter Karen used to be my research assistant, with an SOS request that they come immediately; we all knew Mother wouldn't make a scene in front of them. ("Angel in public, devil in private," my grandmother used to call her moods.)

After that, for several months, it was hospital, then Kessler Institute rehabilitation center, then back to hospital with pneumonia, then back to Kessler. The doctor told me she *must* be transferred to a nursing home (this has to be done directly from a hospital, or Medicare won't cover it). Originally we thought the home would be only temporary, but her "mental orientation" rapidly deteriorated. I had to go to court to be appointed her guardian; the lawyers were so nice, and so was the judge, agreeing to order a psychiatrist sent to the nursing home to evaluate my mother rather than having her brought into court. I asked, "Please, send a good-looking young man, and don't let him tell her he's a psychiatrist," and it worked; he told me later that she was flirting like a very charming young girl from long ago. Mother thought *he* was charming. He diagnosed her with severe chronic depression, which had probably started in her childhood, and old-age dementia.

After that, Kessler wouldn't accept her again, as it was clear her legs were beyond the help of physical therapy. At that time we still hoped she would be able to return home, as she begged every time I visited. I began rehabilitating the house towards her eventual return, and was shocked at what I discovered in her room: piles of newspapers, that she'd forbidden me to move, contained a lot of unopened mail, long-overdue bills, and unwashed plates. With the help of a friend I got it all cleaned out, repainted, and repapered. But it was now clear she could never come back home—her condition, physical and mental, deteriorated week by week. She underwent personality changes; she either didn't recognize me or was furious with me. Clare and Erik took over the visiting, and during her lucid moments Mother told Clare things she'd never shared with me, such as that she'd never felt "safe" except when she was with my father. And that she hated it that her own father had been "so old" when she was born. He'd been a very young and dashing fifty-two, but that had been "old" to her. I realized that one reason she "never felt safe" had been that when she was nine her parents had sold the family homestead (surrounded by uncles, aunts, and cousins) and moved miles away into a boarding-house so they could open a secretarial school (where they worked six days and some nights a week) after my grandfather had lost his court-reporter job following an election upheaval. (I had written about that in *The Keeping Days* and *Glory in the Flower*.)

In the middle of this, *Harriet* was published. I held a small "book party" dinner for all the people who had been helping me, and Mother, and with the book. By then she'd been hospitalized again because her system was what the doctor called "gradually breaking down." On the way to the restaurant I stopped by the hospital to see her, while my editor waited in the car. I'm not sure Mother recognized me, and she could barely speak, but she was being heartbreakingly polite. Her eyes had turned a vivid sapphire blue.

A few days later, early in the morning, her doctor phoned. She had been taken to the operating room during the night for an emergency procedure, but her condition had become so bad they hadn't dared try to anesthetize or operate. Now, shortly after dawn, he'd been to see her, and though she couldn't speak she'd been flirting with him, "with those eyes of hers," when she suddenly passed away. It was the day before her sixty-sixth wedding anniversary. We buried with her the mummified remains of our long-dead parakeet (that I found, wrapped in a handkerchief, in a metal candy box in her lingerie drawer) and the coral sand she'd brought back from her Bermuda honeymoon.

. . .Why am I telling all this? For several reasons: Because family is important, and often we don't understand family members until they're gone. Because depression is a widespread—and *treatable*—illness, and all too often we don't recognize the symptoms. Because *I* had known them—other people close to me had suffered from depression for long periods of time—yet I still hadn't recognized them in my mother, and if she'd been diagnosed earlier her last years would have been happier. Because, although depression does *not* mean a person is "crazy," it can be like a black cloud affecting not just that person but those around, near and dear or not. It's one of those "in the closet" secrets that needs to be brought into the light of day without any shame. Just as I didn't recognize depression in my mother, despite my earlier experience, I didn't realize until rereading *Guinever's Gift* that I have more than once written depression into some of my book characters.

Family is important. That theme has become a running thread in all my books. Kinfolk are kinfolk, and we can't divorce them, though we might feel like murdering them sometimes—possibly because we see in them some aspect of ourselves. The wonderful thing is that "family" needn't only mean those related to us by blood, or whom we know in person. They're also the ancestors from whom we've inherited weaknesses and strengths, dislikes and likes. They're those related to us by marriage, or by adoption. And they're the friends we make who *feel* like family. All of these are a heritage from which we can learn, over which we can laugh or shed a tear, with which we can share good times or bad, from whom we gain wisdom, and strength in our blood and bone that we can pass on.

And that is what most of my books come from, and why I write.

Since my mother died several things have changed. I have wonderful new neighbors next door, including two golden retrievers and a small black-and-tan short-haired pooch who has lots of attitude and must have Doberman somewhere in her genes. Susie, our German shepherd mix (longer than usual hair) died of a stroke, and a year later so did Missie, our almost-Sheltie. Now I have Maximilian Maxwell, a purebred long-haired shepherd—he came from the St. Hubertus Giralda shelter already named Max (all our family dogs have *always* been "pound pups"), but that was too short to yell at him when he was being particularly stubborn, or extra silly (which is often). Everyone who meets him falls in love with him. He insinuated himself into *Feather in the Wind* without my realizing it, just as the grandmother in *Feather* bit by bit became a memorial to my best friend Clare, who had died the year before.

Right now I'm working on a very exciting project—turning my "historic romantic suspense" novel *Guinever's Gift* into an even more suspense-focused filmscript for Hans Kummer of Wild Child Entertainment, which plans to make it into an IMAX film. I'm in the process of seeking a publisher for *Touchstone,* the first book in a detective/murder mystery series featuring Maris Crayle, Ph.D. in Renaissance studies (emphasis: arts, antiquities, jewels, and poisons), who's frequently a witness for the prosecution in murder cases, and is a descendant of the hero and heroine of *The Medici Ring.* I also have some other writing projects in the works.

I'm on the Rutgers University Council on Children's Literature, and act as a mentor, and sometimes speaker, at its annual autumn One-On-One (pairing author-mentors and beginning writers/illustrators of children's books) Conference in New Brunswick, New Jersey. I also do speaking engagements, speak on panels, and teach writing classes, when requested. And I'm involved with a lot of writing-related organizations and conventions, all of which are great inspiration and great fun because you meet so many interesting people—authors and readers. I was co-founder and first president of the NYC/Tri-state Chapter of Sisters in Crime, an organization founded by a group of mystery writers, among them Sara Paretsky, Nancy Pickard, Margaret Maron, and Caroline Hart, to "combat discrimination against women in the mystery field, educate publishers and the general public as to inequalities in the treatment of female authors, and raise the level of awareness of their contribution to the field." Membership is open to anyone, regardless of age, gender, or nationality, who enjoys mysteries and wants to further SinC's objectives. I've learned a lot since being a member, and made some wonderful friends. Its website is http://www.sisters incrime.org/.

I'm a member of Mystery Writers of America and the Authors Guild. When I can, I attend the Bouchercon World Mystery Convention (held all over the world!). I attend the Mid-Atlantic Mystery Convention in Philadelphia, Pennsylvania, whenever it's held. And I *always* go to the Malice Domestic Mystery Conference, held every spring outside of Washington, D.C., because that's my chance to see my Pierce relatives, all of whom (except for the Washington State branch) live in that area.

Which brings me to some important news. Sometime between 2004 and 2006 I plan to move to Alexandria, Virginia, a historic town just across the Potomac from Washington, D.C.—or to a similar town very near. I want to be near my family, and to have a townhouse (the 1780s kind, *not* the kind built in developments far from centers of towns) that can be used for an authors' research center, for holding writing classes and programs with guest speakers, author visits, and for my archives—not just of my book manuscripts, outlines, research notes, contracts, etc., but for the enormous store of materials on the Pierce and Messler (Metselaer) family trees that I'm lucky enough to have. It's a veritable "how middle-class, Middle Atlantic/New England families—of English or Netherlands extraction, at any rate—lived" from the 1630s to today. In addition to all the

The author and her dog, Maximilian Maxwell, Christmas 2002

materials that came to me from my grandparents, my cousin John Pierce's widow Nan has given me the enormous store of Pierce family papers and photographs, including the nineteenth century ones taken by my grandfather Harris Pierce, that he had inherited. I am now having a wonderful time sorting them out and cataloguing them, with help from various cousins. I also now have several enormous nineteenth century family Bibles, with early family genealogy inscribed. What a treasure for a writer, as well as a descendant!

Plus ça change, plus c'est la même chose . . . I got "hooked on books" (especially detective stories and family sagas), on writing, and on history, when I was very young. Family anecdotes true and untrue . . . gossip I wasn't supposed to hear or understand . . . photographs, especially the ones my grandfather had taken, that were a "window" into the nineteenth century world . . . outdated clothing (and my mother's latest evening gowns!) to dress up in, wear for Hallowe'en, or to costume parties (like my grandmother's wedding dress) . . . letters and diaries hidden or unhidden . . . always fascinated me; influenced my life; influenced my books. I probably wouldn't have become a writer without them . . . or without "reading addict" relatives . . . or perhaps, if I hadn't been an only child who spent most of her time with adults. Since then, as a writer of books for young readers, a teacher, and through years of association with young adults in my church and theatre work, things definitely, happily, evened out! Now I'm "passing on" what I learned, to writers young and . . . well, let's just leave it at that!

As I write, the publishing world is still in the boom-and-bust cycle of enormous changes—technological, organizational, and financial—that have been going on for at least twenty years. These are nothing new; they've probably gone on ever since the invention of the printing press. Some authors (Louisa May Alcott and Harriet Beecher Stowe were among them) "ride with the tide," sometimes changing writing styles, genres, or readership demographics; sometimes taking some private-life "time out"; always knowing that "*Plus ça change . . .*" As for my own writing, when I was young and dreaming of being a writer, I always knew there were two kinds of books (and series, but that's another story, dependent on current publishing trends) I wanted to write. One was the "family saga" genre that, historical or contemporary, and whether "best-sellers" of the moment or not, has always been popular in both the adult and young adult demographics. I dreamed of writing these, historical and modern, as Mrs. Lovelace, Janet Lambert, and other favorite writers of mine had done. Happily, that dream came true.

The other genre I wanted to write in was the detective series written, for adults, by Agatha Christie, Ngaio Marsh, Patricia Wentworth, and Dorothy L. Sayers . . . also the Nero Wolfe, Perry Mason, and Sherlock Holmes series that my grandmother and I devoured. I was steered instead into writing historic romantic suspense, when that was in big demand in the adult market. I was taught the genre by my agent, Patricia S. Myrer, who has since retired. What I learned from her led to my writing all my teen-protagonist suspense novels.

Now I want to focus again on my longtime dream; writing classic murder mystery series for the adult market. People have said to me, "Oh, you're deserting your YA fans!" The answer is, *no, I'm not.*

The world has changed since 1963 when *The Wishing Star* was published. Never has this hit home to us as Americans more than on September 11, 2001, when the World Trade Center, the Pentagon, and a patch of land in Pennsylvania were crashed by suicide-mission planes. We all lost what innocence we had left that day. But even before then, commencing with World War II and its aftermath, America had begun to lose its isolation and its innocence. Television, popular music, the Internet, and other media brought the whole world home to us, ugliness, horrors, heroism, and all, and even those of us who were children could not escape it. Just as elementary, middle, and high school curriculums have changed and become more demanding, the reading demographics of preteens and teens have changed since I started writing. They are no longer so innocent either.

And 9/11 changed us all.

And I am going back to what I always wanted to do—write classic crime and murder mystery books. Unlike the horror and otherwise ultraviolent mystery/crime books in which evil triumphs, or at very least lurks in the darkness, soon to pounce again, the classic mystery genre is about normal people among whom, suddenly, murder strikes like a crashing plane. The "civil contract" of the community is broken, and a laser light shines upon all (usually exposing the Seven Deadly Sins within the group) until the perpetrator is identified, wounds healed where possible, and evil removed from the community's midst—if not forever, at least for the foreseeable time. (In a horror/suspense novel, we readers would see it lurking as we leave, whereas the book's characters don't.)

This is what the classic detective mystery is about—the breaking of the unspoken covenant of civilized behavior; the search, identification, and removal of the perpetrator or the murderer; the world of the book's characters beginning to return, not to a state of innocence, but to a state of grace.

Can any of us really believe that middle school and high school readers don't understand this? They can see through adults who can't see through themselves.

After great pain, the world begins again. *There is always hope.* That is what great literature, great art, and faith have always taught us. And it's why I write. It's also why, in addition to writing mysteries, I'm also planning to write more biographies. And to write an anecdotal history of my family which, having braved the Atlantic in small boats in the 1630s, a time of religious and governmental upheaval in Europe . . . and gone in turn through numerous crises, illnesses, wars, and other upheavals . . . have survived, if not always with grace, with a good deal of humor, for some 370-plus years. They were witnesses to northeastern U.S. history (and some served in the military far overseas); what's more, they wrote it down in many cases.

That's what I want to share. (Who was it who said that those who don't understand history are condemned to repeat it?) And I will always write fiction also, because it's often through fiction that the greatest revelations come.

So if you want to be a writer, *write.* Regardless of your age; regardless of what anyone else tells you. You may not get published, but that doesn't matter. Just having written what you wrote will enrich your understanding, even if not your wallet, and will add something to *your* family's archives.

Like many writers, I'm often asked to do school visits, conduct writing classes and seminars, and to speak to organizations. Here are some of the most-asked questions, and my answers:

"How long does it take you to write a book?"

Three days to six months, depending on the length a book is to be, and how well I've thought it out beforehand.

"How do you get started?"

Here's what I was told, modernised for 2002: "Apply seat of pants to seat of chair and turn on the computer."

"How did you learn to write publishable books?"

(Quote from my mentor Maud Hart Lovelace): "Read, *read,* **read! And write,** *write,* **write!** *Nothing* teaches you to write *but* writing!"

*

There are always more stories yet to tell!

Keep reading . . . and writing . . . and I hope to see you someday in Alexandria! You'll know I've moved because my Web site will have changed to http://www.keepingdays.com/.

SAMPSON, Michael 1952-

Personal

Born October 13, 1952, in Denison, TX; son of Roy (a carpenter) and Ida (a homemaker; maiden name, Bon) Sampson; married Mary Beth Glossup (a professor), 1973; children: Jonathan, Joshua. *Education:* East Texas State University, B.S., 1974, M.Ed., 1976; University of Arizona, Ph.D., 1980. *Politics:* Independent. *Religion:* Baptist.

Addresses

Home—Route 2, Box 50-7, Campbell, TX 75422. *Office*—Department of Elementary Education, Texas A & M University—Commerce, Commerce, TX 75429-3011. *E-mail*—Michael@michaelsampson.com.

Career

Educator, author, and storyteller. Commerce Independent School District, Commerce, TX, teacher, 1974-76; Texas A & M University—Commerce, professor, 1979—. International Institute of Literacy Learning, executive director, 1980—. With Bill Martin, Jr., hosted Pathways to Literacy teaching workshops throughout the United States. National Reading Conference, member of technology committee, 2002; vice chair, Texas Education Agency Professional Practices Commission; member of governing board, National Association of Creative Adults and Young Children. Storyteller at schools and libraries.

Member

International Reading Association (member, Las Vegas program committee), National Reading Conference, National Council of Teachers of English, Texas Association for the Improvement of Reading (state board member; state president), Phi Delta Kappa.

Michael Sampson

Writings

FOR CHILDREN

The Football That Won . . . , illustrated by Ted Rand, Henry Holt (New York, NY), 1996.

(With Bill Martin, Jr.) *Si Won's Victory,* Scott Foresman (Reading, MA), 1996.

(With wife, Mary Beth Sampson) *Star of the Circus,* illustrated by Jose Aruego and Ariane Dewey, Henry Holt (New York, NY), 1996.

(With Bill Martin, Jr.) *Yummy Tum Tee,* Scott Foresman (Reading, MA), 1996.

(With Bill Martin, Jr.) *City Scenes,* Learning Media Ltd. (New Zealand), 1997.

(With wife, Mary Beth Sampson) *Wild Bear,* Learning Media Ltd. (New Zealand), 1997.

(With Bill Martin, Jr.) *Football Fever,* Learning Media Ltd. (New Zealand), 1997.

(With Bill Martin, Jr.) *Swish!,* illustrated by Michael Chesworth, Henry Holt (New York, NY), 1997.

(With Bill Martin, Jr.) *Adam, Adam, What Do You See?,* illustrated by Cathie Felstead, Tommy Nelson (Nashville, TN), 2000.

(With Bill Martin, Jr.) *The Little Squeegy Bug* (based on the book by Martin published in 1946), illustrated by Patrick Corrigan, Winslow Press (Delray Beach, FL), 2001.

(With Bill Martin, Jr.) *Rock It, Sock It, Number Line!,* illustrated by Heather Cahoon, Henry Holt (New York, NY), 2001.

(With Bill Martin, Jr.) *Little Granny Quarterback,* illustrated by Michael Chesworth, Boyds Mills Press, 2001.

(With Bill Martin, Jr.) *I Pledge Allegiance,* illustrated by Chris Raschka, Candlewick Press (Cambridge, MA), 2002.

(With Bill Martin, Jr.) *Trick or Treat?,* illustrated by Paul Meisel, Simon & Schuster (New York, NY), 2002.

(With Bill Martin, Jr.) *Caddie the Golf Dog,* illustrated by Floyd Cooper, Walker (New York, NY), 2002.

Sampson's books have been translated into Spanish.

TEACHING MATERIALS

(With T. Kelly) *Signs and Safety,* Kendall/Hunt (Dubuque, IA), 1986.

School, Kendall/Hunt (Dubuque, IA), 1986.

My House, Kendall/Hunt (Dubuque, IA), 1986.

Transportation, Kendall/Hunt (Dubuque, IA), 1986.

Nutrition, Kendall/Hunt (Dubuque, IA), 1986.

Supermarkets, Kendall/Hunt (Dubuque, IA), 1986.

Jobs in the Family, Kendall/Hunt (Dubuque, IA), 1986.

Growing Up, Kendall/Hunt (Dubuque, IA), 1986.

Written in the same pattern as "This Is the House That Jack Built," Sampson's The Football That Won . . . *tells of a* **Super Bowl showdown between the Dallas Cowboys and the Kansas City Chiefs.** *(Illustrated by Ted Rand.)*

I Pledge Allegiance *written by Sampson and Bill Martin, Jr., explains the meaning behind the words in America's national oath. (Illustrated by Chris Raschka.)*

All about Time, Kendall/Hunt (Dubuque, IA), 1986.

Pets, Kendall/Hunt (Dubuque, IA), 1986.

The Zoo, Kendall/Hunt (Dubuque, IA), 1986.

Insects, Kendall/Hunt (Dubuque, IA), 1986.

Also contributor to teaching materials published by Developmental Learning Materials (Allen, TX), 1989.

FOR ADULTS

(Editor) *The Pursuit of Literacy: Early Reading and Writing,* Kendall/Hunt Publishing (Dubuque, IA), 1986.

Experiences for Literacy, SRA Technology Training (Chicago, IL), 1990.

(With Mary Beth Sampson and Roach Van Allen) *Pathways to Literacy: A Meaning-centered Perspective,* Holt, Rinehart & Winston, 1991, second edition published as *Pathways to Literacy: Process Transactions,* Harcourt, Brace (New York, NY), 1995, third edition

published as *Total Literacy: Pathways to Reading, Writing, and Learning,* Wadsworth (San Francisco, CA), 2003.

Contributor of articles and reviews to professional journals and periodicals, including *Reading Teacher, ACT, Tender Years, Reading Improvement, Christian Life, Reading Horizons, Reading Research Quarterly, Living with Preschoolers, Industrial Education* and *Ohio Reading Teacher.* and to books, including *Practical Classroom Applications of Language Experience: Looking Back and Looking Forward,* edited by O. G. Nelson and W. M. Linek, Allyn & Bacon (Boston, MA), 1999.

Sidelights

Michael Sampson is an author and educator who has devoted his career to helping kids read and love it. Both on his own and together with long-time collaborator, children's writer Bill Martin, Jr., Sampson has written humorous titles such as *Swish!, Rock It, Sock It, Number Line!,* and *Caddie the Golf Dog.* Published in 1997, *Swish!* tells the story of two rival girls' basketball teams, and is punctuated by the ebb and flow of an actual basketball game, while in *Trick or Treat?* puns, alliteration, and other wordplay provide fun for novice readers. In the pages of *Rock It, Sock It, Number Line!* a parade of strutting vegetables help teach young readers the numbers one through ten. On a quieter note, *Caddie the Golf Dog* introduces young children to a stray dog who finds not one but two loving homes in a "touching story" by Sampson and Martin that *School Library Journal* contributor Linda Ludke maintained would "resonate with children." *Adam, Adam, What Do You See?* reflects its authors' Christian faith in its descriptions of Bible characters and Christian concepts as well as its inclusion of short verse from both the Old and New Testament. Calling the text "friendly and age-appropriate," a *Publishers Weekly* contributor deemed *Adam, Adam, What do You See?* a picture book that encourages discussion and leads curious "readers to the biblical verses that serve as sources."

Sampson joined collaborator Bill Martin, Jr., to update Martin's first children's book, originally published in 1946. In *The Little Squeegy Bug* a small bug feels less important than the other insects around him, but his efforts to try to be something he's not—a bee with silver wings and a long stinger—only bring failure. Finally, a trip to the wise Haunchy the Spider brings a change to Squeegy: Haunchy weaves the small bug a pair of beautiful silver wings, and instead of a stinger puts a shining star on Squeegy's own tail, turning the formerly nondescript bug into a firefly. *The Little Squeegy Bug* also features the artistic talents of illustrator Patrick Corrigan, whose artwork a *Publishers Weekly* contributor praised as "appealingly stylized."

Martin and Sampson's 2000 picture book *I Pledge Allegiance* is designed to introduce the Pledge that many U.S. children recite at the start of each school day. Including an explanation of many of the Pledge's significant words, as well as a history of the oath since its composition by Frances Bellamy, the book "emphasizes the importance" of reciting the Pledge, according to *School Library Journal* contributor Krista Tokarz.

Sampson once told *SATA:* "During my elementary school years, my first stories were about 'The Hardy Boys' and 'Superman,' while my first publication was a joke published in a national magazine. During the 1980s and 1990s I wrote several books for teachers, including *Pathways to Literacy.* Finally, in 1996, I came full circle in my writing when *The Football That Won . . .* was published by Henry Holt. The story is based on an experience I had as a seventh-grade football player. Actual experiences continue to guide my writing. *Star of the Circus* resulted from watching my kindergarten-aged son's classroom circus show. *Si Won's Victory* is based upon the struggle of a Korean child my son knew in grade school. *Swish!* was written after watching the drama of a cliffhanger finish to a girls' basketball game."

Biographical and Critical Sources

PERIODICALS

Booklist, September 1, 2002, Gillian Engberg, review of *I Pledge Allegiance,* p. 120; September 15, 2002, Stephanie Zvirin, review of *Trick or Treat?* p. 246; December 1, 2002, Helen Rosenberg, review of *Caddie the Golf Dog,* p. 676.
Children's Book Review Service, August, 1996, p. 162.
Kirkus Reviews, August 1, 2001, review of *Rock It, Sock It, Number Line,* p. 1128; September 1, 2001, review of *The Little Squeegy Bug,* p. 1297; October 1, 2001, review of *Little Granny Quarterback,* p. 1428; September 15, 2002, review of *Trick or Treat?* p. 1395; September 15, 2002, review of *I Pledge Allegiance,* p. 1394; October 1, 2002, review of *Caddie the Golf Dog,* p. 1479.
Publishers Weekly, July 29, 1996, p. 87; September 25, 2000, review of *Adam, Adam, What Do You See?* p. 113; August 20, 2001, review of *Rock It, Sock It, Number Line!,* p. 78; October 1, 2001, review of *The Little Squeegy Bug,* p. 63; August 26, 2002, review of *I Pledge Allegiance,* p. 68; .
School Library Journal, October, 1996, p. 105; December, 2000, Patricia Pearl Dole, review of *Adam, Adam, What Do You See?* p. 134; December, 2001, Piper L. Nyman, review of *Rock It, Sock It, Number Line!,* p. 106; December, 2001, Barbara Buckley, review of *Little Granny Quarterback,* p. 106; October, 2002, John Peters, review of *Trick or Treat?* p. 120; December, 2002, Linda Ludke, review of *Caddie the Golf Dog,* p. 108, and Krista Tokarz, review of *I Pledge Allegiance,* p. 127.

ONLINE

Michael Sampson Home Page, http://www.michael sampson.com/ (May 5, 2003).*

* * *

SHANNON, George (William Bones) 1952-

Personal

Born February 14, 1952, in Caldwell, KS; son of David W. (a professor) and Doris (Bones) Shannon. *Education:* Western Kentucky University, B.S., 1974; University of Kentucky, M.S.L.S., 1976. *Hobbies and other interests:* Gardening.

Addresses

Agent—c/o Greenwillow Books, 1350 Avenue of the Americas, New York, NY 10019. *E-mail*—zolizoli@ rmi.net.

Career

Storyteller and author. Librarian at public schools in Muhlenberg County, KY, 1974-75; Lexington Public Library, Lexington, KY, librarian, 1976-78; professional

George Shannon

storyteller and lecturer, 1978—. Guest lecturer at University of Kentucky, 1977. Member, external advisory board, Cooperative Children's Book Center, Madison, WI.

Awards, Honors

Notable Book designation, American Library Association, 1981, and Children's Choice Book, International Reading Association/Children's Book Council, 1982, both for *The Piney Woods Peddler;* Friends of American Writers award, 1990, for *Unlived Affections.*

Writings

FOR CHILDREN

Lizard's Song, illustrated by Jose Aruego and Ariane Dewey, Greenwillow Books (New York, NY), 1981.

The Gang and Mrs. Higgins, illustrated by Andrew Vines, Greenwillow Books (New York, NY), 1981.

The Piney Woods Peddler, illustrated by Nancy Tafuri, Greenwillow Books (New York, NY), 1981.

Dance Away!, illustrated by Jose Aruego and Ariane Dewey, Greenwillow Books (New York, NY), 1982.

The Surprise, illustrated by Jose Aruego and Ariane Dewey, Greenwillow Books (New York, NY), 1983.

Bean Boy, illustrated by Peter Sis, Greenwillow Books (New York, NY), 1984.

Oh, I Love, illustrated by Cheryl Harness, Bradbury Press (New York, NY), 1988.

Sea Gifts, illustrated by Mary Azarian, David Godine (New York, NY), 1989.

Dancing the Breeze, illustrated by Jacqueline Rogers, Bradbury Press (New York, NY), 1991.

Laughing All the Way, illustrated by Meg McLean, Houghton Mifflin (Boston, MA), 1992.

Climbing Kansas Mountains, illustrated by Thomas B. Allen, Bradbury Press (New York, NY), 1993.

Seeds, illustrated by Steve Bjorkman, Houghton Mifflin (Boston, MA), 1994.

April Showers, illustrated by Jose Aruego and Ariane Dewey, Greenwillow Books (New York, NY), 1995.

Heart to Heart, illustrated by Steve Bjorkman, Houghton (Boston MA), 1995.

Tomorrow's Alphabet, illustrated by Donald Crews, Greenwillow Books (New York, NY), 1995.

(Compiler) *Spring: A Haiku Story,* illustrated by Malcah Zeldis, Greenwillow Books (New York, NY), 1995.

This Is the Bird, illustrated by David Soman, Houghton Mifflin (Boston, MA), 1996.

Lizard's Home, illustrated by Jose Aruego and Ariane Dewey, Greenwillow Books (New York, NY), 1999.

Frog Legs: A Picture Book of Action Verse, illustrated by Amit Trynan, Greenwillow Books (New York, NY), 2000.

Lizard's Guest, illustrated by Jose Aruego and Ariane Dewey, Greenwillow Books (New York, NY), 2003.

Tippy-Toe Chick, Go!, illustrated by Laura Dronzek, Greenwillow Books (New York, NY), 2003.

Wise Acres, illustrated by Deborah Zemke, Handprint Books, 2004.

Several of Shannon's books have been translated into Spanish, Chinese, French, and German.

FOLKLORE

Stories to Solve: Folktales from around the World, illustrated by Peter Sis, Greenwillow Books (New York, NY), 1985.

More Stories to Solve: Fifteen Folktales from around the World, illustrated by Peter Sis, Greenwillow Books (New York, NY), 1990.

Still More Stories to Solve: Fourteen Folktales from around the World, illustrated by Peter Sis, Greenwillow Books (New York, NY), 1994.

True Lies: Eighteen Tales for You to Judge, illustrated by John O'Brien, Greenwillow Books (New York, NY), 1997.

More True Lies: Eighteen Tales for You to Judge, illustrated by John O'Brien, Greenwillow Books (New York, NY), 2001.

OTHER

Humpty Dumpty: A Pictorial History, Green Tiger Press, 1981.

Folk Literature and Children: An Annotated Bibliography of Secondary Materials, Greenwood Press (New York, NY), 1981.

(With Ellin Greene) *Storytelling: A Selected Annotated Bibliography,* Garland (New York, NY), 1986.

Arnold Lobel (criticism), Twayne (Boston, MA), 1989.

Unlived Affections (young-adult novel), Harper (New York, NY), 1989.

(Compiler) *A Knock at the Door: 35 Ethnic Versions of a Tale,* illustrated by Joanne Caroselli, Oryx Press (Phoenix, AZ), 1992.

Contributor of articles and reviews to magazines, including *Horn Book, Children's Literature in Education, School Library Journal,* and *Wilson Library Bulletin.*

Work in Progress

Busy in the Garden, illustrated by Sam Williams, and *White is for Blueberry,* illustrated by Laura Dronzek, both for Greenwillow.

Sidelights

Professional storyteller George Shannon combines his interest in folklore and the oral storytelling tradition with his love of literature for children in a series of picture books for the younger set that include *Lizard's Home, Frog Legs: A Picture Book of Action Verse,* and *Tippy-Toe Chick, Go!* the last a "sure pick for story-time" in the opinion of *Booklist* contributor Linda Perkins. In addition to several nonfiction works and a series of popular retellings of folktales, Shannon has written such well-received works as *The Piney Woods Peddler, Dancing the Breeze,* and *Climbing Kansas Mountains,* as well as an award-winning young adult novel titled *Unlived Affections,* which he published in 1989.

Born in Caldwell, Kansas, in 1952, Shannon acquired the knack for spinning yarns early in life, and by the seventh grade was writing his stories down. Throughout middle and high school Shannon's teachers encouraged his efforts at writing, and at college he continued his love affair with books and writing by studying children's literature and library science. He spent several years working as a children's librarian before devoting himself to storytelling and writing his own books for children beginning in 1978.

Shannon's first published work for children, *Lizard's Song,* is the tale of a lizard who sings joyfully of his unique place in the world and, after a foolish bear attempts to set up camp near his rock home rather than in a cave, teaches other animals to be equally celebratory of their own. A *Publishers Weekly* reviewer praised the picture book, which has also been translated for Spanish-speaking children, calling it "a jolly, amiable fancy about the value of finding one's own niche and being one's own self." *Lizard's Song,* which features the colorful illustrations of Jose Aruego and Ariane Dewey, has since been followed by two other sequels, both il-

lustrated by Aruego and Dewey. In *Lizard's Home,* which a *Publishers Weekly* contributor dubbed a "bouyant and affirming" tale, a snake decides that Lizard's rock makes the perfect home—without Lizard. The clever Lizard outwits the snake as easily as he had outwitted the bear in the previous volume, and sings a new song that Patricia Manning commented in *School Library Journal* "will roll off the tongue as trippingly as his original hit tune." *Lizard's Guest,* published in 2003, continues the saga of Shannon's small reptilian homebody.

The Piney Woods Peddler is an adaptation of the story of "Lucky Hans" collected by the Brothers Grimm. A trader on the road doing business resolves to bring his daughter home a silver dollar at the end of his travels; as his luck wanes, each of his trades brings in less than the one before, leaving him with only a silver dime. Fortunately the young daughter is cheerfully pleased with her father's small gift, providing a happy ending to a humorous story Ethel L. Heins described in *Horn Book* as "a repetitive, lilting tale that incorporates elements of traditional American swapping songs."

Shorter folktales also find their way into several collections by Shannon, among them *Stories to Solve: Folktales from around the World,* the sequel *More Stories to Solve,* and *True Lies: Eighteen Tales for You to Judge.* The last book contains short tales from all over the world, each story featuring a character who manages to trick others by twisting or omitting certain facts. Including detailed notes discussing each of the stories, Shannon creates a collection that has enough "brevity, humor, and accessible language" to attract even the most reluctant of readers, in the opinion of *School Library Journal* contributor Grace Oliff.

Relationships between family members are central to many of Shannon's tales for young people. A father and daughter await the moon in their flower garden in the poetic *Dancing the Breeze,* while *Climbing Kansas Mountains* finds Sam and his dad scaling a grain elevator in their native Kansas, from which height they can see the vast prairie stretching out before them. While Carol Fox found the latter story "more description than plot," she praised *Climbing Kansas Mountains* in her review for *Bulletin of the Center for Children's Books,* noting that the story's "tone is warm and intimate with childlike language and viewpoint." And in *This Is the Bird,* described by a *Kirkus* reviewer as "a moving tribute to familial bonds," a carved wooden bird links generations as it is passed from one family member to another. Close friendship is dealt with in *Seeds,* as young Warren moves away from neighboring artist and gardener Bill, but retains ties to his friend by planting a garden in Bill's honor at his new home. *Seeds* "is a warm, satisfying story about a different kind of friendship, about loss, and about new beginnings," noted Stephanie Zvirin in her *Booklist* review.

Animal characters take center stage in several of Shannon's stories. *Dance Away!* finds Rabbit with so much energy that he out-dances all of his friends; he also out-dances cunning Fox, who had planned to trap a rabbit for his supper but ultimately ends up trapped in Rabbit's choreography. And in *Laughing All the Way*, Duck has a pretty awful day, which reaches a low point when Bear decides to pluck the fowl's feathers and make a soft downy bed. Fortunately, Duck keeps his sense of humor and soon has Bear laughing so hard that he accidentally lets Duck go. "Children who love silliness, wordplay, and colorful language . . . will delight in this book," commented Lauralyn Persson in a *School Library Journal* review. Shannon's *Frog Legs* also promises plenty of silliness within its twenty-four poems that "hop, prance, and even can-can across the pages," according to *School Library Journal* interviewer Carol Schene. Enhanced by joyous pastel illustrations by Amit Trynan that depict frogs doing all sorts of child-like things, Shannon's verses more than keep pace, serving as "good fun" packaged in "small doses," according to *Booklist* contributor Stephanie Zvirin.

In addition to penning books for youngsters, Shannon is the author of the young-adult novel *Unlived Affections*, which won the Friends of American Writers award in 1990. It is the story of eighteen-year-old Willie Ramsey. After the death of his grandmother, who raised him since his mother was killed in a car accident when he was two, Willie is determined to break with his oppressive past, sell everything in the family home, and start a new life at college in Nebraska. While cleaning out his grandmother's things in preparation for the sale, Willie comes upon a trove of old letters, many written by his unknown father to his mother. The letters reveal that many things Willie was told about his family were untrue: his father did not desert his family but left because he was grappling with his sexual identity, and Willie's mother never told her husband that he had a son. "Shannon has a story to tell, and it is an unusual and moving one, full of secrets, lies, and dreams," commented Betsy Hearne in *Bulletin of the Center for Children's Books*. A *Publishers Weekly* reviewer called the novel's narrative "honest and concise," adding that "readers will be moved by the sensitive portrayal of each character and the tragedies they endure."

When Shannon tells stories before an audience it is like "writing out loud," with each telling slightly different, slightly unique, he once explained to *SATA*. Several of his books have sprung from the stories he has performed in public, repeated out loud many times prior to being committed to paper. An avid journal-keeper and letter-writer, Shannon also collects impressions, thoughts, and ideas that often make their way into his fiction. "I travel frequently to tell stories," he once noted, "and always at my side is the dog-eared journal filled with dreams, lines, phrases, plot snatches, and impressions that all feed into the next story I tell and the next book I write." "The sounds and rhythms of my stories are of major importance to me," Shannon also explained of his craft, "and I want them to flow on the tongue as if always being said aloud—always new to share."

Biographical and Critical Sources

BOOKS

Children's Books and Their Creators, edited by Anita Silvey, Houghton Mifflin (Boston, MA), 1991, p. 595.
Continuum Encyclopedia of Children's Literature, Continuum (New York, NY), 2001, pp. 712-713.

PERIODICALS

Booklist, December 1, 1981, p. 506; December 1, 1985, p. 574; February 15, 1991, p. 1203; June 1-15, 1994, Stephanie Zvirin, review of *Seeds,* pp. 1844-45; April 15, 1996, p. 1444; January 1, 2003, Linda Perkins, review of *Tippy-Toe Chick, Go!,* p. 910.
Bulletin of the Center for Children's Books, October, 1984, pp. 34-35; September, 1989, Betsy Hearne, review of *Unlived Affections,* p. 20; May, 1991, p. 226; January, 1994, Carol Fox, review of *Climbing Kansas Mountains,* p. 168; April, 1996, p. 279.
Horn Book, February, 1982, Ethel L. Heins, review of *The Piney Woods Peddler,* pp. 36-37; June, 1982, p. 283; September-October, 1990, p. 627; May-June, 1991, pp. 342-43; November-December, 1994, p. 750; May-June, 1995, p. 329; July, 2001, Roger Sutton, review of *More True Lies,* p. 465.
Junior Bookshelf, August, 1982, p. 129; June, 1983, p. 110; June, 1984, p. 120; February, 1986, p. 29.
Kirkus Reviews, April 1, 1981, p. 431; September 1, 1983, p. 155; August 1, 1989, p. 1168; April 15, 1991, p. 539; July 15, 1994, p. 995; April 15, 1995, p. 563; March 1, 1997, review of *This Is the Bird,* pp. 387-388; December 15, 2002, review of *Tippy-Toe Chick, Go!,* p. 1856.
Library Journal, August, 2001, Lucia M. Gonzalez, review of *Lizard's Song,* p. 27.
New York Times Book Review, July 14, 1996, p. 19.
Publishers Weekly, May 1, 1981, p. 67; September 11, 1981, review of *Lizard's Song,* p. 76; July 14, 1989, review of *Unlived Affections,* p. 80; August 9, 1993, p. 477; April 1, 1996, p. 76; September 13, 1999, review of *Lizard's Home,* p. 83; November 18, 2002, review of *Tippy-Toe Chick, Go!,* p. 59.
School Library Journal, October, 1992, Lauralyn Persson, review of *Laughing All the Way,* p. 95; May, 1996, p. 108; September, 1999, Patricia Manning, review of *Lizard's Home,* p. 206; June, 2000, Carol Schene, review of *Frog Legs,* p. 125; May, 2001, Grace Oliff, review of *More True Lies,* p. 146; February, 2003, Joy Fleishhacker, review of *Tippy-Toe Chick, Go!,* p. 122.*

*   *   *

SHEEN, Barbara 1949-

Personal

Born October 8, 1949, in Brooklyn, NY; daughter of Lester (a factory worker) and Marilyn (a homemaker) Sheen; married John Busby (a librarian/musician), August 5, 1980. *Education:* City University of New York, B.A., 1970; Long Island University, M.S., 1973. *Politics:* "Live and let live." *Religion:* Jewish. *Hobbies and other interests:* Swimming, weight training, reading, cooking.

Addresses

Office—905 Conway, #32, Las Cruces, NM 88005. *E-mail*—sheenbusby@hotmail.com.

Career

Freelance writer, 1972. Teacher in Texas and New Mexico, 1970-2003.

Member

International Woman's Writers Guild, Society of Children's Book Authors and Illustrators.

Awards, Honors

Dallas Hispanic Teacher of the Year, nominee, 1999; Disney Teacher of the Year, nominee, 2000.

Writings

Chemical Dependency ("Overview" series), Lucent (Detroit, MI), 2003.
Teen Alcoholism ("Teen Issues" series), Lucent (Detroit, MI), 2003.

"DISEASES AND DISORDERS" SERIES

Attention Deficit Disorder, Lucent (Detroit, MI), 2001.
Arthritis, Lucent (Detroit, MI), 2001.
Hepatitis, Lucent (Detroit, MI), 2002.
Asthma, Lucent (Detroit, MI), 2002.
Diabetes, Lucent (Detroit, MI), 2003.
Cerebral Palsy, Lucent (Detroit, MI), 2004.
Acne, Lucent (Detroit, MI), 2004.

Author of four collections of short stories for adults, two of which were translated into German. Many of her short stories have appeared in magazines and anthologies. Author of *We Learn English,* educational Spanish/English workbooks for Educational Insights, 1975.

Adaptations

The Traveling Animal Mariachi Singers, a bilingual Spanish/English folktale on audiotape, by SHOOFLY, 1990.

Work in Progress

A nonfiction book about Easter Island; a middle-grade novel, books on heart disease, headaches, and ovarian cancer for Lucent; research on herbs and folk remedies.

Sidelights

For three decades Barbara Sheen has been a teacher and writer, publishing works for both adults and children and earning honors for her teaching skills. "I love reading, writing and teaching, so writing nonfiction is a great way to combine my passions. I try to use my teaching ability to make complex material clear and interesting for my readers." At the turn of the millennium, Sheen published a handful of books in Lucent's "Diseases and Disorders" series. Yet, as she told *SATA,* she has plans to expand her scope: "Although, I've written lots of books in the health field, I'm interested in almost everything. I'm a curious person who loves doing research. It's exciting! Consequently, although I plan to continue writing health books in the future, I also hope to write about other subjects too."

Sheen has not limited herself to nonfiction, either. "I also enjoy writing fiction. Everywhere you look, there's a story waiting to be told," Sheen told *SATA.* During the 1970s, she wrote fiction for adults. Her many short stories appeared in magazines and were collected in anthologies and solo collections. Two books of her short stories were even translated into German and sold abroad. Having lived for many years in Texas and New Mexico, it comes as no surprise that Sheen should also be interested in the Spanish language and Southwestern culture. "I also enjoy retelling fairy tales and folk tales from a southwestern point of view," she said. "I use Spanglish, a combination of English and Spanish in these stories because they reflect the culture of the southwest, and because they are fun to read and write. In all my fiction, I try to let my sense of humor shine through. Neither I, nor my characters, take ourselves too seriously."

Biographical and Critical Sources

PERIODICALS

School Library Journal, September, 2001, Margaret C. Howell, review of *Attention Deficit Disorder,* p. 254.

*   *   *

STEWART, Sarah

Personal

Married David Small (an illustrator); children: Ginny, Mark, L.D. *Education:* "Studied Latin and philosophy at an unfortunate number of colleges and universities."

Addresses

Home—(summer) 25626 Simpson Road, Mendon, MI 49072; (winter) 17A Piedras Chinas, San Miguel de Allenda Gto. 37700, Mexico.

When a strange tree begins to sprout dollar bills in Miss McGillicuddy's yard, her neighbors' curiosity turns to greed. (From The Money Tree, *written by Sarah Stewart and illustrated by David Small.)*

Career

Writer; former teacher, speechwriter and ombudsman. Western Michigan University, Kalamazoo, MI, artist-in-residence, 2000.

Awards, Honors

ABBY Award Honor Book, Pick of the Lists, American Booksellers Association, Outstanding Book of the Year, *New York Times,* Notable Children's Book, *New York Times Book Review,* and Best book of the Year, *Parenting,* all 1995, all for *The Library;* One Hundred Titles for Reading and Sharing selection, New York Public Library, Best Books of the Year selection, *School Library Journal,* Blue Ribbon selection, *Bulletin of the Center for Children's Books,* Notable Children's Book, American Library Association (ALA), ABBY Award Honor Book, and First Place Juvenile Literary Award, Friends of American Writers, all 1997, Juvenile Literary Award, Friends of American Writers, 1997, and Caldecott Honor Book, 1998, Christopher Award and Vermont Red Clover Children's Choice Picture Book Award, all for *The Gardener;* Best Books of the Year selection, *Publishers Weekly,* Best Book, *School Library Journal,* Best Book, *Booklist,* Heartland Prize (children's category), Great Lakes Booksellers Association, and Riverbank Book of Distinction, all 2001, all for *The Journey.*

Writings

ILLUSTRATED BY HUSBAND, DAVID SMALL

The Money Tree, Farrar, Straus (New York, NY), 1991.
The Library, Farrar, Straus (New York, NY), 1995.
The Gardener, Farrar, Straus (New York, NY), 1997.
The Journey, Farrar, Straus (New York, NY), 2001.

Adaptations

The Gardener was adapted as an audio recording by Live Oak Media.

Sidelights

The husband and wife team of writer Sarah Stewart and illustrator David Small have collaborated on four books for all ages. Their first book together was *The Money Tree,* which takes place in an unusual garden. Miss McGillicuddy has grown a cash-sprouting tree, whose dollar-bill foliage attracts greedy officials and others hoping to scavenge the "greenery." But Miss McGillicuddy is not interested in the kind of wealth a money tree could bring. Instead, she comes up with a harvest-time solution that brings the town's rampant greed to an end: she chops down the tree and uses its wood to keep her warm all winter. While the message of materialism may evade some of the youngest readers, suggested a *Publishers Weekly* reviewer, the book "will raise worth-while questions for both children and adults."

The Library presents an independent-minded protagonist, Elizabeth Brown, whose affinity for reading begins in childhood and supercedes most other social activities through the years. Told in verse, the book relates how Elizabeth is happiest with a book and how she collects them copiously, hoping to read every book in existence. By the end of her long life, however, she finds that she has too many volumes to handle at home. Her solution is to turn her house into the Elizabeth Brown library and share her love of literature with the entire town. Ilene Cooper of *Booklist* praised *The Library* for its gentle humor and homey illustrations, noting that "reading has

In **The Library,** *Stewart tells the story of Elizabeth Brown, who is so obsessed with collecting books that she eventually turns her house into the town library. (Illustrated by David Small.)*

never looked quite so delicious." *Horn Book Magazine* contributor Ann A. Flowers called Stewart's effort a "deeply satisfying story," remarking that the images of a content Elizabeth sitting by the fire with a friend, working her way through stacks of books, "depict the acme of utter bliss for bibliomaniacs."

"Elizabeth Brown from *The Library* . . . would certainly appreciate Lydia Grace Finch," the protagonist of Stewart and Small's Caldecott Honor book *The Gardener,* declared Susan P. Bloom of *Horn Book Magazine.* "Each of these red-headed, spirited protagonists has a true passion—the one for books, the other for flowers." In the Depression-era tale *The Gardener,* Lydia Grace is introduced as a child in 1935. With her parents out of work, the girl is sent to live with her Uncle Jim, who is a baker in the city. Lydia's letters home comprise the text, which, according to a *Publishers Weekly* reviewer, conveys well "her utterly (and convincingly) sunny personality." Lydia Grace brings color and joy to her uncle's life by indulging in her favorite activity, gardening, though she never accomplishes her key goal, getting her loving but dour uncle to smile. The *Publishers Weekly* writer went on to note that the final scene, with Lydia wrapped in her uncle's goodbye hug as she prepares to return home, "speaks volumes about the vast impact one small individual can make." In the view of

Trish Wesley of *Horticulture,* the child serves a purpose in "sending positive messages about goals, patience, and the rewards of diligence."

A young girl also figures prominently in *The Journey,* which like *The Gardener* is told in epistolary form. The story records a trip to Chicago, which is a new experience for Hannah, an Amish child. Double-spread depictions of the big city are interspersed with memories of the home that Hannah has left behind. While a *Horn Book Magazine* contributor felt that *The Journey* didn't match the "emotional richness" of *The Gardener,* Wendy Lukehart of *School Library Journal* found more to recommend. *The Journey,* she said, "offers so much: a glimpse into Amish culture and Chicago treasures . . . [plus] a fresh authentic voice; and a design perfectly melded to its subtle message."

Stewart once commented: "There are no computers in my home, and the TV lives in a closet. I'm a very private person who writes and gardens (and then reads about writers and gardeners—and everything else under the sun!). I hope that the readers of my books will honor my privacy and understand that I need long periods of aloneness and silence, or I will not be able to hear the muse when she speaks."

A young girl from the country is sent to live with her uncle in the city, where she plants a rooftop garden. (From The Gardener, *illustrated by David Small.)*

In Stewart's The Journey, *an Amish girl named Hannah takes a trip to the city.* (*Illustrated by David Small.*)

Biographical and Critical Sources

PERIODICALS

Booklist, March 15, 1995, Ilene Cooper, review of *The Library,* p. 1338; June 1, 1997, Stephanie Zvirin, review of *The Gardener,* p. 1722; March 15, 2001, Ellen Mandel, review of *The Journey,* p. 1399.

Bulletin of the Center for Children's Books, May, 1995, Roger Sutton, review of *The Library,* pp. 323-324.

Five Owls, May, 1993, review of *The Money Tree,* p. 105.

Horn Book Magazine, January-February, 1992, Hanna Zeiger, review of *The Money Tree,* p. 62; July-August, 1995, Ann A. Flowers, review of *The Library,* p. 454; November-December, 1997, Susan P. Bloom, review of *The Gardener,* p. 673; March, 2001, Susan P. Bloom, review of *The Journey,* p. 202.

Horticulture, April, 1999, Trish Wesley, review of *The Gardener,* p. 98.

Publishers Weekly, April 10, 1995, review of *The Library,* p. 61; June 2, 1997, review of *The Gardener,* p. 70; January 8, 2001, review of *The Journey,* p. 66.

School Library Journal, January, 1992, *The Money Tree,* p. 83; September, 1995, Trev Jones, review of *The Library,* p. 187; September, 1996, Peggy Latkovich, review of *The Library,* p. 156; August, 1997, Virginia Golodetz, review of *The Gardener,* p. 143; March, 2001, Wendy Lukehart, review of *The Journey,* p. 220.

ONLINE

Highlights' TeacherNet, http://www.teachernet.com/ (March 11, 2003), Katherine Romano, interview with Sarah Stewart and David Small.*

STONE, Peter 1930-2003
(Peter Joshua, Pierre Marton)

OBITUARY NOTICE—See index for *SATA* sketch: Born February 27, 1930, in Los Angeles, CA; died of pulmonary fibrosis April 26, 2003, in Manhattan, NY. Author. Stone was best known as the author of books for musicals, winning Tony Awards for *1776, Woman of the Year,* and *Titanic,* though he was also acclaimed for his film and television work. The son of parents who both wrote for Hollywood, Stone earned his B.A. from Bard College in 1951 and his M.F.A. from Yale University in 1953. After graduating, he traveled to Paris, France, where he was a journalist and news reader for CBS radio and television. He returned to the United States in the late 1950s and began writing plays, his first being *Friend of the Family* (1958). He also wrote movie screenplays, and after his first film, the 1963 romantic comedy *Charade* starring Cary Grant and Audrey Hepburn, was produced he won an Oscar for the Grant comedy *Father Goose.* His first big Broadway hit was *1776* (1969) which he adapted three years later to film. Stone became well-known for his skill at adapting works to stage and screen, including the movies *Mirage* (1965) and *Sweet Charity* (1969), and the plays *Sugar* (1972), *Woman of the Year* (1981), and *Titanic* (1998). In addition to the Tonys mentioned above, his *The Will Rogers Follies* (1991) won a Tony for Best Musical, a Grammy, and a New York Drama Critics Circle award, his *Annie Get Your Gun* (1999) won a Tony for Best Musical Revival and a Grammy, and he won Drama Critics Circle and Drama Desk awards for *1776* (1969), as well as numerous other prizes. His most recent work included a play adaptation of *Finian's Rainbow* (2000), and the movies *Just Cause* (1995) and, under the pseudonym Peter Joshua, *The Truth about Charlie* (2002). Stone, who sometimes wrote under the pen name Pierre Marton, also wrote scripts for television, including *Asphalt Jungle* (1961), and the series *The Defenders* (1961-62) and *Adam's Rib* (1973-74).

OBITUARIES AND OTHER SOURCES:

BOOKS

Contemporary Dramatists, sixth edition, St. James (Detroit, MI), 1999.
Contemporary Theatre, Film, and Television, Volume 23, Gale (Detroit, MI), 1999.
Ganzl, Kurt, *Encyclopedia of the Musical Theatre,* second edition, Schirmer Books (New York, NY), 2001.

PERIODICALS

Chicago Tribune, May 1, 2003, Section 2, p. 12.
Los Angeles Times, April 29, 2003, p. B11.
New York Times, April 28, 2003, p. A25.
Washington Post, April 29, 2003, p. B6.

TIRONE SMITH, Mary-Ann 1944-

Personal

Born 1944. *Education:* Graduated from college, 1965.

Addresses

Home—CT. *Agent*—c/o Author Mail, Henry Holt and Co., 115 West 18th St., New York, NY 10011.

Career

U.S. Peace Corps, Washington, DC, volunteer in Buea, West Cameroon, c. 1965-67; writer.

Writings

The Book of Phoebe (young adult novel), Doubleday (Garden City, NY), 1985.
(With daughter, Katie Smith Milway) *Cappuccina Goes to Town* (juvenile), illustrated by Eugenie Fernandes, Kids Can Press (Toronto, Ontario, Canada), 2002.

FOR ADULTS

Lament for a Silver-Eyed Woman (novel), William Morrow and Co. (New York, NY), 1987.
The Port of Missing Men (novel), William Morrow and Co. (New York, NY), 1989.
Masters of Illusion (historical novel), Warner Books (New York, NY), 1994.
The American Killing (mystery novel), Henry Holt and Co. (New York, NY), 1998.
Love Her Madly (mystery novel), Henry Holt and Co. (New York, NY), 2002.
She's Not There: A Poppy Rice Novel (mystery novel), Henry Holt and Co. (New York, NY), 2003.

Contributor to books, including *Going Up Country: Travels Essays by Peace Corps Writers,* edited by John Coyne, Charles Scribner's Sons (New York, NY); and *From the Center of the Earth: Stories Out of the Peace Corps,* edited by Geraldine Kennedy, Clover Park Press.

Sidelights

Mary-Ann Tirone Smith told *SATA:* "I had an idyllic childhood as the first-born of two adoring parents. My father made certain I stayed in touch with his roots, those of a wheat farmer's son. I am certain my summer visits to the farm and my opportunity to ride a cow pony every day have an effect on my writing for children. My parents' faith in God and the words in the Bible have also shaped my life and lifestyle, and in turn, the themes I enjoy developing into children's stories—for example, being happy with who you are, making a true friend, overcoming shyness, being a good sport. *Cappuccina Goes to Town* is my first book coauthored with my dear daughter, Katie Smith Milway, a professional editor."

Biographical and Critical Sources

ONLINE

Mary-Ann Tirone Smith, http://www.tironesmith.com/ (March 7, 2003).

*   *   *

TOLBERT, Steve 1944-

Personal

Born January 3, 1944, in Inglewood, CA; immigrated to Australia, 1969; son of Bill and Marjorie (Robbins) Tolbert; married Sue (a teacher, maiden name, Hedges), January 14, 1978; children: Elise. *Education:* California State University at Long Beach, B.A., 1969; University of Western Australia, diploma of education, 1972. *Hobbies and other interests:* "Reading, viewing films, bike riding, kayaking, swimming, walking the dog and waving to the goldfish."

Addresses

Home and office—3 Honeywood Dr., Sandford, Tasmania, Australia. *E-mail*—stolbert@southcom.com.au.

Career

High school teacher in Sydney, New South Wales, Australia, 1970, Derby, Western Australia, Australia, 1971-74, Tasmania, Australia, 1975-2001. Author, 1991—.

Writings

Channeary, Pearson Education Australia (New South Wales, Australia), 1991.
Settling South, Pearson Education Australia (New South Wales, Australia), 1995.
Eyeing Everest, Pearson Education Australia (New South Wales, Australia), 1996.
Stepping Back, Pearson Education Australia (New South Wales, Australia), 1996.
Escape to Kalimantan, Pearson Education Australia (New South Wales, Australia), 1998.
Tracking the Dalai Lama, Pearson Education Australia (New South Wales, Australia), 2001.

Adaptations

Escape to Kalimantan was recorded by the Hear a Book Service (Tasmania).

Steve Tolbert

Work in Progress

Sorata, a novel of an Aighan asylum seeker.

Sidelights

Steve Tolbert, who grew up in Southern California and Seattle, emigrated to Australia in 1969, where as a high school teacher, he taught English, social studies and Indonesian for thirty years. During his tenure as a teacher, he also began to write successful novels, the first of which, *Channeary,* has become a staple in Australian classrooms for grades seven through nine. While a teacher, Tolbert strove to make his students more interested in Asia because he believes that Australia must take its place as an integral part of Asia. This interest also permeates his writings, a fact he noted at his Web site: "My stories have strong Asian themes and tend to deal with spiritualism, racism, culture clash and cultural adjustment. I often focus on an adolescent who has suffered some traumatic experience and needs some time and a lot of distance to try to come to terms with what has happened." Ever the teacher, Tolbert supplies study units for his young adult novels upon request at his Web site.

During his early years of honing his craft, Tolbert put his experience in the classroom to good use, as he told *SATA:* "Especially with *Channeary,* it's helped me with character models and realistic dialogue. I can remember jotting down notes, often in the middle of lessons, when likely ideas, or words cropped up." In his debut novel, *Channeary,* Tolbert tells the story of a Cambodian girl who must flee her home when the Khmer Rouge (communists) take over her village. In her flight for survival she eventually ends up in Tasmania. In researching his novels, Tolbert visits the settings of his stories. Although he uses published resources of research, he finds "the most important research has always been visiting places where I'd like to set stories." To this end he has traveled in many Asian countries, including India, Nepal, Indonesia, The Philippines, Malaysia, and Vietnam.

Settling South, although set entirely in Australia, has a connection to Vietnam in main character Tim's father, a Vietnam-crazed recluse. Based loosely on a real-life event, the story revolves around Tim, who has gone to live with his mentally ill father after the death of his mother. In a dramatic episode, Tim escapes from his father's bush house, fleeing by motorbike south to Dover, Tasmania. While this novel was based on another's story, Tolbert's next novel, *Eyeing Everest,* was semi-autobiographical and one that remains closest to his heart. In this novel, teenager Meika yearns for her father, who left Australia for Nepal after her parents' divorce. When Meika's mother commits suicide, the girl searches out her long-lost father. About his own life, the author jokingly states at his Web site, "Apparently I cried a lot as a baby and a few months later my parents split up. My father went to Alaska where he has lived a semi-reclusive wilderness life ever since; while my mother stayed to live the big city life." Yet to *SATA* he revealed more tender feelings about *Eyeing Everest:* "Change the Vietnam War to World War II, Nepal for Alaska, and the story closely mimics my own father's life." In researching the setting for the novel, Tolbert walked up the Everest Track to the Tengpoche Monastery.

Published the year after *Settling South, Stepping Back* tells the romantic story of a Cambodian girl, Somaly, who has grown up as a refugee in Tasmania, and a traumatized Cambodian boy, Keo, who return to their war-ravaged homeland. Conversely, in Tolbert's next novel, *Escape to Kalimantan,* the subject is evasion. When

Jack's family is devastated by the accidental death of his sister and separation of his parents, the young man attempts to help his father. Because his father is a wildlife enthusiast, Jack persuades him to visit Kalimantan, one of the world's most impressive sources of animal and plant life. In a similar vein, *Tracking the Dalai Lama* revolves around Jess, who dealing with a tragedy, visits Northern India and Tibet with her father. During their trip the duo meets the Dalai Lama, the exiled spiritual leader of Tibet, whom Jess's father, a journalist, was to interview. In her *Magpies* review of *Tracking the Dalai Lama,* Barbara James noted Tolbert's portrayal of the uniqueness of Tibetan culture and use of a real-life personage in this "quite engrossing" novel.

Tolbert described his writing habits to *SATA:* "I try to write a few hours most every week-day morning. If I'm 'running hot' with an idea, or some revision, I'm likely to extend the time into the afternoon, or to weekends. But by late afternoon, I have to re-engage with the everyday world: the woodfire has to be lit, meals prepared, the goldfish and dog fed, wife and daughter debriefed, drinks provided." He suggests to new writers: "Write for yourself first," and "quickly develop a rhino-thick skin. Set aside a space on the wall for rejection notices. Always have a good bottle of wine available, and enjoy the moment in every conceivable way if a manuscript is praised and/or accepted for publishing."

Biographical and Critical Sources

PERIODICALS

Magpies, November, 2001, Barbara James, review of *Tracking the Dalai Lama,* pp. 41-42.

ONLINE

Steve Tolbert Web site, http://www.southcom.com.au/ ~stolbert/ (June 21, 2002).

W

WAYLAND, April Halprin 1954-

Personal

Born April 20, 1954, in Los Angeles, CA; daughter of Leahn J. (a farmer) and Saralee (a concert pianist; maiden name, Konigsberg) Halprin; married Gary Carlton Wayland (a certified public accountant), October 17, 1981; children: Jeffrey. *Education:* University of California—Davis, B.S. (cum laude), 1976. *Religion:* Jewish.

Addresses

Home—143 South Kenter Ave., Los Angeles, CA 90049. *Agent*—Curtis Brown, Ltd., 10 Astor Place, New York, NY 10003.

Career

Children's book writer and speaker. Worked variously as a farmer, a government housing study worker for the RAND Corporation, a governess for comedian and talk show host Joan Rivers' daughter, and a marketing manager for Pacific Bell. Cofounder, Positive Education, Inc. (nonprofit tutorial agency).

Member

Authors Guild, Authors League of America, PEN, Society of Children's Book Writers and Illustrators, Association of Booksellers for Children, Southern California Children's Booksellers Association, Southern California Council on Literature for Children and Young People, Santa Monica Traditional Folk Music Club (founder, 1978).

Awards, Honors

To RabbitTown was named a Junior Literary Guild selection, 1989, and was selected as a "Book of the Year" by Mommycare.

Writings

To RabbitTown, illustrated by Robin Spowart, Scholastic (New York, NY), 1989.

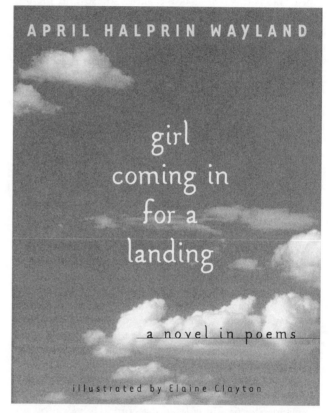

A teen records a year of her life in poems in Girl Coming in for a Landing, *written by April Halprin Wayland. (Book jacket photograph by Craig Aurness.)*

The Night Horse, illustrated by Vera Rosenberry, Scholastic (New York, NY), 1991.
It's Not My Turn to Look for Grandma!, illustrated by George Booth, Knopf (New York, NY), 1995.
Girl Coming in for a Landing: A Novel in Poems, illustrated by Elaine Clayton, Random House (New York, NY), 2002.

Contributor to anthologies edited by Myra Cohn Livingston, including *Poems for Mothers,* Margaret McElderry Books (New York, NY), 1990; *If the Owl*

Calls Again, Margaret McElderry Books (New York, NY), 1990; *Poems for Brothers, Poems for Sisters,* Holiday House (New York, NY), 1991; and *Roll Along: Poems on Wheels,* Margaret McElderry Books (New York, NY), 1993.

Adaptations

Wayland's stories for children were adapted for radio broadcast on *Halfway down the Stairs,* KPFK-FM.

Work in Progress

"A billion books."

Sidelights

April Halprin Wayland is the author of several picture books for young readers, as well as *Girl Coming in for a Landing: A Novel in Poems,* a book for older readers that a *Kirkus* reviewer described as "utterly fresh and winning." In the picture books *The Night Horse* and *It's Not My Turn to Look for Grandma!* she explores children's relationships to animals using humor and whimsy. "I see my books as mixtures of colors," she once explained to *SATA.* "I want each to be as clear and as strong and as beautiful as it can be. I love the picture book format."

"To rebel in my family, you had to join management in a Fortune 500 company and wear a suit every day," Wayland once quipped. The daughter of a farmer and a concert pianist, Wayland grew up in Santa Monica, California, and spent her holidays and vacations at the family farm in Yuba City, five hundred miles north. While she began writing when she was thirteen years old, music was also an abiding interest; she played violin as a child and founded the Santa Monica Traditional Folk Music Club in her twenties.

After graduating from college, Wayland held an assortment of jobs. She helped run the family farm after her father's death, worked as a governess, and co-founded a nonprofit tutorial organization called Positive Education, Inc. She finally entered the corporate world by going to work for Pacific Bell, where she became a marketing manager. Despite the job security, she still held dreams of becoming a writer, and after creating a picture book for her nephew, Joshua, she was hooked. "It wasn't brilliant literature, but I illustrated, xeroxed, laminated, and bound it," she recalled. "The night I finished it, I was so jazzed, I couldn't sleep."

Wayland published *To RabbitTown,* her first book for children, in 1989, and has continued to add to the list in the years since. *To RabbitTown* follows a young girl who is magically transformed into a rabbit, while *The Night Horse* is a gentle tale of another young girl who travels through the night sky on a horse who feeds on the stars. Wayland's 1995 picture book *It's Not My Turn to Look for Grandma!* introduces young listeners to Woolie, whose grandmother can never be found when there is work to be done around the house. While Ma asks Woolie and his siblings to fetch the elderly woman to help with chores throughout the day, each child comes back empty-handed until the evening, when Ma asks fun-loving Grandma to pluck a tune on her banjo—words and music included! Praising the story's "lively mountain twang," *School Library Journal* reviewer Virginia E. Jeschelnig called *It's Not My Turn to Look for Grandma!* a "silly good time for all," while a *Kirkus Reviews* critic dubbed it a story with "so much pep readers will swear it's been handed down for generations."

In 2002 Wayland expanded into the novel format by penning *Girl Coming in for a Landing.* Written in free verse, the book follows a young teen's high school year. In what *Booklist* contributor Gillian Engberg called a "warm and authentic" voice, Wayland describes such universal female coming-of-age experiences as a first crush, boredom, sibling rivalry, shyness, starting to shave one's legs, getting one's period, and dreaming about the future—in a text that Engberg noted "get[s] right to the heart of situations and emotions." Praising Wayland for adding a section on reading and writing verse that provides encouragement to teens who would "otherwise find these tasks intimidating," a *Publishers Weekly* contributor maintained that *Girl Coming in for a Landing* successfully reflects "the voice of a sensitive girl approaching adolescence."

Wayland once remarked, "I can't say enough about the community of children's book writers in Southern California. Teachers have become mentors and friends—everyone generously shares his/her knowledge. I thrive in groups, and this community (in addition to my husband) has had much to do with the joy I find in my career." She added, "I once decided that I wanted to publish 133 children's books by my ninetieth birthday. Then I re-read *Charlotte's Web* by E. B. White and I realized that *one* wonderful book was enough. So my new goal is to write each book as brilliantly as I can."

Biographical and Critical Sources

PERIODICALS

Booklist, October 15, 2002, Gillian Engberg, review of *Girl Coming in for a Landing,* p. 400.

Kirkus Reviews, May 15, 1995, review of *It's Not My Turn to Look for Grandma!,* p. 717; June 15, 2002, review of *Girl Coming in for a Landing,* p. 889.

Publishers Weekly, January 13, 1989, p. 87; June 26, 1995, review of *It's Not My Turn to Look for Grandma!,* p. 106; July 8, 2002, review of *Girl Coming in for a Landing,* p. 50.

School Library Journal, April, 1989, p. 92; April, 1991, p. 104; August, 1995, Virginia E. Jeschelnig, review of *It's Not My Turn to Look for Grandma!,* p. 131; August, 2002, Lauralyn Persson, review of *Girl Coming in for a Landing,* p. 220.

ONLINE

April Halprin Wayland Web site, http://www.aprilwayland.
com/ (June 29, 2003).*

*   *   *

WELTON, Jude 1955-

Personal

Born February 13, 1955, in Hythe, England; daughter
of John and Audrey Welton; partner of David Edgar (a
university lecturer); children: John James. *Education:*
Nottingham University, B.A. (honors first class), 1976
and M.A., 1980.

Addresses

Office—c/o Author Mail, Dorling Kindersley, 9 Henri-
etta St., Covent Garden, London WC2E 8PS, England.

Career

Author of books for young adults. Worked in a
children's home, 1976-78; Marshall Cavendish, London, England, editor, 1981-88; George Philip Ltd., London, editor, 1989; freelance author, 1990—.

Writings

"EYEWITNESS ART" SERIES

Monet, Dorling Kindersley (New York, NY), 1993.
Impressionism, Dorling Kindersley (New York, NY), 1993.
Looking at Paintings, Dorling Kindersley (New York, NY),
    1994.
Gauguin, Dorling Kindersley (New York, NY), 1994.

"ARTISTS IN THEIR TIME" SERIES

Henri Matisse, Franklin Watts (New York, NY), 2002.
Marc Chagall, Franklin Watts (New York, NY), 2003.

OTHER

Impressionist Gardens, Studio Editions, 1993.
Impressionist Landscapes, Studio Editions, 1993.
Mothers in Art, Studio Editions, 1994.
Drawing: A Young Artist's Guide, Dorling Kindersley
    (London, England), 1994.

Contributor to children's literature series *Classic Adventure,* and periodicals, including *Discovering Opera.*

Sidelights

Author Jude Welton has contributed books to several
children's series about art, including "Eyewitness Art"
and "Artists in Their Time." Both series and her non-

series titles intend to introduce children to the basics of
appreciating art and artists, and creating their own art,
as she explained to *SATA:* "My aim is to introduce art
and literature to children and adults who have no specialist knowledge. It is my hope that they will come to
enjoy and truly appreciate the arts."

Several of Welton's books deal with Impressionism,
which is a style of painting that involves expressing
subtle nuances of color and light in the outdoors, and
styles that derived from it. Nineteenth-century French
painter Claude Monet, the subject of her first book, is
remembered as one of the originators of Impressionism
and gave the name to the movement with his 1874
painting *Impressionism: soleil levant* (Impression of a
Sun Rise). Using dabs of primary colors, impressionist
artists sought to approximate the hue of reflected light
and the cheerier aspects of the world. Their paintings
are generally of a light and pleasant nature and are
more concerned with bright emotion than realistic
depiction. Writing about *Monet,* a critic for *Kirkus Reviews* called Welton's book "admirably lucid" and
termed it "invaluable" to those seeking an understanding of art history.

An offshoot of Impressionism was the *fauvism,* or
"wild" use of color employed by such artists as Frenchman Henri Matisse and Russian-born Frenchman Marc
Chagall, who are subjects of later works by Welton.

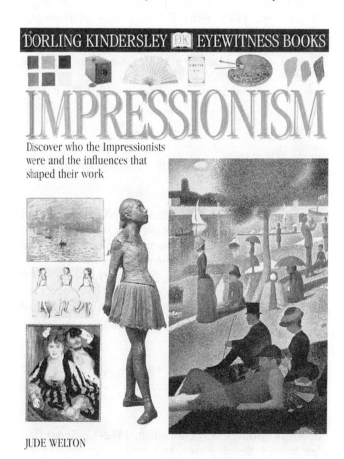

*Jude Welton examines key events in the Impressionist
movement and discusses important artists.*

Frenchman Paul Gauguin, as Welton explains, made an even greater departure from Impressionism in his works, which harked back to European folkloric painting and then to the primitive art of the Caribbean islands, to which he emigrated. With his art, Gauguin demonstrated the validity of using primitive art as a basis for aesthetic experiment.

On a practical plan, Welton created *Drawing: A Young Artist's Guide* to offer children a "creative example that both instructs and inspires," according to *RQ*'s Betty Porter. Using examples from the Tate Gallery in London, she introduces readers to aspects of outline and pattern, color, light and shade, texture, perspective, and composition, as would an art teacher. She encourages children to bring their imaginations to bear on their work as they attempt progressively more difficult art projects.

Biographical and Critical Sources

PERIODICALS

Booklist, May 1, 1993, p. 1562; summer, 1995, Kay Weisman, review of *Drawing: A Young Artist's Guide,* p. 927.
Books for Keeps, March, 1993, p. 21.
Kirkus Reviews, June 1, 1993, p. 729.
RQ, summer, 1995, Betty Porter, review of *Drawing,* p. 526.
School Library Journal, February, 1993, p. 109; May, 1993, p. 144; March, 1995, Alexandra Morris, review of *Drawing,* p. 220.
Times Educational Supplement, February 19, 1993, p. R8.*

*   *   *

WOOLDRIDGE, Connie Nordhielm 1950-

Personal

Born June 16, 1950, in Asheville, NC; daughter of Berndt Evald (a corporate executive) and Naomi (a homemaker; maiden name, Harris) Nordhielm; married Carl Wooldridge (an orthopedic surgeon), July 23, 1977; children: Christina, Scott, Sean, Eric. *Ethnicity:* "Swedish-American." *Education:* Mount Holyoke College, B.A., 1972; University of Chicago, M.L.S. and M.A., 1977. *Politics:* Republican. *Religion:* Lutheran.

Addresses

Home—1831 South B St., Richmond, IN 47374. *E-mail*—connwood@infocom.com.

Career

American Airlines, flight attendant, 1972-73; Seoul Foreign School, Seoul, Korea, first grade teacher, 1973-75; Sieden Prairie Elementary School, Matteson, IL, school librarian, 1977-78; freelance writer, 1978—.

Connie Nordhielm Wooldridge

Awards, Honors

Blue Ribbon Book designation, *Bulletin of the Center for Children's Books,* and best books selection, *School Library Journal,* both 1995, and Irma S. and James H. Black Award, Bank Street College of Education, 1996, all for *Wicked Jack.*

Writings

Wicked Jack, illustrated by Will Hillenbrand, Holiday House (New York, NY), 1995.
(Reteller) *The Legend of Strap Buckner: Texas Tale,* illustrated by Andrew Glass, Holiday House (New York, NY), 2001.
When Esther Morris Headed West: Women, Wyoming, and the Right to Vote, illustrated by Jacqueline Rogers, Holiday House (New York, NY), 2001.

Contributor to periodicals, including *Cricket* and *Highlights for Children.*

Work in Progress

Thank You Very Much, Captain Ericsson, Holiday House (New York, NY); *Elisha the Prophet-Man,* Holiday House (New York, NY); a biography of Edith Wharton, for readers ages twelve to fifteen.

Sidelights

"There are certain characters who flat out demand to have their stories told," Connie Nordhielm Wooldridge once told *SATA.* "Wicked Jack was one of them." After working as a school teacher and librarian for several years, Wooldridge finally brought this folk character to life. With his roots in the Southern folk tales anthologized by such writers as Richard Chase and Zora Neale Hurston, Wicked Jack became the title character of Wooldridge's first picture book.

Wooldridge was first introduced to the story of Wicked Jack while she was attending college classes. A blacksmith so full of spite that he even teaches the Devil a thing or two, Wicked Jack spends his time finding ways to make other people miserable. He finally gets his comeuppance after he slips up and is accidentally nice to a crippled old man who turns out to be Saint Peter. Jack is granted three wishes; they cause so much trouble that the evil-doer ends up getting kicked out of both Heaven and Hell, and Wicked Jack is forced to wander through the swamps for the rest of eternity. "Somebody should write that down," Wooldridge remembered thinking when she first heard this humorous tale. But it would

be years later—after she had written several stories for magazines like *Cricket* and *Highlights for Children*—that she began to imagine the voice of the folk character Jack insisting, "Why don't you write my story?"

"Because I'm a good Lutheran," Wooldridge would always answer the twangy Southern voice inside her head, "and I make it a point to avoid characters like you." That wasn't the end of it, though. "I'd underestimated his persistence," the author explained to *SATA*. "Every time I came upon a collection of Southern folktales, I'd look to see if Jack was in it. Phrases started to come to mind that would be perfect for this or that part of the story . . . if I wrote it down, which I wouldn't."

The summer of 1989 found Wooldridge and her family on vacation in the beautiful Smoky Mountains of North Carolina. "When we wandered into a tourist shop, I walked straight over to the book section and picked up one of Richard Chase's folktale collections as if I knew

In **When Esther Morris Headed West: Women, Wyoming, and the Right to Vote,** *Wooldridge tells the story of Esther Morris, who became a Justice of the Peace. (Illustrated by Jacqueline Rogers.)*

it was there." The story of Wicked Jack was featured in the book, and Wooldridge bought the collection "on the spot."

"He was wearing me down—I recognized that—but I wasn't giving in yet. 'I'll give your story words,' I conceded when I got back home, 'but then you're going straight into my file drawer. I'm not . . . turning you loose on the world.'" She wrote the first half of *Wicked Jack* in a few hours: "I laughed out loud as I typed," Wooldridge remembered. The second half of the story went less quickly. "Even though it was a made-up folktale, I was uncomfortable with Saint Peter as the sole proprietor of heaven. I made some small changes that left the distinct impression Saint Peter got his list of approved entrants from a Higher Power: someone even Jack didn't dare to argue with." *Wicked Jack* was soon in the mail to its future publisher. "I didn't even consider putting it in the file drawer," the author noted. "I think it would have leaped out if I'd tried."

The day *Wicked Jack* arrived in the mail was a special one for Wooldridge—she finally held in her hands her first published book. "On the day I received the brown package that held the finished copies of my book, I felt a moment of panic before I tore it open," she admitted. "What would the illustrator (someone I didn't know and who didn't know Jack) have done to my crusty old friend? When I saw the cover, all I could do was smile. That old coot Jack! When he'd finished bugging me about writing, he must have trucked on over to Ohio and gotten acquainted with his illustrator. I knew from the pictures in the book that his manners had definitely not improved; he had shown [illustrator] Will Hillenbrand his true colors."

Wicked Jack has received much praise from reviewers; Lauralyn Persson noted in *School Library Journal* that *Wicked Jack* is "one of those great spooky-funny books where [readers are] laughing too hard to ever be really scared." And, calling it a "pleasingly tart tale," a *Publishers Weekly* reviewer praised *Wicked Jack* as "intelligent and fun, with a moral thrown in for good measure." A *Kirkus Reviews* critic described Wooldridge's picture book as "stunning," going on to say that she "narrates the story in the voice of a toothless storyteller."

Though Wooldridge had gotten Jack onto paper and out of her head, he wasn't the only folk character who would demand her attention. Soon, Wooldridge was writing the story of Strap Buckner, a "genius" of a man who would knock people down when he met them in *The Legend of Strap Buckner: Texas Tale.* As one of the original "Old Three Hundred" settlers of Texas, Strap Buckner was said to have been a huge man who got into a contest of strength with the devil. Woodridge and

her illustrator, Andrew Glass, "concoct a truly larger-than-life-character," according to a contributor to *Kirkus Reviews,* who continued, "Wooldridge has an excellent way with words." Mary Elam of *School Library Journal* called the book a "faithful interpretation" of the folk tale.

Wooldridge's next subject was a woman out of history rather than out of folk tales. In *When Esther Morris Headed West,* she tackled the story of Esther Morris, the woman largely responsible for getting the vote for women in Wyoming in 1869, years before women could vote anywhere else in the world. Not only did Morris win the right to vote (as doing so had "no ill effects on a woman's health," according to her doctor), but the next year became a Justice of the Peace. "Spicing her prose with a down-home twang, Wooldridge . . . pulls a plum out of the pie of American history," wrote a *Publishers Weekly* contributor. Though Catherine Threadgill in *School Library Journal* noted that some of the historical facts that shaped the story are left out, she noted that "Wooldridge tells Morris's story with wit and dignity." A *Kirkus Reviews* critic praised that the story of *When Esther Morris Headed West* is "told as the rollicking tale it is."

Shortly after the publication of *Wicked Jack,* Wooldridge commented to *SATA* about why she loves writing: "Putting ideas into words can make all sorts of things come out right," she remarked. "Jack got his story told, God was just and in His heaven, and a good Lutheran had made peace with a scoundrel from the swamp. I suppose that's why I'm a writer."

Biographical and Critical Sources

PERIODICALS

Booklist, November 1, 1995, p. 475; July, 2001, Gillian Engberg, review of *The Legend of Strap Buckner,* p. 2015.
Bulletin of the Center for Children's Books, December, 1995, p. 145.
Kirkus Reviews, September 1, 1995, review of *Wicked Jack,* p. 1290.
Publishers Weekly, October 2, 1995, review of *Wicked Jack,* p. 73; August 1, 2001, review of *The Legend of Strap Buckner,* p. 1135; August 15, 2001, review of *When Esther Morris Headed West: Women, Wyoming, and the Right to Vote,* p. 1224; September 10, 2001, review of *When Esther Morris Headed West,* p. 91.
School Library Journal, December, 1995, Lauralyn Persson, review of *Wicked Jack,* p. 101; September, 2001, Mary Elam, review of *The Legend of Strap Buckner,* p. 222; September, 2001, Catherine Threadgill, review of *When Esther Morris Headed West,* p. 222.*

Y-Z

YAGHER, Kevin 1962-

Personal

Born June 23, 1962, in Decatur, IL; son of Charles, Jr. (an electrical engineer) and Carol Y. (a physician's assistant) Yagher; married Catherine Hicks (an actress), May 19, 1990; children: Caitlin M.

Addresses

Office—Kevin Yagher Productions, Inc., 6615 Valjean Ave., Van Nuys, CA 91406.

Career

Kevin Yagher Productions, Inc. (producers of special makeup effects for film and television), Van Nuys, CA, president, 1985—. Also works as film director, producer, and writer; special effects creator and coproducer of the film *Sleepy Hollow,* released by Paramount Pictures in 1999; also creator and designer of the puppets Chucky and Tiffany for the film *Bride of Chucky;* makeup designer for actor Johnny Depp in the film *Blow;* creator of puppet torsos for sequels to the film *Matrix;* creator and designer of all makeup disguises for actor Dana Carvey in the film *Master of Disguise;* creator of phantom makeup for the film *Phantom of the Opera,* creature suits and other effects for *Bill and Ted's Bogus Journey,* makeup effects for Freddy Krueger in sequels to *Nightmare on Elm Street,* and makeup effects for numerous films, including *Glory, Starship Troopers, Face-Off, The Fan, Man's Best Friend, Windtalkers, Cradle 2 the Grave,* and numerous others. Creator and designer of the Cryptkeeper character for the television series and related films based on *Tales from the Crypt* and for the music video "Crypt Jam;" also director of episodes of the series *Tales from the Crypt.* Director of makeup effects for the Aerosmith music video "Pink—1997" and the "Weird Al" Yankovic video "Fat."

Member

International Alliance of Theatrical Stage Employees, Screen Actors Guild, Directors Guild of America, Writers Guild of America.

Awards, Honors

Emmy Award, outstanding direction, National Academy of Television Arts and Sciences, 1992, for "World Championship Boxing," *The Crypt Keeper;* Film Award nomination (with others), achievement in special visual effects, British Academy of Film and Television Arts, 1999, and Hollywood Makeup and Hairstylist Guild Award, best character makeup in a motion picture, 2000, both for *Sleepy Hollow.*

Writings

(And illustrator) *Heverly* (picture book), North-South Books (New York, NY), 2001.

Coauthor (and director) of "Strung Along," an episode of the television series *Tales from the Crypt,* Home Box Office; coauthor (and producer and director) of *Road Hogs,* a television pilot, USA Network.

Adaptations

The feature film *Sleepy Hollow,* released by Paramount Pictures in 1999, was based on a story by Yagher and Andrew Kevin Walker.

Sidelights

Kevin Yagher's Hollywood experience as a master of special effects and his long association with the fantasy/science fiction film genre provided a solid foundation for his first book. *Heverly* is the story of an elf, Prince Eli, who has been exiled from his homeland of Heverly.

When he learns that his father the king is dying and his evil uncle Thornshackle is plotting to steal the throne, Eli decides he must return to save the kingdom. Many perils await him in the Valley of the Skulls through which he must pass, including an evil witch and a three-headed serpent. Eli rides into danger on the tail of a dragonfly who has the power to protect the young prince. After much travail, Eli reaches the kingdom in time to receive forgiveness from his father and ultimately to end the evil threat to his home. A *Publishers Weekly* contributor noted that "the nonstop action generates genuine excitement."

The memorable achievement of *Heverly* may be its unique illustrations. Yagher's characters are tiny, meticulously detailed, three-dimensional models that he created and posed, set against equally realistic backdrops. Yagher's photography, enhanced by computerized effects, adds a cinematic element to the action of the plot, reviewers noted. The *Publishers Weekly* reviewer called it "creepily realistic," from the characters themselves to settings like the "magical tinderwater ice cavern." *School Library Journal* writer John Peters also praised the illustrations: "The tiny, strong-featured figurines are all exquisitely detailed, wonderfully heroic or icky as appropriate."

Yagher told *SATA:* "As long as I can remember, I have been fascinated with folk stories about little people and miniature creatures. As a child some of my favorite books were Beverly Cleary's *The Mouse and the Motorcycle,* E. B. White's *Stuart Little,* and Mary Norton's *The Borrowers.* Other stories that interested me were Irish folk tales of little people such as elves and leprechauns. As a young child I even had a make-believe friend that was only six inches tall. Ever since, I've wanted to write a story of my own that had characters who were small in size. My children's book, *Heverly,* was the outcome of that desire.

"I have made a living as a special effects makeup and creature designer in the motion picture industry. I have worked on such films as *Master of Disguise, Mission Impossible II,* and *Face Off* to name a few. I also directed television presentations, like episodes of the Home Box Office series *Tales from the Crypt.*

"The knowledge and artistic abilities that I have learned in the film industry helped me in illustrating my children's books. Most picture books are illustrated using paintings or pencil drawings. I decided to create three-dimensional models of my storybook characters and miniature sets to place them in. Once everything was completed, I used film lighting to illuminate each illustrated scene, and I photographed them.

"I continue to work in film, but I am currently pursuing what interests me the most . . . children's book projects."

Biographical and Critical Sources

PERIODICALS

Publishers Weekly, August 13, 2001, review of *Heverly,* p. 312.
School Library Journal, September, 2001, John Peters, review of *Heverly,* p. 209.

ONLINE

Kevin Yagher Productions, http://kevinyagher.com/ (September 6, 2002).

* * *

YEE, Paul (R.) 1956-

Personal

Born October 1, 1956, in Spalding, Saskatchewan, Canada; son of Gordon and Gim May (Wong) Yee. *Education:* University of British Columbia, B.A., 1978, M.A., 1983. *Hobbies and other interests:* Cycling, swimming.

Addresses

Home—2 Abermarle Avenue, Toronto, Ontario, Canada M4K 1H7. *E-mail*—paulryee@interlog.com.

Career

Writer. City of Vancouver Archives, Vancouver, British Columbia, Canada, assistant city archivist, 1980-88; Archives of Ontario, Toronto, Ontario, Canada, portfolio manager, 1988-91; Ontario Ministry of Citizenship, policy analyst, 1991-97.

Member

Writers Union of Canada, CANSCAIP.

Awards, Honors

Honourable Mention, Canada Council Prizes for Children's Literature, 1986, for *The Curses of Third Uncle;* Vancouver Book Prize, 1989, for *Saltwater City;* British Columbia Book Prize for Children's Literature, I.O.D.E. Violet Downey Book Award, Sheila A. Egoff Children's Book Prize, and Parents' Choice Honor, all 1990, all for *Tales from Gold Mountain;* Ruth Schwartz Award, Canadian Booksellers Association, 1992, for *Roses Sing on New Snow,* and 1997, for *Ghost Train;* Governor General's Award, Canada Council, 1996, and Prix Enfantasie (Switzerland), 1998, for *Ghost Train;* YALSA, Best books for Young Adult List, 1998, for *Breakaway;* Books for the Teenage List, New York Public Library, 2003, for *Dead Man's Gold.*

Paul Yee

Writings

FICTION FOR CHILDREN AND YOUNG ADULTS

Teach Me to Fly, Skyfighter!, and Other Stories, illustrated by Sky Lee, Lorimer (Toronto, Ontario, Canada), 1983.

The Curses of Third Uncle (novel), Lorimer (Toronto, Ontario, Canada), 1986.

Tales from Gold Mountain: Stories of the Chinese in the New World, illustrated by Simon Ng, Groundwood Books (Toronto, Ontario, Canada), 1989, Macmillan (New York, NY), 1990.

Roses Sing on New Snow: A Delicious Tale, illustrated by Harvey Chan, Macmillan (New York, NY), 1991.

Breakaway (novel), Groundwood Books (Toronto, Ontario, Canada), 1994.

Moonlight's Luck, illustrated by Terry Yee, Macmillan (New York, NY), 1995.

Ghost Train, illustrated by Harvey Chan, Groundwood Books (New York, NY), 1996.

The Boy in the Attic, illustrated by Gu Xiong, Groundwood Books (Toronto, Ontario, Canada), 1998.

Dead Man's Gold and Other Stories, illustrated by Harvey Chan, Douglas & McIntyre (Toronto, Ontario, Canada), 2002.

The Jade Necklace, illustrated by Grace Lin, Interlink, 2002.

NONFICTION

Saltwater City: An Illustrated History of the Chinese in Vancouver, Douglas & McIntyre (Vancouver, British Columbia, Canada), 1988, University of Washington (Seattle, WA), 1989.

Struggle and Hope: The Story of Chinese Canadians, Umbrella Press (Toronto, Ontario, Canada), 1996.

Yee's books have been translated into several languages, including French.

Adaptations

Roses Sing on New Snow was adapted as a videocassette produced by the National Film Board of Canada, 2002.

Work in Progress

Bamboo (picture book), expected publication, 2004; *A Song for Ba* (picture book), expected publication, 2004; *Chinatowns: Chinese Communities Across Canada* (nonfiction), expected publication, 2005.

Sidelights

Paul Yee is a Canadian author whose Chinese heritage and experiences growing up in the Chinatown region of Vancouver, British Columbia, have inspired many of his highly acclaimed books for younger readers. While writing primarily for Canadian children of Chinese ancestry who desire to learn about themselves and their heritage, his books have found audiences with children of many backgrounds from both Canada and the United States. Among Yee's books are the short-story collections *Tales from Gold Mountain: Stories of the Chinese in the New World* and *Dead Man's Gold and Other Stories,* as well as a number of picture books and the novels *Breakaway* and *The Curses of Third Uncle.* Despite his relatively small output, "by fusing the unique details of ethnic experience with the universal concerns for identity and love," a *Canadian Children's Books* essayist maintained, Yee has "made a notable contribution to Canadian children's literature."

Born in Spalding, Saskatchewan, in 1956, Yee had what he once termed a "typical Chinese-Canadian childhood, caught between two worlds, and yearning to move away from the neighborhood." While he wrote short stories as a hobby, he never considered making writing his profession. Instead, after graduating from high school he went on to the University of British Columbia, and ultimately earned his M.A. in history in 1983. Although Yee has taught informally at several institutions in British Columbia, the focus of his career has been on his work as an archivist and policy analyst, organizing and analyzing information to come up with options for government agencies in Canada. 1988 found Yee in Toronto working as multicultural coordinator for the Archives of Ontario.

Although it seems a far cry from archivist/analyst to children's book author, Yee found the step to be a natural one, given his circumstances and interests. "Back in

"...powerful..."
—*Montreal Gazette*

"...a well-written novel with staying power."
—*Quill & Quire*

Breakaway

Paul Yee

Eighteen-year-old Kwok-Ken Wong hopes that a soccer scholarship will help him escape the poverty in his life, but his plans are dashed by racism. (Cover illustration by Laurie McGaw.)

1983, I was involved in doing work for Chinatown, such as organizing festivals, exhibits, and educational programs," he once explained. "Even though I had written some short stories, I had not done anything in children's literature. A Canadian publishing company, Lorimer, knowing about my work in the Chinese community, asked me to write a children's book that would employ my knowledge of Chinese-Canadian life as a background." The result of this request would be *Teach Me to Fly, Skyfighter!, and Other Stories,* Yee's first book for children.

Teach Me to Fly, Skyfighter! contains four interlinking stories about children living in the immigrant neighborhoods of Vancouver. Yee "has succeeded in portraying the personalities, interests, and dreams of four 11-year-

old friends whose voices ring true throughout," according to Frieda Wishinsky in *Quill & Quire.*

Yee's second short story collection, *Tales from Gold Mountain,* was published in 1989 to high praise from critics. Lee Galda and Susan Cox, writing in *Reading Teacher,* wrote that the eight tales included in the book "give . . . voice to the previously unheard generations of Chinese immigrants whose labor supported the settlement of the west coast of Canada and the United States." Yee includes stories about the conflict between the manager of a fish cannery and his greedy boss; a young man who arranges the burial of Chinese railroad workers after he meets his father's ghost; a young woman's gift of ginger root to save her fiancée's life; a wealthy merchant who exchanges his twin daughters for sons; and clashes between old traditions and new influences. Betsy Hearne noted in the *Bulletin of the Center for Children's Books* that "Yee never indulges in stylistic pretensions" in blending realism and legend, and praised the stories for containing "mythical overtones that lend the characters unforgettable dimension— humans achieving supernatural power in defying their fate of physical and cultural oppression." *School Library Journal* contributor Margaret A. Chang praised Yee for "further expand[ing] and enhanc[ing] understanding of the Chinese immigrant experience," while a *Horn Book* reviewer praised *Tales from Gold Mountain* for interweaving "the hardships and dangers of frontier life in a new country with the ancient attitudes and traditions brought over from China" and predicted that the images created "will stay with the reader for a long time."

Published in 2002, *Dead Man's Gold and Other Stories* contains ten tales that combine real life and the supernatural. Against the backdrop of a harsh existence comprised of hard labor in gold mines, on railroads, and in family-run businesses, Yee's protagonists long for home and family as they face prejudices while trying to build a better life. In these stories, each accompanied by an appropriately haunting illustration by Harvey Chan, Yee's characters are also tested by unearthly horrors of one sort or another. Calling the collection "a remarkable piece of literature," Laura Reilly noted in her *Resource Links* review that Yee's tales "all have surprising twists that compel the reader to read on." Praising *Dead Man's Gold and Other Stories, Booklist* contributor Hazel Rochman noted that Yee's "plain, beautiful words speak with brutal honesty" as he writes of immigrant life from the mid-1800s through the 1950s.

Yee's first novel, 1986's *The Curses of Third Uncle,* is a work of historical fiction that deals with the period of the early twentieth century in which Sun Yat-Sen's revolutionary movement fought against the Chinese Empire. Dr. Sun Yat-Sen, called the "Father of Modern China," had led nine uprisings against the Empire by the time he visited Vancouver in 1910 and 1911. Yee's protagonist, fourteen-year-old Lillian, lives in Vancouver's Chinatown and misses her father, who often travels back to China and throughout the British Columbia frontier— presumably to take care of his clothing business. He is actually a secret agent for Dr. Sun's revolutionary movement. At one point in his travels, Lillian's father fails to return. His absence is economically hard on the family, but Lillian will not believe her father has deserted them. Her third uncle, however, threatens to send Lillian's family back to China. In her attempts to locate her father by traveling through British Columbia, Lillian discovers that he has been betrayed by his brother, who has been paid to turn him over to his enemies. Reviewing the novel in *Emergency Librarian,* Christine Dewar called it "a story that is exciting but contrived, with an attractive and reasonably motivated heroine." *Quill & Quire* writer Annette Goldsmith similarly commented that *The Curses of Third Uncle* is "an exciting, fast-pace, well-written tale," and praised Yee for his use of legendary Chinese female warriors to reinforce Lillian's story.

Set in Chinatown in 1932 during the Great Depression, *Breakaway* "explores questions of identity and belonging by detailing conflicts between generations and cultures," according to a *Canadian Children's Books* essayist. A senior in high school, Kwok-Ken Wong hopes a soccer scholarship will save him from an otherwise dismal future working on his father's farm. When his plans are dashed and racism prevents him from playing the sport he loves, Kwok-Ken grows disillusioned but ultimately grows in understanding as he begins to appreciate the strengths of his cultural heritage. Reviewing *Breakaway* in *Quill & Quire,* Patty Lawlor called the book "a well-written novel with staying power" that would be useful in discussions of racism. While noting that the novel's ending is "rather abrupt," *Canadian Materials* contributor Margaret Mackey praised Yee's novel for painting "a valuable picture of a fascinating and complex time and world."

In addition to novels and short fiction for older readers, Yee has also made the Chinese-Canadian heritage come vividly to life for younger readers. Maylin, the heroine of his 1991 picture book *Roses Sing on New Snow,* embodies the difference between the Old World and the New World when she explains to the governor of South China, who is visiting her father's Chinatown restaurant to learn the secrets of her delicious recipes, that "this is a dish of the New World. . . . You cannot re-create it in the Old." Although efforts are made to push Maylin aside and allow the men of the family to take credit for the restaurant's excellent fare, after her father and brothers cannot reproduce the meals served to the governor, Maylin is called forth and ultimately shown to be one of the most talented cooks in Chinatown. Hearne noted

in the *Bulletin of the Center for Children's Books* that "vivid art and clean writing are graced by a neatly feminist ending."

Other picture books by Yee include *The Jade Necklace, The Boy in the Attic,* and the award-winning *Ghost Train. The Jade Necklace* focuses on Yenyee, a young girl whose fisherman father presents her with a necklace with a carved jade fish, then is lost at sea soon after. Giving the necklace to the sea in the hope that it will return her father to her, Yenyee goes on to immigrate to the New World as a nanny before the sea responds to her request in a surprising way. In *Quill & Quire* Sherie Posesorski praised *The Jade Necklace* as "a coming-of-age tale that's both contemporary and timeless, realistic and symbolic," and added that Yee's prose "seamlessly marries the formality of the storyteller's voice with the intimacy of a child's perspective."

Winner of Canada's prestigious Governor General's award, *Ghost Train* focuses on a talented young artist named Choon-yi, whose father, a railway worker, is killed only days before Choon-yi arrives from China to join him. In *The Boy in the Attic* seven-year-old Chinese immigrant Kai-ming discovers the ghost of a boy

After the sea takes her father's life, Yenyee is forced to leave South China and go to the New World. From The Jade Necklace, *written by Yee and illustrated by Grace Lin.)*

difference between nonfiction and fiction is the difference between reliable reporting and imaginative creating," he concluded.

Biographical and Critical Sources

BOOKS

Authors and Artists for Young Adults, Volume 24, Gale (Detroit, MI), 1998, pp. 239-244.

Canadian Children's Books: A Critical Guide to Authors and Illustrators, Oxford University Press (Toronto, Ontario, Canada), 2000, pp. 493-496.

Children's Literature Review, Volume 44, Gale (Detroit, MI), 1997, pp. 156-166.

Oxford Companion to Children's Literature, 2nd edition, Oxford University Press (New York, NY), 1997, pp. 1194-1195.

St. James Guide to Children's Writers, 5th edition, St. James Press (Detroit, MI), 1999, pp. 1148-1149.

Yee, Paul, *Saltwater City: An Illustrated History of the Chinese in Vancouver,* Douglas & McIntyre (Vancouver, British Columbia, Canada), 1988, University of Washington (Seattle, WA), 1989.

Yee, Paul, *Tales from Gold Mountain: Stories of the Chinese in the New World,* Groundwood Books (Toronto, Ontario, Canada), 1989, Macmillan (New York, NY), 1990.

PERIODICALS

Booklist, March 15, 1990, Denise Wilms, review of *Tales from the Gold Mountain,* p. 1464; March 1, 1999, Sally Estes, review of *Tales from Gold Mountain: Stories of the Chinese in the New World,* p. 1212; November 1, 2002, Hazel Rochman, *Dead Man's Gold and Other Stories,* p. 494.

Books in Canada, December, 1983, p. 17; December, 1986, p. 18; May, 1989, p. 5.

Bulletin of the Center for Children's Books, January, 1990, Betsy Hearne, review of *Tales from the Gold Mountain,* p. 178; March, 1990, p. 178; July, 1992, B. Hearne, review of *Roses Sing on New Snow: A Delicious Tale,* p. 307.

Canadian Children's Literature, autumn, 1996, Marie Davis, "A backward way of thanking people: Paul Yee on his historical fiction," pp. 50-68; winter, 1996, James Greenlaw, "Chinese Canadian fathers and sons," pp. 106-108.

Canadian Literature, spring, 1988, "Different Dragons," p. 168; autumn, 1991, pp. 142-143; winter, 1999, review of *The Boy in the Attic,* p. 204.

Canadian Materials, September, 1994, Margaret Mackey, review of *Breakaway,* p. 139.

Emergency Librarian, May-June, 1995, David Jenkinson, "Portraits: Paul Yee," pp. 61-64; May, 1987, Christine Dewar, review of *The Curses of Third Uncle,* p. 51.

Yee's **Dead Man's Gold and Other Stories,** *illustrated by Harvey Chan, contains ghost stories about Chinese immigrants who came to North America.*

who died in Kai-ming's new Canadian home eighty years before. Through the intervention of a magic butterfly, the two boys are able to break through their language barrier and converse, helping Kai-ming make the transition to his new country. Praising Yee's use of the ghost as a metaphor, *Quill & Quire* contributor Freida Ling described *The Boy in the Attic* as a tale of "human courage, resourcefulness, and the adaptability required to uproot yourself from your homeland and start over in a strange country."

Although Yee's primary career was as a historian, he found no difficulty making the switch to fiction. Nevertheless, he once remarked that he finds fiction writing more "arduous because instead of merely reporting what has happened in nonfiction, fiction requires the creation of a story" that will be believable and enjoyable. "The

Horn Book, July, 1990, review of *Tales from the Gold Mountain,* pp. 459-460; March-April, 1992, Elizabeth S. Watson, review of *Roses Sing on New Snow,* p. 196.

Kirkus Reviews, May 15, 2002, review of *The Jade Necklace,* p. 744.

Quill & Quire, October, 1983, Frieda Wishinsky, review of *Teach Me to Fly, Skyfighter!,* p. 16; December, 1986, Annette Goldsmith, "Illuminating Adventures with Young People from Long Ago," p. 14; April, 1994, Patty Lawlor, review of *Breakaway,* p. 39; February, 1997, p. 51; October, 1998, Freida Ling, review of *The Boy in the Attic,* p. 42 ; May, 2002, Sherie Posesorski, review of *The Jade Necklace,* p. 32.

Reading Teacher, April, 1991, Lee Galda and Susan Cox, review of *Tales from Gold Mountain,* p. 585.

Resource Links, June, 2002, Rosemary Anderson, review of *The Jade Necklace,* p. 46; December, 2002, Laura Reilly, review of *Dead Man's Gold and Other Stories,* p. 35.

School Library Journal, May, 1990, Margaret A. Chang, review of *Tales from Gold Mountain,* p. 121; December, 1998, Diane S. Marton, review of *The Boy in the Attic,* p. 96; September, 2002, Margaret A. Chang, review of *The Jade Necklace,* p. 209.

ONLINE

Canadian Children's Book Centre Web site, http://www. bookcentre.ca/ (March 11, 2003), "Paul Yee."

*   *   *

ZONTA, Pat 1951-

Personal

Born March 24, 1951, in Hamilton, Ontario, Canada; divorced; children: Dave, Mike. *Education:* Attended McMaster University; also studied medical radiation technology at St. Joseph's Hospital and Mohawk College, Hamilton, Ontario, Canada. *Religion:* Roman Catholic.

Addresses

Agent—c/o Author Mail, Firefly Books Ltd., 3680 Victoria Park Ave., Toronto, Ontario, Canada M2H 3K1. *E-mail*—p_zonta@hotmail.com.

Career

Worked as a medical radiation technologist in Ontario, Canada, including positions at St. Joseph's Hospital, Joseph Brant Hospital, York-Finch Clinic, McMaster Children's Hospital, and Gamma X-Ray and Laboratories Ltd., for twenty-five years. Also actress and singer, including a singing tour of Italy, 2001.

Member

Ontario Association of Medical Radiation Technologists (education coordinator, 1996).

Writings

Jessica's X-Ray, illustrated by Clive Dobson, Firefly Books (Toronto, Ontario, Canada), 2001.

Also author of *Mikey's Endoscopy,* privately printed. Theater critic, *View.* Contributor to periodicals.

Work in Progress

Short stories and nonfiction.

Sidelights

Pat Zonta told *SATA:* "My idea for *Jessica's X-Ray* germinated when I was a student X-ray technologist, but I did not start writing the book until 1997.

"I began writing the prototype series, 'Xandra's X-Ray: Xander and Xandra Children's Learning Series' after being 'downsized' from my full-time position as an X-ray technician. I self-published the prototype series and, with the permission of Firefly Books, it is currently available exclusively to the Children's Hospital at McMaster Medical Centre in Hamilton, Ontario. The Children's Hospital provided seed funding for the series in 1997, and I have donated the series to the hospital. The 'Xandra' books are given to the children who visit the hospital. Crayola Crayons donated 500 three-packs of crayons to be attached to the black-and-white books so the children can color them.

"With *Jessica's X-Ray* I hope to allay at least a few of the fears children experience about the X-ray process in an entertaining and educational manner while speaking to them respectfully and intelligently. I hope to reach out to as many children as possible. Most people have never seen X-ray, ultra-sound, computer-assisted tomography (CT), or magnetic resonance imaging (MRI) images. I hope to give the public a little insight about how our bodies look from the inside out. I hope *Jessica's X-Ray* will reach children all over the world. I hope it will be translated into other languages. Due to the digital imaging process used to create the original diagnostic images, the book can easily be adapted to an online market or video format.

"The names Jessica and another character, Sarah, are the names of my granddaughters. Sarah, at age three, called the MRI image 'scary guy' and loved to play a game where she opened the book, screamed out his name, closed the book at lightning speed, then laughed at the fun before she repeated the process over and over again.

"Sarah, Jessica, and I are always thrilled when we see the book displayed in bookstores. I have also enjoyed reading *Jessica's X-Ray* to classrooms of children from pre-kindergarten through third grade. They were a wonderful audience and had prepared questions for me to answer after we read the book, such as 'how long did it take to write?' or 'when did you know you wanted to become a writer?' The answer to that question is—when I was in grade five.

"I thoroughly enjoy the interaction with children when I read the book to them. I designed *Jessica's X-Ray* to be interactive. I am very pleased at the fun we have reading it in the classroom. I have performed as an actor in many children's plays, and I can think of no greater thrill than participating with children—in hearing their ideas, enthusiasm, and creativity. I love helping kids in any way I can."

Biographical and Critical Sources

PERIODICALS

Resource Links, April, 2002, Linda Berezowski, review of *Jessica's X-Ray,* p. 58.

School Library Journal, August, 2002, Martha Topol, review of *Jessica's X-Ray,* p. 181.

Illustrations Index

(In the following index, the number of the *volume* in which an illustrator's work appears is given *before* the colon, and the *page number* on which it appears is given *after* the colon. For example, a drawing by Adams, Adrienne appears in Volume 2 on page 6, another drawing by her appears in Volume 3 on page 80, another drawing in Volume 8 on page 1, and so on and so on. . . .)

YABC

Index references to *YABC* refer to listings appearing in the two-volume *Yesterday's Authors of Books for Children,* also published by The Gale Group. *YABC* covers prominent authors and illustrators who died prior to 1960.

Carpenter, Nancy 76: 128; 86: 173; 89: 171; 131: 186; 134: 8; 138: 215
Carr, Archie 37: 225
Carrick, Donald 5: 194; 39: 97; 49: 70; 53: 156; 63: 15, 16, 17, 18, 19, 21; 80: 131; 86: 151;118: 24
Carrick, Malcolm 28: 59, 60
Carrick, Paul 118: 26
Carrick, Valery 21: 47
Carrier, Lark 71: 43
Carroll, Jim 88: 211; 140: 177
Carroll, Lewis
   See Dodgson, Charles L.
Carroll, Michael 72: 5
Carroll, Pamela 84: 68; 128: 214
Carroll, Ruth 7: 41; 10: 68
Carter, Abby 81: 32; 97: 121; 102: 61
Carter, Barbara 47: 167, 169
Carter, David A. 114: 24, 25
Carter, Don 124: 54
Carter, Harry 22: 179
Carter, Helene 15: 38; 22: 202, 203; YABC 2: 220-221
Cartlidge, Michelle 49: 65; 96: 50, 51
Cartwright, Reg 63: 61, 62; 78: 26; 143: 4
Carty, Leo 4: 196; 7: 163; 58: 131
Cary 4: 133; 9: 32; 20: 2; 21: 143
Cary, Page 12: 41
Casale, Paul 71: 63; 109: 122; 136: 28
Case, Sandra E. 16: 2
Caseley, Judith 87: 36
Casilla, Robert 78: 7
Casino, Steve 85: 193
Cassel, Lili
   See Wronker, Lili Cassel
Cassel-Wronker, Lili
   See Wronker, Lili Cassel
Cassels, Jean 8: 50
Cassen, Melody 140: 51
Cassity, Don 104: 24
Cassler, Carl 75: 137, 138; 82: 162
Casson, Hugh 65: 38, 40, 42, 43
Castellon, Federico 48: 45, 46, 47, 48
Castle, Jane 4: 80
Castro, Antonio 84: 71
Catalano, Dominic 94: 79
Catalanotto, Peter 63: 170; 70: 23; 71: 182;72: 96; 74: 114; 76: 194, 195; 77: 7; 79: 157; 80: 28, 67; 83: 157; 85: 27; 108: 11;113: 30, 31, 33, 34, 36; 114: 27, 28, 29; 117: 53;124: 168
Catania, Tom 68: 82
Cather, Carolyn 3: 83; 15: 203; 34: 216
Catrow, David 117: 179
Cauley, Lorinda Bryan 44: 135; 46: 49
Cayard, Bruce 38: 67
Cazet, Denys 52: 27; 99: 39, 40
Cecil, Randy 127: 132, 133
Cellini, Joseph 2: 73; 3: 35; 16: 116; 47: 103
Cepeda, Joe 90: 62; 109: 91; 134: 172
Chabrian, Debbi 45: 55
Chabrian, Deborah 51: 182; 53: 124; 63: 107;75: 84; 79: 85; 82: 247; 89: 93; 101: 197
Chagnon, Mary 37: 158
Chalmers, Mary 3: 145; 13: 148; 33: 125; 66: 214
Chamberlain, Christopher 45: 57
Chamberlain, Margaret 46: 51; 106: 89
Chamberlain, Nigel 78: 140
Chambers, C. E. 17: 230
Chambers, Dave 12: 151
Chambers, Jill 134: 110
Chambers, Mary 4: 188
Chambliss, Maxie 42: 186; 56: 159; 93: 163, 164;103: 178
Champlin, Dale 136: 124
Chan, Harvey 96: 236; 99: 153; 143: 218
Chandler, David P. 28: 62
Chaney, Howard 139: 27
Chang, Warren 101: 209
Chapel, Jody 68: 20

Chapman, C. H. 13: 83, 85, 87
Chapman, Frederick T. 6: 27; 44: 28
Chapman, Gaynor 32: 52, 53
Chappell, Warren 3: 172; 21: 56; 27: 125
Charles, Donald 30: 154, 155
Charlip, Remy 4: 48; 34: 138; 68: 53, 54; 119:29, 30
Charlot, Jean 1: 137, 138; 8: 23; 14: 31; 48: 151; 56: 21
Charlot, Martin 64: 72
Charlton, Michael 34: 50; 37: 39
Charmatz, Bill 7: 45
Chartier, Normand 9: 36; 52: 49; 66: 40; 74: 220
Chase, Lynwood M. 14: 4
Chast, Roz 97: 39, 40
Chastain, Madye Lee 4: 50
Chatterton, Martin 68: 102
Chau, Tungwai 140: 35
Chauncy, Francis 24: 158
Chee, Cheng-Khee 79: 42; 81: 224
Chen, Chih-sien 90: 226
Chen, Tony 6: 45; 19: 131; 29: 126; 34: 160
Cheney, T. A. 11: 47
Cheng, Judith 36: 45; 51: 16
Chermayeff, Ivan 47: 53
Cherry, David 93: 40
Cherry, Lynne 34: 52; 65: 184; 87: 111; 99: 46, 47
Chesak, Lina 135: 118
Chess, Victoria 12: 6; 33: 42, 48, 49; 40: 194;41: 145; 69: 80; 72: 100; 92: 33, 34; 104: 167
Chessare, Michele 41: 50; 56: 48; 69: 145
Chesterton, G. K. 27: 43, 44, 45, 47
Chestnutt, David 47: 217
Chesworth, Michael 75: 24, 152; 88: 136; 94: 25;98: 155
Chetham, Celia 134: 34
Chetwin, Grace 86: 40
Chevalier, Christa 35: 66
Chew, Ruth 7: 46; 132: 147
Chewning, Randy 92: 206
Chichester Clark, Emma 72: 121; 77: 212; 78: 209;87: 143; 117: 37, 39, 40
Chifflart 47: 113, 127
Child, Lauren 119: 32
Chin, Alex 28: 54
Cho, Shinta 8: 126
Chodos, Margaret 52: 102, 103, 107
Chollick, Jay 25: 175
Choma, Christina 99: 169
Chorao, Kay 7: 200-201; 8: 25; 11: 234; 33: 187;35: 239; 69: 35; 70: 235; 123: 174
Chowdhury, Subrata 62: 130
Christelow, Eileen 38: 44; 83: 198, 199; 90: 57, 58
Christensen, Bonnie 93: 100
Christensen, Gardell Dano 1: 57
Christensen, James C. 140: 226
Christiana, David 90: 64; 135: 13
Christiansen, Per 40: 24
Christie, Gregory 116: 107; 127: 20, 21
Christy, Howard Chandler 17: 163-165, 168-169; 19: 186, 187;21: 22, 23, 24, 25
Chronister, Robert 23: 138; 63: 27; 69: 167
Church, Frederick YABC 1: 155
Chute, Marchette 1: 59
Chwast, Jacqueline 1: 63; 2: 275; 6: 46-47;11: 125; 12: 202; 14: 235
Chwast, Seymour 3: 128-129; 18: 43; 27: 152;92: 79; 96: 56, 57, 58
Cieslawksi, Steve 101: 142; 127: 116
Cirlin, Edgard 2: 168
Clairin, Georges 53: 109
Clapp, John 105: 66; 109: 58; 126: 7; 129: 148; 130: 165
Clark, Brenda 119: 85
Clark, David 77: 164; 134: 144, 145
Clark, Emma Chichester
   See Chichester Clark, Emma
Clark, Victoria 35: 159

Clarke, Gus 72: 226; 134: 31
Clarke, Harry 23: 172, 173
Clarke, Peter 75: 102
Claverie, Jean 38: 46; 88: 29
Clayton, Robert 9: 181
Cleaver, Elizabeth 8: 204; 23: 36
Cleland, T. M. 26: 92
Clemens, Peter 61: 125
Clement, Charles 20: 38
Clement, Rod 97: 42
Clement, Stephen 88: 3
Clementson, John 84: 213
Clevin, Jorgen 7: 50
Clifford, Judy 34: 163; 45: 198
Clokey, Art 59: 44
Clouse, James 84: 15
Clouse, Nancy L. 78: 31; 114: 90
Coalson, Glo 9: 72, 85; 25: 155; 26: 42; 35: 212; 53: 31; 56: 154; 94: 37, 38, 193
Cober, Alan E. 17: 158; 32: 77; 49: 127
Cober-Gentry, Leslie 92: 111
Cocca-Leffler, Maryann 80: 46; 136: 60; 139: 193
Cochran, Bobbye 11: 52
CoConis, Ted 4: 41; 46: 41; 51: 104
Cocozza, Chris 87: 18; 110: 173; 111: 149
Coerr, Eleanor 1: 64; 67: 52
Coes, Peter 35: 172
Cogancherry, Helen 52: 143; 69: 131; 77: 93;78: 220; 109: 204; 110: 129
Coggins, Jack 2: 69
Cohen, Alix 7: 53
Cohen, Sheldon 105: 33, 34
Cohen, Vincent O. 19: 243
Cohen, Vivien 11: 112
Coker, Paul 51: 172
Colbert, Anthony 15: 41; 20: 193
Colby, C. B. 3: 47
Cole, Babette 58: 172; 96: 63, 64
Cole, Brock 68: 223; 72: 36, 37, 38, 192; 127: 23; 136: 64, 65
Cole, Gwen 87: 185
Cole, Herbert 28: 104
Cole, Michael 59: 46
Cole, Olivia H. H. 1: 134; 3: 223; 9: 111; 38: 104
Colin, Paul 102: 59; 123: 118; 126: 152
Collicott, Sharleen 98: 39; 143: 29, 30
Collier, Bryan 126: 54
Collier, David 13: 127
Collier, John 27: 179
Collier, Steven 50: 52
Collins, Heather 66: 84; 67: 68; 81: 40; 98: 192, 193; 129: 95, 96, 98
Collins, Ross 140: 23, 24
Colon, Raul 108: 112; 113: 5; 117: 167; 134: 112
Colonna, Bernard 21: 50; 28: 103; 34: 140; 43: 180; 78: 150
Comport, Sally Wern 117: 169
Conde, J. M. 100: 120
Condon, Grattan 54: 85
Cone, Ferne Geller 39: 49
Cone, J. Morton 39: 49
Conklin, Paul 43: 62
Connolly, Howard 67: 88
Connolly, Jerome P. 4: 128; 28: 52
Connolly, Peter 47: 60
Conoly, Walle 110: 224
Conover, Chris 31: 52; 40: 184; 41: 51; 44: 79
Contreras, Gerry 72: 9
Converse, James 38: 70
Conway 62: 62
Conway, Michael 69: 12; 81: 3; 92: 108
Cook, G. R. 29: 165
Cook, Joel 108: 160
Cookburn, W. V. 29: 204
Cooke, Donald E. 2: 77
Cooke, Tom 52: 118
Coomaraswamy, A. K. 50: 100
Coombs, Charles 43: 65
Coombs, Deborah 139: 175

Frankenberg, Robert *22:* 116; *30:* 50; *38:* 92, 94, 95;*68:* 111
Frankfeldt, Gwen *84:* 223; *110:* 92
Franklin, John *24:* 22
Franson, Leanne R. *111:* 57, 58
Frascino, Edward *9:* 133; *29:* 229; *33:* 190; *48:* 80, 81, 82, 83, 84-85, 86
Frasconi, Antonio *6:* 80; *27:* 208; *53:* 41, 43, 45, 47,48; *68:* 145; *73:* 226; *131:* 68
Fraser, Betty *2:* 212; *6:* 185; *8:* 103; *31:* 72,73; *43:* 136; *111:* 76
Fraser, Eric *38:* 78; *41:* 149, 151
Fraser, F. A. *22:* 234
Fraser, Mary Ann *137:* 63
Frasier, Debra *69:* 60; *112:* 67
Frazee, Marla *72:* 98; *105:* 79, 80
Frazetta, Frank *41:* 72; *58:* 77, 78, 79, 80, 81, 82, 83
Freas, John *25:* 207
Fredrickson, Mark *103:* 33
Freeland, Michael J. *118:* 115
Freeman, Don *2:* 15; *13:* 249; *17:* 62-63, 65, 67-68;*18:* 243; *20:* 195; *23:* 213, 217; *32:* 155;*55:* 129
Freeman, Irving *67:* 150
Freeman, Pietri *140:* 223
Fregosi, Claudia *24:* 117
Fremaux, Charlotte Murray *138:* 29; *141:* 95
French, Fiona *6:* 82-83; *75:* 61; *109:* 170; *132:* 79, 80, 81, 82
Frendak, Rodney *126:* 97, 98
Freynet, Gilbert *72:* 221
Friedman, Judith *43:* 197; *131:* 221
Friedman, Marvin *19:* 59; *42:* 86
Frinta, Dagmar *36:* 42
Frith, Michael K. *15:* 138; *18:* 120
Fritz, Ronald *46:* 73; *82:* 124
Fromm, Lilo *29:* 85; *40:* 197
Frost, A. B. *17:* 6-7; *19:* 123, 124, 125, 126, 127, 128, 129,130; *100:* 119; *YABC 1:* 156-157, 160; *2:* 107
Frost, Kristi *118:* 113
Fry, Guy *2:* 224
Fry, Rosalie *3:* 72; *YABC 2:* 180-181
Fry, Rosalind *21:* 153, 168
Fryer, Elmer *34:* 115
Fuchs, Bernie *110:* 10
Fuchs, Erich *6:* 84
Fuchshuber, Annegert *43:* 96
Fufuka, Mahiri *32:* 146
Fujikawa, Gyo *39:* 75, 76; *76:* 72, 73, 74
Fulford, Deborah *23:* 159
Fuller, Margaret *25:* 189
Fulweiler, John *93:* 99
Funai, Mamoru *38:* 105
Funk, Tom *7:* 17, 99
Furchgott, Terry *29:* 86
Furness, William Henry, Jr. *94:* 18
Furukawa, Mel *25:* 42

G

Gaadt, David *78:* 212; *121:* 166
Gaadt, George *71:* 9
Gaber, Susan *99:* 33; *115:* 57, 58
Gaberell, J. *19:* 236
Gabler, Mirko *99:* 71
Gackenbach, Dick *19:* 168; *41:* 81; *48:* 89, 90, 91, 92,93, 94; *54:* 105; *79:* 75, 76, 77
Gad, Victor *87:* 161
Gaetano, Nicholas *23:* 209
Gaffney-Kessell, Walter *94:* 219
Gag, Flavia *17:* 49, 52
Gag, Wanda *100:* 101, 102; *YABC 1:* 135, 137-138, 141, 143
Gagnon, Cecile *11:* 77; *58:* 87
Gal, Laszlo *14:* 127; *52:* 54, 55, 56; *65:* 142;*68:* 150; *81:* 185; *96:* 104, 105
Galazinski, Tom *55:* 13

Galdone, Paul *1:* 156, 181, 206; *2:* 40, 241; *3:* 42,144; *4:* 141; *10:* 109, 158; *11:* 21; *12:* 118, 210;*14:* 12; *16:* 36-37; *17:* 70-74; *18:* 111, 230;*19:* 183; *21:* 154; *22:* 150, 245; *33:* 126;*39:* 136, 137; *42:* 57; *51:* 169; *55:* 110; *66:* 80, 82, 139; *72:* 73; *100:* 84
Gale, Cathy *140:* 22; *143:* 52
Gallagher, S. Saelig *105:* 154
Gallagher, Sears *20:* 112
Galloway, Ewing *51:* 154
Galouchko, Annouchka Gravel *95:* 55
Galster, Robert *1:* 66
Galsworthy, Gay John *35:* 232
Galvez, Daniel *125:* 182
Gamble, Kim *112:* 64, 65; *124:* 77
Gammell, Stephen *7:* 48; *13:* 149; *29:* 82; *33:* 209; *41:* 88; *50:* 185, 186-187; *53:* 51, 52-53, 54, 55, 56,57, 58; *54:* 24, 25; *56:* 147, 148, 150; *57:* 27, 66;*81:* 62, 63; *87:* 88; *89:* 10; *106:* 223; *126:* 2; *128:* 71, 73, 74, 77
Gamper, Ruth *84:* 198
Gampert, John *58:* 94
Ganly, Helen *56:* 56
Gannett, Ruth Chrisman *3:* 74; *18:* 254; *33:* 77, 78
Gantschev, Ivan *45:* 32
Garafano, Marie *73:* 33
Garbot, Dave *131:* 106
Garbutt, Bernard *23:* 68
Garcia *37:* 71
Garcia, Manuel *74:* 145
Gardner, Earle *45:* 167
Gardner, Joan *40:* 87
Gardner, Joel *40:* 87, 92
Gardner, John *40:* 87
Gardner, Lucy *40:* 87
Gardner, Richard
　　See Cummings, Richard
Gargiulo, Frank *84:* 158
Garland, Michael *36:* 29; *38:* 83; *44:* 168; *48:* 78, 221, 222; *49:* 161; *60:* 139; *71:* 6, 11; *72:* 229; *74:* 142; *89:* 187; *93:* 183; *104:* 110; *131:* 55; *139:* 209
Garland, Peggy *60:* 139
Garland, Sarah *62:* 45; *135:* 67, 68
Garn, Aimee *75:* 47
Garner, Joan *128:* 170
Garneray, Ambroise Louis *59:* 140
Garnett, Eve *3:* 75
Garnett, Gary *39:* 184
Garns, Allen *80:* 125; *84:* 39
Garraty, Gail *4:* 142; *52:* 106
Garrett, Agnes *46:* 110; *47:* 157
Garrett, Edmund H. *20:* 29
Garrett, Tom *107:* 194
Garrick, Jacqueline *67:* 42, 43; *77:* 94
Garrison, Barbara *19:* 133; *104:* 146; *109:* 87
Garro, Mark *108:* 131; *128:* 210
Garvey, Robert *98:* 222
Garza, Carmen Lomas *80:* 211
Gates, Frieda *26:* 80
Gaughan, Jack *26:* 79; *43:* 185
Gaver, Becky *20:* 61
Gawing, Toby *72:* 52
Gay, Marie-Louise *68:* 76-77, 78; *102:* 136; *126:* 76, 78, 81, 83; *127:* 55, 56
Gay, Zhenya *19:* 135, 136
Gaydos, Tim *62:* 201
Gazsi, Ed *80:* 48
Gazso, Gabriel *73:* 85
Geary, Clifford N. *1:* 122; *9:* 104; *51:* 74
Geary, Rick *142:* 44, 46
Gee, Frank *33:* 26
Geer, Charles *1:* 91; *3:* 179; *4:* 201; *6:* 168;*7:* 96; *9:* 58; *10:* 72; *12:* 127; *39:* 156,157, 158, 159, 160; *42:* 88, 89, 90, 91; *55:* 111, 116
Gehm, Charlie *36:* 65; *57:* 117; *62:* 60, 138
Geisel, Theodor Seuss *1:* 104-105, 106; *28:* 108, 109, 110,111, 112, 113; *75:* 67, 68, 69, 70, 71; *89:* 127, 128; *100:* 106, 107, 108
Geisert, Arthur *92:* 67, 68; *133:* 72, 73, 74
Geldart, William *15:* 121; *21:* 202

Genia *4:* 84
Gentry, Cyrille R. *12:* 66
Genzo, John Paul *136:* 74
George, Jean *2:* 113
George, Lindsay Barrett *95:* 57
Geraghty, Paul *130:* 60, 61
Gerard, Jean Ignace *45:* 80
Gerard, Rolf *27:* 147, 150
Gerber, Mark *61:* 105
Gerber, Mary Jane *112:* 124
Gerber, Stephanie *71:* 195
Gergely, Tibor *54:* 15, 16
Geritz, Franz *17:* 135
Gerlach, Geff *42:* 58
Gerrard, Roy *47:* 78; *90:* 96, 97, 98, 99
Gershinowitz, George *36:* 27
Gerstein, Mordicai *31:* 117; *47:* 80, 81, 82, 83, 84, 85, 86;*51:* 173; *69:* 134; *107:* 122; *142:* 49, 52
Gervase *12:* 27
Getz, Arthur *32:* 148
Gewirtz, Bina *61:* 81
Giancola, Donato *95:* 146
Gibbons, Gail *23:* 78; *72:* 77, 78, 79; *82:* 182;*104:* 65
Gibbs, Tony *40:* 95
Gibran, Kahlil *32:* 116
Gider, Iskender *81:* 193
Giesen, Rosemary *34:* 192-193
Giffard, Hannah *83:* 70
Giguere, George *20:* 111
Gilbert, John *19:* 184; *54:* 115; *YABC 2:* 287
Gilbert, W. S. *36:* 83, 85, 96
Gilbert, Yvonne *116:* 70; *128:* 84
Gilchrist, Jan Spivey *72:* 82, 83, 84-85, 87; *77:* 90;*105:* 89, 91; *130:* 63, 64
Giles, Will *41:* 218
Gili, Phillida *70:* 73
Gill, Margery *4:* 57; *7:* 7; *22:* 122; *25:* 166;*26:* 146, 147
Gillen, Denver *28:* 216
Gillette, Henry J. *23:* 237
Gilliam, Stan *39:* 64, 81
Gillies, Chuck *62:* 31
Gilliland, Jillian *87:* 58
Gillman, Alec *98:* 105
Gilman, Esther *15:* 124
Gilman, Phoebe *104:* 70, 71
Ginsberg, Sari *111:* 184
Ginsburg, Max *62:* 59; *68:* 194
Giovanopoulos, Paul *7:* 104; *60:* 36
Giovine, Sergio *79:* 12; *93:* 118; *139:* 118
Githens, Elizabeth M. *5:* 47
Gladden, Scott *99:* 108; *103:* 160
Gladstone, Gary *12:* 89; *13:* 190
Gladstone, Lise *15:* 273
Glanzman, Louis S. *2:* 177; *3:* 182; *36:* 97, 98;*38:* 120, 122; *52:* 141, 144; *71:* 191; *91:* 54, 56
Glaser, Milton *3:* 5; *5:* 156; *11:* 107; *30:* 26;*36:* 112; *54:* 141
Glass, Andrew *36:* 38; *44:* 133; *48:* 205; *65:* 3;*68:* 43, 45; *90:* 104, 105
Glass, Marvin *9:* 174
Glasser, Judy *41:* 156; *56:* 140; *69:* 79; *72:* 101
Glattauer, Ned *5:* 84; *13:* 224; *14:* 26
Glauber, Uta *17:* 76
Gleeson, J. M. *YABC 2:* 207
Glegg, Creina *36:* 100
Glienke, Amelie *63:* 150
Gliewe, Unada *3:* 78-79; *21:* 73; *30:* 220
Gliori, Debi *72:* 91; *138:* 82
Glovach, Linda *7:* 105
Gobbato, Imero *3:* 180-181; *6:* 213; *7:* 58; *9:* 150; *18:* 39; *21:* 167; *39:* 82, 83; *41:* 137, 251;*59:* 177
Goble, Paul *25:* 121; *26:* 86; *33:* 65; *69:* 68-69; *131:* 79, 80
Goble, Warwick *46:* 78, 79
Godal, Eric *36:* 93
Godfrey, Michael *17:* 279

Author Index

The following index gives the number of the volume in which an author's biographical sketch, Autobiography Feature, Brief Entry, or Obituary appears.

This index includes references to all entries in the following series, which are also published by The Gale Group.

YABC—*Yesterday's Authors of Books for Children: Facts and Pictures about Authors and Illustrators of Books for Young People from Early Times to 1960*

CLR—*Children's Literature Review: Excerpts from Reviews, Criticism, and Commentary on Books for Children*

SAAS—*Something about the Author Autobiography Series*

Author Index

Author Index